August Tholuck

Commentary on the Sermon on the Mount

August Tholuck

Commentary on the Sermon on the Mount

ISBN/EAN: 9783744745215

Printed in Europe, USA, Canada, Australia, Japan

Cover: Foto ©Lupo / pixelio.de

More available books at **www.hansebooks.com**

CLARK'S

FOREIGN

THEOLOGICAL LIBRARY.

THIRD SERIES.
VOL. VII.

Tholuck's Commentary on the Sermon on the Mount.

EDINBURGH:
T. AND T. CLARK, 38, GEORGE STREET.
MDCCCLXXIV.

COMMENTARY

ON THE

SERMON ON THE MOUNT.

BY

DR A. THOLUCK.

TRANSLATED FROM THE FOURTH REVISED AND ENLARGED EDITION,

BY THE

REV. R. LUNDIN BROWN, M.A.,

TRANSLATOR OF "ULLMANN ON THE SINLESSNESS OF JESUS: AN EVIDENCE FOR CHRISTIANITY."

EDINBURGH:
T. AND T. CLARK, 38, GEORGE STREET.
LONDON: HAMILTON, ADAMS, AND CO.   DUBLIN: JOHN ROBERTSON AND CO.
MDCCCLXXIV.

PREFACE.

I still feel that I owe my dear Friend Rothe warm thanks for having urged me to put forth my exegetical powers in connection with this portion of the New Testament. Although I have no doubts as to the genuineness of the Gospel of John, I must confess that the spirit of Christ finds me most directly in the first three Gospels; and their interpretation has had peculiar attractions for me, because in them the Son of God, at once Divine and human, and the climax of a redemptive process of two thousand years, is presented in a tangible physical shape. The great task of the present age—a task at which men of very different vocations, and with very different aims, are labouring—is to understand the relation in which Christ stands to the form of religion embodied in the Old Testaments: avoiding two opposite errors; that, namely, of degrading Christianity to a mere internal phenomenon of Judaism; and that of representing Judaism as Christianity under a veil, and thus effecting as near an approximation of the two as possible. I am bound to confess that the further my studies have extended, the more clearly have I seen that the religion of the Old Testament and the Gospel constitute one Revelation, and the higher has been my consequent estimate of the loftiness and depth of the Jewish Economy. The present fresh revision of my Commentary on the Sermon on the Mount has contributed to this result.

Many things have presented themselves in a new and clearer light: I have been able to explain several passages more satisfactorily from the Old Testament and from the works of the Rabbins. The compass of the present Edition is indeed little greater than that of the last one, but I have thrown aside much useless material, and replaced it by the results of renewed investigations. I trust also that the arrangement now adopted is in some parts clearer.

When this work first made its appearance, it gave rise to a movement of a practical character in the Church, out of which have grown practical commentaries, commentaries for the use of schools, and sermons on the whole or on particular parts of the Sermon on the Mount. May the present Edition also find its way to practical theologians, and, in these days of the revival of controversy on dogmas and creeds, help to draw the mind to a deeper study of Scripture, and (as this portion of the New Testament is peculiarly adapted to do) quicken and develop that practical spirit, which can alone furnish living stones for the Church, and preserve the plans of the builders of the Church from being mere castles in the air.

A. THOLUCK.

HALLE, *March* 1856.

P.S.—I am indebted to a friend for the translation of pages 207 to 251, and 346 to 362.

R. L. B.

CONTENTS.

INTRODUCTION.

		PAGE
§ 1.	Identity of the Discourse in St Matthew v.—vii. with that in St Luke vi., ...	1
§ 2.	Time of Delivery of Sermon on Mount, ...	8
§ 3.	Occasion, Object, Train of Thought, ...	13
§ 4.	Authenticity and Genuineness, ...	17
§ 5.	Relation to the Evangelical Doctrine of Salvation, ...	34
§ 6.	Exegetical Literature, ...	41

EXPOSITION.

Historical Introduction, ch. v. vers. 1, 2, ... 51
Blessedness of those who in the right way long for the Kingdom of God, and manifest the Fruits of its Righteousness, ch. v. vers. 3—9, ... 59
Blessedness of those who submit to the Reproach which in this World is associated with the Righteousness of the Kingdom of God, ch. v. vers. 10—12, ... 100
Having so high a Vocation, the Disciples of the Kingdom of God must in nowise disavow it, ch. v. vers. 13—16, ... 105
The Righteousness required under the Old Dispensation to be perfected and fulfilled in the Kingdom of Christ, ch. v. vers. 17—48, . . 115
The True Motive in Works of Righteousness, the Eye fixed on Him who sees in secret, ch. vi. ver. 1, ... 293
Warning against a Hypocritical Exercise of Charity, for the sake of the Praise of Men, ch. vi. vers. 2—4, ... 296
Warning against Hypocritical and Unworthy Praying, ch. vi. vers. 5—8, 303
The Lord's Prayer, ch. vi. vers. 9—15, ... 315
Warning against a Hypocritical Use of Fasting, ch. vi. vers. 16—18, . 369
God the Supreme Object of Human Desire and Endeavour, to which all else must be entirely subordinated, ch. vi. vers. 19—34, ... 371

	PAGE
Sundry Admonitions, ch. vii. vers. 1—12, .	395
Epilogue, ch vii. vers. 13—27,	413

INDEXES.

1 Greek Words Illustrated or Explained, .	437
2 Texts of Scripture incidentally Elucidated,	438
3 Principal Matters, .	438

INTRODUCTION.

§ 1. IDENTITY OF THE DISCOURSE IN ST MATTHEW V.—VII. WITH THAT IN ST LUKE VI. 20.

As in the following sections our critical decision must often be determined by a comparison of the discourse in St Matthew with that in St Luke, chap. vi., we must commence with a discussion of the question as to whether these discourses are identical. The Greek expositors decided this question in the affirmative. See *Origen*, in Matt., t. iii. de la Rue, p. 385; *Chrysostom*, hom. 14; *Euthymius, Theoph.* In the Latin Church, on the contrary, St Augustine, in order to meet the charges which the Manichæans founded on the numerous discrepancies in the two accounts, maintained (de consensu Evangelistarum) the existence of two different discourses: one elaborate, which Christ delivered to His Apostles on the summit of the mountain—that which St Matthew reports; and a shorter one, spoken to the people on the plain, given by St Luke. Several Romish writers have followed St Augustine: the author of the Opus Imperfectum, Druthmar, Erasmus, Clarius, and others; on the other hand, Maldonatus, Calmet, and others, have maintained the identity. In the Protestant Church, the view taken was determined mainly by the opinion held on the subject of the Inspiration of Scripture. Those writers who held the narrower view—according to which, Scripture is inspired not only as regards the truth of its religious substance, but even as to its correctness in form and expression—were led to maintain the difference of the discourses. Accordingly, Andreas Osiander, 1530, the author of the stricter harmony founded upon this doctrine of inspiration, held their dissimilarity. The same view was taken by the harmonists, Rus. 1728, Hauber, 1737, Macknight, 1772, Buesching, 1766; also by Socinus, Crell, and more recently by Hess, Storr, Ferf (specim. crit. theol. in ev. Matth., Traject. Batav. 1799). The opposite opinion was supported by Bucer, Calvin, Piscator, Chemnitz, Calov, Clericus, Bengel, and since him by almost all expositors, Stier (Reden Jesu) not excepted. With reference to this subject, Bucer makes some important observations on behalf of a sound system of harmonizing:—"Quanquam moneo diligenter, ut qui de his volunt statuere, quæ Marcus et Lucas habent, cum his nostra conferant atque perpendant, neque velint temere ad nimis vulgatum illud diverticulum in his excurrere, aliam ab illis et aliam a nostro esse historiam positam, præsertim ubi tot eadem leguntur. Frigidis istiusmodi responsis et nihili effugiis aliud nihil efficimus, *quam quod et alia nostra suspecta reddimus eosque, qui ingenio valent, ab illis alienamus.* Præstiterat multo, ingenue fateri, nescire te, quomodo alicubi scriptoribus nostris conveniat, quam incerta adeo et frivola respondere, quibus dissonantiam eorum magis quam consonantiam probes." But, besides the argument drawn from the discrepancies, other arguments for the non-identity of the two discourses were found in the different *periods* to which the discourses in St Matthew and St Luke are assigned, in the locality, and in the external situation of our Lord.

The chronological difficulty will, however, be removed by a correct view of the chronological order in St Matthew generally (on this compare § 2 of Introduction): the other difficulties will be met by a right understanding of the text (compare on ver. 1). We must, on the contrary, maintain the oneness of the two discourses. This is seen, first, from the similarity of their commencement and their close; also from the similar sequence of the parts; next, from the occurrences mentioned as succeeding both—the entrance into Capernaum, and the healing of the centurion's servant (Matt. viii. 5; Luke vii. 1).

If, then, the two discourses be identical, it may be asked, *Whether the two accounts deserves the preference for greater fidelity?* For there are differences between them, not only in the forms of expression, but also in the order of the subjects, and in the greater or lesser fulness of detail. The narrower theory of inspiration would naturally seek to evade such an inquiry, inasmuch as it would imply an amount of incorrectness in the reports—a point to which Clericus directed attention. Accordingly, the question remained unnoticed by the majority of the older harmonists and exegetists. Calvin occasionally gives the preference to St Luke, in regard to the position of the Lord's Prayer (Luke xi. 1): on the whole, however, he would rather leave the question undecided. The learned philologian, Er. Schmidt, writing on Luke vi. 18, gives the preference in every point of view to St Matthew. The supporters of the stricter view of inspiration, however, either show themselves unable to give an opinion on the subject,[1] or else they seek (and among these is even Chemnitz) to escape the admisson of inaccuracies in this way: Every expression in St Luke which in form is different from that in St Matthew, and every clause differently placed, they regard just as so much additional matter, and arrange it harmonistically with the rest.[2] Stier, who attempts to vindicate this last conclusion, is still compelled to make certain admissions which lead to the opposite conclusion.

[1] Cyrill, to be sure (explanatio in Luc. vi. nova bibl. patrum, ed. Maji, t. ii. 1844), after commenting on the differenze between St Matthew and St Luke in regard to the first beatitude, adds the following: οὕτω δέ φασιν οἱ εὐαγγελισταί, οὐκ ἀλλήλοις ἐναντιούμενοι ἀλλὰ μεριζόμενοι πολλάκις τὰ διηγήματα· καὶ ποτὲ μὲν διὰ τῶν αὐτῶν βαδίζουσι κεφαλαίων, ποτὲ δὲ τὸ τῷ ἑνὶ παραλειφθὲν ἕτερος τοῖς ἰδίοις ἐντίθησι συγγραφαῖς, ἵνα μηδὲν τῶν ἀναγκαίων εἰς ὄνησιν λαβεῖν δυνηθῇ τ. πιστεύοντας εἰς Χριστόν. But that the words ἐν πνεύματι in Matthew are the proper supplement to the words in Luke, he does not show; nay, he considers the saying as expressing one idea in St Matthew, another in St Luke. In the former, it speaks of humility; in the latter, it contains an admonition against covetousness.

[2] Most of all would any one, with a sound exegetical feeling, object to regard as different expressions Luke vi. 29, 44, and Matt. v. 40, vii. 16, on account of the difference of the figure; and Luke vi. 31 and Matt. vii. 12, on account of the difference in the arrangement. Yet this has been done even by Chemnitz. The sayings, Luke vi. 44, Matt. vii. 16, and Luke vi. 31, Matt. vii. 12, are regarded by him as different, and are arranged in different places. In the case of Luke vi. 29, Matt. v. 40, however, his exegetical discrimination has not allowed him to follow this course. Having pointed out the distinction between χιτών and ἱμάτιον, he then gives rightly enough the different points of view from which the two Evangelists have apprehended the deed of violence, which also explains the different position of the ἱμάτιον; yet he does not maintain, as one would have anticipated, that there is a repetition of the expression.

He says (S. 70), "The Spirit of the Lord recalled the discourses of Christ to the Evangelists in such a way, that, although they might not record everything with perfect verbal accuracy, they should still give the truth in substance. But the Spirit of truth could not have permitted them to record any essential untruth." "The Apostle Matthew has no doubt given Christ's words more accurately: in St Luke, the Spirit, in a higher form of inspiration, teaches us that, in respect of these minutiæ, verbal exactness is not necessary" (S. 170). "Only once has St Luke been mistaken, ver. 45, where he introduces a passage from another place."

While Stier thus on doctrinal grounds lays claim to greater fidelity on behalf of St Matthew, the writers on the synoptical Gospels, especially since Schulz and Schleiermacher, have given the preference in respect of fidelity to St Luke; for they regarded the Greek version of Matthew as merely an expanded transcription of the Hebrew Gospel of St Matthew, or of the collection of discourses made by him. Thus D. Schulz, Sieffert, Fritzsche, Olshausen; also Wilke (der Urevangelist, S. 685) resp. Neander.—When, in the first and second editions of this work, I expressed myself against this preference of St Luke, I stood very much alone in this opinion. Since then it has become almost universal, especially in respect of the Sermon on the Mount. Already had Strauss observed (Characteristiken und Kritiken, S. 254, in Berliner Jahrbücher): "The other portions of the discourse on the Mount, as well as the Lord's Prayer, need only be perused synoptically in order to show what value is to be attached to the remark commonly made, that in St Luke the separate parts are better put together." De Wette (in the 4th ed. of his Introduction to the New Testament) calls St Luke's account of the Sermon on the Mount a "caricature of St Matthew's;" in the 5th ed. (S. 164), he calls it "a disfigured abridgment." Meyer's opinion (2 Ausg., S. 170) points in the same direction. The school of Baur, which regards the third Gospel as a remodeling of Matthew, taken either by itself or in conjunction with other older documents,—a task undertaken in the interest of the Pauline doctrine,—concludes the same of the account there given of the Sermon on the Mount (Baur, Kritische Untersuchungen, S. 455 f. 472, 589; Hilgenfeld, die Evang. nach ihrer Entstehung und Bedeutung, 1854, S. 173;

Koestlin, Ursprung und Composition der Synoptischen Evangelien, 1853, S. 169, 220).

That the source from which the Gospel according to St Luke is taken is only a secondary one, is a fact which is clearly seen in the Sermon on the Mount, even were it not apparent elsewhere. Yet the discrepancies here are not of such a nature that we must conclude from them that the author has taken the text of Matthew, and wilfully changed it in the interest of some doctrine or tendency. All we are at liberty to conclude from these differences is, that St Luke's informer (whether the information was oral or written) possessed less accurate knowledge. Thus Schleiermacher already remarked (Ueber die Schriften des Lucas, S. 89), "Our reporter appears either to have occupied an unfortunate position for hearing, in consequence of which he failed to catch all that was said, so that here and there he seems to have missed the train of thought; or to have drawn up his account some time subsequently, when a good deal of the discourse had escaped his memory." St Luke's account is, in many respects, more imperfect than the other. Chief among its omissions is that of the statement which contains the theme, not only of St Matthew's 5th chap., but even of the whole discourse, viz., Matt. v. 17—20: a passage whose genuineness is admitted on almost all sides. And here, no doubt, there might appear some warrant for suspecting a wilful change made on behalf of a particular tendency; for it might seem as if the omission had been made in the interest of the "Pauline universality" of this Evangelist (Baur, krit. Untersuchungen, S. 457). But, on the other hand, the occurrence of Jewish-Christian elements in this Gospel militates against such a conclusion. That such Jewish-Christian elements exist, is generally admitted; and Schwegler owns that, on account of them, it is impossible to discover in St Luke a systematic Pauline teaching. Koestlin (S. 220), however, and Hilgenfeld (S. 203) arrive at a different conclusion: they infer that the third Evangelist must have had before him not only Matthew's Gospel, but, besides, some older Jewish-Christian document. The argument of the Pauline tendency of this Gospel having been thus invalidated, the next point was to maintain that the object of the Gospel, equally with the Acts of the Apostles, was conciliatory—to reconcile Pauline with Jewish-Christian doctrine;

but this is a shifting rule, capable of any application. (Baur, S. 521; Zeller, der dogm. Character des III. Evangel., Jahrb. 1843, S. 72, 1851, S. 27; Hilgenfeld, S. 154.)

We find in St Luke, first, certain amplifications of the discourse, such as the fourfold woe (vi. 24—26), which Strauss (with Schleiermacher and Olshausen) characterizes as an "*original* addition;" but which we shall more correctly regard as a transformation made in the transmission of the original from mouth to mouth (as will be more fully seen in the subsequent Introduction to the Beatitudes). Further, in St Luke, the sayings are often disjointed and unconnected, and receive their proper light only from the context in St Matthew, v. 27—30, v. 32—36, v. 31, v. 41, 42, 44.[1] The additions which he makes do not fit in with the context, vers. 38, 39, 40, 46; but manifestly are in their proper context in Matth. x. 24, xii. 35, xv. 14. Expressions occur, as is the case when reminiscences have grown dull and inexact, where the saying is made to take a general form. Instead of the more definite τελῶναι and ἐθνικοί, Matt. v. 46, 47, Luke has (vi. 32, 33) both times ἁμαρτωλοί. The saying in Matt. vii. 21 is by St Luke taken out of its context, and presented (ver. 46) in the form of a general dictum.[2] No doubt St Luke

---

[1] "His disconnected sayings on the love of peace, forgiveness of injuries, benevolence, have a unity and significance only in the contrast between the spiritual exposition of Scripture of Jesus, and the carnal exposition of the teachers of that time."—*Strauss* (Leben Jesu, i., S. 608, 4 Auflage).

[2] Let us compare by this example the merits of the two explanations of the discrepancies in St Luke: that which ascribes them to imperfect recollection, and that which refers them to his so-called Pauline tendencies. St Luke has: "Why call ye Me, Lord, Lord, and do not the things which I say?" Now, was not this evidently the kernel of thought which was remembered when the connection in which it was originally expressed had passed from the memory? And is not the form which it retains here precisely the one which (like Luke xi. 13, compared with Matt. vii. 11) it would so naturally afterwards receive, and under which it would pass current in the Christian Church? Was it not natural, too, that θέλημα τοῦ κυρίου should there come to be substituted for θέλημα τοῦ Θεοῦ; first, as Justin, in quoting the saying as given in Matthew, introduces the explanatory clause: ὃς γὰρ ἀκούει μου καὶ ποιεῖ ἃ λέγω, ἀκούει τοῦ ἀποστείλαντός με (Apol. i. 16)? It must, indeed, be acknowledged that St Luke often gives the sayings of Christ a more peculiarly Christian application. (Koestlin, S. 169.)

And now to apply to this passage the explanation which proceeds upon the basis of a difference of tendency and teaching in the two Evangelists.

in vi. 36 has a more specific expression than St. Matthew (v. 48); the former having οἰκτίρμονες, while the latter has τέλειοι. But then it must be confessed that, viewing the verse in connection with what precedes, οἰκτίρμονες is a predicate which would much more naturally suggest itself to a reporter than τέλειοι; while, on a closer examination of the whole context, we must conclude that τέλειοι is the most worthy of our approval. Again, St Matthew (v. 40) has, "If any man will sue thee at the law, and take away thy coat;" St Luke (vi. 29), "Him that taketh away thy cloak:" the former being evidently the more particular and individualizing figure; the latter, the form it might assume from the lips of a reporter. Finally, certain formulæ of transition in the discourse, occurring here and there in St Luke's narrative, place it beyond a doubt that his reporter loses now and then the thread of the discourse. Thus, Λέγω δὲ ὑμῖν, Εἶπε δὲ πρὸς τοὺς μαθητὰς αὐτοῦ· Luke vi. 27, 39, compare xi. 5, 9, xii. 4, 8, 12, 22, xxiv. 44; further, the expression, εἶπε δὲ παραβολὴν πρὸς αὐτούς, vi. 39, compared with xii. 16.

The decision, then, to which a comparison of these two accounts of the Sermon on the Mount will infallibly conduct us is, that the writer of our Gospel, if not himself an ear-witness of this discourse, must at least have stood in intimate relations with the original hearers of it. And this conclusion is further ratified by the fact, that elsewhere, although the first Evangelist is often inexact in his narrative of events, yet he is most accurate in his report of the sayings of our Lord; nay, more, that some of the most peculiar and most precious utterances of the Redeemer (as, for instance, Matt. xi. 28—30) are handed down to us by him alone.

"Matthew finds fault with the Christianity of his opponents because it does not fulfil the will of God. Luke, on the other hand, who, as a disciple of Paul, attached value only to a confession which is based upon a lively faith in the person of Christ, marks as the great vice of that Christianity which was opposed to his Pauline system, that it did not fulfil the commands of Christ." (Hilgenfeld, S. 173.) If this is not lighting candles by daylight! A similar attempt to show a specific teaching with a view to make out a Petrine Gospel, as an intermediate step between Matthew and Mark, has been made by Hilgenfeld in speaking of the incorrect quotation of Matt. v. 46, in Justin's Apol. i 15; which, however, Ritschl has shown to be altogether unfounded. Zeller's Jahrb. 1851, S. 483.

§ 2. TIME OF THE DELIVERY OF THE SERMON ON THE MOUNT.

It may be asked whether this discourse, which in St Matthew occurs first in order among the discourses of Christ, was also intended by him to be regarded as occupying that place chronologically. This question was answered in the affirmative by Osiander in his Harmony of the Gospels, and it is also maintained by some recent writers (see De Wette, Einleitung ins N. T., 5 Aufl., § 91 c.) Strauss says: "The Evangelists flattered themselves that they were giving a chronological narrative." (Leben Jesu, 4 Aufl., S. 488.) But it has been acknowledged by the greater number of harmonists, ancient and modern, that this Evangelist does not aim at giving a perfectly chronological biography of the Saviour. "The Evangelists," says Bengel (Harmonie der 4 Evv., S. 134), "have not written a daily chronicle, but a history: hence they were at liberty to follow the order of events with greater or less exactness. The more one has kept to that order, the less another deemed it needful to do so; but by a pleasing variation they gave their theme new uses." But although this opinion was thus almost universally adopted, this chronological irregularity was adduced by several as a strong argument against the fact that the Evangelist was himself an eye-witness of what he narrates (David Schulz, Schneckenburger, Schleiermacher, etc.), although Schleiermacher himself says that it cannot be maintained that an eye-witness might not have chosen this irregular method (Hermeneutik, S. 229). On the other hand, an attempt has been made to show that there is at least some method in the division and arrangement of the materials of the history. (Ebrard, wissenschaftliche Kritik, I. S. 86, 2 A; Baur, Krit. Untersuchungen, S. 600; Ewald, Jahrb. für biblische Wissenschaft, 1849, S. 139.)

Now this at least is certain, that the synoptical Evangelists have not jumbled together their materials in chaotic confusion; on the contrary, some plan, if sometimes only in its most general outlines, is traceable in their narrative. But when we speak of the chronological relations of the synoptical narratives, we must never leave out of sight a truth expressed by Planck (see Article by Ebrard in Zeller's theolog. Jahrb. 1845, S. 152), the wise recognition of which would have saved criticism a world of useless labour and ingenuity: "Tho wish to do away with those chronological contradictions, is to mistake the whole spirit of the Gospel narrative. Suppose you had an ancient picture, whereof the great glory was its religious essence, its spiritual idea, but where the form was in many things defective, would it not be folly to wish to deny the faults and imperfections, the incorrectness of the drawing, and so forth? We are not surprised to find these incongruities in those works of art which bear the impress of a simple and childlike spirit. As little, then, need we wonder to find them in the evangelistic record, in which the externals of time and place fade into insignificance before the overwhelming interest of the subject, and come under our observation only in so far as the unfolding of the whole may naturally bring them." (Comp. Delitzsch über Entstehung der Evv., S. 46.)

The most recent criticism (that of Wieseler, Ewald, Koestlin, Hilgenfeld) tends towards the recognition of a certain chronological order. As, however, it considers the Gospel to have originated in two or more sources, or to be the final result of several attempts to remodel the original materials, the question has thus become involved in fresh complications, as we can never know to what extent the later compiler may have considered himself bound to abide by the arrangement of the previous writers or editors. According to Wieseler (Chronolog. Synopse, S. 305), the historical matter was originally arranged in chronological order. This order was disturbed only by the introduction of the unchronological λόγια κυριακά, Matt. v.—vii., x., xiii., by which, however, a more essential unity was imparted to the whole. The clairvoyant criticism of Ewald has discovered four separate treatises out of which the Gospel of St Matthew, as we have it, was composed. According to this writer, the reason why the author of our Gospel assigned to the Sermon on the Mount its present unhistorical position, at the beginning of his narrative, is, because in the large collection of sayings which the Apostle St Matthew had made, and which the author used, this sermon occurred first. It was properly, however, as is seen from St Luke, the inaugural address of Jesus to the Twelve. (Jahrb. für bibl. Wissenschaft, 1849, S. 212; Die 3 Ersten Evang. 1850, S. 208.) Koestlin, who maintains to an extravagant degree the chronological character of the Gospel generally (Ursprung und Composition der Synopt. Evv. 1853, S. 72), sets down this alteration to the account of the last compiler alone. Hilgenfeld (die Evv. nach ihrer Entstehung und geschichtlicher Bedeutung, 1854, S. 109) makes a distinction between an original document, containing both narrative and discourses, and certain passages which have been inserted by a later editor, of a universalizing tendency. To this writer he also ascribes certain transpositions of passages in the original, among which he reckons the Sermon on the Mount, whose original place he holds to have been at chap. x. It is not our business to adjust these differences, this belongs to a critical work upon the Gospel. It must, however, be noted, that there are at least two points on which the opinion of the most recent critics on all sides seems tolerably harmonious: first, that the place which the discourse occupies here, at the commencement of the public teaching of Jesus, is not historically correct; and secondly, that, in all probability, it properly belongs to the time of the calling of the Apostles. And we are led to acquiesce in the former of these conclusions also by a consideration of the historical introduction to the discourse in iv. 24, 25. This introduction represents to us the Saviour as already fully engaged in His mission. It has so summary a character, that the impression conveyed is by no means that the Evangelist intends to intimate that the discourse was held at a certain given period of time. Then, in the discourse itself, we find indications of its delivery at a later period of His ministry. The μὴ νομίσητε (v. 17) clearly presupposes (as remarked by Baur, Calvin, and Chemnitz) that a suspicion hat already been awakened, by His teaching and work, that He meant to overturn the institutions of the country. Great weight has been attached to the fact, that Jesus here so distinctly declares His Messiahship and His office as Judge of the world, vii. 21—23, which, it is said, He could not have done in the commencement of His ministry (Meyer, 3 A. S. 17, and de Wette). The supposition that these avowals of His Messianic dignity are the addition of a later compiler (Koestlin), is quite inadmissible; for the whole discourse betokens one ἐν ἐξουσίᾳ λαλῶν (consider also the ἐγὼ δὲ λέγω and the ἕνεκεν ἐμοῦ, v. 11),—as does the impression which it is reported to have produced upon the hearers (vii. 29). Yet all that this argument proves is, that this discourse was preceded by others, was not absolutely the *first*. "If, now, this full exposition of the truths on which the kingdom of God is founded, and by which it is sustained, is intended not only for the Twelve (for, indeed, it contains no secret doctrines), but likewise for all who do or shall resemble them, it could assuredly have no significance until a certain number of faithful followers was attached to the Person of Jesus." (Ewald.) As to whether Christ intended from the first to fix the thoughts of the people upon Him as the Messiah, that is a question which (after setting aside Strauss' view of the origin of the beginnings of the Gospel narrative, which he ascribes to the law of historical development) we must decisively answer in the affirmative. The baptism of our Lord was, as for the Baptist so for Himself, the seal of His calling: then it was that the consciousness awoke in Him that His time was come. The words, "Mine hour is not yet come," in John ii., need cause no difficulty here; for they only declare that His intention was to begin the manifestation of His Messiahship in Jerusalem, the metropolis of the Theocracy. And after His brief sojourn at Capernaum, He accordingly does appear in the temple of Jerusalem in the capacity of a Restorer of the Theocracy (John ii. 12). Next He reveals Himself to Nicodemus as the Divine Son of Man, and carries on His mission. Leaving, however, out of account St John's history, we find that in St Matthew also Christ designates Himself as the Messianic Bridegroom (ix. 15), as the Son of Man who has power to forgive sins (ix. 6) as One greater than the temple (xii. 6).

The work of judgment, too, was a work which the Messiah was expected to execute, as even the expressions of the Baptist (Matt. iii. 11, 12) show (compare Hilgenfeld, S. 112). Then, too much stress must not be laid upon the $\mu\dot{\eta}$ $\nu o\mu i\sigma\eta\tau\varepsilon$. May not Christ have used the expression to bring out more forcibly the positive character of His mission, and to defend it against the expected attacks of His enemies? In any case, the comprehensive introduction which St Matthew gives is of such a nature, that his intention can never have been to represent this discourse as coming first in order of time. Those harmonists who have found a place for the Sermon on the Mount in St John's order of events, have accordingly fixed its date either a little before that sojourn of Christ in Jerusalem recorded in

John v. (as Paulus and Ebrard), or shortly *after* that (as Chemnitz, Clericus, Beng., Neander, Robinson, Harmony of the Four Gospels, 1845).

Now, it is not difficult, further, to see why the Evangelist should have assigned the Sermon on the Mount this position at the commencement of his Gospel.

Even if our Gospel were to be regarded as a later reproduction of earlier materials, the reason cannot have been any external relation of the author to his materials. On the contrary, as both older and the most recent critics of different schools are agreed, the motive for so doing must have been of a didactic character. Further, it is one which goes to support the tradition, that the Apostle Matthew is the author of the Gospel. For, according to this tradition, the Gospel was written by Matthew the Hebrew, dwelling in Palestine, for Jewish-Christian readers. Now, it is acknowledged that the internal construction accords with this historical notification. Take, for instance, the character of the genealogical register, the allusions to the fulfilment of prophetic sayings, the polemic against the Pharisees as falsifiers of the pure doctrine of the law, and the saying, which occurs only in this Gospel, concerning Christ as the fulfiller of the law (v. 17). Well remarks Koestlin (S. 15), "There cannot be any doubt that *this Gospel stands in a very close and intimate relation to Judaism.* It has a Judaizing character, inasmuch as in it the labours of Jesus are restricted to the Jewish people, and Jesus is represented as standing in a very positive relation to the Old Testament and the Mosaic νόμος: and it has, moreover, an anti-Jewish character, inasmuch as the insensibility of the nation and its rulers towards the salvation offered to them is brought prominently forward, and sternly rebuked; and the superiority of the doctrine of Jesus to the mode of viewing the law then prevalent among the Jews, is most emphatically enforced." In these circumstances, the placing of this discourse at the commencement of Christ's ministry, must plainly have been with the intention of setting forth His doctrine in its relation to the Old Testament economy, on the one hand, and in its antagonism to the falsifiers of the Old Testament religion at that time, on the other. As on the one hand He fulfilled the prophets, so on the other did He fulfil the law. It is a good observation of Bruno Bauer, that the

Sermon of the Mount gives the substance of Christ's teaching according to St Matthew, in as pregnant and significant a manner as the conversation of our Lord with Nicodemus, in the beginning of St John's Gospel, presents the leading thought of the Christian doctrine according to St John.

This view of the object in placing this discourse first, would be still further corroborated, if the idea recently broached by Delitzsch (first in a treatise in the Lutheran Zeitschrift, 1850; then in the "Neuen Untersuchungen über Entstehung und Anlage des Ev. Matthäi," 1853, S. 59), and approved by Koestlin, could be regarded as well founded. That idea is, that the Gospel of St Matthew is throughout constructed on the plan of the five books of the Pentateuch. Now, perhaps it might not appear opposed to the mental tendencies of a Jewish-Christian Apostle to select those books as the plan of his own; but the whole literary character of his Gospel is such as to leave no room for the supposition that he proposed to himself so artificial a method of narrating his story. As for the arguments adduced in proof of this new opinion, they are exceedingly weak. Indeed, with the same means of proof, and the same gift of combination, one might easily demonstrate the existence of an arrangement on the plan of the Pentateuch in many another book of religious history besides. Therefore, great as is the ability which the author has brought to establish his point, we are at last compelled to apply to this attempt the verdict to which the immortal Lücke has given expression: De eo quod nimium artis acuminisque est in ea quæ nunc præcipue factitatur S. Scripturæ maxime evangeliorum interpretatione (Programme, 1853).

§ 3. OCCASION, OBJECT, TRAIN OF THOUGHT.

From the introduction to the Sermon on the Mount, given in Luke vi., we gather that it was delivered after the election of the Twelve, and, as it would seem, on the occasion of their election (which is mentioned only in a participial clause, Luke vi. 13). St Matthew gives us no account whatever of the choosing of the Apostles, speaking of it in chap. x. as a thing which had previously taken place; but even in Matthew, the Sermon was addressed in the first instance to the μαθηταί, a phrase which usually denotes the Twelve: viii. 23, xiv. 19. The import of Matt. v. 2 is the following: "The sight of the great concourse of people induced Jesus to withdraw in order to impart instruction to His disciples. He accordingly ascended a mountain there, that He might teach His disciples." (Meyer on Matt. v. 2.) No doubt, the multitudes must be regarded as hearers (v. 1, vii, 28; Luke vii. 1). But such expressions as v. 12—16 seem to presuppose that in those addressed the life of faith had already begun; and, again, expressions such as v. 12, where those addressed are viewed as occupying the same footing with the prophets (comp. διδάξῃ, vers. 19), and vii. 6, evidently refer to teachers. Hence we must consider the discourse as addressed primarily to the disciples, and secondarily to the people; and the degree of its bearing upon these different classes as expressed by the relative position of the hearers to the Speaker. Thus the Twelve formed a circle in the Saviour's immediate neighbourhood; farther off stood the μαθηταί, whom St Luke, vi. 13, 17, distinguishes from the ἀπόστολοι; and beyond them stood the crowd. Chrys.: ἐπειδὴ γὰρ τὸ πλῆθος δημῶδες ἦν, ἔτι δὲ καὶ τῶν χαμαὶ ἑρπομένων, τῶν μαθητῶν τὸν χορὸν ὑποστησάμενος πρὸς ἐκείνους ποιεῖται τοὺς λόγους, ἐν τῇ πρὸς αὐτοὺς διαλέξει καὶ τοῖς λοιποῖς ἅπασι τοῖς σφόδρα ἀποδέουσι τῶν λεγομένων, ἀνεπαχθῆ, γίνεσθαι παρασκευάζων τῆς φιλοσοφίας τὴν διδασκαλίαν. Piscator: concio quam Christus coram discipulis ad populum habuit. Hase: "The discourse bore immediately upon the disciples, then upon the people, and then upon the whole Christian Church; for it is the constitution of the kingdom in the souls of men."

The occasion of the discourse being thus determined, leads us next to its object, which its position at the commencement of the Gospel has already indicated. The object of our Lord here was, *to exhibit Himself as the Fulfiller of the law, and to enunciate the magna charta of His new kingdom*. What occasion, then, could be better adapted to such a purpose than that early morning on the mountain-side, when He chose out the great pillars of that kingdom in the presence of a great multitude? Yet to call it (with Chemnitz, Harmon. I. p. 112; and after him, Zachariae, Beausobre, Pott, K. Schmid, exeget. Beitraege, Th. II., and many others) simply the address of installation of the Apostles into their office, would not fully express the object of this discourse. Baur calls it an address of instruction for them in their new office (Zeller Jahrb. 1846, S. 529). Now, it was not exactly this; for there is in it no special allusion to the sending forth of the Apostles; on the contrary, in this respect it is distinguished (as Grotius and Neander remark) from the address to the Apostles in chap. x., which is decidedly of this character. Again, to suppose the object to have been merely to combat the errors of the Pharisees, or to crush the prevalent carnal expectations in connection with the Messiah (Jansenius,[1] Rau, Paulus, Hess, Rosenmüller), is to take too restricted and onesided a view. This negative was indeed only the reverse side of the positive object, which was to exhibit the new economy of the kingdom of God as the truest fulfilment of the old: **in this the** condemnation **of the** superficial religion of Pharisaic Judaism was, of course, implied. This has been acknowledged in recent times as the purpose of the Sermon on the Mount by men of all parties,—by Neander and by Baur, by Delitzsch and Meyer, by Ebrard, and by Koestlin and Ewald.

Respecting the division of the Sermon, our decision thereon depends upon our view of the completeness and connectedness of the whole discourse. Some have thought that the most accurate division may be made on the basis of a symbolical arrangement on the principle of numbers. Thus, according to Ewald, the introduction consists first of *seven* benedictions; in the remaining portion of the fifth chap. the true fulfilling of the law is set forth in *seven* main duties; while in chaps. vi. and vii. *seven* means of virtue are treated of. Now, a numerical distribution of this nature is certainly to be found in some portions of the Bible, especially in the poetical books, in the Psalms, the Book of Proverbs, and in Jesus Sirach; and, generally, it is to be found where the language is elevated and figurative; and thus, like the arrangement of rhythm, metre, and parallelisms, it imparts an harmonious and poetic unity to the composition. But precisely on that account we must not expect to **find it** used where the language is simply didactic. Moreover, in the present case, to prove the existence of a numerical division, the text has been subjected to certain artistic operations of a dubious character, such as the gratuitous insertion after ver. 41 of an

---

[1] Jansenius: Justitiam non sitam esse in externis cæremoniis sed in affectu.

original observation. An evidence of the liberty which those writers allow their imagination in effecting their distribution and combinations, may be seen in the arrangement by Delitzsch, which differs widely from that of Ewald. His symbolic system of numbers gives him no less than *ten* benedictions, corresponding to the Ten Commandments. Then v. 21—48 contains twice three antitheses to the teaching of them of old time; vi. 1—18, three antitheses to the conduct to the hypocrite; ch. vii. is passed over; and then attention is directed to the "remarkable parallelism" presented by the conclusion, of which it is said, that "the discourse closes with the parable of the house-building, just as the Book of Exodus, which contains the law of Moses, concludes with the building of the tabernacle!" (S. 78.)[1]

We consider it more advisable to abide by what can be satisfactorily proved. The discourse must have contained throughout a strictly progressive train of thought. We conclude this of the whole, because we find it unmistakeably alike at the commencement, v. 1—20, and the close, vii. 12—27. In both these passages the thoughts are regular and progressive, and of so original a character that they furnish a proof of the genuineness of the discourse.[2] From vi. 19 to vii. 11 the train of thought seems lost. The blame of this attaches, in all probability, to the Evangelist alone. Either, "while retaining the leading points in their consecutive order, he has lost the con-

---

[1] Besides, supposing the numerical division to be right, it must be ascribed, not to Christ Himself, but to the reporter of the discourse. Not so much because such an arrangement were unworthy of Christ, but because the construction of the discourse leaves it uncertain that the whole of it has been handed down to us by the Evangelist. On the supposition that such a numerical arrangement really exists, might it not be accounted for by supposing that it served the reporter as a mnemonic scheme, as the number 14 in the genealogical table, chap. i. ?

[2] De Wette reckons the μακαρισμοί among the most ingenious and profound passages in the Gospel; so that this introduction, he says, "places the genuineness of the discourse beyond a doubt." Baur, indeed, thinks it impossible that so artistic an introduction can have come from Jesus Himself; it must, he supposes, have been the work of a later reviser (Kritische Untersuchungen, S. 586). Perhaps, if the discourse were not, apart even from this artistic introduction—which, however, is only due to the beauty of the train of thought—a model at once of the most popular and the most original eloquence.

necting links," as Ebrard supposes; or he has amplified the sermon by the introduction of foreign materials taken from other discourse of our Lord. As we shall afterwards see, there is more to be said in favour of the former than of the latter opinion.

Our view of the distribution of the discourse is then as follows:—

Chap. v. 3—16. Introduction: Conditions of membership in the kingdom.

17—20. Subject—The Messiah comes to fulfil the law in its depth and breadth.

21—48. The same developed and applied.

vi. 1—18. The motive of Christian righteousness—to please God.

19—34. The righteousness of the kingdom of God the highest good, the end of life.

vii. 1—11. Divers unconnected admonitions.

12. The general canon for our duty towards our neighbour.

13—20. The more difficult the way, the greater the need of faithful guides and teachers.

21—27. Peroration: the Divine doctrine makes blessed only when it is taken up into the will.

§ 4. AUTHENTICITY AND GENUINENESS OF THE DISCOURSE.

We have already seen that the narrative of St Luke has less claim to being considered a faithful account than that of St Matthew. And now the subject leads us to inquire whether there is reason to believe that the discourse, as given by St Matthew, retains in shape and substance the form in which it originally came from the mouth of Christ. Doubts on this point may be held with reference either to the form of the words and the right allocation of the sentences, or to the genuineness of the sayings themselves.

Inquire we first concerning the genuineness of the *form* in which the discourse is here presented. That we have here, throughout, perfect fidelity in form, is a position which has been defended on doctrinal grounds by those who maintain the narrowest theory of inspiration;—some of them, as Stier, regarding as altogether inadmissible, in the case of Matthew the Apostle, inaccuracies which, they think, they may venture to ascribe to Luke, the disciple of an Apostle (see above, pp. 3, 4). But those who held a more liberal theory of inspiration, such as Calvin, Calixt, Roman Catholic, Arminian, and Socinian divines, had no scruple about admitting the existence of inaccuracies in the words, misplacing of some sentences, or interpolation of others, taken from discourses held on other occasions. And here may be compared the free expressions which Luther uses in speaking of the paragraphs, Matt. xxiv. and Luke xxi., respecting which expositors contended as to how much of their contents relates to the destruction of Jerusalem, how mucht to the end of the world: "Matthew and Mark," he says, "mix up and confuse the two, not keeping the order which Luke preserves." (Walch XI. S. 2496.) So, too, Maldonatus (in ch. vii.) remarks: in concionibus Christi nec omnia quæ dixit nec eo quo dixit ordine recensent evangelistæ, contenti præcipua ejus doctrinæ capita commemorare. Owing to the influence of modern opinion regarding the origin of the Gospels, this more liberal view on the formal correctness of the accounts of the sayings of Christ became universally adopted. More particularly, it was generally admitted that insertions of sayings at the wrong place occasionally occurred. And with regard to St Matthew's accounts of the longer discourses of Christ, it was remarked by several divines, following in the footsteps of Calvin—Crell von Corrodi, Eichhorn, Schulz, Sieffert—that it was a characteristic peculiarity of that Evangelist, that he endeavoured to group together sayings of a kindred nature, as in this Sermon on the Mount: at chap. x. in the discourse of direction addressed to the disciples; at chap. xiii. in the collection of parables; at chap. xxiii. in the discourse of denunciation against the Pharisees. In proof of the assertion it was alleged, that many portions of all those discourses occurred in St Luke and St Mark in an historical connection. The question now was, How did this grouping take place? was it accidental, or were the sayings brought into their present order by our Evangelist? The majority held the former view. But Herder, with his critical perception, saw that so thoughtless and accidental an arranging of these sayings was incredible. "St Luke," he observes, "had heard those sayings and parables of Christ singly, one by one, and singly he introduced them into that older, shorter Gospel with which he had been sent forth, and he introduced them in the place which seemed to him to suit best. No wonder, then, that the maxims of the Sermon on the Mount, with other sayings and parables, are found in his Gospel scattered and broken up. Matthew, having a doctrinal object in view, which was foreign to the Gospel of St Luke, collected those sayings, accordingly, and imparted to them the tendency which his whole Gospel was designed to have. In his hands, several of them receive a new point; a few even receive a meaning different from what they originally bore." (Ueber Zusammenstimmung unserer Evv. 1798.) Since the beginning of this century, the conviction has become more general, that there is a connectedness in the discourse of Christ. So Fritzsche, Olshausen, Meyer, Schneckenburger, and especially Baur (S. 587). But, according to them, this order was not given by the original speaker himself, but by the artistic compiler of His sayings. Then, for those who had not yet learnt to regard the greatness of the Founder of Christianity as fading into insignificance before the dialectic progress of His followers, there certainly arose the anxious problem, whether in this case the disciple had gone beyond the Master? So it was held by the other party, that the discourse, as we have it, is a continuous whole (although, doubtless, with some interpolations); and that, as we have it, so it originally came from the mouth of Christ. Compare Neander, De Wette, Meyer (3 Ausg.).

But the genuineness of the discourse was still, to a great extent, recognised by the above-named critics. Since Wilke and Bruno Bauer, however, modern criticism seemed disposed to deny the originality, not only of the form, but even of the thought. As critics thought themselves under the necessity of believing that the original matter had undergone frequent revisions, proceeding from different views of doctrine, it was natural for them to ascribe a considerable portion of the materials to the revisers. Thus already Wilke (der Urevangelist, S. 586)—whose idea was, that St Mark's Gospel was the ground-work of those of St Matthew and St Luke—regarded the account of the sermon in St Matthew as an amplification, in part purely arbitrary, of the text as given in St

Luke. Bruno Bauer endeavoured, by criticising the separate sayings, to show that they all were the offspring of Christian thought in the Church; and that, as such, they were first drawn up by St Luke, then worked up and reproduced by St Matthew. Nay, he regards the Pater noster itself as first "put together by the Church out of the simple and general categories of religion, which, along with the Old Testament, the Church had had transmitted to her." (Kritik der Synoptiker, I. S. 362.) Baur's final decision (as given in his Kritische Untersuchungen, S. 605) is as follows: "Although the historical character of the sayings of Jesus is indubitably beyond all question, so far as their substantial contents are concerned, yet even in their case there has been supperadded a not inconsiderable portion; and this, not only as regards the form, but even the matter of the composition." According to Koestlin, the Gospel is pervaded by three different views of doctrine: "The collection of sayings is still of an entirely *Jewish-Christian* cast; the Jewish-Christian author is already half a Universalist (a '*Petriner*-universalistisch' he calls him), while the last reviser is absolutely a Universalist and a Catholic" (in loc. cit. S. 55). According to Hilgenfeld (in loc. cit. S. 114), "The author of the original document reflects the thought of the earliest Church and the first Apostles, who sought, as in the case of Titus, to make the entrance into the Church of the Messiah dependent on the acceptance of Judaism throught the rite of circumcision, and regarded the ἀποστολὴ τῶν ἐθνῶν as an idea altogether foreign to the mission of the original Jewish-Christians Apostles, or at least as an idea which could only be tolerated." He holds that sayings such as v. 18, 19 must have been introduced in the interest of this Judaizing tendency; for, he says, "the whole ministry of St Paul—the existence of Paulinism at all within the sphere of Christianity—had been an impossibility, if Jesus Himself hat in this way maintained the inviolable validity of the law, and its ceaseless duration. An approximation to a universal Christianity has been made in the revision."

Notwithstanding all this, the most recent criticism has admitted the existence of a genuine historical kernel, especially as regards this sermon. The words of Baur (S. 585) are as follows: "The impression made by the discourse is undoubtedly that of an immediate and original work; and if anything, certainly that anti-pharisaic part, breathing as it does so entirely the spirit of a lively, energetic polemic, belongs to the most genuine sayings which actually came from the lips of Jesus, and are treasured up in our Gospels." Still more exuberant are the words of Ewald, which apply specially to the Sermon on the Mount (Jahrbücher, 1849, S. 197): "Only the more certain must it appear to us that these sayings, in their essence, came to the author as *recollections*. . . . But far more wonderful than this great whole, in which every detail falls into its place so naturally, is that living Spirit which inspires it; that creative power which energizes in every sentence, and in the whole structure and march of the discourse; that vast oratorical sweep which in a few brief words or phrases now rises to the loftiest heights, and now in calm dignity again descends; that sublime force of thought which reaches even the most distant truths, and grows resistless with every step of its onward march."

In order, then, to form a judgment on the question before us, we must first consider what results the critics have arrived at as respects the authenticity of the Gospel in its present shape. Now, critics of the most recent times seem pretty well agreed to assign to St Matthew the position of the first Evangelist. The "ground-work" of our Gospel, Ewald and Koestlin suppose to have consisted in a collection of $\lambda όγια\ κυριακά$—a collection, not of isolated sayings merely, but of whole discourses of our Lord. Even Hilgenfeld maintains the existence of an original document, written in Greek, and comprising both sayings and events, as having formed the basis of the Apostle's history. Baur holds that our Greek Gospel was not written till A.D. 134; but Koestlin, Hilgenfeld and Ewald are of opinion that it must have been written before the destruction of Jerusalem—accordingly, about A.D. 70. These critics, however (as has been seen), are of opinion that the original work was subjected to several revisions, done in the interest of different religious tendencies: we must, on the contrary, maintain that our Greek Matthew is an essentially correct translation of the original document. The genuineness and authenticity of these discourses of Jesus, so far as the *matter* of it is concerned, is to our mind an unquestionable fact.

As regards the *form*, however, in which these sayings have

been handed down to us, its authenticity may well be called in question. The completeness of the discourse, the accuracy of the connection, the correctness of the arrangement of the sayings, are points on which we may well entertain some doubts. This question requires a more searching investigation.

We have already seen, that although in a large part of the discourse a connected train of thought is discernible, yet there are passages where it is difficult to trace one, as vi. 19 et seqq.; and others where there is none at all, as vii. 1—11. There are, moreover, certain amplifications, in which it may be doubted whether they have not been added merely because they treat of a kindred subject: v. 25, 26, 29, 30, vi. 7—15. And, what is of yet greater importance, a large portion of the Sermon on the Mount is found in St Luke in quite a different connection, and the circumstances are there narrated which are said to have occasioned the words: compare Luke xi. 1, etc., with Matt. vi. 9; Luke xii. 32—34 with Matt. vi. 19—33; Luke xi. 9—13 with Matt. vii. 7—11; Luke viii. 16, 17, with Matt. v. 15; Luke xi. 34, 35, with Matth. vi. 22, 23; Luke xii. 58, 59, with Matt. v. 25, 26; Luke xiii. 24, 25, with Matt. v. 13; Luke xvi. 13 with Matt. vi. 24; Luke xvi. 18 with Matt. v. 32; Mark ix. 50 with Matt. v. 13. It is true that, among the moderns, two theologians have, notwithstanding these phenomena, undertaken to defend the authenticity of the whole discourse in its present form. These are Dr Paulus and Stier. Paulus defends the fragmentary nature of the passage in the beginning of chap. vii. (1—11), on the ground that it is in keeping with the didactic style of the East. He says (exegetisches Handbuch, I. 584): "In order that every one might have something to carry away with him, Jesus concludes with sundry weighty maxims, after the manner of Eastern doctors." Stier also (Reden Jesu, I. S. 254) regards these abrupt transitions as precisely "the correct method of spiritual discourse." Not it would not be easy to prove this, especially when one bears in mind the admirable order and connectedness which characterize the beginning and the close of the discourse. In the time when St Luke was the favourite Evangelist (see above, p. 4), it was regarded as a settled point, that the merit of historical accuracy must be conceded to St Luke; and this one is, at first sight, disposed to admit. A different conclusion, however, appears to result from the critical view of more recent times regarding St Matthew and St Luke. And since men of all parties are now agreed that the Gospel of St Matthew stands in a much nearer relation to Christ than that of the third Evangelist, it was natural to expect that the former, not the latter, would contain the original account. The question must nevertheless be determined by a special investigation of the parallel passages in St Luke. We begin with those passages which coincide most exactly with the sayings of the Sermon on the Mount.

One would most naturally expect to find that some of the disjointed sentences in vii. 1—11 were first taken from St Luke's, especially vii. 6. But to vii. 6 no parallel occurs in Luke; and vii. 1—5 is itself found in St Luke's version of the Sermon on the Mount,—a circumstance which establishes the fact of their authenticity. Matt. vii. 7—11, on the other hand, occurs in St Luke in a totally different connection (xi. 9—13); but we have no guarantee whatever that it is there in its *original* connection. There St Luke, after giving the Lord's Prayer, adds several sayings relating to prayer, introducing the first with εἶπε πρὸς αὐτούς (xi. 5), and the others with κἀγὼ ὑμῖν λέγω (ver. 9): *formulæ* used by him when the subjects are not really connected, but are merely strung together; comp. vi. 27, 39, xii. 4, 8, 15, 22, xxiv. 44. The expression πνεῦμα ἅγιον, however, ver. 13, is decidedly more authentic than the vague ἀγαθά of St Matthew.

In the case of Matt. vi. 19 seqq., the connection with the context is not so apparent; and it might appear as if the passage were taken from Luke xii. 22—34. Almost all the words coincide; we cannot, therefore, suppose that they were repeated on different occasions. In St Luke, the passage occurs in a suitable historical context, being preceded by the discourse on covetousness. Delitzsch, too (in loc. cit. S. 78), has recently expressed a leaning towards the opinion that St Matthew, in order to give a specimen of Christ's manner of teaching, has combined sayings which were originally spoken in other circumstances. Yet, if the opinion that Matthew may, in some cases, have lost the connecting links of the sermon be admitted—as must be granted, at least, in the case of vii. 1—5, on account of its coincidence with the account in St Luke—the *matter* of this passage, at least, will not be found out of connection with what precedes. It had been said that the desire to please God is the only right motive to good works (vi. 1—18): how fitly might the thought be added, that the "righteousness of the kingdom of God"—that is, the fulfilment of the Divine will—is the highest end of life, and the only blessedness of the members of that kingdom! Now, let us examine further the context in St Luke xii. Beginning with ver. 13, it appears that the admonition to beware of covetousness is joined to the request of one of the company about the division of the inheritance, by the loose connecting clause, εἶπε δὲ πρὸς αὐτούς; so, too, the parable, ver. 16, commences with εἶπε δὲ παραβολὴν πρὸς αὐτούς (comp. vi. 39, xviii. 1). Now, these are expressions which one is not apt to use when narrating one continuous discourse. No doubt, ver. 22 proceeds with εἶπε δὲ πρὸς τοὺς μαθητὰς αὐτοῦ; and this might imply, that whereas the preceding remarks had been addressed to the ὄχλοι, He now, continuing the same, addressed Himself to His disciples (comp, xvi. 1 with xv. 3, and x. 23, xvii. 22). But the probability is, that here, too, the formula is intended not to carry on the discourse, but to introduce matter of a kindred nature. Such at least is the import of the εἶπε δὲ πρὸς τ. μαθητάς in chap. xvii. 1, in the opinion of most critics (De Wette, Hilgenfeld, etc). Assuredly, the reference further on, vers. 35 and following, to the παρουσία, cannot have been immediately connected with the preceding passage. Further, St Luke's knowledge of this whole passage is manifestly less accurate than that of the first Evangelist. Then, again, in ver. 32 we have a thought introduced out of all connection with the context. The saying which is introduced at ver. 33 is given by St Luke in a more essentially *Christian* form (comp. above, p. 6). Again, in St Matthew, the whole of the previous admonitions are compressed into one weighty sentence, vi. 33; but St Luke makes the sayings, vers. 19—21, come *after* ver. 33, thereby interrupting the current of the discourse; and ver. 21 in St Matthew, which there occupies so important a position, is torn out of its context by St Luke, and made to form the conclusion of the discourse. Nor is this an accidental instance carefully sought out, but one naturally presenting itself, and one of great importance. On the other hand, it cannot be regarded as an instance of individualization, such as would give a greater claim to authenticity to his narrative, when St Luke, ver. 24, substitutes the ravens for "the fowls of the air" of St Matthew. On the contrary, this individualizing was obviously suggested by those passages of Scripture (Job xxxviii. 41; Ps. cxlvii 9) which speak of the young ravens as the most uncared-for of creatures, because they are forsaken by their parents. Immediately after, St Luke has, πόσῳ μᾶλλον διαφέρετε ὑμεῖς τῶν πετεινῶν.

In the position of the Lord's Prayer, most writers have given the preference to St Luke. Thus Calvin, Schleiermacher, Sieffert, Olshausen, Strauss, Neander; according to Ebrard, it is the one solitary instance in which St Luke's arrangement is preferable. Let us examine this opinion. It must be admitted, that the narrative given by St Luke, without any indication as to the date of its occurrence, of an historical occasion for the Pater noster, is not consistent. We cannot, therefore, form any conclusion as to the time when this incident may have taken place, whether before or after the Sermon on the Mount. That it occurred *after* the sermon, on one of the Apostles addressing the request to our Lord, was pronounced incredible already by Socinus; also by Corrodi (Beiträge zur Bef. des vernünftigen Denkens, ix. S. 68), Eichhorn (Allgemeine Bibliothek, ii. 354). That it occurred *before* the sermon was held to be inadmissible, on the erroneous assumption that Luke here narrates acoluthistically. However this may be, our first question must be, whether by the μαθητής we must understand an Apostle, or whether it may not equally well denote a follower from the wider circle of disciples (Euthymius). If the latter, the difficulty at once vanishes. But let it be an Apostle: why, then, may not Christ have, first of all, taught this prayer to an Apostle in private, and then afterwards imparted it as a pattern of right prayer to all the Apostles and people assembled? Or, granted that this incident occurred at a period later than the Sermon on the Mount, it cannot appear incredible that Christ may have recommended the same short and compendious model to an Apostle requesting Him for a verbal form of prayer. To allege that, in such a case, the Saviour would have directed the Apostle to the prayer which He had already given, is to ignore the obvious fact, that, in general, the evangelical annals report only the leading heads of the discourses of Jesus. All the less, on that account, could it be thought right to banish the Lord's Prayer from the Sermon on the Mount on the supposition that it was not there originally, because, in that case, we should have to deny the historical character alike of the verses which introduce it (7, 8), and of those which follow it (14, 15), which yet bear unmistakeably the impress of authenticity. Neander decides the point somewhat confidently. "It is certain," he says, "that the Pater noster does not belong to the Sermon on the Mount, for that was not the place to discuss the whole doctrine of prayer; on the contrary, prayer and fasting are spoken of there only in a very special relation." But the "whole doctrine of prayer" is *not* discussed there, although a sample of a short and pregnant prayer is given. And was not this the very place to introduce such a form of prayer, when He had just been speaking of the prayers of the hypocrites, which were, doubtless, long and verbose? (Matt. xxiii. 14.) The same view was taken by Strauss, and also by Baur, who even regards the historical narrative given by St Luke as an addition made by himself on reflecting upon the contents of the prayer.

These parallel passages are of most importance. The others either are wanting in connection, which even the acuteness of Schleiermacher, Olshausen, Volkmar, have been unable to prove to exist, or they are repetitions of apophthegms spoken at other times. We may readily admit that certain isolated sayings of Jesus, which were handed down by tradition, may have been joined by tradition to different parts of His discourses. But it is equally indubitable that the occurrence of sayings in different connections must often be regarded as repetitions. We cannot, however, with Bengel and Ebrard, admit this to have been the case with large sections of His discourses, as in Luke xii. 22 *et seqq*. These repetitions of sayings are to be found not only in different Gospels, but often in the same. Thus: "He that hath ears to hear, let him hear," occurs in Matth. xi. 15 and xiii. 9: "The first shall be last," Matt. xix. 30, xx. 6: "Many are called, etc.," Matt. xx. 6, xxii. 14: "If thine eye offend thee, etc.," Matt. v. 30, xviii. 9: "A good tree cannot, etc.," Matt. vii. 18, xii. 33: "No man lighteth a candle, etc.," Luke viii. 16, xi. 33: "There is nothing hid, etc.," Luke viii. 17, xii. 2. Similarly, we find certain of the fundamental truths of the Evangelists thus repeated: "Except ye become as little children, etc.," Matt. xviii. 3, xix. 14. "He that taketh not his cross, etc.," Matt. x. 38, xiv. 24. "The Son of Man is come to save that which was lost," Matt. xviii. 11, ix. 13: Luke xix. 10.

"If ye have faith, etc.," Matt. xvii. 20, xxi. 21. "He who findeth his life," Matt. x. 39; Luke xvii. 33; John xii. 25. "The servant is not greater than his master:" this saying occurs in St John twice, and the second time with express reference to the first, John xiii. 16, xv. 20; Matt. x. 24; Luke vi. 40. Similar references occur elsewhere in St John, x. 26, xiii. 33.

Our conclusion is, accordingly, that the arrangement of the sayings of our Lord given by St Matthew, in his account of the Sermon on the Mount, is in the main correct. This result will be further confirmed by an investigation in the other longer discourses of our Lord, as reported by that Evangelist. In Matt. xxiii. we find a considerable portion of a discourse which is historically connected with His conversation at the Pharisee's table, related in Luke xi. 38. No doubt it is St Luke who here gives the occasion of this conversation (vers. 39—46): on the other hand, vers. 47 foll. seem to show that the time was later than St Luke puts it; for these words accord best with the last period of Christ's life, when He had entirely broken with the rulers of the people, when also the other isolated denunciatory discourses and parables were spoken. St Mark and St Luke give the same time as the occasion of a longer discourse, addressed to the people and the disciples at the conclusion of His ministry (Mark xii. 38 foll.; Luke xx. 45 foll.): and the account which these Evangelists give of it is evidently a mere fragment. Christ's discourse in Matthew has, like the Sermon on the Mount, an exordium, and the 49th and following verses in St Luke occur in St Matthew (xxiii. 34 f.)—whose narrative is here also more correct in *form*—as a vigorous peroration: whereas in St Luke, ver. 52, out of all connection, comes dragging after. Let it be further considered that the closing words in St Matthew (vers. 37—39) occur in St Luke at chap. xiii. 34, 35, and there certainly in the wrong place: because they do not fit in with the departure from Galilee, but were spoken as He took a final farewell of the temple, as the mention of the temple, Matt. xxiii. 38, shows.[1] The prophetic denunciation,

---

[1] In this very speech there occur some important differences in form (compare in Luke, vers. 39, 40, 44, 48—52): now a closer investigation will lead to the conclusion, that in all these passages, with the exception of vers. 39, 40 in St Luke, the narrative of St Matthew has greater claim to originality.

with its energetic conclusion (Matt. vers. 34—36), resolves itself at last, in a manner the most impressive, into a solemn, sad apostrophe.

If we turn to the discourse of instruction addressed to the Apostles (Matt. x.), the case cannot be so clearly made out in favour in St Matthew. The whole discourse, with the exception of only a few verses, consists of sayings which are to be found in Luke and Mark in other connections. Besides, attempts have been made to show, from the subject-matter of vers. 15—23, that Christ cannot then have delivered this speech in the shape in which it here lies before us. The Saviour speaks here, vers. 17—23, not only of persecutions, but even of the preaching of the Gospel to the heathen, in opposition to what is stated at ver. 5. Further, He promises (ver. 23) His speedy return. Now such sayings, it would appear, could not form part of a discourse at the first sending forth of the disciples, but must have occurred in an address on their missionary work at some later period. We find, indeed, very similar expressions used on the occasion of a later sending-forth of the disciples, Luke xxi. 12—19; Mark xiii. 9—13. Then, too, even according to Luke, one similar expression was used on an earlier occasion; comp. Luke xii. 11, 12, with Matt. x. 19. And moreover the saying there, Luke xii. 11, 12, occurs in a speech in which the contents of Matt. x. 26—33 are also to be found (comp. Luke xii. 1—9). Nay, Matthew too has something similar to this in chap. xxiv. 9, 13, with reference to the persecutions and to the work among the heathen. If these similar expressions on these subjects occur in Matthew and in Luke at two different places, must we not conclude that Christ expressed Himself similarly on two different occasions? Is it not probable that two sets of sayings on this subject were in existence, one of them from the earlier, the other from a later period? This granted, there remains the question, whether those sayings in Luke xii. 1—12, which coincide with those in Matt. x., are in their right place in the former or in the latter passage? Schleiermacher here gives the decided preference to St Luke, while Neander holds that isolated sayings have been transferred from one discourse to the other. It is difficult to decide with certainty. The following considerations, however, appear to speak in favour of St Matthew. First of all, it must be acknowledged that the discourse on the occasion of the sending of the Apostles cannot have been so short as St Luke (ix. 1 ff.) and St Mark (vi. 7) make it: so far we must incline to ascribe greater authenticity to St Matthew. Further, we find here again, in Luke xii. 4, as it appears, a formula serving for conjunction: λέγω δὲ ὑμῖν τοῖς φίλοις μου. Again, ver. 25 in St Matthew is in its proper place, whereas in St Luke it occurs vi. 40. Finally, the form of the expression in ver. 27 in Matthew, seems more authentic than that in Luke ver. 3. And as for the mission to the heathen, it could not surprise us to find that many things were spoken on the occasion of the first sending which had reference to a future mission. For already, in the Sermon on the Mount, He had spoken of the persecutions of the world, and had called the Apostles the Light of the whole human race; and in the same way, in Matt. viii. 11, 12, had alluded to the rejection of the Jews and the calling of the heathen.

Accordingly, the judgment of the most recent criticism (after the example of Er. Schmid, already quoted, on Luke vi. 18) has agreed to ascribe greater authenticity to St Matthew, also with reference to those apparently historical parallel passages in St Luke. De Wette (on Matt. v. S. 57, 3 Aufl.) remarks: "If the parallel passages in Luke corresponded to those passages in the sermon which are least connected (Matt. vi. 19—vii. 12), that opinion would appear very admissible. But it so happens that St Luke has in his sermon a great deal of the unconnected parts (Matt. vii. 1—5, 12, 16—21; in Luke vi. 37 f., 41 f., 31, 43—46), nay, he adds foreign matter (vi. 39, 40, comp. Matt. xv. 14, x. 24); so that, despite the want of connection, we see ourselves compelled to admit the authenticity of that very part of the discourse (in Matt.) which at first we were disposed to sacrifice. Now, as part of the parallel passages in Luke in nowise commend themselves by fitting connection and occasion, while their position in Matthew is very appropriate (comp. Luke viii. 16, xi. 33, with Matt. v. 15; Luke xvi. 17 with Matt. v. 18; Luke xii. 58 f. with Matt. v. 24 f.; Luke xvi. 18 with Matt. v. 32); as, further, other portions of these parallels are in Luke not less isolated than in Matthew, or at least occur in not better or more necessary connection, or again appear altered in his version (Luke xiv. 34, comp. Matt. v. 13;

Luke xi. 34—36, comp. Matt. vi. 22 f.; Luke xvi. 13, comp. Matt. vi. 24; Luke xiii. 24, comp. Matt. vii. 13; Luke xiii. 25—27, comp. Matt. vii. 22 f.; Luke xii. 33 f., comp. Matt. vi. 19—21); on these grounds, we cannot, for the sake of those passages to which Luke certainly gives the advantage of a better occasion (such as Luke xii. 22—31, comp. Matt. vi. 25—34; Luke xi. 1 f., comp. Matt. vi. 9 f.; Luke xi. 9—13, comp. Matt. vii. 7—11),—we cannot, on account of these passages, acquiesce in the opinion expressed above. All we can admit is, that St Matthew has perhaps amplified the discourse somewhat. The fact, that certain things in the sayings of Jesus occur more than once, may, however, be well explained on the hypothesis that He spoke many things on more than one occasion, which, in some cases,—as, for instance, in the case of such subjects as divorce (Matt. v. 32, comp. xix. 9), and the model-prayer (Matt. vi. 9 f., comp. Luke xi. 1 f.),—appears far from improbable." The conclusions of Meyer (3 A. S. 170) are essentially the same. "The most of the parallel passages in Luke," he says, "occur in such a connection, that to allow them a superior claim to authenticity is impossible. In his version, either they are introduced less suitably, or else they are of such a nature that we may easily believe the special saying to have been spoken by our Lord on different occasions."

How, then, are we to explain this erroneous arrangement on the part of St Luke? The answer to this question is determined by the view taken of the origin of these Gospels. If the discourses of our Lord have been preserved more perfectly by the one Evangelist than by the other, then many of His sayings must have become detached from their original connection,—some of them having been handed down by tradition as isolated utterances, and others having become attached to one or other of His longer discourses. The author of the third Gospel we regard, with Ewald, in accordance with the tradition, as having been the companion of St Paul. According, then, as we suppose him to have been more or less independent in composing his work, we shall have to ascribe this erroneous arrangement to himself, or to the traditions, oral or written, from which he derived his information. From the sources of his Gospel, we must, with Ewald, expressly exclude the Gospel of Matthew: this he cannot have had before him when composing his Gospel. This is evident, among other things, from his imperfect account of this Sermon on the Mount, and from the way in which he breaks up its sayings into mere fragments. To affirm that St Luke has cut into shreds and fragments the perfect web of the discourse, from a mere "fancy for the disconnected and abrupt" (De Wette, Einleitung, 5 A. § 91 c.), in order, as Ewald says (Jahrb. 1849, S. 223), "not to fatigue the readers too much," is gratuitously to ascribe to the author a want of taste, which ill accords with his method in the Acts of the Apostles—a book which even the most recent critics agree to regard as the work of the same writer.[1] The sources from which St Luke drew, appear to have been written. This we gather, partly from his own statement, chap. i. 2, partly from certain recognisable joinings of separate paragraphs, and partly from the Hebraistic character of the language. Yet to some extent the editor retained his independence. This is seen from certain peculiar idioms, occurring not only in the Gospel, but also in the Acts (comp. Zeller, theolog. Jahrb. 1851, S. 256). It is also shown by the circumstance, already referred to, and which is of especial moment in this inquiry, that similar forms of combination occur in different parts of the Gospel, which the writer uses to join together isolated passages whose real connection he did not know. Are we then to refer that erroneous arrangement to the documents used, or to the evangelistic editor who used them? Now, the phenomena which characterize his account of the Sermon on the Mount seem to forbid the former course. The most striking of the parallel passages are precisely those which occur in that original document, which, by universal admission, is peculiar to St Luke, viz., chap. ix. 51—xviii. 14. Now, would it not be a most marvellous play of accident, if, in those sources from which the Evangelist took his Sermon on the Mount, precisely *those* sections were left out, which, in the independent diegesis of Luke

---

[1] We add one more instance, taken from St Luke's account of the Sermon on the Mount, out of many which might be quoted. If the third Evangelist had had before him, as he wrote, St Matthew's Gospel, what in all the world could have induced him to take the saying in Matt. x. 24, "The disciple is not above his master, etc.," out of the admirable connection in which it there stands, and introduce it so promiscuously into the Sermon on the Mount at chap. vi. 40?

ix. 51, etc., are given in quite a different connection? On the other hand, the difficulty will disappear, if we suppose that the Evangelist himself introduced into his narrative of the journey (to Jerusalem) those sayings which had either come to him singly, or had been derived by him from other sources.

Ewald, with all the assurance of a diviner, says that St Luke based his Gospel on no fewer than seven documents, and from these he expressly excludes the Gospel by Matthew. In direct antagonism to his theory, Baur maintains that he made use of St Matthew alone, and explains the discrepancies solely on the ground of his doctrinal tendency. If, however, we inquire concerning the reason which that acute critic adduces why St Luke should have so cut up into fragments St Matthew's Sermon on the Mount—the historical motive for this procedure is supposed to have been merely to give an unhistorical framework to the sayings—we shall find that the answer he gives is one which, if no dogmatical interest can be proved to have influenced St Luke, can by no possibility appear valid to any one but the critic himself. For, according to Baur (in loc. cit. S. 472), Luke ix. 51 is the beginning of the second division of his Gospel, in which the author borrows all his historical materials from Matthew, but gives them an entirely new and peculiar application, and "transplants them, so to speak, out of the soil of Jewish Christianity into that of Pauline Christianity." In this part we are to own the existence of on ardent endeavour on the part of the Evangelist "to make this part of his Gospel the very centre and kernel of the evangelistic history." "And we are especially to notice," he goes on, "how the Evangelist proceeds in carrying out this object. In the first part, he was very sparing in his account of the Sermon on the Mount; but, in the second part, he has taken pains to reproduce the portions of the sermon which he had not yet introduced, and, as occasion offered, to make use of the sayings contained in the sermon in Matthew." And so the sole object of the author, in introducing a number of the sayings of the Sermon on the Mount into the second part of his history, in which he sought to bring in Pauline doctrines, was to gain lectores benevolos for his Paulinistic Gospel! The idea is incredible. And Baur's followers, Koestlin (in loc. S. 141) and Hilgenfeld (in loc. S. 202), have accordingly admitted that, besides the dogmatical use of Matthew, St Luke must have availed himself of other original documents.

But although, with respect to the parallel passages in St Luke, the preference of originality must be accorded to St Matthew, it by no means follows that the latter has given us, throughout, the discourse of Christ as originally delivered. There are, indeed, as has been shown, but few passages (such as chap. v. 29, and possibly vi. 19 f., vii. 6) where there is occasion to suspect an inappropriate interpolation. But the question is not, whether these insertions be many or few, but, whether it is possible that they may exist at all; and that this is partially the case, the discourses in chap. x. and xxiii. seem to show. Now Schnekenburger is of opinion, that to admit this, is to give up the fact that the Evangelist was an ear-witness of the sermon; and Stier even affirms that the admission involves a denial of his apostolic character. "It is impossible," says the former, "that an eye- and ear-witness could, on *any* ground, have introduced entirely foreign elements into the discourse, and could have worked them into a chronologically connected whole." Stier, however, pronounces this peremptory judgment: "We cannot conceive that St Matthew could have wrought up sayings of our Lord, uttered at various times, into one connected whole, as if they had been spoken at one time; for, as the apostolical humility of his own spirit was incapable of such an impropriety, so neither was it possible that the Holy Ghost should guide and instruct him to record any untruth whatsoever for the Church."[1] Both opinions are right, if we are to admit what it is utterly impossible to admit, viz., that the Lord's Apostles and ear-witnesses of His sayings could have attached the same importance to inaccuracies of form as the critics and dogmaticans of a later age have done. That the reverse is the case, is proved by every historical book of the Old and New Testament, and especially by the formal construction of the first Gospel.

[1] Stier, Words of the Lord Jesus, translated by Pope, i. 92. Reden Jesu i. S. 70.

§ 5. RELATION OF THE SERMON ON THE MOUNT TO THE EVANGELICAL DOCTRINE OF SALVATION.

The sermon seems the counterpart of the lawgiving on Mount Sinai. It sets forth the law of Moses in a wider and deeper aspect. At its close, vii. 24—26, it makes the salvation of man depend not on πιστεύειν, but on ποιεῖν. It therefore bears what St Paul, Rom. x. 5 f., indicates as the characteristic features of the law: command, with promise and threatening. This gives occasion to an inquiry concerning the position in which this portion of the Gospel-record stands to the Christian doctrine of salvation.

The Fathers regarded the Sermon on the Mount as, for the most part, simply an amplification of the Mosaic law. Irenæus c. hær. l. 4, c. 13: dominus naturalia legis non dissolvit, sed extendit et implevit; and l. 4, c. 28: quemadmodum in N. T. *fides* hominum aucta est, ita et *diligentia conversationis,* cum non solum a malis operibus abstinere jubemur, sed ab ipsis cogitationibus. Tert. de pœnitentia, c. 3: quemadmodum dominus se *adjectionem* legi superstruere demonstrat, nisi voluntatis interdicendo delicta (and here he adverts to Matt. v.). Jerome: ea quæ ante propter infirmitatem audientium rudia et imperfecta fuerant, sua prædicatione complevit, iram tollens et vicem talionis excludens et occultam in mente concupiscentiam (on Matt. v. 17, opp., ed. Ven. T. vii.).[1] So, too, the great proportion of Roman Catholic writers, among whom Maldonatus expressly characterizes the opposite notion as *heretical.* The Council of Trent, too, declares (Sessio 6, can. 21), that he who teaches Christum Jesum a Deo hominibus datum esse ut redemptorem, cui fidant, non etiam ut legislatorem cui obediant, anathema sit. On the legal view of Christianity, Rationalism is at one with Roman Catholicism. Accordingly the Socinians, the forerunners of Rationalism, side with the Roman Catholic expositors on this subject.[2] They both lay stress upon the ἐγὼ δὲ λέγω,

---

[1] He justifies himself on account of this subordinating of the law against the reproach of Manicheeism made by the moralizing Pelagians (c. Pelag., l. i. c. 31).

[2] Przipcovius remarks on chap. vii. 24, that it follows from this verse, that the belief in obscure mysterious doctrines is a matter of much less importance than the practice of the great moral truths.

which, they say, corresponds to the ἐῤῥέϑη by Moses: so, too, **the Arminians Limborch, Grotius: naturalia legis perfecit Christus,** *præceptis quibusdam exactioribus muniens.* At the beginning of the Rationalistic period, the legal view of **the** Sermon on the Mount became more general also in the Lutheran Church. So far back as 1759, Chr. Crusius laments over this (probatio quod scopus hom. montanæ sit evangelicus neutiquam legalis, p. 2). In the further development of Rationalism, **the** ground it took was most plainly indicated by its preference of **the Epistle of St James to those of St Paul, and of the Sermon on the Mount to the Gospel of St John.** But in this onesided preference, Rationalism had also been preceded by Socinianism. Przipcovius says, in the Introduction to the Sermon on the Mount (cogitationes in ev. Matt.): tria ista capita eximiam sanctæ scripturæ partem et perfectissimam doctrinæ Christi et officiorum atque monitorum nobis præscriptorum descriptionem continent, ita ut, si quo casu reliquæ partes periissent, ex hac una rationem officii nostri plurissime explicati discere licuerit.

It is the fundamental doctrine of the Reformation, that the true light in which the Gospel of Christ is to be regarded, is not as a commanding law, but as a *fulfilled promise.* "Not in merits, sacrifices, and vows"—so speaks the Magus of the North (Hamann, Schriften, vii. S. 58)—"which God requires of man, does the Christian godliness consist; not—but in promises, fulfilments, and acts of self-sacrifice, which God, for the sake of man, has performed and accomplished. Not in the noblest and greatest command which He has enjoined; **but** in the highest blessedness which He has bestowed. **Not in law** and morals, which concern only human dispositions **and human** actions; but in the achievement of **Divine works and deeds for** the salvation of the whole world."

If now we inquire concerning the office which determines the peculiar position which Christ holds towards the **human** race, we shall certainly conclude that it is not that of a lawgiver. Yet the question may arise, whether this may not also form a part of His office, and whether, especially in the Sermon on the Mount, **He does** not appear in this character. Only relatively has an affirmative answer been opposed by the Protestant theology. It denied, 1st, that the Sermon on the Mount forms a counterpart to the Mosaic lawgiving, and affirmed that the former is only the true spiritual interpretation of the latter (comp. especially Vesperæ Groninginæ, Amst. 1698, p. 108 seqq.). 2d, It admitted that Christ has also given laws to the members of His kingdom, and that some of these laws are to be regarded as new, in so far as the law had previously failed to give them their right interpretation; but it denied that, by fulfilling these laws, man can earn blessedness, and that they are able to cause anything more than a knowledge of sin. Thus they applied to the Sermon on the Mount that pædagogical purpose, as a schoolmaster to bring men to Christ, which St Paul ascribes to the Mosaic law (Gal. iii. 24). Hunnius: "nunc ad legis explicationem se accingit Dominus, quam ideo declarandum sibi sumit, ut exquisitissima perfectione legis cognita, homines propriæ suæ justitiæ fiduciam a se abjiciant." 3d, It denied that the $\pi o \iota \epsilon \tilde{\iota} \nu$, in chap. vii. 24—26, refers merely to the fulfilment of the moral law, and affirmed that it refers also to the $\vartheta \epsilon \lambda \eta \mu \alpha \ \tau o \tilde{v} \ \Theta \epsilon o \tilde{v}$ in its highest aspect—that is, to *faith;* John vi. 40.[1] (Zwingli,[2] Calv., the auctor op. imp., Chemnitz, Calov on Luke vi. 46, Chr. Crusius, in loc. cit. Even in vers. 10 and 20, Calov understood the $\delta \iota \varkappa \alpha \iota o \sigma \acute{v} \nu \eta$ to mean the justitia imputata.) The history and illustration of this controversy are given at lenght by Cotta, in Gerhard's Locis Theolog. T. vi. S. 146 f. See also a biblical and dogmatical work by Theodosius Harnack (entitled Jesus der Christ, oder der Erfueller des Gesetzes und der Propheten, Elberfeld 1842), which contains, on the whole, a correct statement of most of the points in question, although there is a want of definite antithesis against those erroneous views which have become historical, and also of adequate dogmatical insight.

Let us examine these conclusions of the older Protestant theology. The *first* has been pretty generally admitted in modern times. Chap. v. 20, as amplified and carried out in the following verses, shows, that what the Saviour opposed was not the Mosaic law, but the false view of that law taken by the Pharisees: the more immediate explanation of that saying, in

---

[1] Bengel acutely compares Matt. xxi 31.

[2] Facere voluntatem Dei discipulum Christi indicat. Qui intus pius est et fructibus fidem prodit, hic vere Christianus est. Quæ sine his fiunt, hypocrisis sunt. Facere vero voluntatem Dei patris, est credere in eum quem misit ipse Joh. vi.

v. 21, must however be compared. The *second* conclusion is also right: it seems, however, opposed by the threatening pronounced against the violation of the law. To this it was indeed answered, that, as generally, the Saviour here speaks more legally, this threatening might also be understood only hypothetically, viz., to indicate how, apart from the Gospel, God would deal even with believers. (Hunnius thes. ev. p. 54; Balduin, qu. 9 on Rom. ii.) But it may be asked, if those who were condemned by the law have had the way of salvation opened to them by Christ, how is it that here there is no mention whatever made of that way? Now the *third* assertion declares that there *is* some allusion to it, if only an indirect one: but it does so in opposition to the context of the verse, and also to the view taken of it in Luke vi. 46. In v. 20 a higher righteousness was required; what that righteousness was to consist in, is shown in the following verses: the fruits required in vii. 16, are to be the outward manifestations of true religion. And if we are to explain the $\vartheta\acute{\epsilon}\lambda\eta\mu\alpha$ $\tau o\tilde{v}$ $\Theta\epsilon o\tilde{v}$ in accordance with the words in St Luke: $\tau\acute{\iota}$ $\delta\acute{\epsilon}$ $\mu\epsilon$ $\varkappa\alpha\lambda\epsilon\tilde{\iota}\tau\epsilon$, $\varkappa\acute{v}\varrho\iota\epsilon$, $\varkappa\acute{v}\varrho\iota\epsilon\cdot$ $\varkappa\alpha\grave{\iota}$ $o\grave{v}$ $\pi o\iota\epsilon\tilde{\iota}\tau\epsilon$ $\tilde{\alpha}$ $\lambda\acute{\epsilon}\gamma\omega$; then this $\vartheta\acute{\epsilon}\lambda\eta\mu\alpha$ must mean that will of God which demands the practical fulfilment of the Divine law. (Compare also Matt. xii. 50.) Besides, the idea, that men shall be judged according to their works, is to be found in other sayings of Christ: Matt. xvi. 27; John v. 29; and especially in the discourse on the judgment, Matt. xxv. 31 ff.,—which some, indeed (Keil, Olsh.), have supposed to indicate the judgment on the *heathen* for their behaviour towards suffering Christians; a view, however, inconsistent with the 34th verse, which shows that the discourse refers to *Christians* only. To seek to isolate from this, and other sayings of our Lord, the truth, that believers are to be judged according to their works, must be but lost labour; since even the Apostle, who most distinctly teaches the doctrine of justifying faith, gives expression to this same truth, Rom. ii. 12, 13, xiv. 10; 2 Cor. v. 10. Hence, too, it must appear a work of supererogation in Olshausen, to attempt, by laying stress on certain expressions in the end of Matt. vii., to prove that the words of Christ respecting works presuppose faith as the basis of these works; and to argue that Christ Himself, and faith in Him, are there pointed out as the foundation of the house; and that what is said in ver. 23, regarding the being known by Christ, is spoken with reference to fellowship with Him, and to the new birth. With greater truth, certain of the older writers (as Calvin, Bengel, Scultetus) have determined that the intention of our Lord, in speaking of the judgment according to works, was to bring out forcibly the contrast between true religion and a religion of mere externals. Infidelitas (observes Bengel, although with a somewhat different application, on chap. vii. 23) proprie damnat, et tamen in judicio magis allegatur lex, c. xxv. 35, 42, Rom. ii. 12, quia reprobi ne tum quidem, quum Jesum Christum cernent, fidei rationes perspicient. Scultetus begins his treatise in the exercitt. Sacræ (l. ii. c. 19) with the words: Non sine stomacho sæpe audivi homiliastas nostros in explicatione versus vigesimi c. v. excurrere in declamationem de justitia *fidei;* and he concludes: ergo justitia superabundans non est justitia fidei opposita justitiæ legis, sed *justitia legis* opposita justitiæ *hypocriticæ Pharisæorum.* So too Stier: "Here is shown the test of true or false profession and life; and not all who have said, 'Lord, Lord,' and done many wonderful things, stand in the judgment. The *fruits* of the grace so freely and graciously offered in the beginning, are inexorably demanded; the one lawgiver, who wills that every man should submit to judgment, and judge himself in order to salvation, appears also as the condemner of all to whom He has not become a Saviour: James iv. 12."[1] Most certainly it is not as merita that those works have any worth in the judgment, but only as documenta fidei. But the measure of the $σωτηρία$ is determined by those manifestations of faith, and will not the degree of the perfection of the former be determined by the latter? This now is admitted, and accordingly different gradations of blessedness are distinguished. One thing, indeed, will be the common inheritance of all the saved, the bona substantialia, that is, the visio essentiæ Dei and the fruitio beatitudinis: the difference will consist in different degrees of the gloria.

If, then, faith is the condition of participation in blessedness; if it is faith indeed which becomes sight; and if the manifestation and exponent of faith is works, according to their quality and quantity; why may not the difference in works determine the difference in the degree of participation in the vision of God,— the difference, too, in the measure of joy and blessedness? And

---

[1] Stier, Words, etc., Pope's trans., i. 97 (Reden, i. 76).

Calov has accordingly made the difference to consist in the measure of fruitio (Syst. Theol. xvi. p. 337). We could not then deny that even believers may inherit a partial unblessedness. This is a point on which our doctrine requires further elaboration.[1]

But although the older theology, by its view of the Sermon as a concio legalis, has not succeeded in solving the difficulty alluded to, it must be owned that it has approached nearer to a correct solution than many another answer proposed to this question of the relation of the Sermon to the doctrine of salvation. Thus, for instance, Hess has written a treatise on the subject (entitled Ueber das Verhältniss der Bergpredigt zur evangelischen Begnadigungslehre, Flatt's Magazin für Dogmatik u. Moral, St 5, 6), in which he is satisfied with the conclusion, that here the Christian doctrine is not stated indeed, but at least the way is paved for it by the removal of the obstructions of pharasaic formalism. When that older view affirms that the Apostle, in passages like those referred to, or Christ in the passages before us, speaks only more legally, *i. e.*, hypothetically (meaning to point out how God would judge, supposing the Gospel not to exist), such an answer is no doubt unsatisfactory. These words of threatening, it is plain, can be no idle words. Yet the view contained an element of truth; for it was based upon the correct belief, that that ancient word of the law, "My judgments, which if a man do, he shall live in them," Lev. xviii. 5, was not abolished by the new covenant, but still forms part of it (Rom. iii. 31, $\dot{\alpha}\lambda\lambda\grave{\alpha}\ \nu\acute{o}\mu o\nu\ \dot{\iota}\sigma\tau\acute{\alpha}\nu o\mu\varepsilon\nu$). If perfect blessedness and perfect communion with God mean the same thing, then perfect blessedness must consist in the perfect fulfilment of the moral commands of God. Now, it is faith in the Redeemer which constitutes the living fountain from which obedience to the will of God flows (Rom. viii. 4; Eph. ii. 10). Accordingly, when faith attains its highest degree and becomes sight, it will necessarily manifest itself in perfect harmony of the human will with the Divine; hence in the perfect fulfilment of the Divine law. In the day of the Lord, believers will appear before God as $\dot{\alpha}\nu\acute{\varepsilon}\gamma\varkappa\lambda\eta\tau o\iota$, as $\dot{o}\lambda\acute{o}\varkappa\lambda\eta\rho o\iota$

---

[1] Compare the essay, "Wie ist das Gericht der Gläubigen nach den Werken mit der vollkommenen Rechtfertigung durch den Glauben zu vereinigen?" Lit. Anz. 1848, n. 38; and Tholuck's Commentar zum Roemerbrief, 5 A., on chap. ii. 6.

(1 Cor. i. 8; 1 Thess. v. 23; Phil i. 6). Referring to this, Hunnius and Calov remark (on 1 Cor. i. 8): "et tandem in die Domini erunt omni ex parte irreprehensibiles, induti jam perfectissimo inhærentis justitiæ habitu."

Now it is from this point of view that we are to determine upon the dependence of blessedness on the condition of perfect obedience to the law, as set forth in the Sermon on the Mount. Doubtless faith in Christ is the means whereby the δικαιοσύνη demanded of us is to be attained; but it is a means which here, as elsewhere, is only partially alluded to by Christ. And the reason was, that His whole ministry was simply of a preparatory character. As Delitzsch says (in loc. S. 75): "This χάρις is, however, veiled here; for only on the completion of the work of redemption was it to be unveiled. The Preacher of the Sermon on the Mount is Himself this χάρις in person. But the relation in which His person and His work stand to that δικαιοσύνη, He here only alludes to, and does not state distinctly." True, the means by which the righteousness was to come, is only alluded to here, but it *is* alluded to in an unmistakeable manner. In those beatitudes which speak of the feeling of spiritual poverty, of hunger and thirst after righteousness, do we not already recognise that Preacher of the Gospel of whom it is said (Matt. xii. 20) that He would not break the bruised reed, or quench the smoking flax, and who (Matt. xi. 29, 30) invites men to Himself, because His yoke is easy, His burden light? If now, on the other hand, He requires, v. 20, a righteousness beyond that of the Scribes and Pharisees, how is this to be reconciled with the other?—how, but by the knowledge that through faith in Him strength is given to fulfil what He requires? "It is certainly not to be denied that Jesus possessed the conciousness of a power of redemption and reconciliation which was to flow through Him. When, in Matth. v. 6, He promises to satisfy them who hunger after righteousness, and in xi. 29, 30, of an ἀνάπαυσις ταῖς ψυχαῖς, of a ζυγὸς χρηστός and φορτίον ἐλαφρόν, He expresses this consciousness." (Plank, in Treatise Judenthum und Urchristenthum, Zeller theol. Jahrb. 1847, S. 278.) From this it follows, that in the words ἦλθον πληρῶσαι more is implied than the mere intimation that He came to impart to the law a deeper theoretical meaning. He could not at His first appearance (Luke iv. 18) have called His doctrine an εὐαγγέλιον, a joyful message for the πτωχοί; He could not have designated His coming as an ἐνιαυτὸς κυρίου δεκτός, as the fulfilment of all the Messianic expectations, had He come only to increase the demands of the law, without also giving an increased measure of strength. If we must believe that He knew that the Messianic promises were to find their fulfilment in Him, then that πλήρωσις νόμου, which He was to accomplish, must have had involved in it a *promise* also.

§ 6. EXEGETICAL LITERATURE.

I. THE FATHERS.—From the Greek Church, the Homilies of St Chrysostom on St. Matthew (ed. Montfauc. T. vii.). They are characterized by careful consideration of text and context, most sound historical exposition, and able application; yet on many points the judgment is wavering or mistaken. Those among the ancients who have constructed epitomes of the Sermon are Theophylact and Euthymius Zigabenus. Expositions of single passages are to be found in the exegetical letters of Isidorus of Pelusium.—In the Latin Church, Hilarius Pictaviensis (in Matt. T. ii. ed. Veron.). As a follower of Origen, he is often mystical and allegorical; on some passages his remarks are accurate and striking. St Jerome (in Matt. ed. Ven. T. vi. p. 1). He is frequently terse and striking; but his criticism is often wavering, and he fails to apprehend the exact shade of thought. St Augustin, de sermone Domini in monte (T. iii. ed Bened.); although not unfrequently erroneous in his interpretation, is yet acute and able. The work of the as yet unknown *auctor operis imperfecti,* who flourished in the time of Theodosius, is to be found among the writings of St Chrysostom (T. vi.), to whom it was at first ascribed. Originally written in Latin, it expounds merely the Latin translation.[1] The author, who was an Arian, has many curious and fanciful explanations, but always characterized by intelligence. Erasmus rightly calls him facundus and eruditus. Finally, rich exegetical contri-

---

[1] On Matt. v. 3, he suggests the question why the word used is mendici and not humilis. His answer is peculiar: ut non solum humiles ostendat, sed etiam indigentes humiles, qui sic sunt humiles *ut semper adjutorium Dei* sint mendicantes. But in the Greek, the word used is not the word corresponding to mendicus, which is προσαίτης.

butions are to be gathered from the letters of Augustine and Jerome.

II. ROMAN CATHOLIC EXPOSITORS UP TO THE 18TH CENTURY.—The Glossa ordinaria by Walafrid Strabo (Opera, Paris 1852), the catena of Thom. Aquinas and Nic. Lyra, are based upon the commentaries of the Fathers, especially St Augustine. In the dark times which preceded, Druthmar deserves to be mentioned with distinction (in Matt., c. 840, bibliotheca maxima Patrum, vol. xxv.): an exegetist who knew Greek. He recognises the importance of *historical* exposition; concise, occasionally original. Radbertus (*ob.* 851, bibl. max. Patrum, vol. xiv.): of allegorizing tendencies; well read in the writings of his predecessors.[1] Erasmus, Annotations on Matthew (critici Sacri N. T.); serviceable philological contributions to the exposition of the text. Maldonatus (*ob.* 1583), Commentarii in quatuor Evangelia, Mussiponti 1596 (cited by Martin, 1852); rich in patristic learning, in ability and exegetical insight.—The most distinguished of the Catholic commentators on St Paul's Epistles is Este: his commentary on St Matthew is, however, short; annot. in difficiliora S. S. loca, 1621. Corn. Jansenius, comm. in harmoniam Evv., Lugd. 1589: not without judgment, yet fettered by his theological opinions. A Lapide, comm. in 4 Evv., Antwerp 1670: dependent on his predecessors, without insight, dogmatically restricted.—For a collection of commentaries, chiefly Jesuitical, vide in biblia magna, de la Haye 1643.

III. EXPOSITORS OF THE LUTHERAN CHURCH IN THE 16TH AND 17TH CENTURIES.—Luther's Commentary on the Sermon on the Mount (in Walch, vol. vii.), despite its manifold digressions and frequent misapprehensions of the exact meaning of a word, must nevertheless, on account of its correct ap-

---

[1] Remarkable is the testimony which Druthmar gives to the historical exposition, and the way in which Radbertus laments the want of historical helps. Druthmar says: Studui plus historicum sensum sequi quam spiritualem ... cum historia fundamentum omnis intelligentiæ sit et ipsa primitus quærenda et amplexanda et *sine ipsa ad aliam non possit transiri*. Radbert complains (l. 2. S. 357): velim perpendant nostri, quantos et quales Græcorum facundia in hoc eodem opere habent tractatores, et tunc potuerint dignoscere, quibus latina paupertas egeat documentis, quia profecto in manus nostras vix perpauca priorum venerunt commenta.

prehension and popular exposition of the thought, be regarded as a masterpiece. Melanchthon's adnotationes in ev. Mtth., 1523, are merely fugitive notes of college lectures, edited against the author's will. The Conciones explicantes integrum ev. Mtth., 1558, in the 3d vol. of the Wittenberg edition (ed. Bretschneider, T. xiv.), are sermons by Froeschel, the materials of which had been prepared by Melanchthon, partly in excursus, partly in entire sermons.—From the 16th century we have the works of Joach. Camerarius, Erasmus Sarcerius, Martin Chemnitz, and Aeg. Hunnius. Sarcerius' scholia in Mtth. (1538) are brief paraphrases of the sense without criticism of the text. Camerarius, notatio figurarum, etc. (1572): notes almost exclusively philological, with scarcely any value now. Hunnius (*ob.* 1603) in Mtth., 1608, in the thesaurus evangelicus, 1706: chiefly traditionally doctrinal.—The principal exegetical work on the Gospels is the harmonia evangelica, Hamb. 1704, 3 voll. fol., published under the name of Chemnitz. Only the first seven chapter of the work, however, are from his pen. The work was continued by Polycarp Lyser, and after his death, with equal ability and learning, brought to a conclusion by Joh. Gerhard. Up to the present time it is the only *elaborate* commentary on the first three Gospels. In this work, the previous expositions are carefully used; the whole compass of Scripture is brought to the elucidation of the separate passages; the exegesis is handled not without a certain freedom from doctrinal and traditional prejudice; philological criticism is more attended to than had formerly been the case in the Lutheran Church; as regards form, however, there is a great want of conciseness.

In the 17th century, Joh. Gerhard, annot. posthumæ in ev. Mtth., ed. Ern. Gerhard, 1663: these are college lectures. Calixt, Concordia evv., 1663, opus posthumum: a short commentary, chiefly in accordance with the traditional Lutheran exposition. Er. Schmid (*ob.* 1637), notæ et animadversiones in N. T. (opus posthumum), 1658: chiefly a philological exposition characterized by learning and insight. Calov (biblia illustrata), a corrector of the heterodox exposition of Grotius; notwithstanding his school dogmatics, he is learned and acute.

IV. EXPOSITORS OF THE REFORMED CHURCH IN THE 16TH

AND 17TH CENTURIES.—Zwingli (opp., T. vi. 1, ed. Schuler and Schulthess, 1836). His editor and faithful colleague, Leo Judaeus, gives him the praise of having expounded Scripture mirâ claritate, brevitate ac simplicitate parique diligentiâ; and even Richard Simon (histoire des commentateurs du N. T., p. 729) seems disposed to acquiesce in this judgment. All that we can say of his exposition, however, is, that although neither carefully worked out nor methodically arranged, it not unfrequently contains a good view of a passage. Conrad Pellicanus (*ob.* 1556, opp., T. vi.): short, often to the point, and not without originality.—The most noteworthy representative of systematic historical exegesis before Calvin, is Bucer in his enarratio quatuor evv., 1536; a work little known, but which has anticipated many a deep thought of modern theology. Bullinger, in Mtth., 1542: elaborately dogmatical, yet not without originality. Calvin (new ed., Berlin 1835—38, voll. i. ii., Harmonia Ev. Matthæi, Marci, Lucæ) is pre-eminently distinguished among the expositors of his century by the religious depth of his criticism, which is based upon rigid grammatical and historical interpretation: his work on the Gospels is not, however, so thorough-going as his commentaries on the Epistles. Beza (Novum Testamentum, 5th improved ed. 1598), the most philological and critical of his fellow-workers. Arctius (*ob.* 1574), discerning, but strongly dogmatical. Piscator (*ob.* 1626), comm. in omnes libros N. T., ed. iii., 1658: exegetical insight, ability in developing the connection of passages. Abr. Scultetus (*ob.* 1625), exercitationes evangelicæ, 1624: a series of able treatises on the first ten chapters of this Gospel, partly historical, partly doctrinal. Fred. Spanheim (*ob.* 1649), dubia evangelica, 3 voll. 1651: to te middle of chap. v. contains an inquiry into doctrinal difficulties, at once learned and concise, clear and acute. Cocceius (opp., T. iv.), a profound and learned but unfinished exposition in disp. xxx. in T. vi. Hammond, Nov. Test. cum paraphrasi et adnotationibus—transtulit et auxit J. Clericus, 1698. Owing to a false originality and a doctrinal superficiality, the learned notes of the author often fail to apprehend the right meaning: the contributions by Clericus, however, are generally useful for the historical interpretation. Jacob. Elsner (com. in ev. Mtth. 1767), Jacobus and Ludovicus Cappellus, Drusius, Ludov. de Dieu, Price, have learned annotations of philological and antiquarian importance, especially in their expositions of the Sermon on the Mount.

V. SOCINIAN EXPOSITORS.—Faustus Socinus (bibl. fratrum Polonorum, T. iv. to Matt. vi. 20). Crell (bibl. fratr. Polon. T. v. only on to the 5th chap. of Matthew). Wollzogen (bibl. T. ii.). Przipcov, cogitationes ad initium ev. Mtth. (bibl. T. iv.). Socinus is the most ingenious.

VI. ARMINIAN EXPOSITORS.—Nothwithstanding his doctrinal superficiality, it cannot be denied that Grotius has, by his rich classical and rabbinical learning, greatly furthered the elucidation especially of the Sermon on the Mount. Episcopius (in Mtth. T. ii.) is serviceable to historical exposition; yet, as elsewhere, so here, although Limborch pronounces this work his best, he is neither precise nor concise. Wettstein's collections from classical and rabbinical authors give frequently, as parallel, passages more apparently than really parallel.

VII. EXPOSITORS OF THE ROMAN CATHOLIC CHURCH IN THE 18TH AND 19TH CENTURIES.—Calmet, opp., T. vii. Commentary on Matth. by Gratz, 2 vols. 1821. Kistemaker's Kurze Anmerkungen zu Matth. Riegler, Bergpredigt Jesu Christi kritisch-historisch-praktisch erklaert, zur Belehrung und Betrachtung dargestellt, Bamberg 1844. All without importance.

VIII. PROTESTANT EXPOSITORS IN THE 18TH AND 19TH CENTURIES.—Curæ philologicæ criticæ, by Christ. Wolf, 1741 (which are to be found as an appendix in Koecher's analecta), are for the most part antiquated now; yet, for the history of the exposition, they form a useful collection. Beausobre (remarques philologiques et critiques sur le N. Test., 1742): independent patristic research, but the quotations often bear but a remote relation to the text. Gottfried Olearius, Observationes in Matth., 1730: characterized by exegetical talent and philological knowledge. Bengel, Gnomon N. T. ed. 1742, new ed. by Steudel, 2 A. Berlin 1854 (Engl. Transl., Edinburgh 1859); remarkable for its profound love and reverence for the Word of God, and careful attention to the very faintest intimations of the text. Heumann, Erklaerung des N. T., I. Band, 1750: a work which, at the outset very incomplete, gains as it progresses, by a diligent use of the labours of others. Kuinoel in Matth., 4th ed. 1837: rich collection of materials from more recent authors, but without philological penetration or theological depth. Paulus, exeget. Handbuch, 1 Th. 1833: exposition from the point of view of the superficial modern illumination. Fritzsche, in Matth., 1826: partially good in its philology and criticism, utterly deficient in its theological comprehension: what is new in it is sometimes more ingenious than true. Olshausen, bibl. Commentar, 1 Th. 3 A. 1838: the first exposition of this century for Christianity and ability. Meyer, Commentar zu Matth., 3 A. 1853: with considerateness, but the sense is sometimes too superficially apprehended. De Wette, Comm. zu Matth., 3 A. 1845, in the Sermon on the Mount, with sententious brevity. Stier, Reden Jesu, 1 Th. 1843: correct views, but without clear and defined perceptions, or sound hermeneutical principles of exposition. The Christian depth, combined with right historical feeling, with which Neander has in his Leben Jesu (5 A. 1852) illustrated the sayings of Christ, has also accomplished much that is meritorious and thankworthy in the interpretation of the Sermon on the Mount.

Separate Treatises on the Sermon on the Mount.—Ferf. Specimen critico-theolog. in ev. Matth., Traj. Bat. 1799. The author is occupied with Evanson's doubts on the authenticity of Matthew, and discusses isolated points in the Sermon on the Mount, yet without profit.—Frotscher (præs. *Iehnichen*) de consilio quod Jesu in oratione quæ dicitur montana, secutus est, Witteb. 1788. The author regards the sermon as one connected whole.—Pott, de natura atque indole orationis montanæ, Helmst. 1789. The author regards the sermon as a collection of apophthegms.—Oertel, de oratione Jesu montana ejusque consilio, Witteb. 1802: an unimportant attempt to determine the occasion, place, and scope of the sermon. Grosse, de consilio quod Christus in oratione montana secutus sit, Gott. 1818: a very feeble attempt to prove one train of thought in the sermon. Jentzen, de indole ac ratione orationis montanæ, Lubecæ 1818: a somewhat better, but still feeble effort of the same description.

The Sermon on the Mount further deserves attention—as

does also, in this respect, the exposition of it by Luther—when considered as a pattern and model of true popular eloquence. As such, it is rightly appreciated by Herwerden, Jezus Christus in de Bergrede beschouwd als een voorbeeld voor den Kanzelrednaar, Gron. 1829.—The following are the most important homiletical works on the Sermon on the Mount: Goess, Reden ueber die Bergpredigt nach neuen Ansichten, Uebersicht und exegetisch. Rechtfertigung, Ulm 1823. Zimmermann, die Bergpredigt in religioesen Vortraegen, Neust. 1836. Mau, die Bergpredigt nach Matth. homiletisch bearbeitet, Hamb. 1836. Arndt, die Bergrede Jesu Christi in 17 Betrachtungen, Magdeburg 1838, 2 B. Harms, die Bergrede des Herrn in 21 Predigten vorgetragen, Kiel 1841. Kling, die Bergrede Christi nach Matth. fuer nachdenkende Christen erklaert, Marburg 1841. Stueler, nachgelassene Predigten ueber die Bergpredigt, Halle 1843. Braune, Bergpredigt ausgelegt (in Bibelstunden), Altenb. 1856.

Works on the Eight Beatitudes.—Gregory Nyss., the Beatitud. in monte, opp., ed. Par. T. i. Rambach, Betrachtungen ueber die 8 Seligkeiten, Jena 1723. Conr. Rieger, richtiger und leichter Weg zum Himmel durch acht Stufen der Seligkeit, Stuttg. 1744. Herder, die Seligpreisungen Christi; in den Werken zur Religion und Theologie, B. iv. G. A. Fischer, Predigten ueber die 8 Seligkeiten, Muenchen 1834. Nielsen, die Seligpreisungen unsers Herrn in neun Predigten, Luebeck 1838.

Works on the Lord's Prayer.—(1.) Origen, **in his** work περὶ εὐχῆς, c. 18, opp., T. i. p. 126 ff.: an elaborate and most able performance, characterized by deep theological insight. (2.) Chrysostom, first in the homilies in Matth., hom. xix. T. vii. p. 149; also in the hom. de instituenda secundum Deum vita, T. ii. ed. Montf. In T. viii. there is a spurious exposition of the Lord's Prayer. (3.) Isidorus Pelusiota epistt., l. iv. ep. 24. (4.) Cyrillus Hierosol. in Cateches. 23, § 11—18, opp., ed. Touttée, p. 329. (5.) Gregory of Nyssa, five discourses de oratione, the last four of which are a commentary on the Lord's Prayer, T. i. ed. Paris, p. 723 seqq. (6.) The anonymous author in the varia sacra of Stephan. le Moyne, Lugd. B. 1685, i. 66. The fragments gathered by Alex. Morus (Notæ in N. T., p. 26), from a codex of St Athanasius in the Medicean library, belong tho same writer.—In the Latin Church: (1.)

Tertullian, in the liber de oratione, T. iii. ed. Paris, p. 501. (2) Cyprian, in his work de oratione dominica, opp., ed. Par. p. 317. (3.) Pseudo-Ambrosius, in the treatise de Sacramentis, L. v. c. 4. (on its spuriousness, see Oudinus, T. i. 651). (4.) Jerome, in his Commentary on Matthew, and in the Dialogus contra Pelagianos, L. iii. c. 51, T. ii. (ed. Ven.). (5.) Augustin, in his exposition of the Sermon on the Mount, and in his sermons on Matth. vi. de oratione dominica: Sermo lvi.—lx., Tom. v. (ed. Bened.). (6.) *Auctor operis imperfecti*. The expositions of the Greek Fathers have been collected and arranged in a scholarly manner by Suicer, Observationes Sacræ, Tiguri 1665, c. vii.—xi.

From the period of the Reformation the most important explanations of the Lord's Prayer are those of Luther's Longer and Shorter Catechisms, together with that in the Heidelberg Catechism by Ursinus and Olevianus. Both explanations, like the catechisms themselves, are masterpieces both in respect of theological depth and of popular expositions. Besides the above-named expositions by Luther, there are yet three others: The first consists in sermons taken down and edited by Sneider in 1518, and afterwards published in the same year by Luther himself, under the title: "Auslegung des Vaterunsers fuer einfaeltige Laien." To this edition he added two short appendices.[1] Next came, in 1529, the exposition in the catechisms; and finally, something was contributed to the illustration of the Pater noster in the sermons on Matt. vi., which he began to hold in 1530. The first more elaborate commentary for laymen bears evidence of less clearness and maturity of thought.

Among later expositions the most remarkable is that of Chemnitz, harmonia evangelica, T. i. c. 51: it is rich in a wide understanding of the text, derived from the Scriptures in their whole extent. The commentary of Socinus is full and carefully worked out. Among the treatises which have been published separately, that which deserves most notice are the exercitationes in orationem dominicam by the learned Hermann Witsius in the exercitationes sacræ, Amst. 3 ed. 1697: they contain much that is useful for exposition, especially culled from patristic

---

[1] Bearing respectively the titles: "Kurzer Begriff und Ordnung aller vorgeschriebenen Bitten," and "Kurze Auslegung des V.U. vor und hinter sich,"—that is, in the right and the inverted way.

literature, but there is a want of a distinct apprehension of the meaning. Gottfried Olearius, observationes sacræ, **Lips. 1713**, p. 176 seqq.; his remarks are ingenious and partly original. The treatise by Nik. Brunner, de præstantia et perfectione orationis dominicæ, in the 2d vol. of the Temple Helvet., Tig. 1736, is worthy of notice. In form, indeed, he follows the strict school of Lampe, but there is considerable insight into the meaning.[1] From modern times we may mention the treatises by Noesselt in the exercitt., Hall. 1803,—which, however, go no deeper into the subject than had been already done in former works; an able exposition of the Prayer by Weber (formerly Professor in Halle), published in the Programme of 1828 under the title: eclogæ exegetico-crit. in nonnullos libror. N. T. locos ii. and iii; finally, Gebser, de oratione dom. comment. 1, Regiom. 1830.—The principal homiletical works on the Lord's Prayer in recent times are the following: John, Predigten ueber das Vater unser, Hamb. 1829, 2 A. 1833. Fikenscher, das Vater unser in 10 Predigten, Nuernb. 1834. Loehe, Predigten ueber das Vater unser, Nuernb. 1834. Zimmer, das Gebet des Herrn, Frankf. 1834. Arndt, das Vater unser in 10 Predigten, Berlin, 2 A. 1841. Zimmermann, das Gebet des Herrn, 11 Predigten, Neust. a. d. Orla 1837. Harms, das Vater unser in 11 Predigten, Kiel 1838. Marheineke, das Gebet des Herrn, 13 Predigten, Berlin 1840. Tholuck, Predigten ueber das Vater unser in B. ii. of the larger ed. of his sermons. Huhn, Predigten ueber das Vater unser, Reval 1842. Niemann, das Vater unser in 10 Predigten, Hannover 1844. Stolz (R. Cath.), das Vater unser und die Zehn Gebote (aus dem Kalender fuer Zeit und Ewigkeit), 1851. Jac. Martin in Geneva, das Gebet des Herrn, from the French, 1852. Veit (R. Cath.), das Vater unser, 4th revised ed. 1852. [Above all, Sermons on the Lord's Prayer, by the Rev. F. D. Maurice, London.]

---

[1] In the first vol. of this collection of dissertations there is an idea suggested by Stapfer, as a counterpart to the notion peculiar to the Hegelian school (which is given by Prof. Sietze in his Grundbegriffe preussischer Rechts- und Staatsgeschichte, Berlin 1829), that the several petitions of the Pater noster express the several periods of the history of the world. Stapfer, namely, suggests that these six petitions express six great epochs in the history of the Christian Church.

EXPOSITION

OF THE

SERMON ON THE MOUNT.

HISTORICAL INTRODUCTION.

Vers. 1, 2.

VERSE 1. In this verse **three things** demand our attention: first, the ὄχλοι spoken of; next, the mountain mentioned; and lastly, the discrepancy with St Luke's account, which the terms ἀνέβη and καθίσαντος αὐτοῦ present. Since, as has been shown, the introduction to the discourse in chap. iv. 24, 25, has merely a summary character, the concourse of people mentioned by St Matthew would be inexplicable, **were it not that the** similar statement of St Luke constrains us to believe **that there** was there a huge and promiscuous crowd assembled. Now, it is intelligible enough that such an assemblage of people should have been gathered together at such a place as Capernaum; for Capernaum was at that time the great emporium for the caravans on their way from Egypt to Damascus, and was **therefore** a place of much resort. Hattin, which tradition points to **as the** spot where the Sermon on the Mount was delivered, lay on the great highway from Mount Tabor: and there may yet be seen, in some cisterns hewn out of the rock, a monument of the great traffic which in old times animated those regions. (Robinson, Palestine, iii. 1019.)

As to the locality of the mountain we have no information: yet ὄρος has the definite article. The opinion that here, as in

Hebrew, it may stand for the indefinite article, a more exact biblical philology must reject. It would seem as if the use of the definite article here could be vindicated only on the assumption, that the Evangelist supposed the mountain he spoke of to be known to his readers, or, as Fritzsche expresses, the meaning: *ascendit montem, quem nostis.* The same supposition must be made, if, with Meyer, we explain the phrase: "the mountain which was to be found there." But not before chap. viii. 5 does the locality of the mountain in question become known to us, viz., the neighbourhood of Capernaum; and there, we know, there was more than one mountain. Moreover, the expression τὸ ὄρος, occurs in the Gospels in passages where it is even more difficult to determine the locality; as in St Matt. xiv. 23, xv. 29; St Luke ix. 28. In the last passage, St Luke, instead of using the indefinite εἰς ὄρος ὑψηλόν of St Matthew, again has the definite εἰς τὸ ὄρος. Compare also St Mark iii. 13, vi. 46; St John vi. 3, 15. The remarkable feature in these passages is not the absence of the name of the mountain. Some of the hills indicated might have no name. The remarkable thing is, simply, the use of the definite article. Accordingly, Schleiermacher has thought he could see in this indefinite notice of the mountain the mark of the later hand of some writer, who, taking as his groundwork the λογία τοῦ κυρίου of Matthew, endeavoured to set these in a framework of history. (Studien und Kritiken 1832, Heft 4, S. 746.) According to Gfrörer, a certain mountain became celebrated from being the scene of the feeding of the multitude (an event credibly reported by the fourth Evangelist), in consequence of which celebrity, other events were reported to have also occurred there. (Heilige Sage, i. 199.) Bruno Bauer has translated the mountain of which the Evangelists speak, and which is one and the same throughout, into the region of dreamland. (Kritik der Synoptiker, i. S. 290 ff.) I had formerly hinted the possibility that, in the cases under consideration, the article might denote the genus, like τὰ ὄρη in St Matt. xviii. 12. Like הָהָר in Hebrew, τὸ ὄρος is used in the sense of ἡ ὀρεινή; the LXX. have sometimes the latter (Gen. xiv. 10; Deut. ii. 37; Josh. ii. 16), sometimes τὸ ὄρος (Gen. xix. 17, 19, 30, xxxi. 23, 25, xxxvi. 8, 9). Compare the indefinite expression ἐν ταῖς ἐρήμαις, St Luke v. 16. This view is further confirmed by Ebrard. In

Palestine, as he remarks, we do not find a plain and several mountains rising up **out of it**; but what we find there, similar to the chalk-formation **of** the Jura, is a plain with valleys cut out of it.¹ Particularly, the Lake of Tiberias is on both sides enclosed with a gradually ascending table-land. "Matthew tells us simply, that the scene of the sermon was the mountain; that is, the scene lay in the region of the table-land, in the upper story of the country so to speak, and not down in the valleys." Meyer objects to this view, that ὄρος can only be a single mountain; thus ignoring the passages of the LXX. quoted above. Is the view itself satisfactory? This is more than questionable. If St Luke (ix. 28) has only τὸ ὄρος where St Matthew (xvii. 1) and St Mark (ix. 2) have εἰς ὄρος ὑψηλόν, then, supposing St Luke not to have meant a single mountain, he must apparently have accepted a different account. When it is said (Matt. xv. 29) that Christ went up εἰς τὸ ὄρος and sat down there, the meaning cannot be, that He seated Himself on the flat table-land. So, too, St Luke's account of the Sermon on the Mount evidently implies a mountain, because it is said there, that He descended from the mountain εἰς τόπον πεδινόν. For we cannot understand by **this** expression the valley-region in contradistinction to the ὀρεινή,—the phrase for that is invariably ἡ πεδινή, ἡ γῆ ἡ πεδινή in the LXX. (compare the τὸ πεδίον of Josephus). By τόπος πεδινὸς we can only understand a level place.² In these circumstances, the only course left open to us is to revert to the former explanation, viz., that He ascended that mountain which was near. And the peculiarity of this mode of expression will very much disappear if we remember that the original narrators had the features of the country present before them,—"a plateau of wavy summits, seldom overtopped by any isolated peaks of remarkable height." (Ritter's Erdkunde, xvi. S. 26.) According to Robinson, there are **in the** immediate neighbourhood of the lake twelve hills from

---

¹ Compare Robinson, iii. 482.
² Jos. ix. 1, x. 40, xi. 16; Judges i. 9; 1 Mac. iii. 40, iv. 21. Dr Robinson, in **a** letter dated Aug. 10, 1844, in which he was good enough to answer some questions regarding the locality of the Sermon on the Mount, which the author had addressed to him, expresses the opinion that τόπος πεδινός may mean a table-land. His idea is, that our Lord descended the opposite side of the hill, and came upon the table-land.

which the Sermon on the Mount might have been delivered (Travels, iii. 485). Thus, wherever that traveller might go, there were hills near him everywhere (compare the word *tell* تَلّ, hill, constantly recurring in names of places in Palestine, in contradistinction to جبل, mountain); and those hills were for the most part without a name, or not well known by the names they had; and this fact renders the vague τὸ ὄρος more intelligible.

In these circumstances, it were not surprising if the expositor should confess himself unable to determine precisely what the mountain here spoken of may have been. Some approximation to a solution of the problem had been sought in the two following considerations: As Christ passed the night upon the mountain, and after the sermon entered Capernaum (St Matt. viii. 1), it follows that this hill must have stood not very far from Capernaum: and further, the hill in question must have been one where there was a considerable space of plain surface, where Christ might heal the sick, gather around Him the circle of his Apostles and disciples, and upon whose slope the crowds of people might have room to sit in comfort.

Now, with regard to the first of these remarks, while it is easy to see that this mountain must have been near Capernaum, it is not so easy to determine where Capernaum itself was. What is the site of the ancient town, is a question, says Ritter, which can scarcely be answered with certainty (Ritter, Erdkunde, xv. 1 Abth. S. 338). According to Robinson, Chan Minie, lying twelve miles S. W. of the mouth of the Jordan, represents Capernaum: other travellers, on the contrary,—Wilson among the rest, —suppose it to be Tel Hum, which lies four miles from there to the N. W., quite at the upper end of the lake. The arguments in favour of this least view are not wholly conclusive; more so, however, than those of Robinson in favour of the first. Still hills, if they cannot be called mountains, are to be met with everywhere. To the N. of Chan Minie, begins a range of rocky hills, of considerable height, descending towards the lake (Ritter, S. 335; Robinson's Travels, iii. 541, 548); and this eminence was pointed out so far back as 1283, by the traveller Brocardus, and in 1483 by Count Solms, as the Mount of Beatitudes (Nuernberger Reisebuch 1659, S. 122, 858). Of the ruins of Tel Hum, however, it is said (Robinson, iii. 2, 555): „Behind them, an extensive tract of country rises in a gentle slope to a considerable height, such as might well be designated with the name of a mountain." This traveller also admits (p. 55), that there are in the neighbourhood of the lake a dozen eminences, any of which might form a fitting locality for the Sermon on the Mount. The tradition of the Latin Church, however, has fixed upon another spot as the scene of its delivery. It is a hill some two miles S. of Chan Minie, called Kurun **Hattin** (*i. e.*, the horns), or Tel Hattin (*i. e.*, the hill). At the elevation of 1000 feet above the level of the sea, it presents a level surface between its two peaks, which rise like two horns 60 feet higher. And, especially since Korte's description of the Holy Land, published in 1741, this tradition has been universally accepted. "Certain it is," says Korte (p. 308), "that the shape of the mountain is suitable: the flat surface on its summit at the foot of its peaks, somewhat in the shape of a huge platter, and the ground gently sloping round, would render the spot very well adapted for a congregation." (Compare Schubert, Reise, iii. S. 223.) This mountain is also regarded as the scene of the feeding of the multitude by most of the ancient travellers, as Adrichomius, Cotovicus, **Brocardus**, etc. And yet it cannot have been well adapted to great assemblages of people, since, according to Pococke, it is only 19 feet long, and 16 broad.

We must therefore despair of attaining to anything like certainty as to the site of this mountain. This much, however, we have seen, may be confidently affirmed, that the locality was not far from Capernaum; consequently, not far from the Lake of Gennesaret: and if this be the case, the scene of the Sermon on the Mount was one of the fairest in nature. The beauty of the environs of the Galilean Lake has been celebrated by all travellers: even Josephus breaks into enthusiasm as he describes the landscape of Gennesaret: "Wonderful is the country that lies over against this lake, both in beauty and in fertility. Its soil is so fruitful that all kinds of trees can grow upon it, and the inhabitants accordingly plant all sorts of trees there; for the temper of the air agrees well with all. There flourishes the walnut-tree, which requires cool air; there is the palm-tree also, which thrives best in a milder atmosphere; fig-trees, also, and olives grow near them, which require an air yet more temperate. One may call this place the triumph of nature, where it forces those plants that are naturally enemies to one another to agree together: it is a happy contention of the seasons, as if every one of them laid claim to this country." (De Bello Judaico, iii. 10, 8.) Travellers have compared this neighbourhood with the best scenery known to them in their respective countries: Hasselquist, the Swede, compares it with East Gothland; Schubert, with the Stahrenberg; Seetzen, with the environs of Lake Locarne; and Clarke, with the romantic valleys of Kent and Surrey. Yet in these comparisons the imagination seems to have added somewhat to the real beauties of this scenery. We have not here the bold and sublime forms of the Alpine mountains; and although Cotovicus justly admired the rich variety of fruit-trees which grow here, yet we miss "the beauty of meadow and of wood; and the eye often sees only naked cliffs, which, almost unadorned with trees, scarcely covered here and there with a scanty herbage, contemplate their dark outline reflected in the black lake below, whose surface no white sail, no tiny bark, enlivens." (Ritter in loc. cit., S. 291.)

To the traveller advancing from the west, the valley first becomes visible from Mount Tabor, although from there the view of the lake itself is intercepted by the heights of Hattin. It is only when, to the east of Hattin, the traveller reaches the steep descent of the mountain, whence an hour's walk down a descent of 1000 feet conducts to the margin of the lake, that from this elevated point the water becomes visible.

In the midst of this scenery the Saviour spoke the Sermon on the Mount. If we realize the beautiful landscape, the cloudlessness of the southern sky, the solemn calm of early morn, when it was spoken, we must feel how all this must have deepened the impression which the discourse produced. "The whole scene," says Hess, "has about it something earnest and sad, something attractive as well as sublime. The cloudless heaven above Him, the rural region around, formed a temple of nature: and no synagogue, not even the Temple of Jerusalem, could make on the minds of the hearers so deep and solemn an impression. Here was nothing of that formality which characterized the disquisitions of the Jewish teachers. He sat down upon the mountain, and, fixing His eye on the disciples standing next before Him, at once began, 'Blessed are the poor in spirit!'"

It remains to consider the two points of difference with St Luke's account. St Matthew says, that after the Sermon, Jesus came down from the mountain: it was accordingly *on* the mountain that He delivered it. St Luke again says, it was delivered "on the plain." St. Matthew, by our Lord sitting; St Luke, standing. To account for the first difference, Chemnitz argued, that our Lord ascended the mountain twice,— once at St Luke vi. 12, and again before ver. 20, this time to escape the pressing of the multitude; but St Matthew (viii. 1) gives us to understand, that the multitude descended the hill along with Jesus. Michaelis, Paulus, and recently Riegler, would translate ἔστη ἐπὶ τόπου πεδινοῦ, "He stood upon a *level country;*" which indeed would have been a fitting place to address the people from, but St Luke proceeds at once, after mentioning this, to speak of the cures He wrought there. But the difference is easily explained; for we are warranted, as has been shown, in maintaining that τόπος πεδινός, a different expression from ἡ πεδινή, means, not a plain, but a level place upon a mountain, upon that very mountain where He was. The other discrepancy, with regard to the position of our Lord, does not exist in the expressions of St Luke. As Calvin, Grotius, Calov, and others, have remarked, St Luke mentions that the Saviour stood upon the plain, merely when he speaks of His healing the people,—a work which, of course, could not be done sitting; but that Evangelist does not say that Christ delivered the discourse standing. We have accordingly no ground for not believing that the Saviour sat when He delivered the Sermon on the Mount; it is not indeed unlikely (according to the supposition of Chemnitz), that, after completing His cures, He went a little higher up the mountain in order to be well heard by all.

Ver. 2. From ancient times, a peculiar significance has been found in the expression ἀνοίγειν τὸ στόμα. Chrysostom and Euthymius think it involves the idea, that speaking was not the only way in which Jesus taught, but that He taught also by His works. From the expression, Luther derives the following advice to preachers: "Stand boldly forward; open thy mouth and begin; have soon done;"—according to him, the preacher is to learn from it a lesson of bold and fearless speaking: "Speak out plainly; respect and spare no man, let the arrow hit whom it may." According to Schmid, the phrase is used, quando aliquid arduum vel diu exspectatum dicendum est. So too Calov, who adds: quod cum vehementia, ardore ac contentione tum animi tum vocis docuerit. On the other hand, Calvin and Beza deny that the phrase has any special emphasis attached to it, and regard it as expressive merely of the introduction to a discourse; Zwingly, κατασκευή est. Since Ernesti, the emphasis has been generally denied. Rosenmüller, Schleussner, and Kuinöl, on the other hand, have condemned the phrase as a pleonasm. The correct view is given by Fritzsche and Meyer. This graphic mode of representation, by telling what precedes the words spoken, excites the interest of the reader in the words themselves. There is thus also something solemn in the expression (comp. Job iii. 1, xxxii. 20; Acts viii. 35, x. 34). Besides, though not implied here, there is the idea of *confident* speaking implied in the phrase, as in Ezra xxix. 21; 2 Kings vi. 11. It is an Hebraism, although it occurs in classical use with various shades of meaning. Οἴγειν στόμα is "freely to tell one's mind, to pour oneself out," in Æschylus, Prometh. Vinct., v. 632, where Droysen translates: as the friend's mouth opens to his friends. In Isocrates (Panathen., ed. Coray, c. 36), λύειν τὸ στόμα is used in the sense of free, courageous speaking-out: ἐπειδήπερ οὖν ἐπελήλυθέ μοι τὸ παῤῥησιάσασθαι καὶ λέλυκα τὸ στόμα, καὶ τοιαύτην τὴν ὑπόθεσιν ἐποιησάμην. In Lucian (Philopseud. c. 33), where, speaking of the column of Memnon, he says that it "opened its mouth and uttered oracles," the expression is used, as in our text, to denote the solemn and the dignified.

Vers. 3—16.

The blessedness of those who in the right way long for the kingdom of God (vers. 3, 4); who themselves manifest the fruits of the righteousness of that kingdom (vers. 5—9); who submit to the contempt of the world (vers. 10—12), without proving false to their high destination as disciples of the kingdom of God (vers. 13—16).

THE BLESSEDNESS OF THOSE WHO IN THE RIGHT WAY LONG FOR THE KINGDOM OF GOD, AND MANIFEST THE FRUITS OF ITS RIGHTEOUSNESS.

Vers. 3—9.

Three questions in reference to these beatitudes present themselves at the outset for solution. 1. The relation of St Matthew's narration to that of St Luke (chap. vi.). 2. The object of Christ in opening the discourse with these beatitudes. 3. The distribution of them.

1. The relation of St Matthew's narration to that of St Luke (chap. vi.). While St Matthew has seven or eight successive and progressive beatitudes, the discourse in St Luke has but four, to which four succeeding woes correspond. While, further, in Matthew πτωχοί and πεινῶντες are followed by an explicative phrase expressive of the spiritual nature of the poverty and hunger, these additions are wanting in St Luke, whose appended νῦν seems rather to point to an intended contrast of the present with the future life. Two questions thus emerge: First, Is the meaning in the two accounts the same, or different? Second, Is the absence in St Matthew of the denunciations of woe an omission on his part, or have they been added in Luke by the reporter of his narrative?

With regard to the first question: Even among the ancients there were some who, like Cyril (see above, p. 3), found a different sense in St Luke's account to that of St Matthew,—a circumstance which appeared to Storr an additional argument against the identity of the two discourses (Vom Zweck Jesu, S. 348). Now, it was first noticed by Credner (Beitraege zur

Einleitung ins N. T. i. S. 307), that the Clementines (Polycarp also) ignore the additional τῷ πνεύματι: further, he declares the view of the Clementines concerning the meritoriousness of poverty to have been the original opinion in the Church, and, accordingly, St Luke's version to have been that originally spoken by Christ. The same opinion, both as to the original meaning of our Lord, and as to the relation of the two accounts, has been adopted by Strauss (i. S. 603), Baur (S. 478), Koestlin (S. 66), Hilgenfeld (S. 62), and Ewald (die ersten 3 Evangelien, S. 211). Baur, however, does not represent so strongly the opinion, that St Luke's is the original account, inasmuch as he regards the sense in St Matt. as unchanged by the addition of τῷ πνεύματι, since the poverty which the Clementines commended was only a *voluntary* poverty, and as likewise those whom Jesus commends are those whose mind does not lust after earthly riches;[1] such are therefore spiritually rich. So the τῷ πνεύματι is to be explained (according to Baur) "symbolically;" that is, their outward poverty is a symbol of their spiritual riches (?). If (he goes on) the τῷ πνεύματι were an addition which altered the original meaning of Christ, and gave it a new spiritual significance, of which only the Evangelist is the author, it must follow that the succeeding beatitudes, which have a spiritual application, were also absent from the original discourse of our Lord. True, this view does not appear in Baur's most recent exposition (das Christenthum u. d. christliche Kirche, 1853, p. 27), according to which, the beatitude of spiritual poverty is made to contain the germ of the new principle of Christianity, which is the victory over finite contraries. If the opinion were admitted, it would still by no means follow, as is maintained, that the same is true of all the beatitudes: moreover, if the τῷ πνεύματι is not authentic, neither can the authenticity of τὴν δικαιοσύνην, ver. 6, be maintained. For, as we read in another passage: "All those beatitudes, different as they may appear, are only so many various expressions for the fundamental tone and character of the Christian consciousness. It is

---

[1] Perfectly similar is the harmonizing of the two accounts in Clem. Alex., Strom. iv. 575, ed. Pott: μακάριοι δὲ οἱ πτωχοί, εἴτε πνεύματι, εἴτε περιουσίᾳ, διὰ δικαιοσύνην δηλονότι· μή τι οὖν ἁπλῶς τοὺς πένητας, ἀλλὰ τοὺς ἐπελήσαντας διὰ δικαιοσύνην πτωχοὺς γενέσθαι, τούτους μακαρίζει, τοὺς καταμεγαλοφρονήσαντας τῶν ἐνταῦθα τιμῶν εἰς περιποίησιν τοῦ ἀγαθοῦ.

the feeling of a need of redemption, simple as yet, and undeveloped, which comprehends in it already the antagonism between sin and grace, which includes in itself the essence of redemption."

Certainly some things appear to argue in favour of St Luke's account. On the one hand, the circumstance, that also in Matthew πενθοῦντες occurs without any addition; on the other, the sentence οἱ πτωχοὶ εὐαγγελίζονται (Matt. xi. 3; Luke iv. 18). Yet the fact, that even those critics ascribe to St Matthew a more exact narrative in general, must of itself awaken a strong suspicion that this general character of his Gospel is borne out in this case too. Now, a very simple solution of the difficulty lies close at hand. It is that which Bucer has set forth with great exegetical ingenuity, adding a reference to the basis of the thought in the Old Testament. It is the well-known Old Testament way of regarding the poor as the pious, the rich as the ungodly, which arose from the fact, that riches have a tendency to lead man astray, making Mammon his god (De Wette, Beiträge zur Characteristik des Hebraismus, in the Studien von Daub, and Creuzer iii. "on the idea of עֲנִיִּים and אֶבְיוֹנִים"): comp. Ps. x. 2, 12, 17, xii. 6, xiv. 6, xxii. 27, 37, lxviii. 11; Is. xli. 14. Further, this Old Testament view of the identity of physical and spiritual poverty furnishes a clue to the explanation of πενθοῦντες, and explains the phrase οἱ πτωχοὶ εὐαγγελίζονται. It is also confirmed by the exposition of πλούσιος (Mark x. 24), and by οἱ πεποιθότες ἐπὶ τοῖς χρήμασι: compare the counsels given in Prov. xxiii. 4, xxviii. 11, 20; Sirach xiii. 2, 4, 22; and, finally, the parallel passages in the Epistle of St James (ii. 5, iv. 9, v. 1) leave no doubt about this view of the distinction between rich and poor. In these circumstances, to go to the Clementines for information, were to go to fetch water from the well when there is a spring in the house. The exposition of vers. 3—5 will show that in the expressions, οἱ πτωχοὶ τῷ πνεύματι, οἱ πενθοῦντες, οἱ πραεῖς, this Old Testament view is also in the background. If now this view was the one held by the first members of the Christian Church, especially in its Jewish-Christian section, can it appear at all strange that the words of our Lord, which St Matthew presents in so admirable an order and distribution, should have been brought into such a form as would best correspond with the common Jewish-Christian notion by the more superficial writer who has handed down to us the narrative of St Luke? Here Bruno Bauer even has not failed to discern the truth (in loco citato, p. 307): "St Luke nowise means to say, that the poor as such are well-pleasing to God; but he speaks of those of them who spiritually pine away in this earthly life, that they may attain to the possession of an eternal inheritance." We will not here again discuss what has been already referred to, viz., as De Wette remarks (on Luke vi. 20), that St Luke's account has more an esoteric character than St Matthew's, and accordingly would be less adapted to the hearers (see above, p. 6). On the side of St Matthew on this passage, are also De Wette, Meyer, Neander.

In this decision our judgment on the Woes is already implied. That, according to Stier (in loc. S. 306), St Matthew has passed these over, because he "makes prominent the progress of development as the main idea of the sermon," is an idea which implies the destruction of the whole rhetorical structure of the discourse in this passage. For the rhetorical effect rests here on climax, but in Luke on antithesis; on which account, it is impossible to conceive of the eight beatitudes being succeeded by eight woes. Unquestionably, these woes must be regarded as an expansion of the thought by the recorder of the narrative; by which, nevertheless (as Schleiermacher observes), the meaning is as little affected as by the omission of $τῷ$ $πνεύματι$, inasmuch as those woes only express the negative side of the ideas which the beatitudes set forth positively.

We have further to inquire concerning the object of our Lord in opening the discourse with these beatitudes. The discourse begins with a joyous $μακάριοι$. Mel.: non quia promerentes sunt vitam aeternam, sed ... ut si diceret: bene est pauperibus, non sunt rejecti a Deo. "Every more elaborate discourse might begin with a salutation, or more solemnly with a benediction." (Ewald, Evv., S. 209.) The very fulness of the beatitudes seems to show that they are purposely placed first. Josephus, and likewise the New Testament, give us to understand that we are to regard the Jewish people, at the time of Christ's appearance, as filled with a desire for the Messianic salvation. The greater portion of them, however, could see in those prophetic utterances of the latter part of Isaiah, upon which especially all eyes were turned, only a promise of political libera-tion, and of Divine vengeance on their oppressors. (Comp. Is. xl. 1, lxi. 1, lxiii. 4, 6). But from these rude multitudes must be distinguished those who, in those prophetic pictures, **borrowed** from the circumstances of the visible theocracy, could not separate the thought from its figure,—and this we must suppose to have been the case with most of the prophets,—and who therefore expected an earthly victory over the oppressors, earthly splendour and power for their nation; but this only as a means towards the establishing of a Messianic kingdom of righteousness, filled with the Spirit of God. Among **those we must include** John the Baptist, still more the priest Zacharias, according to the hymn generally ascribed to him, Luke i. 67 ff.,—whose hopes certainly represented those of the best of the people of Israel at that time. If now Christ's object in this discourse was to describe the true character of the kingdom which He founded, then does the subject of these beatitudes most perfectly accord with this object. For He here pronounces those blessed who strive in the right way after the kingdom of God; and He further teaches, that only by suffering and submission can victory be gained.

The third point which falls to be considered, is the distribution of these beatitudes, and their mutual relations: comp. Burk evang. Fingerzeig, vi. S. 712. Here, the first question is concerning their *number*. Nine times $μακάριοι$ is repeated: but the ninth, ver. 11, has not a special subject, and is therefore to be regarded as an amplification of the $μακάριοι$ of the verse preceding, ver. 10. Accordingly, most commentators reckon the beatitudes as eight in number. Ewald, however, followed by Koestlin, in order to make out the numerical structure of the whole discourse (see above, p. 15), reduces the number to **seven, including** three passive virtues and four active ones,—that **concerning the persecuted he regards as a** mere appendix. The chief point in favour of the number seven is the sevenfold woe pronounced upon the Pharisees, chap. xxiii. Yet, if it can be **shown** that the blessing on those who should suffer persecution from the world, on account of their possessing those qualities which He had just spoken of, is the natural culmination and conclusion of what He had said, it is surely somewhat arbitrary to call that a mere appendix. Delitzsch, **again**, seeks to make the number amount to ten; and, **in order to accomplish this**, takes $χαίρετε\ καὶ\ ἀγαλλιᾶσθε$, in ver. 12, to be the paraphrastic form of a tenth μακάριοι, used with the object of "bringing about a perfect finale." The arbitrariness of this is evident; for ver. 12 plainly contains the *promise* succeeding the μακάριοι of ver. 11.

These eight beatitudes are arranged in an ethical order. The first four are of a negative character: they express the state of spiritual desire which belongs to the indispensable conditions of participation in the kingdom of God. The three following, again, are positive: they set forth what attributes of character are required in the members of that kingdom. The eight shows how the world will demean itself towards the members of the kingdom. This distribution is turned to practical account by Heubner, under the title, Beginning, Progress, and Perfection of Disciples beneath the Cross (Pract. Erklärung N. T. 1855, 1 Th.). The transposition (which will fall to be discussed in its own place) of vers. 4 and 5, adopted, after Code D, by Lachmann and Tischendorf, is here inadmissible.[1] This ethical consecutive order in the beatitudes might now induce us to expect a similar progression in the promises, as each of these exactly corresponds to the blessing desired or the quality possessed. Thus Clemens Alex., referring to these beatitudes, says (Strom. iv. p. 579, ed. Pott), εἰσὶ γὰρ παρὰ κυρίῳ καὶ μισθοὶ καὶ μοναὶ πλείονες: and so Menken, in harmony with the Collenbuschian doctrine of the stages of Christian perfection and reward (Betracht. über d. Matth. 1822, S. 293). But, if we consider the substance of the several promises, we shall find that they are all essentially identical, and that the difference is merely rhetorical: formally, they correspond to the thing desired or possessed, but each of them really comprises all spiritual blessings; as, for instance, the promise

---

[1] Kienlen (ueber die Makarismen) has proposed a peculiar division, which, however, we cannot adopt. According to him, the beatitudes are divided into two groups of four each, which correspond to each other. The first four denote the qualities of those who are desirous of the new birth; the last four, the corresponding qualities of those who have received it. So the first and fifth beatitudes would correspond to each other thus: "They who are aware of their spiritual poverty have already taken the first step towards the kingdom of God, in which all treasures are contained;" and "they who have a pure heart shall, in the vision of God, be made the recipients of these treasures." But even this first correspondence is obtained only by the introduction of thoughts not expressed in the text.

of the βασιλεία τῶν οὐρανῶν, ver. 3, repeated ver. 10, or that of the Divine ἔλεος. Aug.: unum præmium quod est regnum cœlorum pro his gradibus *varie nominatur*. Nay, even the progression among the qualities pronounced blessed is not to be regarded as of such a nature that each stage excludes the rest, or that, in advancing to one, the others are left behind. Rather is that figure true which Origen uses of these virtues (T. xvi. in Joann., Opp. iii. de la Rue, p. 780), "that these different grapes of that vine planted by the heavenly Father in the hearts of believers," ripen one after the other; and also, that when the last of them has come to maturity, the first still remains. Comp. Pseudo-Basilius de bapt. i. 3: Ἴσος ὁ κίνδυνος τοῖς πᾶσιν ἑνὸς ἐλλειφθέντος.

Yet another hermeneutical explanation must prepare the way for our exposition. We must inquire: Are we, in an historical exposition of the sayings of our Lord, to assume that no other meaning is implied in His words than one within the compass of His hearers, and familiar to them, situated as they were; or, may we admit, at least in the case of some of His sayings, that they possessed a significance far transcending the limits of those occasions, and embracing the whole future history of the kingdom of God? The question resolves itself into a Christological one, as to whether we are to regard the Redeemer as restricted within the boundaries of religious thought which characterized that period, or as raised above these limits? The hermeneutist Keil seems to have thought it doubtful "whether the design of Divine Providence (to make the truth which Christ taught the heritage of all time) were known to Jesus, or whether in His sayings He was able to take cognisance of posterity." (Analekten, by Keil and Tzschirner, B. i. St. 1, S. 63.) Eichhorn, who takes the same view, naïvely laments (in a passage in the allgemeine Bibliothek) that "the custom of preaching on texts of the Bible, a custom necessitated by taking the sayings of Jesus in a comprehensive sense, has constantly fettered the progress of exegesis." (He forgets, that were it not for the unfortunate circumstance he deplores, no chairs of exegesis would ever have been instituted.) To restrict the range of vision of a great man within the limits of his particular age, is simply to reduce every prophet and man of genius to the level of commonplace. If he is to apply to Christ the category only of great religious geniuses, still the expositor must not confine His religious consciousness within the limits of His own age; and if so, it follows that many a great saying of His must have far transcended the range of thought of His contemporaries, and have possessed a weight and a breadth which would be measured only by Himself and by posterity. Although this canon has been ignored by some recent expositors, especially by Meyer, its truth cannot be called in question. Yet is there a substratum of truth even in Eichhorn's complaint. So far it is certain, that although the sayings of Christ went beyond the sphere of vision of His hearers, the must still have had some point of contact with the intelligence of His hearers. There can be no doubt—and this should be carefully noted—that all the ideas which meet us, for instance, in this Sermon on the Mount,—those of the kingdom of God, of the righteousness of that kingdom, of the poor in spirit, of the pure in heart, of seeing God, etc.,—were no new ideas, but were, on the contrary, well known to His hearers, and that Christ only opens them up in their deepest meaning. Accordingly, that homiletic treatment of these sayings which makes Christ speak in them to posterity alone, and not at the same time to His own age, can assuredly not be right. And Christ would surely have spoken for the future alone, and in a manner unintelligible to His hearers, if, for instance, all He intended in these consecutive beatitudes, was to develop a religious process which only he could understand who had been born anew by the Spirit of Christ. But the contrary was the case; and hence the expositor will have in every case to look around for some *temporal* relation in each of these sayings, and to set it forth when he has found it. Such a temporal reference is especially discernible in the first of these beatitudes.

Ver. 3. We shall explain, first, the Ascription of Blessedness; second, the promise.

I. THE ASCRIPTION OF BLESSEDNESS: μακάριοι οἱ πτωχοὶ τῷ πνεύματι.

1. *History of the Exposition.*—And, first, the false exegesis must be set aside, which would regard τῷ πνεύματι as a determining clause to μακάριοι, and read thus, "Blessed in spirit are

the poor." This construction, first propounded by Olearius, was approved by Wettstein,[1] Heumann, Michaelis, and Paulus. The spiritual stand-point of the expositor himself is sufficiently marked when Paulus, speaking against the explanation, "the spiritually poor, the inly suffering," makes this reflection: "It is not to be thought for a moment that Jesus wished His followers to be *that*—He, the good-natured friend of mirth and joviality." To this construction there are three objections: (1.) The symmetry of this beatitude in relation to the others would be destroyed. (2.) If the first beatitude has to do only with physical poverty, then the progression in relation to the others would also be abolished. (3.) The construction, καθαροί τῇ καρδίᾳ, in ver. 8, points to the right reading here. If, then, we are to join πτωχοί with τῷ πνεύματι, there is conceivable a twofold reference of the expression: it may refer either to physical poverty or to spiritual poverty. That the poverty are spoken of is physical, is the view held by those commentators who attach greatest weight to the account of St Luke, who leaves out τῷ πνεύματι, the Clementines, and those modern expositors who think that *they* give the original Christian interpretation. (See p. 69.) Some are of opinion that the language used, favours this rendering: πτωχοί meaning *mentici, egeni*; the word for *pauper*, on the contrary, being πένης. So Tertull. adv. Marc. iv. 14, 15: beati mendici (sic enim exigit interpretatio vocabuli, quod in Græco est); in de idolol. c. 12, however, he translates the word *egeni*. In accordance with this is the explanation of a great number of the Fathers, by the majority of whom πνεῦμα is taken in the sense of *voluntate*, ἐκ προαιρέσεως. Thus Clem. Alex. (see above, p. 60), Jerome, Basil (on Ps. xxxiii. 5, Th. 1, p. 147,[2] and reg. brev. interr. 205), Gregory of Nyssa in oratio i. de beatitudinibus. Referring to the passage as viewed in this light, the Emperor Julian, in his 43d Epistle, speaking in derision of the Christians, says, he merely wishes to confiscate

---

[1] Wettstein understood by πνεῦμα simply the Spirit of God; πνεύματι being taken as the dative of judgment, as in Greek, *e. g.*, ὡς ἐμοί (Matthiae, Griech. Gram. 2 Aufl. § 388), thus, "are blessed *in the judgment of God*."

[2] Οὐκ ἀεὶ ἐπαινετὴ ἡ πτωχεία, ἀλλ᾿ ἡ ἐκ προαιρέσεως κατὰ τ. εὐαγγελικὸν σκοπὸν κατορθουμένη· πολλοὶ γὰρ πτωχοὶ μὲν τῇ περιουσίᾳ, πλεονεκτικώτατοι δὲ τῇ προαιρέσει τυγχάνουσιν. Otherwise on Isa. xiv. § 287 (T. i. 597), with reference to the New Testament words: πτωχοὺς δὲ οὐ τοὺς κατὰ χρήματα ἐνδεεῖς λέγει, ἀλλὰ τοὺς τῇ διανοίᾳ ἠλαττωμένους.

their property *in order that, in the character of poor men, they may enter the kingdom of heaven.* Then the majority of Romish writers restrict the phrase to the vow of paupertas voluntaria taken by monks (Jansenius, a Lapide, Zegerus, Maldon., R. Simon, hist. des Commentateurs, etc., 1693, p. 247): the last-named quotes, in support of the signification *voluntas*, Matt. xxvi. 41; Rom. i. 9; 1 Cor. vii. 34; Eph. iv. 3. Some, as Maldonatus, R. Simon, and others, even drag ver. 10 into the service of this doctrine, explaining it of those "who suffer physical hunger for the sake of righteousness." Others, again, while protesting against this limitation to the vows of the convent, still maintain the older more general reference of the text to voluntary poverty: so Bonaventura de profect. relig. 2, 42, Este, Tirinus.—Now, undoubtedly the kindred expressions, ἐκ καρδίας and ψυχικῶς (2 Mac. iv. 37, xiv. 24), denote readiness of will; and this use is legitimate, and is explained by the classical and also Hellenistic use of ψυχή to mean "desire, inclination;" but the adverb πνευματικῶς never bears this interpretation: not to mention that the dative, which is used in our text, cannot be always and at once taken adverbially. This fact also destroys that other interpretation which would understand this dative adverbially in the sense of *patient endurance.* Thus in the Clementine Recognitions, 1. ii. c. 28: pauperes *pro penuriæ tolerantia* adepturos esse regna cœlorum. Melanchthon: *pauperes spiritu*, i.e. *vera patientia* tolerantes paupertatem. If πτωχοί were to be understood of physical poverty, unquestionably the best explanation of it would be that of Clemens Alex. in his Quis dives salvus (§ 14, 15); viz., that riches in themselves are a thing indifferent; the question with regard to them being this, as to whether they are used as an ὄργανον of good; and that, by those whom He praises as poor in spirit, Christ means to denote those who, be they rich or poor, are in heart loosened from worldly possessions, are *therefore* poor: and to this idea an admirable parallel passage might be found in 1 Cor. vii. 29: "They that possess, as though they possessed not" (comp. Jer. ix. 23); and in St James i. 9, 10: καυχάσθω δὲ ὁ ἀδελφὸς ὁ ταπεινὸς ἐν τῷ ὕψει αὐτοῦ· ὁ δὲ πλούσιος, ἐν τῇ ταπεινώσει αὐτοῦ. So among R. Catholic expositors, Kistemaker, who refers to Ps. lxii. 11; 1 Cor. vii. 30, 31; among Protestants, Grotius, Episcopius, Beausobre, Mosh.;

Luther,[1] too, says: "Poverty before God, that is, of the heart, is when one does not place his trust and confidence in temporal things,"—"that one must think of his possessions as though he had them not, and remember that at any time he may lose them." Episcopius: Verba de tali paupertate intelligenda, qua quis proprie animum divitiarum amore vacuum habet, ita ut iis oblectare non velit, aut eas propterea retinere non exoptet, ut habeat semper unde genio suo satisfaciat. It must be observed, that by this application **the ad**vantage which this exegesis would have had, that in this form the **saying** of St Matthew is approximated to that of St Luke, is again lost; and that other **advantage, of** finding an occasion for the subsequent sayings in the historical circumstances by which Christ was then surrounded: and at the same time, of making these sayings have a reference to external necessity. For this view necessarily transfers us to the province of spiritual relations, and in this way it forms the point of transition to the expositions which regard the poverty of the text as a *spiritual* poverty: and this, indeed, must appear the only tenable interpretation to those who feel constrained to recognise a *gradation* in these beatitudes. Those who have understood this saying to denote a spiritual poverty are the following: Origen, hom. v. in **Josuam, T. ii.** ed. de la Rue; Athanasius, quæst. ad Antiochum, quæst. 91; Chrys., Theoph., Euthym., Makarius hom. **xii.,** August., author of opus imperf., Erasmus, Beza, Piscator, Chemnitz, Hunnius, Calov, Spanheim, Knapp, Olshausen, **De** Wette, Meyer. Most of these recognise the dative here as a dat. referentiæ (where the Hebrews **and** Syrians, sometimes the Greeks, would have the genitive), denoting that side of the subject in reference to which the poverty **exists**; comp. 1 Cor. vii. 34: ἁγία καὶ σώματι καὶ πνεύματι.

Nevertheless, many abandon the strict conception of *poverty*, substituting for it the notio adjuncta of *humility* and lowliness of mind: so the Greek commentators (Euthym. bases this **view**

---

[1] The translation in Luther's Bible, "die geistlich arm sind," is not therefore intended to mean: "They who feel themselves poor in *spiritual riches*." In his remarks on Matt. xi. 5, Luther's exegesis wavers: in one place he says, "Thus these poor are certainly not beggars, and those who are physically poor, but the spiritually poor **(in Walch** xii. 120); **at** another, he combines the reference to spiritual and physical poverty. **(Walch xi. 1342.)**

on the etymology of the word from $\pi\tau\acute{\iota}\sigma\sigma\omega$), and several of the superficial expositors of last century, as Bolten: "Blessed are the humble;" Zeller: "Blessed are the modest." The same meaning is attained by a different way by Augustine, Erasmus, Zwingli, who regard the dative here as marking that in which the poverty consists, and take $\pi\nu\epsilon\tilde{\upsilon}\mu\alpha$ in malam partem, as meaning the spiritus elatus, ferocia animi. Against this Fritzsche rightly remarks, that one speaks of poverty only in relation to a good: that poverty, however, which he thinks spoken of here, is of a kind which he was himself least of all disposed to pronounce blessed: fortunati homines *ingenio* et *eruditione* parum florentes.[1]

2. *Exposition.*—That by $\pi\nu\epsilon\tilde{\upsilon}\mu\alpha$, the human spirit, is here denoted the sphere in which the poverty is shown, may also be inferred from the analogy of the Hebrew עֲנִי־רוּחַ. If we are then, with the Peschito, to translate the phrase, "who in their spirit are poor," the only sense in which this can be here said, is with reference to a consciousness of poverty in the blessings of salvation. Some expositors bring prominently forward a desire of *knowledge;* as Stolz: Blessed is the man who has a soul open to the truth. Kuinoel: qui agnoscunt, quam rudes sint divinæ doctrinæ; Fritzsche, substituting for divina doctrina, eruditio and ingenium, makes this exposition a caricature. As, however, hunger and thirst after *true righteousness* is spoken of in ver. 6, we must conclude that what is meant here is the feeling of *moral* poverty. And to this view we are also led by the saying in Matt. xi. 28—30, where the Redeemer invites to Himself those who feel themselves incapable of fully satisfying the law of God. If we would further expand the idea of the text, we might say that the poverty of spirit spoken of is: in knowledge, poor in truth: in will, poor in holiness; and in feeling, poor in blessedness. $\Pi\tau\omega\chi\acute{o}\varsigma$ is used of poverty in spiritual possessions in Rev. iii. 17: of riches in spiritual possessions $\pi\lambda o\acute{\upsilon}\sigma\iota o\varsigma$ is used Rev. ii. 9, iii. 17; 2 Cor. viii. 9; Jas. ii. 5; and in the Ep. of Barnabas, c. 19: $\dot{\alpha}\pi\lambda o\tilde{\iota}\varsigma \tau\tilde{\eta} \varkappa\alpha\rho\delta\acute{\iota}\alpha \varkappa\alpha\grave{\iota} \pi\lambda o\acute{\upsilon}\sigma\iota o\varsigma \tau\tilde{\omega} \pi\nu\epsilon\acute{\upsilon}\mu\alpha\tau\iota.$[2]

---

[1] This view is most closely approached by Epiphanius, in his sarcastic reference to the name Ebionite (hær. 30. 17): πτωχὸς γὰρ ὡς ἀληθῶς (Ebion namely) καὶ τῇ διανοίᾳ καὶ τῇ ἐλπίδι καὶ τῷ ἔργῳ, κ.τ.λ.

[2] Comp. Plato de Repub. vii. p. 521 St.: οἱ τῷ ὄντι πλούσιοι οὐ χρυσίου, ἀλλ' οὗ δεῖ τὸν εὐδαίμονα πλουτεῖν, ζωῆς ἀγαθῆς τε καὶ ἔμφρονος. To speak

But in the exposition of these words, have we not, first of all, to bear in mind that to His hearers the idea of the Poor was no new idea, but a well-known one? (See above, p. 61.) And if, further, we remember that it was, in fact, only the lower classes which gathered round the Saviour, and also consider the ambiguous expression used by our Lord in His first appearance in the synagogue of Nazareth, Luke iv., οἱ πτωχοὶ εὐαγγελίζονται, taken from the Prophet Isaiah (lxi. 1), it will appear highly probable that the same ambiguity is to be found in His use of the expression here, and we shall conclude **that the** idea of physical poverty is here carried over into the sphere of poverty of spirit; that, in a word, those poor are pronounced blessed who are also sensible of their spiritual poverty. Christ **has** given its πλήρωσις to the Old Testament in this respect as well as in others, in that He has unfolded the stamina of great truths which lay slumbering there; this we shall see more fully in ver. 5: but it is also true with regard to those sayings, as Isa. lxi. 1, 2, in which the salvation which the Messiah should bring was promised to the poor, the captive, and the sorrowful (similarly Buzer, Neander, De Wette, O. v. Gerlach).

II. The Promise.

The expression βασιλεία τῶν οὐρανῶν occurs elsewhere in the Sermon on the Mount, in v. 10, 19, 20, vi. 10, vii. 21; and is to be explained by the light thrown upon it by those passages.

Neither the idea nor the expression was first introduced by Christ. A kingdom of God—that **is, an** organic **commonwealth**, which has the principle of its existence in the will of God—had already been established in the Jewish theocracy. But very imperfectly realized. There, the Divine kingdom was confined within the limits of a particular **nation; civil** life became necessarily and immediately religious life, religious truth was conveyed by symbolic representations, and religious life was inculcated by the stern commands of the law. God had especially chosen out the people of Israel among all the nations of the earth—not, indeed, on account of any particular merit

of a feeling of spiritual *poverty* as blessed, had, however, been foreign to Hellenic ideas. Plutarch speaks in one place of πενία ψυχική (de cupiditate divitiarum, c. 4): all that he means by that, however, is the malady of insatiable *covetousness*.

it possessed, but out of pure love—solely in order to manifest Himself in it: Deut. vii. 6—8; Isa. xliii. 21 ff. Hence it is called in this special sense, "His peculiar people," "the people of His inheritance" (Ex. xix. 5; Deut. xiv. 2); "the flock of His heritage" (Micah vii. 14); it is "a nation of priests," "an holy people" (Ex. xix. 6), because it is governed by God as its King (Deut. xxxiii. 5; Isa. xxxiii. 22), and owns itself His by word and deed. Hence Israel stood to the other nations of the earth in the same relation as the priesthood to the laity. Such, at least, was its destination. As it failed to realize it, it too required a special order of priests.

But although in Israel the principle of a Divine theocracy was restricted within the narrow limits of its own nationality, there was yet among the people a certain consciousness of the truth, that the principle itself was of universal application. And as it was evident that the Mosaic religion, as such, could never become the religion of all nations,—to mention only one circumstance, it was plain that all the nations of the earth could not come up to the Temple at Jerusalem to celebrate the feasts, —they believed that the time would come when the spirit of this theocratic principle would be delivered from the symbolical and local forms of Judaism (Jer. xxx. 31). (This is also recognised by Br. Bauer, die Religion des A. Test. ii. 389; Vatke, i. S. 442.) This perfecting and glorification, although at the same time abolition, of the O. Test. kingdom of God, is realized in the Person of the Messiah, who appears as the visible Representative of God Himself, its King. Under Him, the particular kingdom of God becomes a world-kingdom, apprehended in a spiritual sense; and the saints with their King compose this kingdom, of which there shall be no end (Dan. vii. 14, 18, 22). Now, because this kingdom of God was expected to be fully realized in the coming era of the Messiah, when God should take the kingdom upon Himself by a visible Representative, the perfected kingdom of God was called pre-eminently by the name βασιλεία τοῦ Θεοῦ. It was in this sense that the βασιλεία τ. Θεοῦ was expected at that time by many among the Jews (Luke xvii. 20, xix. 11, xxiii. 52). In this sense was the βασιλεία τ. Θεοῦ proclaimed as at hand by John the Baptist: in this sense, too, the Prophet Isaiah (xl. 9) uses the paraphrastic expression, "Behold your God;" אִתְגְּלִיָה מַלְכוּתָא דֶאֱלָהֲכוֹן, "the kingdom of your

God is revealed" (similarly **Targum**, Micah iv. 7). In rabbinical language, it was very common to substitute the term Heaven for the name of God (Luke xv. 21): hence we find in rabbinical writings the mention of the מַלְכוּת שָׁמַיִם much more frequently than of the מַלְכוּת אֱלֹהִים; and in St Matthew almost invariably βασιλεία τῶν οὐρανῶν, while the other Evangelists have all without exception βασ. τ. Θεοῦ. The latter expression does, however, occur in Matt. (vi. 33, xii. 28, xiii. **43**, xxi. 31, 43, xxvi. 29). In rabbinical language the term has a double signification, the spiritual and moral kingdom, and the historical kingdom. (Nitzsch on vi. **10**.) The Rabbins very often understand by מַלְכוּת שָׁמַיִם what we call Divine worship, adoration of God,[1] the sum of religious duties. But they also do understand by it the kingdom of the Messiah, although they do not expressly call it the kingdom of God (Schoettgen horæ Talmudicæ on Matt. vi. 10; and diss. de regno Cœlorum, § 6). The usual expression for the latter conception was עוֹלָם הַבָּא; comp. LXX. Isa. ix. 6, Cod. Alex. πατὴρ τοῦ αἰῶνος μέλλοντος: similarly the expression יְרוּשָׁלַיִם שֶׁל מַעְלָה. (Gal. iv. 25, 26; Rev. xxi. 2, 10.)

Now Christ, in full consciousness of His own Messiahship, declares that the kingdom of God, which men expected should come with Him, was really present; but at the same time He intimates that it is also future: so too His Apostles. As *present* the kingdom of God is spoken of in the following passages: Matt. xi. 12, **xii. 28**, xvi. 19; Mark xii. **34**, Luke xvi. 15, xvii.

---

[1] The passages have **been** collected by Lightfoot and Wettstein, on Matt. iii. **2**, especially Schoettgen **on** Matt. xi. 29. The last also remarks, that between עוֹל מִצְוֹת and עוֹל מַלְכוּת שָׁמַיִם there is no distinction whatever. No doubt, honouring God implies the keeping of the commandments, and so far there is no difference: but the phrase "קִבֵּל מַלְכוּת שָׁמַיִם," taken strictly, appears to have meant, not the fulfilling of duties, nor even keeping the commandments, but inward piety, the submission of rhe **spirit to** God (see the passage Tanchuma, f. **5**, 1, and Cod. **Berachoth**, f. **16**, 1, and the Gemara in Pinner's ed. of the Babylon. Talmud, i. 2 §, S. 2). **Schoettgen** (diss. de regn. cœl. § 6) asserts, that he is not acquainted with any passage in which the Messianic kingdom is expressly called the kingdom *of God*: But surely this is implied in that petition in the **Jewish** prayers: "Thy kingdom come;" as in the solemn prayer Kaddisch, **where** the petitions occur, the one immediately after the other: יַמְלִיךְ מַלְכוּתֵיהּ וְיַצְמַח פּוּרְקָנֵיהּ, "that He **may help His kingdom** to the dominion, and let the Redemption arise."

20, 21; Rom. xiv. 17; 1 Cor. iv. 20; Col. i. 13, iv. 11; Heb. xii. 28. As *future,* in the following: Matt. xiii. 43, xxv. 34, xxvi. 29; Mark ix. 47; Luke xiii. 29, xxii. 16; 1 Cor. vi. 9, 10, xv. 50; 2 Thess. i. 5; 2 Tim. iv. 1, 18; 2 Pet. i. 11; Acts xiv. 22, etc. The idea of this kingdom of God is no other than the Old Test. one: an organized community, which has its principle of life in the will of the personal God. The difference is, that henceforth the Representative of God, through whom He makes known and realizes His will, is Himself present: from this it is also called ἡ βασιλεία τοῦ Χριστοῦ (Eph. v. 5; 2 Pet. i. 11; comp. J. Gerhard, loci theol., T. xx. 122 ff.). Moreover, the manner in which this N. Test. kingdom seeks to realize itself is different. The particular and national limitation exist no longer: civil life becomes detached from the religious; symbols are succeeded by the truth; the law is displaced by grace (John i. 17). Thus the external kingdom of God becomes an inward kingdom (Luke xvii. 20, 21). But since every internal force must have its external manifestation, so must also that living power which has gone forth from Christ, which has inly knit together the faithful in one communion and fellowship, receive its outward expression: accordingly, it does receive it in the ἐκκλησία, Matt. xvi. 18. As regards the import of St Matthew's expression, βασιλεία τῶν οὐρανῶν, it might be supposed that he thereby meant to convey the idea, that this kingdom includes in its embrace the heavenly and the earthly together,—a thought which we find in St Paul and in Matt. vi. 10. But as the phrase is peculiar to St Matthew, and as this phase of the idea is never brought prominently forward, we shall more rightly regard the expression as identical with βασιλεία τ. Θεοῦ.

Further, this New Test. kingdom of God is, both from within and from without, in the individual as in the whole community, a growing, a *becoming* kingdom. Christ calls it an expanding grain of mustard-seed (comp. Matt. xiii. 31, 32; Mark iv. 32): hence the daily petition, "Thy kingdom come." Now, as we have seen that the O. Test. kingdom of God was perfected and completed when it ceased to be external, and became internal by being enthroned in the heart; so, on the other hand, the perfection of the New Testament kingdom will consist in its complete incarnation and externalization,—that is, when it shall attain an outward manifestation adequately expressing, exactly corresponding to, its internal principle.¹ We are also taught to believe that, along with this outward manifestation of the kingdom of God, certain cosmical changes will take place: there will be a new heaven and a new earth (Rom. viii. 19—22; Matt. xix. 28; Col. iii. 4; 2 Pet. iii. 13; Rev. xxi.). According to Rothe, the form of this perfect incarnation of the Church will be the State: that is, the complete moral organism, in which the religious principle which has been nurtured and natured in the Church shall have become an all-permeating and pervading soul. If so, then the end would be like the beginning, a religious state; only with this unspeakable difference, that whereas at the beginning the natural was immediately regarded as the religious, in the end the natural shall have mediately become the religious.²

Owing to the comprehensiveness and many-sidedness of this conception, it is a matter of the first importance to gain the true point of union under which all its different elements may be combined; in attaining which, nothing can better assist us than a careful consideration of the genesis and history of the conception. By neglect of this method, commentators, ancient and modern, formed a partial idea of the expression βασ. τ. Θεοῦ, and mistook one or other of its many phases for a comprehensive view of the whole.³ Since the time of Semler, how-

---

¹ "It follows, that when the Church becomes outward, then will also be connected therewith something untrue to its idea."—Nitzsch.

² The chief mistake in Rothe's view appears to be, that he speaks of a *gradual* transition of the Church into the State in its present form. On this point we agree rather with Stahl. It is indeed impossible to restrict the State to the sphere of justice; but an important element in the State certainly are its relations to crime, to law and discipline. Rothe, however, is uncertain if law and discipline are to be regarded as forming an element in the perfected State (Anfaenge der christ. Kirche, i. S. 32). But if this element is wanting, the idea of the State retained in this 'perfected state' is only of the most general character. Further, Rothe (S. 11) admits that cosmical changes will take place, which cannot be regarded as the result of a natural development. Can we then think that in the perfect state there will be an influence put forth upon nature analogous to the present, to be regarded as proceeding with it in progressive order? In any case, we must say, that as the Church in its present specific manifestations and working will disappear, so also will the State. Only, the question remains, will action, in the perfected kingdom of God, be simply a manifestation of goodness, or as the putting forth of a power over nature?

³ Euth. in Matth. iii. 2: in that passage he understands βασιλ. τῶν οὐρανῶν to mean Christ Himself. He goes on to say: ἢ βασ. οὐρ. λέγει τ. πολιτείαν

ever, exegesis has been led more to take into consideration the Old Testament and Jewish point of connection with New Testament ideas. Still, modern expositors have fallen short of a right apprehension of this conception. Either they have taken too superficial a view of what is the point of unity between the Old Testament and the New in this connection—as Wahl, who (even in his 3d edition) is satisfied with the abstract common element, felicitas nunc et olim per Jesum obtinenda; or they have altogether lost sight of the idea of any common element in the Old and New Testament views, and found in this most vital biblical thought nothing more than an *accommodation* to Jewish notions. Thus Semler himself, who substituted for the "little, local, Jewish idea" of the kingdom of God, that of a doctrine destined for the moral improvement of man (elsewhere "the new plan of salvation" is the substitution he proposes). Zeller would substitute the meagre idea of the "character of the Christian religion." [1] Others have given the view correctly, with this exception, that, ignoring the existence of a kingdom of God in this world, they have restricted the expression to a designation of the perfected state hereafter: so the old expositors of the Western Church (se on vi. 10); and among the moderns, Koppe (exc. 1, ad ep. ad Thess.), Keil (hist. dogm. de regno Messiæ, 1781), and Storr (Opusc. i.)—the latter includes in the expression the dominion of Christ from the time of His elevation to the right hand of God. [2] The idea

τῶν ἀγγέλων, ἣν ὁ Χριστὸς ὅσον οὔπω νομοθετεῖν ἔμελλε διὰ τῶν εὐαγγελικῶν ἐντολῶν· λέγεται δὲ βασ. οὐρ. καὶ ἡ ἀπόλαυσις τῶν ἐν οὐρανοῖς ἀγαθῶν. δηλοῖ δὲ καὶ ἄλλα πλείονα τὸ ὄνομα τῆς βασ. τ. οὐρ., πολυσήμαντον ὄν, ὡς προϊόντες εὑρήσομεν. Zwingly on John iii. 5: capitur hic regnum Dei pro *doctrina cœlesti* et prædicatione evangelii ut Luc. 18, capitur aliquando pro *vita æterna* Matt. 25, Luc. 14, quandoque pro *ecclesia* et congregatione fidelium ut Matt. 13. 24.

[1] Bahrdt (das Neue Testam. u. s. w., S. 6): "Because the Jews expected a Messiah who should appear at the head of the nation as their king, Jesus found it expedient to conceal His benevolent intention (to unite men in one general moral religion), and to represent the adherents of the better religion under the figure of a kingdom, etc." This accommodation-evasion is also to be found in the 3d edition of Bretschneider's Lexicon.

[2] In Fleck de regno divino, Chr. Gottfr. Bauer de causis, quibus intuitur rectum super ratione regni divini judicium (comm. Theol., ed. Rosenmüller and Maurer, i. 2), the view given is wanting in unity and definiteness: comp. Baumgarten-Crusius bibl. Theol. S. 149–157. From recent times, comp. Neander,

of the βασιλεία τοῦ Θεοῦ was most fully apprehended and most explicitly set forth by Origen. In his treatise, περὶ εὐχῆς, T. i. 238, we read: δηλονότι ὁ εὐχόμενος ἐλθεῖν τὴν βασιλείαν τοῦ Θεοῦ, περὶ τοῦ τὴν ἐν αὐτῷ βασιλείαν τοῦ Θεοῦ ἀνατεῖλαι καὶ καρποφορῆσαι καὶ τελειωθῆναι, εὐλόγως εὔχεται. παντὸς μὲν ἁγίου ὑπὸ Θεοῦ βασιλευομένου καὶ τοῖς πνευματικοῖς νόμοις τοῦ Θεοῦ πειθομένου, οἱονεὶ εὐνομουμένην πόλιν οἰκοῦντος αὐτόν· παρόντος αὐτῷ τοῦ πατρὸς καὶ συμβουλεύοντος τῷ πατρὶ τοῦ Χριστοῦ ἐν τῇ τετελειωμένῃ ψυχῇ κατὰ τὸ εἰρημένον, οὗ πρὸ βραχέος ἐμνημόνευον· πρὸς αὐτὸν ἐλευσόμεθα καὶ μονὴν παρ' αὐτῷ ποιησόμεθα. After a few explanations, he goes on to say that the more God's name is hallowed, the more will His kingdom come, and that which we read of, 1 Cor. xiii. 9, 10, will be fulfilled, and adds: τῇ οὖν ἐν ἡμῖν βασιλείᾳ τοῦ Θεοῦ ἡ ἀκρότης ἀδιαλείπτως προκόπτουσιν ἐνστήσεται, ὅταν πληρωθῇ τὸ παρὰ τῷ ἀποστόλῳ εἰρημένον, ὅτι ὁ Χριστὸς, πάντων αὐτῷ τ. ἐχθρῶν ὑποταγέντων, παραδώσει τ. βασιλείαν τ. Θεῷ κ. πατρὶ, ἵνα ᾖ ὁ Θεὸς τὰ πάντα ἐν πᾶσι. Regarding the conception from another point of view, he observes elsewhere (T. 14, in Matth. T. iii. p. 929), that what is promised to the poor is really Christ Himself, as their αὐτοβασιλεία.

Among the Reformers, Luther, taking the passage in connection with Phil. iii. 21, regards the life of Christians in the kingdom of heaven as an anticipation in *faith* of the perfected kingdom of God (Auslegung des viii. Psalm., § 22, 23, in Walch v. 296): "Through the power of the Holy Ghost, our heart has, with faith in the Word, laid hold of life in heaven. But now the flesh hangeth yet upon us, and our soul remains as it were in a gloomy prison-house, so that she cannot behold the glory of our civil life (πολιτεία) and inheritance in heaven. But when the body falls to pieces, then she will see no more in parts, but face to face, as St Paul says, 1 Cor. xiii. 12." In his beautiful sermon on the kingdom of God (Walch xii. S. 1938 ff.), he brings out the truth, that in this kingdom God governs, not by the law, but by the forgiveness of sins; and that Christ is there appointed to be the Healer of the sick, the infirm, and the poor. In his exposition of the Larger Catechism, he brings together the two phases of the kingdom

---

Leben Jesu, 5 Aufl. S. 126; Rothe, die Anfänge der christlichen Kirche, i. § 1, 2, 35.

of God, the present and the future, when he says: "God's kingdom comes to us in two ways: first, it comes to us in a temporal way in the Word, and in faith; again, it comes to us eternally in revelation. Now, we pray for both, that it may come to those who are not in it as yet, and to us who have received it, ever increasingly from day to day, and at length in life eternal." Calvin dwells more upon the ethical signification of the term; when, however, he refers to the growing realization of the kingdom of God, viewed in this sense, the future historical significance is brought forward. Falluntur, he says on John iii. 3, qui regnum Dei pro cœlo accipiunt, cum potius spiritualem vitam significet, quæ fide in hoc mundo inchoatur, magisque indies adolescit secundum assiduos fidei progressus (comp. on Matt. vi. 10 and iii. 2).

Now, when we read here that the kingdom of God is bestowed upon the poor in spirit, we can understand that, to the hearers, as apprehended from their point of view, what was promised did appear as that kingdom of the Messiah which was expected and looked for by them; and that what the Saviour meant, was the kingdom of God, in the widest compass of that conception as a kingdom, beginning in the present, and to be perfected in the future. So, too, in vers. 10, 19, 20, although in ver. 19 the use of the Future tense shows that the reference there is principally to the consummated future kingdom; as likewise in vii. 21. As the blessings and the promises corresponds to each other, we are to understand the kingdom of God (ver. 3), as promised to the poor in spirit, as implying the fulness of riches. In ver. 10, side by side with this idea, is a reference to that kingdom as a sure refuge for the persecuted.

Ver. 4. Wettstein asserts, and in this he is followed by Griesbach and D. Schulz, that Cod. D, the Vulgate, Clem. Alex. (Strom. iv. 376), Origen (in Matt. xxi. 3), Eus., Gregory Nyss., Jerome, and others, make vers. 4 and 5 change places: so also Lachmann, Tischendorf, whom Neander follows; comp. Griesbach, comment. critica in text. græc. N. T., i. 45. With regard to Origen, certainly in one passage (T. iii. p. 740, de la Rue) he urges this order, on the ground that it is intended that heaven should be first promised, and then, after it, the earth. Yet he himself elsewhere (p. 780) follows the usual order: Chromatius also has both. It was thus uncertain what was the proper arrangement of the verses; but as Cod. D. alone is in favour of placing the πραεῖς first, we must aside by the received version. That the change is recommanded by the sequence of thought, as Neander and O. v. Gerlach think, cannot be said. On the contrary, the probability is, that the change was introduced on certain *mystical* grounds: either it was thought, with Origen, that the promise of the earth, as the *lower* good, should come immediately after the promise of heaven; or because some mystical meaning was attached to γῆ, as forming a *higher stage* of blessedness (Gregory of Nyssa, T. i. p. 772). Chrysostom also notices, that by some it was understood as the γῆ νοητή; and in Matthäi (edit. maj.) a scholiast explain it thus: γῆν δέ τινα λέγομεν ἀγαθὴν, ῥέουσαν λογικὸν, ἄδολον γάλα καὶ μυστικὸν μέλι, ἧς σκιὰ ἡ ἐν τῷ νόμῳ ὀνομασθεῖσα τοῖς κατὰ σάρκα Ἰουδαίοις.

I. The Ascription of Blessedness.

Πενθεῖν, frequently conjoined with κλαίειν (Mark. xvi. 10; James iv. 9; Rev. xviii. 15, 19), is a stronger expression than λυπεῖσθαι. Chrys.: τοὺς μετ' ἐπιτάσεως λυπουμένους. In James iv. 9, κατήφεια is placed in antithesis to χαρά; to loud γέλως again, is opposed πένθος. Here a question arises, as to whether there is any temporal reference implied in this sorrow, as in the cas of the πτωχεία of ver. 3, or whether the mourning spoken of is exclusively the grief of repentance. The latter is the view usually taken: the mourning spoken of is the sorrow of penitence immediately flowing from a felt poverty of spirit (Clem. Alex., Strom. iv. p. 580; Hilary, Chrys., Basil, Ambrose, Jerome, Zwingli, Bucer, Calov, and many others). This λύπη, experienced with reference to the soul's relation to God, works μετάνοια, 2 Cor. vii. 10. This penitential grief is not, however, to be regarded as confined to the period of conversion, but ought to be viewed as a continuous condition of the soul (see above, p. 64). Zw.: qui enim sese ad Dei lucernam examinat, semper invenit, quod displiceat, semper, quod fleat. Other views are not so worthy of adoption, as being not so well in keeping with the context; such as that which makes the cause of sorrow to consist in persecution for Christ's sake (Mel., Mald., Wett., Hunn.), or, less definitely, in the loss of earthly possessions, endured in persecution on account of Christ (Aug., Greg. Nyss.). Such a cause of sorrow would be here too isolated; and, moreover, this subject is not mentioned in order till ver. 11. If with regard to the πτωχοί the reference to temporal concerns was admitted, and if such a reference is natural with regard to the πραεῖς in ver. 5, we shall naturally expect to find it here also, in this idea of mourning which must have been so familiar to the hearers. These three predicates will then be regarded as an analysis of one and the same idea— that, namely, which is expressed in Isa. lxi. 1, 2, by various related predicates, especially as in that passage the corresponding expression לְנַחֵם כָּל־אֲבֵלִים occurs. That kingdom of God, which those promises of Isaiah contemplate, Christ is seeking to establish (Luke iv. 18): but of the two points of view included in the predicates which Isaiah there employs, the external and the internal, Christ brings the latter into prominence, and retains the former merely as forming a background to it. Luther also, in accordance with his view of πτωχοί, explains πενθοῦντες of the probation of sorrow borne by the Christian in a true spirit of faith and patience: "Just as not that man is called poor in spirit who has no money, but he who covets none, and places not in riches his trust and confidence: not *he* is called a mourner who outwardly hangs his head, but he who does not fix his confidence on the hope of having here only good days, and living in mirth and revelling like the world." Similarly O. v. Gerlach: "All these blessings are at the same time exhortations; and the mourning here spoken of is mourning with the consciousness that, in our sorrow for earthly need, no earthly succour can deliver us."

II. The Promise.

The promised consolation corresponds to the mourning which is called blessed: and here the consolation is not given by mere words, but in fact (Luke vi. 24; Sir. vi. 16, xxvi. 4). This consoling efficacy is only one of a thousand virtues which come forth from the kingdom of God to bless men. In hearing this μακαρισμός, the hearers must have had brought before their view the consolations promised for the Messianic time: for comfort and consolation were expected to come to men with His kingdom (comp. the prophetic passages, Isa. xl. 1, lxi. 2, lxvi. 11), nay, the Messiah and His kingdom were expressly called ἡ παράκλησις τοῦ Ἰσραήλ (Luke ii. 25, the Targum of Isa. iv. 3, xxxiii. 20, Jer. xxxi. 6; comp. Buxtorf lex. talm. s. v. נֶחָמָה and the rabbinical name for the Messiah מְנַחֵם. See Lightfoot on John xiv. 16). Such a παράκλησις was the portion of the anxious mourner Simeon when he cried: νῦν ἀπολύεις τὸν δοῦλόν σου ἐν εἰρήνῃ (Luke ii. 29). In the sense in which Christ spoke, the promise is to be regarded as fulfilled already in this life, but perfectly in the perfected kingdom of God in the life to come.

Ver. 5.

I. THE ASCRIPTION OF BLESSEDNESS.

In this beatitude we may clearly discern the Old Testament foundation on which the thought is based. It is only a repetition of the promise of Ps. xxxvii. 11; the LXX. also translates the עֲנָוִים of the Psalmist by πραεῖς.

Πραΰς, classically, is only the opposite of ὀργίλος, θυμοειδής: but the Hebrew עָנִי unites the significations of meek and humble, as, according to its etymology (from עָנָה to bow down), it means the bowed-down by sorrow, the patient endurer; so that עָנִי also often includes this idea, as in Isa. lxvi. 2, where, co-ordinate with עָנִי, is the phrase נְכֵה־רוּחַ and חָרֵד עַל־דְּבָרִי. In Hellenistic language πραΰς is used as the opposite of ὑψηλοκάρδιος. The LXX. translate עָנָו and עָנִי by πραΰς: the Peschito Version has here ܡܟܝܟܐ, which means generally "humble"[1] (for the proper word for meek is ܢܝܚܐ Matt. xi. 29): Ar. Polygl. المتواضعين "to the humbled." When St James (iii. 13. ff.) opposes πραΰτης to ζῆλος and ἐριθεία, and exhorts (i. 21) to receive ἐν πραΰτητι the Christian truth, what he means by the expression is, that unassuming disposition which is opposed to a quarrelsome temper. In 2 Cor. x. 1, πραότης and ἐπιείκεια are co-ordinated with ταπεινὸν εἶναι; and elsewhere this virtue appears in close connection with ταπεινοφροσύνη (Matt. xi. 29;

---

[1] Comp. עָנָיו in rabbin. language; also the use of ܡܟܝܟܐ in the Syriac, in the sense of "pious," may be compared.

Eph. iv. 2). The older commentators, however, even of the most diverse schools (Clem. Alex., Mel., Calv., Chemnitz, Episc., Cocc., Bengel), hold to the ancient classical signification, and explain πραΰς here: non cupidus vindictæ. If, now, we are to retain the view of a gradation in these beatitudes, the idea intended to be brought more prominently forward here will be that of Humility. According to Rambach, Stier: it is that lowly disposition of heart which has in it the susceptibility of being moulded by the Spirit of God, in contradistinction to the opposing, defiant inflexibility of natural self-will.

II. The Promise.

What surprises here, is the apparent contrast between the benediction and the promise: the meek and the humble, the very persons of whom one would least expect it, are to attain to supremacy and power. Here especially a temporal reference of the word forces itself upon us. In the world, that principle holds good which is expressed by the insurrection-loving Britons in Tacitus (vita Agricolæ, c. 15): nihil profici patientia nisi ut graviora tanquam ex facili tolerantibus imperentur. This was also the principle of the Jewish nation at that time. Luther, too, remarks: "Particularly He refers in these words to the Jews, who supposed they should suffer no wrong from any heathen, and thought they did well when they quietly avenged themselves, and used to defend the practice by quotations from Moses, such as Deut. xxviii. 13: 'The Lord shall make thee the head, and not the tail; and thou shalt be above only, and thou shalt not be beneath.' That would be all very well. But we read: When God Himself doeth it, then it is well done." This temporal reference of the text is dwelt upon exclusively by Clericus (by Gratz also): felices judicandi mansueti, quia mansuetudine sua grati erunt rerum potientibus nec solum vertere cogentur ut (illi) qui sunt indolis ferocioris. If, however, we inquire more minutely into the meaning of that Old Testament passage on which the Saviour's words are based, Ps. xxxvii. 11, we shall see here a notable instance of the manner in which the Saviour deepens and develops the Old Testament ideas, and imparts to them the N. Testament πλήρωσις. The original expression in Ps. xxxvii. 11 is: עֲנָוִים יִירְשׁוּ־אָרֶץ, and ver. 29: צַדִּיקִים יִירְשׁוּ־אָרֶץ וְיִשְׁכְּנוּ לָעַד עָלֶיהָ, comp. vers. 9—29, and

Ps. xv. 13. In contrast to this promise, it is said of the מְרֵעִים, vers. 9, 10, 22, that they shall be rooted out and destroyed from their place. Comp. especially vers. 34—37. Also in Prov. ii. 21, 22, we read in the LXX.: ὅτι εὐθεῖς κατασκηνώσουσι γῆν καὶ ὅσιοι ὑπολειφθήσονται ἐν αὐτῇ· ὁδοὶ ἀσεβῶν ἐκ γῆς ὀλοῦνται, οἱ δὲ παράνομοι ἐξωσθήσονται ἀπ' αὐτῆς. According to their most general idea, those sayings foretold the open and final victory of the patient sufferers over the ungodly. More specifically, they were understood the announce the future perfecting of a kingdom of God in the Holy Land, from which those who were alienated from God were to be excluded: this is also implied in Ps. i. 5 (see Ewald), and more clearly by the Prophets Isaiah (lxii. 12, lx. 21) and Zechariah (xiv. 21). As regards the use which our Saviour makes of the words, it is first to be taken generally as a reference to the truth (which the history of individuals and of communities alike so amply corroborates, Rom. xii. 21), that humility and meekness are a victorious principle in the history of the world. Æsop makes Chilo ask what was the occupation of God, and the answer is: He abases the high and exalts the lowly; a reply which Bayle calls an abrégé de l'histoire humaine. Now, even taken in this general sense, the expression involves a thought of deep significance. But its import is not yet exhausted. The developed doctrine of the kingdom of God discloses to us the final terminus which the prophets dimly discerned: a cosmical change, introducing a new earth in which righteousness shall dwell, in which the heavenly Jerusalem shall be established among men. (See above, p. 75.) Then shall they who have suffered with the Redeemer also with Him inherit the kingdom, as Old Testament prophecy (Dan. vii. 29) had foretold: Matt. xix. 28, xxv. 34; 2 Tim. ii. 10; Rev. iii. 21, v. 10. If we believe at all that the Saviour foresaw the fulfilment of the kingdom which He founded, we can entertain no doubt that He had it before His eye when He spoke these words. Accordingly, we see that in this promise humility and meekness are by Him pronounced to be the truly world-conquering principle, with reference to their ultimate victory in the history of the future.

Here, too, the various expositors have appropriated to themselves each a different phase of this many-sided conception. Some have viewed this victory of meekness in its commencement and progress; others, in its perfection: a few have regarded the promise to be of earthly possessions; others, again, of spiritual. The expression $γῆ$ is taken for the sum of all that earth can bestow of possessions, by Chrysostom, by Theoph., Euthym., and Luther. The last observes: "As above He has promised the kingdom of heaven and an eternal inheritance, so here He promises an inheritance upon earth." Beza enlarges this idea, and at the same time retains the genetic and historical connection with the Old Testament representation when he thus comments on the passage; pacifice hac vita et bonis suis fruentur eaque ad posteros suos transferent. (Similarly Hunnius.) Grotius, on the contrary, narrows the idea when he observes: $τὴν$ $γῆν$ dicere videtur firmas et constantes amicitias quæ in terris optima longe est possessio. Some, abstracting from the connection the concrete eschatological idea (as regards the expression $κληρονομεῖν\ τ.\ γῆν$, they quote Rom. iv. 13), retain merely the general idea of a spiritual inheritance of the world; as Cocceius, Heidegger (exercitationes), Heumann (poecile sive epistolæ miscellaneæ, T. iii. p. 376), Michaelis, Paulus. Neander too; at least he lays greatest stress upon this view: "The inheritance of the earth is that world-dominion which Christians, as organs of the Spirit of Christ, are ever more and more to obtain, as the kingdom of God wins for itself ever increasing sway over mankind and the relations of society, until, in its final consummation, the whole earth shall own its dominion."[1] But with regard to the passage Rom. iv. 13, which Wettstein also brings to bear upon our text, precisely the application which St Paul there makes of the promise of Canaan, shows that here too the eschatological view is the correct one. Other expositors, in direct antagonism to the spiritualistic view, adopt the eschatological view absolutely and immediately: a few of whom even take $γῆ$, as meaning the new earth, to denote simply the regnum gloriæ, as Jerome, Zwingly, Calov. Basil (hom. in Ps. xxxiii.) explains $γῆ$, $ἡ\ ἐπουράνιος\ Ἱερουσαλήμ$. Gregory Nyssenus, influenced by a consideration of the gradation in the beatitudes, speaks of the "land of the living" (Ps. cxlii.), which in the future world is heaven, where grows the true tree of life. Others come to the same conclusion, whilst retaining the genetic con-

---

[1] Life of Christ, translated by J. M'Clintock, Bohn 1852, p. 243.

nection of the passage with Ps. xxxvii. 11. Origen and the Greek scholiasts had already found in γῆ (see above p. 78) a typical reference to the promised land, "flowing with milk and honey." Vitringa connects the passage with the promise of dominion over the world, given in Dan. vii. 27, which he says is to have its fulfilment in the kingdom of a thousand years which shall precede the judgment. Nevertheless, by many commentators it is acknowledged that different phases are combined in the promise of the verse. Chemnitz: pertinet promissio ad hanc, potissimum vero ad futuram vitam: already on this earth is to them a sure portion awarded; chiefly, however, in the life to come will their full inheritance be vouchsafed. With Jansenius, Bengel thinks that even now, although here the meek must often succumb, the victory takes place, inasmuch as all things must work together for their good, while the absolute and perfect triumph promised (Rev. v. 10) is yet to come. Calvin, also, calls attention to that Divine justice manifesting itself throughout the whole **course of the** world's history, to which the humble Christian may safely entrust his cause; but at the same time he opens up the **view of the** future judgment. Erasmus (and similarly Glassius) ranges together various elements of the fulfilment of this promise: Sed hæc est nova dilatandæ possessionis ratio, ut plus impetret ab ultro largientibus mansuetudo, quam per fas nefasque paret aliorum rapacitas. Placidus autem, qui mavult sua cedere quam pro his digladiari, tot locis habet fundum, quot locis reperit amantes evangelicæ mansuetudinis. Invisa est omnibus pervicacia, mansuetudini favent et ethnici. Postremo si perit possessio miti, damnum non est, sed ingens lucrum, periit ager, sed incolumi tranquillitate animi. Postremo, ut omnibus excludatur mitis, tanto certior est illi cœlestis terræ possessio, unde depelli non poterit.

Ver. 6. From this verse the reference to the Old Testament background ceases. Neither have we any more to note, as hitherto, any allusion to the outward circumstances of poverty, sorrow, or abasement. This must have rendered it all the more apparent to the hearers, that equally in the preceding verses the principal stress was laid on the spiritual phase. The three verses have expressed under various forms the sense of want: this verse intimates the *object* of that want. It is δικαιοσύνη.

δίκαιον, in accordance with the Arabic derivation of the Hebrew צָדִיק, and with the classical meaning of the word in Aristotle, means that which corresponds to a rule or law, which is right or straight in reference to it. Arist. Ethics, v. 1, 8, τὸ μὲν δίκαιον τὸ νόμιμον καὶ τὸ ἴσον. Accordingly צְדָקָה, δικαιοσύνη, in the state of mind which corresponds to the moral requirements of God's righteousness, Deut. vi. 25; as we read in Josephus, de Maccabæis v. 24: καὶ δικαιοσύνην παιδεύει (ὁ νόμος), ὥστε διὰ πάντων τῶν ἠθῶν ἰσονομίαν καὶ εὐσέβειαν διδάσκειν, ὥστε μόνον τὸν ὄντα Θεὸν σέβειν μεγαλοπρεπῶς. Now it is this righteousness, uprightness before God, which in the time of the law could only partially be realized, that the disciples are to attain in the kingdom of Christ: in vi. 33, Rom. xiv. 17, we read of a δικαιοσύνη τῆς βασιλείας τοῦ Θεοῦ.

Now, this perfect righteousness belongs to the eschatological kingdom of God, in its future perfect development. 1 Cor. xv. 28; 2 Pet. iii. 13. Gl. ord.: hæc justitia non plene implebitur *donec Deus sit omnia in omnibus:* ideo hic possumus esurire, non saturari. The end which all healthy religious striving proposes to itself, is to attain this righteousness in fellowship with God; and it can be perfectly realized only when the will is entirely united with God. This condition of perfect oneness of will with God is essential to full self-contentment, that is, blessedness. Therefore, when this righteousness is attained, then, and not till then, will perfect blessedness enter. This righteousness Old Testament prophecy regarded, accordingly, as the highest blessing which the Messianic kingdom would bring with it: Isa. iv. 4, iii. 4, xi. 9, lx. 21; Zech. xiv. 20, 21, etc. At the period of Christ's coming, too, the better people in Israel looked forward with longing to the ὁσιότης and δικαιοσύνη of the Messianic kingdom (Luke i. 75). This pure desire the Saviour meets in this verse. He designates this spiritual longing by expressions borrowed from the strongest physical wants. Thirst was, especially for the inhabitants of the East, the figure for the most intense desire. In this sense it is used of spiritual things, Amos viii. 11; Ps. xlii. 1; Isa. lv. 1, lxv. 13; John vi. 35, vii. 37: and, further, to reinforce the thought, hunger is added, Ps. xxxiv. 11; Ps. xlix. 10; John iv. 34. Now let it be observed, those whom the Saviour calls blessed are not those who possess this righteousness, but those who desire it:

and this is intelligible only on the supposition, that at His appearing this desire was to be satisfied. Only on this supposition, too, could He, whose commands went so far beyond the pharisaic fulfilment of the law, invite to Himself those who groaned beneath the burden of the law, and speak of the easiness of *His* yoke (Matth. xi. 30). In what way His appearing was to satisfy this earnest longing after righteousness, is not here disclosed (vide supra, p. 40); but in Rom. viii. 4, 5, we will find this more particularly set forth: it is the Spirit of life which proceeds from Christ, and which is received by faith in Christ, which can effect what the law could not do,—that is, can make us free from the law of sin and death.

It is surprising that so obvious an explanation should have nevertheless escaped not a few expositors. And, first, it has been overlooked by those who have attempted to establish a oneness of thought between St Matthew and St Luke, in whose account the τὴν δικαιοσύνην is wanting. According to Bucer, Calvin, Mald., the reference to the אֶבְיוֹנִים is continued in this verse: compare such expressions as Ps. lxxii. 4, "He shall keep the simple folk by their right, and defend the children of the poor." The hunger and thirst of which the verse speaks is thus supposed to be the desire of the poor for right usage on the part of others. But the figure is so commonly used to express a desire for spirituall things, and this δικαιοσύνη is so manifestly presented here as the final goal of the members of God's kingdom, that it is impossible to adopt this view. A different exegesis leaves the connection of the passage altogether out of sight, and introduces here the type of doctrine subsequently developed by St Paul. It would understand the δικαιοσύνη spoken of here as justitia imputata: thus Calov; to which conclusion Sarcerius also comes by the by-way of a metonymy: justitiam, says he, ponit pro causa justitiæ, pro *verbo;* est igitur sitire justitiam flagrare pro cognoscendo *verbo*, e quo postea fides, ex qua tandem ipsa justitia. This view is also referred to by Melanc. Chemnitz recognises it as one of the interpretations we may choose from. Bullinger connects the righteousness spoken of here with the justitia inhærens. Hunnius, on the contrary, rightly regards it as the justitia novæ obedientiæ attained by the justitia fidei. Luther, who says expressly that "the righteousness spoken of here is not that which makes a man accepted before God," passes on from the immediate idea of the verse to the secondary thought implied in it, viz., the desire to see righteousness obtain dominion among men. So, too, Zuingl. and Mel.; Jansenius also acknowledges that this idea is implied. Another exposition, which likewise restricts the meaning of the verse, and introduces an idea foreign to the order of thought, is that which Chrysostom, Theoph., Euthym. support, which makes out δικαιοσύνη to be the virtue of justitia rependens, as a preparatory step to the following virtue of mercy.

Others were led to an essentially different interpretation, by considering the construction of διψῆν with the accusative. It usually governs the genitive. Both constructions are in use, however: indeed, Josephus uses them indiscriminately. (See examples quoted by Kypke, in loco.) This circumstance, combined with the recollection that πεινῆν and διψῆν are used elsewhere in the service of the Gospel (1 Cor. iv. 11; Phil. iv. 12), and the comparison with Luke vi. 21, μακάριοι οἱ πεινῶντες νῦν, ὅτι χορτασθήσεσθε, gave occasion to some to take the accus. δικαιοσύνην *adverbially*, as meaning "*as to,* or, *on account of,* righteousness." Thus Clem. Alex. (Strom. l. iv. p. 444), who, however, also adds the common opinion; Valla (who quotes the LXX. in Ps. li. 16, cxlv. 7), Maldon., Rich. Simon (histoire des comm. du N. T., p. 248), Olearius, and Jansenius, who even went the length of basing upon the passage an argument for the meritoriousness of fasting.

Ver. 7. From this verse the discourse is addressed, not, as hitherto, to those who desire, but to those who possess. De Wette's exegesis of ver. 8 is not correct, when he refers it to those "who have a pure *longing* ofter spiritual health." There follow three virtues of possession: pity, purity, and peace. Carefully considered, these will be found to be not accidental ethical virtues, but characteristic Christian graces, the possession of which presupposes, as the exposition will show, the possession of salvation. Here, too, there is thus a latent announcement of salvation (see above, p. 40).

Ὁ ἔλεος, ἐν Hellenistic Greek, τὸ ἔλεος, denotes sympathy with the suffering, also with those who suffer through *sin*. Augustine and Gregory Nyss. subject the conception to an unjustifiable restriction, when they understand it simply as a benevolent or charitable disposition; for this is only one way in which this Christian virtue manifests itself. It is characteristic of the Saviour, that, in opposition to Pharisaism, He proves the moral worth of this ἔλεος in the sight of God, even from the O. Test. Scriptures, Matt. ix. 13, xii. 7, xxiii. 23. But He also gives expression to the conviction, that it is, above all, the experience of the mercy of God in a man's own soul which is fitted to call forth this virtue in him, Matt. v. 23 (compare the apostolic word, Eph. iv. 32). Moreover, in that prayer which men who are already Christians are supposed to pray, human compassion for sin is made the condition of receiving compassion from God (vi. 14, compare v. 23). In accordance with this idea is the promise given here. Thus the remark of Calov is substantially correct: hic aphorismus fructus fidei iustificantis cum omnibus consequentiis complecitur. On the other hand, to make the saying refer to that compensation which takes place in the sphere of human life, through the return of good offices (Calvin, Pisc., Cocc.), is a view opposed equally by the context and by the analogy of the passages above quoted.

Ver. 8. The exposition of this profound saying is begun by Gregory. Nyss. with these spirit-stirring words: ὅπερ παθεῖν εἰκὸς τοὺς ἔκ τινος ὑψηλῆς ἀκρωρείας εἰς ἀχανές τι κατακύπτοντας πέλαγος, τοῦτό μοι πέπονθεν ἡ διάνοια, ἐκ τῆς ὑψηλῆς τοῦ κυρίου φωνῆς οἷον ἀπό τινος κορυφῆς ὄρους εἰς τὸ ἀδιεξίτητον τ. νοημάτων βλέπουσα βάθος.

I. THE ASCRIPTION OF BLESSEDNESS.

The idea of a pure heart was also for the hearers no new idea. The Psalmist had required that he who would approach the sanctuary should have a בַּר לֵבָב, Ps. xxiv. 4. This בַּר לֵבָב distinguished the true Israelite from the false, Ps. lxxiii. 1. And David had prayed for a pure heart, Ps. li. 12. The question arises, as to whether the Saviour understood the expression in the Old Testament acceptation. Now, in Ps. lxxiii. it is evident that the purity of heart spoken of is in opposition to that impurity which manifests itself in appearances inconsistent with the truth of things. Then, in Ps. xxiv., after purity *deceit* is expressly spoken of; and also in Ps. li., the succeeding כון; a correct exegesis must conclude to imply, that in that passage purity is identical with sincerity (comp. Hengstenberg in loc.). In the Classics, *καθαρόν* means the *ἀκήρατον*, "the unmixed" (Jamblichus, vita Pyth. p. 129); hence also, sincerity in opposition to hypocrisy; and so, too, in the New Testament, where *καθαρός*, combined with *καρδία* and *συνείδησις*, forms the antithesis to *ὑπόκρισις*, 1 Tim. i. 5, iii. 9; 2 Tim. i. 3, ii. 22. The most restricted view that could be taken of the idea would be, if, with Baum.-Crusius, we understood it simply of uprightness in the dealings of man with man; a wider view, if understood principally of sincerity towards God; the widest, however, if we took it generally to denote moral purity, whether in the objective sense—of justification and forgiveness of sins, or in the subjective—of the possession, on the part of man, of a cleansed and purified heart; and the latter, either understood here in contrast to the outward legal purity of pharisaic morality (Luther, Bull., Chemn., Storr); or, apart from any such contrast, generally; or again, with a special limitation to the lusts of the flesh (Mel., Pisc., Mald., Calmet). The choice between this more limited view and the more general one is left open by Chrys., Theophylact, and Euthymius. The widest acceptation is the one which has been most generally adopted. Origen (hom. 73 in Joann. § 2) *οὐ τοὺς ἀπηλλαγμένους πορνείας, ἀλλὰ τοὺς πάντων ἁμαρτημάτων· πᾶσα γὰρ ἁμαρτία ῥύπον ἐντίθησι τῇ ψυχῇ*. Thus, generally, Clemens Alex. also (Strom. iv. p. 381): *ὅτ᾽ ἂν μηδὲν ἔχῃ νόθον τὸ ἡγεμονικόν*. Jerome: quos non arguit ulla conscientia peccati. Greg. Nyss., Zw., Grot., Calov, De Wette, Meyer, etc. Nor is this view opposed to the O. Test. usus linguae, as will appear if it be remembered that the divided לב (comp. לב ולב) is also spoken of with reference to God, and then it is called a spiritual *μοιχεία* (James iv. 5), the serving of two masters. Viewed in relation to God, this purity of heart is accordingly that undivided love which regards God alone as the highest good. So, too, in Ps. lxxiii., where this purity of heart is made the test and touchstone of the true Israel, this undivided love to God is expressed, ver. 25, "Whom have I in heaven but Thee?" Undoubtedly St James views doublemindedness in the light of impurity, when he requires the *δίψυχοί* to *ἁγνίζειν τὴν καρδίαν*. This is acknowledged by Bucer and Pellican, the former of whom remarks: Ne quid aliud corde volutes, aliud verbis et externa specie præ te feras, sed ex puro simplicique corde in gloriam Dei et salutem proximorum instituas omnia.

It has, indeed, been objected, that in the connection in which this verse occurs with ἐλεήμων before, and εἰρηνοποιός coming after it, it would be expected to relate only to a single virtue. But this objection will disappear if it can be shown here, as in the case of the first and third virtues mentioned, that, in the sense in which Christ used them, they are to be regarded as graces produced by the working of the new principle of faith. This καθαρότης τῆς καρδίας also, as explained by the light thrown upon it from the πλήρωσις τοῦ νόμου in this chapter, is possible only as the fruit of a life of faith. (Acts xv. 9.) Augustin: quis non quærat unde mundet quo videre possit, quem toto affectu desiderat? Expressit hoc divina testatio: "fide, inquit, mundans corda eorum." Sed quali fide? quæ per dilectionem operatur. (Gal. v. 6.) Druthmar applies the expression to a state of freedom from the reproaches of conscience: quos non remordet conscientia criminalis peccati; others to the justitia forensis attained through faith: any such reference, however, is opposed to the context. Also the view of Aug., Mald., Calv., who regard this καθαρότης as identical with the ἀκεραιότης required in Matt. x. 16, the opposite of which would be merely astutia, must be rejected: and that for the simple reason, that by these three virtues we must believe the Saviour to indicate so many special fruits of Christian faith.

II. The Promise.

The promise of the vision of God would not strike the hearers as something altogether new to them. To see the face of the earthly sovereign had been held by the Jews as the highest privilege (1 Kings x. 8; 2 Kings xxv. 19; Esth. i. 14); to behold the countenance of the heavenly King was with them an object of highest desire (Ex. xxxiii. 18; Josh. xiv. 8), and expressed a state of perfect blessedness: Ps. xi. 7, xvii. 15. Indeed, the appearance before the Lord in His temple on earth was itself an object of inward longing and delight. (Ps. lxiii. 3.) The last, the רְאוֹת אֶת־פְּנֵי יְהוָֹה, is, according to Lakemacher (observ. philol. P. i. p. 96) and Michaelis, *all* that the text means to allude to. Directly in contrast with that longing and the promise of its fulfilment, would now appear to be that axiom of the

O. Test. religion, that mortal man cannot see God and live, for at the sight of Him he dies. (Ex. xxxiii. 20.) According to Hupfeld (on Ps. xi. 7), all that this expression implied, was the idea that the unclean are forbidden a near approach to God. We must, however, take a wider view of this axiom, as implying finitum non esse capax infiniti: a thought which (without, however, any denial of the doctrine of the communication of the Divine Spirit to mortals) was the prevailing opinion of the Old Test. stage of development as respects the relation of God to man, an idea which continued to be held by the Ebionites. Then the expression, Num. xii. 8, does not appear to coincide with this axiom, and to present, over and above, the difficulty that a bodily form, תְּמוּנָה, seems to be ascribed to the Deity, and therewith a seeing of God with the bodily eyes seems to be affirmed. But, to begin with this saying concerning Moses, if we compare this תְּמוּנָה with the same word used in Job iv. 16, we shall easily bring Num. xii. 8 into harmony with Ex. xxxiii. 20. What Job speaks of is a vision, a picture of the imagination: now, if, similarly, Moses' תְּמוּנָה is only a sensible manifestation of God, not identical with His very nature, a theophany like that of which Ex. xxxiii. 23 speaks, then this expression תְּמוּנָה is no more a contradiction of the general canon than the manifestation that immediately followed on that occasion. Further, as for the expressions used Ps. xi. 7, xvii. 15, and the similar words, to "stand before God's face for ever" (Ps. xli. 13, cxl. 14; Job xxxiii. 26), all that can be said is, that they contain the utterance of a devout longing which lies beyond the sphere of dogmatic science, and has its root and spring in the very being and inmost soul of man—a longing for absolute fellowship with God; and this the New Testament clearly points out as the goal of humanity. Consequently, these expressions are not to be explained according to the canon of doctrine, but from the overflowings of the pious consciousness.[1] In Ps. xvii. 15, however, we may explain the difficult

---

[1] Even the Mohammedan religion, zealous as it is for the spiritual character of God, has allowed itself to borrow from Judaism the expression, النظر الى وجه الله, "The vision of the countenance of God," to denote Divine fellowship after death. (Reland, de religione Muh. l. 2, § 17; Pococke, Miscellanea ad Portam Mosis, p. 304.) The philosophic Gasali,

תְּמֻנָה after the analogy of Num. xii., to which it seems to allude, as a longing after a theophany of God: unless it appears better to regard this as simply an expression of overflowing desire after an "as-it-were bodily intercourse with the Godhead" (Hupfeld). Yet we find in the Old Testament theology intimations, which go on increasing in clearness and force, of the Godhead one day becoming visible and accessible to man in the תְּבוּנָה, in the כָּבוֹד of God. Here now the New Testament joins the Old with its doctrine of the Logos, in which the Θεὸς ἀόρατος visibly manifests Himself to His creatures, and takes upon Himself their nature, and **appears** personally amongst them. (John i. 18; Col. i. 15.) Only in 1 Tim. vi. 16 we find again the Old Testament idea that God is infinitely beyond the apprehension of finite man: "Whom no man had seen, nor can see;" an expression, however, which must be regarded as modified by the words 1 Cor. xiii. 12, concerning the limited nature of our knowledge.

Now the Old Testament forms of expression, above quoted, have passed over to the New Testament. The Apostles speak of a vision of God, Heb. xii. 14; 1 John iii. 2; and "to be before the throne of God, to see His face and to serve Him," is represented in the Revelation of St. John as the height of the blessedness of the perfected children of God (Rev. vii. 15, xxii. 4). As now, for the Christian layman, these phrases are nothing more than a figurative expression for the fulfilment **of** the desire after communion with God, so too this alone can **have** been the meaning which the hearers attached to the promise of this verse. For Christ, however, who ascribes to Himself as distinct from all other mortals a special vision of God (John vi. 46), the expression must have had a much deeper significance, and was no mere indefinite longing. **And** it is now the office of the expositor, first from apostolic sayings, next from a general view of the Christian knowledge of God, to determine, in so far as possible, what was implied in these **words** of our Lord.

In St Paul, we find the phrase "to see" used figuratively

---

however, in his dogmatical work كتاب الاربعين في اصول الدين explains the phrase to mean توحيد, which is the "becoming one with God."

as a phenomenological designation of that higher degree of knowledge which is characteristic of eternity, 2 Cor. v. 7; 1 Cor. xiii. 12. So, too, philosophy has availed herself of this term to denote a sphere of knowledge which goes beyond mere logical thinking, and is of the nature of intuition (Schelling, Billroth, Weisse; Goeschel, Aphorism. S. 139; Conradi, "die Unsterblichkeit und das ewige Leben," S. 144). In the two passages from St Paul above cited, the object seen is not particularly defined; the words $\kappa\alpha\vartheta\grave{\omega}\varsigma\ \grave{\epsilon}\pi\epsilon\gamma\nu\acute{\omega}\sigma\vartheta\eta\nu$, however, in 1 Cor. xiii. 12, lead us to regard God as the object. The phrase of the Apostle, like that in Ps. xvii. 15, is based upon those Old Testament words in Num. xii. on the relation of the knowledge of God possessed by Moses to that which the prophets enjoyed. Now what is there ascribed to Moses, is in a higher sense to be fulfilled in the perfected Church. It might seem as if in that passage the phrase $\kappa\alpha\vartheta\grave{\omega}\varsigma\ \kappa\alpha\grave{\iota}\ \grave{\epsilon}\pi\epsilon\gamma\nu\acute{\omega}\sigma\vartheta\eta\nu$ were meant to imply, that a power of knowing is promised adequate to the complete knowledge of the Divine: carefully considered, the passage will be found not to convey that idea; all that it says is, that the form or manner of the knowledge will be the same. The contrast to the knowing $\pi\varrho\acute{o}\sigma\omega\pi\sigma\nu$ $\pi\varrho\acute{o}\varsigma\ \pi\varrho\acute{o}\sigma\omega\pi\sigma\nu$ is, that knowledge which is $\grave{\epsilon}\kappa\ \mu\acute{\epsilon}\varrho\sigma\nu\varsigma$ and $\delta\iota'$ $\grave{\epsilon}\sigma\acute{o}\pi\tau\varrho\sigma\nu$, in parts and fragmentary: that is, to *discursive* knowledge is opposed that which is simultaneous and intuitive, which is the knowledge of the part by the whole, and the whole in each several part (comp. Rothe's Ethik, ii. S. 153).

Further than this the apostolic sayings will not take us, in our endeavour to attain a fuller comprehension of the expression. The Protestant discussion of the question studiously avoided any decision respecting the modus of the visio Dei (Gerhard, T. xx. S. 394; Bullinger on John i. 18; Pareus on 1 Cor. xiii. Voetius: de visione Dei per essentiam disputationes selectæ, T. ii. p. 1193.) Expositors simply noticed that point of the comparison which the relation of the eye to the other senses naturally suggests, viz., that this knowledge shall resemble vision in its *clearness* and *distinctness*. Chrys., hom. 75 in Joh.: $\grave{\epsilon}\pi\epsilon\iota\delta\grave{\alpha}\nu\ \gamma\grave{\alpha}\varrho\ \tau\tilde{\omega}\nu\ \alpha\grave{\iota}\sigma\vartheta\acute{\eta}\sigma\epsilon\omega\nu\ \tau\varrho\alpha\nu\sigma\tau\acute{\epsilon}\varrho\alpha\ \grave{\eta}\ \ddot{o}\psi\iota\varsigma,\ \delta\iota\grave{\alpha}$ $\tau\alpha\acute{\nu}\tau\eta\varsigma\ \grave{\alpha}\epsilon\grave{\iota}\ \tau\grave{\eta}\nu\ \grave{\alpha}\kappa\varrho\iota\beta\tilde{\eta}\ \pi\alpha\varrho\acute{\iota}\sigma\tau\eta\sigma\iota\ (\grave{\eta}\ \gamma\varrho\alpha\varphi\grave{\eta})\ \gamma\nu\tilde{\omega}\sigma\iota\nu$. The schoolmen penetrated deeper. According to the doctrine of Thomas Aquinas, the visio is intuitiva; that is, it is not through the medium of arguments, but direct, immediate. It is apprehensiva, not comprehensiva; that is, not a knowledge of the totality of God, but still a real knowledge of His present essentia; further, it is an operatio intellectus non voluntatis (Summa, P. 1, qu. 12, art. 1, and on 1 Cor. xiii. 12). The last point, which was called in question by the Mystics and Scotus, rests on the Aristotelian conception of θεωρία, in which the spirit has pure αὐτάρκεια, whereas in desire there is always a sense of want. That this height of knowledge could be gained by men by no mere phenomenological process, but only by a course of moral perfecting, was, however, the common conviction of all Christian writers.

Now, this truth is expressed in Heb. xii. 14, 1 John iii. 2, and in our passage. Here, however, a question arises, as to whether the promise stands in a merely external relation to the fulfilment of the promise, or whether the relation be inward and causal. The answer depends on the view taken, on the one hand, of the nature of God; on the other, of the corporeity of men after the resurrection. A visio spiritualis was alone admitted by Augustin (ep. ad Paulin. 147, T. 1, Ben., Sermo liii. in Matth. T. V. 220), Ambrose, Jerome. The Protestant dogmaticians regarded the glorified bodies of the saints as somewhat similar to the present, and could therefore maintain of this vision that it will be videre mentibus et *oculis* (Chytræus, de vita et morte æterna, 1583, p. 157, Calov, Hollaz). Among the moderns, this view is held by Menken and his school, who quote Ezek. iii. 12 as a proof that God fills a certain space (Homilien ueber Hebr. ix. x. S. 45). If such an external vision of God were meant, it is plain that the relation between the promise and the fulfilment need be no more than an outward relation; that is, the vision would be a reward bestowed from without. But the relation of moral purity to a perception of God is not outward, but inward. This was recognised even by the old popular belief, and the language of the Mystics: comp. Elsner, observ. s. in locum; Priçæus, comm. in N. T. in loc.; Callimachus, hymn. in Apollin. v. 9: Ὠπόλλων οὐ παντὶ φαείνεται ἀλλ' ὅτις ἐσθλός (see also Spanheim on the passage, and compare Isa. vi. 7). Further, the analogy of the other beatitudes, in which there is a manifest correspondence between the promise and the predicate, leads us to expect that here the relation will be inward and causal, that the purity is the condition of the vision of God; and we must accordingly conclude, further, that the organ of vision here is not the eye, but the pure heart. Aug.: quemadmodum si corporalia opera membris corporalibus coaptarentur ac diceret quisquam: beati qui pedes habent, quia ipsi ambulabunt, etc., sic: beati qui oculos habent, ipsi enim videbunt. *Sic tanquam spiritualia membra componens, docuit quid ad quid pertineat.*

But another question emerges, as to the sense in which a *pure* heart is to be regarded as the medium of the most intimate fellowship with God. And here, what Claudius says will naturally suggest itself, about the sun never mirroring itself upon the face of ocean in storm. Yet the expression, carefully weighed, leads us further than the mere negative condition of inward repose and dispassionateness. The beautiful expansion of the figure of a mirror in Gregory of Nyssa will, if we bear in mind the visio per essentiam defended by Thomas Aquinas, carry us further: Μακάριος γίνεται ὁ καθαρὸς τῇ καρδίᾳ, ὅτι πρὸς τὴν ἰδίαν καθαρότητα βλέπων ἐν τῇ εἰκόνι καθορᾷ τὸν ἀρχέτυπον. Ὥσπερ γὰρ οἱ ἐν κατόπτρῳ ὁρῶντες τὸν ἥλιον, κἂν μὴ πρὸς αὐτὸν τὸν οὐρανὸν ἀποβλέψωσιν ἀτενές, οὐδὲν ἔλαττον ὁρῶσι τὸν ἥλιον ἐν τῇ τοῦ κατόπτρου αὐγῇ, τῶν πρὸς αὐτὸν ἀποβλεπόντων τοῦ ἡλίου τὸν κύκλον· οὕτω, φησί, καὶ ἡμεῖς, κἂν ἀτονῆτε πρὸς κατανόησιν φωτός, ἐὰν ἐπὶ τὴν ἐξ ἀρχῆς ἐγκατασκευασθεῖσαν ὑμῖν χάριν τῆς εἰκόνος ἐπαναδράμητε, ἐν ἑαυτοῖς τὸ ζητούμενον ἔχετε. καθαρότης γὰρ ἀπάθεια καὶ κακοῦ παντὸς ἀλλοτρίωσις ἡ θεότης ἐστίν· εἰ οὖν ταῦτα ἔν σοί ἐστι, Θεὸς πάντως ἐν σοί ἐστιν. And if it be said that these remarks lie beyond the sphere of Scripture, we have at least an answer expressly founded upon a saying of Scripture, if we take the idea of purity of heart in the sense in which it has been unfolded from the Scriptures themselves (p. 90). If the pure heart is the heart whose love is not divided between God and the world, the heart which can say with the Psalmist, Ps. lxxiii., "My flesh and my heart faileth, but God is the strength of my heart and my portion for ever," is it not manifest that that by which this highest union with God is accomplished is *Love?* Hence it follows, that the promised reward cannot be merely such as will be attained after death; and that (if not exactly in the Pauline sense) the seeing of God shall, even here, be realized according to the measure of self-surrendering love: as

St Paul, in 2 Cor. iii. 18, speaks of the soul mirroring itself in Christ, and becoming glorified by the reflection of His light.

Ver. 9. A third characteristic virtue of Christianity. This also is quite at variance with the spirit of the Jewish people at that time, whose expectations of a worldly Messiah disposed them to expect rather a summons to war and tumult. The character, which is here **pronounced** blessed, is the very reflection of the character **of Jesus Himself**, in its threefold attributes **of pity**, purity, and **peace**.

I. THE ASCRIPTION OF BLESSEDNESS.

Various opinions have been held regarding the philological acceptation of εἰρηνοποιός. The Vulgate translates it by pacefici, which combines the meanings "peaceable" and "peacemaker;" Socinus, Grotius, Wettstein, "the peace-lovers." Pape owns that the word is used in this sense, but only in the N. **Test.; Wahl, not even** there; whereas Stephanus (Thesaurus), **on the** contrary, remarks: apud Mtth. *nove*, **ut** opinor, dicuntur pacifici, *i.e.*, qui sunt *pacis amantes*. The opposite, πολεμοποιός, does certainly **occur** only **in the sense** of making war, beginning hostilities; and in Greek not only εἰρηνοποιός occurs, but also εἰρηνοποιέω, εἰρηνοποίησις, εἰρηνοποιΐα, in Greek usage, **only of** "*making* peace." (See examples by Hase in Steph. Thes.) For the signification "peaceable," reference is made by Wettstein to Isocrates de pace, c. 16, and Pollux onomasticum, T. i. L. i. § 41 and 152. **The passage** in Isocrates, φημὶ δ' οὖν χρῆναι, ποιεῖσθαι τὴν εἰρήνην μὴ μόνον πρὸς Χίους κ.τ.λ., ἀλλὰ πρὸς πάντας ἀνθρώπους, does not prove the **point**: for there war was already kindled; **so it** is of making peace that he speaks. **In the** first passage in Pollux, certain honourable titles of a king are collected: βασιλεὺς εἰρηνικὸς, εἰρηνοποιὸς, εἰρηνοφύλαξ; but "peacepreserver" appears here to correspond better both to the royal title of honour and to its synonymes. In the second passage a title is quoted: περὶ συμμάχων εἰρηνοποιῶν καὶ πολεμοποιῶν: here both the synonymous expressions given, συμπολεμοῦντες, κοινωνοὶ πολέμων, ἔνσπονδοι, and the contrasted predicates, **seem** unquestionably to point to **"peace-holder, or preserver,"** as the true meaning. **And** this meaning was **natural to** classical usage, for the translation **of a verb** by its subject with ποιεῖσθαι

7

was a wide-spread Grecism: as ἀρὰν ποιεῖσθαι for ἀρᾶσθαι, θαῦμα ποιεῖσθαι for θαυμάζειν. So, too, in Hellenistic Greek, after the Hebrew usage of עָשָׂה, ποιεῖν εἰρήνην, Jas. iii. 18. Thus the rendering "peace-loving" appears classically admissible: as in Latin pacificus has, since Ennius, had this meaning. Yet the reading of peace-maker seems here the most warrantable—in which sense εἰρηνοποιεῖν occurs in the LXX., Prov. x. 10. Moreover, this comprehends also the former idea, as Phavorinus in his Lexicon remarks; compare Nyssenus: βούλεται τοίνυν πρότερον εἶναί σε ἀλήρη τῶν τῆς εἰρήνης καλῶν, εἶθ᾽ οὕτως ὀρέγειν τοῖς ἐνδεῶς ἔχουσι τοῦ τοιούτου κτήματος. Also the Hebrew gnomology praises the peace-maker, Prov. xii. 20: οἱ βουλόμενοι εἰρήνην εὐφρανθήσονται, where the Hebrew has: יוֹעֲצֵי שָׁלוֹם. So too the Talmudical treatise, Peah § 1: "Of the following, man reaps the fruits alike in the present life and in that to come, viz., honouring father and mother, doing good, הבאת שלום בין איש לרעהו, making peace among people." In Luther's translation, by the "peaceable," he means more than merely the "peaceful;" in the margin he explains: "those who make, further, and preserve peace among one another. And they are more than the peaceable."

Since, then, peace-making is what is here spoken of, which is that inward peaceable temper which seeks to spread itself all around, we are to regard certain particulars thereof, on which some have exclusively dwelt, as possibly included in the idea, although not as thought along with it. Thus, for instance: the making of peace in one's own heart among the contending passions, is an idea which Clemens, Str. iv. 579, discovers in the expression, οἱ τὴν ἄπιστον μάχην τὴν ἐν τῇ ψυχῇ καταπεπαυκότες. Aug.: pacifici in semet ipsis sunt, qui omnes animi sui motus componentes et subjicientes rationi, carnalesque concupiscentias habentes edomitas fiunt regnum Dei. Others, as Pellic. find here a reference to Reconciliation, according to the use of εἰρήνην ποιεῖσθαί τινι, Isa. xxvii. 5. Many refer the εἰρήνη specially to that which Christ has procured (Col. i. 20; Eph. ii. 15); thus Chrys., Cocc.: operam dantes ut habeant homines pacem cum Deo in justitia per fidem. So too Alting, Elsner, Stier.

II. The Promise.

The disciples of Christ are called, on account of this peace-making, the children of God. If now the correspondence between the promise and the predicate holds good in this case too, it seems to be implied that the diffusion of peace is to be regarded as a characteristic of God Himself. Now the predicate ὁ Θεὸς τῆς εἰρήνης recurs constantly in the writings of St Paul, and the question is, in what sense is it used? The common salutation, in which εἰρήνη occurs conjointly with χάρις, the εἰρήνη ὑμῖν in John xiv. 27, xx. 26, and the use of the osculum pacis among the early Christians (Tertull.; 1 Pet. v. 14; 1 Cor. xvi. 20), leave no doubt that the principal reference is to the peace of reconciliation, although at the same time the idea of mutual peace specially enters into the general thought, as Rom. xvi. 20 shows; comp. 2 Thess. iii. 16: δώῃ ὑμῖν τ. εἰρ. διαπαντὸς ἐν παντὶ τρόπῳ.— Υἱός, according to Hebrew usage, implies the ideas of origin and of resemblance, for which reason, at ver. 45, a few codices have, instead of υἱοί, the gloss ὅμοιοι. The idea of a resemblance springing from inward relationship is also implied in the υἱὸς ὑψίστου of Sirach iv. 10: γίνου ὀρφανοῖς ὡς πατὴρ, καὶ ἀντὶ ἀνδρὸς τῇ μητρὶ αὐτῶν· καὶ ἔσῃ υἱὸς ὑψίστου, καὶ ἀγαπήσει σε μᾶλλον ἢ μήτηρ σου.—As the ἐλεημοσύνη, called blessed in vers. 7, denotes, in Christ's view, that which flows from redeeming ἐλεημοσύνη, so we must conclude with regard to this love of peace among the members of God's kingdom, that, rightly viewed, it is a fruit of peace with God through Christ.— Κληθήσονται (comp. v. 19), after an Hebraism, which occurs chiefly in the two parts of Isaiah,—נִקְרָא with appellation following, as *e.g.*, "Thou shalt be called the holy city,"—is used in cases where, together with *being*, the idea of *being owned* is intended to be expressed; Beza, Beng.: erunt et celebrabuntur. To the distinction implied in this title, St John touchingly refers, 1 Ep. iii. 1. This promise will be fully realized only with the perfected δόξα of the children of God as joint heirs with Christ, Rom. viii. 17. Gl. ord.: cum Deus erit omnia in omnibus, tunc beatitudo adoptionis dabitur.

7*

BLESSEDNESS OF THOSE WHO SUBMIT TO THE REPROACH WHICH IN THIS WORLD IS ASSOCIATED WITH THE RIGHTEOUSNESS OF THE KINGDOM OF GOD.

Vers. 10—12.

Vers. 10, 11. Although the disciples were to labour to bring peace to the world, yet the world was to offer them opposition and wage war against them. The body, says the Epistle to Diognetus, ought to love the spirit, from which it receives life; nevertheless the contrary is the case, there is hostility between them. Moreover, these sayings were utterly opposed to the carnal Messianic expectations of His hearers. There is clearly a reminiscence of the 10th and 11th verses in 1 Pet. iii. 14, ἀλλ' εἰ καὶ πάσχοιτε διὰ δικαιοσύνην, μακάριοι, and in 1 Pet. iv. 14, εἰ ὀνειδίζεσθε ἐν ὀνόματι Χριστοῦ, μακάριοι: the similarity of expression can scarcely be accidental. The relation that vers. 10 and 11 bear to each other is, that ver. 11 is a further explanation of ver. 10: this is seen by the μακάριοί ἐστε ver. 11, and by the absence of the promise in that verse, this having been already given in ver. 10.

Those whom He addresses are regarded as already in possession of the δικαιοσύνη, which goes forth from Christ, as ἕνεκεν ἐμοῦ shows. The persecution consists in three things (ver. 11): in abuse, in violence, and in slander. In ver. 11, διώκειν is not used generally as in ver. 10, but rather specifically; yet there is no occasion, with Beza, Pricæus, Raphel, to accept here the classical signification, persequi judicio (comp. the rhetorical use of ὁ διώκων and ὁ φεύγων), for that idea is expressed in Hellenistic Greek by κατηγορεῖν. In 1 Cor. iv. 12, διώκειν occurs along with λοιδορεῖν as its climax. Perhaps in allusion to our text, Cod. B. D., and several translations, especially the Vulgate, omit ῥῆμα: this must have arisen from the idea that it might be dispensed with (comp. Acts xxviii. 21); a few other codices omit πονηρόν, probably on similar grounds. But ῥῆμα is as little to be dispensed with as πονηρόν, contrary to Meyer's opinion: we cannot, therefore, with Lachmann and Tischendorf, consent to its abolition. For ῥῆμα, conjoined with πονηρόν is in fact the LXX. translation of רעה, Num. xiv. 36; so that εἰπεῖν πονηρὸν ῥῆμα is a Hebrew phrase, as κραταιοῦν λόγον πονηρόν, Ps. lxiv. 6, and ἐπιφέρειν τινὶ λόγον πονηρόν, Judith viii. 8.

That the Christian principle, as such, would encounter the most determined opposition in the world; that the bitterest hostility would be directed against the disciples, simply on account of **their connection with the Redeemer; is** expressed in various forms (John xv. 18, xvii. 14). It is **striking to** reflect how the history of the coming ages must have stood before the Redeemer when He spoke these words.[1] The cause of this antagonism we find expressed in John iii. 20: Every one that doeth evil hateth the light. The Christian is, by his very appearance, a moving conscience to excuse or condemn the children of the world. On the other hand, John vii. 7 discloses another reason of this enmity: the Christian, and, above all, the Apostles, must by the testimony of their word condemn the nature of the world. That there is a special reference here to the stated ministry, to apostolic labours, is seen from the comparison of those whom He addresses with the prophets. If now the persecution is endured as the natural result of the manifestation of the Spirit of Christ in His disciples, it follows as matter of course that the reproaches must be false: and so ψευδόμενοι appears superfluous. And it is in fact wanting in Cod. D. and in the Itala (Cod. A. does not count, as it only begins at Matt. xxv. 6). In the Peschito, Philox., and in three codices of the Itala, it occurs in a different order, namely, after ἕνεκεν ἐμοῦ (which, however, in the Syriac does not imply a varying reading). If, now, we could add the authority of Origen, which has been quoted in favour of its omission, the word might, with Griesbach, be regarded as doubtful. **To expunge it altogether from the text** (Fritzsche, Lachmann, and Tischendorf), appears, considering the overwhelming weight of testimony both of eastern and western witnesses, unjustifiable (so too De Wette). But the **testimony of Origen happens to** be more than doubtful;[2] and the only warrantable ground for

---

[1] Addison, Truth of the Christian Religion, § 8.

[2] In his Commentary on Jeremiah xxiv. 9 (T. iv. S. 272), ἐγενήθη λόγος κυρίου ἐμοὶ εἰς ὀνειδισμόν, he quotes our saying as a parallel passage, adding: ἡμεῖς οἱ τάλανες ἔχομεν ὀνειδισμοὺς διὰ τὰ ἁμαρτήματα ἡμῶν. In antithesis

the omission of the word would be that it is superfluous. But superfluous it is not: it serves as a determining clause to ὅταν ὀνειδίσωσι κ. τ. λ. No doubt it is somewhat strange to find the ἕνεκεν ἐμοῦ placed after ψευδόμενοι: in its position there, the ἕνεκεν ἐμοῦ must relate, not immediately to ψευδόμενοι, but to the whole preceding sentence, ὅταν——ψευδόμενοι. Glossa ord.: *mentientes.* Hoc addit, ne glorietur de quo vere mala dicuntur. So also Olsh., B.-Crusius.

The Promise.—It may appear surprising to find the promise already given in ver. 3 repeated here. Were there a gradation in these promises, this would be inadmissible. This is not, however, the case; and the only question is, whether in this case also there is a correspondence between promise and benediction. The despised and persecuted are to receive some compensation: in this view the kingdom of God, which is the μισθὸς πολύς, is promised them, as for them the sum of all blessings, and as their sure asylum. The repetition of the promise was noticed already in early times; and in order to bear out the idea of gradation in the promises, a different reading was proposed. Τινὲς τῶν μεταιιθέντων [1] read τὰ εὐαγγέλια, as Clement has it, Strom. l. iv. p. 49: ver. 10: ὅτι αὐτοὶ ἔσονται τέλειοι, and ver. 11: ὅτι ἕξουσι τόπον, ὅπου οἱ διωχθήσονται.

The encouragement to rejoice and be exceeding glad, given in ver. 12, can only be regarded as a further amplification of the substance of the promise in ver. 10. It is a summons not only to patient endurance, but to joy, nay, to the highest expression of joy (comp. ἀγαλλιᾶσθαι in conjunction with χαίρειν in Tob. xiii. 13, and St Paul's καυχᾶσθαι ἐν θλίψεσιν, Rom. v. 3). The next clause intimates the reason for this joy as consisting in the greatness of the reward, corresponding to the severity of the ordeal of persecution through which they were to pass. Ἐν τοῖς οὐρανοῖς. *Heaven* may, without any arbitrary symbolizing, be regarded as denoting, as well in the Bible as throughout the whole ancient world, a condition of free and

---

to this ἡμῶν, he wished to bring out especially the ἕνεκεν ἐμοῦ in the words of Christ, and therefore he omits ψευδόμενοι, by quoting which he would only have weakened the antithesis.

[1] By which we are to understand not (as Millius and Lardner suppose) the Glossatores, but such persons as unscrupulously introduced their own particular opinions into the text of Scripture.

blessed life, as opposed to the constrained and sorrowful condition which belongs to the mortal and the finite. The Lutheran doctrine, also, considers that οὐρανός is not to be understood τοπικῶς but τροπικῶς: see on chap. vi. 9. There is, indeed, an allusion to the future in this expression, as also in Col. i. 5, 1 Pet. i. 4, the reward is represented as reserved in heaven. But it is not implied that the reward exists only in the future: what is meant is rather that the δόξα (John xvii. 22), present and inward now, shall then be openly made manifest: Col. iii. 3, 4.

Μισθός. The expectation of a recompense is represented in Heb. xi. 6, as a characteristic feature of a true faith in the living God. Good things received and enjoyed by a nature which has been brought into perfect unison with the Divine will, and has thus fulfilled the idea of humanity, can only conduce to perfect harmony without, to perfect contentment and blessedness within. Legally speaking, a reward is some good thing which has been *deserved,* and is received on account of some *service performed.* In this sense, it is plain, we cannot use the term in reference to man and God.. It is inconceivable that man can render by his virtues any service to God, any more than in taking a draught of the fountain the thirsty traveller renders that fountain a service. Moreover, this juridical view of the reward is expressly excluded by such passages as Luke xvii. 18, and in the Pauline doctrine, Rom. iv. 4. Now the apparent discrepancy between the passages of Scripture which speak of a reward, and those which show even that reward to be of grace, is reconciled in the **Protestant doctrine,** according to which the merces is merces gratiæ, as we read in the Apologia, p. 137, ed. Rech.: "But Scripture calleth eternal life a reward, meaning, not that God oweth us eternal life for our works' sake, but that, whereas this life eternal is given for other reasons, by it is at the same time recompensed to us all our labour and pain, albeit the treasure is so great that for these works God oweth it not. Even so are the inheritance of a father and all his goods given to his son, and are an ample **recompense** for **his** obedience; yet does he not inherit them on account of his deserts, but because his father, as an father, vouchsafes to make him his heir." Accordingly μισθός is to be understood in this limited sense in those passages where it occurs as a promise to the faithful: chap. v.

46, vi. 1, 2; Luke vi. 35; Matt. x. 41; 1 Cor. iii. 14; 2 John 8; Rev. xxii. 12. So, too, in the N. Test. the Christian reward is said to spring from the faithfulness and justice of God, —it is given because God is "faithful" and "just," namely, in fulfilling His promises: 1 Thess. v. 24; 2 Thess. iii. 3. The Roman Catholic doctrine—held, however, under various limitations of the idea by various writers—maintains a meritum in the merces, according to Moehler's definition (Symbolik, S. 201, 5 ed.): "Meritorious works are those done by human liberty in *the strength of Christ.*" But if this strength of Christ depends upon faith in His receiving and justifying grace; if it is from this faith as an impulsive principle that good works spring, then the believer's relation to God is not a relation of right, but of faith, and consequently the recompense of these good works can no longer be regarded as a matter of right, but only as the gift of grace. And, indeed, many explanations of the Romish dogma veer towards this conclusion. Jansenius of Ypern, for instance, represents the merces as following not ex pacto but ex liberalitate; and cites the analogy of a father who promises his children a reward to encourage them in rendering that obedience which they are already bound to render. Hence the reward in the Protestant acceptation is to be regarded as consisting in the communication of a condition agreeable to the faith which has been exercised in the grace of God. Again, it is denied in the Protestant doctrine that the vita æterna can be really merited as a $\mu\iota\sigma\vartheta\acute{o}\varsigma$: on the contrary, it is maintained that this is true alone of the gradus beatitudinis, to be attained by each (comp. Gerhard, on this passage, T. viii. S. 127, and passim loci, T. viii. l. 18, c. 8). The maxim of Spinoza: beatitudo non est præmium virtutis, sed ipsa virtus, is not, indeed, destroyed by the doctrine of the Bible, but rather (as Billroth rightly observes) receives from the Christian eschatology its full significance. It is true of every force, that it can attain its full realization only when it becomes *manifest:* so, too, of this reward resting in the disposition of the heart; whenever the disposition is perfected, the reward will be no longer hidden, but will become manifest. The manifestation, then, is the $\delta\acute{o}\xi\alpha$ which in the N. Test. is promised to the redeemed (comp. Col. iii. 3, 4).

The value of those persecutions for righteousness' sake is

seen from this, that they are classed with the sufferings endured by the prophets (Heb. xi. 35): and how great the reward of the prophets was, may be inferred from Matt. x. 41. No doubt, this parallel with the prophets shows that the Saviour addressed Himself here, in the first instance, to the Apostles: we learn, however, from x. 41 that every disciple of the kingdom of God is even more than a prophet. The occasion of persecution was in both cases the same: the prophets, too, testified from their own point of view that the works of the world were evil. (John vii. 7.) How sustaining is the consciousness of suffering and contending in company with others! (1 Thess. ii. 14) how encouraging must it have been for that little fearful band of disciples to be joined to that "cloud of witnesses" (as they are called, Heb. xii. 1), who had given up all the possessions of this world that they might fight a good fight for the world unseen!

HAVING SO HIGH A VOCATION, THE DISCIPLES OF THE KINGDOM OF GOD MUST IN NOWISE DISAVOW IT.

Vers. 13—16.

Ver. 13. That strength which God has vouchsafed to the disciples for a high purpose, must be by them sacredly preserved (ver. 13); and they must never withdraw themselves from the world from fear of its hostility (ver. 14—16).[1]

The dignity of the disciples of Christ is expressed by a twofold figure: as a spiritual salt, they are to season humanity and preserve it from moral corruption; and as a spiritual light, they are to be to humanity what the physical sun is to the world. By the first metaphor they are characterized as a power of life; by the second, as a power of light. The first includes the negative idea of preserving the world from insipidity and from decay; the second is purely positive. Directly, the vocation

---

[1] Bruno Bauer, who regards this as one of the sayings worked into the discourse, taken from St Mark ix. 50, still confess (in loc. S. 319): "Matthew must have worked hard, but also with rare good luck, to turn that saying (Mark ix.) into an admonition to the disciples to always show themselves worthy of their vocation as the salt of the earth."

alone of those addressed is spoken of, and their destination as concerning other men. Indirectly, however, reference is also made to their own gifts: the possession, on their part, of a spiritual salt and a spiritual light is presupposed. Now, as it is their vocation that is spoken of—their universal vocation for the whole world (Matt. xxviii. 19), and as the loss of this vocation is signalized as equivalent to the loss of all their value to the world, it has been held that the verse applies exclusively to the Apostles, and to the ministries of the word. Salmero (T. v. tract. 27) even says: sal ipsum, videlicet Prælatos ut tales, minime doceri neque corrigi, quia quatenus tales sunt, ut apostoli et summi pontifices, haud saliuntur.[1] Also Luther, Bucer, and Chemnitz make out that here is spoken proprie de officio ministerii. Undoubtedly the principal reference is to those whose *vocation* it is to season and illuminate the world: in so far, however, as all Christians have part in the universal priesthood, they all have part likewise, in a limited degree, in this vocation. This will appear especially from a comparison of Phil. ii. 15 with ver. 14, and of 1 Pet. ii. 9 with ver. 16.

Even in antiquity salt was highly valued as an important nutritive substance; it denotes proverbially one of the most essential necessaries. Nil sole et sale utilius, says the Roman proverb (Plinius, hist. nat. 31, 9, comp. 41). It is mentioned, Sirach xxxix. 31 (26), among the necessaries of human life; and in Mark ix. 50 it is said, $\kappa\alpha\lambda\grave{o}\nu$ $\tau\grave{o}$ $\ddot{\alpha}\lambda\alpha\varsigma$. In Homer, either because it cannot be dispensed with, or with reference to its symbolical import, it is called $\vartheta\varepsilon\tilde{\iota}o\nu$, and in Plato $\vartheta\varepsilon o\varphi\iota\lambda\grave{\varepsilon}\varsigma$ $\sigma\tilde{\omega}\mu\alpha$ (Timæus, ed. Stephan. p. 60). The idea which the metaphor here employed accordingly suggests, is that the disciples of Christ are a noble and indispensible element in the world. Yet this is a point of comparison which salt has in common with many other things, although Fritzsche supposes that this alone is implied: quanta salis ad alias res comparati, tanta est vestra inter cæteros homines dignitas.—Salt, however, presents certain peculiar points of comparison. We hold it erroneous to suppose

---

[1] The same words are used by Calvin in support of exactly the opposite opinion: qui se pro apostolis nullo jure venditant, hoc operculo tegunt, quidquid abominationum ingerere libuit, quia Petrum et similes Christus vocavit salem terræ, nec interea expendunt, quam gravis et severa addita sit comminatio, omnium esse deterrimos, si insipidi reddantur.

(as some writers, led astray by Luke xiv. 35, have done) that reference is here made to a fructifying power in the salt: as in that case the salt alluded to must be alkali, potass, or marl, as common salt has no such property (so Calmet, Deyling observ. sacræ, i. 204). On the contrary, the distinctive properties of common salt are purity and a conserving power, preserving from corruption. On account of its dry and cleanly whiteness, it is the emblem of purity: purior salillo, says the Latin proverb; and in Persius (sat. iii. 25) we read, est tibi far modicum, purum et sine labe salinum. Pythagoras, too, has this property in his mind when he speaks of salt as the emblem of righteousness: comp. Diog. Laert. hist. phil. viii. segm. 35, περὶ τῶν ἁλῶν ὅτι δεῖ παρατίθεσθαι πρὸς ὑπόμνησιν τοῦ δικαίου· οἱ γὰρ ἅλες πᾶν σώζουσιν ὅ τι ἂν παραλάβωσι. καὶ γεγόνασιν ἐκ τῶν καθαρωτάτων, ὕδατος (ἡλίου) καὶ θαλάττης. Still more peculiar to salt is its seasoning and conserving power, which Pythagoras also mentions, by virtue of which, on the one hand, it seasons food (Job vi. 6, with which compare Isidorus Pelusiota, epp. iv. ep. 49), and on the other hand, preserves it from corruption (2 Kings ii. 20, with which comp. Spanheim, dub. ev., p. iii. 457). Generally speaking, the ideas of purity and incorruptibility are closely allied: in the Mosaic writings, corruption and death are frequently viewed as denoting one and the same idea (Baehr, Symbolik des mos. Cultus, i. S. 299). In one of Plutarchs's dialogues, where sea and land contend whether of them is the most indispensable to man for the maintenance of his life, the following is said in praise of salt (Sympos. l. iv. quæst. 4): κρέας δὲ πᾶν νεκρόν ἐστι καὶ νεκροῦ μέρος· ἡ δὲ τῶν ἁλῶν δύναμις ὥσπερ ψυχὴ παραγενομένη χάριν αὐτῷ καὶ ἡδονὴν προστίθησι. It was from this pungent property of salt that it came to be used figuratively for *wit*, both in Greek and Latin: compare the *urbani sales,* and the proverb: ἅλμη οὐκ ἔνεστιν αὐτῷ: the expression in Col. iv. 6 has at least some affinity.

Now, in virtue of these two properties of purity and incorruptibility which appertain to it, salt became also a religious symbol.[1] Maxime autem in *sacris* intelligitur ejus auctoritas, quando nulla conficiantur sine mole salsa (Pliny, hist. nat. 31,

---

[1] Comp. Majus, de usu salis symbolico in rebus sacris, 1692.

41). Salt is the oldest and simplest form of sacrifice. Before the use of incense, salt was offered; as Ovid describes (Fasti i. 337):

<blockquote>
Ante deos homini quod conciliare valebat,
Far erat et puri lucida mica salis.
</blockquote>

In the Jewish meat-offerings, too, whilst leaven and honey, on account of their tendency to engender decay, were expressly excluded, salt was commanded to be used. And just in this way, as symbolic of continuance and constancy, this salt is called the Salt of the Covenant of the God of Israel (Lev. ii. 11, 13; Ezek. xliii. 24). At the same time, the meat-offerings were made to symbolize the idea of *purity,* inasmuch as honey as well as leaven were to be removed, because these substances promote decay, and seasoning salt was to be added, together with the fructifying oil and the sweet-savoured incense. (Vid. Hofmann, Schriftbeweis, ii. 1, S. 154.) In accordance with this, Theodoret says, with reference to Ezek. xvi. (Opp. T. ii. p. 11): τὸ ἅλας τὴν πνευματικὴν σύνεσιν καὶ τὴν θείαν διδασκαλίαν (σημαίνει), τὴν διαστύφουσαν τὰ σεσηπότα καὶ σῶα φυλάττουσαν: comp. Origen, hom. vi. on Ezek. xvi. 4, Opp. T. iii., where, comparing Matt. v. 13 and Col. iv. 6, he says: Grande opus est insaliri, qui sale conditur, gratia plenus est. Further, in Mark ix. 49, the sacrificial salt is spoken of as a symbol of the seasoning and cleansing efficacy of the Holy Spirit in the soul of man, preserving the good that is therein, and consuming all that is unclean and unholy, and making thus the human spirit a fitting and well-pleasing sacrifice to God; comp. πυρί used along with πνεύματι ἁγίῳ, Matt. iii. 11. Theophylact on Matt. ix. 49 says: τὸ ἅλας ἤγουν τὴν νόστιμον χάριν τοῦ πνεύματος καὶ συνεκτικήν.—With regard to the use of salt in the case of new-born children, alluded to Ezek. xvi. 4 (to which Galenus refers) it is impossible to say whether the object was merely the dietetic one, of drying and constricting the skin, or whether the custom had besides some symbolical significance: comp. Hævernick, Commentar. in loc. Augusti (Denkwuerdigkeiten, B. vii. S. 300) connects with that Jewish custom the symbolical usage in the Christian Church, of putting salt into the mouth of the baptized child, with the words: Accipe sal sapientiæ in vitam æternam.

When, therefore, Christ calls His disciples the salt of a

world which is alienated from God, the point of the comparison which most naturally presents itself is precisely that effect of salt which is most peculiar to it, viz., its seasoning property. The expositors accordingly, with few exceptions, are content to refer to *this* point in the comparison. In support of this, Col. iv. 6 may be compared, and also the rabbinical saying, that alms-giving are the salt of riches. (Buxt. lex. Talmud. p. 1218.) But if we are at liberty to explain our passage by Mark ix. 49, and if these words in St Mark are to be regarded as containing a reference to Matt. iii. 11,—we may view the salt still more concretely as denoting the πνεῦμα ἅγιον. It will then be found to involve a special reference to the sacrificial ritual, and the thought will be: that the whole of humanity is here contemplated as a sacrifice presented to God, which, although not in itself well-pleasing to God, becomes so through the efficacy of the Holy Ghost going forth from Christian men. (So J. Moeller, in a commentary on this passage, Erfurt 1832.)

Now, with regard to the question, whether in the following metaphor of the light a different thought is expressed, we say not necessarily so. (Comp. Maldonatus, Bengel.) Still, as the seasoning power certainly denotes the life, it so far seems distinguishable from the light. True, Stier calls such a distinction superficial, and says, "Rather is salt the *inner* essential power and virtue from which the efficacy proceeds by natural laws: light, on the contrary, is the *outward expression of testimony* viewed in itself." (Sayings, i. 119.) But when it is said, Ye *are* the light of the world, the expression surely implies that they actually possess in themselves something which energizes outwardly in a manner as natural as the salt does. St Chrysostom, and especially Luther, dwell upon another distinction: the salt, they say, is the emblem of spiritual discipline, and the light of spiritual doctrine: the distinction, however, would imply that the saying was spoken with reference exclusively to the ministry.[1] If the disciples possess a seasoning efficacy for the world, if they have a power which is rooted in the Holy Ghost, for the benefit of men, then they must of necessity possess that power, that efficacy, also for themselves (comp. οὐδὲ

---

[1] The auctor operis imperfecti finds in the salt which preserves, a reference to the working of the Apostles upon the Jews, in the light which illumines, to their working among the heathen.

καίουσι, ver. 15, and μωρός): only, this point is not brought prominently forward.

The idea expressed in the succeeding words is, that the high trust which had been committed to the disciples must be carefully guarded. If the Apostles, and with them all Christians, lose this seasoning power, they shall not be able to obtain it again through any other organ, and will forfeit that Divine appointment for the world to which they have been specially called. Μωρός [connected with μῶλυς, μωλυρός, weak, insipid, stupid (comp. the use of ἀμβλύς, תָּפֵל, הִפְכָה, the Italian *matto* from the German *matt*)] is, with botanists and physicians (Hippocrates, Dioscorides), the technical term for insipidity: ἄναλος, Matt. ix. 50, may illustrate it. The Vulgate renders μωρανθῇ incorrectly by *evanuerit;* Valla: *desipuerit;* the best rendering is that of Erasmus and Beza: infatuerit.—It may be here asked, what is the subject of the verb ἁλισθήσεται, and whether it be not *meat?* If so, the Greek proverb might be compared: ὅταν τὸ ὕδωρ πνίγει, τί ἐπιρροφήσομεν; At first Luther translated the words thus: "What can be salted with it?" Subsequently, however (in ed. of 1538), thus: "What shall we salt with?" With the latter reading accords the Dutch translation: *waarmede zal man dan zouten;* the latter edition, however, has *het* instead of *dan*. The vulgate "in quo salietur" is ambiguous; but Augustin and Jerome make salt the subject: so too the English, Spanish, and Italian translations. The Peschito and Philox. have ܡܠܚܬܐ ܡܠܚܐ; ܡܠܚܐ is gen. fem.; so likewise the Persian translation in the Polyglott, which is based upon the Peschito Version. That this is the right translation may be seen from Mark ix. 50: ἐν τίνι αὐτὸ ἀρτύσετε; Further, the continuation of the subject in our passage is decisive upon this point. No writer in modern times has controverted this opinion, with the exception of Br. Bauer (in loc. S. 314). But a *physical* objection has been raised by many to this reading. It has been urged that salt does not in fact lose its salifying virtue (unless, perhaps, chemically) when brought into contact with sour substances. Moved by this difficulty, Hermann von der Hardt, followed by Schoettgen, has maintained that the substance alluded to is asphalt, mixed with salt (Ephemerides philologicæ, diss. xi.). Asphalt is a pitch-like substance; so he brings this meaning out of the passage: "Yet are to make the world at peace with one another, ye are to be the peace-makers." For the refutation of this, see J. D. Michaelis: de mari mortuo, de nitro Plinii, de nitro Hebræorum. Nor need we, in order to vindicate the statement of the text in its physical aspect, to call to our aid the passage from Maundrell, quoted by Macknight and others, to the effect that salt was found by that traveller in the plain of Aleppo, which had lost the taste of salt.[1] In that case the saline taste was lost through the action of the sun causing chemical decomposition. But as the taste remaining in the salt which has been exposed to the influence of the weather is flat and somewhat bitter, and in any case such as renders it unavailable for seasoning meat, there is no necessity so to understand the epithet ἄναλον as if it meant that every trace of the peculiar taste of salt were wanting.

Such tasteless salt is thrown out of the house, and is no more heeded by the passers-by. Καὶ καταπατεῖσθαι, Bengel: adeoque. Nil est tritius, quam qui vult divinus haberi, ac non est. Merum sæculi hominem non tantopere dedecet sua vanitas. While other substances, which are no longer available for their own special use, may still be turned to account for some other purpose, this salt is "fit neither for the land nor yet for the dunghill," Luke xiv. 35. Compare what is said of the wood of the vine, Ezek. xv. 2 seqq. Bucer makes this application: neque ad aliam quamlibet minimam atque abjectam functionem, quæ ad Christianismum quidem pertineat, idonei essetis. Compare the same necessary limitation of the οὐδέν in John xv. 5.—As the phrase βάλλεσθαι ἔξω, ἐκβάλλειν, in various figurative applications, is used to denote exclusion from the kingdom of God (John vi. 37; Luke xiii. 28; Matt. viii. 12, xxii. 13), it would be natural to suppose that the figure contains this special allusion here also (Hilarius, Huther, Chemnitz, and others). Even καταπατεῖσθαι might seem to indicate this, as it might be re-

---

[1] Maundrells Journey to Palestine, p. 162. "In the valley of salt at Dschebal, some sixteen miles from Aleppo, there is a declivity of twelve feet high which has been formed by the continual removal of the salt. I broke off a piece where the surface is exposed to the action of the rain, air, and sun, and found that although it contained the mica and particles of the salt, it had entirely lost the **taste of salt**. **The inner** portion, however, which was more joined to the rock, still **retained the peculiar taste**."

garded as implying a reference to what was a custom in the Jewish synagogues (and indeed still is), to make the $\pi\alpha\tau\epsilon\tilde{\iota}\sigma\vartheta\alpha\iota$ part of the Punishment of apostacy. This custom was also prevalent in the early Church: and Hecebolius the rhetorician, the teacher of Julian, who was a Christian under Constantine, under Julian became a heathen, and, after Julian's death, once more a Christian, relates, that part of his penance was to throw himself down at the threshold of the church, with the exclamation: $\pi\alpha\tau\acute{\eta}\sigma\alpha\tau\acute{\epsilon}\ \mu\epsilon\ \tau\grave{o}\ \ddot{\alpha}\lambda\alpha\varsigma\ \tau\grave{o}\ \dot{\alpha}\nu\alpha\acute{\iota}\sigma\vartheta\eta\tau o\nu$.[1] Yet to suppose that there is here a reference to this custom, which was quite special, and, moreover, only occurred here and there, were manifestly arbitrary. Besides, the $\ddot{\epsilon}\xi\omega\ \beta\lambda\eta\vartheta\tilde{\eta}\nu\alpha\iota$ will not bear this special application, inasmuch as it is here used only to bring out vividly the contrast to the profitable use of the article in household economy: this the fuller passage in St Luke plainly shows. Now, if by this salt, which, having once lost its taste, cannot recover it again, is signified the gift of the Holy Ghost, the passage might appear to confirm the doctrine of the possibility of the lapsus finalis sanctorum; especially if its application is not to be restricted to the Apostles: thus accordingly Stier. Spanheim, on the other hand, contends for the Calvinistic dogma, although only by means of manifold distinctions (dub. evang. iii. c. 93). It might be answered, that the $\ddot{\alpha}\nu\alpha\lambda o\nu$ does not, as already remarked, imply the denial of some remaining taste in the salt; but then the taste here supposed to be lost is the taste of *salt*. We must note in what respect those whom Christ addresses are called the salt of the earth: it is solely with reference to their destination with regard to other men. Luther derives this idea immediately from the figure: "By the word *salt* He shows what their office is to be. For salt is not salt for itself; it cannot salt itself; but its use is to salt meat, and for that it is used in the kitchen, to give the meat a taste, and to keep it from decaying." The thought is accordingly as follows: If the men who are designed by God to be the organs of the reformation of the world lose their capacity to be so, then there exists no human instrumentality by which they may regain this power: as to whether it may be possible for them to recover it by the working of God, that is a point on

---

[1] Comp. Suidas s. v. Ἐκηβόλος, Socrates histor. ecclesiast. L. iii. c. 2.

which nothing is said here. Accordingly, in the sequel the ἐν τίνι ἁλισθήσεται is further dwelt on only under this one aspect: that those who have lost their salt thereby also lose their position in the body of the human race.[1]

Ver. 14. The medium through which that new life which, as ver. 13 has shown, it was to be the mission of the Apostles to diffuse, was to be conveyed to men, is a new knowledge. It is a knowledge based upon feeling, that is, on experience; and which must therefore also prove efficacious in the life, as ver. 16 shows, in which καλὰ ἔργα are mentioned as the fruits of the φῶς. The central point of this knowledge, this light, is in Christ: He is pre-eminently τὸ φῶς τοῦ κόσμου (John viii. 12, ix. 5, xii. 35); through Him His followers become υἱοὶ φωτός (1 Thess. v. 5), φωστῆρες (Phil. ii. 15), φῶς ἐν κυρίῳ (Eph. v. 8); also, ver. 15, the fact is alluded to, that the light of the disciples is kindled from a light not their own. In virtue of the dignity of their destination, the disciples dare not withdraw from the world. They *cannot* do so, as the words οὐ δύναται, κ.τ.λ., imply: but neither *dare* they; for to do so were to op-pose the Divine purpose, as ver. 15 states. Erasmus: hæc est evangelicæ doctrinæ natura, non *sinit*, sui professores latere, quamvis ipsi famam hominum fugitantes quærant latebras. Cur autem abscondatur, quod *in hoc ipsum paratum* est, ut ex æquo prosit omnibus? It belongs essentially to that power, that it should manifest itself outwardly; which is true also of Christian faith, that active element in the world's history. And it is in this energizing quality, this impossibility to remain silent or concealed, that the dignity of the Christian vocation consists: which is not, however, expressed in the words ἐπάνω ὄρους κειμένη, as many suppose, who regard ὄρος as denoting the dignitas apostolica, or something similar. The comparison to "a city set on an hill" would be all the more vivid to the hearers, as towns and villages, crowning the summits of the surrounding eminences, might be seen from where they stood, especially the mountain-city of Saphet.

Vers. 15, 16. As in a house a candle is not lighted for the

---

[1] Chemnitz: illi, qui sal infatuum, non blandiantur sibi, si aliis donis polleant et virtutibus, quasi alia ratione possint usui esse ecclesiæ.

purpose of putting it under the bushel, but with the object of giving light to others, so the light of the disciples was kindled as the light of Christ for the sake of men walking in darkness. —Λύχνος is the lamp which was fastened upon the λυχνία or λυχνοῖχος. As only the lower tables of the East were used at meals, the candlestick was usually placed on the floor. If a person leaving the room wished to retain the light, he would cover it with some hollow vessel, frequently with that used for measuring corn, which was to be found in every house (hence τὸν μόδιον, i.e., the one belonging to the house; so too ἡ λυχνία). St Luke has less definitely: οὐδεὶς καλύπτει αὐτὸν σκεύει, ἢ ὑποκάτω κλίνης τίθησιν (viii. 16). A passage in Fulgentius (mytholog. iii. 6) illustrates this custom: novaculam sub pulvinar abscondit lucernamque modio contegit; and afterwards: lucernaque modii custodia eruta. The loosely added καὶ λάμπει is not, with the Itala (ut luceat), to be regarded as denoting the object, but the effect. In the two passages in St Luke where the same saying occurs, we miss the connection of subject, viii. 16, xi. 33: the latter passage clearly shows that many apophthegms, joined together on account of some outward similarity, had in this shape been handed down by tradition.

As therefore the light is so placed in a house that all may have the benefit of its light, so, too, must Christ's disciples be. Accordingly, they must not withdraw themselves from men, but must openly appear among them (comp. x. 27). And their testimony must be delivered not only in words, but also by the life: comp. 2 Cor. viii. 21, προνοούμενοι καλά, οὐ μόνον ἐνώπιον κυρίου, ἀλλὰ καὶ ἐνώπιον ἀνθρώπων. The καλὰ ἔργα are the outward manifestation of the light; Bengel: non vos, sed opera vestra. The exhortation is not opposed to the warning given in chap. vi. 1, 5, against φανῆναι, θεαθῆναι τοῖς ἀνθρώποις: for there it is acting from a desire of self-glorification that is condemned; here, it is the καλὰ ἔργα which spring from a desire to honour our heavenly Father that are approved: comp. John xv. 8, ἐν τούτῳ ἐδοξάσθη ὁ πατήρ μου, ἵνα καρπὸν πολὺν φέρητε. (On ὁ πατὴρ ἐν τοῖς οὐρανοῖς, see on chap. vi. 9; on δοξάζειν, comp. Matt. ix. 8: Luke xxiii. 47.) Besides, what is required here is not an intentional show of good works, but only the intentional appearance of the disciple in the society of men; and if he appear there, his good works will of necessity become manifest.

And the object is, that men, seeing these works, may "glorify your Father which is in heaven." It had, indeed, been said, ver. 10, that the world would hate the Christian δικαιοσύνη, and would persecute it; yet this does not imply that some will not be susceptible so as to be gained out of the κόσμος (comp. John xvii. 9 with 20). Among these would be men who from the first were men bonæ voluntatis, as the centurion; Luke xxiii. 47: ἐδόξασε τὸν Θεόν. Among them others, too, who had before been scandalized, or had even blasphemed: 1 Pet. ii. 12: ἵνα ἐν ᾧ καταλαλοῦσιν ὑμῶν ὡς κακοποιῶν, ἐκ τῶν καλῶν ἔργων, ἐποπτεύσαντες, δοξάσωσι τὸν Θεὸν ἐν ἡμέρᾳ ἐπισκοπῆς: these words have almost the air of a distinct reminiscence. And even of those who do not own these works, what St Chrysostom says is true: κατὰ τὸ συνειδὸς ὑμᾶς θαυμάσονται καὶ ἀποδέξονται, ὡσπεροῦν οἱ φανερῶς κολακεύοντες τοὺς ἐν πονηρίᾳ ζῶντας κατὰ νοῦν διαβάλλουσι. Luther: "This is said quite in St Matthew's fashion, who often speaks of works in this way. For he and the other two Evangelists, Mark and Luke, do not build their Gospels upon the high doctrine of Jesus Christ, like St John and St Paul. Hence it is that these Evangelists discourse and exhort so much about good words and works; and so it was to be in Christianity, that men were both to speak the first and perform the last. But let everything have its proper place and value: the first thing is to have faith in Christ, and after that comes the doing of good works."

III. THE RIGHTEOUSNESS REQUIRED UNDER THE OLD DISPENSATION TO BE PERFECTED AND FULFILLED IN THE KINGDOM OF CHRIST.

Vers. 17—18.

Ver. 17. A saying of the greatest importance in the original history of Christianity. The works to be compared on the subject are the following: Spanheim, dubia evang., dubium 105—118. Vesperæ Groningianæ, 1698, the treatise contained therein: an Christus addiderit Veteri Testamento, p. 103. Bialloblotzky, de legis Mosaicæ abrogatione, 1824. Harnack, Jesus. der Christ oder der Erfueller des Gesetzes, 1842. Mich.

Baumgarten, doctrina Jesu Christi de lege Mosaica ex oratione montana hausta et exposita, 1838. Baur, Kritische Untersuchungen, S. 613. Nagel, Ueber Melchisedec, Stud. u. Kritiken, 1849, S. 348. Planck, das Princip des Ebionitismus (in Zellers theologisch. Jahrbuch, 1843, S. 14). "Judenthum und Urchristenthum," in Zellers theol. Jahrb. 1847, S. 268. Ritschl, die altcatholische Kirche, S. 27. Baur, das Christenthum u. die christliche Kirche, 1853, S. 25. E. J. Meyer, Ueber das Verhaeltniss Jesu und seiner Juenger zum alttest. Gesetz, 1853. Hofmann, Schriftbeweis, ii. S. 75. Lechler, das Alte Testament in den Reden Jesu, Stud. u. Kritiken, 1854, S. 787.

Inquire we first concerning the point of transition from ver. 16 to ver. 17. Some writers are of opinion that the same subject is continued; others again think that a new subject is here entered upon. The former is the view taken by the auctor op. imperf., Bucer, Mald., Menoch.: "They are to exhibit their light and their doctrines in the same way as Christ Himself did, who had not come to destroy the law." Luther: "Having assigned to the Apostles their office, the Lord Christ next proceeded to show them by an example what they should preach." Similarly August.: Posteaquam cohortatus est audientes, ut se præpararent ad omnia sustinenda .... incipit eos jam docere, quid doceant. Gloss. ord., Gloeckler, Ernesti, Episc.: "That they were not to conclude from what He had said that He meant to introduce innovations." The majority, however, have rightly regarded this verse as forming the commencement of a new subject, to which the foregoing stands as an *introduction*. Τίς γὰρ τοῦτο ὑπώπτευσεν; (St Chrysostom, referring to the μὴ νομίσητε, begins in this way his explanation:) ἢ τίς ἐνεκάλεσεν, ἵνα πρὸς τοῦτο ποιήσηται τὴν ἀπάντησιν; and he replies that it is a *præoccupatio*, in respect of the antagonistic position towards the law of Moses, which He assumes in the following verses. More correctly Socinus observes that vers. 17—21 form the exordium to the New Testament lawgiving which follows. Coccius: The exordium to the following exposition of the Christian δικαιοσύνη. Stier: "A sublime porch with the inscription: 'I am He who maketh and fulfilleth all things.'"

With regard to the question as to what gave rise to the subject here introduced: many hold it to have been occasioned by the suspicions thrown out by the Pharisees, that Jesus was an enemy of the law: suspicions which arose from the fact, that He neither taught nor obeyed those observances which they had themselves enjoined upon the people. (Matt. xxiii. 23.) So Bucer, Calv., Chemn., De Wette, Michael., Baumg., Stier, Neander. It was very natural to the Reformers, in opposition to the Genevan libertinism and Saxon antinomianism, to suppose that here such an apology of the law was intended: and even Olshausen supposes that there were antinomian tendencies among the disciples themselves. Calvin remarks on ver. 17: Putabant igitur vetus et usitatum regimen aboleri, quæ opinio multis modis valde noxia erat, pii enim Dei cultores nunquam evangelium amplexi essent, si fuisset a lege defectio. Leves autem et turbulenti spiritus ansa arrepta totum religionis statum convellere cupide aggressi essent, scimus enim quam proterve in rebus novis exultet temeritas. If, however, the remarks made in § 3, on the object of the Sermon, be correct, the occasion of the introduction of this subject was, not so much the suspicions of the Pharisees, as the desire to explain to the Apostles, whom He had so recently called, what was the relation in which He stood to the Mosaic economy. But although the subject was not occasioned by those suspicions, no doubt the antithetical introduction μὴ νομίσητε may have been. It is not, indeed, absolutely necessary so to explain this antithetical form of introduction (see p. 10): compare, for instance, οὐκ ἦλθον διακονηθῆναι ἀλλὰ διακονῆσαι, Matt. xx. 28, and μὴ νομίσητε ὅτι ἦλθον βαλεῖν εἰρήνην, Matt. x. 34.

E. J. Meyer, assuming that Christ here speaks only of the *prophetical* contents of the law and the prophets, is of opinion that the words were spoken in opposition to the carnal expectations of the Messiah of the *disciples:* an opinion which must stand or fall with that assumption. According to Lightfoot and B. Crusius, the antithesis was with reference to the prevalent idea, founded, B. Crusius thinks, on Jer. xxx. 31, that the Messiah would reform the law. Bucer, too, says: Prophetas sciebant prædixisse, innovanda esse per Christum omnia. And there is one remarkable fact which these commentators have omitted to notice, viz., that although the Jews of every age and sect maintained emphatically that the law was to abide for ever (see on ver. 18), there are yet many passages which speak of the substitution of a new law by the Messiah, particularly the abrogation by Him of the ceremonial law: in which passages allusion is repeatedly made to Jer. xxxi. 31. (They are to be found in Schoettgen, Jesus der wahre Messias, S. 882; Roeth, cp. ad Hebr. p. 85; see especially Gfroerer, Jahrh. des Heils, 2te Abth. S. 341.) But the verse can contain no such allusion to *this* Messianic expectation on the part of His audience, supposing it to have existed; for, so far from *opposing* such an expectation, the verse exactly *fulfils* it. There is, however, no reason to believe it to have existed; for it would be certainly rash to make isolated sayings, gathered from the Rabbis of the 3d to the 10th century, the opinion current among the Jews at the time of Christ. The probability is, that all that the Jews generally understood by the passage in Jeremiah (xxxi. 31) was, that the covenant was to be renewed and established by the inscription of the law on the hearts of men. Thus Kimchi explains it: והיה התורה הדשה שחדש להם תשובתם ..., זאת הברית לא יפרוח כי אתן תורתי בלבב, that the renewal of the covenant consists in its קיום, in the confirmation of the law by its being inscribed in their heart.

The genuineness of this saying of Christ has been more generally recognised than that of any other. (Planck, "Ueber das Princip' des Ebionitismus," in loc. cit.) Few there are who, like Gfroerer,[1] have called in question its authenticity. In recent times it has come to be regarded as the key to the new principle of Christianity in the first phase of its development. Taken along with vers. 18 and 19, this saying appears to claim for Christianity only the character of a more profound Judaism, or as being merely a reformatory manifestation, not as a distinctly new stage of religious development. It was natural that it should prove a stumbling-block to Marcion: he accused the Catholic Judaizers of altering the text, and thus confirmed it himself: τί δοκεῖτε; ὅτι ἦλθον πληρῶσαι τὸν νόμον ἢ τοὺς προφήτας; ἦλθον καταλῦσαι, ἀλλ᾽ οὐ πληρῶσαι. (Isidorus Pelus. epp. i. 371; Origen, dialogus de recta fide, T. i. 830, ed. de la Rue; Tertull. contra Marc. iv. 9, 36.) The

---

[1] Gfroerer ("die heilige Sage," 2 Abth. S. 84) and Roeth (ep. ad Hebræos, 1836, p. 214) announce their discovery, that the only reason for which the supposititious Matthew put this saying into the mouth of Christ, was in order that he might in ver. 19 combat St Paul, whom it is he means when he there speaks of the "least in the kingdom of God."

Manichæans also took exception to it; either doubting its genuineness, or declaring that if genuine it was unintelligible. (Aug. contra Faust. i. 17, c. 1, 5, 6.[1]) On the other side, heathens, Jews, and deists found in it a proof that the Author of Christianity held merely Jewish opinions, and that it was Paul who first proclaimed the peculiar doctrines of the Christian religion. (Julian, in Cyrill i. 10, 351; the Talmud tr. Schabbath, f. 116, 2; R. Isaac, Chissuk Emuna, or Defence of the Jewish belief, c. 19, ed. Wagenseil; Mendelsohn, "Jerusalem oder die religioese Macht des Judenthums;" the deist Toland, "Nazarenus;" the Wolfenbuettler Fragment. vom Zweck Jesu, § 7, against which see Bialloblotzky, de legis Mosaicæ abrogatione, Gott. 1824, and Tobler, "Gedanken zur Ehre Jesu," S. 63.) Even Fritzsche regards the liberal doctrine of St Paul as foreign to the original purpose of Christ: as does also Strauss in the first and fourth editions of his Leben Jesu (4 ed. i. 528), although he does not state this categorically, but only hypothetically. Previous to Fritzsche, this saying had been commonly regarded by the Rationalists as simply in direct antagonism to the *Pauline* phase of Christianity. But the investigation of the subject, in its philosophical and historical bearings, led to the conclusion, that in Him who spoke these words there must have been at least the germ of that system which bears His name. Strauss admits that this is to be inferred from the importance attached by Christ to the state of the heart and disposition, in opposition to the external view of the requirements of the law which the Pharisees took. Here, however, no more is acceded to Christ than what Rationalism itself allowed. Planck, however (in his essay "ueber Judenthum und Urchristenthum"), goes beyond this position: according to his view, the state of mind and heart which Christ required, is a readiness on the part of man to surrender himself wholly to God, as Matt. vi. 24 strongly testifies. No doubt even this view makes the relation of God to man entirely objective: there is nothing of that principle of χάρις which is the Divine bending in mercy towards the human, of which St Paul speaks; man is directed only to his own prac-

---

[1] Faustus (like the modern criticism) argues: quod Joannes non testatur, qui fuit in monte, Matthæus hoc scripsit, qui longo intervallo, postquam Jesus de monte descendit, secutus est eum; testis idoneus tacet, loquitur **minus** idoneus.

tical relation towards God. Baur, in his latest work, argues from the saying μακάριοι οἱ πτωχοί, which he calls "the most pregnant expression of the original Christian consciousness." That saying, he remarks, which represents Christians as sensible even here, in the midst of outward poverty, that they are in possession of heaven, reconciles and unites this world and the next, and thus destroys and transcends the position which the old economy held. Although Baur believes himself constrained to maintain that Christ Himself adhered to the law in its widest compass, he holds that He still possessed a most distinct consciousness, that the new doctrine must of necessity advance beyond the limitations of its commencement. (Christenthum und Kirche, S. 30.) He observes: "That He was fully conscious not only of the antagonistic character of His doctrine, but of the effects which would attend its promulgation, may be seen from Matt. ix. 16. In that passage He not only points out the unaccommodating spirit of the new doctrine, but gives plainly to understand, that although He Himself adhered as much as possible to the old traditional forms, and thus put the new wine into old bottles, yet He did so in the distinct consciousness that soon enough the new substance would destroy the old forms, the new wine burst the old bottles. But what was it which could thus impart to the new principle a momentum which should destroy the old forms and go beyond everything, but that He went back to the state of man's heart and soul, to that in a man which makes him a man, which constitutes his own true self?" (Baur, Christenthum und Kirche, S. 27.) Here it is the *doctrine*, upon whose dialectical development the new principle is built up; while the *person* of Christ, it is expressly stated, remains in the background in the Sermon on the Mount. Ritschl holds, however, that it is the *person* of Christ which triumphs over the Old Testament position. "When," he remarks (S. 44), "Christianity comes forth as a new religion, what, it may be asked, is the point where the new principle appears no longer as a latent germ, but as a reality, and detaches itself definitely from all the representations of Old Testament piety?" "*The answer to this question*, we read further, *is that the perfect righteousness which, in opposition to the Pharisees, Jesus required as the condition of entrance into the kingdom of heaven was represented as a reality in Himself.*"

We proceed to the exposition. We have to determine the meaning of νόμος καὶ προφῆται on the one hand, and πληρῶσαι on the other. Νόμος and προφῆται, the two principal portions of the Old Testament, denote the codex in its widest extent (chap. vii. 12, xxii. 40; Luke xvi. 16; Acts xiii. 15; Rom. iii. 21), and by transposition, the *religion* of the Old Testament. For in them are expressed the main elements of the Old Testament, and indeed of all religions; **to** wit, *commandment* and *promise*. But neither of these is exclusively allotted to one or the other part of the codex: even the νόμος contains a prophetic and typical element, and the prophets are preachers of the law. Hence ὁ νόμος καὶ οἱ προφῆται is sometimes used to denote the Old Testament dispensation in its legal (Matt. vii. 12, xxii. 40), sometimes in its prophetical, aspect (Matt. xi. 13, Rom. iii. 21). Sometimes, however, we find all the parts of the Old Testament comprehended under the term νόμος, as the pars potior codicis (Rom. iii. 19; John x. 34).

Ἤ in this passage has *essentially* the meaning of καί. The only difference would be, that in the one case (if καί was used) the writer's object would be to bring both ideas simultaneously before the reader, as forming together but one idea; whereas, in the other case, the one idea would come up after the other. Thus a law says: "Whoso slandereth the King *and* Queen," or, "whoso slandereth the King *or* the Queen." The reason for the use of the one or the other cannot, therefore, lie in the construction of the clause, as Fritzsche thinks, who, in his Commentary on Rom. iv. 13, lays down the canon, that ἤ occurs **in** negative, καί in positive, sentences. Exceptions to this may be found, in a negative sentence, in chap. vi. 25, where, according to preponderating testimony, the proper reading is καί: in positive sentences, where ἤ is used, in 1 Cor. xi. 27; 1 Pet. i. 11; James ii. 15, iv. 11. In the last passage, as in many others, the codices hesitate between καί and ἤ. In our own passage, Cod. 125* has καί. The reason for putting καί or ἤ here cannot like in the construction of the sentence, any more than the reason for adding or omitting the disjunctive before the first clause is to be found therein (Bornemann, on Xenoph. Mem. L. 1, c. 6, § 9, and on exped. Cyri, L. 6, c. 4, § 2). Chrys. has here: ἢ τὸν νόμον ἢ τοὺς προφήτας. Nothing therefore can be definitely determined as to the meaning of the passage from the use of καί or ἤ: although, in the Roman Catholic controversy on the Lord's Supper, the ἤ in 1 Cor. xi. 27 was regarded as decisive. On the one hand, we cannot, with Meinel (Treatise on the passage in Bertholdt's Journal d. neuesten Theolog. Litt. 1822, B. xiv. S. 22) and with Wieseler (Stud. u. Krit. 1839, 4 H., S. 1122), maintain, that by the ἤ the prophetic part is brought into distinct prominence as an independent conception; for ἤ is used sometimes to unite ideas which are quite synonymous: comp. e.g. ἰῶτα ἓν ἢ μία κεραία, ver. 18; Acts i. 7, χρόνους ἢ καιρούς; Herodian, vii. 3, 8: τιμὴν ἢ δόξαν ἐπὶ τροπαίοις προσγενομένην. As little can it, on the other hand, be said, with Usteri (paulinischer Lehrbegriff, 4 A S. 197), that by the ἤ the Prophets are expressly designated as supplementary to the idea of νόμος, i.e., as the expounders of the law. Such being the state of the case, it follows that there are possible two different explanations of the *thing* itself, and a third different view of the *form*. The Law and the Prophets may denote the Old Testament economy apprehended as an unity—either (1.) in its *ethical*, or (2.) in its *prophetical* character; or (3.) the prophetical part may be viewed as independently annexed by ἤ to the ethical. The first view is that prevalent in modern times (Bucer, Calv., Mel., Socin., Grotius, Episc., Rosenm., Paul., Kuinoel, Usteri, Mich., Baumgarten, B.-Crus., Meyer, De W., v. Gerlach, and, though not articulately, the critics of Baur's School). The *second* is found in Clemens Alex., Strom. vii. 532, ed. Pott.: πληρῶσαι δὲ τὸν νόμον οὐχ ὡς ἐνδεῆ, ἀλλὰ τῷ τὰς κατὰ νόμον προφητείας ἐπιτελεῖς γενέσθαι κατὰ τὴν αὐτοῦ παρουσίαν· ἐπεὶ τὰ τῆς ὀρθῆς πολιτείας καὶ τοῖς δικαίως βεβιωκόσι πρὸ τοῦ νόμου διὰ τοῦ λόγου ἐκηρύσσετο. Hilar.: lex operum posita est et omnia in fidem eorum, quae in Christo erant revelanda, conclusit... lex autem sub velamento verborum spiritalium nativitatem Domini nostri et corporalitatem et passionem et resurrectionem locuta est. Also Olshausen, E. J. Meyer: the last in this sense, that the pedagogical character of the ethical law is presented under the point of view of the prophecy. Meyer thus sums up his explanation: "Christ has come to allow that which the Old Testament, in its Law and in its Prophets (at once prophetical and typical), intended, to become realized." The *third* view, which disjoins the two members of the clause, and thus is also *formally* different from the other two, is, that Christ expresses His fulfilling of the prophetical predictions on the one hand, and of the law on the other hand. This interpretation is the one most generally adopted in ancient and modern times (Chrys., Theoph., Aug., Euthym., Bullinger, Beza, Chemnitz, Hunnius, Calov, Bengel, Meinel, Strauss, Neander, Bleek (Stud. u. Krit. 1853, S. 303), Ewald, Lechler in loc. cit.).

The opinion, that the reference is exclusively to the legal portion of the Old Test., is based mainly on two arguments, chiefly insisted on by De Wette and Baumgarten. First, it is alleged that no one could ever have ascribed to Christ the intention of abrogating the Prophets; and second, that in the succeeding passage there is no allusion to the Prophets. In opposition to the former argument, it has been rightly adduced by E. J. Meyer, that such an idea was by no means unnatural in men who witnessed the appearance of Jesus, so utterly at variance with the carnal Messianic expectations which they cherished. But the second argument holds its ground; and it is corroborated not only by vers. 18—20, but by the parallel passage in Luke xvi. 17. The reason why the majority of expositors, ancient and modern, have held that there is also a reference to the Prophets, was not so much on account of the disjunctive form of the phrase,—not so much the ἢ τοὺς προφήτας—as the idea that Christ, having intimated the πληροῦν as His special mission, could not, in so doing, leave wholly out of account the prophetical portions of the Old Test. Many too, like Bleek (in loc. cit., S. 304), have allowed their opinion to be determined by the 18th verse.

Under this impression apparently, E. J. Meyer has been led to deny all reference to the Law viewed in its injunctions and commands, and to explain the saying exclusively of "the realization of the *intention* of the Law and the Prophets." His *discursus* is occasionally very ingenious in its polemical portions, but it is vitiated by the want of a sufficiently clear apprehension of the concept *intention*. For he ascribes an intention, with regard to the future, not only to the Law, but also to the predictions in the Prophets; whereas there can only be an intention where there is a purpose to be attained. Then, again, failing adequately to distinguish between the practical and the theoretical, he lumps together the *pedagogical* and the *typical* characters of the νόμος, under the idea of an intention (S. 63, 64); whereas the two are distinct: the law, in its pedagogical character, must prepare the way for the new religion in a practical manner, whilst in its typical character it does so by instruction and insight. Joined to this is the mistake [of supposing], that the *literal* fulfilment of the Law must fall to the ground, the pedagogical institution of Moses be given up, in order that that which was *intended* by it (under which expression he again comprises both the moral preparation and the antitypical realization), viz., the spiritual kingdom of Christ, may be obtained. This erroneous view is next made the basis of a new and utterly mistaken exposition of those verses, which makes the prophetical interpretation of this 17th verse simply impossible,—viz., the 18th and 19th. According to this author, the command there given, to keep even the least commandment, only means the keeping of these commandments in their spirit and *intention*, while in the *letter* obedience to them is done away with. "If you do the commandments like the Pharisees, *i.e.*, in the letter, without thinking of their intention, you shall never attain to the kingdom of heaven. Ye have heard, for example, the Mosaic law: Thou shalt not kill. This command exists no longer in the kingdom of heaven; and if you do not get beyond these words, you will never reach the kingdom of heaven. But what that command intends, the idea upon which it is based, viz., true brotherly love,—*that* is of account in the kingdom of heaven." So here an intention is ascribed to the *commands* of the law,—although, from the terms in which his conclusion is given, one would not expect it. As the typical method of preparation cannot be the right one, all that remains is the pedagogical; that is, the lower moral requirements pave the way for the fulfilment of the higher. But this writer goes on to argue, this higher fulfilment cannot stand in an antagonistic relation to that lower fulfilment; consequently, that the higher may be fulfilled, the lower must be abolished: but the *tollere* here is rather a *conservare*.

Yet the thought which this author develops so obscurely, is one which we hold is at the root of a correct interpretation of the saying under consideration. It is already to be found in Augustin (con. Faust. T. viii. 220): Impletur lex (so he does not take νόμος and προφ. disjunctively) vel cum fiant, quæ ibi præcepta sunt, vel cum exhibentur, quæ ibi prophetata sunt, lex enim per Moysen data est, gratia et veritas per Jesum Christum facta est (Joh. i. 17). Gratia pertinet ad caritatis plenitudinem, veritas ad prophetiarum impletionem. So, too, Neander, Stier, Lechler, in loc. cit. As the prophecy *theoretically*, so was the law *practically*, a shadowy outline of μέλλοντα ἀγαθά (Heb. x. 1). It is a σκιαγραφία, ὑπογραφή (Stallbaum on *de repub.* ii. p. 60, 179), to which the Christian economy supplies the ζωγραφία or ἀπεργασία. In its constituent ethical elements, alike as regards its incentives and its requirements, it contains the germs of that δικαιοσύνη which is fully realized in the Christian economy as δικαιοσύνη τ. βασιλείας τοῦ Θεοῦ (vi. 33). In its ritual elements, it has on the one side an ethical and pedagogical import, on the other, a symbolical and didactical character. Hence νόμος καὶ προφῆται must be viewed as forming together an unity: for the νόμος contains the element of prophecy (Acts xxvi. 22); and the Prophets *expound* the Law, —nay, more, they CONTAIN THE LAW *in a series of progressive revelation, they give it a deeper meaning*, and bring it nearer and nearer *to the Christian revelation. So Christ has come to perfect, to fill up with religious knowledge and life, all that in the Old Testament revelation existed only in outline.* Compare the striking saying of Synesius, homil. on Ps. lxxv. 9: ἐν γὰρ ἔπνευσε πνεῦμα καὶ εἰς προφήτην καὶ εἰς ἀπόστολον καὶ κατὰ τ. ζωγράφοις πάλαι μὲν ἐσκιαγράφησεν, ἔπειτα μέντοι διηκρίβωσε τὰ μὲν τῆς γνώσεως. Nor is it a proof that we are at fault in taking this comprehensive view, that in the sequel only the one side, the relation to the ethical law, is brought prominently forward. St Paul, likewise, when he speaks of fulfilling the law, dwells principally upon the fundamental law of Israel, the ethical Decalogue (Rom. ii. 14, 15, iii. 20: comp. Author's commentary, 5 A., S. 141). "The Decalogue," says Hengstenberg (Beitraege, iii. 597), "gives the essence of the whole law. This is shown already by the number of *ten* commandments, on which stress is laid in the law itself (Exod. xxxiv. 28; Deut. iv. 13). [The number ten, the highest of simple numbers, was the decisive number in the old Symbology.] It is shown, further, by the fact, that the ten commandments are called the words of the covenant, Exod. xxxiv. 28; **and** the circumstance, that the Decalogue alone was deposited in the ark of the covenant, while the Book of the

Law, as merely supplemental to it, was placed beside the ark."[1] But "although Christ referred to the whole of the Old Testament, in both its parts, He might afterwards bring *one particular aspect* into greater prominence," (Neander).

And with this we have already given our view of the meaning of πληροῦν. With regard to its lexical signification: that given by Vitringa, followed by Hottinger, Schoettgen, Heum., = ־בד to "*teach*," is not to be mentioned. Πληροῦν, in its secondary sense, is "to make up the full numbers:" πληρουμένης τῆς ἐκκλησίας, Arist. Eccl. v. 89; to "supplement:" τό, τε ἐν ἡμῖν νέον σεμνότητος πληρώσετε τῇ τῶν ὑμετέρων ἔργων ἀνδραγαθίᾳ (Herodian, i. 5, 25); "what owing to my youth is wanting to my authority, you will make up by your bravery." Thus the word is used of the filling-up of a measure, Matt. xxiii. 32, and of the full realization of a symbolical institution like the Passover, Luke xxii. 16. Πληροῦν νόμον, ἐντολήν, in classic and Hellenistic use, means: implere, explere legem, peragere quae sunt officii. (Herodian, iii. 11; Arrian. diss. Epict. 4, 8; Rom. viii. 4, xiii. 8; Fritzsche ad Rom. ii. 472.) The praeceptum, as Mel. observes, is a simulacrum so long as its fulfilment is wanting. Λύειν (comp. on v. 19), καταλύειν νόμον, in Hellenistic and classic Greek, is equivalent to ἀκυροῦν (Matt. xv. 6; Gal. iii. 17), καταργεῖν (Rom. iii. 31, iv. 14):, comp. 2 Macc. ii. 23, iv. 11; Joseph. Antiq. xx. 4, 2, xviii. 3, 1; Demosth. Timocr., ed. Reiske, p. 700: λύει καὶ ποιεῖ τοῦ μηδενὸς ἀξίαν ὁ τουτουΐ νόμος. The antithesis to λύειν in ver. 19, schows that the theoretical and the practical negation are to be regarded as conjoined.

The question which next presents itself is, whether the clause is to be supplemented from the context by the object of the fulfilment, "the Law and the Prophets," a course grammatically admissible (see Krueger's Griech. Gramm. § 60, 7),— or, whether we are to take the infinitive absolutely as in Luther's translation [and in the English authorized version]; as Stolz: "I am not come to weaken, but to make perfect." Neander, Harnack. Such an energetic declaration appears still more in keeping with His full consciousness of being the Redeemer. How much or how little is implied in the idea of *fulfilling*, must depend, first, on the dogmatical stand-point of

---

[1] Mel.: Quid est lex? Respondeo pueris breviter: est decalogus.

the expositor, and next, on the view taken, as to whether the prophetical element has here any significance. The act of fulfilment may be regarded either as comprehended in the work done by Christ Himself, or as only begun by Him and completed by the disciples as His agents. Again, the fulfilling may be restricted to the sphere of His teaching, or it may be extended to His practical agency, the fulfilling by His life and sufferings. That the fulfilment is accomplished by Christ alone, is held by the Fathers mentioned in p. 34, by the Catholic, Socinian, and Arminian expositors (Socinus, Wolzogen, Crell), who, assuming the imperfection of the law, explain $\pi\lambda\eta\varrho o\tilde{v}\nu$: defectum legis explere; Wettst.: perfecit legem Christus, tum addendo promissa vitæ alterius, tum ea auferendo, quæ obstabant, quominus gentes cum Judæis in unam societatem coalescere possent. The more this supplementing is regarded as *not* of a mechanical and quantitative character, so much the more does this explanation approach that other which regards the fulfilment as consisting rather in an *unfolding* and *deepening*, than a supplementing, of the Old Testament economy. The Rationalists make it out to be merely an *explaining*: Teller, "to explain and enforce the law in all its extent;" Barth, "I am come to amplify and make honourable that ancient doctrine of Wisdom;" Doederlein, "Sancire nova decreta et vetera melius explicare" (Institt. ii. p. 405); even Heubner (praktische Erklaerung des N. T.): "to explain more accurately, and to recommend by practising it." With a profound apprehension of the law in its relation to the Christian doctrine of salvation, Luther explains it thus: "to show the real kernel and true significance of the law, that men might learn what it is, and what it requires;" and Meyer: the $\pi\lambda\acute\eta\varrho\omega\sigma\iota\varsigma$ of the law is the perfect development of the real essence of its precepts, and the deliverance of their substance from that positive form in which it had hitherto been confined: so Olsh., De Wette, Ewald.

That the fulfilling was merely and external supplementing or improvement of the law, cannot be admitted. It is disproved by the deep pedagogical and economical view of the Old Testament held by Christ and by St Paul (see on ver. 21): further, by the allusion to the Prophets, if that is recognised as an independent element; by the $\mathring{\epsilon}\omega\varsigma\ \mathring{a}\nu\ \pi\acute{a}\nu\tau a\ \gamma\acute{\epsilon}\nu\eta\tau a\iota$, ver. 18; by the important position of $\pi o\iota\epsilon\tilde{\iota}\nu$, ver. 19; and by what is said of the moral superiority of the members of the kingdom of God, ver. 20. As rightly observed by Augustin, Christ annexes greatness in the kingdom of heaven, not to the observance of commands which had yet to be given, but to obedience to those already in existence. (Comp. also Philippi, ueber den thaetigen Gehorsam Christi, 1841, S. 33.) Certainly there is implied in what follows, a *deepening* of the Divine requirements in the law, if by this be understood the introduction of a deeper significance than it ever had before. And not alone in this expression, but everywhere in the Gospel, that the Saviour had no intention to teach anything entirely new, anything for which some point of contact might not be found in the Old Test., and for which the Old Test. had not prepared the way. It is not with rabbinical hair-splittings, but with simple depth of insight (as every unprejudiced reader must admit), that He points out, in Old Test. sayings and facts, truths which seem entirely to transcend the stage of religious development which the Old Testament had reached. He vindicates the right of the heathen to God's messengers by the examples of Elijah and Elisha, Luke iv. 25, 26; the incomparably superior importance of the fulfilment of the moral law to that of ritual observances, is shown by a quotation from Hosea, Matt. ix. 13, xii. 7; the right even to break the Sabbath, when its claims come into collision with moral self-love or love of our neighbour, is proved from the example of David and the priests, Matt. xii. 3, 4; the summing-up of all the commandments of the moral law in love to God and to thy neighbour, Matt. xxii. 40; a future life for the departed patriarchs is demonstrated from the words of Moses himself, Matt. xxii. 32. (Compare Lechler's admirable disquisition in the treatise already quoted, "das Alte Testament in den Reden Jesu," S. 792.)

Now, although we have little sympathy with the attempt to fathom the deep things of Holy Writ with an exegetical plumbline, yet, with the interpretation as hitherto determined, we cannot content ourselves. We are carried beyond it by that consciousness in the Saviour, in virtue of which He promises, in the Beatitude, ver. 6, the possession of $\delta\iota\varkappa\alpha\iota\sigma\sigma\acute{\upsilon}\nu\eta$ to those who longed for it; by the expression in Luke iv. 18, in which Christ applies to Himself the words of the prophet, $\varkappa\eta\varrho\acute{\upsilon}\xi\alpha\iota\ \tau.\ \alpha\grave{\iota}\chi\mu\alpha\lambda\acute{\omega}\tau\sigma\iota\varsigma\ \ddot{\alpha}\varphi\varepsilon\sigma\iota\nu,\ \tau\sigma\widetilde{\iota}\varsigma\ \tau\upsilon\varphi\lambda\sigma\widetilde{\iota}\varsigma\ \dot{\alpha}\nu\acute{\alpha}\beta\lambda\varepsilon\psi\iota\nu,\ \dot{\alpha}\pi\sigma\sigma\tau\varepsilon\widetilde{\iota}\lambda\alpha\iota\ \tau\sigma\grave{\upsilon}\varsigma\ \tau\varepsilon$-

θραυσμένους, adding the words: σήμερον πεπλήρωται ἡ γραφὴ αὕτη; further, by the allusion in our passage to the prophetical element; and by the comprehensiveness of the expressions, ver. 18, ἰῶτα ἓν ἢ μία κεραία, and ἕως ἂν πάντα γένηται.—In the first place, we must regard the πληροῦν as applying, not only to the teaching of Christ, but to the whole of His ministry in doing and in suffering: nor can the circumstance, that no reference is made to the latter in the sequel, deter us from this conclusion (vide *supra,* p. 126). Here at the outset, we are met by the view, which would restrict the πληροῦν τ. νόμον to the resolution of Christ to submit personally to obedience to the law, in order to reconcile the Jews (Spanheim; Reinhard, Plan Jesu, 5 A. S. 15; Planck, Einführung des Christenthums, i. 175: Amthor, de Apostasia, 1833, p. 7). This opinion, however, is antiquated, and has no longer any supporters. Not so, however, that according to which these words contain the expression of our Lord's perfect ὑπακοή, the union of His will with the will of the Father embodied in His actions and sufferings. This opinion has still its representatives: it is held by some with a reference to the Church dogma of the satisfactio activa; by others, apart from any such reference. Without this reference, by Socinus, Bleek, v. Gerlach, Lechler; with it, by Chrys., Bucer; and since the introduction of the dogma of the obedientia activa into the Reformed and Lutheran Churches, by several theologians of both communions (see Aretius [1]), and Cocceius, Hunnius, Calov, Er. Schmidt (in loc.): comp. Quenstedt, theol. didactica, iii. p. 282; among recent writers, Philippi, vom thaetigen Gehorsam Christi, S. 34, Mich. Baumgarten (in loc. cit. S. 15). The only objection to the opinion that this element of His own personal obedience formed part of His idea, is in the words, ἕως ἂν πάντα γένηται, in the following confirmatory verse. In these words, He alludes to a future fulfilling of the law by the members of His kingdom, a fulfilment rendered possible only through Him. Yet it must be admitted, that this may form one aspect of the many-sided conception. But for the supposition that this πλήρωσις includes the idea of a satisfactio activa, there is

---

[1] Piscator, the opponent of the doctrine of the obedientia activa, here, remarkably enough, declares himself in favour of it: Ut vita quoque sua et actionibus atque adeo etiam perpessionibus illa ipsa præstet, quæ Moses et prophetæ facienda præceperant.

very little warrant. It must be remembered, that the idea of an *obedientia vicaria activa* is a foreign to the Old Testament and rabbinical conceptions of the Messiah, as that of an *obedientia passiva* is peculiar to them; and the former, even if it can be gathered from St Paul's Epistles, has no support anywhere in the words of Christ. As we are compelled by the expression, ἰῶτα ἓν ἢ μία κεραία, in ver. 18, to understand the νόμος as comprehending not only the moral, but also the ritual law,—the Jews regarded the two as forming one indivisible whole,—we must, with Bleek, acknowledge that the highest act of fulfilment of the *ritual* law was the sacrificial death of the Redeemer: thus we may place beside this ἦλθον πληρῶσαι that other saying: ἦλθον διακονῆσαι κ. τὴν ψυχήν μου λύτρον δοῦναι, Matt. xx. 28.

But even now we have not exhausted the full meaning of the words. To establish a βασιλεία τῆς δικαιοσύνης, to conduct the members of His kingdom to a perfect fulfilment of the law, was to be the great work of the Messiah (Isa. xi. 9, lx. 21, lxii. 12; Jer. xxxi. 31, etc.). We infer, too, from the quotation with which He accompanies the announcement in St Luke iv. 18, that He did not regard this πληρῶσαι of the law as terminating in His own person: He must have had before Him a βασιλεία τ. Θεοῦ as the final goal, Matt. vi. 33; comp. also 1 Cor. vii. 19. Then to this πληροῦσθαι in the Church, we find an allusion in ver. 18, in the ἕως ἂν πάντα γένηται, and in ver. 20. Hence we must, with Aug. (in loc. citato, p. 124), interpreting the saying by John i, 17, ἡ χάρις καὶ ἡ ἀλήθεια διὰ Ἰ. Χ. ἐγένετο, conclude that it contains a distinct *promise of grace* to His followers. How, indeed, could He have omitted all allusion to the great doctrine of χάρις, in a passage like this, which, even more unmistakeably than Luke iv. 18, contains a declaration of the whole scope of His mission? In this sense, the saying is explained repeatedly by St Augustin. Quia venit dare caritatem et caritas perficit legem, merito dixit: non veni legem solvere, sed implere (Sermo 126 in Johann. T. v. Opp. 427; T. viii. 2, 705, etc.). By His very fulfilment of the commandments, he says (T. viii. 229), Jesus has abolished them; as if, instead of nasciturus est, passurus est, one put natus est, passus est. So the greater number of Catholic exegetists; Este: principaliter venit, ut per gratiam ejus observatio legis impleretur.

Among the Protestants, Bullinger, **Bucer**: ut ergo consummatam expectamus felicitatem, ita pariter absolutam oportet speremus et in nobis legis impletionem, quæ continget, cum exstincta morte Deus fuerit omnia in omnibus. 1 Cor. xv. 28; comp. Stier.

The promise here made is precisely that of which Jeremiah holds out the prospect (xxxi. 33), that the law of God would be written in the *hearts* of men by the Spirit of God, and that, according to ver. 34, through the forgiveness of sins. Ritschl (in loc. cit. S. 32) observes, that the contrast is not between fulfilment in the letter and fulfilment in the spirit. This is so far correct, as Christ certainly ascribes to the law authority, not only over the outward actions, but over the inward spirit which prompts them: wrong, however, if he would exclude the power which goes forth from Christ to impart that new spirit.

Commentators, ancient and modern, enumerate, from the stand-point of an elaborated doctrinal system, the various ways in which this πλήρωσις νόμου has been accomplished. St Chrysostom, who (Homil. in Joann. v. 19, ed. Montf. T. vi., p. 662) designates the Sermon on the Mount the διόρθωσις of the νομοθεσία of the Father, says on our text: τὸν δὲ νόμον οὐχ ἑνὶ ἀλλὰ καὶ δευτέρῳ καὶ τρίτῳ ἐπλήρωσε τρόπῳ, and mentions the following threefold πλήρωσις: (1), in that Christ fulfilled the law Himself, John ii. 17, viii. 46, xiv. 30; (2), in that He fulfils it *through us*, Rom. x. 4, viii. 3, iii. 31: (3), in that He has used, not an ἀναίρεσις τῶν προτέρων, but an ἐπίτασις and πλήρωσις. Nicolas a Lyra enumerates accurately the various fulfilments of the law *and* the prophets, with reference to the different classifications of the law. Maldonatus: 1, Christ has fulfilled the law in His own person, and by causing the Apostles also to fulfil the ceremonial law; 2, in that He has explained its meaning; 3, inasmuch as He has given us grace to fulfil it; 4, inasmuch as the types of the law were realized in Himself. Melanchthon speaks of a fourfold fulfilment, giving special prominence to the second: 1, By the obedience of Christ in His own person; 2, *inasmuch as He endured for us the penalty of the law*; 3, inasmuch as He fulfils the law in us through the Holy Spirit; 4, inasmuch as He confirms the law, and asserts the necessity of obedience to it. Morus, in his treatise de discrimine sensus et significatus, even adduces this saying as a proof of how comprehensive the signification of a word may be (diss. theol. et philol., P. 80 seqq.).

Ver. 18. Confirmation and closer definition of the thought of the preceding verse: the special allusion to the Prophets is not further dwelt upon, although in itself the νόμος may certainly be regarded, according to the well-known abbreviation, as inclusive also of the προφῆται (vide supra, p. 125).—The νόμος, in its full extent, endures for ever: the whole of its extent being expressed by the smallest portions of the contents of the codex. Ἰῶτα, the smallest Hebrew letter; κεραία (*cornicle*, from κέρας), a *stroke* (of a letter), such as, *e.g.*, that which distinguishes ד from ר or ך from ן, for which the Rabbis have קוץ or עוֹקֶץ, a *thorn*.[1] Tanchuma, P. 681, in Wettstein: dixit Deus: Salomon et mille similes illi peribunt de mundo et apicula una de littera Jod non peribit. As, however, νόμος κ. προφ. does not denote the codex as such, but its substance, and the Old Testament religion founded thereon, so here, by the elements of the letters, we are to understand the elements of that religion, the ἐντολαὶ ἐλάχισται of ver. 19.

Here we may inquire how the determination of the time, ἕως ἂν παρέλθῃ ὁ οὐρανὸς καὶ ἡ γῆ, is to be understood, and in what relation ἕως ἂν πάντα γένηται stands to that phrase. Παρέρχεσθαι, like παραδραμεῖν, παραφέρεσθαι, παράγειν, means to "pass by," to "pass from view," hence, to "perish" (vide Wettstein in loc.): comp. Aristid. i. 216, παρῆλθον ὥσπερ μῦθοι, and the phrase παρέρχεταί μέ τι,, "I forget something." Comp. in Hebrew עָבַר, Ps. xxxvii. 36; Nah. i. 12; Job. xxxiv. 20. Of the passing away of the heavens, Matt. xxiv. 35; 2 Pet. iii. 10; Rev. xxi. 1; παράγεται, 1 John ii. 17; the intransitive παράγει, 1 Cor. vii. 31. Now the heavens, with their stars, are represented both in the classics and in the Old Testament as that which, amid all earthly change, remains imperishable: in the classics we even find this proverb: θᾶσσον ἂν τὸν οὐρανὸν (in Hesiod, ἕδος ἀσφαλὲς αἰεί) συμπεσεῖν, donec coelum ruat. Comp. in the Old Test., Ps. lxxii. 7, lxxxix. 37, 38; Job. xiv. 12; Jer. xxxiii. 20, 21; Baruch i. 11. So also Luke xvi. 17: εὐκοπώτερόν ἐστιν, τὸν οὐρανὸν καὶ τὴν γῆν παρελθεῖν, ἢ τοῦ νόμου μίαν κεραίαν πεσεῖν. Accordingly, the period indicated has been regarded as one which will never come; so that the verse

---

[1] Most carefully on this point, Iken dissert. philol. theol. T. i., diss. xx.—Augustine, who thought of the Latin *i*, understood κεραία to denote the dot.

declares that the law is imperishable. Thus Calv., Zwingli, Luther, Pisc., Chemn., Grot., Wettstein, and with few exceptions, recent critics. But what in this case does the second clause mean: ἕως ἂν πάντα γένηται? Kuinoel and Gratz, in despair of finding a suitable signification for these words, conclude that they are merely added from memory, from Luke xxi. 32, and are here out of place. The older expositors, Chemn., Grot., Cler., translate as if there was an ἀλλά: quin imo penitus implebuntur. Fritzsche (in the New Theological Journal by Winer and Engelhardt, v., S. 14, and in his commentary in loc.) thinks this a case where, as in James ii. 14, and also occasionally in classical authors, the sentence has a double apodosis,—one before the protasis, the other after it,—and both expressing the same sense, and that πάντα has here the signification of quælibet; so that the meaning would be as follows: donec omnia, *quæ mente fingere queas*, evenerint. Winer seems not disinclined to adopt this view, referring to 2 Cor. xii. 7; Rev. ii. 5: yet he does not think it satisfactory (Gramm., 6 A., S. 540). Fritzsche believes himself to have been the first to propose this syntactical rendering: quod neminem videre memini. But it was suggested first of all by Episcopius;[1] after him, by an anonymous writer (in den *freiwilligen Hebopfern*, 5ter Beitrag, S. 409), with the same translation of πάντα as in Fritzsche; by J. C. Schulz (in den Erinnerungen zu D. Michaelis Bibeluebersetzung, S. 39); by Rosenmueller (Schol.); by Vater. Undoubtedly πάντα occurs in the sense of παντοῖα in many connection: πάντα γίνεσθαι = to assume any shape, Odyssey, iv. v. 417; πάντα εἶναί τινι, Herod. i. 127, Thuc. viii. 95: vide Pape.[2] But, as Meyer remarks, with this meaning the ἕως ἂν πάντα γένηται would drag heavily after the concrete and vivid expression, ἕως ἂν παρέλθῃ ὁ οὐρανὸς καὶ ἡ γῆ.

---

[1] Episcopius ad locum: quæ sequuntur verba ἕως ἂν πάντα γένηται idem mihi continere videntur, quod præcedentia et ad confirmandum magis id quod dictum est, adhiberi, hoc pacto: imo vero dico vobis, priusquam omnia ista pereant, nihil omnino in lege mosaica immutandum erit; πάντα γένηται itaque est idem, quod ὁ οὐρανὸς παρέλθῃ, quia cœlum et terra omnia sunt. The latter obsure expression seems to indicate a view similar to Fritzsche's.

[2] A similar meaning is expressed by the formula οὐδὲ ἂν εἴ τι γένοιτο, ne si omnia quidem fiant, which has been elucidated by the annotators on Plutarch, de educ. puer. P. 78, ed. Oxon.

Therefore ἕως ἂν πάντα γένηται is now correctly regarded as a closer determination of the period of the παρέρχεσθαι, as Chrysostom explains: ἀμήχανον ἀτέλεστον μεῖναι, ἀλλὰ καὶ τὸ βραχύτατον αὐτοῦ πληρωθῆναι δεῖ. There will thus come to pass, what under the Jewish religion never could come to pass, a ποιεῖν of the whole contents of the law, as ver. 19 also declares. That, when this is attained, the νόμος shall cease, is not necessarily implied in the words: for an indication of time with ἕως sometimes marks a terminus without decidedly negativing the continued existence of that which is expressed in the previous clause: comp. Matt. i. 25; Ps. cx. 1. Keeping in view the way in which the law is fulfilled through Christ, we shall conclude that, in its *form*, the law ceases as a requirement so soon as the πνεῦμα implants its principle in the heart (Rom. viii. 4): in its *substance*, it continues. If by ἕως ἂν παρέλθῃ ὁ οὐρ. κ. ἡ γῆ a terminus be denoted which shall never be reached, as in Luke xvi. 17, the νόμος is here characterized as imperishable, its imperishability is the leading thought of the verse; and the second clause with ἕως comes in only in a secondary way, to give assurance of the subjective realization of the law, and in so doing, to indicate the manner in which it is called imperishable. This view is strongly supported by Luke xvi. 17. And here a second question arises, which has not been always—not, for instance, by Chrys.—carefully distinguished from the first.[1] Like the νόμος, heaven and earth might be regarded under both points of view, both as perishable and as imperishable: for it is only the σχῆμα τοῦ κόσμου τούτου which shall pass away (1 Cor. vii. 31), while a new heaven and a new earth arise in its place (Isa. lxv. 17, lxvi. 22; 2 Pet. iii. 13; Rev. xxi. 1; Rom. viii. 21).[2] There is therefore no contradiction when St Luke (xvi. 17) alludes to the passing away of the heavens and the earth as the most improbable occurrence and St Matthew, on the other hand, peremptorily asserts (xxiv. 35), ὁ οὐρανὸς καὶ ἡ γῆ παρελεύσεται. Now, if Christ here refers to the fact, that heaven and earth are to pass away, ἕως must determine a certain point of time after which, although not before having been

---

[1] Notwithstanding that his ἀμήχανον ἀτέλεστον μεῖναι presupposes the imperishability of οὐρ. καὶ γῆ, Chrys. yet adds: ἐνταῦθα αἰνίττεται, ὅτι ὁ κόσμος ἅπας μετασχηματίζεται.

[2] Comp. the learned disquisition in Spanheim, dubium 132.

fulfilled, the law shall pass away. How is this? Peculiar is the answer of the author who was the first to propose this view of ἕως (yet see the translation of Ulfilas), to wit, Socinus: The law was to pass away by the abrogation of certain parts of it after the death of Christ, *after that He had Himself perfectly satisfied the law* (vide infra). According to Stier: "Inasmuch as the fulfilling of its substance and the development of the kingdom of Christ will last until that time." Lechler (in loc. cit. S. 797): "It will pass away in so far as it is comprised in *word* and *letter;* it will continue inasmuch as it will be perfectly realized in history (in what takes place, γενέσθαι)." Substantially of the same opinion, although not taking the same view of the ἕως, Cocceius: Christus dum dicit, nullum Jota aut apiculum præteriturum, significat nihil in vanum scriptum esse, quod scriptum est etiam mansurum esse, ut intelligatur non in vanum scriptum esse quod scriptum est. Ut multis aliis testimoniis, ita etiam hoc, potest nobis constare, Dei providentiam vigilaturam esse, ut non intercidat scriptura et lectio scripturæ vera et genuina. With reference to the words we have quoted from Stier, speaking of the substance of the law: it is difficult to see how, in *this* respect, we can speak of the passing away of the law. Stier in these words regards the development of the substance of the law as coincident with the development of the kingdom of Christ. But in the perfect kingdom of Christ, the law will pass away only as a fragment may be said to pass away which becomes part of a whole: it will be abolished only in the sense of being therein contained. Further on, however, Stier's view seems to approach nearer to that of Cocceius and Lechler, inasmuch as he speaks of "a passing away of the letters and points in which the law must till then be contained." Thus the theme of that solemn assurance would be, that the law, as a written **word, is to endure up to the period of** the perfecting of the kingdom of God: a view, however, which is attended with more than one difficulty. It has already been shown that the letter is here used figuratively for the Old Testament religion. But if it is also granted that He is speaking of the codex as such, surely the prediction of its continuance to the end of the world would be here out of place,—especially when one considers that the codex of the New Testament would then be excluded. Erasmus remarks concerning a Bibliolatrical application: neque laboratur de literarum apiculis, cum constet *non pauca etiam volumina* V. T. (and so also of the New) *intercidisse.* True, Lechler finds in these words a promise that the λόγοι Χριστοῦ were to last beyond that time, as in Matt. xxiv. 35; but surely a consideration of the latter expression, which affirms the eternal continuance, not of a written codex, but of the substance of the sayings of Christ, would lead one to suppose the same thing to be affirmed equally of the Old Testament codex.

If heaven and earth are considered as here denoting the transient and the perishable, and ἕως as marking a limit of duration, the only view of the verse which fits in with what is expressed, ver. 17, of the purpose of Christ's coming, is that indicated by Bucer (who here refers to 1 Cor. xv. 28). "As an incontrovertible witness for God against sinful man, the law will continue to exist; and by its commands it will continually hold up to him the will of God, even until it passes over into the freedom of subjectivity, and is written in men's *hearts;* until the time of eschatological perfecting of the redeemed, when they shall all be united in the kingdom of God: then, and not before, its mission will be accomplished, and it will pass away." Νόμον οὖν καταργοῦμεν διὰ τῆς πίστεως; μὴ γένοιτο, ἀλλὰ νόμον ἱστάνομεν: Rom. iii. 31. This appears also to be Olshausen's view, although less clearly expressed. Now, this view would have some historical foundation, if the opinion above referred to (p. 114), regarding the relation of the Messiah to the law, could be proved to have been prevalent at the time of our Saviour. In that case, the expectation with regard to the Messiah which is expressed in those rabbinical sayings we have quoted,—viz., that He would substitute for the Mosaic law a new and entirely moral law,—would have been adopted by Christ, who would, however, have referred men for the fulfilment of that expectation to a fixed future period.

The modern view of the passage is based upon the historical foundation of these rabbinical expectations, although, singularly enough, this, the strongest support of the opinion, is not taken into consideration. According to this view, Jesus was still entangled in the Jewish notions of His time. With this idea, Paulus (Exeget. Handbuch) gives the following explanation: So long as the Messianic theocracy lasts on this earth and under these heavens. Moses, although improved and perfected, shall still hold his own. Whenever the Messianic theocracy should have attained its object, they expected that there would be a new heaven and a new earth, when, as all would the thoroughly improved and perfected, there would be no longer any need of an external law. Πάντα is then understood indefinitely to mean, "everything which was to happen in order to the attainment of the Messianic kingdom of God." So, too, Gfroerer,—who, however, regards the saying as unauthentic,—Strauss, Usteri (Paulin. Lehrbegriff, 4 A. S. 201), Planck ("das Princip des Ebionit." in loc. cit. S. 15), Ritschl ("altkatholische Kirche," S. 28), Koestlin (S. 55), Hilgenfeld (in loc. cit. S. 62). "This explanation is rendered incumbent by the parallel form of the clause, ἕως ἂν πάντα γένηται, by which, on the one hand, the continuous validity of the law is made to depend upon '*all its enactments being perfectly accomplished and fulfilled at a certain definite period;*' and, on the other hand, the duration of the present state of the world is fixed accordingly. Therefore, although Jesus predicts a material alteration of the law and the abolition of single portions of it, it follows nevertheless, from the fact that He makes this event take place only after the perfect fulfilment of the law, that Jesus, notwithstanding His dignity as Messiah, did not consider Himself justified in abolishing the law." No satisfactory reply to the arguments in favour of the opposite opinion is here given, and still less in the superficial argumentation of Planck. And with regard to the positive side of this opinion, we confess our inability to make out its meaning. If Jesus is speaking from a Jewish point of view, what kind of "legal enactments" can they be which must be "fulfilled" before the near approach of the close of the earthly economy? Is it a requirement of the law, that it must be realized also in respect of the spirit and disposition? So we might suppose from the tenor of Ritschl's view of the whole passage,—although the expression. "to fulfil the legal enactments," seems opposed to this idea of his meaning. But if, on the other hand, Jesus is supposed to have expected the παρουσία to take place within a lifetime (Matt. xxiv. 34), how can He have ever anticipated such results? With Planck's explanation of the ἕως ἂν πάντα γένηται, we miss the issue entirely. In view of the dilemma which awaits this criticism in the 18th and also the 19th verses, so hard to bring into harmony with it, it has next proceeded to deny the authenticity of both sayings. They were introduced, it is alleged by the author in support of his anti-Pauline doctrine, in opposition to the great opponent of the law, St Paul: Koestlin (S. 54), Hilgenfeld (in loc. cit. SS. 62, 115); to which opinion the master has also gone over (Baur, "Christenthum und Kirche," S. 29).

But neither in this rationalistic sense, nor yet in that other Christian sense, can this interpretation of the passage, as intended to represent the heavens and the earth as transitory, and ἕως κ.τ.λ. as a period of time, be the right one. If the Redeemer had intended to express the future abrogation of the law in the sense of the rabbinical expectation, would not the thought which He would have brought prominently forward have been the *fulfilment* of the Messianic expectation, and *not* that of a limited duration: for which, besides, the expression, ver. 17, is much too strong? If, on the other hand, He had intended to proclaim the abrogation of the law in the Christian sense,—that is, in its character as a series of requirements,—He might doubtless have spoken in ver. 17 as He has done; for this abrogation of the form (as Kimchi rightly perceives on Jer. xxxi) was in reality a confirmation of the substance. But could Christ speak here of a future abrogation without—I will not say being unintelligible, but—without awaking the suspicion of a derogative feeling on His part with regard to the law, which would be entirely at variance with the 17th verse? Moreover, it must be especially noted, that He does not refer this spiritual γενέσθαι to His own efficacy. It is true, certain far-seeing Rabbis might speak of an annulling of the law in the time of the Messiah; but in the doctrine of all parties, the *eternity* of the law was a locus communis. Comp. Baruch iv. 1, ὁ νόμος ὁ ὑπάρχων εἰς αἰῶνα. Philo (Vita Mos. ii. 656, ed. Mang.): διαμενεῖν ... ἕως ἂν ἥλιος καὶ σελήνη καὶ ὁ σύμπας οὐρανός τε καὶ κόσμος ᾖ. Bereschith R., f. 10, 1: "Everything has an end; heaven and earth have an end: one thing alone has no end, and that is the law:" and many similar passages. Our conclusion then is: *that the heavens and the earth, and even so the law, are here regarded as enduring for ever.* This conclusion, which is also supported by the parallel passages, Luke xvi. 17 and Matt. xxiv. 35, has been adopted among modern writers by Neander, Mich., Baumg., Meyer, De Wette, Bleek. In Luke xvi. 17, heaven is considered as imperishable; in Matt. xxix. 35, eternal continuance is predicated of the words of Christ, *even if* the heavens and the earth were to pass away.[1] Christ always spoke as if His doctrine was one with the law: is it then to be supposed that He denied to the law what He affirmed of His own words? Therefore the one as well as the other shall in substance endure for ever.

But what did Christ consider the substance of the law, and what is the significance of this γενέσθαι, *which* also occurs in Matt. xxiv. 34, where it indicates the coming to pass of something predicted? About the substance of the ethical commandments, there can be no difficulty. As already observed, it can only be that which lies at the foundation of the Christian moral law, and which is developed from ver. 21. The sum of the Old Testament precepts was discerned by Christ as indicated in the Old Testament itself, Matt. xxii. 37, 39, consisting in *supreme love to God, and love to one's neighbour as one's self.* It must not be left unnoticed, that even rabbinical wisdom made some efforts to obtain a similar compendium of the law: most remarkable in this connection is the passage in the Gemara (at tr. Maccoth, f. 236, ed. Cocc.): דרש ר' שמלאי תר"יג מצות נאמרו למשה בסיני
שס"ה כמנין ימות החמה דמ"ח כנגד איבריו של אדם רב המנונא
ומאי קרא תורה צוה לנו משה תורה בגימטריא חרי חכי תורה שית
מאה וחד סרי הויין אנכי ולא יהיה לך מפי הגבורה שמענום בא דוד
והעמידם על יא" דכתיב מזמור לדוד יי' מי יגור באהלך ומי ישכון
בהר קדשך הולך תמים ופועל צדק ודובר אמת בלבבו וגו' בא ישעיהו
והעמידן על שש שנ' ה לך צדקות ודובר מישרים וגו' בא מיכה והעמידן
עלג' שנ' הגיד לך אדם מה טוב ומה יי" דורש ממך כי אם עשות משפט
ואהבת חסד והצנע לכת עם יי' אלהיך וכו' חזר ישעיהו והעמידן על
שתים שנ' כה אמר יי' שמרו משפט ועשו צדקה בא עמוס יהעמידן על
אחת שנ' כה אמר יי' לבית ישראל דרשוני וחיו היו מתקיף לוה רב נחמן
ודילמא דרשוני בכל התורה כולה אלא בא חבקוק והעמידן על אחת שנ':
וצדיק באמונתו יחיה. Samlai taught: "Six hundred and thirteen commandments were given by Moses on Mount Sinai: 355

---

[1] Lechler, in loc. cit. S. 797, reproaches Stier and Olshausen with inconsistency in maintaining, with most writers, that the same assertion is made respecting the words of Christ in Matt. xxiv. 35, as concerning the law of Moses in Matt. v. 18: whereas, according to him, the converse is unmistakeably expressed. This reproach is justified by the circumstance, that these expositors agree to take the same view of the ἕως and the παρέρχεσθαι with Lechler; but it applies only to them.

according to the days of the sun-year, 248 according to the number of the generations of man. How may we prove that there are 613 commandments? By the saying, Deut. xxxiii. 4: Moses has given you תורה, the law. The word Thora contains the number 611. To this we must add the two commandments, Exod. xx. 2 and 3 (so that the number 613 is complete). Then came David, and reduced these commandments to eleven, according to the passage, Ps. xv. 1 f.:

"'Lord, who shall abide in Thy tabernacle?
Who shall dwell in Thy holy hill?
(1.) He that walketh uprightly,
(2.) And worketh righteousness,
(3.) And speaketh the truth in his heart:
(4.) He that backbiteth not with his tongue,
(5.) Nor doeth evil to his neighbour,
(6.) Nor taketh up a reproach against his neighbour:
(7.) In whose eyes a vile person is contemned;
(8.) But he honoureth them that fear the Lord.
(9.) He that sweareth to his own hurt, and changeth not:
(10.) He that putteth not out his money to usury,
(11.) Nor taketh reward against the innocent.
He that doeth these things shall never be moved.'

"Afterwards Esaias came, and reduced the eleven to six, according to the saying, chap. xxxiii. 15:

"'(1.) He that walketh righteously,
(2.) And speaketh uprightly:
(3.) He that despiseth the gain of oppressions,
(4.) That shaketh his hands from holding of bribes,
(5.) That stoppeth his ears from hearing of blood,
(6.) And shutteth his eyes from seeing evil:
He shall dwell on high.'

"Then came Micha, and reduced the six to three, according to the saying, chap. vi. 8:

"'He hath showed thee, O man, what is good,
And what the Lord requireth of thee, namely:

>   (1.) To keep the word of God,
>   (2.) To love mercy,
>   (3.) And to walk humbly with thy God.'

"Once more, Isaiah brought down the three to two, according to the passage, chap. lvi. 1:

>   "'Thus saith the LORD:
>   (1.) Keep ye judgment,
>   (2.) And do justice.'

"Lastly came Habakkuk, and reduced them all to one, chap. ii. 4: '*The just shall live by his faith.*'"

But more than the *moral* law is included here, as the expression, ἰῶτα καὶ κεραία, shows; while ver. 19 shows that the fulfilment here spoken of extends to all the ἐντολαί. To limit the meaning of the verse to the ethical law, is accordingly inadmissible. Such a limitation, however, is at the foundation of the paraphrase of Erasmus, and the exposition of Luther, Chemnitz, Calov; while it is expressly laid down by Melanchthon and Hunnius. In the 18th century, after the example of the Socinians and Arminians (Episcop., not Grotius; Socin., Przipcov, not Wolzogen), the fulfilment spoken of was usually regarded as applying merely to what Michaelis calls "the eternal doctrine of morals taught by Moses and the Prophets." The ceremonial law is, however, included here. Yet this view of the saying nowise favours the idea, that Christ was still under the limits and restrictions of the Jewish religion of His day. So far is this from being the case, that on this supposition not only would the saying be unintelligible, as shown above (p. 137), but it is irreconcilable with such a supposition. For if it was only in the *Jewish* sense that Christ spoke of the ritual law as continuing valid till the end of the world, could He have spoken of its fulfilment as a work which should gradually be accomplished in the course of time? For was it not, at the very period in which He spoke, scrupulously observed, especially by the Pharisees? Once more, therefore, we must inquire: What does ἕως ἂν πάντα γένηται signify?

The Redeemer can have spoken of the necessity of a fulfilment of the ritual law only *in its pedagogical and typical-symbolical character*. We are in a position to prove, historically, that the ritual law was contemplated by the Redeemer under both these aspects. In Mark ii. 27, He speaks of the Sabbath-law as instituted for the sake of man, *in order to his education*. "Man was not made for the Sabbath;" that is, not by keeping the Sabbath, and not by fulfilling the ritual law in general, can the eternal destination of man be attained, as, by fulfilling the moral law, it can (comp. 1 Cor. vii. 19): ὥστε κύριός ἐστιν ὁ υἱὸς τοῦ ἀνθρώπου καὶ τοῦ σαββάτου: the Son of Man, who stands in no such need of pedagogical commands, is therefore Lord also of the Sabbath. There exists but one example of our Lord's regarding the ceremonial law in its typical point of view. The Saviour wishes to celebrate the Passover with His disciples: He changes it into the sacramental feast in commemoration of the spiritual Passover, and announces at the same time that this sacrament is itself again a type of the perfect celebration which will take place in the kingdom of God: Luke xxii. 16 (comp. Lechler in loc. cit. S. 841). Allusions, however, to the typical character of Old Testament history frequently occur in the discourses of Christ: it will suffice to refer to John iii. 14 as an example. Under these circumstances, we are perfectly justified in supposing in our passage a reference, not only to this typical, but also to that pedagogical view of the institutions of the Old Testament. The whole ritual law must also come to pass, be fulfilled, be *realized*. And this realization, which is appointed to take place at some future time, is, in the first instance, to be accomplished in His own person. And where shall we look for this fulfilment, this realization, of the ritual law, but in His own sacrificial death, in which the shadowy outline of the Old Testament sacrifices was filled up, and their idea realized? (Heb. x. 1.) But the ritual law was to be accomplished also by His Church. The Saviour, as we have seen, contemplated the ritual law in its pedagogical aspect. In this sense, that law is fulfilled when it reaches its τέλος by bringing men to Christ; and when the object of the pedagogical commands is gained by the fulfilment of them by the Church in the spirit of Christian liberty. When the educational object of these observances is thus fulfilled, there will be no need anxiously to inquire whether every the least of the ritual laws has been typically, *i.e.*, spiritually, fulfilled in the Christian Church. The outline of the picture has reached the end contemplated, equally educational in its character, when it has furnished the basis of the finished picture, albeit many lines in it are now effaced. So, too, a pedagogical institution has done its work when it has conducted its pupils to the appointed goal. Undoubtedly, however, these pedagogical commands are, in the main, such as have also received an antitypical realization in the Church of Christ. The idea of the theocracy is realized in the Church; of the priesthood, in the Christian people, the Passover in the Lord's Supper; Circumcision, in Baptism; the command to avoid the dead and the ceremonially unclean, in avoiding the morally dead and unclean; and so on. "The true negation becomes again the most pregnant affirmation, when each appointment of the old times is rightly appreciated. True, the letter of the olden time is not, as such, elevated to a position of authority, but its idea is: this idea will, however, apprehend its own destination from itself alone, which (the destination) is parallel to the jot and tittle of the old." —Bruno Bauer, Synoptiker i. S. 327. As was remarked above (p. 132), the προφῆται may certainly be regarded as included, although, as vers. 19, 20 show, only referred to by the way.

The explanation of γενέσθαι had already to be touched upon in explaining πληρῶσαι. Many of the ancients fail to give here a clear and definite statement. In Jerome, still more in Hilary, Euthymius, the typical fulfilment is most prominently brought forward. This first says: Ex figura litteræ ostenditur, quod etiam, quæ minima putantur in lege, sacramentis spiritualibus plena sint et omnia recapitulentur in eo: in support whereof he afterwards refers to the sacrifices,—presupposing, therefore, the fulfilment of the ceremonial law. In Augustine, who, however, includes also the prophetical fulfilment, the fulfilment of the moral law in believers by love is chiefly dwelt on (vide supra, p. 125). A few, such as Beda, Rupertus, Druthmar, regard the ἰῶτα as denoting the number ten; and accordingly find here a special reference to the Decalogue. According to the Glossa ordinaris, the expression refers alike to *command* and *promise:* donec spiritualiter impleantur vel imperfecta perficiantur et significantia, i. e. impletio consummentur. Similarly Este, Menoch., Tirin. The older Lutheran exegesis restricts the lex to the Decalogue alone, and finds here only the concio legalis hypothetica (vide supra, p. 39); so that the Mosaic utterance: maledictus qui non permanserit in omnibus, quae scripta sunt in libro legis, is adduced as a parallel passage: see Chemnitz, Gerhard, loci V. T. 65. Hunnius, Sarcerius: *exaggerat Christus difficultatem legis et æternam Dei voluntatem in servanda lege stabilit, ut sciamus legis impletionem non esse in nostris viribus.* Bucer and Bullinger lay stress upon the view of St Augustine: so likewise Bengel: *facta sunt et fiunt, etiam in Christianis: non erant facta ante illum.* On the other hand, the ethical and prophetical fulfilment is maintained by Calvin, Beza, Piscator. Aretius holds that the fulfilment is by Christ Himself. Socinus hit upon the idea already alluded to, that ἕως ἂν γένηται marks a period of time of which the fulfilment of the law by Christ Himself was the commencement, after which the abrogation of the ceremonial law took place: *is autem sensus est, quod non prius futura esset abrogatio ulla præceptorum illorum, quam illis plenissima aliqua ratione obtemperatum fuisset, nempe ab aliquo homine præstitum perfecte vel minimum præceptorum istorum, id quod ab ipso Christo factum sine dubio est, dum hic in terris ageret, quo facto et ipso in cœlos sublato, tum demum abrogatio facta est . . . cæremonialium omnium.* Wettstein, E. J. Meyer, explain the saying of the fulfilment of the prophetical portion of the law. According to Clericus, who understands ἕως in the sense of *sed*, the proper translation is, not as Grotius asserts: donec omnia facta erunt, but (as γίνεται νόμος is equivalent to integer manet): sed omnia præcepta erunt. The idea would thus be, not that of *being fulfilled*, but that of *continuing valid*. The rendering is adopted by most of Clericus' successors: Elsner, Heum., Mich., Bahrdt, Rosenmueller, and many others. Meyer adds the connecting thought: that "this fulfilment of every part of the law would never take place;" but comes to the same conclusion: that the passage asserts that "the νόμος is continually binding." But, even to go no further than the prophetic anticipation of a Jeremiah (xxxi. 33), was not that anticipation to be realized in the Church of Christ? But Meyer, as well as Olsh. and De Wette, has essentially gone over to the ethical and typical interpretation of the passage. Only Ewald explains: "until the end of the world, before which a great deal of what was *predicted* in the Old Testament must take place."

Ver. 19. There follows a universal inference with respect to the way in which the members of the kingdom are to demean themselves with regard to the law. As the connection with ver. 20 shows, there is here a special allusion to the Jewish teachers of the law. The antagonism to the *Pharisees,* in this verse and at ver. 20, is so plain, that when here, and at ver. 20, Hilgenfeld (see above, p. 147) and Koestlin, after the example of Gfroerer, assert that the opposition is to St Paul and his doctrine, all we can do is to ask a second time, if this is not to light a taper in full day-light?—Bullinger: accusationem sibi intentatam tanquam per Antistrophen convertit in Pharisæos. The ἐλάχισται ἐντολαί, the ἰῶτα κ. κεραία, are then to have full recognition both theoretically and practically. And how? Inasmuch as they receive their due in the sense explained in ver. 18. Accordingly, λύειν cannot here be taken to signify a *transgressing* of the commandments (as Cast., Beza, Piscator, Fritzsche think). Usage is not indeed opposed to such a rendering. but, even if, in the instances adduced by Bos, Schleusner, and others (such as John v. 18, vii. 23) (Palæphatus de incred. c. 53), λύειν τὸν νόμον is equivalent to ἀκυροῦν,—yet transgressing is only one species of irritum reddere; and λύειν τ. νόμον and τὸν ὅρκον are found connected together, Dion. Halic. hist. Rom. 5, 10: οὐδὲν καταλέλυται διὰ τ. ἐμὴν ἐπιείκειαν οὔτε νόμοι οὔτε ὅρκος. The only meaning it can have in this verse, is (as before καταλύειν) to *declare invalid;* comp. οὐ δύναται ἡ γραφὴ λυθῆναι (John x. 35). Now, as nothing of this nature can be thought to have been intentionally uttered by the Scribes, the object of the expression can only be to indicate what was the opposite to the πληροῦν of which Christ had spoken, that external observance of the law, which was really practically to destroy it altogether. Τούτων refers back to the lesser portions of the law indicated by ἰῶτα and κεραία. The thought swells: if the annulling of even *one* of them is so important an act, what consequences would not the abrogation of many or all of them involve! In Matt. xxv. 45, ἑνὶ τούτων τῶν ἐλαχίστων, the same form of expression. There is therefore no occasion to hold either, with Alberti, that the demonstrative pronoun is here out of its proper place, or, with Krebs, B.-Crusius, to regard τῶν ἐλαχίστων as a more closely determining apposition, in the sense of "were it even the least;" although in poetry this construction does occur (Kuehner, ii. S. 145).

Some writers, measuring the ἐλάχιστα by the Christian standard, have supposed that it could only mean the commands of the ceremonial law.—Thus the saying would contain an admonition to the effect, that *for the present*, the ceremonial law was to be left untouched, still to be enforced and observed.[1] Thus Tobler (Gedanken zur Lehre Jesu, S. 69) gives this meaning: "Whoever will, *for the present*, keep all the commands of Moses, and will teach them, giving to each its proper place, as I do, who yet know the higher spiritual law, he shall be counted among the greatest of the citizens of the kingdom of God both here and hereafter." But the ἰῶτα ἢ κεραία comprehends the totality of the law. Again, it might be thought that the reference here is tho the *moral* law. As Christ was thinking of the Pharisees when He spoke, He might be here alluding to their evisceration of the law through their tradition and their glosses: comp. vers. 21, 33, 43; Matt. xxiii. 23. It were false, however, to conclude that He is speaking here of the ten commandments of the Decalogue,[2] any of which He calls "small," only in speaking ex mente Pharisaeorum (Mel., Calv., Beza, Chemnitz, Spanh., Rosenm., Mich. Baumgarten); for He is here expressing *His own* opinion on the legal institution. Neither may we say, with Er. Schmid, partim ex mente sua, partim ex mente Scribarum. Mel.: Quid vocat minima? Profecto maxima sunt, dubitatio in corde de Deo, securitas etc. Sic loquebantur (tamen) Pharisæi et Dominus utitur verbo ipsorum. No doubt, the fact that the casuistry of the Pharisees made a great deal of their distinction of the קלות וחמורות, of the easier and more difficult commandments, the greater and less, has something to do with the passage. The fact itself is seen from the question of the Scribe, Matt. xxii. 36, and numerous corroborations by Wettstein and Schoettgen, on this passage and on xxii. 36. Generally speaking, there was a strong tendency, as in the Romish Church in our own day, to magnify the importance of the observance of

---

[1] This *for the present* is also expressed by Ulfilas qui *nunc* abrogat; but only in antithesis to the abrogation of these laws which is to take place at the end of the world, according to *Divine* appointment.

[2] Gloeckler even finds here a *direct* reference to the Decalogue, which are called ἐλάχιστοι on account of the little space they take up! "Τῶν ἐλαχίστων, i.e., not 'the least important,' but the least in compass, namely, the so-called ten commandments."

the ceremonial injunctions. The קלים were, according to the canon of external distinction, those things which negatively and positively were forbidden: the difficult, those which were punishable by death.[1] Now, Christ Himself recognises that the commandments are not all of equal importance; but here, and at ver. 22, He shows how great is the guilt of the non-observance even of the least important among them. Those commentators who have left out of account the fact, that here the moral law of Christ is assumed to be identical with the law of Moses (vide on ver. 21), have supposed that the commandments of which Christ speaks are the Christian commandments, because He is speaking of participation in, or exclusion from, the kingdom of heaven. They have accordingly referred the τούτων, not to the νόμος, but (as Schoettgen) to the preceding Beatitudes, or else they have regarded it as referring to the succeeding commands of Christ. So Chrysostom, who thinks the ἐλάχισται merely a predicate applied by Christ, out of humility, to all His commandments. So too, many others; the auctor op. imp., for instance: **talis est** mos loquendi in Scripturis, quæ post modicum dicturi sunt, quasi jam dicta demonstrantur Ps. xlviii.; Mald., Grot., according to whom, it relates to those of the Christian precepts which are actually of inferior importance: a distinction in support of which Origen acutely adduces the canon of the greater or less compass of the moral injunctions therein contained (in Matt. Opp. iii. 831). The auct. op. imp. concludes from what follows, that by the ἐλάχισται, the affectus **is to be** understood; from which he adduces also the following in explanation of **the** ἐλάχιστος κληθήσεται: mandata Moysis in *actu* facilia et ideo in *remuneratione* modica, in *peccato* magna, mandata Christi in *actu* difficilia adeoque in remuneratione magna, in *peccato* minima. Hilary and others, who also hold this view of the τούτων, on the other hand, find in the minima even a reference to *doctrine:* minimum autem **est** omnium Domini passio **et crucis mors,** quam si quis tanquam erubescendum non con-

---

[1] In the Tanchuma, fol. 72, 2, we read: "He who does not wash his hands after food, is like him who kills a man." On the other hand, the pentateuchal Midrash קְהַל בְּנֵי, sect. 6, explains the expression, Prov. v. 6, אֹרַח חַיִּים פֶּן תְּפַלֵּס, rather as meaning that the way of life, *i. e.*, the law, was not to be levelled, inasmuch as men knew not what reward God had distined for each.

fitebitur, erit minimum, confitenti vero magnæ in cœlo vocationis gloriam pollicetur: an application which would be all the more natural to those who, as Theoph. and Jerome, thought that the $ἰῶτα$ and $κεραία$ contained an allusion to the cross of Christ: "$ἰῶτα$, the upright beam: $κεραία$, the cross-beam." Recent expositors are much at one with regard to the meaning. Stier: "He who, in his exposition of any one commandment, which was written for Israel in the books of Moses, has nothing else to set out with than, 'This is now obsolete,' is one of those who destroy the law. But he who discovers in the whole, for himself and for others, an inner abiding meaning and import which even yet applies to us all, is the genuine teacher of Holy Scripture. He only who interprets it in harmony with the Old, is a true interpreter of the New Testament."[1] De Wette: "If we contemplate the law as an organic whole, in which everything is of importance, all difficulty vanishes. Even the least of its precepts must receive its due, and the idea to which it belongs be perfectly realized: this can be proved, *e.g.*, in the case of the laws of purification."

That there is an allusion here to the religious teachers of that time, may be seen, among other things, from the fact, that the warning against false and enfeebling teaching is brought prominently forward in the former half of the verse; compare the words of Bullinger quoted above (p. 145). $Ἐλάχιστος$ without the article denotes, as the antithetical positive $μέγας$ shows, "*one* very small:" Luke xii. 26, xvi. 10; on the other hand, $ὁ ἐλάχιστος$, 1 Cor. xv. 9. Compare also $ἔσχατος$ without article, chap. xix. 30. Coccejus presses the distinction of degree with the utmost possible strictness: 'nominabit eum minorem *pueris* in Christo, in quibus est æque pretiosa fides ut in adultis, 2 Pet. i. 1. On $πληθήσεται$ compare on ver. 9. But it may be asked, is such an apportioning of transgression and retribution conformable to the requirements of righteousness? If for the least offence one of the most inferior positions of reward is assigned, what then in the case of a *great* offence? Accordingly, it was thought that the $ἐλάχιστος$ could have been used only ex mente Pharisæorum. This issue we have, however, already seen to be inadmissible. On the other hand, if

---

[1] Stier, Words of the Lord Jesus, i. 146. Pope's Translation.

by the βασιλεία τῶν οὐρανῶν be meant the perfect kingdom of God, the question must suggest itself: Can such as declare a commandment of the law to be null, have any place at all in that kingdom? This is a difficulty which is not allayed by a milder view of the offence, such as Olshausen gives: "The Lord is speaking of a point of view which belongs to the principles of Christianity; and men holding these principles are represented as treating the word of God without becoming reverence, and going on to annul many apparently unimportant ordinances of the law." Yet is the offence considerably aggravated by the διδάξῃ (as M. Baumgarten observes); and it now becomes of such a nature, that it might appear very questionable whether such members of the Church can have any participation whatsoever in the kingdom of God. Hence Aug. and Hilary: fortasse omnino *non erit, quia ibi nonnisi magni esse poterunt:* so likewise Luth., Chemnitz, Calixt (who refers to οὐ μὴ εἰσέλθητε in ver. 20), Episc., Wolf, Kypke, and many others. That this expedient is altogether arbitrary may be seen from the antithetical μέγας, instead of which we must have expected to find οὐδὲν κλη9.; the ascent from μικρότερος to μείζων ἐν τῇ βασιλ. τῶν οὐρ. is to be found also in chap. xi. 11. Still more manifestly erroneous is E. J. Meyer's explanation: ἐλάχισται, he thinks, denotes, "that which every isolated command of Moses is, in itself considered: in itself, that is, it is of the *least;* that is, in its literal sense, and viewed apart from its idea: in itself, consequently, it deserves to be done away with. But seeing that the idea of every Mosaic commandment is a great one, he who destroys the least of them destroys something great; and such an one may therefore be called ἐλάχιστος ἐν τῇ βασιλ. τ. οὐρανῶν." But that there is a distinction in the commandments, the ἰῶτα κ. κεραία had already indicated; and can we suppose that all the Mosaic precepts would have been characterized as αἱ ἐλάχισται without any reference to that *point of view* under which they are so regarded?

Others accordingly understood the βασιλεία τῶν οὐρανῶν to mean, not the kingdom of God in its final state of perfection, not the regnum gloriæ but the kingdom of God as it exists among men—in a word, the Church. In this view, the judicial sentence certainly assumes a more lenient aspect. Gregory M.: doctor qui solvit mandatum minimum, minimus in ecclesia vocatur, quippe cujus vita despicitur. Thus Zwingly, Beza, Bengel on the German translation: regni coelorum hæredes ubi de tali quaestio inciderit, dicent: parvus est, nullus est; M. Baumg., who collates ἐξουθενημένοι ἐν τῇ ἐκκλησίᾳ, 1 Cor. vi. 4. There is the same difference of opinion as to the meaning of the phrase βασιλ. τ. οὐρ. in other passages where it occurs, as ver. 20. Now, wherever in the New Testament, in speaking of the *judgment*, the Future is used, there can be no doubt that the judgment alluded to is that ἐν τῇ ἐσχάτῃ ἡμέρᾳ: so expressly in Matt. xii. 41, 42; compare the οὐ μὴ εἰσέλθητε, ver. 20; ἔνοχος ἔσται, ver. 22; ὁμοιωθήσεται, vii. 26; κρινεῖ, Rom. ii. 27; δικαιωθήσεται, Rom. iii. 20; κληρονομήσουσι, 1 Cor. vi. 9; ζημιωθήσεται, 1 Cor. iii. 15, etc. Now it is no less evident, from many passages, that the idea in the view presented to us of the last judgment is that alone of a judicial sentence, based upon the moral worth of each individual. It is owing to this that the reading varies between the Future κρινεῖ, and the Present κρίνει, as, *e.g.*, 1 Cor. v. 12; that Luther sometimes translates it as if it were Future, sometimes as if it were the Present, Rom. iii. 30; sometimes, as Rom. iii. 20, thus: "may (*mag*) no flesh be justified." (Comp. Author's Comment. on Ep. to the Romans on chap. ii. ver. 6.) Under these circumstances, the question, in what stadium of the kingdom of God the judgment will be completed, is one which, in passages like that before us, really cannot be raised at all. For there is here no reference whatever to time. What we have here, is only a general declaration of the estimation in which a certain line of conduct towards the Divine law is regarded. An index to the object aimed at is to be found, in the first place, in a remark already made by Calvin, Spanheim, that there is an allusion, an ἀντανάκλασις between τῶν ἐλαχίστων and ἐλάχιστος: as Bengel well remarks: est ploce. Pro eo ac nos tractamus verbum Dei, Deus nos tractat, Joh. xvii. 6, 11; Apoc. iii. 10. Luther: "He that counteth it a small thing to despise God's commandment, shall be himself likewise despised and rejected." Therefore the correspondence between punishment and offence is not to be too minutely insisted on; besides, ἐλάχιστος without the article, "a very small," is only a relative idea: consequently, all that is involved in the expression is the thought, that in the judgment of God upon men, the position of God towards men corresponds to the position which men take up in reference to the law of God; or, in other words, the law of God is the absolute standard (norma) of the moral judgment of man (1 Cor. vii. 19).

Ver. 20. This verse is joined to the preceding by γάρ, which shows that the thought that the perfect πλήρωσις of the law could not be effected by the teachers of that time, but only by Christ Himself, is here confirmed. There πλήρωσις in question is that of the law, both as a doctrine and as a life: comp. previously the ποιεῖν and the διδάσκειν. It is impossible, with Olshausen, to regard the point of transition from ver. 19 to ver. 20 as consisting in this, that from the prohibition arbitrarily to destroy the law, He here passes on to the prohibition of arbitrarily adhering to it: because ver. 20 does not speak of *adhering* to the law.—Πλεῖον τῶν γραμματέων, an abbreviated comparison for τῆς δικαιοσύνης τ. γρ., as, *e. g.*, in John v. 36. Winer, 6 A. S. 219; also in classic Greek, Kuehner, ii. § 749. Περισσεύειν πλεῖον conjoined, instead of the Gen. of comparison, or instead of παρά or ὑπέρ, as it usually occurs.—There is some unimportant testimony in favour of placing ὑμῶν before ἡ δικαι.: no doubt it would bring out the antithesis better; but that object has evidently given occasion to the reading.

The Scribes and Pharisees were, in the eyes of the people, the models of piety under the law. Indeed, it is a universal fact that in the eyes of the multitude, with their traditional religion, orthodox teaching is regarded as the standard of character, virtue is supposed to be in proportion to knowledge, excellence to orthodoxy. Comp. Matt. xxiii. 23. The Scribes, in St Luke νομικοί, belonged mostly, although not all, to the party of the Pharisees (Luke xi. 44, 45; Acts xxiii. 9). The latter were regarded as the ἀκριβεστάτη αἵρεσις τῆς Ἰουδαϊκῆς θρησκείας, Acts xxvi. 5. According to Josephus, they enjoyed the greatest reputation among the people. Τοσαύτην ἔχουσι τὴν ἰσχὺν παρὰ τῷ πλήθει ὡς καὶ κατὰ βασιλέως τι λέγοντες καὶ κατὰ ἀρχιερέως εὐθὺς πιστεύεσθαι (Joseph. Antiq. xiii. 10, 5). Moreover, they did not form a *sect* in our sense of the word, but a αἵρεσις, in the Greek: the expression used by the Jewish writers is merely חלק, a division; nor can they be supposed to have been a numerous body; in the time of Herod there were only 6000 of them (Josephus, Antiq. xvii. 2; 4). The Sadducees and the Essenes were still less numerous. And the questions which here suggest themselves are these: To what party did the rest of the people belong, and what was their tendency? and out of which party did Christ gain the majority of His followers? This is a question of great interest, and, even for the history of the origin of Christianity, of importance. I have endeavoured to answer it in the Commentary on the Epistle to the Hebrews (3 A. Einleitung, cap. v.). The result arrived at is, that we are forced to admit the existence of another party of men, pious according to the law, who belonged to none of the leading schools, the forerunners of the Careans; and for this, we have also the evidence of the Talmud. These were the $\pi\rho o\sigma\delta\epsilon\chi\acute{o}\mu\epsilon\nu o\iota\ \tau\grave{\eta}\nu\ \pi\alpha\rho\acute{\alpha}\kappa\lambda\eta\sigma\iota\nu\ \tau o\tilde{v}\ \textrm{'}I\sigma\rho\alpha\acute{\eta}\lambda$, spoken of Luke ii. 25, 38. Many of them we must suppose to have been present at the preaching of the Sermon on the Mount: gladly would their heart respond to this and other descriptions of a spiritual fulfilment of the law. But even among the Pharisees there were a number of true-hearted Israelites, who, although enveloped in the mists of tradition, like many a Roman Catholic in the system of his church, did yet honestly seek to please God by striving spiritually to fulfill the law. This is evidenced, for instance, by the case of Nicodemus, of Joseph of Arimathea, of Gamaliel, and of the lawyer mentioned in St Mark, xxii. 28, if we are at liberty also to reckon him among the Pharisees. The Talmud also bears witness to this fact in a certain passage, after summing up the many kinds of mock-piety then in vogue. There are seven classes of Pharisees enumerated in the remarkable passage of the Gemara, tract. *Sota*, f. 22, 2 (comp. the rabbinical commentary in Surenh. Mischna, iii. 219). They are as follows: (1.) The Sichemites, who did their work for the sake of men, as the inhabitants of Sichem, who let themselves be circumcised to please not God, but the Israelites. (2.) The Sneaks, who from false humility scarcely ventured to lift their foot. (3.) The slow-worms, who kept their eyes shut lest they should behold a woman. (4.) The bowed-down, who always kept their head bent. (5.) The men of superfluity, who made it their boast that they did more than the law required. (6.) The Pharisees for the sake of gain. (7.) The Pharisees from fear of punishment. But in that very passage there is quoted the following saying of King Jannaeus, who on his death-bed said to his wife: אל

תהיראי מן הפרושים ולא ממי שאינן פרושים אלא מן הצבועין שדומין
לפרושין "Fear not the Pharisees, nor those who are not Pharisees;
but beware of the dissemblers who look like the Pharisees."

Are we then to understand, by the righteousness of the
Scribes and Pharisees of which the Saviour here speaks, the
righteousness of that better part of the Pharisees? (Thus Chrys.,
Euthym., Episc., Jansen., Wettst.) In support of this opinion
it may be alleged, that if Christ meant only to say that the
righteousness of His disciples must be something better than the
mock-piety of the mass of the Pharisees, which even the Talmud
does not omit to rebuke, this was not to require of them a very high
grade of excellence. Besides, that better portion of the Pharisees
need to have gone beyond these requirements which are afterwards referred to as the prevalent interpretations of the law. But,
in the first place, a limitation of this nature is not justified by the
simple meaning of the text. Moreover, the object was merely
to turn the regards of the people away from that class which
they had hitherto looked to as their examples. Further, it must
not be left out of account, that the object here, and in the sequel,
is to vindicate the conduct of Jesus towards the law, against
those who laid especial claim to serve and to preserve it, and who
in this consciousness directed their attack against Christ. Hence
we can only regard the accusation of Jesus as directed against
the class in general,—the exceptions to it not being here taken at
all into account. Calvin, who strictly maintains that the verse
relates, on the one hand, to the Pharisees, as the previous instruc-
tors of the people, on the other hand, to the Apostles, as those
who were about to take their place, would restrict the meaning
of the $\delta\iota\varkappa\alpha\iota\sigma\sigma\acute{\nu}\eta$ to orthodox teaching. But it is manifest from
the whole context of vers. 17—19, and from the $\pi o\iota\varepsilon\tilde{\iota}\nu\;\varkappa\alpha\grave{\iota}\;\delta\iota\delta\acute{\alpha}$-
$\sigma\varkappa\varepsilon\iota\nu$, ver. 19, that the false teaching is regarded only as the
obstacle which stood in the way of the true fulfilment of the
law, and prevented its true fulfilment. Besides, we cannot think
that $\delta\iota\varkappa\alpha\iota\sigma\sigma\acute{\nu}\eta$ means merely theoretical irreproachability. Still
less is it possible,—seeing that such is the tendency of the dis-
course (comp. p. 162),—to suppose that the higher righteousness
here required is the justitia imputata, which Glass., Calov, Cru-
sius would here drag in.— $O\grave{\upsilon}\;\mu\grave{\eta}\;\varepsilon\grave{\iota}\sigma\acute{\varepsilon}\lambda\vartheta\eta\tau\varepsilon\;\varepsilon\grave{\iota}\varsigma\;\tau.\;\beta\alpha\sigma.\;\tau.\;o\grave{\upsilon}\varrho$.
Here too Beza explains the $\beta\alpha\sigma.\;\tau.\;o\grave{\upsilon}$. of the ecclesia militans:
indigni estis, qui in ecclesia doceatis. It is clear, however, that

the idea is that of participation in the kingdom of God in its perfected state, the βασιλεία ἑτοιμασμένη ἀπὸ καταβολῆς κόσμου, Matt. xxv. 34.

THE IDEAL RIGHTEOUSNESS AND FULFILMENT OF THE LAW, AS OPPOSED TO THE NARROW PHARISAIC OBEDIENCE.

Vers 21—48.

First, generally, we must here investigate more fully a question already touched upon in the Introduction, § 5. *In what respect is the νομοθεσία of the Redeemer in antagonism to the dicta of the law?* Is the antagonism merely *relative*, or is it *absolute;* or is it merely opposed to the mode of explaining and understanding the law which was at that time in vogue?

The first is the view taken by the expositors of the Greek Church, and by the majority of the R. Catholic, Socinian, and Arminian commentators. They hold, namely, that the antagonism is merely a relative one, in the sense in which the imperfect appears in contrariety to the perfect. The writer who expresses himself most strongly and most unequivocally in favour of this opinion is St Chrysostom, who insists, that the speaker here is no other than He who gave the pedagogical law from Sinai: δύο ταῦτα δεῖξαι βουλόμενος, ὅτι τε οὐ μαχόμενος τοῖς προτέροις, ἀλλὰ καὶ σφόδρα συμφωνῶν ταῦτα νομοθετεῖ, καὶ ὅτι εἰκότως καὶ σφόδρα εὐκαίρως τὰ δεύτερα ἐκείνοις προστίθησιν. ὅπερ ἵνα καὶ σαφέστερον γένηται, αὐτῶν ἐπακούσωμεν τῶν τοῦ νομοθέτου ῥημάτων· τί οὖν αὐτός φησιν; ἠκούσατε, ὅτι ἐρρέθη τοῖς ἀρχαίοις, οὐ φονεύσεις. καίτοι δ καὶ ἐκεῖνα δοὺς, αὐτός ἐστιν· ἀλλὰ τέως ἀπροσώπως αὐτὰ τίθησιν. εἴτε γὰρ εἶπεν, ὅτι ἠκούσατε, ὅτι εἶπον τοῖς ἀρχαίοις, δυσπαράδεκτος ὁ λόγος ἐγίνετο καὶ πᾶσιν ἂν προσέστη τοῖς ἀκούουσιν· εἴτε αὖ πάλιν εἰπὼν, ὅτι ἐρρέθη τοῖς ἀρχαίοις παρὰ τοῦ πατρός μου, ἐπήγαγεν, ἐγὼ δὲ λέγω, μείζων ἂν ἔδοξεν εἶναι ὁ αὐθαδιασμός. διὸ δὴ ἁπλῶς αὐτὸ τέθεικεν, ἓν μόνον ἀπ' αὐτοῦ κατασκευάζων, τὸ δεῖξαι ὅτι εἰς καιρὸν ἦλθε τὸν προσήκοντα ταῦτα λέγων ... ἐρωτήσωμεν τοίνυν τοὺς τὸν νόμον ἐκβάλλοντας, τὸ μὴ ὀργίζεσθαι τῷ μὴ φονεύειν ἐναντίον, ἢ μᾶλλον ἐκείνου τελείωσις τοῦτο καὶ κατασκευή; εὔδηλον, ὅτι τοῦτο ἐκείνου πλήρωσις καὶ μεῖζον τούτου ἕνεκεν. ὁ γὰρ πρὸς ὀργὴν οὐκ ἐκφερόμενος, πολλῷ μᾶλλον τὰς χεῖρας καθέξει παρ᾽ ἑαυτῷ. Origen, protesting on the one hand against those who, in expounding Scripture, rigidly adhere to the letter, and on the other hand against those who, in their zeal for the deeper meaning, **look away** from the letter altogether, refers to the words: dictum est antiquis, non occides; and adds: hoc observant et Pharisæi; to which, however, is subjoined for **the** disciples: si quis iratus fuerit, etc.; and **this**, he says, is the abundantia justitiæ (in Num. hom. xi. T. ii. p. 305). Basil, with reference to the apparent contradiction between Matt. v. 34 and Ps. xv. **4**, observes, of all the commandments of the Sermon on the Mount: πανταχοῦ τοῦ αὐτοῦ σκόπου ἔχεται ὁ κύριος, προλαμβάνων τ. ἁμαρτημάτων τ. ἀποτελέσματα, καὶ ἐκ τῆς πρώτης ἀρχῆς ἐκτέμνων τ. πονηρίαν (Hom. in Ps. xiv. T. i. p. 356). In the same sense Gregory of Nyssa remarks, that in order to do away **with** perjury, the oath is at the same time forbidden: and in order to prevent murder, anger is also prohibited (Hom. xiii. in Cant. Cant. T. i. p. 657).[1] In accordance with this, the Socinian Przipcov (bibl. fratr. Polon. T. ix. p. 7): ex dictis patet, quanto plenius et perfectius lex Christi quam Mosis delictis homicidiorum occurrat, quæ non tantum arboris hujus infelicis truncum, sed **imas** ejus radices earumque fibras exscindit. The Manichæans and anti-judaistic Gnostics substituted for this improvement an actual antagonism: thus Ptolomæus, the Valentinian, says on Matt. v. 39: τὰ δὲ ἐναντία ἀλλήλων εἰσὶν ἀναιρετικά; (ad Floram, in opp. Iren., ed. Massuet. p. 360.) This, however, is as little the meaning of the Socinians as it **is of** the Fathers. Socin.: opponit non ut contraria sed ut perficientia eam legis partem. Yet are these Socinian expositors not always consistent; for on ver. 28 Socinus remarks: sic **plane demonstrat,** se illud non explanare velle, sed aliquid diversum ab isto proponere; with reference to the command about oaths, Voelkel remarks, de vera religione, L. iv. c. 13: in antecedentibus verbis e Mose depromptis, quibus sua Christus ita opposuit, ut quod in illis

---

[1] Such is his explanation in the paragraph: πῶς πληρωτὴς τοῦ νόμου γέγονεν ὁ Χριστός· καὶ τίνα τούτου ἔπαυσεν, ἢ ἐνήλλαξεν ἢ μετέθηκεν; in the constit. apost. l. vi. c. 23. But in what sense does the sentence subsequently occur there: οὐ νόμον οὖν περιεῖλεν ἀφ᾽ **ἡμῶν**, ἀλλὰ δεσμά? **The legal view of Christ**ianity **so predominates** in this paragraph, that it does not seem to be spoken in the Pauline sense.

conceditur, in his prohibeatur, etc. Moreover, this opinion of the Socinians and Arminians was in keeping with their view of the whole Old Testament economy; thus Voelkel next goes on to prove that the imperfect requirements of the law corresponded to the imperfect nature of its promises, viz., of only earthly goods.—Against this view the Protestant Church protested energetically. It had been preceded by St Augustine in his controversy with the Manichæans, who remarks: non ait donec *addantur quæ desunt,* sed *donec omnia fiant* (T. viii. 220); and by Jerome and Hilary. It maintained the absolute character of the moral law of the Old Testament. It based this opinion partly on such Old Testament dicta as declare the *perfection* of the law (as Ps. xix. 8; Deut. xxx. 19), partly on such sayings of Christ as presuppose this perfection of the law (as Luke x. 28). Let it be noticed how Luther, for instance, in the Larger Catechism, unfolds the deepest doctrine of morals out of the ten commandments: although occasionally it may be seen that he is sensible of forcing the text. We may see how decidedly the two parties opposed each other in the early times, from the introductory words of Chemnitz on the one side, and of Wolzogen and Maldonatus on the other. Chemnitz commences with the words: totus hic locus obscuratus, imo forde depravatus fuit ab illis, qui existimarunt, Christum hanc suam explicationem opponere ipsi legi divinæ. Wolzogen again says: antequam ipsa verba explicemus, indicandus nobis est crassus valde et perniciosus error, qui fere omnibus interpretibus a Papismo alienis communis est veræque pietati, quam evangelium exposcit, vim omnem adimit, quod scilicet Christus nova sua præcepta, de quibus in hac parte agit, non Mosaicæ legi, sed tantum falsis interpretationibus scribarum et Pharisæorum opposuerit; and Maldonatus: omnes hæreticorum interpretes pro comperto habent (spiritus enim sanctus illis, opinor, revelavit) Christum non legem, sed scribarum et Pharisæorum traditiones interpretationesque corrigere; eaque de re impudenter veteres auctores, quod aliter senserint, reprehendunt.[1] Modern expositors, with few exceptions (as Neander, Bleek in loc. cit., Hofmann, Schriftbeweis i. 524), follow the Protestant view: Kuinoel, Fritzsche, Olsh., Meyer, De Wette,

---

[1] How can Cornelius *a Lapide* have come to maintain, that Maldonatus finds here only an antagonism to pharisaic interpretations? He remarks in answer to him: verius est, Christum *tam legi quam* scribis se opponere.

B.-Crusius, M. Baumg., Stier, Nagel in loc. cit., Rischl (altkath. Kirche, S. 31), Ewald, Lechler. Lechler observes: "This opinion presupposes two things: (1.) That Jesus found the principles of all true religion already laid down in the Old Testament: and therefore sought to set down **nothing** that was opposed to it; and, indeed, thus He ever spoke. (2.) That Christ directly opposed Himself to the method of explaining and applying the Old Testament which till then was **in vogue**; that He had an entirely different idea of the perfect religion,— an idea, however, which was fully accordant with the Old Testament itself; only hitherto it had never been realized or carried out into life." We have already expressed ourselves against the opinion of an external limitation, a *correction* of the Mosaic law (p. 127). The whole position assumed by the Saviour towards the law is directly opposed to such an opinion. When He argues against the Pharisees and their traditions, it is the law itself with which He confronts them: Matt. xv. 3; ver. 6: ἠκυρώσατε τὴν ἐντολὴν τοῦ Θεοῦ διὰ τὴν παράδοσιν ὑμῶν. John v. 45: μὴ δοκεῖτε ὅτι ἐγὼ κατηγορήσω ὑμῶν πρὸς τὸν πατέρα, ἔστιν ὁ κατηγορῶν ὑμῶν Μωϋσῆς, εἰς ὃν ὑμεῖς ἠλπίκατε. So too, in the 18th verse, He had said that the law must be fully realized; in ver. 19, had declared that the law in its whole extent is holy; and in ver. 20, had said that the righteousness of His disciples must go beyond—*not the Messiah law, but the legal religion of its representatives*. In the Saviour's view, the whole law is, in its principle, contained in the one command to love God above all things, and our neighbour as ourself. The position of St Paul too, with reference to the law, is simply this, that he regarded the whole of the New Testament doctrine of salvation, especially the Christian moral law (Rom. xiii. 9), as contained in germ in the Law and the Prophets (Rom. iii. 21, xvi. 26). Some may regard this view of the Old Testament as the consequence of a superstitious veneration for the codex; but it is unquestionably the view taken by Christ, and of the Apostles (**see above**, Lechler). What is there that could make this doubtful? The objections originally mooted by Socinus, and further insisted on by Neander and Bleek, are these: (1.) That the Old Testament commandments are, for the most part, cited in their literal form. But if at vers. 21, 35, 43, this is not the case, as is admitted, but, on the contrary, the pharisaic interpretation is there subjoined; if at ver. 31 an omission occurs in the interest of the relaxation of the command,—are we not entitled to suppose that where this does not take place, as at ver. 27, 38, the Old Testament command had been misinterpreted in the lax manner indicated by our Lord's antithesis? (2.) That the only possible interpretation of the words ἐῤῥέθη τοῖς ἀρχαίοις is, "it hath been said to them of old time," that is, to the Fathers at the time of the promulgation of the Sinaitic law; because, if the meaning were "*of* them of old time," the phrase used would be τοῖς πρεσβυτέροις (?). Of this objection we shall speak presently. The most striking difficulty is precisely that which Neander passes over in silence, viz., that ἐγὼ δὲ λέγω, in ver. 32, seems to introduce, not merely a relative, but an absolute antithesis: as if it were said, that divorce was sanctioned in the Old Testament, but entirely prohibited in the New. But is it not apparent, from the manner in which Christ pronounces upon this Mosaic law of divorce in Matt. xix. 8, 9, that He felt that on this point He was giving no new commandment, but was merely *liberating from its temporal fetters a thing which already in principle existed, and unfolding it from its germ?* He does not represent His categorical prohibition of divorce as being an improvement upon the law, which He propounded in virtue of His own omnipotent authority: He sets it forth as a *requirement of the Word of God:* οὐκ ἀνέγνωτε, κ.τ.λ. The Mosaic command, He shows, was merely a permission, and a temporal concession to the infirmity of that period (ἐπέτρεψε, not ἐνετείλατο): He Himself, however, whose mission was to "fulfil," reveals theoretically as well as practically what was the original *intention* of God. "In this respect also, what Christ does, is not to 'destroy,' but to 'fulfil,' inasmuch as He carries out perfectly and completely the great purpose of the Mosaic law, which was to set bounds to the sinful caprices of men,—a purpose hitherto only partially realized on account of the hardness of their hearts." (Lechler, in loc. cit. S. 809.) It surprises one to find this view first enunciated by an expositor of the Middle Ages, by Druthmar. He remarks, that Christ places Himself in opposition to Moses only in those commands where *antiquis* is wanting in the text; but even then, he says, our Lord is not in antagonism to the *intention* of God and of the lawgiver: non *præcipit Deus* sed *concessit Moyses* populo adhuc rudi et carnali. Further, Przipcov, whilst contending, with equal decisiveness and ability, that Christ opposed Himself not only to the Scribes, but to the law itself, yet maintains that the intentio legis Mosaicæ belongs to the moral law taught by Christ, and that in virtue of the command to love God above all, and our neighbour as ourself: vid. bibl. fratrum Polon. T. ix. p. 210, 231.

Hofmann's view is somewhat different. Yet, in the main, it coincides with that indicated above. Only, he dwells upon the idea, that by His allusion to the Scriptures as a whole, our Lord was seeking to lead men to apprehend each separate commandment in its deeper sense and significance.[1] "In opposition to the pharisaic interpreters of the law, who restricted duty to each separate injunction and prohibition viewed in its isolated and literal aspect, He teachers what is the one will of God concerning man, as attested by the Scriptures considered as a whole." But this antithesis of the Scriptures in their totality, and the command in its isolation, is never once referred to: and if it were, it is scarcely likely that it would be expressed in this form of contrasting the general and the individual; rather would it have sufficed to refer to the highest command of supreme love to God, as the canon for the understanding of the individual precepts; and, finally, may not the vindication of the prohibition of divorce, given in Matt. xix., be cited as a proof, that the Saviour regarded the isolated precept as involving a call to understand it in its deeper sense? When, however, he speaks of the relation of this injunction to the power to fulfil the same, Hofmann expresses himself both ably and truly. He observes: "Faith, as the power to fulfil the law, is not indeed spoken of here; but faith in Jesus is presupposed to exist in those, to whom the Lord designs to reveal a righteousness better than that of the Pharisees. Because they believe in Him, therefore addresses He His word to them. Their faith in Him renders possible in **them a** state of mind and feeling, which He would in vain expect in the inquisitive crowd around. Yet would not their faith in Him, if dissociated from that state of feeling which He required, be of avail to **render** them partakers of the kingdom of heaven; for it were not then that faith which His person demands." (Schriftbeweis

---

[1] This too is the opinion of Bucer, on ver. 21. Quemadmodum consummatio legis adeoque et germanæ justitiæ *dilectio* est, ita hanc Christus ubique unice urget . . hinc est quod et in præsenti ea præcepta explicanda potissimum desumit, quæ ad eandem **propius pertinent.**

i. S. 526.)—'Ηκούσατε, ὅτι ἐρρέθη τοῖς ἀρχαίοις. It has been already shown, that what Christ opposed was not the law, but the prevailing pharisaic mode of interpreting the law. The words first quoted seem to express the contrary, if, with the Vulgate, Peschito, and Luther, they are to be translated, "Ye have heard, that it was said to the ancients;" for who could the ancients denote, if not the men ot the time of Moses?—First, as for ἠκούσατε: the interpretation of the word prevalent among the older Protestant expositors was, that it refers to the assurances which the Scribes gave the people, that what they taught was a tradition from the Mosaic period. Thus Bucer, Chemnitz, Er. Schmid, Cocc., Calov, and Este. Priæus compares Ps. xliv.: τοῖς ὠσὶν ἡμῶν ἠκούσαμεν, οἱ πατέρες ἡμῶν ἀνήγγειλαν ἡμῖν. Spanh.: vestris doctoribus illud frequenter in ore, dictum esse jam olim majoribus vestris (there is, however, no ἠκούσατε in ver. 31) But the rabbinical use of language might rather have been referred to, in which שמע, שמועה, is used for oral tradition: comp., e.g., אם עקר דבר מן דברים שלמדנו מפי שמועה, "He who rejects anything of that which we have learnt by tradition." But to teach this tradition was the business of the Scribes alone. Drusius and Clericus adduce the various methode of Jewish exposition regarding the literal interpretation מִשְׁנֶה or משנה; according to them, the allusion here is to the literal interpretation of the Decalogue known by the name מִשְׁנֶה. The reference here is, however, quite out of place. The expression is rather to be explained by the circumstance, that to the people and the Apostles (who are here addressed) the Mosaic law was know solely and simply by the reading in the synagogue of the 54 portions of the law (comp. Acts xv. 21; John xii. 34; Rom. ii. 13): hence, too, it arose that the Biblical text was called the מִקְרָא, i.e., the accepted Bible-text (see Buxtorf, lex. talm. s. h. v., and Bashuysen, clavis talm. p. 208). The expression in our passage, then, refers to the fact, that it was only through a medium that the people were acquainted with the law, which medium moreover was not the right one.

But the simplest way of obviating the difficulty in question, would be to take (if one might) the Dative, in ἐρρέθη,[1] τοῖς ἀρχαίοις,

---

[1] On ἐρρέθη, Cod. D.E., and ἐρρήθη (the latter used, probably, only by unclassical writers), compare Lobeck ad Phrynichum, p. 447; Buttm. ausf. Grammatik, ii. 121.

ablatively, as has been done, after the example of Camerarius,[1] by Beza, Piscator, by many commentators ancient and modern, by Kypke, Krebs, Kuinoel, Fritzsche, Olsh., Mich., Baumg., Stier, Ewald. Several, as Socin., Capellus, Alberti, Ernesti, Neander, have accused this construction of hardness.[2] Now this is incorrect. The Greeks frequently use the Dative with a passive in the sense of the Ablative: εἴρηται ἡμῖν, λέλεκταί μοι; a use which has been carried over into Latin: comp. Palairet, Raphel, Annotat. Herod., Kypke in loc., Winer 6 Auf. S. 196. This construction is found also in the Hellenistic writers of the New Testament; comp. Wahl, s. v. ἀγνοέω: and it is current in the Hebrew, Syriac, Chaldee, and rabbinical languages (Ex. xii. 16; Prov. xiv. 20, comp. Ewald, 3 Auf., S. 326; Hofmann, gr. Syriaca, p. 373). Thus, in this view, the term ἀρχαῖοι in the text is regarded as denoting the older Rabbis, and corresponds to the formula תָּקְנוּ קַדְמוֹנֵינוּ אָמְרוּ or אָמְרוּ רִאשׁוֹנִים קַדְמָאִין: see Edzard on tr. Avoda Sara, cap. ii. p. 284; Schoettgen in loco. In support of this view, it might be alleged that this interpretation afforts a distinct antithesis to the ἐγώ; but then in vers. (27) 31, 38, 43, the τοῖς ἀρχαίοις is wanting. But then there are these objections:—First, from the almost necessary ambiguity of the phraseology, this construction is not to be expected here: in other passages where ἐρρέθη occurs, whether in the New Testament or in the LXX., the Dative invariably denotes the persons addressed, as in Rom. ix. 12, 26; Gal. iii. 16; Rev. vi. 11, ix. 4. Further, if the object were to present an antithesis to the ἐγώ, should we not rather have expected to find the words in this order: τοῖς ἀρχαίοις ἐρρέθη? This argument cannot, however, be strongly insisted on, as cases do occur in which the emphasis rests, not only upon the first part of the clause, but also upon the last (Acts xxvi. 5; 1 Cor. xiv. 22, iv. 14; Theod. on Rom. x. 14: δεῖ γὰρ πρῶτον χειροτονηθῆναι τοὺς κήρυκας . . . ἔπειτα τῶν κηρυγμάτων

---

[1] The first author who has this construction is the Persian translator in the Polyglott, ver. 27: که اولیان کفتند "that the ancients said;" at vers. 21 and 33, again, he has که با پیشینیان کفته شد "that it was said to the ancients." Wheloc's Persic translation (Lond. 1657) has invariably پیشینیان را "to the ancients."

[2] Alberti obs. philol., p. 38: ea enim phrasis est insolens.

ἀκούσαι: comp. Author's Commentary on Romans, 5 ed., on chap. x. 19). Then we must add the consideration, that οἱ ἀρχαῖοι never occurs in the New Testament, nor does the corresponding word קַדְמוֹנִים occur in Josephus, as a designation of the older Rabbis: the word did not come into vogue in this acceptation, until a period when the learned in the law could look back through more than a century to a line of authorities. The New Testament name for the older teachers of the law is οἱ πρεσβύτεροι (Matt. xv. 2; Mark vii. 3, 5; Heb. xi. 2), *seniores*,—used, however, only as a designation of honour, like οἱ πατέρες (see Bleek on Heb. xi. 2): comp. Gal. i. 14, αἱ πατρικαὶ παραδόσεις, and in Joseph. Antiq. xiii. 10, 6, ἐκ πατέρων διαδοχῆς. For this we have in the Talmud אמרו זקנים, also רבנן קשישי מינן, "our ancients before us," tr. Berachoth, f. 30, 1.

There is, therefore, little probability that the ablatival view is the correct one; and we have now to inquire whether, regarding τοῖς ἀρχαίοις as a bona fide Dative, we can accept that old Protestant exposition of it, already indicated, which in recent times has met with support from such writers as B.-Crusius, De Wette, Ritschl in loc. cit., Neander, and Bleek. Now, if ἀκούειν can mean nothing else but the hearing of the law through the medium of the readings in the synagogue, then something may be urged in favour of the opinion lately represented by Neander and Bleek, that the ἀρχαῖοι are the contemporaries of Moses to whom the law was promulgated. For this opinion has in its favour the philological use of ἀρχαῖος, and equally the use of the rabbinical קַדְמוֹנִים. For ἀρχαῖος is used in the sense of *priscus*, ancient, Aristoph. nubes v. 974: ἀρχαῖα καὶ διπολιώδη: comp. Luke ix. 8, 19; 2 Pet. ii. 5; Rev. xii. 9. Felbiger, the Socinian translator of the Bible, has "zu den Uralten, to the ancients." So in a ספר תפלות in Capell.: זכר אהבת הקדמונים אברהם יצחק ישראל.

Yet the word ἀρχαῖος is used not only of remote antiquity, but likewise of the recent past: comp. Acts xxi. 16; 2 Cor. v. 17. (Sir. ix. 10; Polyb. hist. I. c. ix. 3. See also Doederlein's lateinische Synonymik, iv. S. 89.[1]). Therefore, philologically, οἱ ἀρχαῖοι might certainly denote the generation immediately preceding that of our Lord,—a view which is proposed by the author

---

[1] Jacob, on Lucian's Toxaris, p. 72, observes of πάλαι also: saepius ad paulo remotiora refertur.

of the Vesp. Gron., p. 112, and adopted by B.-Crusius and Ritschl. In which case the expression in John x. 8, οἱ πρὸ ἐμοῦ, might be compared, which indeed cannot well be understood in any other sense. No doubt, as Socinus already remarks, it might appear surprising to find that, which the men of that day were wont to hear, characterized as that which was heard by their forefathers. But to this objection it might be replied with some reason, that the fact, that the doctrine was set forth to their ancestors, lent the doctrine itself greater weight. Add to this, that in this sense ἠκούσατε must obtain another signification, and must be understood, not as referring to the public reading in the synagogue, but only to the *learned* instruction of those days, or any means of communication then in use; a view to which Baumgarten-Crusius also seems to incline. But as it was, in fact, only by means of the readings in the synagogue that the law became known to the people, as these readings were in use *at least* a century before Christ, and as they again were based upon the paraphrastic Targums,[1] we may ask, Had not the people been taught to understand that the law had been delivered to the ancients of the time of Moses precisely in the form in which it was expounded to them by the Scribes?

In the succeeding antitheses the object of the Saviour is consequently twofold. On the one hand, He seeks to exhibit the Mosaic law, in its deeper import, as the moral norm of the righteousness of His kingdom. On the other hand, He aims at an exposure of the laxer pharisaic righteousness of His cotemporaries, showing how inadequate it was to attain the high end in view. Before, however, proceeding to an exposition of the details, we must indicate two hermeneutical canons, through neglect of which misunderstandings of a radical and practical nature have been occasioned.

1. In this section, as indeed everywhere, not the *literal*, but the *spiritual*, interpretation is the true one. Inasmuch as the spirit of an author is expressed by means of the word and the letter, we must, of course, set out from an exposition of the letter and the word. As, however, on the other hand, the letter is of importance only as regarded as an element in the word, the word only when viewed as a member of the sentence, the

[1] See Zunz, die gottesdienstlichen Vortraege der Juden, 1832, S. 352 f., and infra on ver. 43.

sentence only considered as part of the organic whole, criticism, in order to obtain an understanding of the word, must press forward to an understanding of the whole work; and the correctness of the interpretation of a sentence and an isolated clause must be determined by the consistency of that interpretation with the idea of the whole work.[1] It is from the neglect of this hermeneutical principle that those false, merely literal, and hence unspiritual, views of such commands as those in vers. 29, 34, 39—42, which are to be found principally in the sect of the Quakers, have arisen. That otherwise highly respectable Christian sect has added to a false spirituality, a literal method of viewing Scripture, which is equally erroneous. On the ground of the precept in ver. 34, they have rejected the oath; in literal obedience to ver. 39—41, they resist all opposition to evil, whether by means legal or personal; from Luke x. 4, they have learnt to give up salutations in the streets; from Matt. xxiii. 8, to abjure titles. This literal obedience springs no doubt from reverence for the words of Christ; but they who observe it, fail to mark how this clinging to the particular tends to the lowering of the general, how this veneration of the letter leads to depreciation of the spirit—the summum jus degenerating into the summa injuria.[2]* If the maxim, ἀντιστῆναι τῷ

---

[1] Origen observes truly—although he afterwards makes no right application of his rule—that it is according to this norm that we must also determine where the sayings and commands of Christ are to be taken literally, and where not, de principiis iv. c. 19: διὰ τοῦτο δεῖ ἀκριβῶς τὸν ἐντυγχάνοντα τηροῦντα τὸ τοῦ σωτῆρος πρόσταγμα τὸ λέγον· ἐρευνᾶτε τὰς γραφὰς, ἐπιμελῶς βασανίζειν, πῇ τὸ κατὰ τὴν λέξιν ἀληθές ἐστιν, καὶ πῇ ἀδύνατον, καὶ ὅση δύναμις, ἐξιχνεύειν ἀπὸ τῶν ὁμοίων φωνῶν τὸν πανταχοῦ διεσπαρμένον τῆς γραφῆς νοῦν τοῦ κατὰ τὴν λέξιν ἀδυνάτου. What specially concerns us is, that shortly before Origen had cited vers. 22 and 34 of our chapter as commands, concerning which the question could not once be raised as to whether they were to be understood κατὰ λέξιν.

[2] It is true also in the domain of law, that he alone realizes the idea of a judge who knows how to interpret the letter of the law in the spirit of the law. It is necessary, says, e.g., Holweg (Einl. zum Grundriss des Civilprocesses, 1832, 3 A. S. iv.), that the lawyer be a vir bonus: "not alone to theologians may the well-known phrase be applied; we may also say, 'pectus facit Ictum!'"

* [Follows in the text a quotation from an old German Prince, which we give in the original:] "Die heilige Schrift ist eine Mutterbrust, aber zu sehr gepresst, laeuft Blut heraus."

πονηρῷ, is from a principle of love renounced in *every* case, then, by encouraging others to fresh deeds of violence, we endanger the rights of those committed to us, and so from a principle of love do injury not only to the evil-doers themselves, but also to the innocent. If the precept, τῷ αἰτοῦντι δίδου, be in *all* cases fulfilled, then we strengthen the hands of beggary and indolence, and support vice. If the command of obedience to parents, given in Col. iii. 20, be in all circumstances obeyed, then must children sometimes commit sin. If Luke xiv. 12 be absolutely complied with, then must we never bid our friends and relations to our table. But these examples will suffice. Besides, when the letter is thus strictly followed, it happens ordinarily that even the letter does not receive its due; and if the spirit of Christ is discarded, at least common sense is left, and compels the rigid letter-server to perpetrate rational inconsistencies. The man who will not allow himself to resist evil by deeds, will not hesitate to oppose it at least by words: he who gives to every needy man that asks, will distinctly refuse to grant the request when his child asks a knife, or when a murderer begs poison; and so on. So, then, with regard to the sayings of Christ which we are about to consider, we must never forget that they are to be interpreted according to the analogia fidei, according to the whole scope of the Christian doctrine, according to the *spirit* of Christ.

2. Our Lord's mode of address is that of the popular orator; the language He uses is not that of the school. Hence we find here no minute distinctions, no juridical interlocutors; hence, too, we have no right to take the letter of what He says in a strict literal sense, and to press it unduly. The popular orator gives forth his utterance in concise and terse language, trusting to the common sense of his hearers as his interpreter, which with intuitive skill curtails or supplements his sayings, according as the intention of the speaker and the connection of the discourse require. Especially characteristic of the popular speaker (particularly so of the Oriental orator) is the concrete expression, the *example*[1] drawn from life, the figure. Now,

---

[1] More Hebraico, says Chemnitz, i. 441, doctrina generalis in uno aliquo exemplo proponitur, ut eadem ratione ad similia, quæ ejusdem generis sunt, accommodetur. There is a treatise by Ernst Walch, entitled: ἐγχώριον ἦθος in stylo populorum oriental.; and another by C. Ernesti: de usu vitæ communis ad Interpr. N. T., 1779.

an example is seldom of universal force, a figure has seldom universal application. Hence the spiritual interpretation is here seen to be a paramount necessity. Especially in the Sermon on the Mount, which is the great model of popular rhetoric of a truly spiritual kind, the thought is often set forth in a special concrete example (as in vers. 22, 29, 40, 45), and in a figure (as in vii. 4—6, 13, 14, 16, 24, et seqq.[1]). And these passages cannot fail to impress us with the conviction, that this mode of address has many advantages, and that it helps greatly to make the Scriptures a popular work; although it is to be expected that the more such expressions occur, the greater is the danger that literary pedants, who cling to the mere letter, will wander from the green meadows of a lively and spiritual interpretation into the barren tracts of scholastic abstractions. The inaugural address to the Apostles in chap. x. furnishes illustrations of the fact, that a concrete example imparts vividness and life to a thought,—illustrations which are also very instructive for the expositor of the Sermon on the Mount. Take, for instance, the injunction given in Matt. x. 9, 10: it is given in Mark vi. 8 and 9 in a form so completely different, that, according to the letter, these verses express precisely the converse of St Matthew's words, whilst the thought is really the same; for under both forms of expression the thought may be clearly traced, that the heralds of the faith are to count upon the loving care and provision of those who receive their message.

These observations are strikingly illustrated by the works of Luther. He was a man of the people, and, as such, he speaks like Scripture itself. No clausulæ or subtle distinctions does

---

[1] It is whorty of notice to what an extent the spirit of the Saviour Himself exercises and influence upon the parabolical expressions of which He makes use. Then, several parabolical expressions of the Sermon on the Mount are related to rabbinical sayings. These have been collected together by Corrodi (Beitraege zur Befoerderung des vernuenftigen Denkens, Heft v. S. 90); but some of them are of so questionable a character that the translator has not thought proper to give them always unaltered. Thus a parallel to the words of Christ, "Whosoever shall smite thee on thy right cheek," etc., is found in the rabbinical dictum, "If thy neighbour calls thee an ass, put on thee an ass's saddle!" The hyperboles (גוזמא) of the Rabbis, which the Talmud often uses in such bad taste, also furnish, in many instances, matter for comparison with the sayings of our Lord (e.g., Matt. v. 29, 30, compared with Gemara tr. Niddah, f. 13, 2).

he use; his language is forcible and direct, requiring to be understood according to the purpose of the speaker and the connection of his discourse. Frequently, too, does he avail himself of concrete examples, of proverb and parable. Hence, in his writings, as in the Bible, there are for the reader who will not look beyond the mere letter, contradictions without number, pointed weapons which may be dangerously misused. Surely those of his followers who have understood his peculiarity, ought to have been the last men to insist upon a rigid adherence to the letter.

Christ, like certain of the more enlightened Scribes of that time, regarded the sum of the whole law as consisting in the command to love God supremely, and our neighbour as ourself (see above, p. 139). Now, if the Sermon on the Mount—the magna charta of the kingdom of God—is to contain the moral rule of life for the members of that kingdom, might this object not be attained by fully setting forth this fundamental law, and liberating it from all partial and particular limitations? (as is done, for instance, at least in one of its phases, in the parable Luke x, 36). This must, indeed, have been the course taken by our Lord, had He appeared in the character of a teacher of systematic theology. But what if, in their pharisaic treatment of those two precepts, the Scribes, through their lax method of interpreting the law, were wont to obscure the practical application of those precepts? Yet might we perhaps anticipate that Christ would supply a spiritual exposition of the Decalogue, the fundamental law of Israel (see above, p. 125); subjoining perhaps, as in Matt. xix. 18, 19, those two leading commands. But neither has Christ satisfied *this* desire on our part after a systematic treatment. Only the two first laws which He speaks of, vers. 21, 27, are taken from the Decalogue; in ver. 33 there is not even the semblance of a reference to the Mosaic Tables. In the opinion of Ewald (see above, p. 16), who thinks ver. 42 meaningless in its present connection, we are to imagine inserted after ver. 41 a new antithesis, containing a third reference to the Decalogue: ἠκούσατε ὅτι ἐρρέθη· οὐ κ λ έ ψ ε ι ς, ἀποδώσεις δὲ τὸ ἱμάτιον τῷ πτωχῷ. But in acting thus, the "positive" criticism is as arbitrary as it is self-assured: for ver. 42 furnishes not the slightest pretext for such a proceeding. According to Stier, the order is determined by the object, of presenting the various relaxations of the law by the Pharisees in a culminating series: first, in vers. 31, 32, their literal mode of understanding the law; next, in vers. 33—48, their false exposition of it; and, lastly, chap. vi. their false conduct and mock-holiness. But is not a *literal* exposition at the same time a *false* exposition? Moreover, the omission with which ver. 31 is cited, is based entirely on a wrong exposition. We scorn the expedient of supposing repeated omissions in the narrative (see above, p. 32): it remains, therefore, that we assume that only those examples were selected by our Lord, which illustrated most forcibly, on the one hand, the earthly element in the prevalent interpretation, and, on the other, the deep spiritual character of His own.

There remains that we glance at the order in which the prohibition of murder and that of adultery are cited. In St Matthew the former is mentioned first, and that not only here, but in xix. 19. In this he follows the division of the Masoretic text, which has been in use in the Western Church. The reverse order is that of the LXX. in Exod. xx., Deut. v.; Mark x. 19; Luke xviii. 20; Rom. xiii. 9; James ii. 11; as likewise in Philo de decal., Clem. Alex., Theoph. ad Autol. etc. Philo maintains the precedence of adultery, on the ground that it is the worst transgression against our neighbour. On the same ground, Grotius (ad Ex. xx. and Explic. decal., p. 45) even demands a transposition in the Hebrew text: matrimonium enim totius civilis societatis fundamentum est. It might be asked, Was this the reason for the transposition in the LXX.? A circumstance which we notice in the version of the Decalogue given in Deuteronomy, from the prophetic era, appears to favour this view. There, together with various other changes, we find in the tenth commandment, that whereas in Ex. xx. the *house* occurs first, in Deut. v. the wife is first mentioned among the objects which must not be coveted. This was possibly done for the reason which Philo refers to; for the LXX. appear to have been so convinced that this order is the right one, that in their translation they have also introduced it into the older version of the law in Exodus. Were the ingenious argument of Meyer ("die urspruengliche Form des Dekalogs," Tueb. 1846) borne out, it might be maintained that the arrangement in use before the Exile was generally very different from the Masoretic order,—was, in fact, such an one, that in it the prohibition of adultery preceded that of murder. As the order in which St Matthew places the two prohibitions is common to him with the Targums and with Josephus, we may add this circumstance to the many arguments in favour of the Palestinian origin of his Gospel.

Vers. 21, 22. The fifth commandment is quoted by the Saviour in conjunction with its rabbinical gloss. This, as indicating the punishment assigned to the actual breaking of the commandment, offered a welcome occasion to our Lord to show the infinitely higher dignity of His own requirements, inasmuch as He visits the offence in its faintest beginnings with that very punishment which, in the pharisaic statute, was decreed against its open outbreak.

We shall illustrate,

(1.) The commandment.
(2.) The antithesis, ἐγὼ δὲ λέγω.
(3.) The degrees of transgression of the commandment.
(4.) The degrees of punishment.[1]

(1.) The commandment.—The Future in Hebrew, as jussive, always in the law-passages; whereas in Greek and Latin it commonly expresses the milder form of command—expectation (Bernhardy Gr. Syntax, S. 378): but sometimes also the more peremptory command (Rost Gr. Gramm. 4 A. S. 639; Krueger Lat. Gramm. ii. § 463, 2 A.); comp. the Future v. 48, vi. 5. Here the older Protestant exegesis sets out from the supposition, that even Moses did not direct his prohibition against the deed alone, but that along with the deed he comprehended the temper and disposition. Calvin: Quod si tyrocinium dumtaxat traderet veræ justitiæ, frivola esset illa Mosis contestatio: Cælum et terram testor, quod tibi ostenderim hodie viam vitæ et mortis. Item: Et nunc Israel, quid abs te postulat Deus tuus, nisi ut sibi penitus adhæreas. Inanis etiam ista esset promissio et frustratoria: Qui fecerit hæc, vivet in ipsis. . . . Nec aliunde tam ipse quam Apostoli pie sancteque vivendi præcepta deducunt: et sane atrocem Deo legis authori faciunt injuriam,

---

[1] Grulich's treatise on Matt. v. 20, in the "Annalen der Gesammten Theologie," 1833, which affects to be a profound investigation of the words of Christ, is, however, without value.

qui tantum oculos, manus et pedes illic componi fingunt, ad fucosam bonorum operum speciem, in solo autem evangelio doceri amandum ex corde esse Deum. Facessat igitur error ille, legis defectus hic a Christo corrigi. Luther, in a manner as ingenious as it is popular, shows that the Mosaic commandment involved the meaning which Christ educed from it: "Do you suppose," he says, "that He spoke only of murder by the hand when he said, '*Thou* shalt not kill?' *Thou*, what does *thou* mean? Not only thy hand, foot, tongue, or any other member, but thyself, all that thou art in soul or body. Just as when I say to any one: 'Thou shalt not do such and such a thing,' I speak not with the hand, but with the whole person." But did the Lawgiver Himself comprise in the ten commandments of His covenant all the spiritual meaning which has been evolved out of them? This we will not believe, if we consider that those laws were intended to be the foundation of a *civil* and religious law for a Theocracy; *i.e.*, for a religious state in which the civil was at the same time a religious commonwealth. (See above, p. 72.) But would not the ninth and tenth commandments lead to a different conclusion, at least if they are interpreted as Augustine, the Reformed Church, since the seventeenth century the Lutheran and the majority of modern expositors, Ewald among the rest, have understood them? If חָמַד denotes *inward* coveting (or lusting after, as Luther translates), may not the others also refer to something inward,—may there not be implied in the commandments, Thou shalt not commit adultery, Thou shalt not steal, a prohibition of the *desire* to do these things? The question is an old one; it is already raised in the Glossa ordinaris from Isidorus Hisp. on Ex. xx. 14: quæritur quoque, quomodo differat non *mœchaberis* ab eo, quod paulo post dicitur: Non *concupisces* uxorem proximi tui? In eo enim quod dictum est: non mœchaberis, poterat et illud intelligi, nisi forte in illis duobus præceptis non mœchandi et non furandi, ipsa opera notata sint, in his vero extremis concupiscentia ipsa. Calvin endeavours to get rid of the difficulty by a piece of refinement which is certainly foreign to so primitive a law. The commands against the *deed*, he says, include the consilium, the deliberata assensio; on the other hand, what is forbidden in this tenth commandment is the subjective titillatio concupiscentiæ. (Instit. ii. 8; 49.) Even Calov gives the same explanation (on Ex. xx.), without heeding the opposite opinion of Luther. Leo Judæus says (groesserer Katechismus herausgegeben von Grob, S. 48): "Since killing, stealing, etc., had been already forbidden in the outward deed, so are here the evil desires and thoughts themselves forbidden." Now, it may well be called in question whether that Calvinistic view is the right one, or whether the true interpretation be not rather that of the Jewish expositors, whom Luther professes to follow. According to it, the covetousness forbidden in the tenth commandment **is** of a practical character, and consists in "overreaching and injuring our neighbour under the pretext of right." This view has been ably defended by Geffken ("die Eintheilung des Decalogs," 1838), who is also followed by Meier. Or, does not the truth lie somewhere between these views? May not the covetousness forbidden be of such a kind as, on a given opportunity, may seek to appropriate to itself in some indirect way that property of another towards which it goes forth in longing and desire? Grot. (explic. decalog. p. 48): ideo in V. T. vocibus illis (חָמַד, הִתְאַוָּה) plerumque non motus *solos*, sed permanens studium propositumque significari. So was the commandment understood by Josephus: μηδενὸς ἀλλοτρίου ἐπιθυμίαν λαμβάνειν (Antiq. iii. 5, 5). The Rabbis too, with the exception of Abarbanel, explain the לֹא תַחְמֹד of Exodus to be a desire tending towards action (Vitringa, Observ. iii. 605 seqq.). In the first instance, however, the desire is considered as an inward one, as is expressly stated by Aben Esra. He says, that man, knowing that God always does the best that can be done, while man by his own strenght can attain nothing, ought not to covet the property of others, but to rejoice in that which he possesses: כי ידע שהשם לא רצה לתת לו לא יוכל לקחתו בכחו ובמחשבותיו על כן יבטח בבוראו שיכל כלני ויעשה הטוב בעיניהו (Bibl. Bomb. ad Ex. xx.). Thus we are certainly led here to something inward, as distinguished from the mere outward act; although, on the other hand, we cannot suppose that all that is spoken of is the titillatio concupiscentiæ. The לֹא תִתְאַוֶּה of the tenth commandment in Deuteronomy points also to the same inward sphere, as the Rabbis have observed. St Paul, in Rom. vii. 7, has also taken the words of the law in this sense. But although this commandment extends to the prohibition of sinful desire, this cannot be affirmed of the remaining nine, at least in the view of the **Lawgiver**. It is true, they are anything but mere police regulations, but are throughout laws of religious and theocratical administration. This may be seen not only from the commandments themselves, but above all from the motive to obedience by which they are prefaced, viz., gratitude to God, the Saviour of Israel.

And shall we then be justified in accusing Christ of putting a meaning into the words of the law which did not historically belong to them? Not so, if we will only rightly understand the character of the Sinaitik lawgiving as part of the *Divine* education of man. All that is here admitted is, that in the case of the Jewish nation, and specially at that period of its development, the will of God towards the human race flowed forth in a finite and a national channel; and this is just the view which we find in the words of Christ Himself in St Matt. xix. (see above, p. 159). Even Grotius has here discerned the truth (de jure belli et pacis, 2, 20, 39, 3): nam illud, non concupisces, quod in Decalogo est, quamquam si scopum spectes legis, id est τὸ πνευματικόν, latius patet (vellet enim lex, omnes etiam mente esse purissimos), tamen ipsum præceptum externum ἐντολὴν σαρκικὴν quod attinet, ad motus animi pertinet, qui *facto* produntur. The argument, however, which E. Meier (in loc. cit. S. 71) brings against this view is not very cogent. Christ, he maintains, cannot have used the word תַחְמֹד in a spiritual sense; for then He would have made use of it in expounding the command, οὐ μοιχεύσεις. Indeed, it might be said that Christ might, in expounding any of the commandments, have used the tenth commandment as the key to the spiritual interpretation of them all. This He might have done, undoubtedly. He might have equally chosen that commandment and the one which He did choose, viz., the command to love God and our neighbour. But what if He sought to gain the same end by another method? Moreover, had He chosen this commandment, the thought would have received quite a different turn; for here the point of it is turned against the pharisaic gloss: "The punishment, such is the idea, which ye visit upon the deed of murder, I visit upon the faintest beginnings of the crime."

(2.) The antithetical ἐγὼ δὲ λέγω.—Clem. Alex.: ἡ τοῦ ἐγὼ προσθήκη προσεχεστέραν δείκνυσι τῆς ἐντολῆς τ. ἐνέργειαν. What impression must this antithesis have conveyed to the hearers? If they discovered in it any, were it only a partial, opposition to the Lawgiver of Sinai, they might doubtless understand that here was One who could say of Himself, "A greater than Solomon and the temple is here" (xii. 6, 42). But then the solemn declaration of the converse which had just gone before, must have appeared to them simply illusive. If however, they understood the words merely as expressing opposition to the doctrine of the law currently taught by the Scribes, then His declaration was only such an ואני אומר as we find in the Talmud one teacher so frequently using in **confronting another**. We see, however, from vii. 29, that the discourse seemed to them not like the doctrine of the Scribes, but as of one ἐξουσίαν ἔχων, of one who had received Divine authority and power; therefore, as of a *Prophet*.

(3.) The degress of transgression of this law.—The transgression of this law begins not with the actual deed, of which human tribunal take cognizance, but with the lawless desire within the breast.

(a) Ὀργίζεσθαι, like the Hebrew זעם (غ_ۭ to foam), חמה, and others, denotes, first (according to its root, ὀργάω, ὀρέγω), any passionate emotion; next, it came to mean one who does **evil to his** neigbour.[1] On the other hand, ἀγαπάω (ἀγάω, γάω = χάω, χανδάνω, to open out to any one), אהב (connected with אנה, אבה, cupere, capere), denotes a passionate affection of the mind which strives to possess another, to be absorbed in another. The affection, as ἄλογον, is in every case reprehensible so soon as it is no longer penetrated by λόγος, which is true of the affection of love no less than of that of anger. In the case of anger, however, we naturally think especially of that blind, unreasoning affection of the mind which in self-revenge seeks to injure another. This is the ordinary usage of the word, not only in biblical language, but also in philosophical and common parlance. Hence in St James i. 20 we read: ὀργὴ ἀνδρὸς δικαιοσύνην Θεοῦ οὐ κατεργάζεται; and, among other vices, ὀργή

---

[1] Originally, it denoted any impulse—indeed, even the ebullition of *love!* Thus ὀργὰς or ὀργὴν ἐπιφέρειν τινί, "to turn one's affections towards any one;" see the annotators on Thucyd. l. viii., ed. Bip., p. 592: τὸ ἐπιφέρειν ὀργὴν ἐπὶ τοῦ χαρίζεσθαι καὶ συγχωρεῖν ἔταττον οἱ ἀρχαῖοι. In Latin, *ira* likewise denotes in the poets simply "spirit;" comp. Statius, ed. Markland, Dresd. 1827, p. 258.

is prohibited to Christians, Col. iii. 8; 1 Tim. ii. 8. Yet not only does Bible language, but also the peripatetic philosophy and common life, acknowledge that there is such a thing as an anger which is guided by reason, and is therefore right. Such an anger is predicated of God, and is also ascribed to the Saviour in St Mark iii. 5. In Eph. iv. 26, too, it is assumed that anger is not necessarily sinful. The Stoics, of course, condemned anger, as they did every πάθος: brevem insaniam, Seneca calls it: procul absit ira, says Cicero (de off. i. 38), cum qua nihil recte fieri nihil considerate potest. But Aristotle rightly owned that, when under the control of reason, this affection is moral: ὁ μὲν οὖν ἐφ᾿ οἷς δεῖ ὀργιζόμενος, ἔτι δὲ ὡς δεῖ καὶ ὅτε καὶ ὅσον χρόνον, ἐπαινεῖται (eth. Nicom. vii. 7). Nic. a Lyra rightly and tersely remarks: ira injusta, quando appetitur pœna ejus, qui non meruit, aut plus quam meruit, vel si appetatur ordine debito prætermisso, vel quum appetitur propter indebitum finem, ut quando appetitur solum propter vindictam, non propter justitiam.

The received version reads εἰκῆ, in this passage. If rightly, then this saying too would recognise the possibility of a legitimate anger. Regarding the meaning of the adverb, it is best rendered temere, inconsiderately, blindly. In Polyb. L. i. 52, 2, it occurs along with ἀλογίστως; Lucian says of a blind rivalry, that it is χαλεπαίνειν εἰκῆ (dial. meretr. c. iv.); Arrian (Epict. i. 9) contrasts εἰκῆ χρῆσθαι φαντασίαις with ἐπακολουθεῖν λόγῳ. Now the context does not require this εἰκῆ, since without it the anger spoken of can only be understood to mean a blind affection of the mind (vid. Bode cv. sec. Matt. ex vers. Æthiop., p. 41). Indeed, the introduction here of the idea, that there is such a thing as lawful anger, would rather weaken the condemnation passed, in the passage, upon passionate wrath. Moreover, there are so many and weighty authorities against the word, that it has been omitted from the text by Erasmus, Luther, Zwingli, Mill, Bengel,[1] Schulthess, Gersdorf, Lachmann, De Wette, Neander, and Tischendorf.[2] The word is wanting in Cod. Vat. in 48, 198, in the Ethiopic and Arabic

---

[1] Bengel: plane humanum hæcce glossa sensum redolet: ne pharisæi quidem sine causa irasci fas esse contenderunt.

[2] Comp. Gersdorf, Beitraege zur Sprach-Characteristik des N. T., S. 479 f.; Schulthess in his essay: "Ist die Vorschrift Jesu, Matt. v. 22, stoisch oder peripathetisch?" in Winer's Zeitschrift fuer wissensch. Theolog. H. 3.

versions of the Polyglott, in the Anglo-Saxon translation, and in the Vulgate; in Justin, apol. i. 16; Origen, T. i. p. 112 and 181 (ed. de la Rue); Ptolem. ep. ad Floram (opp, Iren., ed. Massuet, p. 560). According to Augustine (retract. L. i. c. 19), it was omitted in the codices Græci; according to Jerome (contra Pelag. L. ii. c. 5.), it was omitted in plerisque codicibus antiquis, and in *veris* codicibus, he says in his comm. in Matt. Evidence in its favour is given by all the Greek codices, with the exception of the above mentioned; by the Itala, the Peschito, Philoxen., the Coptic, Armenian, Gothic, and Slave translations; by Irenæus (L. iv. c. 13, and ep. ad Zenam et Ser., ed. Paris, p. 414), Chrys., Theod., Cyrill, Hilary, auctor op. imp., *constit. ap.* vi. 23, ii. 53, etc. On the strength of this testimony, Wettst., Matthaei, and Griesbach have decided in favour of its authenticity, particularly as the omission of εἰκῆ would be more easily accounted for by the mode of thought of the first century than its insertion. (Griesbach, comm. crit, in textum N. T., part. i. p. 46.) In fact, according to the antiquity and number of the external testimonies, these would seem to decide in favour of the retention of the word: undoubtedly it was read in the second century, but in the East and the West; the Itala and the Peschito, the oldest translations in the East and the West, both have it; it is to be found in Fathers of the second century,— Irenæus (see Lachmann, præf. to ed. 1842, p. x.), auctor ep. ad Zenam,—testimonies which Gersdorf and Schulthess have assailed, but not with satisfactory success. On the other hand, the omission of the word in Justin and Origen has by no means the same weight, as in those citation the stress is laid on the ὀργίζεσθαι; so that the absence of εἰκῆ there, is no proof that it was not commonly read: Eusebius, for instance, in dem. ev. i. 9, uses εἰκῆ; while in quoting the verse at i. 7, he omits the word. The passage from the Epistle of Ptolemy ought in future never to be cited in this connection: when he says, τί γὰρ· οὐ φονεύσεις, ἐν τῷ μηδ' ὀργισθῆναι περιείληπται, this is anything rather than a quotation. True, there is unfortunately wanting here, to enable us to conclude the decision, the authority of Cod. A and C, which have it not; yet we must regard the testimonies we have from the second century in favour of the word, as outweighing the negative testimony of the Codex Vaticanus from the fourth century.

Notwithstanding all this, however, the internal grounds indicated above constrain us to agree with the most recent critics in removing the word from the text; the fact, namely, that its insertion would weaken the sense. For when Griesbach tries to account for its omission on the ground of ethical prejudice, of the stoical rejection of every kind of anger, this opinion, although borne out by a reference to Jerome and Cassianus, to whom Griesbach chiefly alludes, is yet unsupported by the writings of the rest of the Fathers. Jerome says in his Commentary: radendum est ergo *sine causa*, quia ira viri justitiam Dei non operatur. Cassianus (de instit. Cœnob. viii. 20) says, that *sine causa*, although unnecessary, was added by those qui amputandam iram pro justis causis minime putaverunt, *cum utique nullus, quamlibet absque ratione commotus, sine causa dicat irasci*. In these cases, of course, the εἰκῆ was rejected because anger of every kind was repudiated. But then it must be remembered that these two are the very Fathers who have done most to establish the rigorous monkish morality, which was permeated with the notions of the Stoics (compare Jerome on ver. 27, the distinction between *passio* and *propassio*). It were therefore unfair to conclude that they represent the opinions of all the Fathers; the majority of whom, on the contrary, recognised a righteous anger. True, they speak sometimes as though they viewed all kinds of anger as illegitimate (vid *e.g.* Hermas ii. 5); yet most of them justify it. Thus St Augustine (in the retract., comp. Olshausen) makes a distinction between anger against a brother and against the sin of a brother, and acknowledges the former as inadmissible. The constit. apost. (ii. 53), speaking of Eph. iv. 26, say that the object of the Apostle is merely to prevent anger from being kept up, and so becoming μνησικακία. The Clementina recognise the lawfulness of anger when it does not become an irrational affection (recogn. x. 48[1]). In Euth. it is said, with great truth: ἔστι δὲ εὔκαιρος ὀργὴ ἡ γινομένη κατὰ τῶν πολιτευομένων ἐναντίως τῶν ἐντολῶν τοῦ Θεοῦ, ὅταν μὴ πρὸς ἐκδίκησιν ἡμετέραν, ἀλλὰ πρὸς ὠφέλειαν τῶν κακῶς βιούντων ἐξ ἀγάπης καὶ φιλαδελφίας ὀργιζώμεθα: compare also other passages in Suicer's Thes. s. v. ὀργή. In these circumstances, the

---

[1] The same is implied in that passage, Clem. Alex. Strom. v. p. 239; where, moreover, as Potter remarks, that Father attaches himself to stoical doctrine.

most probable conclusion is, that hesitating Christians thought it necessary to modify the statement of our Lord, and so added this εἰκῇ. But whatever critical judgment we may pass on the word, in its *sense* at least, it of course belongs to the passage. For if the deed of murder is to be followed up to its first beginnings, how could the anger spoken of here be anything but a blind and irrational anger? In the same sense as our Saviour here, St John says, 1st Epistle iii. 15, Whosoever hateth his brother is a murderer; hatred being essentially on the same level with murder.

(β) Saying, 'Ρακά. Here the passion is regarded as rising until it breaks out in language, in an idle word of abuse such as might be thrown out in common life. As the object is to gain a fitting gradation, the view of Augustine, which is adopted by Gregory, Rupert, and Calvin, commends itself, that the word was, as that Father had been informed by a Jew, a meaningless interjection of the indignatio commoti animi; corresponding to the Latin hem! Hence, too, in the Vulgate it is given untranslated. Similar is the opinion of St Chrysostom when he says, that among the Syrians the word has the same meaning as the meaning σύ of the Greeks. The root is רקק, to "spit out;" it might therefore correspond to our "pshaw!" Thus we should gain the following climax: ὀργίζεσθαι denoting the ira restricti animi (χαλεπαίνειν), as Tertullian calls it; ῥακά denoting the anger just breaking out (ῥήγνυσθαι); μωρέ, the real word of insult (κακολογία); so Aug., Erasmus; and Beza. As, however, the adoption of the meaning rests only upon an hypothesis, we must give some surer indications of the grounds for it. The derivation of the word from the Greek ῥάκος (a rag, ragamuffin [?]), given by St Augustine and adopted by the Ethiopic translator, is an absurd mistake: to this derivation Ewald also inclines, referring to the Aramaic רקא.[1] The opinion most prevalent, especially since Grotius, is one which is to be found in Jerome, Hilary, auct. op. imp., and in the Greek Scholia; viz., that the word expresses the Hebrew ריק, ריק, with Aramaic ending ריקא, used *not* in the Old Testament sense, nequam, but rather in that of "cerebro

---

[1] In a fragment from Nicostratus we find the exclamation, ὦ κατάπτυστον ῥάκος! There, however, it is not a term of abuse, but it is of an actual rag he is speaking: see Suidas, s. v. κατάπτυστον.

carens."¹ Two things appear to decide in favour of this opinion: (1.) the fact, that רֵק מֹחַ, "empty of brain," was really very frequently used as a term of abuse, as conveying a *mild* reproach (comp. Wettstein and Lightfoot in loc., but especially Drusius comm. ad vocabula Hebraica N. T., and proverbia classis ii. L. iv. § 16); (2.) the fact, that in the Greek text the Aramaic word is introduced unaltered, like ῥαββί. No doubt there are difficulties in the way of this derivation, which are, however, capable of removal.² A greater difficulty arises from the connection in which the word occurs; namely, that if ῥακά = ἄφρων, κενόφρων, it would not differ from μωρός. It depends accordingly upon the view taken of the meaning of the latter.

¹ Luther has, with the Vulgate, "Racha," which is apt to mislead the German reader from its resemblance to Rache (revenge). The word is written with χ also in the Cod. Cantab., ῥαχά. In the New Testament, also sometimes in other writings, the χ has been put, though not correctly, wherever in the Aram. כ occurs; thus Matt. xxvii. 46, σαβαχθανί for שְׁבַקְתַּנִי.

² 1. If ῥακά is the Chaldaic רֵיקָא, why is it not spelt ῥηκά, just as קֵיפָא in Greek is spelt Κηφᾶς, and all words compounded of בֵּית, *e.g.* Βηθλεέμ, Βηθσαϊδά, Βηθφαγή; or why not ῥαικά according to the analogy of Βαιθήλ, Γαιβάλ (עֵיבָל), Καινᾶν (קֵינָן)? No doubt the Greek spelling is abnormal, but it is well known that great irregularity prevails in the rendering of the Hebrew vocals in the LXX. The Hebrew ־ֵי is sometimes written with the short vowel ε, as in 'Ελάμ (עֵילָם); there is even a case in which it is rendered by an α: the Levitical town יַעְצֵר (Josh. xxi. 37) is spelt Μαφά, whereas in Josh. xiii. 18 it is Μαιφαάθ, and in Jer. xlviii. 21, Μωφάς (there, however, the Kethib reads מֵיפַעַת). Perhaps, too, in the old time the pronunciation varied: the people of Jerusalem, for instance, used to pronounce בֵּן, the son, בֵּיר; besides the form בַּר, בַּן was also in use; the Galileans, we know, pronounced the Scheva like οα, see Βοανεργές, Mark iii. 17.

2. How comes it that the Peschito has here ܪܰܩܳܐ? This is not equivalent to רִיק, which would rather have been rendered by ܣܪܺܝܩܳܐ. It rather seems to be derived from the root רָקַק, "to be thin, to spit." in Arabic رَزَقَ, whence also the subst. ܪܰܩܺܝܩܽܘܬܳܐ, ܪܰܩܳܐ, levitas, contemptibilitas. To this derivation seems also to point the circumstance, that ῥακκά is spelt with double κ in Cod. 13, 106, in Wettstein, Gloss. Alb., in Theodoret (Opp. T. iv. 946); also in the Philoxenian translation. Cod. Ridley has ܪܰܩܳܐ; Cod. Par., on the other hand, has ܪܰܩ, and Cod. Barsal. ܪܰܩܳܐ (see Eichhorn's Repert.

(γ) Μωρέ. If ῥακά has the meaning "brainless," how, in what sense can the word μωρέ express a climax in the manifestation of this passion? To say, with St Chrysostom, that it is so because reason is the highest gift of man, is vain, if we take ῥακά, as he himself does, in the sense of "brainless." Now the climax need not lie in the word in itself, if it can only be shown that it existed in the common usage of speech; for it is particularly true of terms of abuse, that everything turns upon custom and the use of language. But rabbinical passages show plainly that the term רֵיק מוֹחַ was used only as a mild reproach, and that chiefly in discourses which were meant to set matters right. When, *e.g.*, Aben Esra, on Ex. xxxi. 18, speaks of those who wondered that Moses could have found to do all that time

vii. 26, x. 21). The word has been also derived in this way by those whose gloss Theophylact gives: τινὲς δὲ οἱ ῥακὰ συριστὶ κατάπτυστόν φασι σημαίνειν. That, besides the common term of abuse רקא, another was in use in the Aramaic, viz., רקא, vilis, is what cannot be proved (Castellus and Schaaf have taken this adjective from the New Testament alone). Probably the Syriac translator has slavishly adhered to the spelling of the Greek word, what indeed he does not always do comp. Ἀκελδαμά, Pesch. Acts i. 19.

We may here ask in passing: How comes it that the Aramaic words in the New Testament have invariably the *a*-sound, whereas in Galilee the Syriac was, as in generally supposed, the language of the country (Michaelis, Einleitung ins N. T. i. 145); the Tiberians read the Kametz as an *o* (Gesenius, Lehrgebaeude, S. 39); and it is admitted, that under the government of the Seleucidæ generally, the Syrians had a great influence upon that Chaldaic dialect which the Jews brought home with them from the Captivity? Some say that this was the pronunciation of the more refined dialect of Jerusalem; others seek the reason in the mountainous nature of the country of Palestine, which made the *a*-sound popular with the inhabitants of that, as it is with those of all mountainous countries. It is, however, more natural to suppose that the Hebrews, who had brought this pronunciation from East Aram, retained it almost unaltered in the time of which we speak. Must not even the corrupt language of the Talmud Jeruschalmi be called Chaldee rather than Syriac? Besides, did the West Aramaic language *possess* the *o*-sound at the time of Christ? The beginnings of our diacritical marks in the Syriac go back no further than the sixth century (see Hupfeld, Stud. u. Krit. iii. 4, 796). Now, that is just the time when the oldest information we have occurs, as to the difference between West and East Aramæans in their pronunciation of the *a*-sound (Assemani bibl. orient. ii. 407); and with this information the investigation on the origin of the vowelsigns accords. (Hupfeld in loc. cit. S. 808; comp. the same, on the difference between the two dialects, Stud. u. Krit. iii. 2, 293.)

on the mount, he calls them דּוֹרֵי רֵיקִים; so too on Ex. xxxiv. 8, and elsewhere. In the Book רוּת, c. xi., where a woman upbraids her husband for an inconsiderate speech, she begins with רֵיקָא; and so in many other similar cases. The *familiar* character of the reproach, and the small importance attaching to it, may be seen from these references; and at the same time they show that it indicated merely a weakness of understanding. The author of the op. imperf. shows himself to have been well-informed when he writes: vulgare verbum erat apud Judæos, quod non ex ira neque ex odio sed ex aliquo motu varie dicebant, magis *fiduciæ* causâ, quam iracundiæ. The Arabic has also in this passage the milder جَاهِل, which occurs not unfrequently in the Arabic in explanatory speeches; while in the subsequent clause, for μωρέ it has the offensive حـقـو. Μωρός is a very different word. It is a *moral* reproach. Hengstenberg remarks on Ps. xiv. 1, that נָבָל there denotes the atheism of the *heart*. Hupfeld gives on Ps. xiv. a minute investigation of נָבָל and its synonyms, כֶּסֶל, לֵץ, פֶּתִי; and he shows, by an admirable collation of passages, that נָבָל is used only in a *spiritual*—that is, a *religious* and *moral*—sense, in Deut. xxxii. 6; Ps. lxxiv. 18, 22; Josh. vii. 15; 2 Sam. xiii. 12. In Sirach l. 28 the Samaritans are called λαὸς μωρός. He who is acquainted with the use of language, both of the Old Testament and of the rabbinical writings, can have no doubt whatever that between the two words a real distinction exists, and that they form a decided gradation. It can only have been from overlooking this consideration that Neander could have thought of removing from the text the words ὃς δ' ἂν—τῷ συνεδρίῳ, or that certain writers (as Paulus and Schulthess) could have regarded μωρέ as, equally with ῥακά, an Hebrew word, supposing it to be equivalent to מֹרֶה, "the froward against God." The truth is given already in Phavorinus: εἴρηται καὶ ἐπὶ τοῦ ἀθέου καὶ ἀπίστου: thus Lightfoot and Dilherr (farrago rituum sacrorum, p. 171); thus, in more modern times, E. A. Schulze, Spec. in Matth. Frankf. 1758, D. Michaelis, Nachtigall (neues Magazin ueber Religionsphilosophie, etc., by Henke, iii. S. 190), and several others. In the other passages, also, where the word is used by our Lord, it expressess the opposite of the religious property of σοφία and φρόνησις: chap. vii. 26, xxiii. 17, 19, xxv. 2, 3, 8. A kindred rabbinical saying, in which the word used is רֵקָא, occurs in the Talmud, tract. Kidduschin, f. 28, 1: הַקּוֹרֵא לַחֲבֵרוֹ רָשָׁע יוֹרְדִין עִמּוֹ לְחַיָּיו, "He who calls his neighbour רֵקָא does a thing worthy of death."

With regard to the predicate ἀδελφός, it may be remarked, that it frequently occurs in such a connection that it must mean generally one's neighbour: thus vers. 23, 24, chap. vii. 3, 4, 5, xviii. 15, 21. This is the Hebrew usage, after which Erasmus and Grotius translate in our passage: alteri cuivis. Yet it is very possible that the word was used by Christ with very much of its original force, as really denoting brotherhood; who was regarding the original union and relationship of the human family among one another and with God: Acts xvii. 26.[1] St Jerome: frater noster nullus est, nisi qui eundem nobiscum habet patrem. So likewise Euth.; B.-Crusius says: there can be no doubt that in the New Testament the name is used in connection with the Father-name of God.

(4.) The degrees of punishment assigned.

The first thing in these which strikes one is this, that the second appears plainly to be a civil punishment, while the last seems as plainly to be a Divine punishment. Neander, usually so wary a critic, has allowed himself to be moved by this difficulty to an act of critical violence, and has declared the words ὃς δ' ἂν εἴπῃ—τῷ συνεδρίῳ to be an interpolation. Κρίσις and γέεννα he regards as equivalent expressions of a *Divine* punishment. The meaning which, in his view, is alone defensible, is: "The man who suffers revenge to spring up in his heart, or to find vent in a word of abuse, is as guilty of the Divine judgment of the γέεννα as he who allows the feeling to become action." The same sense has been gained by Este and Episcopius, who, however, have not had recourse to the same critical coup-de-main. The latter argues thus: In all the three cases, the punishment assigned is simply death; no greater punishment is assigned to the deed of murder than to the murderous affection: to suppose, then, that there is a gradation of punishments, the κρίσις (decreed against murder) being less, and the γέεννα

---

[1] Epictetus also uses the word in this deeper sense, L. I. c. xiii. § 3: ἀνδράποδον, οὐκ ἀνέξῃ τοῦ ἀδελφοῦ τοῦ σαυτοῦ, ὃς ἔχει τὸν Δία πρόγονον, ὥσπερ υἱὸς ἐκ τῶν αὐτῶν σπερμάτων γέγονε καὶ τῆς αὐτῆς ἄνωθεν καταβολῆς;

greater, would involve this absurdity, that the punishment with which the transgression by word is visited is *greater* than that decreed against the transgression by deed. Hence, he says, the idea must be this, that he who sins against the love of his neighbour either by his feelings or by his words, is *equally* deserving of death with the actual murderer. Stier also assures us that "it is only in *expression* that these three punishments rise to a climax: the punishments by no means indicating different degrees of culpability." Yet it is difficult to see what else they can be, when Stier himself paraphrases the meaning thus: "*he* deserves the judgment, *yes, and more* than the judgment."

But when we consider that the outbreak in language marks a higher degree of the passion than the inward affection, and further notice that in the text the punishments decreed are expressed in different terms, can we believe that $\kappa\rho\iota\sigma\iota\varsigma$ and $\gamma\epsilon\epsilon\nu\nu\alpha$ $\tau o\tilde{\upsilon}$ $\pi\upsilon\rho\acute{o}\varsigma$ signify the same thing, or, with Este and Episc., that $\sigma\upsilon\nu\acute{\epsilon}\delta\rho\iota o\nu$ also conveys exactly the same idea? There are four possible methods of determining the question, one or other of which has been adopted by the various expositors. The most natural thing would seem to be, to suppose *all* the punishments to be civil, since $\kappa\rho\iota\sigma\iota\varsigma$ and $\sigma\upsilon\nu\acute{\epsilon}\delta\rho\iota o\nu$ refer to such. According to Paulus, we have here the three kinds of civil punishment which "Christ, in the event of His recognition as Messiah, intended to introduce into His theocratical kingdom:" by the $\gamma\acute{\epsilon}\epsilon\nu\nu\alpha$ $\tau o\tilde{\upsilon}$ $\pi\upsilon\rho\acute{o}\varsigma$ was meant the kingdom of Belial, that is to be excluded from the theocracy. (Pfaff goes still further on this false exegetical track, notæ exeget. in ev. Matth. p. 90 seqq.) Schoettgen and Lightfoot take the same view, *in so far* as they also recognise the appointment of a civil punishment merely. Their view is, that as in those days, on account of the frequent occurrence of the crime of murder, murderers were no longer visited with the extreme penalty of the law, so Christ, showing the high morality of His law, decreed that, while the malicious were given up to the judgment of God, the offenders with the tongue should be dealt with by the law of the land: $\emph{ἔνοχος εἰς}$ $\tau. \chi.$ is explained: so guilty that he were even deserving of the Gehenna; $\emph{εἰς συνέδ.}$ would thus be the leading idea. This view might be carried out still further, if we could also regard the $\gamma\acute{\epsilon}\epsilon\nu\nu\alpha$ $\pi\upsilon\rho\acute{o}\varsigma$ as a civil punishment: whereof more afterwards.

Naturally, this view did not suggest itself to the Fathers; **for it is based upon a conception of** the Messianic work which was quite foreign to their ways of thinking. Moreover, affections can surely never be a subject of judicial cognizance. It was therefore natural that the ancient writers should regard the punishments as future. Few of them, however, have clearly carried out this idea. Chrys. is obscure **upon this** point. Theoph. states more articulately his opinion, that κρίσις is the condemnation by God, συνέδριον a judgment by the Apostles: ἔνοχος ἔσται τῷ συνεδρίῳ τῶν ἁγίων Ἀποστόλων ὅτε καθίσουσι κρίνοντες τὰς δώδεκα φυλάς. So Calvin, who says of the second punishment: gravior pœna coram toto cœlesti consessu. **Yet** he, like Piscator, has felt it a difficulty, that on this view the two first classes are not visited with the punishment of γέεννα, a circumstance which Bellarmine and a Lapide have not failed to turn to account, in order to show the difference between peccata venialia, which per se deserve only the fires of purgatory, and mortal sins, which merit per se the flames of hell. The majority, however, could **not** fail to see that these several appointments of Divine punishment can only be spoken of here according to human analogy; that the estimate which God **forms of** the offence is here presented in a palpable form by reference to the civil punishments common among men (as is also the case in Matt. xviii. 6). If this is the case, then the Future ἔσται, used here, serves as a corroboration of what has been remarked above (p. 150) concerning the view of the judgment-day; because, if the decrees of punishment are simply taken from the relations of the present, it follows **that** the judgment itself cannot be restricted to a given **future** moment **of** time. St Augustine has expressed himself ably on this subject: gradus itaque sunt in peccatis, ut primo quisque irascatur et eum motum retineat corde conceptum. Jam si extorserit vocem indignantis ipsa commotio non significantem aliquid, sed illum animi motum ipsa eruptione testantem, qua feriatur ille, cui irascitur, plus est utique quam si surgens ira silentio premeretur: sin vero non solum vox indignantis audiatur, sed etiam verbum, quod jam certam ejus vituperationem, in quem profertur, designet et notet, qui dubitet amplius hoc esse quam si sonus indignationis ederetur? Itaque in primo unum est, id est ira sola, in secundo duo, **et ira et** vox, quæ iram significat, in tertio

tria, et ira et vox, quæ iram significat, et in voce ipsa certæ
vituperationis expressio. Vide nunc etiam tres reatus, judicii,
consilii et gehennæ ignis. Nam in judicio adhuc defensioni
datur locus. In consilio autem quamquam et judicium esse
soleat, tamen quia interesse aliquid hoc loco fateri cogit ipsa
distinctio, videtur ad consilium pertinere sententiæ prolatio,
quando non jam cum ipso reo agitur, utrum damnandus sit, sed
inter se qui judicant, conferunt, quo supplicio damnari oporteat,
quem constat esse damnandum. Gehenna vero ignis nec dam-
nationem habet dubiam sicut judicium, nec damnati pœnam,
sicut consilium, in gehenna vero ignis certa est et damnatio et
pœna damnati. Videntur ergo aliqui gradus in peccatis et in
reatu, sed quibus modis invisibiliter exhibeantur meritis animarum, quis potest dicere? So the Glossa ord., Bullinger,
Luther, Chemnitz, Mald., Menoch., Spanh., Socin., Calov, Mares,
in the hydra Socin. iii. p. 657, Bengel, Mich., and the majority
of writers. Bengel: reatus civilis denotat reatum spiritualem ad
culpam et pœnam. There remains, however, a difficulty, which
De Wette has chiefly urged: the abrupt transition to the punishment of hell introducing quite a new range of ideas. It behoves
us, then, to subject the three classes of punishment to a more
minute investigation.

Ἔνοχος ἔσται τῇ κρίσει. Ἔνοχος = ἐνεχόμενός τινι,
"subject to, liable to," so that the civil power has right over
him. Elsewhere also it occurs with the Dative and Genitive of
the penalty, LXX. Gen. xxvi. 11; Matt. xxvi. 66 (with the
Genitive, because the idea "guilty of a thing" is implied in it:
Kuehner gr. Gramm. § 536 b.): subsequently, with reference
to the punishment, ἔνοχος εἰς γέενναν, elliptically for ἔνοχος βάλλεσθαι εἰς γέενναν (comp. ἔνοχος ἀναιρεθῆναι, Num. xxxv. 31);
εἰς here indicating the local motion, as in ἐς κόρακας, ἐς μακα-
ρίαν, ad Gemonias scalas.[1] (Winer, 6 A. S. 191.) As subsequently συνέδριον occurs as enhancing the κρίσις, κρίσις must
represent a special tribunal, the Jewish sub-tribunal. The Jews,
according to the rabbinical records, had three courts of judgment:—(1.) In places of less than 120 inhabitants, a court composed of three men, which had power to sit in judgment only
on money cases, דִּינֵי מָמוֹנוֹת. (2.) In places of more than 120 in-

---

[1] According to Lightfoot, Vriemoet, Fritzsche, εἰς denotes the farthest limit, usque ad: but in that case we should have ἕως or ἕως εἰς, Matt. xi. 23.

habitants, a court of twenty-three men, which decided also on capital cases, דין שׁל עשׂרים: this is the συνέδρια of Matt. x. 17. That the decisions of this court required to be confirmed by the Synedrium by no means follows from what Josephus says, Antiq. xiv. 9, 3, to which Mich. refers. (3.) The Synedrium of seventy-two, which sat in judgment on the most important matters,—on questions of law, on false prophets, on war and peace, and on the general affairs of the country.[1] Now, **as only the second court could punish capital crimes, and as the penalty of murder was death by the sword, it follows that the** κρίσις **spoken of here is the second court of judgment; and the word denotes at once the court and the punishment which it decreed.** The fact, that murder could be punished by an inferior court, made the

---

[1] Josephus differs somewhat from these accounts: according to him, the second consisted only of seven judges (Antiq. iv. 8, 14 and 38, comp. de bell. Jud. ii. 20, 5). In Moses no number is given, and it thus remains uncertain whether the account of Josephus or that of the Rabbis is to be followed. There are few writers who, like Selden, accuse Josephus of a direct error. The majority reject absolutely the rabbinical tradition; and, indeed, it is difficult to believe that a public man like Josephus should have been ignorant of the constitution of his country, with which he had himself a great deal to do. Besides, one is disposed to suspect the rabbinical tradition, when, on reading the oldest evidence on the subject, that in the Mischna tr. Sanh. chap. i. § 6, one finds the proof that there must be twenty-three judges, and the reasons alleged for this necessity, accompanied with absurd and manifestly fabulous statements. Grotius and Bernardus have attempted to reconcile the two accounts, though in too artificial a way. **We regard the rabbinical statement as erroneous. As to its origin, it** may have been as follows: The number twenty-three was a sacred number in the Jewish administration of justice in the later times. Ten votes formed the municipality, eleven votes were necessary for an acquittal, twelve for a conviction: thus the number twenty-two was made up. But as the number of judges must be an odd number (Selden de synedriis, p. 926), the number twenty-three was taken. According to the statement of the Talmud, this was the number of members which must be present in order to pass judgment: behind the half-moon of regular Synedrists there sat three rows of twenty-three scholars, from whose numbers the Synedrium was supplied (Selden de syned. L. ii. c. vi.; Jost, Geschichte der Juden, iii. S. 87). Now, if in the constitution of the Synedrium this importance was attached to the number twenty-three, we may suppose that in later times the opinion was entertained, that this was the number of the judges of those inferior courts. Comp. especially Selden, L. ii. c. v. and vi.; Voisin in Pugio fidei, P. ii. c. iv. Wagenseil Sota, p. 15; Leusden philologus hebræo mixtus, p. 344; Krebs ad h. l., and others. Hartmann has also spoken on this subject (in his Zusammenhang des N. and A. T., S. 400), **but without any results.**

crime appear in a less evil aspect. The moral earnestness of the Saviour is shown, however, in this, that He visited the very germ of the crime, the passionate affection, with the same punishment with that court inflicted upon the deed itself. The allusion to the higher board of the Synedrium implies a reference to the severe penalty which it inflicted upon the worst offences,—of atheism, blasphemy, etc., on which it alone sat in judgment,—viz., to the penalty of death by *stoning*. As we have already seen that the mention of the different courts of judgment implies a reference to the different kinds of death they decreed, we cannot be surprised that in the third case only the punishment and not the court is named. What, however, is very questionable is, that ἡ γέεννα τοῦ πυρός must necessarily be understood as indicating the Divine punishment after death. Two considerations induce us to call this in question: *First*, the incongruous nature of the gradation in the penalties spoken of, if, while the two first plainly refer to civil courts and penalties, the third carries us at once to the Divine. *Second*, the difficulty as to whether the two first punishments also would then have to be regarded as occurring anywhere but in the Gehenna. These considerations are important enough to induce the expositor to examine whether the Gehenna of fire may not also be understood to denote a civil and temporal punishment.

It is to be desired that this word γέεννα were subjected to a fresh investigation, in both its antiquarian and theological aspects. The learned lectiones variae of Sam. Petitus (L. i. c. v., also in vol. xii. of the Frankfort edition of critici sacri) are not sufficient. Expositors, in their comments on the word, attach themselves for the most part to the words of Kimchi on Ps. xxvii., with which the statement of R. Jehuda Levita (in the Book Kosri, ed. Buxt., p. 72) accords. They are as follows: גֵּיהִנָּם סָמוּךְ לִירוּשָׁלַיִם וְהוּא מָקוֹם נִמְאָס וְיַשְׁלִיכוּ שָׁם הַטּוּמְאוֹת וְהַנְּבֵלוֹת וְהָיָה שָׁם אֵשׁ תָּמִיד לִשְׂרֹף הַטּוּמְאוֹת וְהָעֲצָמוֹת: "Gehinnom, a place near Jerusalem, a place held in abhorrence, whereinto the bodies of animals and all manner of impurities were thrown, where there was also a fire constantly burning to consume the filth and bones." Beza doubts the accuracy of this statement, but in the main it is probably true. From the Old Testament we gather the following data on the subject. The place גֵּיא,[1] in the ravine of the Valley of the children of Hinnom, had been desecrated by the idolatrous Israelites, by the sacrifice there by fire of children to Moloch. As an expression of his abhorrence of the act, King Josiah defiled the place with dead bodies (2 Kings xxiii. 10); and since then, to be thrown there, or to be buried there, was the most hateful of indignities (Jer. vii. 32, 33). Now, when the word γέεννα (גֵּיהִנֹּם) is used by the Rabbis (Bartolocci bibl. rabb. ii. 28) and in the New Testament, also with the addition of **the words τοῦ πυρός**, as a designation of the place of future torment, how in this circumstance to be reconciled with those historical data? Thus: We may easily suppose that the carrion and refuse collected in Gehenna were periodically burnt. There were thus these three ideas connected with the place: first, the bloody historical reminiscence of the idolatry, which was in fact the worship of demons (LXX. Ps. xcvi. 5); next, the worm of corruption; and once more, the fire: three things which certainly made the place a not inappropriate type of the place of damnation. The point of transition to this symbolic view is to be found in Isa. lxvi. 24: without the Holy City lay the dead bodies of the transgressors, whose worm dies not, and whose fire is not quenched; a passage apparently referred to in Sirach vii. 17; Judith xvi. 21: or we may even say (as Gesenius also thinks it probable), that in this description in Isa. lxvi. 24, the prophet borrowed his language from the state of the Valley of Hinnom, while the Saviour made use of the words of the prophet in describing γέεννα, Mark ix. 48. If this view be correct, it is a confirmation of what was previously thrown out as a supposition, viz., that at least the carcases of beasts were thrown there, and that fire was kept burning there.

The word βληθῆναι εἰς γέενναν τοῦ πυρός, in the mouth of Christ, must accordingly be understood in the sense indicated in Jer. vii. and Isa. lxvi.; viz. thus: "He shall be slain, and his body thrown on that place of horrors." Thus Petitus in loc.

---

[1] Touching the name בְּנֵי־הִנֹּם, or גֵּי הִנֹּם, there does not appear to be any ground to doubt its derivation from a proper name, or to go back to the meaning, "groaning," according to נָהַם, as Winer does in his Reallexicon.— גֵּיא is correctly stated by Lorsbach to be from the Persic بَانْتَن to consume: the Sanscrit root is *tap*.

cit., B.-Crusius.[1] If it be said that such a punishment of criminals was unheard of, the answer is, that it might nevertheless have been mentioned by our Lord as an extreme one, as in St Matt. xviii. 6 He speaks of drowning in the sea, a punishment equally unknown to the law. Yet it should not be left out of account, that the law of Moses had decreed the penalty of death by fire against a certain kind of incest, sinning with mother and daughter, Lev. xx. 14. To this vivicomburium Chem., Calixt, Spanheim, Calov, refer. Little use, however, can be made of this circumstance for the passage before us. There is no foundation for the idea of Michaelis (Mos. Recht, v. S. 235), that it is of the burning of the corpse after death by stoning that Christ is speaking. And generally, we cannot suppose that there is any allusion to a burning in the Valley of Hinnom. It is difficult to see how such an act of criminal justice could have been carried out in a place which was legally unholy; such a thing could never have been done originally in the time of Moses, and probably not in later times. Moreover, the laws which the Talmud lays down as to the procedure in the punishment of death by fire, are of such a nature that they exclude burning in the Valley of Hinnom. The Gemara on the Sanhedrim (c. vii. 1, ed. Cocc.) seeks to prove that the condemned is not to be burnt to ashes; and in the כפר זקן, that is, the Catechism of R. Levi Ascher († 1293) (a work which is the basis of the Jus Hebraeorum by Hottinger), it is given as a tradition of the ancients, that the punishment of fire was to be concluded by the infusion of burning lead. (Hottinger, p. 334.)

It remains that we say something of the ethical deductions which may be drawn from this saying. The passionate affection is introduced in several stages of its development on to the deed of murder itself, and to each degree the proper penalty is assigned. Thus, for different degrees of the sin, there are different measures of guilt. But it is not merely with a view of terrifying men that these different degrees of guilt are accompanied with different degrees of punishment, as Zwingly seems to imagine: In summa, tria docet Christus. Primum, quod est

---

[1] Baumgarten-Crusius even maintains, that with the sole exception of St Luke xii. 5. "the word Gehenna is never once used by our Lord to denote merely a *future* state, but that it always signifies *present* exclusion from the communion of saints."

perfectissimum, ut sine affectu simus iræ. Hoc vero quum impossibile esse novit, sese nostræ imbecillitati attemperans, præcepta alia ponit, quæ cohibeant affectuum impetum effrenem ne impudentius erumpat. Si ab ira vobis omnino temperare non potestis, quod tamen maxime urgeo, hoc tamen curate, ne signa iræ et rancoris, ne contumeliosa verba effundatis. Quodsi affectus iræ vos et huc impulit, manum tamen cohibete, ne ferociat et sæviat. Mallem ego vos omnino puros esse et sine omni affectu, et hoc lege mea requiro, tales discipulos volo et amo. Veruntamen non abjiciam vos, etiamsi primis assultibus cesseritis, modo ne quid petulantius et impudentius, modo ne frena affectibus nimium laxetis. Modus servandus in omni re. But the object is not thus to make allowances; what we have placed before us in the words of Christ is rather the *objective* law of the Divine judgment. On the other hand, the common doctrinal opinion was, that the degree of guilt determined the measure of *future* punishment. This view was held in a form modified according to the general doctrine of each peculiar creed; thus several theologians of the Romish Church regarded the punishment assigned to the two first degrees of guilt to be purgatory, these being venial sins; whereas that of the third, a mortal sin, was hell (see above, p. 182). Otherwise, however, thought Este, Maldon., Menoch., Tirin. The Protestant Church rejected the doctrine of venial sins, and also that of their temporal expiation, but yet used the words in proof of gradus pœnæ infernalis (Gerh. loci theol. T. v., 73; Quenstedt theol. didactico-polem. iv. 565; Spanh. dubia T. ii., dub. 140). In accordance with what has been set forth above (p. 183), we are not at liberty to make this temporal application of the words. Moreover, the final issue of human development is not, we hold, determined by individual sins, but by the presence or absence of faith; according to that saying of Luther, that the only sin which condemns men is the sin of unbelief, John iii. 36.

In the process of the climax from the inward affection to its outbreak in words, at first in a weaker, then in a stronger form, we note the absence of the ultimate culmination, and inquire. What punishment does the Lawgiver, who visits the word with the same penalty with which the Pharisees visited the actual deed, Himself assign to the deed? But here (as in ver. 28), it was not His design to speak of this: His design was merely to show that the actual sin takes its commencement from the sinful feeling. Its commencement, we say; and therefore we must regard the following view of Este, which has been already criticized in its *exegetical* aspect (p. 182), as equally erroneous in an *ethical* point of view: unde non alia apparet differentia, quam quod concilium sit plurium, judicium esse possit unius tantum. Hic sensus etiam ex eo probatur, quia infra quoad reatum non distinguit inter moechantem et eum, qui vidit mulierem ad concupiscendam eam; quem dicit jam moechatum in corde suo. Neither, on the other hand, must we educe from the words (particularly as the *deed* is not contemplated) any general decision on the degree of guilt in the affection in relation to the word, or of the word in relation to the deed. Rightly was it remarked by Luther, in his polemic against the Romish distinction of peccata venialia and mortalia, that the guilt is determined not according to the species facti, but according to the persona. Thus, in certain circumstances, the affection may involve more guilt than the angry word, and the word than the deed. The *white* devil, says Luther, is oftentimes worse than the black one; and, as Hamann observes: "Our Lawgiver is one who makes the lustful leer a sin, and who acquits an adulteress." The cases which our Lord contemplates here, are only those *into which there enters a degree of that passion, which, under given circumstances, would result in the deed of murder*. So too Mald. Other cases, we must suppose, are therefore acknowledged, in which (and the auct. op. imp. also expresses himself to this effect) the affection is morally as bad as the deed, because it is restrained solely by external circumstances or considerations; or again, cases in which the affection, without the intervening expression in words, passes at once to the deed. So too, on the other hand, it is implied that cases may exist in which the same manifestations which are spoken of here, may exist, and be characterized by little criminality, or even be entirely free from guilt. There is such a thing—and the εἰκῆ expresses this—as an ὀργίζεσθαι which is unpunishable, and there is also a guiltless saying ῥακά, μωρέ: so that Chrys. is right, so far as the sense is concerned, in adding εἰκῆ also to both these clauses. Proofs of this occur in the New Testament itself. Anger is ascribed to Christ, St Mark iii. 5: in John ii. 15 and Matt. xxiii. 13 it must be presupposed. St Paul speaks of an anger which is without sin, Eph. iv. 26. St James calls ῥακά, when to the man who has no works he addresses the words ὦ ἄνθρωπε κενέ (ii. 20). Μωρέ is spoken by Christ not only to the Pharisees, but to His own disciples (Matt. xxiii. 17, 19; Luke xxiv. 25, comp. Gal. iii. 1, 3). Therefore, in the case of this saying too, we must beware of that mistaken literality which induced some, even in the time of St Chrysostom, to fancy that they satisfied the command of Christ if they succeeded in avoiding the use of the identical word μωρέ (Chrys. de compunctione, L. i. c. ii.).

Vers. 23, 24. Connected with the foregoing by οὖν (as in v. 30, vi. 14, 15), two thoughts are added, which show that when anger has arisen, that sin against all moral earnestness must be at once atoned, and thus tend to enforce the command. The most sacred engagement must be interrupted, if an offence against a brother remains unrepented of: nor must the demand of such haste be deemed extravagant, for who can tell how shortly life may close, and then the injured will appear as the accuser before God!

But whether these additional verses formed part of the *original* discourse—whether they belonged originally to our Evangelist, or have been taken from some other source,—that is a question which has been differently answered, according to the different opinions held regarding this Gospel. Not only Wilke, Br. Bauer, but even Neander has held that vers. 23—26 have been taken from some other source and added in here. According to Br. Bauer, the 23d verse is simply an "expansion" of the saying found in St Mark xi. 25 (B. i. S. 336). Wilke, however, thinks that Mark xi. 24—26 is a later addition to the original Gospel (Wilke, der Urevangelist, S. 666): nay, it is even maintained (and surely the force of arbitrary assumption could no further go) that the words in Mark xi. 25 stood originally before Matt. vi. 14!—But the vers. 23, 24 connect themselves admirably with what precedes; and it would be difficult to decide agains them in their present place, unless, indeed, we had a right to insist upon a popular speaker keeping strictly to the didactical enunciation of his subject, and absolutely to prohibit him from adding any elements of a practical and hortatory character. With regard to ver. 25: it, too, fits in well with the context, yet in its case there is a greater possibility of its having been taken from some other place. It is found likewise in St

Luke xii. 58, 59. Yet, that there it stands in its *original* place, even Schleiermacher has not undertaken to prove (die Schriften des Lukas, S. 191). This has been done by Aug. and Grotius: according to them, what is meant by reconciliation with the adversary, is reconciliation with God and the accusing conscience; so Olsh., Neand., Meyer Comm. zum Ev. Luc. 3 A. in loc., Hilgenfeld, etc. If it be true that the Evangelist has gathered together the floating elements of the Sermon and connected them together, giving the words *this* signification, we must assuredly recognise the ability of the combination: the saying, however, is not there in its original place, and on this the above critics are agreed. Baur (S. 475) is of opinion that this saying belongs to the compilation made up out of Matthew with the object spoken of at p. 19: according to Koestlin, it is taken from the Gospel of St Peter. Now, as the third Evangelist gives elsewhere other sayings of the Sermon on the Mount in a detached form, showing that he was but imperfectly acquainted with that Sermon (see above, p. 31), and as vers. 23—26 occur only in the Sermon on the Mount, we must regard these sayings as here in their original place.

The Redeemer spoke not to Christians, but to Jews: no marvel, then, if His discourses bear traces of being addressed to those among whom the Jewish worship and ceremonial were still maintained.[1] So here He speaks of the sacrificial rite: comp. vi. 5, 17, vii. 15, x. 41, xviii. 17. The words were received in the Christian Church, and applied in an easy unconstrained way to its relations: what is here said of the altar, was applied to the Lord's Supper; and so arose that beautiful custom of the early Church, of the mutual act of forgiveness among members of Christian families before the celebration of the Holy Communion.[2]

---

[1] So when Planck, Ritschl, and others, quote passages like this to prove that Jesus never contemplated the abolition of the law, the idea is not less mistaken than when Papists base on the same passages an argument for the perpetuity of the sacrifice of the mass, and of the altar. (Spanheim, dubia ev. iii. 832.)

[2] Dion. Areop. de eccles. hierarchia, 3, 3, 8: οὐ γὰρ ἔνεστι πρὸς τὸ ἓν συνάγεσθαι, καὶ τῆς τοῦ ἑνὸς μετέχειν εἰρηναίας ἑνώσεως τοὺς πρὸς ἑαυτοὺς διηρημένους, comp. Corderius catena in Psalmos T. iii. p. 322, in Ps. cxlvii. 3, a passage which he referred to this. On the principles of the Rabbis on the subject of reconciliation, see L'Empereur on Maimónides de legibus Hebr. forensibus, Lugd. Bat. 1637, p. 221.

The picture is drawn from life. It transports us to the moment when the Israelite, having brought his sacrifice to the Court of the Israelites, awaited the instand when the priest would approach to receive it at his hands. He waits with his gift at the rails which separate the place where he stands from the Court of the Priests, into which his offering will presently be taken, there to be slain by the priest, and by him presented upon the altar of sacrifice.[1] Now, for a man to interrupt himself in so solemn a moment as this, is to recognise the supreme importance of the engagement for which he allows his worship to be disturbed.[2] Valerius Maximus (L. iii. c. iii.) tells how, on one occasion, a youth who was holding a censer to Alexander at sacrifice, rather suffered his arm to be consumed than interrupt the sacred ceremonial.—And the command to break off this sacred occupation points, further, to this truth, that the means of reconciliation with God can have no efficacy without reconciling love towards man; as in vi. 14, 15. When this duty towards man has been discharged, then, and then only, may the sacrifice be offered—then, and then only, does it become efficacious: τότε, it is said, ἐλθών, κ.τ.λ.: comp. the admonition in 1 Tim. ii. 8. St Chrysostom: ἐκκοπτέσθω, φησὶν, ἡ ἐμὴ λατρεία, ἵνα ἡ σὴ ἀγάπη μείνῃ· ἐπεὶ καὶ τοῦτο θυσία ἡ πρὸς τὸν ἀδελφὸν καταλλαγή· διὰ γὰρ τοῦτο οὐκ εἶπε, μετὰ τὸ προσενεγκεῖν ἢ πρὶν τὸ προσενεγκεῖν· ἀλλ' αὐτοῦ τοῦ δώρου κειμένου καὶ τῆς θυσίας ἀρχὴν ἐχούσης πέμπει διαλλαγησόμενον τῷ ἀδελφῷ. From this first reason Chrys. then educes the second: that otherwise thine own offering has no efficacy.

Ἐὰν προσφέρῃς, κ.τ.λ., is not to be understood of the sacrificial act itself: ἔμπροσθεν, ver. 24, shows that the sacrifice does not yet lie upon the altar; hence, too, ἐπί ought not to be translated, with Luther, "auf,"—it was the priest who placed it *upon* the altar,—but, with the Vulgate, "to the altar," or "be-

---

[1] Since the later times of the Hebrew monarchy, it had been the duty of the priest to slay the sacrifice.

[2] The sacrificial ceremonial might be interrupted in certain circumstances; e.g., on account of a legal flaw in the sacrificial beast; then, to prevent the guilt of a transgression of the law,—as, for instance, if in the time of the Passover a man suddenly recollected that there was some leaven in his house. See Schoettgen and Lightfoot. The opinion of the latter, that private sacrifices were postponed to the great festivals, is refuted, e.g., by Luke ii. 22.

fore the altar" (Engl. trans.).[1] Δῶρον = κορβᾶν, used of any kind of sacrifice (Matt. viii. 4, xv. 5, xxiii. 18). The whole representation is vivid and striking. At the altar of God (ἐκεῖ), in the very moment when man seeks forgiveness, the recollection of the wrong he has done rises up in his soul. Bengel: inter rem sacram magis subit recordatio offensarum, quam in strepitu negotiorum.—For the further determining of the sense, the phrase ὁ ἀδελφός σου ἔχει τι κατὰ σοῦ is of importance. The indefinite τι is to be taken in the sense of ἔγκλημα, κατηγόρημα, as elsewhere we have μομφὴν or μέμψιν ἔχειν πρός τινα, Col. iii. 13; Eurip. Orest. v. 1069; Sophocles Ajax, v. 180; Æschylus Prom. vinctus, v. 444: and similarly, ἔχειν τι κατά τινος and πρός τινα, Mark xi. 25: Rev. ii. 4, 14, 20; Acts xxiv. 19. The Peschito has ܣܢܐܬܐ (ed. Trost incorrectly ܐܢܐ); supply, "a hatred." We may now inquire at whose door does the wrong lie,—that of the offerer or of the brother? Has the offerer suffered, and the brother committed, the wrong, so that the τι would express the unrighteous accusation of the former by the latter? Or, is it rather the brother who has suffered, and the offerer who has done, the wrong, so that τι denotes a righteous accusation by the former against the latter? Chrys. first says, that in ch. vi. 14 it is the offended party who is addressed, but here the offender; but then he allows himself to be influenced by the διαλλάγηθι, which he takes not as a middle, but a passive (were it the offender who is addressed, the reading must, he thinks, have been: κατάλλαξον σεαυτὸν τῷ ἀδελφῷ σου). He accordingly holds that it is the injured person who is here addressed. Theoph., from the words, "if he have aught against thee," adopts the same conclusion. So likewise Zwingli, Pellican, Bucer, and Beza, who, however, adds: simulque innuit, plerumque accidere, ut difficiliores sese ad reconciliationem præbeant, quos potius petere veniam oportuit. But it is not easy to see how the admonition can be complied with, if by the ἀδελφός we are to understand the offending party. What reason should we have to expect that, in any given case, such an one would be

---

[1] De Wette (even in his third edition) quotes erroneously as Beza's the words: si offerendo tuo dono occupatus sis. He takes them from Fritzsche, who gives this as the sense of Beza's comment, which, however, it is not, as the later gives the idea thus: si ad altare veneris munus oblaturus.

ready at once to lay aside his animosity on the occasion of such a visit? Michaelis, speaking of the impossibility of *literally* fulfilling the precept, even if the person addressed is the offender, says in his homely way: "The injured man would be apt to resent the intrusion of such a visit, fresh words would ensue," etc. etc.: all of which applies much more, if we suppose that the person *visited* is the offender. But the context decides the question, as the auctor operis imperfecti has already well observed: it shows that the person in question is one who has been guilty of saying the ῥακά and the μωρέ to his brother. So also Augustine, Jerome, Calvin, Luther, Calov, and the majority of critics. Aug.: Si in mentem venerit, quod aliquid habeat adversum nos frater, id est: *si nos cum* in aliquo *læsimus,* tunc enim ipse habet adversum nos. Nam nos adversum illum habemus, *si ille nos læsit*—ubi non opus est pergere ad reconciliationem, non enim *veniam postulabis* ab eo, qui tibi fecit injuriam, sed tantum *dimittes,* sicut tibi dimitti a Deo cupis, quod ipse commiseris. Only Euthymius and Olshausen would have both the ἀδικήσας and the κακῶς πεπονθώς included. Yet for the former view we have also the authority of the use, in Mark xi. 25, of the phrase, εἴ τι ἔχετε κατά τινος, where the τι relates to a wrong suffered by the subject of the clause through the conduct of another.

Thus, in the word διαλλάγηθι, it is the *offender* who is called upon to take the first step towards reconciliation. The passive Aorist, here as frequently with middle signification (Krueger, § 52, 6); used, too, with the Dative of the direction, as in Plut. Themist. c. vi., διαλλάξας τὰς πόλεις ἀλλήλαις. Instead of the Dative, we have elsewhere πρός with this verb; Dionysius Halicarn. ant. Rom. ix. 27: τοῦ διαλλάξαντος (τὸν δῆμον) πρὸς τοὺς Πατρικίους. It may be asked whether any conclusion may be drawn from the lexical meaning of διαλλάσσω, as to whether the enmity is to be regarded as one-sided or reciprocal. Tittmann thought to: according to him, διαλλάσσειν signifies, efficere ut quæ fuit inimicitia *mutua,* ea esse desinat,—καταλλαγή proprie non est mutua reconciliatio, sed *alterius* (de Synon. N. T. 102). The question has since been investigated afresh, first, in the earlier editions of this commentary, then by Fritzsche on Rom. v. 10; and with the result, that between διαλλάσσειν and καταλλάσσειν there exists no essential difference. A distinction does, indeed, appear to be made between the words in a passage in the Scholium to Thucydides, i. 120, ed. Poppo, which Tittmann seems to have overlooked,—a distinction, however, exactly the opposite of that which Tittmann draws. What the Scholiast (whom Suidas also follows) remarks on ἐναλλάγησαν is as follows: ἀντὶ τοῦ συνέμιξαν καὶ ὡμολόγησαν· ἐναντίον δέ ἐστι τῷ διαλλάγησαν. διαλλαγῆναι γάρ ἐστι τὸ δι' αὐτοῦ τοῦ ἐχθροῦ παρακληθῆναι καὶ φιλιωθῆναι αὐτῷ· ἐναλλαγῆναι δὲ τὸ ἀπὸ φιλίας εἰς φιλίαν ἄλλον μεταπηδῆσαί τινος, ἐχθροῦ ὄντος τῷ πρώτῳ φίλῳ. This use would very well suit our passage, where the reconciliation is made to begin with the offender. A number of passages might be quoted in support of it. Ἡρώδην δὲ παρεκάλει (Cæsar) πᾶσαν ὑπόνοιαν ἀφελόντα διαλλάττεσθαι τοῖς παισίν (Jos. Antiqu. xvi. 4, 4): here the anger was on the father's side. Dionys. Halicarn. antiqu. Rom. vii. 51: τί οὖν παραινῶ; ὅσα μὲν ἐχαρίσασθε καὶ συνεχωρίσατε τῷ δήμῳ, τὴν ἔχθραν διαλλατιόμενοι ὅπως δήποτε φυλάττειν κύρια. Here the patricians are exhorted not to take back from the people anything that they had once surrendered them, for the sake of peace. So in the instance in ix. 27. Thus also in the LXX., 1 Sam. xxix. 4, where διαλλάττεσθαι corresponds to the Hebrew הִתְרַצָּה: captavit gratiam alicujus.—Yet the word itself does not really involve any allusion to the ultimate issue of the disposition to be reconciled; for, in the active, it simply means, "to establish a change of feeling between two persons," and in the middle, "to change one's feelings with regard to another." Thus the middle is used also where *two* irritated parties are called upon to make peace with each other. Aristophanes, Aves, v. 1683: σφὼ νῦν διαλλάττεσθε καὶ συμβαίνετε, and precisely in a case where the offended party invites the other to be reconciled. Euripides (Helena, v. 1231 ff.): Helen calls upon Theoclymenos to make peace and to forget the past. The latter asks: on what conditions? χάρις γὰρ ἀντὶ χάριτος ἐλθέτω. Helen, making the overture of reconciliation, says: σπονδὰς τέμωμεν καὶ διαλλάχθητί μοι; whereto Theoclymenos replies: "I let my wrath against thee vanish: let it pass into the air." Further, Euripides, Medea, v. 898: διαλλάχθητ᾽ ἅμα τῆς πρόσθεν ἔχθρας ἐς φίλους μητρὸς μετά. Here the mother, who has laid aside her own anger, calls upon her yet incensed children to abandon their unrighteous hatred of their father. Καταλλάσσεσθαι is used similarly by Aristotle, Rhetor. i. 9: *διὸ τὸ δίκαιον κακόν· καὶ τὸ τοὺς ἐχθροὺς τιμωρεῖσθαι μᾶλλον, καὶ μὴ καταλλάττεσθαι· τό, τε γὰρ ἀνταποδιδόναι δίκαιον.* Moreover, according to an observation of Thomas M., later writers used *καταλλάσσειν* in the place of *διαλλάσσειν*; as in the passage quoted above from St Chrysostom, he says, not *διάλλαξον σεαυτόν*, but *κατάλλαξον*—an interchange of idiom which also goes to show that the words cannot be lexically different.—The question, **whether, in the case** before us, we are to **suppose** animosity or ill-will to exist on **the** port of the offended person, does not fall within the province of an expositor. **We may** merely observe that, as human nature goes, there are few cases where this will be wanting: thus, in **the call** to reconciliation in **1 Cor. vii. 11**, it is evidently supposed to exist.[1]

As regards the *πρῶτον*, **it may be asked** whether it is to be joined with *ὕπαγε* (Chrysostom, Erasmus, Luther, Castellio, Bengel, Meyer) or with *διαλλάγηθι* (Beza, Erasm., Schmid, De Wette). In so far as the position of adverbs generally is concerned, they may in Greek either precede or **follow** the verb. Grammarians tell us that the original place of the adverb and of the adjective was *before* the verb or substantive: *τὸ δέον ἡ πρόταξις*. When it comes after, Apollonius, de adverbio, p. 535 (Becker's Anecd. ii.), considers it an hyperbaton. But what those grammarians consider is merely the logical law, not the euphonistic aspect of the clause. Where the relation of the adverb to the verb is less exact, there is more scope allowed for euphony. The placing of the adverb at the end of sentences can, indeed, be accounded for only on euphonistic considerations. Thucydides, ii. 5: *ἀπέκτειναν τοὺς ἄνδρας εὐθύς*; ii. 18: *ἀφίκετο τῆς Ἀττικῆς ἐς Οἰνόην πρῶτον*, etc., vid. Krueger, Comm. on Dionys. Halicarn. Historiographica, S. 299. **On** the customary transposition of certain particular **adverbs,** see Winer Real-

---

[1] The call contained in 2 Cor. v. 20 presupposes that the first step towards reconciliation has already been taken by God, to which man is invited to respond. When, again, such phrases as *καταλλάσσεσθαι τοῖς θυσιαστηρίοις, τῷ Θεῷ, τῇ ἐκκλησίᾳ* were used in the language of the Church, their meaning was simply equivalent to *δεκτὸν γενέσθαι τῷ Θεῷ*, and they presupposed the existence of repentance on the side of man (vid. Suicer and du Cange Gloss. graec. med. aevi s. h. v.; and the Latin reconciliari, du Cange Gloss. lat. med. aevi s. h. v.). So likewise in the passages which occur in 2 Maccabees, i. 5, vii. 33, viii. 29,—in which last we read: *τὸν ἐλεήμονα κύριον ἠξίουν καταλλαγῆναι τοῖς αὐτοῦ δούλοις*.

woerterbuch, 6 A. S. 488.¹ Winer himself, however, accounts for the non-logical position of the adverb here on the ground of inaccuracy. The reason which Meyer gives for combining πρῶτον with ὕπαγε is, because ὕπαγε expresses the leading idea: he is not to be afraid to go directly out of the temple. If the word were the more definite ἄπελθε, the reason might have weight; but ὕπαγε, in such a case, like לֵךְ, means no more than *age* (vide Matt. xviii. 15, xix. 21; Rev. x. 8). The combination with διαλλάγηθι is very much preferable from the antithesis which τότε the forms: "then, and not before, will God be reconciled to thee." Auctor op. imp.: tanquam si dicat ad illum: vade, ego libenter contemnor, libenter honoris mei patior damnum, libenter exspecto dominus servos, tantumodo ut *vos* in amicitiam veniatis.

Vers. 25, 26. The demand might appear too urgent: its urgency is justified by the thought of the brevity of life, of the greatness of the punishment of unrepented anger.—The use of the term εὐνοεῖν may surprise; usually its meaning is: bene velle, bene cupere alicui. But few would, with Erasmus, translate: habeto benevolentiam; the majority make it express the thought that reconciliation is demanded: in gratiam redi, compone. (Vulgate, Syr., Luther, Beza, English, "agree.") Beza even asks whether the proper reading may not be συννοῶν, which, however, hat not the meaning of ὁμονοεῖν. Εὐνοεῖν and κακονοεῖν τινι are correspondent terms, meaning to be well, and ill-disposed towards any one; compare Xenophon Cyrop. viii. 2, 1: οὐ ῥᾴδιόν ἐστι φιλεῖν τοὺς μισεῖν δοκοῦντας, οὐδ' εὐνοεῖν τοῖς κακονόοις. Polybius: εὐνοϊκῶς διακεῖσθαι πρός τινα, L. v. c. 50; μεσιτεῦσαι τὴν διάλυσιν εὐνοϊκῶς, L. ii. c. 34; when hostile powers make terms of peace, they swear for the future ἀδόλως εὐνοήσειν τῷ ἄλλῳ. See Elsner ad locum.

Let us first understand clearly the judicial relations of what is here presented. The matter under discussion is a legal question of debt (comp. ver. 26, and ὁ πράκτωρ Luke xii. 58), and

---

¹ Gersdorf (Sprachcharacteristik des N. T., S. 107; and similarly Bornemann Scholia in ev. Lucam on Luke xii. 1, S. 80) says that the New Testament writers followed idiosyncrasies of their own in their position of the adverbs; that, *e.g.*, St Matthew puts the adverb after the imperative. But what possible reason could there be for such a habit as that of putting the adverb after the imperative? Gersdorf himself admits that there are exceptions.

as such it might have come under the judgment of the Court of Three. Ἀντίδικος, in a judicial sense, is also with classical writers the technical term for both appellant and respondent (Reiske, index ad orat. græc.): from the language common in the legal administration of the provinces it passed also into rabbinical usage אַנְטִידִיקוֹס. Accuser and accused are represented as being in the way together. This might be best explained by Attic and Roman customs. According to the former, on the occasion of certain flagrant crimes the ἀπαγωγή took place at once (Heffter die athenaeische Gerichtsverfassung, S. 206 ff.; Meier and Schoemann, der attische Process, S. 227 ff.). The Roman custom was, that an endeavour should first be made to have reparation made, inter parietes, inter disceptatores domesticos: if the attempt was fruitless, the reus was summoned, and, if necessary, coerced by the actor to appear before the prætor (rapere in jus; see Adam's Roman Antiquities, i., 405[1]). Yet the reference is not to Roman customs, as Burder (in Rosenmuellers Altes und Neues Morgenland, v. 23) erroneously supposes; because even under the Romans the Jews retained their own legal administration. Still, even Jewish law forbade the hearing of a case in the absense of the accused (Gemara of tr. Sanhedrin, ed. Cocc., c. i. § 10, and Hottinger: jus Hebr., p. 104). The pharisaic party was wont to plume itself on its judicial leniency, the Sadducees on their judicial strictness (Josephus, Antiqu. L. xiii. c. x.; Jost, Gesch. der Juden iii. S. 85). Some judges of the Pharisees used even to attempt arbitration between the parties: against them was adduced the saying of a stricter party: כָּל בּוֹצֵעַ הֲרֵי זֶה הוֹשֵׁא, "he who sets afoot an arbitration sins," for "the judgment is God's," הַמִּשְׁפָּט לֵאלֹהִים (see Gemara *Sanhedrin*, ed. Cocc., c. i. § 2, 3). If a case once came before judges of this temper, there would be small chance of any subsequent accommodation. Chrys.: πρὸ μὲν γὰρ τῆς εἰσόδου σὺ κύριος εἶ τοῦ παντός· ἐὰν δὲ ἐπιβῇς ἐκείνων τῶν προθύρων, οὐδὲ σφόδρα σπουδάζων δυνήσῃ τὰ καθ' ἑαυτὸν, ὡς βούλει, διαθεῖναι. So much for the attendant circumstances of the act.

It is the opinion of Chrysostom, Theoph., Euthymius, and

---

[1] There is a passage similar to that under consideration in Jambl. vita Pythag. c. xxvii., where we find the arbiter μεθ' ἑκατέρου τῶν ἀντιδίκων ὁδῷ προάγοντα.

Zwingli, that our Lord here passes over to *earthly* relations. Chrys.: ἀπὸ τῶν παρόντων ποιεῖται τὴν συμβουλὴν, ἃ καὶ τοὺς παχυτέροις τῶν παρόντων μᾶλλον κατέχειν εἴωθε. The idea is, that the injured person, who makes perhaps the rejoinder, "But am I to suffer myself to be robbed of my rights?" is admonished to yield to violence on worldly considerations,—on the ground, namely, that going to law with his adversary may make his case even worse. This advice is applied more particularly by Dr Paulus to the circumstances of that time, when Jewish Christians going to law before Roman or Jewish judges stood scarcely any chance of obtaining a favourable verdict. But mere utilitarian motives find no place in the discourses of our Lord. We have seen, moreover, that the person addressed is the offender, not the injured party. Accordingly, the majority of commentators, even those who, in general, are sufficiently ready to bring down the sayings of Christ into the sphere of everyday life, have agreed to regard the words as parabolical: this is the view no less of Socinus, Grotius, Michaelis, Gratz, than of Jerome, auctor op. imp., Hilary, Luther, Calvin, Chemnitz, Bengel, and modern expositors. When a saying is of such a character as to be at once recognised by a discerning critic as parabolical, its application is not usually added: comp. Matt. xii. 43—45; Luke xii. 42—48: John xi. 9. Supra, ver. 22 may be compared.

Some think that it is the injured party who is now spoken to (Luther, Bucer, Chemnitz, Hunnius, Calov on ver. 25). There is, however, no ground for this supposition. On the contrary, the address to the offender is here continued, to him who is guilty of the ῥακά and the μωρέ: this is admitted by Hilary, Jerome, auctor op. imp., a Lapide, and recent critics. The application is accordingly this: Be not surprised at the urgency of My command to be reconciled; for should it so be that you were to pass from this life with an unforgiving heart, the passion of which you have not repented, the wrong you have not atoned, will meet you as an accuser before the judgment-seat of God. The wrong done and unforgiven is thus represented as the accuser before God. Similarly it is said, Matt. xii. 42, that the Queen of the South should condemn the people of the time of Christ, inasmuch as her desire for wisdom would serve to shame and confound them. So too, in John v. 45,

Moses is called the accuser of the unbelieving, because they should be judged with reference to him.

The sense in which this passage is introduced, Luke xii. 58, has been already indicated (p. 22). St Augustine observes, that then the *adversary* could not deliver the offender, because he was himself subjected to the judgment: accordingly, he thought that in this passage, **too**, the adversary must be understood to be God, or the law of God, with which the sinner must make his **peace** in this **life (comp.** also his Sermo 251, vol. v. 722). This surmise Hilary well answers: adversario tradente nos judici, *quia manens in* **eum** *simultatis nostræ ira nos arguit.*[1]
—"The way:" in the Old Testament, too, the path of our life is called "the way of all men;" "the way whence I shall not return" (1 Kings ii. 2; Job xvi. 22). He who is called from that way is not the injurer, but the injured, who is to appear in the other world as the accuser. Whether by the *officers* **our** Lord meant specially the angels (Matt. xiii. 49, xxiv. 31), **or whether these are** mentioned merely **to render the sense** of judgment more vivid, is uncertain.

Those who viewed the words apart from the **context found** them capable of manifold allegorical interpretation. As the name ἀντίδικος is given in 1 Pet. v. 8 to the evil (comp. κατήγωρ, Rev. xii. 10), it has been supposed to refer to him by Clemens **Alex.** (Strom. iv. p. 605), Tertull., Ambrose; who have, however, failed to give the opinion any intelligible application (compare the censure passed on it by Jerome). Origen (hom. 35 in Lucam) understands it to be the evil angel of each man; others, the principle of evil' in man: Isidore of Pelusium (L. i. ep. 80), the body; the εὐνοεῖν he makes out to be a careful watching of it. Others, mentioned by Hilary and Jerome, approach more nearly Augustine's view, inasmuch as they understand by the adversary the πνεῦμα; which becomes the accuser **of man** whenever its claims are not satisfied.

In order to impress the scene more forcibly upon the audience, the judicial transaction is placed before them piece by piece. **The accuser gives over the accused** to the judge, **to receive** his

---

[1] Coccelus: sunt, qui possunt suspirare adversum nos aut **etiam** desiderare nostram charitatem, qui, si non fiant nostri patroni et benedicant nobis (Luc. xvi. 9; Job xxxi. 20), erunt accusatores nostri Deo illorum causam suscipiente (Matt. xxv. 45).

fitting punishment, who, in his turn, surrenders him to the ὑπηρέτης. The latter in St Luke (xii. 58), more definitely, is called the πράκτωρ. Dio Cassius lx. 10: πράκτορας τῶν τῷ δημοσίῳ ὀφειλομένων κατέστησε; also the LXX. Isa. iii. 12, λαός μου, οἱ πράκτορες ὑμῶν καλαμῶνται ὑμᾶς. In another form, ὁ πράκτωρ = ὁ φορολόγος (comp. Thes. Steph., ed. Par.). Not therefore to the δεσμοφύλαξ, Acts xvi. 27, but to the law-officer (Acts v. 22) whose duty was to enforce the execution of the sentence, and who could, if necessary, consign the condemned person to prison.[1] Euripides Troad.: ἀπέχθημα πάγκοινον βροτοῖς, οἱ περὶ τυράννους καὶ πόλεις ὑπηρέται.—Κοδράντης: Latin, quadrans, comp. Mark xii. 42, λεπτὰ δύο ὅ ἐστι κοδράντης, —equal, accordingly, to two mites; the still smaller coin, the mite, is named in Luke xii. 58, τὸ ἔσχατον λεπτόν. The phrase is proverbial, like our expression, to "pay every farthing." Augustine compares the phrase usque ad fæces. The corresponding expressions in Latin are, ad nummum solvere, ad extremum assem solvere, in assem vendere (Cicero ad Atticum, L. v. ep. 21; Horace, epp. ii. 2, 21[2]).

Now, in the case of any book but the Bible, criticism would have taken the meaning of this passage to be simply, that the judicial proceedings were to be executed against the offender according to the utmost rigour of the law. But theology has endeavoured to draw from the words some doctrinal deduction. Thus they seem to imply the possibility of the debt being eventually paid off; consequently the Roman Catholic Church makes use of the dictum in vindication of a doctrine of purgatory. On the same ground, certain Universalists infer from it the doctrine of an ἀποκατάστασις. Others in the Protestant Church, again, suppose the words to corroborate the theory of endless damnation.

Only a few, however, of the R. Catholic dogmaticians and critics understand φυλακή distinctly to mean purgatory. This is done by Bellarminus de purg. i. 7, Salmero, Tirinus. Some think it may apply either to purgatory or hell (de Sa., a Lapide). The greater number take it to mean the *infernum*. Glossa ord.,

---

[1] May not the βασανισταί of Matt. xviii. 34, which have so puzzled commentators, have also been such as these πράκτορες?

[2] Gronovius investigates with profound antiquarian research the proverbial character of the expression, de sestertiis, L. iv. S. 336. Here is another proverb: Crœsi pecuniæ teruncium addere.

Lyra, Maldon., Jansenius: non posest ex hoc loco recte urgere quis probationem purgatorii.[1] Origen is adduced by the defenders of purgatory as a supporter of their doctrine, but not quite correctly, although he certainly regards the φυλακή of St Luke as a place of purification, intended to prepare for final restoration. He says: quodsi magnum præmium debuerimus sicut ille qui dicitur decem millia debuisse, quanto tempore claudamur in carcere donec reddamus debitum, non possum manifeste pronunciare ... utique qui tanto debito fuerit obnoxius, *infinita ei ad reddendum debitum sæcula numerabuntur* (hom. 35 in Luc. T. iii. 975). Petersen rejects the idea of expiation in the R. Catholic sense, but he holds φυλακή to mean "the imprisonment of the first death, intended for the further education of men." On the other hand, he regards the "pit of the second death" as the place into which those spoken of, Heb. x. 26, as "sinning wilfully" are to be cast; and this place he considers to be "the place of punishment," which, however, equally with the other, is designed for the further education of men.[2] The same view was more fully developed by L. Gerhard (Systema ἀποκαταστάσεως, 1727), who vindicates (§ 693) this interpretation of the passage before us. Olshausen has also adopted this view. His grounds are, that φυλακή denotes, not Gehenna, but only Scheol; that ἕως indicates a set limit; and that it is a believer that is spoken of, not an unbeliever. This last argument, however, leaves out of account, what ought ever to be kept in mind, that all the legal threatenings in the New Testament, especially those in the Sermon on the Mount, must be regarded solely from the legal point of view. Φυλακή Olshausen regards as the common designation of Scheol, and Scheol he considers to be a middle state. But the word is not always used in this definite sense. It occurs in 1 Pet. iii. 19; Rev. xx. 7. The Peschito, which in one passage translates ܫܝܘܠ *Scheol,* has in the other places ܒܝܬ ܐܣܝܪܐ *prison.* Gueder's opinion appears to be the right

---

[1] **The** most recent commentator **on this** Gospel of the Romish Church, Arnolde, 1855, remarks, regarding the explanation of φυλακή as purgatory, that the word is not necessarily to be so interpreted.

[2] Petersen, The Triumph of Truth in restoring the children of disobedience (Sieg der Wahrheit, etc.), 1709, in the "Wiederbringung aller Dinge" ("Restoration of all things"), T. iii. 36, comp. T. i. 67.

one (Die Erscheinung Christi unter den Todten, 1853, S. 44): the word is the local expression for a condition in which all the energies are bound and fettered.—To this view the passage Rev. xx. 7 points (taken in connection with ver. 3): compare also 2 Pet. ii. 4; Jude 6; Wisdom xvii. 17. Now there can be no question that a state of this kind is represented in 1 Pet. iii. 19 (comp. 2 Pet. ii. 9) as the condition of the ungodly previous to the final judgment: accordingly, the existence of a middle condition is there assumed. But from this it cannot be proved that such is the state of which our text speaks, because of the ἕως ἂν ἀποδῷς. For although there is nothing in the language to imply that the terminus indicated by ἕως may not at length be reached (see p. 133), still it is also possible that that terminus may not be reached. And an analogous passage, in the parable in Matt. xviii. 30, 34 (ἔβαλεν αὐτὸν εἰς φυλακὴν ἕως οὗ ἀποδῷ τὸ ὀφειλόμενον [comp. ver. 25]), seems to show that in our text this is represented as impossible. If *any* eschatological inference were intended to be drawn from the passage, there is more to be said in favour of its application to the doctrine of everlasting damnation. (Gerhard Confessio Catholica, iii. 494.)

II. THE COMMANDMENT AGAINST ADULTERY. VERS. 27—32.

Vers. 27, 28. The command against murder is followed by the one which came next in the law, that against adultery. As in the former case a corollary was subjoined to the Old Testament ordinance in vers. 23—26, so likewise here in vers. 28—30. This is, however, expanded by the addition of the Old Testament law of divorce, ver. 31. That the latter *was* a law, is also indicated by the phrase ἐρρέθη, δέ. It is only by the New Testament πλήρωσις of this commandment that the sacredness of marriage is seen in its true light, and at the same time the prohibition of divorce rightly apprehended. There is a preponderating evidence against the words τοῖς ἀρχαίοις, added in the Received Version: they are therefore to be removed here, and in vers. 38 and 43; in ver. 31, even the ἠκούσατε is wanting.

As the commandment is quoted without the addition of any alleged pharisaic comment, we must suppose that the Pharisees, in their exposition of it to the people, took it simply in the sense of the words as they stand (see above, p. 163). Assuredly the tenth commandment, according to which, even coveting a man's wife was accounted a sin, might have led to a deeper understanding of the seventh (see above, p. 172, and on ver. 38). But as there was no such deeper apprehension of the other commandments, so neither was there of this. To this fact St Paul bears testimoy, Rom. vii. 7. So too we find in the Talmud, tr. Joma, f. 29, 1, the sayings: הרהורי עבירה קשין מעבירה, "Thoughts of transgression are worse than the transgression itself:" a dictum to which Maimonides (More Nevoch. iii. 8) alludes as one well known. In regard to demeanour towards women, even a monkish reserve is required (comp. what has been already said on the name "slow-worms," used of certain of the Pharisees, p. 152). The Rabbi Levi Ascher (in the thirteenth century, it is true) prohibits setting eyes on a woman, seeing so much as a hair, even of the betrothed (Hottinger, Jus Hebr. p. 279). But also in the Talmud we read, in tr. Nedarim, f. 20, 1: כל הצופה בנשים סופו בא לידי עבירה וכל המסתבל בעקבה של אשה הוויין לו בנים שאינן מהוגנין, "He who looks on women falls at last into transgression. If a man sees so much as the heel of a woman, that man's children are not honest." How different in dignity of expression the words of the Saviour from these! But the difference is more than a formal one. For even in the best cases, the object of those admonitions **was merely to prescribe prophylactic regulations as a safeguard against the** *deed*, which alone was dreaded. This is seen from the quotation from the Nedarim, and the R. Levi expressly states it. Our Lord, on the contrary, declares the truth, that the transgression in deed takes its rise in a transgression in a region **whither the human eye cannot penetrate.** The Rabbis were not, by any means, all in the habit of making so much of evil thoughts. The accomplished Abarbanel, who himself declares, in the introduction to the Decalogue (ad Ex. xx.), that the commands relating to the לֵב are the foundation (the עִקָּרִים) of all the rest, says nevertheless: רבים חשבו כי אין עון במחשבת לב רק בדברי ע"ז, "Many are of opinion that thoughts of the heart are not sinful, except in the matter of idolatry." Tr. Kidduschin, f. 40, 1, declares: מחשבה רעה אין הק"בה מצרפה למעשה, "Evil thoughts God reckons not as deeds." And even Kimchi expresses himself in the spirit indicated by Abarbanel, on Ps. lxvii. 18 (ed. Isny, 1543): כלומר לא יחשב לי לעון שהמחשבה רעה אין הק"בה מצרפה למעשה אלא אם כן באמונת האל, "As though he would say: God will not reckon it to me as sin; for God considers not **evil thoughts like deeds, except** in those thoughts against faith in God." The same opinion is expressed by Josephus, Antiqu. xii. 9, and there, singularly enough, in opposition to Polybius, the heathen historian. And this lax view did not necessarily come in collision with the tenth commandment; for, as we have seen (p. 171), the rabbinical interpretation of the לֹא תַחְמֹד did not apply these words exclusively to the sphere of the heart.

The μοιχεύειν which came under the prohibition of the law, many commentators regard as including every species of fornication[1] (Augustine, Cornelius a Lapide, Calov, Chemnitz, Rosenmueller): then must γυνή be translated, with the Vulgate, *mulier* (so Euthymius, Beza, Schmid, Rosenmueller, Fritzsche). In classic Greek the two are distinguished: Dio Cassius, lx. 31, says of Messalina, ἐμοιχεύετο καὶ ἐπορνεύετο: μοιχεύειν, however, included also certain kinds of fornication (see Meier and Schoemann der attische Prozess, S. 327). In Hebrew, however, נָאַף is clearly distinguished from זָנָה and so too in Hellenistic Greek is μοιχεύειν from πορνεύειν, as the species from the genus; in the LXX., and also in the New Testament, μοιχεία and πορνεία occur together: Hos. iv. 14; St Matt. xv. 19; Gal. v. 19; Heb. xiii. 4. We must, therefore, here take the word in the more restricted sense in which it was commonly used; and all the more so, as in ver. 31 only nuptial relations are treated of: so that γυνή is here to be understood in the sense of γαμετή, uxor: comp. Erasmus, Piscator, Grotius, Wettstein, Maldonatus. In taking γυνή in the sense of mulier, Beza, Fritzsche, Baumgarten-Crusius, Stier, and others following the Vulgate, have been led astray by the idea that the πλήρωσις of this command must necessarily extend to every species of unchastity, or the erroneous assumption that μοιχεύειν denotes every kind of incontinence. It is true that several Rabbis have included זָנָה in נָאַף, as Aben Esra on Ex. xx.; Jarchi, on the contrary, says on Deut. v. 18, "נָאַף is only of married persons:" Gesenius also, in his Thesaurus, and E. Meier, know of no other signification but *mœchari*.

But the first beginnings of adultery are, according to our Lord, in "looking on a woman to lust ofter her;" not the evil

---

[1] The Persic Polyglott translates it even زني وفسادي "fornication and rioting."

desire accidentally arising within, but the glance intentionally thrown out. *Βλέπειν*, distinguished from its synonym, means to "look" (Doederlein lat. Synonyme, iv. 317), and may be explained, "to cast a glance on a woman" (so 1 Cor. i. 26, x. 18); not necessarily an intensified glance (ἀτενίζεσθαι ὀξύτερον), or a prolonged look, as the glosses ὁ ἐμβλέπων or ἐμβλέψας would indicate. In classic Greek the special terms for such lustful glances are ἐποφθαλμιᾶν, κακοσχόλως ἰδεῖν, περιέργως ἰδεῖν. LXX., Gen. xxxix. 7: ἐπιβάλλειν τοὺς ὀφθαλμοὺς ἐπί τινα. Such glances are the forerunners of sensuality: the saying, sunt oculi in amore dulces, is corroborated by many passages in the classics, which may be found collected in Pricæus, Grotius, Wettstein. Similar passages from the Old Testament are the following: Job xxxi. 1; Ezek. vi. 9, xxiii. 16; Prov. xxiii. 33; Sirach ix. 5, 8; from the New Testament: 2 Pet. ii. 14; from the Talmud Jerusch. the passage Berachoth, c. 1, f. 3: עֵינָא וְלִיבָּא סַרְסוּרֵי דַחֲטָאָה, "Eye and heart are the two handmaids (agents) of sin;" from Ben Syra's Proverbs: וַי לְמִי שֶׁהוֹלֵךְ אַחַר עֵינָיו כִּי בְנֵי זְנוּנִים הֵמָּה׃, "Woe to him who goes after his eyes, for they are adulterous." Ἐπιθυμεῖν γυναικός, used in Greek of sensual desire, comp. Plutarch terrestriane an aquatilia, etc., c. xviii.: τὸν δὲ ἐν Αἰγύπτῳ παιδεραστοῦντα χῆρα καὶ τὸν ἐπιθυμήσαντα Γλαύκης τῆς κιθαρῳδοῦ κριόν . . . . . ἀφίημι. Artemidorus Oneirocrit. i. c. 76: ἐρωτικῶς διακείμενός τις καὶ ἐπιθυμῶν τῆς γυναικός. Xenoph. conviv. c. 4, § 63, 64: ἔναγχος δὲ δήπου καὶ πρὸς ἐμὲ ἐπαινῶν τὸν Ἡρακλεώτην ξένον, ἐπεί με ἐποίησας ἐπιθυμεῖν αὐτοῦ, συνέστησάς μοι αὐτόν.[1] Also of beasts: see Dio Chrys. i. 503, οἱ ὄνοι οὐκ ἐπιθυμοῦσιν ἵππων. The testimony is overwhelming in favour of reading the Accusative αὐτήν, which occurs occasionally in the classical authors (see Chilo in Stobæus' Floril. iii. 511, μὴ ἐπιθύμει ἀδύνατα), and in the Septuagint (see Ex. xx. 17). Reference is therefore made to a κινεῖν καὶ διαγριαίνειν of the πάθος. But is it an intentional or an unintentional reference? This depends on whether πρός (= ὥστε) designates the *eventus*, as Calvin,

---

[1] In Hebrew the word corresponding is שִׁיק, from which comes חֲשׁוּקָה, Gen. iii. 16. The translation הַתְאָוָה, given in the Muenster Hebrew version of the New Testament, and in the two recent London versions, is not so good.

Calov, Hunnius, Glassius, Kuinoel, and Paulus suppose, or the *aim*, the final purpose. Πρός may undoubtedly designate the result and issue: for example, ἡ ἀσθένεια, ἡ ἁμαρτία πρὸς θάνατον (John xi. 4; 1 John v. 16); and, πρὸς τ. ἰδίαν αὐτῶν ἀπώλειαν (2 Pet. iii. 16). But before the infinitive, where actions of men are spoken of, in all passages pertinent to this subject, πρός denotes the final aim: compare Matt. vi. 1, xiii. 30, xxiii. 5, xxvi. 12; and in the Septuagint for לְמַעַן, Jer. xxvii. 10, xxxii. 29, 35. Ἐπιθυμεῖν consequently is described not as the consequence, but as the aim of βλέπειν.[1] Among moderns, Bruno Bauer has been the only one to take a different view, based on the notion that the context requires the specification of the lightest transgression of the commandment; whereas, wilfully to cherish lust, is "one of the worst sins" (see p. 341). Undoubtedly, a continued cherishing of lust is so; but Christ here speaks of a single look in the service of lust. Chemnitz says, "quando libidine aestuans oculis se prodit." So also do the Rabbins (see in Hottinger) hold to the הבטה בכוונה, that is, the "aspicere cum intentione." Chrysostom makes the remark, that in this case εἰκῆ is not subjoined for the same purpose as it had been previously; because the words of themselves express the idea of the immorality of ἐπιθυμία, and that the βλέπων is here ὁ μηδενὸς ἀναγκάζοντος τὸ θηρίον εἰσάγων ἠρεμοῦντι τῷ λογισμῷ; a συλλέγων ἑαυτῷ τὴν ἐπιθυμίαν. Gregory of Nyssa says: οὐ τὸν ἐπιθυμήσαντα κατά τινα συντυχίαν εἶναι κατάκριτον, ἀλλὰ τὸν ἐκ πονηρίας τὸ πάθος ἐπισπασάμενον: Augustine, "qui *hoc fine* et *hoc animo* attenderit ut eam concupiscat quod jam non est titillari delectatione carnis, sed plene consentire libidini." So also Jerome and the Auctor op. imp., who remarks, that man has a voluntas carnis and a voluntas animae; that from this latter the συγκατάθεσις proceeds; and that the anima is here addressed. He is followed by the Catholic, Socinian, Arminian, and Rationalistic interpreters.[2] Jerome first attempted to formularize the

---

[1] With the Genitive it might signify "on account of," and designate the inward impulse: πρὸς τοῦ πάθους κινεῖσθαι, "proceeding from the πάθος" (Herm. on Viger, p. 862).

[2] Episcopius, however, distinguishes more accurately: "Christ does not speak of that consensus with ἐπιθυμία which is intended in the examples drawn from classical writers, where the evil deed is already determined on, and only waits for a fitting opportunity, but of that consensus where, with-

matter: "*propassio* (he employs the terminology of the Stoics, who treat πάθος as νόσημα) licet initii culpam habeat, tamen non tenetur in crimine; ergo qui viderit mulierem et anima ejus fuerit titillata, hic propassione percussus est; si vero consenserit et de cogitatione affectum fecerit—de *propassione* transivit ad *passionem* et huic non *voluntas* peccandi deest, sed *occasio*." Luther also shared the same view, and made use in this connection of the questionable idea of the "peccatum veniale," which had already proved itself so very dangerous in Catholic theology.[1] Compare the following passage, which in other respects is excellent:—"Here, however, we must not go so far as to say that if any one is thus assailed, even though he himself feels that one lust and desire awakens another, he is therefore to be damned. For I have often said, that it is not possible to live in flesh and blood without having sinful and evil inclinations, not in this particular alone, but also in reference to all the commandments. Teachers have therefore made a distinction, with which I shall not meddle, to wit, that an evil thought to which one does not consent, is not a deadly sin. When a man is insulted, it is impossible that his heart should not feel, or be moved and begin to stir in order to get revenge. But that is not damnable, if he only do not resolve and purpose to do the wrong, but resists the temptation. And even supposing the devil not to stir up evil thoughts and lusts in our hearts, it is not possible to avoid them: but see thou to it that they do not tarry and grow there, but cast them out, and do as one of the Fathers of old times taught, 'I cannot prevent a bird flying over my head, but I can prevent its nestling in my hair, or biting off my nose.' Thus also it is not in our power to prevent this and that assault, to avoid this and that thought occurring to us; if it only stops there, if we do not admit it to our hearts when it knocks for entrance, if we do not suffer it to take root, for fear of its resulting in a purpose or an approval. Notwithstanding it is *sin*, although included in the

out any intention of committing a criminal action, the emotions of sin are yielded to."

[1] Even in Protestant works on dogmatical theology the idea retained its elasticy: "peccatum veniale venia dignum vel ratione *causæ*, quod ex infirmitate, vel ex ratione *objecti* seu ex *passivitate materiæ*, vel ex levitate *actus* ut est verbum otiosum, vel ex *imperfectione* consensus." Only there was added the important limitation, that these "venialia" apart from Christ are all "mortalia" (**Quensted**, theol. did. ii. 72).

general forgiveness." So the more recent exegesis: compare Stier, "Only active lust, to which the *will* consents, is sin [—the Protestant dogma would here, and with good reason, insert, "in him who participates in the grace of Christ"], not the impulse involuntarily awakened in the flesh which now belongs to our *nature*." Strictly speaking, even the opinion of Melanchthon is different from this. He regards the words as containing a prohibition of all "motus inordinati" whatsoever; and to the question, "Cur prohibentur inordinati motus, cum nemo possit eos prorsus exuere?" he replies, "hæc dicta Christi non sunt inutilia, quia sunt prædicationes pœnitentiæ, ut dixi: vult Deus nos agnoscere quod simus mersi in peccatis." The end in view here is the same as that mentioned in p. 36. Both Lutheran and Reformed interpreters contend that even the motus involuntarii of concupiscentia are here meant.[1] But even this idea retains somewhat of the uncertainty of the other, as the expression, "imperfectio consensus," used by Quenstedt in his discussion of the matter (vide supra, p. 209), shows: he allows, too, that the regenerate sin with a "consensus semiplenus." Chemnitz also expressly concedes the existence of this same vagueness. Calov thinks that the awakening thought ought here to be included: "suave fore se hac muliere potiri;"—but is such a thought conceivable without a degree of consensus? We judge, therefore, that no clear line of separation can be drawn; and we must content ourselves in this case, as in the previous commandment against murder, with Völkel's remark (de vera rel. iv. 17), "habet cupiditas illa gradus suos, quorum *licet quilibet adulterinum quoddam contineat,* quo tamen propius quis ad externum adulterii effectum accedit, eo graviorem culpam sustinet,"—in so far, namely, as the will also more vigorously co-operates.

Hence it is a great and important mistake when a great number of commentators, leaving entirely out of sight the closing words, interpret the expression, ἐμοίχευσεν αὐτὴν ἐν τῇ καρδίᾳ αὐτοῦ, in the spirit of the ethics of the Stoics, as embodied in

---

[1] The Old-Lutheran, W. Franz of Wittenberg, constitutes on this point an exception (see his work de interp. Sc. S. 1619, p. 552). From the fact that a preliminary stage to actual μοιχεία is here spoken of, and that reference is made to that "concupiscentia, cui nihil deest nisi occasio," he rightly concludes, "longe est phantastica imaginatio adulterandi," and then adduces the words of Luther just quoted.

the saying of Seneca, "latro est antequam inquinet manus." In three citations Clemens Alex. omits the ἐν τῇ καρδίᾳ as unnecessary: and the versio Syr. Hierosol. takes no notice whatever of it. So Grotius, Episcopius, Paulus, Fr., Riegler, Meyer, Stier, and others: formerly also Göschel, in the interest of an interpretation of the words παρεκτὸς λόγου πορνείας extended so as to favour divorce. The same misunderstanding led Este, Episcopius, and Neander astray in the interpretation of ver. 22. Even Justin Martyr estimated aright the importance of ἐν τῇ καρδίᾳ, for he quotes the saying as follows: ἤδη ἐμοίχευσεν τῇ καρδίᾳ παρὰ τῷ Θεῷ. Rightly Zwinglius: "dicet aliquis, si sic se res habet, ut æque sit peccatum, si affectus premitur et si erumpit, erumpam ergo, et adulterium opere explebo. Absit. Nam minus est cum ignis accensus intus opprimitur et extinguitur, quam si erumpens omnia vastet et devoret; at nihilominus ignem intus esse aut fuisse (etiamsi non erumpat) infitiari nemo sanus potest."

Ver. 29, 30. That it is exceedingly difficult to fulfil, in every particular, the requirements laid down in ver. 28, is clear enough: but the Saviour demands even the utmost degree of self-denial. This is the connection, which is here very much more manifest than is the case with the cognate saying in chap. xviii. 8, especially as evil desires are there represented at the same time under the aspect of a σκανδαλίζειν τὸν πλησίον (Köstlin, p. 48). The present maxim also suits the connection more exactly, in so far as hand and foot are not first mentioned here, as they are there, but the eye; and as no allusion whatever is made to the foot; finally, δεξιός is here employed in both cases,—a circumstance which might lead to the adoption of a different view of the saying in the two passages. As it does not strictly suit the context in Matt. xviii., it might readily be supposed that the Evangelist there adopted it, because at the first transmission of the preceding words respecting σκάνδαλον, it had been connected therewith on account of the general relationship of the subject. In analogy with ver. 23—25, and chap. vi. 14, 15, a parænesis is appended to the πλήρωσις of the command concerning adultery.

Δέ might be used merely conjunctively: but it is better, with Bucer, Grotius, and others, to take it as originating in a reference to the answer to an unmentioned objection. As in chap. xix.

10, the disciples, being shocked at the strictness of the Christian command concerning marriage, reply, "It were better, then, not to marry at all," and the Saviour in a measure confirms their judgment; so also here does He confirm their opinion, that the fulfilment of His requirements necessitates the utmost strictness towards ourselves. $\Sigma\varkappa\alpha\nu\delta\alpha\lambda\iota\zeta\varepsilon\iota\nu$, "to serve for a $\sigma\varkappa\alpha\nu\delta\dot{\alpha}\lambda\eta\vartheta\varrho\text{o}\nu$," *i.e.*, for a trap or snare, is used both of evil and of good things which act as a temptation: of the former, an example may be found in Mark ix. 42 and Ps. Sal. xvi. 7, $\dot{\varepsilon}\pi\iota\varkappa\varrho\dot{\alpha}\tau\eta\sigma\acute{o}\nu$ $\mu\text{o}\iota$ $\dot{\alpha}\pi\grave{\text{o}}$ $\pi\acute{\alpha}\sigma\eta\varsigma$ $\gamma\upsilon\nu\alpha\iota\varkappa\grave{o}\varsigma$ $\pi\text{o}\nu\eta\varrho\tilde{\alpha}\varsigma$ $\sigma\varkappa\alpha\nu\delta\alpha\lambda\iota\zeta\text{o}\acute{\upsilon}\sigma\eta\varsigma$ $\ddot{\alpha}\varphi\varrho\text{o}\nu\alpha$: of the latter, in Matt. xi. 6, xiii. 57, xxvi. 33.

The word "right"—"right eye"—is a designation of superiority. Augustine says: ad augendam vim dilectionis valet. Quanquam enim ad videndum isti oculi corporis communiter intendantur .... amplius tamen formidant homines, dextrum amittere. Even the ancients accustomed children not to use the left hand: Plutarch de lib. educ. c. 7, and Aristotle de animalium incessu, c. 4, $\varphi\acute{\upsilon}\sigma\varepsilon\iota$ $\beta\acute{\varepsilon}\lambda\tau\iota\text{o}\nu$ $\tau\grave{\text{o}}$ $\delta\varepsilon\xi\iota\grave{o}\nu$ $\tau\text{o}\tilde{\upsilon}$ $\dot{\alpha}\varrho\iota\sigma\tau\varepsilon\varrho\text{o}\tilde{\upsilon}$. Specially strong in support of this figure are the biblical parallels, Zach. xi. 17, and 1 Sam. xi. 2. On the construction $\sigma\upsilon\mu\varphi\acute{\varepsilon}\varrho\varepsilon\iota$ with $\tilde{\iota}\nu\alpha$ instead of the infin., compare Winer, 6 ed. 301, Tittmann, de usu part. in N. T. synon. l. ii. Were we to assume a paraenesis strictly limited to ver. 28, the eye might be regarded as the organ of the $\dot{\alpha}\varkappa\text{o}\lambda\dot{\alpha}\sigma\tau\omega\varsigma$ $\beta\lambda\acute{\varepsilon}\pi\varepsilon\iota\nu$, and the hand of the $\dot{\alpha}\nu\alpha\iota\sigma\chi\acute{\upsilon}\nu\tau\omega\varsigma$ $\ddot{\alpha}\pi\tau\varepsilon\sigma\vartheta\alpha\iota$. The hand was not, however, mentioned previously; this second illustration serves, therefore, only to expand the thought expressed by the first: the hand is the organ of action: compare, for example, פשט יד לבזל (Gemara Sota), "to stretch out the hand for prey."—That the fires of Gehenna, in Christ's discourse, are only an image, is most clearly demonstrable from the substitution of other images afterwards: for instance, in Matt. viii. 12. we find $\sigma\varkappa\acute{o}\tau\text{o}\varsigma$, and $\beta\varrho\upsilon\gamma\mu\grave{o}\varsigma$ $\dot{o}\delta\acute{o}\nu\tau\omega\nu$, a physical condition produced by *cold* (Hesych., $\beta\varrho\upsilon\gamma\mu\acute{o}\varsigma\cdot$ $\psi\tilde{\omega}\varphi\text{o}\varsigma$ $\dot{\varepsilon}\nu$ $\dot{\varrho}\acute{\iota}\gamma\varepsilon\iota$).

Not without justice does Grotius say, in his interpretation of the saying, "in hunc locum, ni valde animi fallor, multa congeruntur subtiliora quam ferat sermonis popularitas." Zwinglius goes farthest astray; for he mistakes the connection with ver. 28, and goes back to vers. 23—26: "It do not mean," he says, "that under all circumstances forgiveness will be dispensed: on the contrary, those members shall be destroyed without mercy whose sin does injury to the entire body of the Church." The idea of the figurative, proverbial sentence is, "Better sacrifice the smallest limb, than lose the whole body," or, viewed generally, "better sacrifice a little good, than risk eternal salvation." This figurative character is overlooked by Pricæus in his interpretation; as also by Fritzsche, and by Ch. F. Fritzsche the elder, vide Nova Opuscula Fritzschiorum, p. 347. They affirm: "Jesum *vere* exstirpari oculum voluisse," and that, primarily, "quia tanta præcipiendi asperitas severo honestatis magistro belle convenit." But when an expositor has ceased to recognise the obligation of obeying this "honestatis magister," there is nothing to prevent his ascribing to Him even an *absurd* degree of strictness. That would be an absurd degree of strictness; for when the right eye had been plucked out, the left would take its place; and when the left eye had also been plucked out, lust would still keep its place in the heart, which, as Christ recognised in Matt. xv. 19, is its real seat. In such a case, Origen ought not to have been blamed for his act by the Church.[1] Should we say, with Paulus and Michaelis, that Christ only meant to put them to the test—"The slave of his passions objects, 'I cannot avoid directing mine eye to this and that thing.' Christ answers, Well, then, put it out. But the man will first try whether he cannot give it up in some other way, and will find it possible,"—the admonition would assume a ludicrous aspect. The saying would undoubtedly lose its repulsiveness in an ethical point of view, if one might say, with Menoch., V. Löscher (decimæ ev. ii. p. 68): si aliter fieri non potest, potest tamen aliter fieri. Pricæus takes in reality the same view, when he remarks that what Philippus says in Frontinus 4, 7, holds good: "si partem ægram corporis haberem, abscinderem potius quam curarem." In any case the saying would be somewhat hyperbolical; for, strictly speaking, things never go so far that in order to root out lust we must deprive ourselves of an eye: it is otherwise with ver. 39, for the case

---

[1] This παρερμηνεία occurred even at a latter period. The Nicene Synod saw itself compelled to lay down a canon forbidding those to become priests who ὑγιαίνοντες ἑαυτοὺς ἐξέτεμον. In the Canon. Apost. it is justly said of such an one: αὐτοφονευτής ἐστιν ἑαυτοῦ κ. τῆς τοῦ Θεοῦ δημιουργίας ἐχθρός.

there mentioned, really did presens itself. There is more of a comparison, then, in the expression than in Matt. xviii. 6, and in many similar rabbinical sayings (vide supra), *e.g.:* "better for him to be cast into the furnace of fire than to put his neighbour to shame" (Gemara Sota, Wagenseil, p. 195); and in the classical sayings, for example, "profice, quæcunque cor tuum laniant, quæ si aliter extrahi nequirent, cor ipsum cum illis evellendum erat" (Seneca, ep. 51); βέλτιον ἦν θατέρου με τῶν ὀφθαλμῶν ἐλαττωθῆναι, ἤπερ ἐπὶ σοὶ φροντίζειν (Heliodor. Æthiop. ii. 16). So that, in an extreme case, the most precious of the two eyes should be sacrificed. The condemnation to the fire in the case of the "body" is alone spoken of, because the subject of discourse is the loss of offending members, in comparison with the loss of the whole body.

This literal view might, consequently, perhaps be justified. One expression in the text, however, throws doubt on it, namely, the predicate δεξιός applied to the eye and the hand. Is not the explanation just discussed more emphatic without it? "If thine eye be a source of constant temptation to thee, better lose thine eye than thy whole life." An expositor may, therefore, feel himself necessitated to take the expressions "eye" and "hand" figuratively; and the first suggestion is to take them as significative of the corresponding lusts. The organ, the member is frequently employed to denote the lust which works through it; most strikingly in Col. iii. 5: compare also the German proverbial sayings: "cut off a man's long fingers; draw his sweet tooth." So Jerome, "per dextram autem et cæteras corporis partes voluntatis et affectus initia demonstrantur;" Theodoret, Heraclitus (in the Cat. of Cramer), ὀφθαλμὸν λέγει τὸν λογισμὸν τῆς ἐπιθυμίας; Glossa ordinaris, Luther, Calvin, Bullinger, "affectus sunt animi membra;" Coccejus, Bengel. Stier forcibly observes: "Every absolute 'thou shalt not' involves the addition, 'even though thou shouldst die in consequence,'—as may actually be the case when a man suddenly breaks off from vicious habits." The appended words, βάλε ἀπὸ σοῦ, might appear to confirm this view of the evil desire. And were it to be objected that the word δεξιός renders such a view inadmissible, we might say, with Bucer and De Wette, that the Lawgiver looks at the desire itself as a good; as though He said, "Thy desires which are so dear to thee, and the source of so much enjoyment." Calvin's opinion, that, on this view, the expression would be somewhat hyperbolical, is incorrect. The denial even of the dearest pleasure is required;[1] but **according to** Augustine (**see** de civ. Dei, **xvi.** 21) the hyperbolical element is, "iste tropus fit, quando id quod dicitur longe est amplius, quam quod eo significatur." Against this view it might notwithstanding be urged, that the duty to root out evil lusts is self-evident, and that, consequently, it could not be mentioned as something extreme: further, also, that then the comparison evidently drawn between the part and the whole would be lost; for, according to it, the *minus* is not a merely apparent good and really an evil, but, in its measure, a genuine good. The same difficulties arise if we understand, with Jansenius, a Lapide, Tirinus, external things apparently good, such as, "lascivientes sodales, adspectus, contactus," which are, strictly speaking, of evil. Olshausen refers the eye and hand to actual organs of the body,—limiting, however, in his explanation, the "plucking out," and "cutting off," to "withholding ourselves from, or restraining ourselves in, **their use.**" In chap. xviii. 8, 9, where the same saying occurs, Olshausen thinks that the members, as contrasted with the whole body, are intended to denote the intellectual powers and capacities, which ought not further to be developed, as soon as it is felt that they are a hindrance to the highest and all-embracing principle of life. Now, such an admonition might indeed be approved of, if what is spoken of were some unimportant faculties or capacities, but not where the question is of **decided** talents and gifts. To suppress such gifts from fear of sinning, would be conduct like that of the servant whom the Lord so severely censured, who said, "I was afraid, because thou art a hard man: therefore have I kept thy

---

[1] Commentators have in general made a false use of the figure of hyperbole. Much that is erroneous in this respect may be found in the writings of Flacius, Glassius, Mascho ("Unterricht von den biblischen Tropen und Figuren," 1773), Tzschucke (Commentarius rhetoricus de Sermone Jesu Christi, p. 256); the last mentioned, however, **lays down correct principles.** Flacius, for example, in his "Clavis," characterizes the description of love in 1 Cor. xiii. **as** hyperbolical; so Reinhard the formula, "unio mystica," in his "Dogmatik;" **according to** Ammon (see his observation on Ernesti's "Instit. hermeneut.," ed. 5, p. 130), even the expression ἄνθρωπος Θεοῦ is a "formula hyperbolica." Even Wilke's "Rhetorik" is not satisfactory on this point (see p. 843).

pound in a napkin" (Luke xix. 20). Imperfect and unessential dilettante gifts, however, could not be said to stand to the very "kernel of life," in the same relation as a member to the whole body.

The question might now be asked, whether the *lesser* good does not rather lie outside the individual; and whether Christ does not mean *real possessions,* which, in case they become a snare, must be abandoned. So Chrysostom, Augustin, Isidorus Pelusiota, Pellicanus, Flacius: "Friends, spouse, relatives, counsellors,—*e.g.,* the eye, the counsellor to wisdom; the hand, to action (St Augustin),— these it is that are spoken of here, whenever they become an occasion of temptation." No further objection can be raised against this figurative view, than that this *outward* good is not so well fitted to form a contrast to the body: we prefer, however, to recur to the first-mentioned opinion of Pricæus and Löscher, and to understand the expression literally,—only adding, that the case specified is an extreme one, such as can never actually occur.

Vers. 31, 32. But few interpreters have recognised the close connection between this command and the preceding; yet it is suggested even by the very abbreviated expression, ἐῤῥέθη δέ. We cannot, with Beza, explain the omission of τοῖς ἀρχαίοις —presupposing the ablative view—on the ground that the Old Testaments words are here quoted literally; for there is a change in the words here as well as in ver. 43, where τοῖς ἀρχαίοις is also omitted.[1] Chrysostom remarks correctly: οὐ πρότερον ἐπὶ τὰ ἔμπροσθεν πρόεισιν, ἕως τὰ πρότερα ἐκκαθάρῃ καλῶς· ἰδοὺ γὰρ καὶ ἕτερον δείκνυσιν ἡμῖν πάλιν μοιχείας εἶδος. The indissolubleness of the bond of marriage is also a proof that the sphere of μοιχεία is much wider. Consequently there exists here a clear connection. But that the discussions on divorce in chap. xix. 3—19 could not have occurred if Jesus had not here given utterance to such a saying, is not so evident as Köstlin (p. 47) asserts. Why could not the Pharisees have found some other opportunity, and some other place, for making this question a matter of dispute?

---

[1] Druthmar, taking τοῖς ἀρχαίοις as a Dative, thinks that it is omitted in the present instance, in order to indicate that the ordinance in question was not of God, but was merely a concession of the Lawgiver.

Literature of the Subject.

Ugolini, "Thes. Antiq." T. xxx.; Selden, "Uxor Hebraica," Wittenb. 1712; Maimonides, "de Hebr. juribus divortii," ed. Sonneschmid, 1718; Michaelis, "Mosaisches Recht," ii.; Danz, "Uxor maritum repudians," in Meuschen's "N. T. e Talmude illustratum," p. 688; Beza, "de repudiis et divortiis, 1573," in the "tract. theol. ii.;" Gerhard, "loci theol." T. xv., xvi.; Daub, "System der theol. Moral," ii. 2. Abth. 1843, p. 3 f.; Schleiermacher, "die Christliche Sitte," 1843, p. 336 f.; Harless, "Christliche Ethik," § 52; Rothe, "Theol. Ethik," § 1089 f.; Liebetrut, "Die Ehe nach ihrer Idee und ihrer geschichtlichen Entwickelung," 1834; Märklin, "über die Ehe, eine dogmatisch-kirchenrechtliche Abhandlung," in Klaiber's "Studien der Würtembergischen Geistlichkeit," B. v. H. 2, B. vi. H. 2, B. vii. H. 1.—In R. Catholic theological literature, see Klee, "die Ehe, eine dogmatisch-archäologische Abhandlung," 1833; Pabst, "Adam und Christus, zur Theorie der Ehe," 1835; Oischinger, "die christl. Ehe," 1852.—Fichte, "Naturrecht," p. 174 f., "Sittenlehre," p. 443 f.; Schleiermacher, "Entwurf des Systems der Sittenlehre," § 258 f.; Hegel, "Grundlinien der Philos. des Rechts," § 161—167; Martensen, "Grundriss des Systems der Moralphilosophie," 1845; Wirth, "System der speculativen Ethik," 1841, ii. § 12 f.—In Ecclesiastical Law, see v. Moy, "von der Ehe und der Stellung der Kath. Kirche in Deutschland," 1830; Uhrig, "System des (Kath.) Eherechts," 1854; Strippelmann, "das Ehescheidungsrecht," 1854; Göschen, the article on "Marriage" in Herzog's "theol. Realencyklopädie."—For an historical view of the question, see Stäudlin's "Geschichte und Vorstellungen von der Ehe," 1826; which, however, is but a collection of facts and data.

Ver. 31. (1.) *Marriage and divorce according to Moses and the tradition of the Pharisees.*

The very remarkable saying recorded in Gen. ii. 23, 24, as uttered in the earliest period of the world's history, represents marriage, in its true idea, as an indissoluble bond of union between two individuals of different sexes. Notwithstanding, we find polygamy practised in the time of the patriarchs, as well as in that of the Mosaic legislation. Jewish tradition, and following its example, the Koran also, limits the number of wives to four; the high-priest was only allowed one; kings, eighteen. Here and there a higher view of marriage was defended: Gamaliel enjoined monogamy, under penalty of excommunication (Selden, 1, 9). Even in the time of Justin we find the Rabbins practising polygamy (dial. c. Tryph., p. 226, ed. Par.): the Emperor Theodosius enacted a special law, anno 393, forbidding polygamy to the Jews. Higher requirements respecting the marriage-tie are not mentioned, either in the law or by the Rabbins. According to the latter, the three conditions laid down in Ex. xxi. 9, 10, for a maid married to the son of her master, apply also to wives generally. In addition, seven other obligations are enumerated, the majority of which have reference to money affairs. So also the matrimonial duties of the wife are limited to cooking, nursing, and other similar things (tr. Gittin, ed. Surenh., P. iii. p. 73). In juridical treatises, such as the two which treat of matrimonial affairs, "de libellis matrimonialibus," and "de libellis divortii," we should naturally expect to find only legal distinctions; but, although in other parts of the Talmud the juridical and ethical elements are not kept very strictly separate, in this the latter altogether fails. Still, the Book of Tobit sets before us a pleasing picture of married life in ancient times; and that a knowledge of the nature of true conjugal love was not lacking, is evident especially from various tender expressions concerning a first marriage, and from warnings against the divorce of the first wife. We may see this even from Mal. ii. 14, 15, where reference is made to Abraham's married life as a model. (Sir. vii. 21; Gemara, tr. Sanhedrin, f. 22, 1, לכל תמורה חוץ מאשת נעוריו, "Everything may be gained back again save the wife of one's youth.") In marriage, however, the husband is the κύριος (1 Pet. iii. 6); and as such he alone has the right to send away his wife (שלח, ἀπολύειν,[1] ἀποπέμπειν), but not the

---

[1] The word ἀπολύειν is used of the wife who divorces her husband in Diod. Sic. 12, 18. The expression employed in Attica for a husband separating from his wife, was ἀποπέμπειν, ἐκβάλλειν; that for the wife separating from her husband, ἀπολείπειν (see Meier and Schömann's "der Attische Process," S. 413). Other expressions are, in Paul and Josephus, χωρίζεσθαι, διαζεύγνυμι, ἀφιέναι; in Philo and Plutarch, ἀπαλλάσσειν; in the ecclesiastical writers, ἐκβάλλειν, ἐξωθεῖν (see Cotel. "Patres apost." i. 463).

wife the husband.¹ This discharge was effected by means of
a letter of divorce, written in the presence of witnesses: it was
designate סֵפֶר כְּרִיתֻת in the Septuagint, βιβλίον ἀποστασίου;²
and in the Talmud, גֵּט. This right of the husband was not,
however, entirely uncontrolled. By way of punishment, it was

---

¹ In these circumstances, Mark x. 12, where the prohibition is extended to
the wife also, is somewhat remarkable. Cases did indeed occur, during the
time of the Herods, when the Jewish people was sunk in coarseness and immorality, of women deserting their husbands: *e. g.*, Herodias; a Salome also,
who sent her husband, Kostobaras, an Idumæan proselyte, a letter of divorce
(see Joseph. antiq. xv. 7, 10). Grotius is of opinion that a separation of
this kind is alluded to in John iv. 18; but on the case reported by him Josephus remarks: οὐ κατὰ τοὺς Ἰουδαίους νόμους. The wife is, of course, not
slavishly—that is, utterly without rights—bound to her husband. Adulterers,
for example, were to be punished with death for their breach of conjugal faith.
Moreover, wives were permitted to sue for divorce on certain charges. If a
husband failed to fulfil the ten conditions laid down by Josephus, his wife
might lay a complaint. Amongst these conditions, the due fulfilment of connu-
bial rites occupies so decidedly the first place, that the Mishna decides how
often it ought to take place in each different class; it further commands that
legal proceedings be instituted, and divorce granted, in cases of non-fulfilment,
or even when there is **a change of rank (see Ketuboth** 5, 6, ed. Surenh. iii.
74). There were other conditions besides; such as leprosy, ten years' impotence, cruelty, etc. (Danz, "uxor maritum repudians," in Meuschen's "N. N.
e Talm. illustr.;" Selden, iii 16, 17; Michaelis, "Mos. Recht," ii. 270). But
no use can be made of these ordinances in connection with Mark x. 12. The
words of the Lord refer to an ἀπολύειν τὸν ἄνδρα: in the cases just alluded
to, the wife instituted legal proceedings in order to *get a letter of divorce from
her husband.* The reading adopted by Fritzsche, from Cod. D, ἐὰν γυνὴ
ἐξέλθῃ ἀπὸ τ. ἀνδρός, is evidently a mere escape from a difficulty It would
be a far readier and less questionable course to admit **an** expansion of the
words of the Lord, borrowed by evangelical tradition from Paul (see 1 Cor. vii.
13: γυναῖκα ἀπὸ ἀνδρὸς μὴ χωρισθῆναι). Still, how is **this** possible, when it
is universally allowed that the expression παραγγέλλει ὁ κύριος contains an
allusion to an historical tradition of the Lord? And must we not, therefore,
assume that, either in His conversation with the Pharisees (see chap. xix.),
or in this place, the prohibition was expressed with greater completeness, and
in application to both **man** and wife, for the purpose of exhausting the idea
of the indissolubleness of marriage? Separation on the part of the wife
appears to have occurred but rarely in the time of St Jerome, the fourth century; **for** Jerome was obliged expressly to justify Fabiola, who had been divorced from her adulterous husband, and had married again: "quidquid viris
jubetur, id consequenter redundat in feminas" (ep. 77, ad Oceanum).

² The form τον, instead of τα, belongs to the later period of the language
(Lobeck, "Phrynichus," p. 517); still, the phrase δίκη ἀποστασίου was employed

ordained that the marriage should be indissoluble whenever the wife had been dishonoured before marriage, or her conduct as a wife calumniated (Deut. xxii. 19, 24). Otherwise, the *moral* right to divorce a wife was limited to the case specified in Deut. xxiv. 1.

This ground of divorce, however, was interpreted more or less strictly, according to the greater or less laxness of the tendency that prevailed in the rabbinical schools. Some few raised a warning voice against divorce on frivolous pretences (see Prov. vi. 32; Sirach vii. 21, 28). Compare, however, also Sirach xxv. 26, εἰ μὴ πορεύεται (γυνὴ πονηρὰ) κατὰ χεῖρά σου, ἀπὸ τῶν σαρκῶν σου ἀπότεμε αὐτήν: Ben Syra sententiæ, n. 3, גָרְמָא דְּנָפִיל לְחוּלָקָךְ גְּרָדִיהּ, "Gnaw the bone which has fallen to thy share;" on which the Hebrew Commentary edited by Fagius remarks: "If he send her away, he doeth not well; for he will never more have an hour of gladness, but constant sadness." At that time there existed two schools of pharisaic Rabbinism,—one rigid and casuistical, the other more lax. Trigland, in his "de secta Caræor.," p. 98, reports the saying of a Caræan: בֵּית שַׁמַּאי לְעוֹלָם מַחְמִירִים וּבֵית הִלֵּל מְקִלִּים, "The Shammaites always make the law severer, the Hillelites relax it." In regard to the ground of divorce now under consideration, the one party were too rigid, and the other to lax. By עֶרְוַת דָּבָר, which the Talmud calls בִּעוּר, the Shammaites understood an *indecorum,* whoredom, going out without veil, with arms entirely uncovered, etc., appealing to Deut. xix. 15—"an impropriety which rests on the evidence of two witnesses;" the Hillelites explained it "an impropriety, or on account of something else" (Selden, "uxor Ebræa," 3, 16—21; Buxtorf, "Spons. et divort.," p. 85, 122). The Hillelites had the Halacha, the current view, of what was allowable, in their favour; so that, as we are informed in the Gemara, the Shammaites, although they clung firmly to their own opinions in all other matters of dispute, finally gave way on this one point, and the Caræans alone remained true to the stricter view (Wolf, "notitia Caræorum," p. 98), until, in 1290, R. Levi

even in the early Attic legal style of the charge brought by a master against a servant who sought to escape from his power (see Heffter, "die athenäische Gerichtsverfassung," S. 249).

ben Gerson brought even the Talmudists to the same rigid judgment. The baseness of the motives which the Mishna allows may be learnt from the following: "If his wife falls sick, the husband must cure her; but if he is unwilling, then let him give her a letter of divorce, and say, Cure thyself" (tr. Ketuboth 4, 9, Surenh. iii. 71). It is but a **natural consequence** of Hillelism, when R. Akiba, whose opinion is usually adduced as a third one, following the Mishna, **considers any reason whatever a sufficient justification of divorce**: "**even if the wife have** only **put too** much salt into the food;" or, "if another please me better;" and quotes the Scripture as an authority in his favour, because it is said at the beginning of Deut. xxiv. 1: אִם־לֹא תִמְצָא־חֵן בְּעֵינָיו. In accordance with the Halacha, Onkelos, and also Targum Jonathan, translate עֶרְוַת דָּבָר by עֲבֵירַת פִּתְגָם, that is, "trespass is some matter." Josephus also ("Antiq." iv. 8, 23) was not acquainted with any other view: γυναικὸς τῆς συνοικούσης βουλόμενος διαζευχϑῆναι καϑ᾽ ἃς δηποτοῦν αἰτίας (πολλαὶ δ᾽ ἂν τοῖς ἀνϑρώποις τοιαῦται γένοιντο) γράμμασι μὲν περὶ τοῦ μηδέποτε συνελϑεῖν ἰσχυριζέσϑω. Concerning his own second wife, **he says** that he sent her away μὴ ἀρεσκόμενος τοῖς ἤϑεσι ("vita," § 76). We read also in Philo ("de leg. spec.," p. 781, ed. Fr.), ἐὰν δὲ ἀνδρὸς ἀπαλλαγεῖσα γυνὴ καϑ᾽ ἣν ἂν τύχῃ πρόφασιν, κ.τ.λ. It is therefore fair to conclude that the question put by the Pharisees in Matt. xix.: εἰ ἔξεστι τ. γυναῖκα αὐτοῦ ἀπολῦσαι κατὰ πᾶσαν αἰτίαν, expressed the **view** then prevailing in the school of Hillel. **The law is adduced** in that passage as if the **only condition of divorce** were the giving of the usual letter: and, practically, this was so; for in the letters of divorce nothing was said with regard to the **cause of the divorce**. Here, therefore, the law was wrested by means of lax omissions, as, in other cases, by means of superadded limitations.

Ver. 32. (2.) *Marriage and divorce according to the Christian* πλήρωσις. We have already directed attention to the consideration, that, in the present case, the πλήρωσις **cannot be regarded as** a mere deepening of a superficial view of the law, but only as **a** *correction* (p. 158). Precisely here, however, we derive help from the more detailed explanation in chap. xix.;— from it we learn that the Mosaic permission of divorce was rather regarded as a temporary adaptation of the original idea of marriage to the needs of the Jewish nation; and that Christ sought to restore it to its original position. It must certainly have caused a nation, whose laws sanctioned polygamy and divorce, the greatest astonishment to find in the very earliest pages of its history a view of marriage expressed, of a far higher character, to which the Redeemer was able to refer, and which He at once appropriated as His own. "Because God in the beginning created man and woman for each other, they shall enter into so close a fellowship with each other, that the man shall subordinate his filial relationship to this, shall leave his father's house in order to found a family of his own (so even Targum Jonathan), and they two shall become one flesh." So far as these words contain the reason of the ordinance concerning marriage laid down in the Sermon on the Mount, the commentator ought to take them into consideration at the very outset. As regards form, the citations from Gen. i. 27, and ii. 24, are—apart from the omission of αὐτοῦ after πατέρα, and the writing of κολληθήσεται instead of προσκολληθήσεται— taken verbatim from the Septuagint, by which, as also by the Samaritan version, the words οἱ δύο, which are not in the original text, were added. Bleek's observations lead him to the conclusion, that the reported discourses of Christ display, at all events for the most part, this dependence on the translations ("Beiträge zur Ev. Kritik," S. 57; Ritschl in Zeller's Jahrb. 1851, S. 520). The saying, ἕνεκεν τούτου, κ.τ.λ., is introduced by the Saviour as spoken by God, by means of the formula καὶ εἶπεν, sc. ὁ ποιήσας αὐτούς. Commentators have therefore differed as to whether it is Adam who there speaks, assuming the tone of a prophet, or whether it is the historian who adds a reflection of his own. Augustine took the former view (i. 9, 13, in Gen. ad litt.); and his example was followed by Bengel, and more recently by Baumgarten in his "Commentary on the Pentateuch:" "At the sight of the woman, the mystery of marriage was revealed to Adam's clear vision." Calvin's observation is true: "postquam historice retulit, quod gestum a Deo erat, finem quoque divinæ institutionis demonstrat." This deduction contains nothing that was not already involved in the words, "flesh of my flesh." But relative to the quotation of the words as spoken by God, Calov's remark, "Spiritu S. per Mosen loquente," holds good: the Epistle to the Hebrews adduces sayings as words of God, in which God is spoken of in the third person (i. 6, 7, 8). The words of the historian did but give utterance to that which was implicitly contained in the Divine act of the creation of the two sexes. Now, although the words ἕνεκεν τούτου point back to Adam's saying, "flesh of my flesh," still the Saviour did not intend to quote them: He referred to the original account of the creation in Gen. i. 27, to the fact of the creation of the two sexes,—in which fact it was involved that they were destined for each other, and destined for each other in such a way, that the γίνεσθαι εἰς σάρκα μίαν might be predicated thereof. In defining the true idea of marriage, it is of no little importance accurately to weigh the phrase εἰς σάρκα μίαν: Delitzsch and many other commentators pass it over. Beginning with the derived idea of "affinitas," Le Clerc explains, "intima affinitate conjuncti;" referring to the words, "flesh of my flesh," Tuch translates, "one body:" so also Chrysostom, ὥσπερ οὖν σάρκα τέμνειν ἐναγές, οὕτω καὶ γυναῖκα διαστῆσαι παράνομον: the "Constit. Apostol." (vi. 14), ἡ γὰρ γυνὴ κοινωνός ἐστι βίου, ἑνουμένη εἰς ἓν σῶμα ἐκ δύο παρὰ Θεοῦ, Mercerus and Elsner; Baumgarten-Crusius renders, "life, existence;" Maldonatus and Stier, "one person;" Neander and De Wette, "one organism, one life-unity." These expositors, for the most part, are satisfied with the *sensus,* and pass by the *significatus:* most writers have not gone beyond that general idea of close union, which is expressed in such classical sayings as, συντῆξαι καὶ συμφῦσαι εἰς τὸ αὐτὸ (Plato, "Sympos." 192); ἐρῶντας γενέσθαι ἐκ δύο ὄντων ἀμφοτέρους ἕνα, adduced by Arist. (Pol., 2, 2) as the view of Aristophanes; ὥστε δύο ὄντας ἕνα γεγονέναι (Plut., "Sympos." i.). The context leaves little room to doubt that there is an allusion to the words, "flesh of my flesh," which had preceded: consequently, commentators were undoubtedly justified in contenting themselves with the general idea of close relationship. In any case, however, it would be quite another question whether the interpretation of the Saviour, and of the Apostle in 1 Cor. vi. 16, does not put a more definite construction on the words—a construction expressing the real nature of marriage. This is the opinion of those interpreters who consider that the main element of the intimate union is indicated by the particular terms chosen. According to the majority of rabbinical commentators, the expression directs attention to the concrete unity of the paternal and maternal principle, manifesting itself in the child as the fruit of marriage: according to Maimonides, attention is drawn to the fact, that man limits the satisfaction of his sexual instincts to one and the same individual of his kind, whereas to animals this is a matter of indifference. To this kind of vinculum conjugale refer also, Chrysostom, Jerome, Calvin, and others: Isid. (Pel. 4, ep. 129), on the contrary (he quotes 1 Cor. vii. 4), Olevian, and Hemming, understand the expression of the copula conjugalis.[1] If the interpretation given by the Apostle may be taken as a standard, thee unquestionably the last-mentioned view is first suggested by the words of 1 Cor. vi. 16, οὐκ οἴδατε, ὅτι ὁ κολλώμενος τῇ πόρνῃ ἓν σῶμά ἐστιν (to which, according to Krüger's Greek Grammar, § 60, 7, αὐτῇ should be supplied), for which a foundation is adduced in ver. 17 from Gen. ii. 24. This unity of the two is so real and entire, that it manifests itself even in the physical sphere. Such is the opinion of Olshausen, Harless, Stier, and Meyer. But when Stier replies to Olshausen,—who considers the primary element in marriage to be the unity of souls, and the physical oneness but as the complement to the former,—"No; that is marriage as idealized by man, but by no means as actually instituted by God. Were this fantastic notion of marriage a just one, there could be no actual marriage without unity of soul, and then the discovery of want of affinity and sympathy would furnish a valid ground of divorce,"—his polemical zeal evidently carries him too far. When he on his side declares that "physical community is not only the basis, but also the only essential element of marriage," he overlooks what even a Maimonides hinted at, namely, that the distinction between the satisfaction of a man's sexual impulses and that of a beast's, consists in the former's choosing *one individual*—a choice presupposing a certain spiritual attraction. The same writer is perfectly in the right, however (compare Harless, "Ethik," S. 269), as opposed to such spiritualistic views as those advanced in an

---

[1] Uniting these various references, Calov explains: "sunt una caro, (1.) per dilectionis consensum (Eph. v. 28); (2.) per indissolubile vinculum (Matt. xix. 6); (3.) per individuum vitæ consortium (1 Cor. vii. 20); (4.) per copulæ conjugalis officium (1 Cor. vii. 3); (5.) per copulæ conjugalis *fructum*."

article on the "Indissolubleness of Marriage," published in the "Evangelische Kirchenzeitung" of 1837. That article says: "There has never been a doubt (?) in the Church that the marriage-bond is tied as soon as the spirits of both parties have become one; and that, on the contrary, whenever only the flesh has become one, no marriage is concluded." To such a Platonic love, not only the Church, but also Scripture, is opposed. The teachings of Christ and the Apostles leave no room to doubt that spiritual oneness, be it perfect or imperfect, reaches its completion in physical oneness; then also the two persons are permanently appropriated to each other. Were it otherwise, why did Christ pronounce merely the **marrying** again, and not also the separation, $\mu οιχεία$? Why did even Moses forbid a reunion with a divorced woman, only in cases when she had in the meantime become the wife of another (Deut. xxiv. 1 f.)? St Paul evidently regards the matter thus, when he describes the carnal union with a harlot as a surrender of one's own personality to her; when he characterizes fornication, in quite a different sense from drunkenness or even suicide, as a sin against a man's own body, in so far as it ceases to be his own property (1 Cor. vi. 16, 18, compare 1 Cor. vii. 4). And inasmuch as persons who enter into sexual union with each other make a mutual surrender of themselves, a "oneness of life" is established, like that which subsists between body and soul: it can therefore be said, $\dot{o}\ \dot{\alpha}\gamma\alpha\pi\tilde{\omega}\nu\ \tau\dot{\eta}\nu\ \dot{\epsilon}\alpha\upsilon\tau o\tilde{\upsilon}\ \gamma\upsilon\nu\alpha\tilde{\imath}\kappa\alpha$, $\dot{\epsilon}\alpha\upsilon\tau\dot{o}\nu\ \dot{\alpha}\gamma\alpha\pi\tilde{q}$ (Eph. v. 28, 29). To be divorced from one's wife, is consequently, as Sirach says in chap. xxv. 26, equivalent to being rent $\dot{\alpha}\pi\dot{o}\ \tau\tilde{\omega}\nu\ \sigma\alpha\rho\kappa\tilde{\omega}\nu\ \alpha\dot{\upsilon}\tau o\tilde{\upsilon}$. Accordingly, the Biblical idea of marriage, so far as it is to be learnt **from** the saying before us, is the following: Marriage **is a Divine** institution, having for its aim, to bring man and woman to an indissoluble unity of body and spirit, that they may thus mutually complement each other, and lay the foundation of a family. The philosophers and jurists of the seventeenth and eighteenth centuries were long in error on **this** subject; and first, in recent times, have Fichte and Hegel[1] brought to light the true nature

---

[1] Hegel was the first to reassert the true idea of marriage, as opposed both to that which represents it as having its final purpose in the increase of the population, and to that which represents it as originating in an urbitrary contract: "Under the category of a *contract*, marriage cannot be placed;

and importance of the idea of marriage. There are, however, some traces of its not having been wholly unappreciated, even in classical antiquity. It lies at the foundation of the Platonic myth of the Andregyne in the Symposium: and this myth may perhaps be referred to an older Asiatic tradition (compare in Bopp's "Conjugations-system," S. 284, the passage from the "White Veda," and Fortlage's "Philosoph. Meditationen über Plato's Symposium," 1835, S. 132). Specially remarkable is the following saying of Antipater (probably the Stoic of Tarsus), from the work περὶ γάμου in Stobæus' "Floril." tit. 67, 25: συμβέβηκε δὲ καὶ τὸν μὴ πεῖραν ἐσχηκότα γαμετῆς γυναικὸς κ. τέκνων ἄγευστον εἶναι τῆς ἀληθινοτάτης κ. γνησίου εὐνοίας. Αἱ μὲν γὰρ ἄλλαι φιλίαι καὶ φιλοστοργίαι ἐοίκασι ταῖς τῶν ὀσπρίων κατὰ τὰς παραθέσεις μίξεσιν. Αἱ δ' ἀνδρὸς καὶ γυναικὸς ταῖς δι' ὅλων κράσεσιν ὡς οἶνος ὕδατι, καὶ τοῦτο ἔτι μὲν μίσγεται δι' ὅλων. Οὐ γὰρ μόνον τῆς οὐσίας καὶ τῶν τέκνων καὶ τῆς ψυχῆς, ἀλλὰ καὶ τῶν σωμάτων οὗτοι μόνοι κοινωνοῦσιν. Compare, besides, other unexpectedly deep sayings in the section of Stobæus' work entitled, ὅτι κάλλιστον γάμος.

The judgment pronounced by the Saviour on the subject of divorce, is based on this idea of marriage. In relation to the original institution of marriage, the Mosaic permission of divorce was a relaxation. On ch. xix. Jerome remarks: "considera, quod non dixit: permisit vobis *Deus* sed Moyses, ut juxta ap. 1 Cor. vii. consilium sit hominis, non imperium Dei." Attention should also be drawn to the consideration, that from Deut. xxiv. 1, the passage in question, the letter of divorce does not appear to have been a peculiarly Mosaic institution. The structure of the unusually long antecedent (vers. 1—3) is rightly analyzed by Abarbanel (see Buxt. "de divortiis"); by the Vulgate and Luther, on the contrary, it is misunderstood. This latter indeed has translated the words as if Moses commanded or conceded the writing of letters of divorce; whereas the existence of the custom of doing so is presupposed. The ground for allowing this custom to continue, was the σκληροκαρδία of the people, which would have manifested itself in murders and violence had the laws rigidly upheld the indissolubleness of marriage. A lawgiver, who can only maintain the authority of the law by means

although it is so placed by Kant, *scandalously* we must say."—Hegel, Philosophie des Rechts. § 75.

of punishments, shows his wisdom in so attempering his enactments to the moral condition of the nation, that he may never have to order punishments which it is impossible to execute. Plutarch well remarks on the impossibility of carrying out the bloody Draconian laws: δεῖ πρὸς τὸ δυνατὸν γράφεσθαι τὸν νόμον, εἰ βούλεται χρησίμως ὀλίγους, ἀλλὰ μὴ πολλοὺς ἀχρηστῶς κολάζειν. Still, both the institution retained, and the command added by Moses, imposed three restrictions on any disposition to act arbitrarily in this matter. In the *first* place, the letter of divorce was to be executed before witnesses, and with certain formalities: *secondly,* after its despatch, a renewal of the bond once severed was not possible (Deut. xxiv. 4)—a condition which constituted no slight hindrance to separations from momentary excitement: *thirdly,* the limitation to the case of עֶרְוַת דָּבָר. By the interpretation of the school of Hillel, this last restriction was rendered illusory. By substituting adultery for the עֶרְוַת דָּבָר, the Saviour gave the Mosaic restrictions their πλήρωσις. The school of Shammai recognised no other valid ground of divorce than unchaste conduct; this restriction was enforced by Christ to its full extent, and shown to be a matter of necessity and not of arbitrary appointment. "Quodcunque enim," so taught the old Protestant theologians (see Gerh. conf. cath. iv. 248), "ipsam conjugii formam" (in the terminology of the present day, forma is essence, idea), "tollit, propter illud separatio quoad vinculum fieri potest. Atqui adulterium formam conjugii tollit, quia solvit unitatem carnis." Theodoret says, in his "disp. 9, de græc. affect. curatione" (N. T. ed. Hal. p. 944): μίαν μόνον ἀφορμὴν διαλύσεως ἔδωκε, τὴν ἀληθῶς διασπῶσαν τὴν ζεύγλην. If, according to 1 Cor. vi. 16, the προσκολλᾶσθαι τῇ πόρνῃ is equivalent to ἓν σῶμα γενέσθαι αὐτῇ, then an unfaithful husband or wife enters into a new bond of marriage in the very act of unfaithfulness, and must naturally for a time feel bound thereby. He therefore who seeks a divorce except on this ground, drives his wife, in case she marry again without being loosed from the first bond, into adultery; and he who marries the wife divorced in such a way, also commits the same sin. It follows also, that he who has thus divorced his wife is guilty of μοιχεία if he marry again, as is declared in Matt. xix., 9, καὶ γαμήσῃ ἄλλην. Socinus says: "quo loquendi modo magis ob oculos ponit et quantum sit delictum dimittere citra prædictam causam uxorem suam, et quod hac dimissione non efficiat, ut non amplius sit sua uxor." The saying is therefore directed non against divorce on other grounds than πορνεία, but against separation followed by a new and unjustified marriage.

Παρεκτὸς λόγου πορνείας. An exception which is omitted in Luke xvi. 18, Mark x. 11, 1 Cor. vii. 10, 11; not however, for the reason assigned by Grotius, "exceptiones ex naturæ æquitate venientes tacitæ insunt omnibus legibus quantumvis generaliter pronunciatis," but because the actual separation which takes place in adultery is not so much a ground for divorce as a divorcing of oneself. Λόγος, in Hellenistic and classical Greek, is equivalent to the word αἰτία used in Matt. xix. 3, and to πρόφασις used by the Septuagint in Ex. xviii. 16, xxii. 8; see also Acts x. 29 (compare Kypke on the last passage.) That it is a mere periphrasis, as Schwarz (see Olearius, "de Stylo N. T." p. 270) and Palairet think, cannot be shown from examples such as εἰς ἀργύριον λόγον. Selden and Kypke defend the meaning "proportio," "analogy;" but Matt. xix. 9 is opposed thereto. Hackspan and Wolf take λόγος in the sense of πρᾶγμα, and λόγον πορνείας, therefore, as equivalent to πρᾶγμά τι πορνικόν: but that λόγος is used in this way as identical with דָּבָר, notwithstanding that Bretschneider (Lex. N. T.) grants it, cannot be proved from the New Testament. There is properly a distinction between πορνεία and μοιχεία: Theodoret, on Rom. i. 29, defines the former, ἡ οὐ κατὰ γάμον συνουσία. Greg. Nyss. remarks, in his "Epist. canon." ii. 118, πορνεία ἐστὶ καὶ λέγεται ἡ χωρὶς ἀδικίας ἑτέρου γενομένη, τισὶ τῆς ἐπιθυμίας ἐκπλήρωσις. The word, however, signifies extra-conjugial satisfaction of the sexual appetite in general, and therefore includes μοιχεία. Clemens Alex. "Strom." iii. 552 (Ed. Pott.): ἡ ἐκ τοῦ ἑνὸς γάμου εἰς τοὺς πολλοὺς ἔκπτωσις. Thus have the translators, without intending to indicate a difference of meaning, expressed now πορνεία, and then μοιχεία. Itala, Ulf., Luther, have the latter; the Vulgate and Syriac, the former. But the reason why πορνεία is selected, is not so much, as De Wette thinks, "because it is at the same time used in a wider sense," but because the moral aspect of the transgression is more distinctly indicated by the *genus*. In order to gain a larger warrant for divorce, the lexical meaning of the expression has been widened. Paulus was of opinion, that it referred only to unchastity before marriage; but, apart from other considerations, that offence was punished by stoning (see Deut. xxii. 21). Another extension is suggested by the use of the expression, "whoredom," in regard to God, both in the Old and New Testament. Hence Hermas says (see "Pastor," 2, 4): "non modo mœchatio est illis, qui carnem suam coinquinant, sed et is qui simulacrum facit, mœchatur;" Augustine: "omnino quaslibet illicitas concupiscentias quæ animam corpore male utentem a lege Dei aberrare faciunt et perniciose turpiterque corrumpunt." [1] Origen, who suggests the doubt as to whether poisoning, child-murder, secret pilfering of her husband, are not as great crimes as adultery, seeks to escape from the difficulty by means of an unnatural explanation of παρεκτός ("in Matt." iii. 648): "Whoso separates for every other reason than adultery." Augustine struck into the same path: in his view, παρεκτός and εἰ μή (chap. xix. 9) are to be understood, not as *negative*, but as *exceptive* (see his "de adult. conj." l. i. c. 4). His example was followed by Bellarmine, by the most recent Catholic commentator, Arnoldi, and by others (see Gerh. conf. cath. iv. 261). Zwingli thinks that the **ground** of divorce here specified, is adduced merely by way of illustration: "hic enim mos est Sacræ Scripturæ, ut uno exemplo contenta universa ejusdem generis exempla comprehendat." Grotius was disposed to extend the application of πορνεία to "omnis modus imminutæ pudicitiæ;" was further inclined to follow in Origen's footsteps, but finally drew back to the position, that in the **interpretation** of the law, due regard must be paid to the *analogia juris*. So De Wette also, without properly considering why sexual union with another person, and this only, is a ground for divorce:— he says, "In so far as He allows one actual ground of divorce, He allows more than one." More might be urged in favour of those who maintain that πορνεία should be interpreted in the sense of ver. **28**, and that "there is a reference to every deeper disturbance of the unity existing between husband and wife." So Stier, who thus surrenders the consequence necessarily flowing from his view of marriage: he asks, "Shall we limit the words of the Lord here to the coarser aspect of the

---

[1] At a later period he vacillated, and wrote in his "Retract." i. 19: "nec volo in re tanta tamque ad dignoscendum difficili putare lectorem istam sibi nostram disputationem debere sufficere, **sed legat et alia,**" etc.

matter, when He Himself shortly before gave another view thereof?" So all those who defend the spiritualistic view of marriage before alluded to, which mistakes the significance of the copula carnalis: for example, Baumg.-Crusius, in his comments on this passage; and Daub, in his "System der Moral," ii. 1, S. 25, who, after quoting the saying before us, remarks: "The sole condition of the indissolubleness of marriage is, that the marriage be a real one,—that is, be based on the virtues of unlimited confidence and faithfulness." Marheineke says, in his "theol. Moral" (1847, S. 508), "The words of Matt. xix. 6 refer not only to the actual fact of adultery, which is unchastity, but to everything that strikes at the very roots of marriage." Heumann ascribes the strictness of the prohibition to temporary causes, to opposition to the excessive license of the Jews: Schleiermacher, on the other hand, regards the considerate exception of the single case πορνεία, as a concession to the Jews, to whom Christ spake (see his "Christliche Sittenlehre," S. 340). In general, it has been thought possible to elude the application of the words under consideration to our own relations, by pleading that the New Testament speaks of divorces which were effected without the supervision of a court of justice (see Michaelis on the passage; Reinhard's "Moral," iii. 396, 4 A.; Flatt, "Moral," S. 579; De Wette, "Sittenlehre," iii. S. 249, and many others). It is undoubtedly true that public authoritative decisions on divorce, according to fixed laws, afford a sure guarantee against arbitrariness; but, the decision being left to the judgment of the magistracy, can it, if it be really Christian, take any other standard than the command of Christ? With the least ceremony, Märklin thus cuts off all further inquiries: "The Saviour may have been acquainted with the fundamental view of marriage, but He was not aware of the necessary consequences thereof" (see the "Studien der Würtemb. Geistlichkeit," B. iii. H. 1, S. 119).

After the preceding investigation, our conclusion can be no other than this: that, according to Christ's view of marriage, there is but one valid ground of divorce a vinculo, the ground expressed in the words, "until death you part." Adultery, as has been said, is not so much a reason for divorce, as itself an actual divorce (Marheineke, "Moral" S. 507; Rothe, "Ethik," iii. 637). Nay more, were the copula carnalis so unessential an element of marriage as the spiritualistic view represents it, one might agree with Rothe in his opinion, that divorce is not accomplished even when husband and wife are outwardly separated by death. But if a marriage is dissolved when the natural sexual conditions thereof are done away with, then surely our own view receives confirmation from Matt. xxii. 36.

We may now pass to the consideration of St Paul's doctrine on this subject. To all appearance, he allows at least one other valid ground of divorce; and if there be *one* other, why not *several* others, analogous to the one?

Let us first endeavour to determine the relation in which St Paul's own explanation, introduced by the words, τοῖς δὲ λοιποῖς ἐγὼ λέγω, οὐχ ὁ κύριος, stands to the command of the Lord, introduced by the words, τοῖς δὲ γεγαμηκόσι παραγγέλλω οὐκ ἐγώ, ἀλλ' ὁ κύριος:—the command, namely, γυναῖκα ἀπὸ ἀνδρὸς μὴ χωρισθῆναι καὶ ἄνδρα γυναῖκα μὴ ἀφιέναι. Theologians of the greatest variety of opinions have arrived at the conviction, that the Apostle did not intend to institute a subordinating contrast between his own command and that of Christ (see Usteri, De Wette, Meyer, Baur, v. Gerlach). According to chap. xiv. 37, the Apostle considers the ἐντολαί communicated to him by revelation as equally binding with those historically given by the Lord. The relation is rather the following:—The general principle was laid down by the Lord; and in virtue of the *revelation* which he had received, the Apostle applies that general principle **to the particular** cases occurring in the course of his experience. Accordingly, those who are united to unbelievers are dissuaded from seeking a divorce even on the ground of difference of religion. If the spiritualistic view of marriage were the Apostle's, how could he fail to regard *this separation of soul in the most inward region of the spirit as a justification of divorce,* as, in fact, the Roman Catholic Church has done? He says: εἰ δὲ ὁ ἄπιστος χωρίζεται, χωριζέσθω· οὐ δεδούλωται ὁ ἀδελφὸς ἢ ἡ ἀδελφὴ ἐν τοῖς τοιούτοις: and proceeds, ἐν δὲ εἰρήνῃ κέκληκεν ἡμᾶς ὁ Θεός. Τί γὰρ οἶδας, γύναι, εἰ τὸν ἄνδρα σώσεις, κ.τ.λ. Here arise two questions: namely,—1. Are the words, οὐ δεδούλωται, equivalent to δέδεται in ver. 39, which forms a contrast to ἐλευθέρα ἐστὶν, ᾧ θέλει γαμηθῆναι, as Ambrosiaster, Calvin on ver. 12, and Beza on ver. 15, explain it? 2. Do not the words, ἐν δὲ εἰρήνῃ, contain an indirect exhortation rather to dissolve the union and to seek another?

In regard to the first question, Nitzsch is of opinion (see his "System der christlichen Lehre," § 200), that the view quoted is unavoidable, inasmuch as "in the case supposed by St Paul, it was self-evident that the one who was wickedly forsaken could not be under obligation to continue outwardly living with the other. Ultra posse nemo obligatur." But could not the wife beseech and strive, in the various ways which love would suggest, to prevent her husband from carrying out his purpose? The evidence drawn from the language used by the Rabbins in their marriage-contracts appears to be stronger: for example, שֵׁיעֲבַד is used of the vinculum matrimonii; but as we are unable to determine the period to which such words belong, the proof for the contrary from ver. 11 is much stronger: ἐὰν δὲ καὶ χωρισθῇ, μενέτω ἄγαμος. If it be conceded that St Paul sets forth the words of our Lord, with his own parenthetical explanation, as expressing a general principle, how could he afterwards, in carrying it out, speak in opposition to it? Besides, we must bear in mind that the words, ἐν δὲ εἰρήνῃ, κ.τ.λ., show what spirit guided him in his injunctions. Here, however, there is a still greater divergence amongst interpreters. Luther, Este, Bengel, Semler, De Wette, and Meyer explain: "What thinkest thou then, that thou"—; consequently, as an admonition to peaceableness in such a sense that, in order to avoid quarrels, the bond should *not* be too anxiously maintained. On the other hand, Chrysostom, Calvin, Grotius, Calov, Billroth, Rückert, Olshausen, and most others, render: "But cling to the bond of concord, for thou canst not know whether thou shalt not," etc. Every one will at once feel constrained to admit that such a negative idea of peaceableness, consisting in a mere "going out of the way," is little in accordance with the spirit of Christianity. The question may, however, be asked, whether the meaning given to the words by the last explanation is grammatically justifiable. I had at first referred to the Hebrew מִי יוֹדֵעַ, which, like the German phrase, "wer weiss, ob" (who knows, whether), is used in Eccless. iii. 21, viii. 1, to express doubt or denial: but in 2 Sam. xii. 22; Joel ii. 14; Jonah iii. 9, it is used to express hope, like the German, "wer weiss—er kommt" (who knows but he will come)? Of Meyer I have here the complaint to make, that he has left unnoticed the arguments I advanced in favour of the affirmative sense. He satisfies himself with the dictatorial remark, "εἰ cannot be used for εἰ μή—not even in 2 Sam. xii. 22: Joel ii. 14; Jonah iii. 9." De Wette grants that מִי־יוֹדֵעַ, in the passages quoted, are "expressive of modest hope:" Hitzig also is of the same view (see his remarks on Joel ii. 14). The former, however, next goes on to say: "But this does not justify an explanation opposed alike to usage and to the immediate context." What the context requires, is matter of dispute: and an explanation which has those Old Testament passage in its favour cannot be opposed to usage. An as example of מִי יוֹדֵעַ אִם, which De Wette failed to discover, I adduced Esther iv. 14, translated by him: "Who knoweth whether thou art not come to the kingdom for the sake of this time?" I have also in my favour the classical use of the formula in the Heraclitical fragment from Euripides, frequently quoted by Origen and others: τίς εἶδεν, εἰ τὸ ζῆν μέν ἐστι κατθανεῖν, τὸ κατθανεῖν δὲ ζῆν; It is allowed that Euripides here, in his Oriental manner, simply suggests an affirmation: hence Aristophanes parodied the unhellenic sentence in his "Frogs" (see Küster on Suidas, s. v. τίς οἶδεν, and Conz and Bergler on Aristoph. "Ranæ," v. 1514). Even οὐκ οἶδα εἰ, which corresponds not to the Latin "haud scio an," but to "vereor ut," leaves the matter, at all events in some instances, quite undecided; so that it might occur (see Elmsley's Medea, v. 911, ed. Lips., p. 239, and Bornemann's Xenophon, conviv. 8, 9). In these circumstances, it cannot be disputed that the explanation of ver. 16 given above is admissible. Finally, there is this consideration,—is it not clear from vers. 17 that the general tendency of the Apostle's admonitions is to induce every one to remain in the condition in which he was when called?

A justification of second marriages we cannot therefore find in the case of so-called "desertio malitiosa" adduced by the Apostle, but rather a dissuasion therefrom, conjoined with a reference to Christian hopes.—St Paul also held the words, "till death you part," to have validity for Christian marriages (Rom. vii. 3). Among the early writers of the Church, the same result was arrived at by Clemens Alex. ("Stromata" ii. 506), Chrysostom, Hilary, Jerome. The last-mentioned remarks on

St Matt. xix. 10: "grave pondus uxorum, si excepta causa fornicationis eas dimittere non licet, quid enim si temulenta fuerit, si iracunda, si malis moribus, si luxuriosa, si gulosa, si vaga, si jurgatrix, si malefica, tenenda erat hujusmodi? *Volumus nolumus sustinenda est. Cum enim essemus liberi, voluntariæ nos subjecimus servituti.*"

With respect to the re-marriage of those who have been divorced for adultery, whether of the innocent or the guilty party, Scripture says nothing definite. Amongst the Jews, there could be no question of the guilty party marrying again, inasmuch as adulteresses and husbands committing adultery with wives were punished with death. Nor could it be thought of under Christianity, inasmuch as such characters were either excluded from the Church for seven years, or (after monastic establishments had been founded) adulteresses were compelled to retire to a convent for life. The legislation of the State having been permeated by Mosaic-Christian elements, Constantine enacted that both the adulteress and he who committed adultery with her should be punished with death: Justinian punished only the latter with death; the adulteress he banished into a convent. The "Bambergensis" followed Justinian; the "Sachsenspiegel" and the "Schwabenspiegel," Constantine. To the same strictness the Reformers inclined;[1] so also the Protestant provincial laws. Both the adulterer and the adulteress were punished with death by the Police Regulations of the Elector Moritz in 1542, of the Elector Augustus in 1572, and

---

[1] The question as to what is to be done with a divorced adulteress in case she cannot preserve her chastity, is answered by Luther, in the Short Catechism on the Ten Commandments (published in the year 1520: see Walch x. S. 723), as follows: "Answer—In order that there might be no need of asking this question, God commanded in the law to stone adulterers. The secular authorities should therefore use their sword to kill adulterers: but if the authorities are dilatory and careless, then may the offender flee into another land, and there wed if he cannot contain. It were better, however, for the sake of avoiding a bad example, that he should be put to death." Melanchthon also, in his Comm. and the Loci theolog., decides in favour of death or perpetual banishment. Calvin and Bucer frequently complain against the authorities for not punishing adulterers with death; and Beza joyfully narrates, in his work, "de divortiis et repudiis." op. theol. ii. 89, how that at last, "communi suffragio," the citizens of Geneva had decreed to punish adultery with death.

of the State of Mecklenburg in 1572. As far as the Church is concerned, its sole primary business is to awaken the guilty one to penitence, and to press upon the innocent one the duty of receiving the offender when penitent, even as God receives him. Clear intimation would thus be given of the duty of the innocent party in a case of adultery. In the early Church, opposite views on this subject prevailed. Some not only allowed the innocent to marry again, but also forbade the offender to be taken back.[1] But milder views became generally prevalent. In Hermas (Pastor, mand. 4, c. 1) we read: "si scierit vir, uxorem suam deliquisse et non egerit pœnitentiam mulier et permanet in fornicatione sua et convivit cum illa vir, reus erit peccati ejus et particeps mœchationis ejus.—Et dixi illi: quid, si mulier dimissa pœnitentiam egerit et voluerit ad virum suum reverti, nonne recipietur a viro suo? Et dixit mihi: imo, si non receperit eam vir suus, peccat, et magnum peccatum sibi admittit, sed debet recipere peccatricem, quæ pœnitentiam egit, sed non sæpe, servis enim Dei pœnitentia una est." Only as exceptions to the rule does Origen (t. xiv. in Matt.) mention cases in which bishops permitted wives to marry again during the lifetime of their husbands (and, though Erasmus in his observations on 1 Cor. vii. calls it in question, they where certainly such as had been divorced). The Council of Nantes, in can. xii. (see Cotelerius on the Patres Apostolici i. 86), ordained that

---

[1] According to Attic and Roman law, a husband who omitted to divorce his wife taken in adultery fell into ἀτιμία. The "Constitut. Apost." appear to sanction **the same** legal severity (see l. vi. c. 14): ὁ κατέχων τὴν παραφθαρεῖσαν, φύσεως θεσμοῦ παράνομος· ἐπείπερ ὁ κατέχων μοιχαλίδα, ἄφρων καὶ ἀσεβής. 'Ἀπότεμε γάρ αὐτὴν (Prov. xviii. 12) φησίν, ἀπὸ τῶν σαρκῶν σου. Οὐ γάρ ἐστι βοηθὸς ἀλλ' ἐπίβουλος πρὸς ἄλλον ἀποκλίνασα τὴν διάνοιαν. Possibly, however, only the continuation of the marriage-relationship with an impenitent adulteress is here spoken of: compare the passage from Hermas quoted above. St Jerome is against re-marriage in his remarks on chap. xix. 9, although he defended Fabiola: so also Tertullian ("de monog." c. 9) and Basil. The latter pronounces in "Can. 26 ad Amphib." against the marriage of a **paramour** and his mistress; in Can. 31 against re-marriage in a case of "desertio malitiosa," so long as the death of the deserter remained uncertain; in Can. 21 **he strictly requires of wives that they should receive again their** adulterous husbands, but imposes not the same duty on husbands in relation to adulterous wives. He then adds: καὶ τούτων δὲ ὁ λόγος οὐ ῥᾴδιος, ἡ δὲ συνήθεια οὕτω κεκράτηκε. Then stricter view prevailed in the Council of Elvira (A. 325), and of Carthage (A. 407).

an adulteress should do penance seven years, after which her husband might take her to himself again, provided he did penance with her, and both came to the table of the Lord in company. Augustine's judgment had great influence in this matter. In his work, "De Fide et Operibus," c. 19, he confesses, "venialiter falli quemque," who thinks that Christ's words warrant the innocent party in a divorce to marry again; and in his "De conjugiis adulterinis" he declares that the innocent party ought to remain unmarried, and to await the repentance of the guilty; for that man verily will neither reap damage nor disgrace who unites himself again with an adulteress like her to whom Christ said, "Therefore neither do I condemn thee; go hence and sin no more." In the "De nuptiis et concupiscentia" (l. i. c. 10) he says: "manent inter viventes semel inita jura nuptiarum ut potius sint inter se conjuges, qui ab alterutro separati sunt, quam cum his quibus aliis adhæserunt." The same divergence is observable also in the ecclesiastical regulations of a later period: the Church of ancient Britain forbade the divorced to marry again; the Anglo-Saxon and Frankish Church allowed them (see Richter's "Kirchenrecht," § 268, Anm. 12). After the ninth century, the papal prohibition as it exists at the present time in the Romish Church, gained more and more the upper hand (see Richter, p. 569, 4 ed.).—The Evangelical Church reasserted afresh the right of the innocent party in a divorce to marry again: Calvin says: "si innocenti personae non concederetur aliud conjugium, id esset *nomine* divortium, non re;" the guilty party was delivered over to the civil authorities.

Now, though we may have shown this to be the Christian $\pi\lambda\acute{\eta}\rho\omega\sigma\iota\varsigma$ of the idea of marriage, the question is not yet answered, whether we are to consider it as an ecclesiastical law laid down for all who are baptized in the name of Christ, or only as a moral admonition: still less is the question answered, whether these narrow limits relate only to the Church, or also to the State? On the former question, let us first note the decided expressions of Stier: "Both the secular laws of the State (which is in fact Christian), and even ecclesiastical law (which cannot be independent of the State), not only *may* observe a Mosaic considerateness ($\pi\rho\grave{o}\varsigma\ \sigma\kappa\lambda\eta\rho o\kappa\alpha\rho\delta\acute{\iota}\alpha\nu$), but must do so, when the same conditions present themselves. We can no more do away with divorce than with oaths." So also Daub, Marheineke, Nitzsch, Rothe. At the same time, as the latter shows (iii. 635), among Christians "measures must be taken to prevent arbitrary divorces;" that is, they must not depend on the inclination of individuals, but on the judgment of the recognised authorities. Marheinecke says (see p. 505): "No true marriage can be annulled. It may, however, happen that the true idea of marriage is not realized in a particular instance: then the relation in which the two sides stand to each other is an abstract one, and no true marriage has been effected. In such a case, the judicial annulment is but the outward and formal declaration of the reality, of that which is,—to wit, of the unreality of the marriage." But that the appeal to the Mosaic $\sigma\kappa\lambda\eta\rho\omega\kappa\alpha\rho\delta i\alpha$, in this case, renders the argument "somewhat unsound," is allowed even by Rothe. On the members of His kingdom, Christ made the high claims embodied in the Sermon on the Mount: how, then, can they plead for a relaxation which had force only for the pedagogic, that is, the Mosaic, economy? If, according to Matt. xxviii. 20, baptism pledges us to the $\tau\eta\rho\epsilon\tilde{\iota}\nu\ \pi\acute{a}\nu\tau\alpha\ \ddot{o}\sigma\alpha\ \dot{\epsilon}\nu\epsilon\tau\epsilon\iota\lambda\acute{a}\mu\eta\nu\ \dot{\upsilon}\mu\tilde{\iota}\nu$, why should it not pledge us also to the observance of this particular $\dot{\epsilon}\nu\tau o\lambda\acute{\eta}$? If it is incumbent on the Church to exercise discipline at all, how can it refrain when a separation takes place contrary to the command of Christ, or when such Christians as have been divorce in defiance of the Christian idea of marriage, claim the blessing of the Church on their second marriage? On this ground, earnest-minded theologians have of late emphatically protested against the Church's bestowing its blessing in cases of that kind. (See Jul. Müller's "Christus und unser Zeitalter in Bezug auf die Ehebündnisse Geschiedener," in the "Evang. Kirchenzeitung," 1829, n. 22, and his "Zwei Vorträge über Ehescheidung," 1855; O. v. Gerlach, "Ueber das Gutachten der Bonner Facultät über Ehescheidungen," in the "Evang. Kirchenzeitung," 1836, and his "Welches ist das Recht der ev. Kirche in Bezug auf Ehescheidungen?" 1839). We sympatize with the moral earnestness to which these protests owe their origin; but still we do not see how they can be put into practice, without the most formidable moral dangers to the family and the State, so long as there is withheld from the Protestant Church the right to that kind of separation, without which even the Roman Catholic Church would be in no position to carry out her absolute prohibition of second marriages to the divorced,—the right, namely, to the "separatio secundum torum et mensam."

We are thus compelled to regard the Church as bound by the letter of the Scriptures; but it is otherwise with the State, even with a Christian State. The State, being the administrator of law, takes up, even as Christian, the position of the lawgiver of the Old Testament theocracy; and what was allowed to the latter, out of regard to the σκληροκαρδία of the people, must also be allowed to lawgivers in Christian states. (Compare what has been said on this point above.) Even a Moses could only realize the idea of marriage within the limits imposed by the rudeness of the condition of the Jews; and the Christian lawgiver is in a precisely similar position. Hence, from the very first establishment of a Christian State down to the present day, legislators have allowed other grounds of divorce besides those sanctioned by Scripture. So far now as the Church is unprepared to submit to State-legislation, and as the people are not *church-like* enough to submit to Church-legislation, this want of agreement between the principles of the latter and the actual procedure of the former, cannot fail to end in the introduction of civil marriages. This the Church certainly cannot desire; though, on the other hand, in the present ecclesiastical condition of the people, as experience proves in those countries where civil marriages are permitted, she has, so far, no cause for alarm.

Finally, by way of supplement to our exegetical observations, let us take a survey of the history of opinion on marriage and divorce. We begin with the classical world. From the heroic age onwards, monogamy was the rule among the Greeks:—bigamy only the doubtful exception. On the other hand, however, concubinage was sanctioned, both by law and custom, alongside of marriage. For the legal permission of the παλλακία, see Diog. Laertius l. ii. c. 26: a paramour found with the παλλακή might be slain just as an adulterer (see Lysias, de cæde Erat. § 31). Characteristic is the relative purpose assigned respectively to Hetæræ, concubines, and wives in the (Pseudo?) Demosth. c. Neæram 1386, 19: τὰς μὲν γὰρ ἑταίρας ἡδονῆς ἕνεκ᾽ ἔχομεν· τὰς δὲ παλλακὰς, τῆς καθ᾽ ἡμέραν θεραπείας τοῦ σώματος· τὰς δὲ γυναῖκας τοῦ παιδοποιεῖσθαι γνησίως, καὶ τῶν ἔνδον φύλακα πιστὴν ἔχειν. This was the prevailing view of the purpose of marriage; its proper aim was παιδοποιεῖσθαι (see Xenoph. Memorab. 2, 2, 4): hence in Sparta— in Athens also, according to Plutarch—marriage was a duty legally binding on citizens. By mutual agreement, marriages could be at once dissolved: the husband also could ἀποπέμπειν his wife, on returning her dowry: the wife had to lay her complaint of κάκωσις in a legal form (see Meier's "att. Process," S. 413; Becker's "Charicles," ii. 488). If a husband caught his wife in the act of adultery, he was at liberty to take revenge; in other cases, severe penalties awaited the crime (see Meier's "att. Process," S. 330). Nobler views of the nature of marriage may be found in Plutarch (γαμικὰ παραδείγματα), who, to the shame of Christian legislative chambers, specifies oneness of religious faith as essential to a prosperous marriage (c. 19). Compare Lasaulx, "Zur Phil. der Ehe b. d. Griechen" in the "Abh. der Münchner Akad." 1853.—The austerity of ancient Roman manners may be seen even in their marriage-relationships. The idea of marriage set forth by the Roman jurists surpasses that of many of the jurists and philosophers of Christendom. In the Pandects, Modestinus explains it to be, "consortium omnis vitæ, divini et humani juris communicatio" (de ritu Nupt. l. 1); he also says, "nuptiæ sunt viri et mulieris conjunctio individuam vitæ consuetudinem continens" (see "Instit. de patria potest." § 2). It is related by Tertullian (apol. c. 6), that in the first 520 years after the foundation of the city, no case of divorce had ever arisen; this statement, however, is not quite reliable (compare Savigny, in the "Abhandl. der Berliner Akad." 1814 and 1815; and Göttling's "Geschichte der röm. Staatsverfassung," S. 99). When a man and his wife had quarrelled, a conference in the sacellum of the Dea Viriplaca effected their reconciliation, and they returned from the abode of the deity in amity (Valer. Max. ii. 1, 6). With old-fashioned simplicity, Cato declares that he counts it far more praiseworthy to be a good husband than a great senator (Plutarch, "Vita Catonis," c. 20). Still, with all the honour paid her at that time, the wife was placed in the most entire dependence: only for the husband did the right to divorce exist, and that too on very slight grounds. Not even in a case of adultery had a wife this right. This sanctity of the relationship between the sexes was weakened, however, by the express legalization of concubinage, as a kind of subordinate marriage for the unmarried. Romulus permitted husbands to dissolve the stricter marriage (by *confarreatio*) on four conditions. On the whole, however, this appears to have been as uncommon, as the dissolution of free marriages was frequent in the later ages of the Republic. Emilius Paulus put away his wife without being able to give any reason; Cicero divorced Terentia because she had contracted a trifling debt, and Publilia because she appeared to rejoice at the death of his daughter Tullia. Wives also, at that time, began to separate themselves from their husbands, and that with such levity, that Juvenal in his day says, "fiunt octo mariti quinque per autumnos" (vi. v. 228).

After Christianity became the religion of the people and of the State, the regulations of the State ceased to be coincident with those of the Church. We have seen above, that the only ground of divorce recognised by the Christian Church as allowable, was adultery: even the case mentioned by St Paul in 1 Cor. xii. 15 is so commented on by the Fathers, with the single exception of Ambrosiaster, that it is evident they thought of a divorce without the right of marrying again. Nay more, as we have already shown, even in cases of divorce for adultery, it was the rule for the innocent party to renounce all claim to a second marriage. When the Emperors had adopted Christianity, and Christians customs had obtained supremacy amongst a large portion of the population, the earlier laws were no longer able to keep their ground, and the regulations concerning marriage-relationship were altered in various respects. Under Constantine the prohibition of concubinage to married people was renewed, that of celibacy was abrogated, and restrictions were put on divorce. Divorces, cum bona gratia—that is, by mutual agreement—remained; and the right to move for a divorce was conceded to wives, under the following circumstances: 1. if the husband be a homicida; 2. or a medicamentarius (poisoner); 3. or a sepulchrorum dissolutor:—the husband had the same right if his wife were, 1. adultera; 2. medicamentaria; 3. conciliatrix, that is, a procuress (cod. Theol. l. i. de repudiis 3, 16). As a large portion of the population were still heathens, one cannot be surprised at the moderateness of the restrictions imposed: even adultery on the part of the husband does not appear among the causes for divorce. The later legislation was even more indulgent in regard to the grounds for divorce. Under Theodosian I., thirteen grounds of separation were valid for the wife, seventeen for the husband. Both the Gothic, Burgundian, and other legal codes, sanction divorces on such pleas as witchcraft, spoliation of graves, etc. (see Strippelmann's "Ehescheidungsrecht," S. 52).

Thus arose collisions with the laws of the State, which, as the secular authorities still maintained their supremacy, were not infrequently a source of great distress to the Church. When Fabiola was blamed for availing herself of the right of divorce, which, according to the ancient Roman notion, belonged only to the husband, Jerome replied: "aliæ sunt leges Cæsarum, aliæ Christi, aliud Papianus, aliud Paulus noster præcipit." This disagreement with the civil law is shown by Gregory Nazianzen, when he says (Ep. 176, [211]): τὸ ἀποστάσιον τοῖς ἡμετέροις ἀπαράσκει πάντως νόμοις, κἂν οἱ Ῥωμαίων ἑτέρως κρίνωσι. At the time when the lax laws of Theodosian were still in force, St Ambrose said (l. viii. in Luc. xvi.): "Dimittis uxorem quasi jure sine crimine, et putas id tibi licere, quia lex humana non prohibet; sed divina prohibet. Qui hominibus obsequeris, Deum verere." Still, even within the Church itself, different opinions were held, and different decrees were passed relative to the grounds of divorce. Councils and provincial synods in the East and the West sometimes admitted such grounds of divorce as the following: attempts at assassination, desertio malitiosa, leprosy, etc. (see Cotelerius' "Patres apost." i. S. 88). From the time when the re-marriage of divorced persons was prohibited, the Church escaped all collisions with the State, in so far as, for the idea of *divortium*—an idea capable of so wide an application—that of *separatio secundum torum et mensam* was substituted. After Lombardus had classed marriage among the Sacraments, the doctrine in relation to it took the form in which it was afterwards expressed by the Council of Trent. The justification of the prohibition of the marriage of the innocent party in a divorce on the ground of adultery, was still a source of difficulty, showing very clearly how, in the face of certain immoveable assumptions, the plainest statement of Scripture may be made to give way. Kistemaker thinks that the Saviour only intended to define the intention of the *Mosaic* law (see his work, "Ueber den Primat Petri und das Eheband," Münster, 1806, S. 113); Hug regards the exception given in St Matt. xix. 9 as spurious, and the mention of this exception in Matt. v. 32 as a temporary accommodation, preparatory to the stricter decision (see his Essay, "de conjugii vinculo indissolubili," in the Freiburger theol. Zeitschrift). Jäger resorts to the most vigorous measures, and declares the words in question, in both passages, to be interpolations (see his "Untersuchung, ob die Ehescheidung nach der Schrift und der Kirche ältester Zeit erlaubt sei," Arnstadt, 1804). Waibel recurs to the desperate expedient, adopted by Paulus Burgensis, of maintaining that Christ gave the command only for the Jews ("Von dem Sacramente der Ehe," Augsburg, 1830, S. 44). Maldonatus, Jansenius, and Cornelius a Lapide conceive that the reference is to a lifelong separatio quoad torum et mensam; and, taking the words, ὃς ἐὰν ἀπολελυμένην, κ.τ.λ., by themselves, they argue that ἀπολύειν does not loosen the vinculum even in a case of πορνεία. In this, however, they overlooked, on the one hand, the fact, that the inquiring Pharisees and Jews were unacquainted with such separatio quoad torum et mensam: and, on the other hand, the new difficulty arising from the fact, that other reasons might suffice to justify such a separation as this. The latest Catholic exegesis has fallen back on the explanation of Augustine (see Arnoldi "Ausleg. d. Matth.," 1855): "Whoso putteth away his wife, save for the cause of fornication, *and the like,* etc. And whoso marrieth *a* woman put away (—not *the* woman put away; not, therefore, as if the words, παρεκτὸς τοῦ λόγου πορνείας, required to be supplied from the preceding context, and this particular case were excepted), etc." *Three* reasons justified a lifelong separation secundum torum et mensam,— namely, the adultery of either the husband of the wife, the crime of sodomy, and apostasy from the true faith: *six*, a temporary separation,—namely, great moral corruptness, irresistible aversion, mental aberration, a voluntary determination on the part of both to devote their life in a higher way to God, persistent infectious disease, and malicious desertion. (See Uhrig's "Eherecht," S. 800. Compare also Chemnitz's attack on the doctrine of the Council of Trent, in his "Examen conc. Trid." P. ii. can. 7, and that of Gerhard, in his "Loci theolog." T. xvi.)

The polemic of the Protestant Church was directed, in the first instance, against the sacramental view of marriage, and in connection therewith, against its being treated exclusively as a matter for Church-legislation. At the commencement of his career, Luther also made a distinction amongst baptized Christians, between the great "heathenish mass," and those "who wished to be really Christians." "'T were better to put such as are not willing to obey Christ under the law of Moses, rather than see them quarrelling with each other continually. They ought, however, to be told that they never were Christians, but are under a heathenish law. But if thou be a Christian, thou mayest not seek a divorce" (Walch's Ed. iii. 411). "For this reason we will not go further, inasmuch as we see what ought to be the conduct of such as mean to be true Christians. As to those who are no Christians, they do not concern us, inasmuch as they are to be ruled, not by the Gospel, but by force and penalties" (see "Bergpredigt" in Walch, iii. 668). Whereupon Otto von Gerlach remarks (see his "Kirchenrechtliche Untersuchung der Frage: welches ist die Lehre und das Recht der evang. Kirche in Bezug auf Ehescheidungen?" 1839), that if Luther had carried this distinction into practice, the result must have been the institution of civil marriage; and, as a final consequence, exclusion from the Evangelical Church. But nothing further came of an opposition which originated in a first impression.[1] In his work, "Vom ehelichen Leben," 1522, Luther enumerates the following as grounds on which a Christian may justly seek divorce:—1. Adultery; 2. Impotence; 3. Refusal to discharge the functions of marriage; 4. Malicious desertion. In his work, "Von Ehesachen," 1530, on the contrary, the grounds of divorce are limited to two, namely, adultery and malicious desertion. Dishonourable casti-

---

[1] It was some time before Luther arrived at a clear and definite judgment on the marriage-question. In his treatise, "De captivitate Babylon." 1520, he went so far as to sanction marriage even with a heathen! "I will not consent to such hindrance as difference of religion, which will not permit a man to marry a wife who is unbaptized, even with the hope of converting her, much less without such a reason. Who has forbidden it? God, or man? Who has given man the authority to forbid such marriages? Patricius, the heathen, married Monica, the mother of St Augustine, a Christian: and why should it not be allowed at the present day?" (see Walch, xix. 8. 123.)

gation, for example, he did not count a sufficient reason, but judged that it was a "mishap which they should be content to endure; for, having become one body, they must continue such, come honour or disgrace, poverty or wealth." Attempts on life he did regard as constituting a valid ground, but declares that a husband must run the risk of concealed danger, and against open dangers the authorities can defend him (Walch, x. 950). Luther's view is shared by Calvin (in Matt. xix.), with this exception, that he hesitates somewhat in regard to the desertio malitiosa. Melanchthon, on the other hand, appealing to the *lex Theodosiana* (de conjugio), adds *sævitiæ* (attempts on life): Zwingli allows several reasons equivalent to πορνεία (vid. supra, p. 229).

Consistories and marriage-tribunals having been once established in the Protestant Church, marriage affairs were subjected to the jurisdiction of the clergy, as in the Romish Church. Only in the eighteenth century, and first of all in Prussia, did the claims of the Church in this respect begin to be disregarded; Hesse, Baden, Bavaria, Saxony, and others followed: and until the late Concordat, even the R. Catholic Church was compelled, in Austria, to stand by and see marriage affairs subjected to the control of the civil power. Until about the middle of the eighteenth century no grounds of divorce, save the two allowed by Luther and Calvin, were generally sanctioned by the statutes of the Protestant Church, the Consistories, and the writers on ecclesiastical law. The only exceptions were the following:—In the Swiss Church, the Zürich marriage statutes of the year 1525, and the Basle Church Canon of 1529, which allowed such grounds as cruelty, insanity, and the like; in Prussia, the consistorial ordinance of 1584, which also included cruelty, and attempts on life; in Wirtemberg, the marriage law of 1687, which approved such grounds as denegatio debiti conjugalis, sodomy, incest. Similar grounds commended themselves also to the private judgment of individual theologians of the sixteenth and seventeenth centuries: for example, Sarcerius and Danäus considered morbus insanabilis a sufficient reason; Henning, immanis violentia, or deportatio propter crimen; Hunnius, denegatio debiti conjugalis.

A new epoch in the opinions held regarding this moral relationship began with that so-called period of "Illumination," the way for which, even in the sphere of law, was prepared by Thomasius. The delegation of the ecclesiastical power to the civil rulers was followed by the investment of the civil courts with authority in marriage affairs, as being *civil* affairs. Such is the view advocated by Kayser in his "disp. de jure principis ev. circa divortia," held in Halle in 1715, under the presidency of J. H. Böhmer. Hereupon a number of new reasons for divorce were insisted on; such as, "uncongeniality of disposition," "irreconcileable enmity," and the like (compare Strippelmann's "Ehescheidungsrecht," S. 88). After the middle of the eighteenth century, the influence of this laxity began to extend even to the statute-books. Not only crime, but even misfortune, was accepted as a valid ground for divorce. At last the Prussian legislation, having arrived at the highest pitch of "illumination," sanctioned divorce by mutual consent where the marriage was childless, thus changing it into a matter of contract and private law.

III. THE PROHIBITION OF OATHS. VERS. 33—37.

Literature of the Subject.

On the oaths in vogue amongst the Greeks and Romans, compare, Valckenaer's Opuscula, ed. Lips. T. i.; Lasaulx's "Ueber den Eid bei den Römern," 1844: on those of the Northern nations, see Grimm's "Rechtsalterthümer," Th. ii. On Mohammedan oaths, compare the excellent dissertation by Mill, "de Muhammedismo," etc., in the dissertat. selectæ, Ludg. Bat. 1743, p. 113. On oaths amongst the Jews, see the Tractate "Shebuoth," with the observations of Maimonides and Bartenora (Mischna, ed. Surenhus. T. iv.); Maimonides "Constitutiones de jurejurando," Ludg. Bat. 1706; Zeltner's "de jure vet. Hebr." Jen. 1693; Haltermann's "de formulis juram. Jud." Rost. 1701; Seb. Schmid's "fasc. disp.," disp. xi.; Leue "von der Natur des Eides," 1836; F. Bayer's "Betrachtungen über den Eid," 1836; Göschel's "Princip, Begriff und Gebrauch des Eides," 1837; W. Bauer's essay, "Ueber den Eid," in the "Denkschrift des theol. Seminars von Herborn für 1846." Amongst works on Ethics written from a theological point of view, compare especially Rothe's "Theologische Ethic," iii. 576. For the history of oaths, see Malblanc's "Doctr. de jurejurando e genuinis legum fontibus illustr.," 1781; and Stäudlin's "Ueber den Eid," 1824.

Ver. 33. In regards to both parts of the command adduced, it may appear doubtful whether distinct passages are quoted from the Old Testament. If this be the case with οὐκ ἐπιορκήσεις, then the command is based either on the third of the Decalogue (Ex. xx. 7), according to the Septuagint, οὐ λήψῃ τὸ ὄνομα κυρίου τοῦ Θεοῦ σου ἐπὶ ματαίῳ, or on Lev. xix. 12, לֹא־תִשָּׁבְעוּ בִשְׁמִי לַשָּׁקֶר, LXX. οὐκ ὀμεῖσθε τῷ ὀνόματί μου ἐπ' ἀδίκῳ. The antithetical words, ἀποδώσεις, κ.τ.λ., must refer to such passages as Num. xxx. 3; Deut. xxiii. 21. In the other passages, all the commandments, which Christ sets forth in their πλήρωσις, are from the Old Testament: we should therefore expect this to be the case here also, and be disposed to assume rather that the command is taken from the Decalogue, than from Leviticus. It is questionable, however, whether in Christ's day the words were understood of perjury, i.e., ἐπιορκεῖν—a point which commentators have neglected to investigate. Philo and Josephus (Antiq. iii. 5, 5) took the command in this sense: ἐπὶ μηδενὶ φαύλῳ τὸν Θεὸν ὀμνύναι. So also Socinus, Grotius, Rosenmüller (ad Ex.), and Ed. Meier (see his "Die Form des Dekalogs," S. 27): Ewald has advanced a new and arbitrary view in his "Geschichte Israels," ii. 152. That it is grammatically defensible is unquestionable, for לַשָּׁוְא alternates with לַשָּׁקֶר; whereas, in the command concerning bearing false witness, reported in Ex. xx. 16, the latter is employed; in Deut. v. 18, we find the former. At the same time, however, as Calvin rightly urged, we must allow that there is a decided difference between this latter and the third command. Hence both Calvin and Luther, in their exposition of the Decalogue, treat the third command as relating to sin against the majesty of God, whether through false or idle swearing. For this reason, among the Rabbins, Aben Ezra alone has taken לַשָּׁוְא and לַשָּׁקֶר as identical: he declares them to be בְּנֵי אָב אֶחָד, "children of the same father." Abarbanel, on the contrary, explains, הוא כולל לשקר ולכזב או לבטלה, "it includes at once the false and the frivolous oath." Jarchi and Kimchi limit the third command to frivolous oaths alone,—the former explaining it by לְחִנָּם, and the latter (in "Rad.") by שֶׁלֹּא תִשָּׁבַע בִּשְׁמִי כִּי אִם בִּיָּכוֹל, "thou shalt only swear when it is *necessary.*" Even the Septuagint rendering, ἐπὶ ματαίῳ, appears to have this sense, which Onkelos also has expressed by לְמַגָּנָא, and Jonathan by עַל מַגָּן, which is equivalent to חִנָּם, that is, temere, frustra. Maimonides, too (see his "constit. de jurejur." c. i. § 7), refers the command of the Decalogue to empty, wordy oaths, which it is impossible to carry out, or whose object is self-evident; as, for example, "that the heavens are the heavens:" the prohibition in Lev. xix. 12 he refers to practicable oaths. It can also be shown that the words, "the *Name* of Jehovah, thy God," in this third command, strengthened, if they did not originate, the superstitious fear of using the title "Jehovah" amongst the Jews. Jarchi observes on Lev. xix. 12, that there Moses writes only בִשְׁמִי, because in Ex. xx. he had written אֶת־שֵׁם־יְהֹוָה אֱלֹהֶיךָ, and that, since a man may possibly sin by using שֵׁם הַמְיֻוחָד, that is, "the name peculiar to God," it was necessary to bring together here all the names of God.—Inasmuch, then, as the application of the third commandment to frivolous oaths is so ancient and universal; as, moreover, a correct interpretation must include this reference, and the Saviour, therefore, probably included it; we are necessitated to conclude that the expression οὐκ ἐπιορκήσεις is based on Lev. xix. It may, of course, be asked: If, in the mind of Christ, the command in the Decalogue included trivial oaths, whilst He (as we think), by His antithesis, condemns *only* such oaths, why did He not rather unfold the true significance of the words, "to take the name of God in vain?" To this we reply: Because in this, as in other cases, our Lord Christ censured, not so much the *transgression* of the commandments, as the *weakening* of them.

In the present case, the command was weakened by means of the additional clause, ἀποδώσεις, κ.τ.λ. Though conceived in Biblical phraseology, it is evident that the only object of the clause was to restrict the application of the command either **to** *religious* vows, whose fulfilment was for the advantage of the hierarchy (Mark vii. 10, 11), or to *promissory* oaths, in which self-interest plays a larger part (see Grotius and Beza), **or to oaths in which the** name of *God* was expressly mentioned. **Both** here and in chap. xxiii. our Lord raises His protest against this **last evasion of** conscience; our second supposition has therefore the greater probability in its favour, as, in fact, most writers **acknowledge.**

Ver. 34, 35. If the words now before us are opposed to oaths in general as a πονηρόν, then is this command (which, however, Neander and Bleek neglect to quote in support of their views) most decidedly opposed to the Mosaic system, in which an oath was a religious act, a solemn confession to the true God. This opposition is most distinctly set forth by Theophylact: he says, μάθε ὅτι τότε οὐκ ἦν πονηρὸν (τὸ ὀμνύειν), μετὰ δὲ Χριστόν ἐστι πονηρὸν, ὥσπερ καὶ τὸ περιτέμνεσθαι καὶ Ἰουδαΐζειν! At first sight, one would undoubtedly conclude that the πλήρωσις of the Old Testament command consisted not merely in the prohibition of ἐπιορκεῖν, but even of εὐορκεῖν; not merely in the prohibition of *perjury*,[1] that is, a perversion of truth in a religious aspect, and of *violating* an oath, that is, not being true to a religious promise, but also of *all oaths in themselves*.—It will be necessary to take into consideration the meaning and construction of ὅλως. It is equivalent to τὸ ὅλον, τὰ ὅλα, τοῖς ὅλοις, used adverbially: compare πάντη, πάντως, πάντι, πᾶσι. Epictetus says, in his Enchir. (c. 33): ὅρκον παραιτήσαι, εἰ μὲν οἷόν τε, εἰς ἅπαν, εἰ δὲ μὴ, ἐκ τ. ἐνόντων. Ὅλως contrasts the genus with the individual, and forms the antithesis to κατὰ σμικρὰ and κατὰ μέρος (compare 1 Cor. v. 1, vi. 7, xv. 29; Plato, "Sophistes," § 22, ed. Heind.; Xenoph. "Memorabilia," vi. 1, 17, i. 2, 35; Wettstein on 1 Cor. v. 1). The question is, accordingly, What is the particular to which the general term, ὅλως, is here opposed? As our Lord's precept relates to the Old Testament command immediately preceding, the *species* of that, ἐπιορκεῖν, must be the individual to which the *genus*, ὀμνύειν, is opposed. Concisely and aptly does Bengel remark: "omnino utrumque, falso et vere jurandi genus, non tamen verum juramentum universaliter prohibet."[2] The antithesis would therefore be incorrectly understood, were we

---

[1] The German word "Meineid" (perjury) is derived from a substantive "Mein;" perfidia (Nibelungen, 3896). Compare Grimm's "Rechtsalterthümer," ii. 904. Originally, ἐπιορκέω = ὄμνυμι. As ἐπί in composition denotes also repetition, it has been thought that the change from the one meaning to the other arose from the "*frequent* swearing" (comp. Sirach xxiii. 10, ὁ ὀμνύων διὰ παντός, ἀπὸ ἁμαρτίας οὐ μὴ καθαρισθῇ). But it is more accurate to take ἐπί in the hostile sense.

[2] Ἁπλῶς, "without side-purpose," would have the same meaning: ἁπλῶς ἐκφέρειν, Dion. Halic. de Thucyd. 53, 2; Arist. "de mundo," 6, 12, μετὰ ἁπλῆς κινήσεως.

to suppose, with the opponents of all oaths, that all species of εὐορκεῖν are opposed to ὅλως: the words μὴ ὀμόσαι ὅλως which are dependent on λέγω, express nothing more than μὴ ὀμνύετε in James v. 12.

They do not, however, express less. The construction resorted to by many of the older writers, in order to connect ὅλως with the succeeding verses as forming a kind of summary of them, is forced and unnatural; and, besides, it renders ὅλως quite unnecessary. According to this construction, the translation would be, veto ne *quocunque modo* sic juretis: so Dan. Heinsius (see his "Exercitationes sacræ," Lugd. Bat. 1639), Beza, Chemnitz, Sarcerius, Er. Schmid, and Flatt ("Moral," S. 382); Heumann renders, "Ye shall not swear at all in that sense." The view which has been expounded by Maldonatus is similar: that ὅλως refers exclusively to the *form* of the oath,—hence "neither by God, nor even by any creature." This construction is possible, but there would then be no contrast to ἐπιορκήσεις. This last-mentioned construction was adopted without a consideration whether it gave a sense more favourable to the permissibility of oaths. Such a sense, however, would be obtained were we to translate ὅλως by "in general" (compare Gusset in "Vesp. Gron." S. 119, and Göschel, in Herzog's "Realencycl." under the word "Eid;"—"swear not on every occasion, and by everything"). In fact, to this meaning the formulas, ὅλως δέ, τὸ δὲ πᾶν, in the sense of "ne multa, denique," approximate: further, also ὅλως εἰπεῖν, τὸ δὲ ὅλον, τὰ ὅλα, τοῖς ὅλοις (compare Bremi on Demosth. "Olynth." iii. S. 187). In one passage of Aristotle ("Polit." ii. 2, § 4), it cannot be otherwise understood. The question there argued is, whether it be better to adopt the system of communism or of private property; and the philosopher decides, ὅλως, that is, in general, private property must exist.[1] The words, "in general, swear not," would therefore only be a warning against that usus promiscuus and temerarius of oaths which occurs in common life. But where an antithesis is subjoined, as in the present instance, not

---

[1] The passage runs as follows: ἕξει γὰρ τὸ ἐξ ἀμφοτέρων ἀγαθόν· λέγω δὲ τὸ ἐξ ἀμφοτέρων τὸ ἐκ τοῦ κοινὰς εἶναι τὰς κτήσεις καὶ τὸ ἐκ τοῦ ἰδίας· δεῖ γάρ πως μὲν εἶναι κοινάς, ὅλως ἰδίας. Garve paraphrases, "*as a general rule, on the whole,* everything must be some one's in peculiar;—in special circumstances, however, and in a partial respect, it must be regarded as common."

mentioning particular cases in which it is allowable to use oaths, but requiring in all cases the simple "yea, yea," such an expedient is plainly unallowable.

It would appear, then, that this πλήρωσις is in opposition to the Old Testament lawgiver: *he* prohibits perjury and violation of oaths: Christ forbids oaths themselves. Such an opposition must, to the highest degree, have excited surprise, on account of its variance with the Old Testament view of oaths. In Ex. xxii. 11 and Deut. vi. 13, x. 20, oaths by God are *commanded:* according to Isa. xix 18, lxv. 16; Jer. iv. 2; Ps. lxiii. 12,- they are a mark of the true worshippers of God; in Gen. xxii. 16; Isa. xlv. 23, God is represented as swearing by Himself. Jewish theologians have therefore ranked oaths among the rites of Divine worship, and amongst acts of confession of God. Maimonides says, in his "Constit. de jurejur." (see c. 11, § 1), השבועה בשמו הגדול מדרכי העבודה היא והדור וקדוש גדול הוא לחשבע בשמו, "an oath in the name of God is a kind of worship, it is an act of great reverence to swear in the name of God." With this compare the beautiful comment of Kimchi on Jer. iv. 2, the closing words of which are, "Not every man is fit to swear truly, אלא יראי השם יאהביו, but only such as fear and love God." Whereas, then, under the Old Covenant an oath was an act of worship, He who came to fulfil that covenant is held to have declared all oaths to be of the evil one, of the devil (ἐκ τοῦ πονηροῦ).[1] Were this so, we ought to inquire very zealously into the reason of this New Testament condemnation of oaths. It must have been based either on a deep and true knowledge of the nature of an oath, or on the immoral condition of him who takes an oath, or of him who requires an oath, or in both at once.

Recent theological writers on ethics, such as Sailer, Reinhard, De Wette, Harless, Rothe, and others, have unanimously decided that the Christian idea of an oath[2] is, "an affirmation of the

---

[1] Chrysostom felt that the expression, ἐκ τοῦ πονηροῦ, brought him into collision with the authority of the Old Covenant, if it is to be applied to oaths as such: he takes refuge this difficulty in the figure of hyperbole: ἐκ τοῦ πονηροῦ ὤμησεν αὐτὰ εἶναι, οὐχ ἵνα δείξῃ τοῦ διαβόλου τὴν παλαιὰν οὖσαν, ἀλλ' ἵνα μετὰ πολλῆς τῆς ὑπερβολῆς ἀπαγάγῃ τῆς παλαιᾶς εὐτελείας.

[2] By way of explanation of the German "Eid" (oath), Adelung adduces "ᾰ: Grimm compares "aiva, eiva," that is, "law;" in the Swedish laws, "Lag" (lex) signifies "oath." Jus and jurare are one word. Ὅρκος, from εἴργω,

truth under appeal to God, the avenger of untruth." Cicero defines it, "affirmatio religiosa" (de off. 3, 29). The school of Kant naturally set itself in opposition to oaths in this sense; but this polemic, which was rooted in an abstract Deism, we may now pass by as antiquated (see the "Religion innerhalb der Grenzen der blossen Vernunft," 2 A. S. 240; Pott, "de jurisjurandi natura morali," in the "Sylloge comm. T. V.;" K. Ludwig Nitzsch, "de judicandis morum præceptis in N. T. a communi omnium hominum ac temporum usu alienis comm. vi.;" Gutbier, in Augusti's "Theolog. Blätter," 1 Jahrgang, No. 24, S. 374). Rothe's view also, in agreement with Reinhard, Marheineke, and others, is, that "an oath is rather a religious confession of the highest solemnity, an act of worship in the strict sense, and ought always to be regarded as such."

The immorality of the oath could only consist in the untrustworthiness of the person swearing, and the want of confidence on the part of the person requiring him to swear. In this way the oath was rejected, as being opposed to self-respect, by the Essenes (Josephus, de bello Judaico, ii. 8, 6), by the Pythagoreans (Diogenes Laert. c. viii. § 22), and by the Stoics (Epictetus, "Enchirid." § xxxiii.; Marcus Aurelius, εἰς ἑαυτόν, iii. 5): the last allowed it at least to be used only in extreme cases. Generally speaking, the principle of the more moral Greek was such as Isocrates expresses (ad Demonic. c. xxiii.): "An upright man must lead such a life as will gain more confidence in him than an oath can do. Only in order to free himself from a base calumniation, or to deliver a friend, may he swear: thou mayest not do so for the sake of money, even if thou swearest truly." Plato also requires the oath to be used but rarely; and in Philo we accordingly read (de decem orac. ii. 194, ed. Mang.): κάλλιστον καὶ βιωφελέστατον καὶ ἁρμόττον τῇ λογικῇ φύσει τὸ ἀνώμοτον, οὕτως ἀληθεύειν ἐφ᾽ ἑκάστου δεδιδαγμένῃ, ὡς τοὺς λόγους ὅρκους εἶναι νομίζεσθαι. Sirach xxiii. 9, warned those who would speak wisely against much swearing; and even Maimonides comes to the conclusion: "It is a great blessing for men not to swear at all" (de jurejur. c. xii. § 12). The oath is regarded as inconsistent with the highest place of the Christian life by Clement of Alexandria,

ἀρκέω; see Scheidius in Lennep's "Etymol." ii. 685; Heb. vi. 16 might also be compared.

by Origen, and by Augustine.[1] While, as will be seen from subsequent references, from the earliest times of Christianity, many regarded the oath as absolutely unchristian.

In modern times, Erasmus, who also regarded the prohibition of divorce as required only of those who had attained to Christian perfection, was the first to express the opinion, that, in giving this command, our Lord's intention was to show that the Christian character ought to be so perfect that no oaths should any more be required of Christians. This view was supported by Pelicanus and Bucer among the Reformers. The latter remarks: ita fidos inter vos mutuo et veritatis studiosos esse addecet, siquidem cives vultis esse regni cœlorum, ut simplex sive affirmatio sive negatio ad faciendam fidem quacunque in re cuique satis sit.—At si quis agat cum iis, qui ea dilectione præditi non sunt ut simplici affirmationi fidem habeant, possitque illis jurando fidem facere rei ad gloriam Dei facientis, nequaquam peccabit jurando. The same view is maintained by Stirm in the treatise, "Revision der Gruende für und wider den Eid;" in Klaiber's Stud. der würtenb. Geistlichkeit, I. Band, 3tes H.; Olshausen, De Wette (Christliche Sittenlehre, iii. S. 121 ff.), Baumgarten-Crusius, Neander. Olshausen says: All the commands given here have their full significance in the kingdom of God: apart from that kingdom, however, not one of them can be applied literally. Ἐκ τοῦ πονηροῦ has been accordingly supposed by many to denote, *the evil which necessitates oaths:* Augustine, Glossa ordinaris: tu non malum facis, qui bene uteris juratione, quæ, esti non bona, tamen necessaria est, ut alteri persuadeas quod utiliter suades, *sed a malo* est illius, cujus infirmitate cogeris jurare: so Stirm, S. 107. But if here the stress were laid upon the fact that the immoral element consists in *requiring* an oath, it were strange that the command

---

[1] Clement, in the Paedag. iii. 299, contents himself with warning people against the use of oaths in common life. In the Strom. vii. p. 729, 861, f. ed. Pott. he allows their use on rare occasions (σπανίως), but bids Christians aspire to such a character for veracity that oaths would not be required of them. Origen exhorts first of all to strive to swear ἐν ἀληθείᾳ, κρίσει καὶ δικαιοσύνῃ (Jer. iv. 2), ἵνα μετὰ τοῦτο, προκόψας τις, ἄξιος γένηται, τοῦ μὴ ὀμνύειν ὅλως (hom. v. in Jer. T. iii.). Augustine condemns not the swearer so much as the person requiring him to swear; of himself he says: quantum ad me attinet, juro—sed magna necessitate compulsus (his thought is admirably expanded in Sermo 180. in ev. Joh. c. ix. opp. T. v.),

is directed against *taking* an oath. There is, therefore, much more to be said in favour of the opposite opinion held by Rothe, that the command is directed against unnecessary, thoughtless swearing, not against taking a REQUIRED oath.[1] Yet the majority of critics consider that the command of Christ refers really to an ideal kingdom, where oaths are neither required nor given: because, although it is only swearing that is forbidden, this presupposes a condition in which **oaths are not demanded**. It is, of course, taken for granted **that oaths are** permitted where this ideal kingdom does not yet exist. But if this command does not relate to the present sinful, earthly state, if it is really to be regarded as a prophecy in the form of a command, would it not bear a character entirely different from the other commands of this discourse? For, which of the other commands does not suppose that the **world in** which it is to be obeyed is a world full of sin, in which men **are angry, in** which lustful looks are cast, in which divorces occur, and blows are given? It is, indeed, surprising that even the most recent expositors have overlooked this consideration.

In the circumstances in which we are actually placed, the use of the oath is necessarily conceded in certain cases. That the absolute prohibition of swearing does not extend to our present circumstances, may be seen most clearly from the **conduct of Christ Himself and His Apostles** in relation to oaths. St Paul frequently makes **use of** asseverations, "as we must **regard as** essentially of the nature of swearing;" this Rothe himself admits: *e.g.,* 2 Cor. i. 23; Rom. i. 9; Phil. i. 8; **1 Cor. xv. 31** (it may be otherwise in the case of 1 Thess. ii. **5, 10**; 2 Cor. xi. 11, 31; Gal. i. 20; 1 Tim. v. 21). Then there are those other expressions which approach very nearly to the form of an oath, Rom. ix. 1; 2 Cor. ii. 17, xi. 10; Eph. iv. 17; 1 Thess. v. 27. The Christian idea of the oath was not essentially different from that

---

[1] Just so, Luther observes: "We know well that our Lord is not here laying down rules for the management of worldly affairs, or what concerns the magistracy, **but** that He speaks only for the **guidance of** each Christian man, and shows **how** he ought to live." To this also Melanchthon refers in his answer to the objection of the Anabaptists, viz., **that they** did not know how to distinguish the law from **the** Gospel. The majority of English theologians—Hammond, Clarke, Doddridge—take **the same** view, only they regard the oaths required by the magistracy **as forming exceptions**.

of the Old Testament: this is proved by Heb. vi. 13—16. And those formulas in St Paul have this peculiarity, that there is no allusion in them, whether direct or indirect, to a *required* oath; a circumstance which is also unfavourable to Rothe's distinction quoted above. Very truly observes St Chrysostom on Phil. i. 8: οὐχ ὡς ἀπιστούμενος μάρτυρα καλεῖ τὸν Θεὸν, ἀλλ᾽ ἐκ πολλῆς διαθέσεως τοῦτο ποιεῖ· καὶ τῷ σφόδρα πεπεῖσθαι καὶ θαῤῥεῖν. It is very true, that in a state of mind free from such vacillation and disturbance, the necessity would not arise to give expression in certain moments to this state, in such phrases as, "God is my witness etc.;" but equally certain is it, that in a soul in which religion and the world are striving for the mastery, the necessity may at times arise to give distinct expression to the feeling of his dependence upon God, and, by expressing, to strengthen that feeling. W. Bauer (in loc. cit., S. 13) truly says, that "for the religious man, every confirmation is of the nature of an oath:" only that the oath is simply the *express* realizing of the presence of God; and there would be no need of this, if the consciousness of God were never liable to wax feeble and dim. To those passages from St Paul we may now add the oath of our Lord before the civil ruler, St Matt. xxvi. 63: because the words, "thou hast said," are really a judicial oath; for among the Hebrews, as among ourselves, it was often the judge who stated the form of oath, whilst the accused made it his own by the word אָמֵן.[1]

For the reasons already given, we cannot regard the words of the text as containing an absolute prohibition. We may, therefore, inquire if it is possible to find in them another meaning. Many of the commentators do nothing more than make assertions which they do not attempt to prove. Menochius adds, without further comment, to the non jurate omnino of the Vulgate: scil. *nisi causa sufficiens subsit* (this recalls the above-mentioned addition to the marriage-formula, p. 248). Melanchthon, Bullinger, Este, Coccieus, and many more, also leave the ὅλως entirely out of account. One of the most usual expedients was to suppose that the ὅλως referred merely to the common modes of swearing. Two explanations have been given by those

---

[1] The oath, חֵי יְיָ, and the oath prompted by others חֵי אֱלֹהִים, were equivalent: Maimonides, constit. de jurejur. c. xi. § 10; Selden, de Synedr. ii. 11, p. 830; Saalschütz, Mosaisches Recht, S. 615.

critics who defend the oath. Either the saying has been viewed as a prohibition of the *promissory* oath, the subject of which is not in the power of men; or as a prohibition of the *thoughtless* oath. The former view has been held by Socinus, Grotius (compare de jure belli et pacis, L. ii. c. xiii. § 21), Episcopius, Wolzogen, and in modern times, Gloeckler. According to Grotius, the pharisaic gloss had limited the Old Testament command to promissory oaths: allusion to which is made, according to him, in ver. 37, which, after James v. 12, he explains thus: "Your promise in answer to questions, such as **Dabisne? should** be the simple dabo: it is unseemly because the future is not in the power of man, comp. ver. 36." But as the exposition of ver. 37 will show, this view is ungrammatical. Besides, it cannot be seen that oaths of asseveration are more permissible than oath of promise: accidents may occur over which man has no control, as sickness or death; and then the oath ceases to be binding.

The Redeemer speaks alone of those irrelevant oaths which are made in common life. In this view, Roman Catholic, Protestant, Socinian, and Rationalistic expositors are for the most part agreed. So Luther, who remarks, that, in itself, swearing is as little immoral as cursing: Calvin, Zwingly, Bullinger, Bucer, Przipcov, Calixt, Calov, Bengel, Elsner, Paulus, Fritzsche, Stier, Ewald. The latter remarks: "The name of God is omitted in Matthew and James simply because in those times men usually feared to swear by Him, except in courts **of law,** which are not here alluded to." If this is the meaning of the text, then its fulfilment by Christ is analogous to that of the other commandment: in the Old Testament, there was to be so great a reverence for God, that perjury was prohibited; in the New Testament, there is to be so great reverence, that even each *thoughtless* oath must be avoided. In proof of the correctness of this view, Zwingli remarks, that the oath mentioned is **not** the oath required by God in courts of law, but the substitutions for it used in common life. If this be true, it would certainly strongly confirm our view. Let us inquire. If, as Euthymius, Grotius, Neander suppose, the ὀμνύναι ὅλως includes the oath by God, it would not be so; for then the division which follows, ver. 34, etc., would stand to what precedes in the relation of a climax. Grotius: *ne quidem* per cœlum—graviter falluntur qui a Christo improbari putant consuetudinem jurandi per res alias extra deum. Neander: "Our Lord mentions only certain figurative forms of oath, in order more expressly to show that He would banish every from of asseveration out of His kingdom." Grotius calls in to support his view the saying in James v. 12, "Neither by any other oath." With regard to the last passage, however, it is not easy to see (and this Stirm admits) that the most important oath, the direct oath by God, should be loosely added to the indirect oath by God: we must rather suppose those other oaths ($\mathring{\alpha}\lambda\lambda\omicron\iota\ \tau\iota\nu\grave{\varepsilon}\varsigma\ \mathring{\omicron}\varrho\varkappa\omicron\iota$) to be of the same nature with those already mentioned. Further, if the phrase, "swear not at all," included swearing by God, should we not rather expect to have here the conjunctive $\mu\eta\delta\grave{\varepsilon}$ instead of the disjunctive $\mu\acute{\eta}\tau\varepsilon$ (as Br. Bauer remarks, Synoptiker, 345)? With greater appearance of truth, De Wette remarks: "The form of swearing by God did not require to be mentioned, as the sin of it is self-evident; and it is implied both in the previous $\mathring{\alpha}\pi\omicron\delta\acute{\omega}\sigma\varepsilon\iota\varsigma\ \delta\grave{\varepsilon}\ \tau\tilde{\omega}\ \varkappa\upsilon\varrho\acute{\iota}\omega$, and in what succeeds. The ground of the condemnation of all those oaths in which God is not immediately invoked, implies the condemnation of the oath by God." But from the phrase, $\mathring{\alpha}\pi\omicron\delta\acute{\omega}\sigma\varepsilon\iota\varsigma\ \tau\tilde{\omega}\ \varkappa\upsilon\varrho\acute{\iota}\omega$, we should be forced to conclude that the $\mathring{\omicron}\mu\acute{\omicron}\sigma\alpha\iota$ refers to swearing by God, only if we are to take the word in the sense of præstare jus jurandum (Kypke), not if it means servare jus jurandum. However, as, in the subsequent statement concerning indirect oaths, these are placed on the same footing with direct oaths, the question is still an open one, on what ground only the former, and not the latter, are mentioned in the condemnatory clause. It cannot certainly be said that the condemnation of the one presupposes the condemnation of the other; the reason why only the indirect oaths are mentioned, and not swearing by God, may be learnt from the Jewish practice with regard to swearing. From Matt. xxiii. 26 seqq., as well as from numerous sayings of the Talmud and the Rabbins, and even from the testimony of so accomplished a Jew as Maimonides, it may be, and has been shown, that not one of all the indirect forms of oath which are enumerated here, was valid in a court of law, because they were not regarded as binding. Even vows made in human affairs were not regarded as binding if the name of the person to whom the vow was made was not distinctly expressed: tr. Nedarim, with the comments of Maimonides, in Surenhus Mischna iii. 122. The same principle was maintained also in the case of oaths. Maimonides declares (according to the Halacha) that oaths by heaven, by the earth, by the Prophets, and even when the swearer intended to refer to the Creator of all things, were not binding, and that the judges acquitted people of them (Constit. de jurej. c. xii. § 3). The only oath which was valid in courts of law, and which was binding, was the oath by the name or by one of the titles of God (comp. Maimonides and Selden De Synedriis, 2, 11, S. 801). Now the opponents of the oath admitted that the words, "Thou shalt perform unto the Lord thine oaths," had been added by the pharisaic expositors of the Scriptures, simply with the object of vindicating the sanctity and obligation of those direct oaths which were valid in courts of law. In these circumstances, the command of Christ can be understood only in this sense: "Ye must, from fear of God, abstain not only from perjury, but from swearing at all: from such swearing as you are wont to use in common life." With regard to the practice of swearing in common life, some allusion is made to it in Lev. v. 4: "If a soul swear, pronouncing with his lips to do evil, or to do good, whatsoever it be that a man shall pronounce with an oath, and it be hid from him." In explaining this precept, Aben Esra speaks of the practice of swearing as universal in his day, so that he says, men swear daily countless times, and swear that they have not sworn. He adds, רק זאת העברה תספיק להאריך הגולה, "This offence alone makes our exile yet longer last." From the New Testament we have instances of thoughtless swearing and repeated swearing in the case of St Peter, Matt. xxvi. 72—74; and an illustration of the evasive forms of swearing in Martial x. ep. 95, ecce negas, jurasque mihi *per templa Tonantis*, non credo; jura, verpe, per Anchialum (אֱלֹהֵהּ חַי).

Let us now take an historical view of the various opinions upon the subject of oaths held in the Christian Church. First of all, we are met by the precept of St James, which is almost identical with the words of Christ in St Matthew: St James v. 12, πρὸ πάντων δὲ, ἀδελφοί μου, μὴ ὀμνύετε μήτε τὸν οὐρανὸν, μήτε τὴν γῆν, μήτε ἄλλον τινὰ ὅρκον· ἤτω δὲ ὑμῶν τὸ ναί, ναί, καὶ τὸ οὔ, οὔ· ἵνα μὴ ὑπὸ κρίσιν πέσητε. Some explain this to mean: "that your yes be a true and veritable yes,—that is, a yes of deeds." Thus Zwingly, Grotius, Theile, Kern, and Hilgenfeld (Kritische Untersuch. ueber die Evv. Justins, S. 175). Thus regarded, the words of St James would be somewhat different from our passage. We are, however, of opinion that the sense of both passages is the same, namely this: "Let your λόγος καταφατικός be a simple Yes, and your λόγος ἀποφατικός be a simple No." For, first, it is natural to suppose that the idea of the two passages is the same; then it must be noted that Justin Martyr, Apol. i. c. xvi., the Clementine Homilies, iii. 55, xix. 2, Clemens Alex., Strom. v. p. 596, ed. Pott, and Epiphanius adv. haer. xix. 6, all agree to regard the second half of the saying of St James as the words of Christ (Semisch Denkwuerdigkeiten des Justin, S. 375). No doubt Hilgenfeld says that the quotations in Justin, and this among the rest, are not taken from our Gospel; and he even expresses the suspicion that the form of the tradition in St Matthew "is an attempt again to introduce a mode of asseveration similar to an oath" (comp. also his "Entstehung der Evv." S. 63). That, however, Justin was acquainted with our Gospel, is a position which, to our mind, has been proved by Semisch; comp. also Ritschl in Zellers Jahrb. 1851, S. 486 f.[1] If, now, we are to maintain that St James quoted the words of our Lord, although with a modification similar to that presented by those passages in St John, where he has a double ἀμήν, while the other Evangelists have but one, it might yet appear questionable, when we bear in mind the wide-spread feeling in the early Church touching the absolute character of the command against swearing, if the Apostle gave the words of his Master the relative signification which we have shown them to bear.

If our Lord Himself intended to express an absolute condemnation of the oath, He does not place it in the category of moral imperfection, but He regards it as a positive *sin*. This is implied in the words, "lest ye fall into condemnation." His decision is therefore that expressed by the believing Jews in the ev. Nicod. c. ii. S. 532, ed. Thilo: ἡμεῖς νόμον ἔχομεν μὴ ὀμνύειν, ὅτι

---

[1] With reference to the quotation of the passages in the Const. apost. v. 12, even Hilgenfeld observes (Krit. Unters. S. 177) that the author of the Constitutiones, although he had before him the text of St Matthew, yet says, using the words of St James: ἔστω δὲ τὸ ναὶ ναί, καὶ τὸ οὒ οὔ, τοῖς πιστοῖς παράγγυα.

ἁμαρτία ἐστίν. It must be confessed that such a view is rather out of keeping with the Old Testament complexion of the Epistle, especially when we consider the practice of St Paul and the decision of Heb. vi. 16, which is so entirely opposed to this view. In no case, however, can we suppose that the oaths spoken of refer to the oaths of courts of law: the context forbids it. In ver. 9—11 men are exhorted to submit to injustice without murmuring, in hope of the speedy judgment of God. Can, then, the oaths spoken of here be any other than those which are called forth by the spirit of impatience or of revenge?

Moreover, it can scarcely be proved that oaths were universally condemned as sinful in the Church of the first two centuries: this was done rather in the third and fourth centuries, and in yet later times,—only, it is true, by limited circles, but for that reason all the more decidedly. The oldest testimony against swearing is that in Justin, from the second half of the second century, Apol. i. c. xvi: περὶ δὲ τοῦ μὴ ὀμνύναι ὅλως, τἀληθῆ δὲ λέγειν ἀεί, οὕτως παρεκελεύσατο· μὴ ὀμόσητε ὅλως, κ.τ.λ.: the words sound very decise; yet they must be understood in the sense of Clement Alex., Origen (see above, p. 252), viz., as expressing what ought to be the end and aim of Christians; so that swearing would be regarded as an imperfection rather than a sin. In this sense, too, we may understand the general expression of Irenæus (c. haer. ii. 32): non solum non perjurare, sed nec jurare præcepit Deus. That this opinion of ours is no arbitrary assumption, may be seen from the fact, that in the Constitutiones apostolicæ vii. 3, we have first the quotation of the words of Christ, οὐκ ἐπιορκήσεις, ἐρρέθη γὰρ, μὴ ὀμόσαι ὅλως, and then come the words: εἰ δὲ μήγε, κἂν εὐορκήσῃς. In the Martyrdom of Polycarp (c. xi.) the latter declares, in answer of the summons of the Proconsul, that it was not permitted him as a Christian to swear by the Genius of the Emperor. Tertullian also regards this as unchristian,—not so, however, to swear by the *health* of the Emperor (apolog. c. xxxiii.). In the third century, Novatus makes his followers swear by the body and blood of Jesus that they would remain faithful to him. (Eusebius h. e. vi. 43). The Clementines, in the second half of the second century, hold that our Lord Himself swore, and regard the phrase, "Verily I say," as an oath (Recognitiones vi. 9, Hom. xi. 26; Hilgenfeld, crit. Unters. S.

342). Although Gregory Nazianz., on becoming a Christian, made a rule to live ἀνώμοτος, he yet allowed weaker Christians to swear (ed. Par. i. 760, ii. 18, 224 ff.). Also Athanasius swears in the presence of the Emperor (Opp. i. p. 525). The author of the opus imperfectum speaks of clergy who, holding the New Testament, swore on it: he finds fault with this practice himself, because he says that it makes them responsible for the consequences of the oath. Hilary regards the oath as given for the rudiores: in simplicitate viventibus jurandi religione opus non est, cum quibus semper quod est est: from this, however, it does not follow that he absolutely condemns swearing. Jerome more decidedly (ad locum): he says that the oath by God in the Old Testament was merely a concession, the object of which was, to prevent the people from swearing by idols: Evangelica autem veritas non recipit juramentum, cum omnis sermo fidelis pro jurejurando sit. So Pelagius, in accordance with his moral characteristics (ad Demetr. c. xxii.). The milder view of Augustine has been already alluded to (p. 253). The most rigorous are the view of the Antiochians,—above all, that of Chrysostom.[1] The same strict view is also to be found in Theophylact and Euthymius. In the Western Church also, as Druthmar observes, the oath was regarded as not permitted to the perfectiores, neither to the clergy (in the Synod of Tribur, a. A. 895). The old difficulties were raised again by those sects which insisted upon going back to the letter of Scripture: the followers of Wickliffe, the Mennonites, the Quakers, and the Russian sects of the Raskolnikes, Duchoborzens, and Philipponites.

Very unsatisfactory are the attempts which these opponents of oaths have made to elude the Biblical argument. Augustine characterizes several of them as ridiculous,—as, *e.g.*, that the *per* Deum is essential to an oath; and he lays special stress upon the νή in 1 Cor. xv. 31, as showing that oaths are permissible (ep. 157, T. i. 424, Sermo 181, c. v. in Joh. i.). Chrysostom expounds 1 Cor. xv. 31 incorrectly, and passes over in silence 2 Cor. i. 23, where the Apostle calls God to record

---

[1] Τί οὖν, he says on our passage, ἂν ἀπαιτῇ τις ὅρκον, φησί, καὶ ἀνάγκην ἐπάγῃ; ὁ τοῦ Θεοῦ φόβος τῆς ἀνάγκης δυνατώτερος. The strongest expression is as follows: ἐπιορκεῖν οὐκ ἀνέχονται (οἱ τοῦ Χριστοῦ), μᾶλλον δὲ οὐδὲ ὀμνύειν· ἀλλὰ τὴν γλῶτταν ἐκτμηθῆναι ἂν ἕλοιντο πρότερον, ἢ ὅρκον τινὰ ἀπὸ τοῦ στόματος προέσθαι (hom. x. ad Antioch. T. ii. Montf.).

Pseudo-Basil., in Ps. xiv. (Opp. i. 346), makes the following pointless observation on 1 Cor. xv. 31: οὐ παρήκουσε τῆς εὐαγγελικῆς διδασκαλίας ὁ εὐαγγέλιον πεπιστευμένος, ἀλλὰ λόγον ψιλὸν ἐν σχήματι παραδέδωκεν ὅρκου, κ.τ.λ. The remark of Pelagius on the same passage is almost childish: *per non semper significatio juramenti est. Nam si dicam, per puerum misi: non statim per puerum jurasse recte putabor.* Origen (Opp. T. iii. p. 910) seeks to weaken the force of Matt. xxvi. 64, by maintaining that Christ there neither affirms nor denies a question, which Origen yet recognises as an adjuration; but that the words, "Thou sayest it," are merely a reproachful retort. Barclay, the apologist of the Quakers, says (Apol., Propos. xv. § 12): The question is not what Paul or Peter did, but what their own Master taught to be done; and if Paul did swear (which we believe not), he had sinned against the command of Christ. The expositors of the English Church understood the words of Christ as an express admission of the propriety only of legal oaths: they were not so decided in adducing the instances from St Paul in their argument against the Quakers; Clarke (Paraphrase of the Four Gospels, 1750, 10th ed.), "Swear not at all in common conversation." In a recent polemical treatise ("der Eid, eine religiöse Abhandlung," Barmen, 1830), the Pauline passages are got over by holding that the words, "I swear," form an essential element in an oath: they are, however, of course implied. To swear, meant originally nothing more than to say, to answer (Svaran, English "answer").

Vers. 35, 36. The μὴ ὀμόσαι is rendered more special by a fourfold division. In the last of these, ἐν τῇ κεφαλῇ, the verb ὀμόσῃς is repeated, to which a clause is appended: in consequence of this, Fritzsche thought that μηδέ must there be the right reading. This is not *necessary*, as the ὀμοσῇς stands last; so that it is not the idea of the verb that is oppended, but the whole of the negative saying (comp. Meyer). As, however, the negative particles (μηδέ and μήτε) are frequently interchanged in the codices (Winer, S. 435, 6 A.), we may admit the reading, as there is really a difference between the last clause and the three previous ones. It is this: the three first refer to mighty objects in nature regarded as representing the power of God: the last to a precious object, which is lightly staked.—

The construction ὀμνύναι with ἐν and εἰς is Hebraistic, like ב נשׁבּע. Herodian, to be sure, uses it in speaking of a military oath (Hist. ii. c. ii.): εἴς τε τὸ ἐκείνου ὄνομα τοὺς συνήθεις ὅρκους ὀμόσαντες; this Irmisch (Herod. T. ii. § 58) regards as an imitation of the Latin in nomen jurare: the classical phrases occur in St James v. 12, verbs of swearing with the Accusative, in St Matt. xxvi. 63, with κατά and the Genitive, and elsewhere.

The oaths by created things, which are found in the East, among the Greeks, the Romans, the Germans, may be divided into two classes: Either the swearer invokes sacred symbols as representative of God: the altar; the rod of the Judge (among the Greeks and Romans); the red ring of the god Ullr (among the Scandinavians); the graves of ancestors (among the Nasamonians); or certain exalted objects of might in nature.[1] Or, on the other hand, he refers to some valuable and sacred object, which he stakes upon the truth of what he is asserting; *e.g.*, his head (by which the Homeric Zeus swears), his beard, his hair, his sword. In both these kinds of oath, there is the physical contact by which that spiritual relation expressed by the preposition, εἰς, in, per, and by, is rendered sensibly vivid. With a deep psychological insight, our Lord expresses in high, figurative language that which psychological reflection discovers to be the ground of these oaths. An ancient view, based upon the feeling of the immanence of God in Nature, was, that the sun, the earth, and the elements are animated by the Divine Spirit. This view might have partially sprung from a religious awe, which sought to rise to the First Cause of all things. Our Lord, in allusion to those oaths, shows, that what gives those created things their significance, is only what they possess as reflections of God Most High. Quia nulla est pars mundi, says Calvin, cui Deus non insculpserit gloriæ suæ notam. Further, it was natural that the swearer should refer to, and expressly mention, something that was valuable to him, and which he was prepared

---

[1] Instances of the forms of swearing current among Jews and heathen are given by Grotius, Wettstein, Schöttgen, Scheidius (in Meuschen N. T. ex Talm. illustr.) Compare the remark of Aben Esra on Ex. xx. 7, on the oath by the head of the king: מנהג אנשי מצרים עד היום אם ישבע אדם באאש המלך ילא יקיים את דבריו הוא בן דית יאלי נתן בידו משקלו זהב לא יחיה בעבור כי היא בזוה את המלך בזדחביא.

to stake; with regard to such oaths, the Saviour shows how that everything is in the mighty hand of God. Thus even the indirect oaths are really oaths by God, and the thoughtless use even of these is not without sin. These thoughts are clothed in a noble figure of speech. The idea here, that in heaven the glory of God is especially manifest, and that earth is the reflection of the same, is one which had been expressed in Hebrew poetry, in which heaven is called God's throne, and earth His footstool (Isa. lxvi. 1). In this figure the Saviour expresses the same thought. Jerusalem is an holy city, because, according to Ps. xlvii. 3, it is קִרְיַת מֶלֶךְ רָב, the city of the Great King (not of *one* great king, as Luther translates in Matt.) (Matt. iv. 5). The same argument is used xxiii. 21, 22. How little the head is in the power of men, is shown by the fact that they cannot even give one single hair a colour different from that which it has received from Nature. Now, as the art of dyeing the hair ($\beta\acute{a}\pi\tau\varepsilon\sigma\vartheta\alpha\iota\ \tau\grave{a}\varsigma\ \tau\varrho\acute{\iota}\chi\alpha\varsigma$) was known to the ancients, the expression does not seem to hold good; on which account, Luther, Wettstein, Kuinoel, expound: to *produce* a single white or black hair. It is clear, however, that our Lord did not refer to artificial but to natural changes: this is seen from the fact, that He mentions also the *white* hair, that of *age*. How miserable, then, is the observation of Ottius, in the Spicilegium ex Josepho (ed Haverc. 1741), that Christ is alluding to Herod, who, according to the account of Josephus, had the vanity to dye his hair: Christus servator sapientissime et sanctissime hoc monito Herodis taxavit vanitatem!

Ver. 37. The fear of God, as well as the self-respect of a truthful man, requires him, instead of using those thoughtless oaths, rather to confine himself to an earnest assurance or denial. In the same sense an Arabic proverb says (Erpenius proverb. centur. ii. 40): فلتكن كلمنك نعم او لا لتكن حقافا عند جميع الناس, "Let thy discourse be Yes or No, that thou mayest prove thyself to all people as a lover of truth." The repetition of $\nu\alpha\acute{\iota}$ and $o\check{v}$ is the expression of lively feeling: with the Rhetoricians, $\dot{\eta}\ \dot{\alpha}\nu\alpha\delta\acute{\iota}\pi\lambda\omega\sigma\iota\varsigma$ (Demetrius de elocutione, § 66), comp. Theocr. 4, 54: $N\alpha\acute{\iota},\ \nu\alpha\grave{\iota}\ \tau o\widetilde{\iota}\varsigma\ \dot{o}\nu\acute{v}\chi\varepsilon\sigma\sigma\iota\nu\ \ddot{\varepsilon}\chi\omega\ \tau\acute{\varepsilon}\ \nu\iota\nu;$ Aristoph. nub. v. 1457: $\nu\alpha\acute{\iota},\ \nu\alpha\acute{\iota},\ \varkappa\alpha\tau\alpha\iota\delta\acute{\varepsilon}\sigma\vartheta\eta\tau\iota\ \Pi\alpha\tau\varrho\widetilde{\varphi}o\nu\ \varDelta\acute{\iota}\alpha.$ So, too,

2 Cor. i. 17: ἵνα παρ' ἐμοὶ τὸ ναὶ ναὶ καὶ τὸ οὒ οὔ. In the Old Testament, יֵשׁ יֵשׁ, 2 Kings x. 15; with the Rabbis, הֵן הֵן, see Buxt. lex. talm. s. v. הֵן; and with the Arabs, frequently, *e.g.*, in the Arabian Nights, نعم نعم. The very repetition shows that it is not intended to restrict men to the use of the *word* Yes: were it so, the "Verily" of Christ himself would be a violation of His own command.—Τὸ περισσόν, well translated by Luther: "was darüber ist." Chrys.: τὸ πλέον καὶ ἐκ περιουσίας προσκείμενον. And Beza: superflua, redundantia. These ideas, however, are not so much expressed in the words as implied in the sense.

Ἐκ τοῦ πονηροῦ is explained to mean the devil, not only here, but at ver. 39 and vi. 13, by Chrys., Theoph., Euth., Tertullian. A Codex has a gloss: ἐκ τοῦ διαβόλου; thus Zwingli, Beza, Piscator, Maldonatus: similarly Luther, in his first edition of 1522, "vom Argen;" then, in the edition of the same year, which followed a few months later, he has "vom Uebel." The more recent expositors have again taken the word as a masculine (Wettstein, Semler, Fr., Wahl, Meyer); in support of which Beza notices the use of the definite article. But this cannot decide the question; for the neuter of the adjective, used substantively, may be with or without the article, according as the idea is more or less regarded as a *whole* (see Plato de republ. l. v. p. 476, A.; comp. the adverbs ἐκ περισσοῦ and ἐκ τοῦ περισσοῦ, ἐξ ἐμφανοῖς and ἐκ τοῦ ἐμφανοῦς). Indeed, in these circumstances, the article is commonly used. The question must then be decided on doctrinal grounds, or according to the analogy of language. As regards the latter, we find in St John in the forms, ἐκ τοῦ διαβόλου, ἐκ τοῦ πονηροῦ εἶναι (viii. 44; 1 John iii. 8, 12); further, ὁ κόσμος ὅλος ἐν τῷ πονηρῷ κεῖται (1 John v. 19). On the other hand however, he also uses the formula, εἶναι ἐκ τῆς ἀληθείας, John xviii. 37; 1 John ii. 21, iii. 19; in St Paul, ἐξ ἐριθείας, Rom. ii. 8. To these expressions the phrase, ἐκ τοῦ πονηροῦ or ἐκ τῶν ψευδῶν εἶναι, a denoting *origin* or *sphere*, might be analogous; but it cannot suffice, with Meyer, to refer simply to the common adverbial usage ἐκ δόλου, ἐκ φανεροῦ. Philologically, either view is admissible. With regard to the doctrinal point of view, the expression would indeed appear very strange if it contained the opinion of Jesus on oaths in general (see above, p. 249). This would be the case if we viewed the word as a neuter, as in Matthaei on James v. 12, ἐκ τοῦ πονηροῦ ἐστιν, ὅπερ ἐστὶν ὁ ὅρκος. How much more if He had declared that the oath, the act of the most intense religious self-determination, was of the *devil!* But if it is of oaths of impatience, frivolity, and passion, such as occur in common life, that He is speaking, our Lord might have referred them to the devil, in the same sense as He ascribes to him that thoughtlessness which steals away the seed of the word from the heart, Matt. xiii. 19. According to the New Testament doctrine, all evil has its centre of union in Satan; and whether the Speaker refers one evil deed to Satan or to an evil nature, the difference can be merely a rhetorical one. He would refer the evil deed to the one or to the other, according as He wished to present its evil with a greater or less degree of intensity. Now, in the present case, there was no occasion for characterizing the evil so emphatically: hence also De Wette, Baumgarten-Crusius,[1] Ewald retained the neuter view. In chap. vi. 13, also, ἀπὸ τοῦ πονηροῦ is to be regarded as the neuter.—A different philological view was occasioned by St. James v. 12: in accordance with that passage our text is thus explained by the Ar. Polygl. في النعم نعم ; the Persic Polygl. درای رای, "in or by the Yes, let yes be the answer:" so too Zwingli, Beza, Grotius, Piscator, Paulus, and others. Many expositors feel it a difficulty, that the repeated Yes or No is already something "more" (περισσόν): or, as Hilgenfeld says, "an attempt to introduce again an asseveration similar to an oath." But the repetition of the Yes is merely a concrete expression or a strong assurance. A philological objection to this explanation is, that (without connecting it by the article ὁ ναί) the idea of ναί could not be added to the λόγος, in order to give it the signification of ὁ λόγος ὁ καταφατικός. St James writes: ἤτω ὑμῶν τὸ ναὶ ναί, κ.τ.λ.

---

[1] B.-Crusius: "It is simply referred to evil; there is no necessity to suppose the idea of Satan to be introduced into this plain and clear statement."

IV. AGAINST RETALIATION. VERS. 38—42.

Ver. 38. That was a wide-spread but false idea of the Old Testament economy, according to which the God of justice of the Old Testament was regarded as a God of cruelty, whilst the God of love existed only in Christianity; and the command to love one's enemies was viewed as a distinctive principle of the New Testament. Those who held this idea believed, like the Marcionites and Manichæans (vide Aug. c. Faustum Manich. L. xxxii. c. 76), that in this part of the Sermon on the Mount, from ver. 38 onwards, the contrast of our Lord's teaching to that of Moses comes out most strongly.

The Old Testament saying with which our Lord commences, was the rule given to the magistrates in the courts of justice, Ex. xxi. 23—25; Lev. xxiv. 19, 20; Deut. xix. 21. As some well-known law passages show, the dictum is often quoted elliptically, with omission of the subject and part of the predicate, for which only ἀντί stands; in the LXX., δώσεις precedes. This command of Moses is based on the jus talionis (τὸ ἀντιπεπονθός), which lies at the foundation of the oldest code of law. A violation of the law demands compensation: as the law has been dealt with by the transgressor, so does it deal with him, in order to let him see what his action deserves. In a ruder state of society, this retribution takes the form of a qualetale as a compensation in kind (talio); in a more developed state, the compensation is in *proportion* to the defence: the punishment then is quantum-tantum, by imprisonment or by fines; thus it was amongst the Jews in the time of Christ. [Very instructive for theologians is here Aristotle's Eth. Nicom. v. 78, and Hegel's Rechtsphilosophie, § 99 f. 211 f.; comp. also the learned treatise by Danz, origo talionis in Meuschen N. T. e Talm. illustrat.] This law of the civil courts was not, however, a rule to guide the conduct of individuals. They, on the contrary, are forbidden to seek for compensation in so far as passion or revenge is their motive.[1] Compare Lev. xix. 18, "Thou shalt not avenge, nor bear any grudge against the children of thy people; but thou shalt love thy neighbour as thyself: I am the Lord." Further, Prov. xxiv. 29, "Say not, I will do

---

[1] "Revenge is the right in itself, but not in the form of the right," but proceeding from selfish passion; hence also it goes *beyond* the right.

to him as he has done to me: I will render to the man according to his work." Lam. iii. 27—30, "It is good for a man that he bear the yoke in his youth; that he sit alone, and keep silence, because He hath laid it upon him; . . . that he give his cheek to Him that smiteth him, and be filled full with reproach."

The bad sense in which the command had been applied by the Scribes, is to be learnt from the contrast drawn in the passage which follows. It seems that what is there spoken of is private intercourse: the majority of commentators have accordingly regarded the false exposition of the Scribes as consisting in this, that they applied in private intercourse a law which was given only for the administration of courts of justice: thus Luther, Bucer, Piscator, Calov, Tirinus, Bengel, B.-Crusius, and others. Some of them, as Luther and others, expressly remark, that our right to seek for the protection of the law, at least in the case of those whose interests are committed to us, is not withdrawn. The later Lutheran commentators, however, expressly confine these injunctions of Christ to those cases, ubi magistratus (sc. Paganus) non vult vos ab injuria defendere et malos punire. Thus Bucer, Chemnitz, Scherzer, and others; according to whom the words of Christ apply properly only to the Apostles, as going out among the heathen. From this limitation Dr Paulus further concludes, that it is only "the provocations of the heathen" that are here spoken of; that the Apostles were not to seek redress for them from heathen courts of law,—redress which, indeed, they would have small chance of obtaining.

The view taken by the Fathers is one opposed especially to this last limitation. They do not hold that the words quoted are merely the expression of the law for the civil courts. The phrase, "an eye for an eye," they regard as expressing the **nature** of the retributive *Law* in contrast to *Grace*. Hilary: lex infidelem Israel intra metum metu continebat et injuriæ **voluntatem** injuriæ vicissitudine coercebat. Fides autem nullius **tam** gravem dolorem esse patitur injuriæ, ut ultionem expetat et illatæ sibi quisquam vindex sit contumeliæ. Tertullian de patientia, c. 6: olim oculum pro oculo, nondum enim patientia in terris, quia nec fides. Jerome: in lege *retributio* est, in ev. *gratia*. St Augustine ably shows that even talio implies a limitation of the desire of revenge; for this desire would most readily return a *double* portion to the offender. Two lesser degrees of the πλήρωσις of the moral requirement are passed over by our Lord: *first,* requiting *less* than has been received; and *next,* not requiting at all: our Lord at once passes to the highest stage. His followers are to be ready even to suffer *more*. St Chrysostom also remarks, that in the Old Testament, bounds are set to the desire of vengeance: the offender who deserved a double requital was, he said, to receive only a single one; the feeling of revenge was further restrained by the thought, that the offence was the work not of the offender, but of the devil acting by him (τῷ πονηρῷ is thus taken in the masculine). Euthymius also regards the law as intended for private intercourse: he has failed to apprehend the distinction which the Latin Fathers have noticed between Law and Grace; so that he only mentions that the Old Testament lawgiver sought to deter men from sin by the ταὐτοπάθεια, the New Testament Lawgiver by the μέλλουσα κόλασις. Ernesti is the first to notice that this law was given for the judge, and not for people in their private intercourse. He says, that the Mosaic court of law did, within certain limits, give satisfaction to the desire for revenge, whereas our Lord has made it the duty of the offended person to deny himself this legal compensation; so too Maldonatus, Este, a Lapide, Grotius, Episcopius: recently, Meyer, De Wette. Roman Catholics ano Socinians regarded this as the correction of the Mosaic law: the Socinian writers went so far as to say that a *Christian* court of law is not to be resorted to, even in cases where capital or other grievous punishments are decreed; vide Gerhard loci, T. xiii. 274, xv. 139; Scherzer, Coll. anti-Socin., p. 1098.

We cannot so limit the antithesis of our Lord. The word which marks the legal transaction is κριθῆναι: there can be no reference to anything legal in the compulsion spoken of in ver. 41, still less in ver. 42. It will be more correct to regard the antithesis as an admonition against a revengeful temper, and against a selfish desire for compensation, whether privately or through a legal proceeding (comp. Ewald); for although, as Grotius observes, magistrates are appointed to maintain justice and grand compensation, and each man has a *right* to avail himself of them, it yet by no means follows that it is his *duty* to do so. The Pharisees, however, as can be shown, made this right a duty, not even admitting private arbitration (vide supra, p. 199). From this it follows that the phrase, "an eye for an eye" (although there is no express gloss to it), must be quoted here in the same sense in which the Pharisees used to apply it in the interest of private retaliation. That phrase expressed a revengeful and retaliating spirit, which at least demanded *as much* as had been lost; while the words of Christ inculcate an unavenging and loving disposition, which is ready to submit even to a greater share of injury. But, as even the disciple of the Old Testament was bound to exercise this forgiving disposition, the censure implied in the words of Christ would apply not merely to the Pharisees and His contemporaries, but to all in the Old Testament who had not complied with those requirements (vide supra, p. 266). Accordingly, even a prophet like Elijah would come under this censure, who called down fire from heaven on the innocent instrument of an idolatrous king. Luke ix. 55: οὐκ οἴδατε οἵου πνεύματός ἐστε ὑμεῖς.[1]

As regards the abuse of the application of this precept, we must first recall the canon with which we set out (p. 164). We saw that the commands in vers. 39—42 are to be regarded as only concrete illustrations of the state of mind and heart required,—as extreme cases, which no doubt, under certain circumstances, may occur.[2] So thinks Augustine, when he remarks

---

[1] We must inquire here, not only whether another exposition may not be possible, but whether the text is genuine. There is doubt about the fact that the words of the text which follow: ὁ γὰρ υἱός, κ.τ.λ., are unauthentic; but modern criticism has seen fit to decide also against those first quoted. If they are genuine, the question arises (and it is also one of importance for our text): "Is the opposition to the whole of the Old Testament stage of religious development, or merely to the passionate temper of the prophet in that particular instance?" There are arguments in favour of both views: comp. Calvin, Bengel, Meyer, and Keil, Commentary on 2 Kings i. In the text we have followed the latter, to which also the remark of Bengel seems to point: retunditur provocatio ad Eliam; but it is easy to understand, that if the original text ended with the words ἐπετίμησεν αὐτοῖς, the Christian transcriber may have supplemented them with the words, οὐκ οἴδατε κ.τ.λ., and later the words ὁ γάρ, κ.τ.λ., were subjoined.

[2] We need not fear, says St Chrysostom, that a man of such self-denying love would have to starve or go **naked**; because, for one thing, a man of such a noble temper would not be **likely** to be assaulted, and if he were, there would be many ready to cover his nakedness and assist him in his distress.

on vers. 39, 40: hoc ad præparationem cordis, no ad ostentationem operis præcipitur. In St John xviii. 23, we have a case where the Saviour had an opportunity of literally fulfilling the command of ver. 39, and has not done it. It is only the *spirit of revenge* that our Lord condemns: it is therefore not inconsistent with His command to seek the protection of the law. The man who is capable of literally fulfilling these injunctions, is also morally capacitated to leave them externally unfulfilled; and may, without disobeying the command, seek for the protection of the law. The right view had been fully recognised by Augustine and by Luther: comp. the limitationes of Gerhard, loci xiv. 138. Augustine says: Neque hic ea vindicta prohibetur, quæ ad correctionem valet; etiam ipsa enim pertinet ad misericordiam; nec impedit illud propositum, quo quisque paratus est ab eo, quem correctum esse vult, plura perferre. Sed huic vindictæ referendæ non est idoneus, nisi qui odium, quo solent flagrare qui se vindicare desiderant dilectionis magnitudine superaverit. Non enim metuendum est, ne odisse parvulum filium parentes videantur, cum ab eis vapulat peccans, ne peccet ulterius. And again: teneatur in secreto animi patientia cum benevolentia, in manifesto autem id fiat, quod eis videtur prodesse posse, quibus bene velle debemus. Luther requires from the Christian, as a Christian, that he should be ready to act in all things as the text requires: only as father, neighbour, subject, he must maintain the right which is entrusted to him. "He who would here teach that it is right to present the other cheek, or to throw away the cloak, would be as great a fool as that mad saint of whom it is said, that he allowed himself to be eaten up of lice, and would not kill one of them on account of this verse, saying that one must not resist evil." "So it is not forbidden to go to law, and to proffer an accusation against an unlawful assault, if only the heart is not false, but continues as patient as before, and if it is done only in order that right be maintained, and that wrong be put down." It cannot, therefore, surprise us to find, that the same Apostle who in 1 Cor. vi. 7 exhorts rather to suffer wrong than to go to law, himself invokes the judicial authority of the civil power, Acts xvi. 35, 40, xxii. 23—29, xxv. 9 et seqq.

Ver. 39. We have first to consider the order of sequence on

to ver. 42. If τῷ πονηρῷ be taken as a neuter, the phrase μὴ ἀντιστῆναι τῷ πονηρῷ may be regarded as the general maxim which is amplified and carried into details in the following clauses. But it seems preferable to regard the 39th verse, which speaks of physical injury, as the first contrast to the carnal view of the laws of Moses. This is then carried further: The forgiving disposition is required to be exercised with regard to *robbery* (ver. 40); in the case of forcible *constraint* (ver. 41); and (though the connection here is not so close) also in the case of an importunate *request* (ver. 42). Accordingly there are these three cases of offence against the body, the property, or one's personal liberty. This view of the relation of the sentences need not prevent τῷ πονηρῷ from being regarded as a neuter in the sense of injuria (Augustine, Calvin, Castellio, Chemnitz, Wolf, Stier). That the antithesis is formed by the masculine ὅστις is not against it, as ἐάν τις and ὅστις are often used for each other (comp. Mark viii. 34, with Matt. xvi. 24); and accordingly Codices 1, 3, 5, 8, in Matt. have here ἐάν τις. The classical commentators remark: ἐάν τις is the urbanior forma loquendi for ὅστις ἄν: Stallbaum on Euthyphr. S. 17; Apol. Socr. S. 67. On the other hand, nothing can be concluded from this view against regarding the word as a masculine: only that then we must not (with Chrysostom and Theophylact) understand πονηρός as meaning the *devil* as working by the instrumentality of men of violence. Ἀνθίστημι denotes opposition in *word* (St Luke xxi. 15; Acts vi. 10), as well as in *deed*: it is equivalent to ἀντιτάσσεσθαι (Rom. xiii. 2; St James v. 6); Justin, quoting the passage, uses the synonymous term ἀνταίρειν. Thus, according to the literal view of the saying, the resistance of evil by *words* is also condemned.

Our Lord is not speaking of injuries involving danger to life, such as the commandment of the law speaks of; but of a common unprovoked insult: a point of importance in expounding the text. Would He have said, "Whoso knocks out the right eye, let him also knock out the other?" A blow on the cheek was the utmost mark of contempt, such as few would dare to inflict on any one but a slave. Seneca de constantia, c. 4: sic invenias servum, qui flagellis quam colaphis cædi malit; hence the proverbial expression: os præbere, offerre contumeliis (comp. Clericus in loc. cit.; Gronov. on Grotius de jure belli ac pacis, i. 2, 7). In the Old and the New Testaments too we find κολαφίζειν, almost like καταπτύειν, used to denote extreme contempt: Isa. l. 6; Lam. iii. 30; 2 Cor. xi. 20. Striking with the right hand, one would naturally hit the left cheek; but the right cheek is mentioned first, because, as Maldonatus remarks, non *cædendi* consuetudinem sed *loquendi* secutus est; thus in the Hebrew לְהֵימִין always stands first, and then לְהַשְׂמִאִיל. Augustine resorts to allegory; suggesting that the right cheek is Christian excellence, by which the world is offended; the left is excellence in the world, which is to be surrendered. Beza: quos contemnimus, eos solemus averso ictu, nimirum in sinistrum latus verberare.—Instead of τὴν ἄλλην, ἕτερος should have been used, as, according to the grammarians, ἕτερος ἐπὶ δυοῖν, ἄλλος ἐπὶ πολλῶν: yet this distinction is not always observed by classical writers; vide Sallier on Thomas M. s. v. ἕτερος. The illustration expresses the willingness to suffer a *double* amount of injury, as ver. 40, the willingness to give double, and ver. 41, to *do* double.

Ver. 40. The second illustration is given somewhat differently by St Luke: see Introduction p. 20. In Luke (vi. 29) it is said, "Him that taketh away thy cloak, forbid not to take thy coat also:" it is accordingly a violent robbery that is referred to. In St Matthew, again, it is a judicial proceeding that is spoken of; this the Vulgate expresses: qui vult tecum in judicio contendere; and Chrysostom expounds: ἐὰν εἰς δικαστήριον ἕλκῃ καὶ πράγματά σοι παρέχῃ. Κρίνεσθαι in the Middle, with the Dative of direction, or with πρός, to judge: it might certainly refer to any extra-judicial contest (Beza, Grotius, Kuinoel), but the order in which the garments are mentioned is against it. Χιτών—in the Old Testament כְּתֹנֶת, with the Rabbis חָלוּק—was the narrow under-garment, composed of cotton or linen, which came next the body (Vulgate, tunica); ἱμάτιον—in the Old Testament שִׂמְלָה, with the Rabbis טַלִּית (Vulg., pallium)—is the loose *overcoat*. On account of its size, as well as the material, the latter was the more expensive article: Mark xiii. 16. The poor Oriental made use of it as a covering by night; on account of which, the humane law of Moses was, that one should not retain the overcoat in pawn over night (Ex. xxii. 26). The greater value of this overcoat may be seen also from the saying, Bava Meziah, "When one gives a beggar a coin to buy a חֲלוּק, let him no buy טַלִּית." The obliging disposition must accordingly be so great, that, rather than go to law, the man must be willing to give not only the cheaper garment, but also the more valuable one. The garments are mentioned in St Luke in a different order: his informant thinking that what was alluded to was an aggressive assault (here also the Ethiopic has deprædari), the upper coat was, of course, mentioned first. On both views, the idea of the saying remains the same.

Ver. 41. An instance of compulsion. Ἀγγαρεύειν is the specific word for legal requisitions, quartering upon,—ἐπισταθμία, vid. in Suidas ἀνεπιστάθμευτος,—forcing to serve as a messenger, etc.: thus of Simon, who was compelled to bear the cross, Matt. xxvii. 32. Christ here speaks, not of legal requisitions, but of acts of constraint in private life. In the rabbinical writings, בְּאַנְגַּרְיָא, *by constraint*, is opposed to בִּשְׂמְחָה; Suidas also says: ἀγγαρείαν ἀνάγκην ἀκούσιον λέγομεν καὶ ἐκ βίας γινομένην ὑπηρεσίαν.[1] The mile is a Roman mile, the fifth part of the German mile. Here too the spirit of ministering love shall be prepared, instead of declining the simple request to perform the double of what is asked.

Ver. 42. In asking and borrowing, the liberty of the giver to grant or withhold the request is acknowledged: it may, therefore, appear doubtful whether this saying belongs to this context: but St Luke (vi. 30) has it also in this connection. We think that the looser form in which ver. 42 is added, and the consideration that the command requires no twofold fulfilment, point to the conclusion, that in this saying, the thought pre-

---

[1] There can be no doubt that the Persic etymology given by Lorsbach is the right one, viz., from انگاشتن to write, which is possibly connected with a Semitic root, as Winer thinks. انگار‌ه means dispatch, and the ἄγγαροι were originally dispatch-carriers (Herodotus viii. 98; Xenophon Cyrop. viii. 6, 17; Suidas, οἱ ἐκ διαδοχῆς γραμματοφόροι); hence those dispatch-bearers were themselves called dispatches. The word angariare came into the later Latin in the sense of, "to force to service" (Du Cange glossar. lat. med. s. h. v.). It may also be noticed, that Suidas also uses the name Ἀστάνδαι for the ἄγγαροι. This word may also be explained from modern Persic, as equivalent to fixing the posts, by استاندن.

viously expressed is presented in an extreme case: we are not, accordingly, to expect here the mention of an act of constraint. What is spoken of, is an unjustifiable asking, which almost amounts to taking (comp. Luke vi. 30), and of an importunate borrowing: and these are mentioned as the smallest degree of injury against the rights of one's neighbour. It is very evident here, that the literal fulfilment of the isolated command may become a transgression of the general principles of morality: hence Jerome seeks to confine the asking and giving to spiritual gifts (and these, too, must not be given to every one, according to ch. vii. 6): Jerome says, what in itself is true enough: *si de eleemosyna tantum dictum intelligamus, in plerisque pauperibus hoc stare non potest; sed et divites, si semper dederint, semper dare non poterunt.* As we may conclude from δανείσασθαι, the Saviour is speaking of the giving of earthly gifts; that, however, also in the case of these, certain considerations are to be attended to, may be seen from 2 Cor. viii. 12; Gal. vi. 10; 1 Tim. v. 8. The command, "Be willing to lend," occurs with a different application in St Luke vi. 35, δανείζετε μηδὲν ἀπελπίζοντες.[1] Others have inferred that our Lord condemns lending upon interest; of this, however, He is not speaking (Calvin). Ἀποστρέψεσθαί τινα is also used in the classics (*e.g.* Sophocles Oed. Col. v. 1236) of turning away ungraciously from any one; in the LXX. especially it is the translation of הֲסָתֵּר פְּנֵי, הַעֲלִים בֵּן. Of a similar meaning are the Old Testament precepts: ἐὰν δὲ γένηται ἐν σοὶ ἐνδεὴς ἐκ τῶν ἀδελφῶν σου . . . οὐκ ἀποστέρξεις (vulg. ἀποστρέψεις) τὴν καρδίαν σου; Sir. iv. 5: ἀπὸ δεομένου μὴ ἀποστρέψῃς ὀφθαλμόν, καὶ μὴ δῷς τόπον ἀνθρώπῳ καταράσασθαί σε.

It is, accordingly, the part of Christian love, when one's rights are violated, to abstain from any selfish feeling of vengeance, and rather to seek to gain over one's enemy by acts of ministering love; and, according to Rom. xii. 20, overcoming the evil with good, to heap fiery coals of shame upon his head. This has become one of the most remarkable fruits of the Christian spirit, in the world. True, a similar conduct in regard to injuries is enjoined elsewhere than in the Old and New Testament: but rarely indeed is it said that it should proceed

---

[1] This μηδὲν ἀπελπίζοντες, Meyer (Comm. on Luke, 3 A.) would explain thus: *nihil desperantes sed—mercedem cœlestem exspectantes.* (?)

from the spirit which the Saviour assumes, namely, that of ministering love. There are, indeed, even in the Talmud, expressions which, in a figurative form, appear to present parallels to our passage (comp. above, p. 166): the Stoics especially enjoin æquabilitas animi in cases of insult. But the passages quoted from the Talmud show that its admonitions are dictated by a spirit of arrogance: and the Stoics would not allow themselves to be moved by injury, simply because they sought to rise above everything unreasonable. B.-Crusius remarks on ver. 23: The "Greeks and Romans always, in passages of this nature, regard the matter in the spirit of pride, of proud magnanimity."

Here, too, the Christian conscience has, even in the early Church, allowed itself to be led astray by a too literal interpretation, although the cases are not so numerous as in the matter of oaths. Of this number, are, among the Fathers, Origen, c. Cels. 8, 10; 7, 3; Tertullian, de idolol. c. 18; Lactantius, inst. div. vi. 18, 29; vi. 20, 15. Even martyrdom was not avoided in order to escape enlistment (Neander, Denk. i. S. 123, 2 Ed.) But those who held these views had many opponents; and Tertullian himself reminds the heathen that Christians enlisted for the service of the State (Apol. c. 42). Yet the same Father thinks it inconsistent with the priestly vocation of Christian to allow themselves to be invested with magisterial honours, on account of the necessity, thus entailed upon them, of executing criminal justice: comp. G. Arnold, Abbild der ersten Christen B. v. 5; Barbeyrac sur la morale des pères, c. v. 25; vii. 20, and others; Neander, Kirchengeschichte, i. 1, 464, 2 Ed.; and especially M. Pfaff de eccles. sanguinem non sitiente, Tub. 1740. On account of the hostility of those principles of the State, Celsus (Orig. contra Celsum vii. 3) and the Emperor Julian (Gregory Nazianz. oratio c. Jul.) blamed and reproached the Christians for holding them; Marcellinus also mentions, as a reproach of the Pagans (Augustine, ep. 136): quod (hujus religionis) prædicatio atque doctrina reipublicæ morbus multa ex parte conveniat. This accusation was also proffered by the spies upon the Persian Christians (Assemani acta Martyr. i. 181). Jewish adversaries, of a later time, reproached the Christians with not strictly adhering to the precepts of the Sermon on the Mount (Wagenseil, Sota, S. 822).

The sound view of St Augustine, which is now generally held in the Church, is thus expressed in the Glossa ordinaris: nec in his vindicta prohibetur, quæ fit ad correctionem, quæ et ipsa pertinet ad misericordiam, nec impedit propositum mansuetudinis. Sed hoc non conceditur nisi ei, cui potestas ordine data est, et sine ira, ut pater in filium.

In the testing period of the Reformation, this result also was called in question. Erasmus quotes this verse as opposed to the general practice of Christians, and exclaims: quid facient huic loco, qui lites, qui bella *calculis omnibus* approbant inter Christianos? Christus absolute vetuit resisti malo *nimirum vulgari via* ut malum malo repellatur. In the time of the Reformation, a sect of the Anabaptists, following literally the maxim of the text, and not heeding the tradition of the Church, went the length of abolishing magistrates and soldiers; the same views were held by the Mennonites; the Quakers carried them so far as to condemn every kind of resistance; many of the Socinians held that the words of the text extend only to civil processes. The English Deists, assuming that this maxim alone expresses the original spirit of Christianity, repeated the accusations of the Pagans: Mandeville's "Fable of the Bees" has for its object to show what would become of a State from which judges, advocates, soldiers, and sellers of articles of luxury, were excluded. Finally, Wislicenus, in his work, "Ob Schrift, ob Geist," 1845, expounds the words more in the spirit than in the letter: referring to Matt. v. 39—42, he says (S. 18): "These words, taken in their simple and natural sense, without the ordinary comment, are by us not only not followed, but are not even held as a moral requirement; for we know well, that to obey them would be to giver over the world to wickedness."

Compare Luther's Treatise, "von den Pflichten der Obrigkeit und Unterthanen," "Bedenken, ob Kriegsleute auch in einem seligen Stande seien," "von der Gegenwehr in puncto religionis" (Walch x. 398, 572, 622); Melanchthon, loci loc. de magistratu; Calv. institt. 4, 20; Grotius, de jure belli et pacis 2, 7; Episc. de magistratu, Opp. i. 71; Gerhard's loci T. xiv.; K. Ludwig Nitzsch, de judicandis morum præceptis, etc., S. 187.

V. The Command to Love One's Enemies.

Vers. 43—48.

Vers. 43—45. The command of the previous verse is carried still further in the present precept, from which we see that the two passages were originally connected. The offenders of whom He has been speaking, belong to the category of the "enemies" (comp. τῷ πονηρῷ, ver. 39, if that be a masculine). **Not** only must the disciple of **Christ be** so free from a spirit of revenge, that he shall be **ready even to receive** a double amount **of** injury, but he must actually return *good for evil*. Augustine: **sine ista** dilectione . . ea, quæ superius dicta sunt, implere quis potest! And, further, there is a correspondence between the manifestations of enmity and those of love, to one's enemies: against the hostile disposition, love shall prevail; the word of cursing shall be met by the word of blessing; hatred by deeds of kindness; and, for the actual manifestations of hatred, reproach and persecution, shall be returned the highest manifestation of Christian love, which is, *intercession*. St Chrysostom points out the gradual progression towards a climax, in this statement, of the **demands** of love, beginning at ver. 22: εἶδες ὅσους ἀνέβη βαθμοὺς, καὶ πῶς εἰς αὐτὴν ἡμᾶς τὴν κορυφὴν ἔστησε τῆς ἀρετῆς; σκόπει δὲ ἄνωθεν ἀριθμῶν· πρῶτός ἐστι βαθμός, μὴ ἄρχειν ἀδικίας· δεύτερος, μετὰ τὸ ἄρξασθαι τὸν ἀδικοῦντα τοῖς ἴσοις μὴ ἀμύνεσθαι· τρίτος, μὴ δρᾶσαι τὸν ἐπηρεάζοντα ταῦτα ἃ ἔπαθεν, ἀλλ' ἡσυχάσαι· τέταρτος, τὸ καὶ παρασχεῖν ἑαυτὸν εἰς τὸ παθεῖν κακῶς· πέμπτος, τὸ καὶ παρασχεῖν πλέον, ἢ ἐκεῖνος βούλεται ὁ ποιήσας· ἕκτος, τὸ μὴ μισῆσαι τὸν ταῦτα ἐργαζόμενον· ἕβδομος, τὸ καὶ ἀγαπῆσαι· ὄγδοος, τὸ καὶ εὐεργετῆσαι· ἔννατος, τὸ καὶ Θεὸν ὑπὲρ αὐτοῦ παρακαλεῖν εἶδες ὕψος φιλοσοφίας.

At it is the *disposition* of which the Saviour is speaking in this, as well as in the previous paragraph, **it** follows, that here, as **well as** there (see on ver. 38—40), this disposition will often be manifested in the precise manner which is indicated here, and similarly 1 Pet. iii. 9; Rom. xii. 20—21; 1 Cor. iv. 12. At the same time, however, the principle of love may, in certain circumstances, manifest itself in a different way. It can be shown also, in the case of this command, that neither our Lord nor the

Apostles always literally fulfilled it. In His prayer, our Lord says, John xvii. 9, "I pray not for the world;" to the hypocrites, He exclaims, "Ye serpents, ye generation of vipers, how can ye escape the judgment of hell!" Matt. xxiii. 33; and of the condemned addressed in Matt. xxv. 41, it is said, "Then shall He say to them on the left hand, Depart from Me, ye cursed, into eternal fire." When He is rejected and despised, He by no means answers with blessings (not at least with *apparent* blessings), but occasionally in terms of stern denunciation: comp. Matt. xvi. 3, 4; John viii. 44; Matt. x. 33, xi. 20, xii. 34; and in the writing of the Apostles: Gal. i. 8; 1 Cor. v. 5; 2 Tim. iv. 14; 1 St John v. 16; 2 St John 10.

Ver. 43. The first half of the saying is in Lev. xix. 18. Τὸν πλησίον is not from the masculine ὁ πλησίος; in the LXX., and with κοινή in Diog. Laert. i. 69, Antoninus xi. 1, and others, we find merely ὁ πλησίον. The words "as thyself" are omitted: had the Pharisees done so with the object of enfeebling the precept, as in ver. 31? So Socinus and Stier. We need not imagine this, as the object here is merely to bring out the contrast between the *neighbour* and the *enemy*. The words, καὶ μισήσεις τὸν ἐχθρόν σου, are a rabbinical addition; and, taken in connection with the following antithesis, given in the words of Christ, and with vers. 46, 47, they show in what sense the words, "thy neighbour," in the law ought to have been understood. The addition of the clause makes it sufficiently plain, that what our Lord is opposing is the false exposition of the Scribes. Socinus, indeed, takes a different view, thinking that here the intention of effecting a reformation of the law is more openly expressed than in what precedes: Maldonatus (who is opposed to Este, a Lapide, Tirinus), Grotius, Neander, Bleek, and also Delitzsch (vide supra, p. 159). Neander says: If the neighbour denotes one's fellow-countryman, it necessarily implies hatred of the enemy. Delitzsch (Entstehung des ersten Ev. S. 78): "In the words, 'Thou shalt hate thine enemy,' a phrase which has nothing whatever to do with rabbinical teaching (!), is expressed the principal feature of the position of Israel with reference to other nations." Thus already Tertullian adv. Marc. 1, 23: disciplinam diligendi *extraneum* vel *inimicum* antecessit præceptum diligendi proximum (Lev. xix.). Augustine quotes the words as actually words of the law: nec quod in lege dictum est: *oderis inimicum tuum,* vox jubentis justo accipienda est, sed permittentis infirmo. Similarly Luther: "The saying given here by our Lord occurs in no one passage of the Old Testament, except, occasionally, in Deuteronomy, where it refers to their enemies, the heathen; and although it is not expressly stated that they are to hate their enemies, yet this follows from what is said in Deut. xxiii. 3, that they are never to do any good thing to the Ammonites and Moabites," etc. The Socinian Osterod thought even that the words μισήσεις, κ.τ.λ., had fallen out of the Old Testament codex. But it is impossible not to admit the view which Socinus holds, and Luther dilates upon, viz., that the antithesis is directed also against a false opinion of the Scribes.[1] For the antithesis of our Lord relates not alone to the *heathen* enemies, as ver. 46 shows (comp. Fritzsche). In the pharisaic interpretation of the word, ἐχϑρὸς must accordingly have denoted, if not exclusively at least inclusively, the private enemy. Now it is unquestionable that this is a false application of the law. Everywhere in the law רֵעַ is equivalent to ἕτερος: and even the man whose murder is contemplated is so designated, Deut. xxii. 26. And, although it is further a very common prejudice that love to one's enemies is a virtue peculiar to the New Testament (even Olshausen in loco), still it is certain that the law itself condemned the cherishing of a hostile temper in private intercourse: Lev. xix. 18: "Thou shall not avenge, nor bear any grudge against the children of thy people;" comp. Exod. xxiii. 4, 5. To this we must add many sayings of the gnomic, lyric, and didactic poetry, from which we may infer that this command was no dead letter, but really penetrated the spirit of godly men: Prov. xxiv. 17, 29, xxv. 21, 22; then there is that beautiful saying which St Paul appropriates, Rom. xii. 20, Ps. vii. 5, Job xxxi. 29, Sir. xxviii. 1; further, the noble example of Joseph, Gen. xlv. 1; of David, 1 Sam. xxiv. 7, xviii. 5; and of Elisha, 2 Kings vi. 22.

---

[1] Jonathan adds, on Lev. xix. 18: "So that thou do nothing to him which thou hatest thyself." But such explanations and illustrations as the Targums contain are to be regarded only as bearing upon the lectures held in the synagogue, which were written at least a century before Christ; and it is from them that those expositions of Scripture are taken to which our Lord here refers (Zunz, die gottesdienstlichen **Vortraege der Juden,** 1832, S. 332 f.).

But we must inquire, whether the rabbinical exposition, as understood to refer to national hatred, had a right to regard the rabbinical gloss as essentially implied in the positive clause, ἀγαπήσεις τὸν πλησίον σου, as the commentators above quoted hold. This has been maintained, on the ground that in the Old Testament law ὁ πλησίον denotes never a fellow-man, but a fellow-countryman (Socinus, Grotius, Maldonatus, Wettstein, Fritzsche, Meyer). The correctness of this view may be determined by comparing several passages, in which the law is addressed especially to the עַם, *e.g.*, Exod. xxii. 24, 27; comp., with reference to this passage, Lev. xix. 17, where it is said, בְּעַמֶּיךָ, and ver. 18, אֶת־בְּנֵי עַמֶּךָ. So too אָח and עֲמִית, both which words are in the law convertible with רֵעַ, refer to the fellow-countrymen of the Jews. In the command of Lev. xix. 18, only the Israelite was included in the רֵעַ: this is clearly shown by the fact, that the command is repeated expressly for him in vers. 33, 34, כְּאֶזְרָח מִכֶּם יִהְיֶה לָכֶם הַגֵּר הַגָּר אִתְּכֶם וְאָהַבְתָּ לוֹ כָּמוֹךָ.

On the other hand, it is true, that even this saying appears to extend the privilege of neighbourly love to those who were not Israelites, as in Num. xv. 16 it is expressly said: "*One law, and one manner, shall be for you and for the stranger that sojourneth with you*" (thus D. Michaelis; L. Bauer, Biblische Moral des A. T. i. 105; Steudel, Alttest. Theologie, S. 131). But it must not be forgotten, that the foreigners who lived in Israel had all gone over to Judaism; on account of which the word προσήλυτος, by which the LXX. characterized those strangers, also denotes one who has gone over to a religion. The Syriac translation has: ܐܢܐ ܘܡܬܦܢܐ ܠܘܬܝ "he who turns himself to me." Maimonides (constit. de cultu peregrino, c. x.) states, that a heathen was not permitted to sojourn in the Jewish kingdom, for mercantile purposes, if he did not become a proselyte; and (constit. de regibus, c. viii.) he says: כל גוי שלא קִבֵּל מִצְוֹת שֶׁנִּצְטַוּוּ בְּנֵי נֹחַ הוֹרְגִין אוֹתוֹ אִם יָשַׁב תַּחַת יָדֵינוּ "Every גוי who dwells among us without accepting the seven laws of Noah (among which Monotheism was the chief) is *slain*." It appears from this statement, which is confirmed by Exod. xii. 48, that the heathen who dwelt in Israel were no longer *entirely* heathen; whilst, on the other hand, not being circumcised, they were not entirely Jews: not גֵּרֵי בְרִית, גֵּרֵי צֶדֶק, but only גֵּרֵי שַׁעַר

(like as those who stood at the gate, Lev. xxv. 48): they were afterwards called by the Rabbis the Proselytes of the gate, חֲסִידֵי גּוֹיִם; and, in the New Testament, οἱ σεβόμενοι τὸν Θεὸν sc. ἐκ τῶν ἐθνῶν. Only in so far as they were not perfect Israelites **we** have at least a relative extension of the πλησίον to the heathen.[1] Nor is there any ground for the opinion, that the heathen beyond Palestine were to the Jews only an object of hatred. No doubt, there was a common feeling of national hostility, as many **expressions** in the Prophets and in the Psalms show; but not in private intercourse. In 2 Kings vi. 22, we have an instance of magnanimous feeling towards the heathen, who are not assailed with weapons. In the Rabbis we find, no doubt, examples enough of personal hatred towards heathen, and of a lamentable limitation of the command of love to one's enemies, Prov. xxiv. 29, to the Israelites (vide Wettstein, Meuschen, Lightfoot, in loco). All the more remarkable are the instances of liberality towards the poor among the heathen in foreign lands, which occurred frequently in the later days of Judaism. Of these the rabbinical compilers, whom we have quoted, make no mention: vide Maimonides de jure paup. et peregrini, ed. Prideaux, Oxon. 1769.[2]

But we must further see whether we are entitled to suppose that the Jewish people understood the expression, one's neighbour, as contrasted with, and exclusive of, foreigners. We must here take into account that the words רֵעַ, אָח, עָמִית, nowise denote exclusively the Jewish countrymen, but are equivalent to ἕτερος, with which word St Paul (Rom. xiii. 8) translates the ὁ πλησίον of the LXX. in Lev. xix. 18. Even *before* the promulgation of the law רֵעַ occurs in this sense, and in relation to the heathen: Exod. xi 2; Gen. xxxviii. 20. It must be remembered that

---

[1] Besides, it is with the Rabbis a contested point as to whether there is any distinction between רֵעַ and תּוֹשָׁב.

[2] According to the law of Moses, a corner of the field was left for the גֵּר and the poor of Israel: in this the later Jews permitted also the heathen to share (vide Maimonides in loc. cit. c. i. § 9). There we also read (c. 9, § 6) that alms were collected in a special box "for the poor of the world:" there, too, it is expressly ordained, c. 7, § 7: מפרנסים ומכסים עניי כותיים עם עניי ישראל מפני דרכי שלום, "Let the poor who are not Israelites be fed and clothed equally with those of Israel, for the saks of the ways of salvation."

the law was not a law for all mankind, but only for a small exclusive nation: so that "another" might mean a fellow-countryman. It therefore by no means follows, that the lawgiver intended expressly to exclude the heathen from the operation of his laws: who would ever maintain that when he forbade the bearing of false witness against thy neighbour, and the coveting of his wife, that he meant to declare that these things were permitted when that neighbour was not a Jew? Some Rabbis, as the author of the Aruch, have indeed laid down the canon: הוציא כל אמות באמרי רעך, "When he says רעך, he shuts out all the heathen. Yet some of them took a more intelligent view, as Kimchi, who remarks on Ps. xv. 3, רעהו וקרבו הוא שיש לו משא ומתן עמו או שכנו: "His neighbour is every one with whom he has intercourse in giving and taking, that is, in daily life, or who dwells near him." The writers of the Talmud were also well aware what evil results would follow from understanding the רֵעַ in a sense hostile to the rest of mankind. Alluding to the command, Exod. xxi. 37: "If one man's ox hurt another's (רֵעַ), that he die," etc., the Gemara on Bava Kama, fol. 38, 1, says: What thinkest thou, if רעך be taken strictly, *i.e.*, if it means one's neighbour, then must the ox of the heathen, if it pushes the ox of the Israelite, be acquitted: if it is not taken strictly, then must the ox of the Israelite, if it push the ox of a heathen, be also pronounced guilty (Bava Kama, ed. l'Empereur, 1737, p. 74). The word ὁ πλησίον occurs in the sense of fellow-man already in Sirach xiii. 15: πᾶν ζῶον ἀγαπᾷ τὸ ὅμοιον αὐτῷ καὶ πᾶς ἄνθρωπος τὸ πλησίον αὐτοῦ. πᾶσα σὰρξ κατὰ γένος συνάγεται κ. τ. ὁμοίῳ αὐτοῦ προσκολληθήσεται ἀνήρ. Even Abenezra gives this remarkable sentence as the principle from which obedience to the law should flow: "For I, who have created you, am one God:" a saying which necessarily implies the relation of universal brotherhood among men —שעם כי אני אלוה אחד בראתי אתכם.

We must finally notice the answer which our Lord gave to the question, "Who is my neighbour?" Luke x. 30. In the first place, the very question is a proof that it was a controverted point in what sense רֵעַ was to be understood. For, it was understood by many, as in the gloss of our passage; but also by many, such as Sirach, in the wider signification of fellow-man. Now our Lord, in His answer, takes the question out of the domain of the school, and transfers it into common life. His reply is: "Even a Samaritan, as thou canst not help acknowledging, would in a case of necessity, prove himself by deeds *thy* neighbour." From the preceding remarks, it is impossible to doubt that our Lord did not intend to establish a new interpretation of רֵעַ as one opposed to the Old Testament, but sought only to deliver it from the unnecessary limitations which it had received on account of the peculiar circumstances of the theocracy.

It follows, then, that the Scribes had rendered themselves guilty of a falsification of the law, even if they understood the words added (Thou shalt hate, etc.) only in a *national* sense. It follows, further, that although now רֵעַ is generally explained to mean a fellow-Jew, this translation is, to say the least of it, inaccurate. Equally so, however, is the old explanation of it, as meaning simply a fellow-man (Bucer,[1] Calvin, Spanheim, Coccejus, Calov, Scherzer Coll. Anti-Socin. p. 1079, Hacksp. Notæ misc. ad h. l., and others). The word was unquestionably given among the laws which were intended to direct the people in their intercourse with each other; and, accordingly, it denotes simply the Jewish fellow-contryman.

Ver. 44. We have seen that the command to love one's **enemies** is not given as an antithesis to the law of Moses, but that it was also commanded to the Jewish people, and also practised by them. Even beyond the pale of the Bible-religion, it was not wholly unknown to the moral consciousness of other nations. Here we may compare the very unsatisfactory, incomplete, **misleading, writings of Fischer**, quid de officiis et amore erga inimicos Græcis et Romanis placuerit, Halae 1789; **Huepeden, de amore inimicorum**, Gottingen 1817; Klippel; Meyer, doctrina Stoicorum ethica atque Christiana, 1823; and Grotius, Pric., Wettstein, in loco. Generally speaking, **the stand-point of the ancient world is less elevated than that of the** Old Testament law: ὠφελεῖν μὲν τοὺς φίλους, βλάπτειν δὲ τοὺς ἐχθρούς, was the maxim even of the wise men of the

---

[1] Bucer considers it as a singularis providentia, that the Hebrew word has been translated ὁ πλησίον. This word, he thinks, was intended to prevent a narrow misunderstanding, inasmuch as it necessarily suggests the wider thought of fellow-man.

people.[1] This egotism is very plainly put in some verses of Hesiod, which Plutarch was inclined to consider unauthentic on account of their illiberality: τὸν φιλέοντα φιλεῖν καὶ τῷ προσιόντι προσεῖναι, καὶ δόμεν ὅς κεν δῷ, καὶ μὴ δόμεν ὅς κεν μὴ δῷ. Δώτῃ μέν τις ἔδωκεν, ἀδώτῃ δ' οὔτις ἔδωκεν (Op. et dies v. 353). In a passage in Plutarch (de sera Num. vind. c. 22), where there is a description of the moral transformation of an immoral man, it is said, in his praise, that since him there had been no one among the Cilicians who was more useful to his friends or more dangerous to his enemies. Socrates, Plato, and the other Stoics, opposed these maxims: according to Plato, nothing but good ought to proceed from a good man; according to the Stoics, the wise man ought to imitate the Deity in loving his enemies (Xenoph. Memor. ii. 3, 16; Plato de Republ. p. 134 seqq.). But what distinguishes the doctrine of morals taught by the philosophers from the Christian doctrine, are the different motives prescribed.[2] Why does Socrates condemn hatred of one's enemies? It is on account of the evil which the hater entails upon himself. What Plato blames, is the custom of determining who is a friend, or who an enemy, by the power the man possesses to aid or to injure. The Stoic, again, condemns hatred of one's enemies, on the ground that the wise man ought not to allow himself to be moved by any passion.[3] What the motive of *Christ* is, is expressed in ver. 45. The thought which is there set forth, in popular language, is expressed by Clement of Alexandria (Strom. iv. 605, Pott.): τὸ δὲ ἀγαπᾶν τοὺς ἐχθροὺς, οὐκ ἀγαπᾶν τὸ κακὸν λέγει, οὐδὲ ἀσέβειαν ἢ μοιχείαν ἢ κλοπήν· ἀλλὰ τὸν κλέπτην καὶ τὸν ἀσεβῆ καὶ τὸν μοιχὸν, οὐ καθὸ ἁμαρ-

---

[1] The Emperor Julian is conscious of saying a thing opposed to the prevalent opinion, when he remarks (Fragm. ed. Spanh. p. 290), φαίην δ' ἂν εἰ καὶ παράδοξον εἰπεῖν, ὅτι καὶ τοῖς πολεμίοις ἐσθῆτος καὶ τροφῆς ὅσιον ἂν εἴη μεταδιδόναι.

[2] What a counterpart to the Christian love of enemies is presented in what Basil narrates of Socrates, giving it as a parallel to ver. 39 (de legendis libris gentilium, c. v.)! Having been struck in the face by a drunken man, the wise man was content to set over the wound the words, "N. did this;" as the name of the sculptor is inscribed on his statue.

[3] Seneca de benef. iii. 26, vii. 31: Revenge is doloris confessio. Ille ingens animus et verus æstimator sui non vindicat injuriam, *quia non sentit*—ille magnus et nobilis est, qui more magnæ feræ latratus minorum canum securus exaudit.

τάνει καὶ τῇ ποιᾷ ἐνεργείᾳ μολύνει τὴν ἀνθρώπου προσηγορίαν· καθ᾿ ὃ δὲ ἄνθρωπός ἐστι καὶ ἔργον Θεοῦ. Chemnitz gives the following limitations for the application of this principle: Simplicissima responsio sumitur ex verbis Christi: *ita diligendos scilicet esse inimicos, sicut deus diligit malos*, longanimitate sua parcens, et benefaciens illis in opere providentiæ, non ut illos confirmet in impietate, sed ut hac sua bonitate illos ad pœnitentiam adducat, ad Rom. ii. 4. Sæpe vero freno et hamo coercet ipsos, ut ita eos convertat, Ps. xxxii. 9; Jes. xxxvii. 29. Ex hac collatione multæ quæstiones recte et expedite possunt explicari. . . . Optanda sunt etiam inimicis bona gratiæ et gloriæ, quibus nemo potest male uti, bona vero naturæ et fortunæ eatenus ipsis optanda sunt, quatenus ipsis salutaria sunt ad pœnitentiam. The rule given by St Augustine on ver. 39 applies here: Non ad operis ostentationem, sed ad cordis præparationem hæc dicta sunt. The command to love one's enemies may be obeyed in spirit, even when it is one's duty to proclaim the course of God instead of His blessing, and to withhold instead of granting and benefit.

The words εὐλογεῖτε τ. καταρωμένους ὑμᾶς are omitted in Codex B., the Vulgate, seven times by Origen and other Fathers, by Griesbach, Lachmann, Tischendorf. Despite this strong testimony, it is uncertain whether the words ought not to be retained. The meaning of the clauses is so similar, that omissions in their citation might easily occur.[1] The conclusions, which are so similar, might occur in the transcriptions. Further, in Luke vi. 28, from which the words might have been introduced into our passage, καλῶς ποιεῖτε comes after the rest. Finally, the words in our Gospel mark a fitting progression from the *spirit* to the *word*, the *deed*, and the *prayer*.

The first clause, expressing the spirit, Thou shalt love, etc. has placed over against it, Thou shalt hate, etc., and is then carried out in the special commands which follow. The word used in the Law-passages is ἀγαπᾶν and not φιλεῖν; for the former is equivalent to diligere, moral love; the latter, to a more instinctive natural love. This distinction is well observed in St John xi. 5, where the word used of the love of Jesus to the sisters in ἀγαπᾶν; whereas, for His love to the brother, φιλεῖν is used in

---

[1] Origen omits five times the succeeding ἐπηρεαζόντων ὑμᾶς καὶ, but twice he quotes it. Tertullian, de patientia. c. vi., omits καλῶς ποιεῖτε.

vers. 3, 36. But the distinction in the case of φιλεῖν is not always observed in classical usage.[1] Not τοὺς μισοῦντας, but the Dative μισοῦσιν, is the right reading, as in Luke vi. 27, according to the Hellenistic construction of εὖ, κακῶς ποιεῖν; the Accusative, however, occurs in Mark xiv. 7, and the LXX., Gen. xxxii. 9, 12, Job xxiv. 21, etc. With the exception of Codex B., there is almost an equally great amount of testimony against ἐπηρεαζόντων ὑμᾶς καὶ. But here, it might be said, that the words were, originally, merely a marginal note inserted by a transcriber from Luke vi. 28. Ἐπηρεάζειν, "to injure by word, to slander;" "and to injure by deed, to maltreat:" the Vulgate takes it in the former sense: calumniari; Ulf. and Luther in the latter.

The Peschito has ܠܐܝܠܝܢ ܕܕܒܪܝܢ ܠܟܘܢ؟؟ "who drag you on by force;" Philox.: ܕܛܠܡܝܢ ܠܟܘܢ؟ "who plunder you." Διώκειν is not to be understood here, any more than in ver. 11, of legal persecution, as Beza, Elsner, have done.

Ver. 45. Bullinger: non modo quid sui faciant, ostendit Christus, sed stimulos admovet, quibus incitet. The motive adduced for this behaviour is, that it best corresponds to their character, as "sons of God" (comp. on ver. 9). The remark of Bengel is founded upon an incorrect translation of the Aorist γένησθε: Ita fiunt filii, he says, cum inimicos amant, ut jam antea habeant Patrem. Filii fiunt filii, sicut discipuli fiunt discipuli, Joh. xv. 8. Meyer is equally wrong: "That they man *become* the children," etc., that is, in the kingdom of the Messiah. Rightly the Vulgate, Luther, the English translation: "That ye may *be* the children." Maldonatus translates the υἱοί by similes merely. Beza, however, observes: Valet regula: tunc dici aliquid esse, cum esse intelligitur (comp. κληθήσονται, ver. 9); Hunnius: *re* et *facto* probabitis vos esse. Here expositors are in the habit of quoting brilliant parallel passages from the classics (comp. Grotius, Pricæus, Wettstein). Reference is made to the phrase, ὁμοιοῦσθαι τῷ Θεῷ κατὰ τὸ δυνατόν, in Plato Theæt. 176

---

[1] In later Greek, ἀγαπᾶν, as well as φιλεῖν, means to kiss: Eustath. p. 1935, 35; du Cange, gloss. græcit. med. ævi s. v. ἀγάπη; comp. the later inexact use of φιλεῖν, ἐρᾶν, ποθεῖν, Creuzer on Plotinus de pulchritudine, p 213

A.; and Plutarch (de sera N. vindicta, c. 5), bids the revengeful remember the πραότης and μεγαλοπάθεια of God. Si Deos imitaris, says Seneca (de benef. iv. 16), da et ingratis beneficia. Nam et sceleratis sol oritur et piratis patent maria (comp. vii. 31). Εἰ μὲν δύνασαι, so speaks Antoninus ix. 11, μεταδίδασκε (teach te enemy something better), εἰ δὲ μή, μέμνησο, ὅτι πρὸς τοῦτο ἡ εὐμένειά σοι δέδοται· καὶ οἱ θεοὶ δὲ εὐμενεῖς τοῖς τοιούτοις εἰσίν· εἰς ἔνια δὲ καὶ συνεργοῦσιν, εἰς ὑγίειαν, εἰς πλοῦτον, εἰς δόξαν· οὕτως εἰσὶ χρηστοί· ἔξεστι δὲ καὶ σοί.

Now, although the profoundly religious Plutarch and the childlike Antoninus have here made a beautiful application of the religious doctrine of their system, yet we must not forget that in the system itself the matter was viewed in a very different aspect. The Platonic ὁμοιοῦσθαι τῷ Θεῷ meant nothing more than that men should take refuge from sensuality in the domain of philosophic thought, and in a life in harmony therewith; and the God of the Stoic, whose good-will even the wicked experience, is nothing else but that εἱμαρμένη which, unconcerned about individuals,[1] guides the course of the world according to the principle of an eternal law of reason. The decision respecting the relation of the New Testament doctrine of love to enemies, to that of the classics, is rightly given by Marheineke, Moral S. 491.

The benign, all-enfolding light of the sun, which shines alike on all (Sirach xlii. 16), who do not withdraw themselves from its beams, and the fruitful blessing of the raincloud (Ps. cxlvii. 8), which, stretching far over all lands, pours its treasures upon all,—what beautiful images of the all-embracing love of God, which visits even His enemies! For the evil are regarded as the enemies of God. Chrys.: καὶ γὰρ καὶ αὐτοὺς οὐ μόνον οὐ μισεῖ, φησιν, ἀλλὰ καὶ εὐεργετεῖ τ. ὑβρίζοντας.

But, inasmuch as a capacity to receive the blessings of God is the condition of participation in them, the blessings here spoken of are limited to the external and sensible blessings, as in Acts xiv. 17. The Divine justice is nowise diminished by this forbearance, Rom. ii. 4, 5. The author of the Opus imperfectum ably touches upon other points besides that adduced in the passage of St Paul: Quemadmodum in *bonis* non separat pec-

---

[1] Seneca nat. quæst. ii. 46: singulis non adest (Jupiter), sed signum et vim et causam dedit omnibus.

catores a justis, sic nec in *malis* justos a peccatoribus . . ne mali separati cognoscant se abjectos esse et desperent, neve boni separati cognoscant se electos et glorientur, maxime *cum nec malis bona prosint sed noceant magis, nec bonis mala noceant, sed prosint magis.*

In St. Luke's narrative the beautiful concrete form of the saying is lost: ὅτι αὐτὸς χρηστός ἐστιν ἐπὶ τοὺς ἀχαρίστους καὶ πονηρούς. Ὅτι, which the Vulgate and Peschito translate as a relative, gives the point of comparison. Ἀνατέλλειν since Herodotus was used only intransitively; but in the κοινή, and in Homer and Pindar, it occurs transitively; also in the LXX., Isa. xlv. 8, Gen. iii. 19. According to the ancient view of the world, the phenomena of nature were referred immediately to the author and Lord of nature; and accordingly the sun is here called "*His* sun," τὸν ἥλιον αὐτοῦ. Augustine: solem *suum* i.e., quem ipse fecit atque constituit et a nullo aliquid sumsit, ut faceret. The subject of βρέχει must be regarded as God, according to ancient Greek and Hebrew usage: comp. in Latin, Jove tonante; even Josephus writes ὄντος τοῦ Θεοῦ, νίφοντος τοῦ Θεοῦ, although Aristophanes (Nubes, v. 367) jests at the ancient phrase, ὁ Θεὸς ὕει. Justin Martyr quotes accordingly: φέρει τὸν ὑετόν. Another instance of the manner in which the religious mind, in contemplating nature, rises at once beyond all second causes to the great First Cause, may be seen from St Matt. vi. 26, 30.—Βρέχειν for ὕειν occurs before the time of Alexander only in the poets; in prose, however, it is found in the κοινή, in the LXX., in Arrian, and Polybius.

Vers. 46, 47. That manifestation of love to which the religion of the Pharisees was wont to confine itself, is characterized as a merely natural feeling, such as is found in the lowest stage of the moral life. It is the love of those who love us, of our φίλοι. Φίλοι and ὠφέλιμοι are, in the ancient view, corresponding expressions, as already observed (p. 283). Auctor op. imp.: qui amicos diligit, *propter se* diligit, non propter Deum, et ideo nullam habet mercedem. Of course there were noble exceptions among the Pharisees. Thus, we have a saying from the sentences of the Pirke Aboth of the Talmud, c. v. § 10, which date from ante-Christian times, and are in some respects excellent. According to this saying, that disposition whose maxim is, "What is mine is mine, and what is thine is thine," is called the מִדָּה בֵּינוֹנִית; whilst only *he* is called חָסִיד whose motto is, "What is mine is thine."—Parallel to τ. ἀγαπῶντας ὑμᾶς, Cod. E, K, L, M, S, Ulf., and others, have φίλοι, but B, D, and the translations have ἀδελφοί, or the corresponding word. Φίλοι, as Griesbach observes in his Critical Commentary, is a word corresponding to the Hewrew ἀδελφοί; and φιλοῦντας in Codex 17 of Matthew confirms this: but in order to have a proper antithesis to ἐθνικοί (for which, indeed, those codices, Peschito, Ar. Erp., Pers. Pol., have again τελῶναι), we must take τοὺς ἀγαπῶντας in the sense **of fellow-countrymen**.

Here the Saviour assumes the pharisaic point of view and mode of address; like them, He speaks of a reward: they themselves had an eye to a reward in all their conduct (ch. vi. 2, 3). He speaks of the περισσόν by which they sought to distinguish themselves from others, as their very name indicates, פְּרוּשִׁים (ch. xix. 16, 20). He selects, as representatives of the lowest class of society, the τελῶναι and ἐθνικοί, as they themselves used to do. (On μισθός, vide supr., p. 103.) For ἔχετε, Codex D and the Vulgate have ἕξετε. But also in ch. vi. 1 the Present tense is used to express a certain future; here, the Present shows that the reward is regarded as already existing, as a κληρονομία τετηρημένη ἐν οὐρανοῖς (1 Pet. i. 4; Col. i. 5). For τελῶναι, and also for ἐθνικοί, St Luke has the general word ἁμαρτωλοί. Justin (Apol. i. 15) quotes: εἰ ἀγαπᾶτε . . . . . καὶ οἱ πόρνοι τοῦτο ποιοῦσιν. But it was precisely the class of tax-gatherers which, **among the Jews, had the worst character**, being regarded as occupying the same moral level with the heathen: Matt. xviii. 17. Their business was to collect the personal and income taxes, the duties on **wares at the harbours, and on articles of food** in the towns. According to the testimony of Appian (Syr. c. l.), they were felt to be peculiarly oppressive and tyrannical **in Judea** at the time of the Roman rule. Even under its **Grecian masters, it was the practice in Palestine to let on lease** the right of collecting the customs to men of opulence (Josephus, Antiq. xii. 4, 1. 4). Those *lessees* of customs, along with the tax-*gatherers*, are designated by the comprehensive term מוֹכְסִים; in tract. Schabbath, fol. 78, 2, the large are distinguised from the small. But both classes were regarded with the aversion

19

and contempt which everywhere and at all times is apt to meet a class which, in the discharge of its functions, takes upon itself to make domestic inquisitions, to open locked-up places, and so forth (vide Plautus, Menaech. i. 2, 6; Trin. iii. 3, 64, 80; Terence, Phorm. i. 2, 100). They were also addicted to the practice of exacting and embezzling funds for their own enrichment (Luke iii. 13, xix. 8). Hence also among the Greeks they are called καπήλοις, λῃσταῖς, πορνοβοσκοῖς, μοιχοῖς (Artemidorus, Oneinocr. iv. 59; Lucian, Necyom. c. 11; Theophrastus, Charact. c. 7); and the terms applied to them are φορτικός, λῃστεύων, ἀπάνθρωπος, etc. (Pollux, Onom. ix. 5). Also in the Talmud they are classed with robbers and murderers (comp. Buxt. lex. s. v. מוֹכֵס). It as frequently been asserted (Wettstein, Lightfoot; also Winer, Realwoerterbuch), that they were incompetent to act as witnesses, and that the oath taken by them was invalid; this is, however, incorrect.[1] This dislike to the publicans must have been increased when Judea became a Roman province; for the taxes then went immediately to the heathen, and the duty of collecting them fell to be discharged by heathen officers, מוֹכְסִין נָכְרִי. This was not, however, universally the case, as may be seen from the instances of *Jewish* tax-gatherers which occur in the New Testament; and these men, by favouring their countrymen, won their good-will (comp. the Gemara on Sanhedrin in loc. cit.). From what has been said, we may gather to how great an extent our Lord, by His intercourse with these men, and by sayings like that in Matt. xxi. 32, must have provoked and scandalized the self-righteous Pharisees.

As regards the parallel clause, ἐὰν ἀσπάσησθε, κ.τ.λ., no doubt the reading of φίλοι instead of ἀδελφοί may possibly be correct, as אָח denotes the "friend," as well as the relation and the

---

[1] The Sanhedrin Exc. ex Gemara, ed. Coec. p. 194, says, that they were not always incompetent, but only when they could be proved to have been guilty of exactions. In the Nedarim Mischna iii. 4 (Surenh. iii. 112) it is merely said, that promises and declarations made to murderers, robbers, and tax-gatherers were not binding. According to Maimonides and Bartenora, this did not hold with regard to those tax-gatherers who had been appointed by a just ruler. The statement from the Bava Kama. c. 10, 1, that alms could not be taken from the coffer of tax-gatherers, must also be taken with limitations. The fear was, that the money might have been exacted; but from his private resources the publican was permitted to give to the poor (comp. l'Empereur).

"fellow-countryman." Nor is the antithesis of ἐθνικοί against this view, as the latter, equally with τελῶναι, denotes the lowest moral grade (Matt. xviii. 17; comp. τὰ ἔθνη, vi. 32). Yet same have preferred the meaning of "fellow-countryman" on account of that antithesis (Piscator, Paulus, Griesbach, and others). In this case, the antithesis in ver. 43 would also refer to *this* meaning of ἐχθρός. But would our Lord have thus pointedly required the people to be well-disposed towards the *heathen?* No similar expression of His occurs: on the contrary, there are numerous passages in which He strictly observes the national line of demarcation (ch. x. 5; Mark vii. 24, 28). We accordingly prefer the meaning, "friend, relation."

Ἀσπάζεσθαι has been recently again taken in its proper sense of, to salute, to greet, by Paulus, Fritzsche, Meyer, De Wette: as by the Vulgate, Peschito, Ulfilas, Chrysostom, Erasmus, Grotius. Now it is quite possible that the uncharitable, bigoted Jews refused to salute the heathen: but did they refuse the salutation to all whom they did not count among their brethren? And would our Lord think it worth while to notice this, the smallest and most customary of the signs of ἀγάπη? It is true, no doubt, that the Oriental mind attaches considerable importance to the salutation (Sir. xli, 20; 2 John 10), and that to this day the Arabs meet Christians with the salutation السلام عليكم, which corresponds to the Hebrew שָׁלוֹם לָכֶם (Harmar, Beobacht. ueber den Orient, ii. 36; Rosenmueller, Altes und Neues Morgenland, v. 31). But is the salutation here spoken of, one of a peculiarly significant character? if so, would not such a salutation have been mentioned? Now it is proved that ἀσπάζεσθαι has also the secondary signification of φιλοφρονεῖσθαι (Muenthe, Palair., Loesner ad locum, Kypke on Heb. xi. 25). We have, therefore, no hesitation in accepting the sense in which Beza and Luther understand the phrase, viz., "to act in a friendly manner towards one."—Περισσόν, well rendered by Luther "Sonderliches," special, "more than others." Plutarch often combines ἴδιος and περιττός (Wyttenb. Mor., ed. Lips. i. 368[1]).

---

[1] Justin, Apol. i. 15, quotes instead, τί καινόν, in which Hilgenfeld scents an anti-Judaizing tendency; on the contrary, compare Ritschl in Zeller's Jahrb. 1851, S. 490.

Ver. 48. It is a question whether οὖν denotes the inference from the verses which immediately precede, or the result of *all* the foregoing πληρώσεις. The nature of the saying itself would seem to indicate the latter, if there is implied an allusion to the words, Lev. xix. 2: ἅγιοι ἔσεσθε, ὅτι ἅγιός εἰμι ἐγὼ κύριος ὁ Θεὸς ὑμῶν. It would then correspond to 1 Peter i. 15, κατὰ τὸν καλέσαντα ὑμᾶς ἅγιον καὶ αὐτοὶ ἅγιοι γενήθητε. Τέλειος = תָּמִים, already in the Old Testament used not of metaphysical, but of moral perfection, Deut. xviii. 13: τέλειος ἔσῃ ἐναντίον κυρίου τοῦ Θεοῦ: comp. Matt. xix. 21; Rom. xii. 2; Col. i. 18. It is used of God, 2 Sam. xxii. 26; Deut. xxxii. 4. This is the view of Aretius, Beza, Maldonatus, Er. Schmid, Calvin, Kuinoel, Fritzsche, Olshausen. Bruno Bauer asserts, that the reason the Evangelist had, in selecting τέλειοι instead of οἰκτίρμονες, as in St Luke, was that he might have a word which would form a good conclusion; and Ewald's idea is, that Matt. vii. 12 ought to come in here, in order that the duties to God and man may be both comprehended here. Now none of the preceding Christian antitheses speak directly of duties towards God, in the sense in which moral philosophy is wont to place them in juxtaposition to duties towards man. If τέλειοι were to be understood in a general sense, what is spoken of would be the imitation of God in the fulfilment of the so-called indirect duties towards God. But the commands contained in the verses which precede ver. 42 could not well come under the category of the imitation of the Divine perfection. Moreover, there does not exist, as alleged, any necessity for a comprehensive formula to conclude with, for there is no reason for the exclusion of the commands in chaps. vi. and vii. We hold, accordingly, that the right view is what is expressed in the οἰκτίρμονες of St Luke; that the τέλειοι in St Matthew is therefore to be restricted to those virtues (and ver. 45 implies this) in which especially resemblance to God is manifested. Among the Fathers this view was universal (Justin, Origen, Clemens Alex. vii. 752, Tertullian, Chrysostom, Hilary, Augustine; so too Erasmus, Bucer, Calvin, Luther, Chemn., Sarcer., Calixt, Bengel, Stier, Meyer, De Wette; comp. also Spener in opposition to the extravagant views of Christian perfection, theol. Bedenken iv. 103). Justin, dial. c. Tr. c. 96, quotes thus, taking in ver. 45: γίνεσθε χρηστοὶ καὶ οἰκτίρμονες ὡς καὶ ὁ πατὴρ ὑμῶν ὁ οὐράνιος· καὶ γὰρ τὸν παντοκράτορα Θεὸν ὁρῶμεν, τὸν ἥλιον αὐτοῦ, κ.τ.λ.: so too Origen quotes, de princ. ii. 4, 1. Schol. Matthæi, with allusion to Plato, τοῦτο δὲ ποιοῦντες ἐξομοιούμεθα κατὰ τὸ δυνατὸν τῷ Θεῷ ἐν τῷ ἀδιακρίτως εὐεργετεῖν.

CHAPTER VI.

THE TRUE MOTIVE IN WORKS OF RIGHTEOUSNESS, THE EYE FIXED ON HIM WHO SEES IN SECRET.

Ver. 1. First, as regards the point of transition from the previous chapter. Maldonatus thinks we have here the commencement of a new discourse: after the Saviour had on the mountain taught His Apostles the consilia of perfection (chap. v.), He now begins in the plain a discourse of instruction in the Christian virtues in general. According to Ernesti (similarly too De Wette), chap. v. shows wherein Christian righteousness must exceed the righteousness of the Pharisees; chap. vi. points out wherein the Christian ought to surpass others in those virtues which were common to both Christians and Pharisees. Luther and Chemnitz think that chap. v. contains the correction of wrong *doctrine,* chap. vi. the reformation of *life;* Chrysostom again regards chap. v. as unfolding the true doctrine of morals, whilst chap. v. sets forth the dangers which arise from wrong motives (especially pride) in putting it in practice. So, especially, a Lapide: postquam explicuit legis præcepta, hoc capite modum docet, ea rite sancteque faciendi sc. ut ea faciamus *recta intentione.* This system of logical categorizing may seem to belong rather to the reflecting expositor than to the speaker himself: moreover, these divisions apply no further than the 17th verse. Still we must suppose that the thoughts of our Lord did make this transition (comp. Ebrard). Stier's idea is, that in the 6th chapter there follows the rebuke of that false religion which was the result of their literal method of expounding the law. But it is not clear in what way that false *obedience* to the precepts of the law could have resulted from a carnal *apprehension* of those precepts. Surely many a Pharisee may have honestly obeyed the law, in so far as he understood it, without regard to the praise of men.

That false piety is exposed in those three kinds of good works, of which the Jews in the later days of the nation were especially proud; and which also occupy the most prominent position in the religious practice of the Greek and Romish Churches. Special value is attached to alms-giving already in the Apocrypha (Berthold on Dan. iv. 24; Cramer, Moral der Apokryphen in Keil and Tzschirner's Anal. ii. 83), were it is even declared to be able to save from ruin and from death (Tobit iv. 6—12, xiv. 9—12, xii. 9, 10; Sir. iv. 2, xxix. 15, 16; whether also in Dan. iv. 24 is doubtful; comp. on the passage, Michaelis, Haevernick, Lengerke). Numerous proverbs express the great importance attached to alms-giving by the Rabbis: "Alms are the salt of the kingdom." "As once expiation was made on the altar by the sacrifice, so now it is made on each man's table by alms-giving." "Prayer is a winnowing shovel; for as this winnows the corn, so does that the wrath of God." "Alms-giving and doing good are the fulfilling of the whole law." (Buxt. Florilegium hebr. p. 88; Otho, lex. Rabbin. p. 164).

Owing to this high estimation of alms, they were called in the dialect of Jerusalem צִדְקְתָה (Buxt. lex. Talm. s. h. v.); also צְדָקָה according to its meaning, "benevolence," "goodness." So too in Samaritan ᴣᴘᛋᴔ (Gesen. carm. Sam. S. 61), Arab. ܨܕܩܬܐ, Syr. ܙܕܩܬܐ. In the Greek language of apocryphal and Christian writers, we find ἐλεημοσύνη used for "alms," the abstract for the concrete; so too in the Romaic languages, la carità, la charité. Here the ed. rec. has also ἐλεημοσύνη. The testimonies in favour of this reading have been but imperfectly given by the critics: they are, Cod. Z. Dubl. rescr.; Ulf.; Philox.; the Coptic, which has donum vestrum (ed. Schwarz, 1846); the Ethiopic translation; Origen in the Greek text ad Matt., T. iii. 501 (in the Latin translation it is twice rendered justitia); then Chrysostom, who considers that what is said in the close of chap. v. on love to enemies, relates to almsgiving, and so makes *this* idea the point of transition to chap. vi.; so too the auctor operis imperfecti in the Latin text. On the other hand, for δικαιοσύνῃ we have the following authorities: Cod. B, D,

Itala, Vulgate, the Syriac translation of Jerusalem, and others.[1] Several critics, as Wettstein, Matthæi, Elsner, contend for the reading ἐλεημοσύνη with great decision, on the ground that the οὖν in ver. 2 must refer back to ver. 1. But it is difficult to see how δικαιοσύνη could come to be read, if it had not been the word which stood originally. It is very unlikely that a *definite* term, ἐλεημοσύνη, would have been supplanted by the more *general* one, δικαιοσύνη: while, on the other hand, it is easy to conceive that the more definite word was introduced to explain the more general term. Thus in the Philoxenic version, to the word ܙܕܝܩܘܬܐ the gloss ܙܕܩܬܐ is added, meaning "alms." We therefore give decided preference to the reading δικαιοσύνη.

In what sense, then, is the word used? Drusius understands it in the rabbinical acceptation of "alms." In this sense, however, the word is never used in the Old Testament or the Apocrypha. Yet, in later Hebrew usage, the idea of charity, deeds of mercy, "doing good," came to be mainly associated with the word. We may therefore (with Grotius and others) take the word here in that sense; so that ver. 1 will contain the general reference to works of kindness and mercy; ver. 2, the special admonition on the subject of alms-giving. Meyer contests this meaning of δικαιοσύνη; and De Wette says that it has this meaning only as the general includes the special, the word itself implying much more than "doing good." This is true even where the *leading* idea of the word is benevolence, as may be seen from Tob. xiv. 11: καὶ νῦν, παιδία, ἴδετε, τί ἐλεημοσύνη ποιεῖ καὶ [πῶς] δικαιοσύνη ῥύεται. But it is incontestable that in later parlance the idea of kindness, mercy, charity, became the leading idea of the word. Compare, *e.g.*, the use of δικαιοσύνη Θεοῦ, Baruch v. 2: "Wrap the righteousness of God around thee like a garment;" compare also δίκαιος, Matt. i. 19, which Chrysostom explains by χρηστός; and Prov. xi. 4, Ps. cxii. 9, where δικαιοσύνη stands for "liberality." Besides, the rabbinical use of the word for "alms" could not otherwise be accounted for. The transition to this use is indicated by the phrase ποιεῖν ἐλεημοσύνην. Yet, if we consider the arrangement

---

[1] The Peschito version has ܙܕܩܬܐ, but as the vocalization is uncertain, it does not count.

of the three sections, vers. 2—17, in which three sorts of good works are spoken of, we are forced to conclude that ver. 1 treats not of any one *species,* but of the *genus* of good works. For in each of these sections we find, first, a reference to the nature of pharisaic work; next, in contrast therewith, the corresponding Christian work; and as a finale, the section concludes with the full-toned ἀπέχουσι τὸν μισθὸν αὐτῶν. They are thus illustrations of the general sentence which introduces them, and which finishes with the words, εἰ δὲ μήγε, μισθὸν οὐκ ἔχετε. So Augustine, Beza, Grotius, Bengel, Olearius, observations in Matt., and the modern commentators. The "righteousness" is accordingly that "righteousness of the Pharisees" spoken of in v. 20; the phrase, δικαιοσύνην ποιεῖν, ἐργάζεσθαι, for τὰ τῆς δικαιοσύνης, Acts x. 35; 1 John ii. 29; Heb. xi. 33. To this correspond exactly the phrases, ἐλεημοσύνην, and ἐλεημοσύνας ποιεῖν, in Sirach vii. 10, xxxii. 2; Tobit i. 3, 16. Wettstein objects: qui juste vivit, dicitur δικαιοσύνην ποιῶν, non vero δικαιοσύνην ποιεῖν αὐτοῦ. The objection, however, does not hold; for it is precisely that righteousness to which the disciples of Jesus were to aspire that is the subject of discourse: comp. v. 20: ἡ δικαιοσύνη ὑμῶν; Gen. xx. 13: "The kindness which thou shalt show unto me," זֶה חַסְדֵּךְ אֲשֶׁר תַּעֲשִׂי עִמָּדִי.

What is forbidden, is not that these works should be done in conspectu hominum, as what follows might lead us to suppose. The Ethiopic version falsely translates ἔμπροσθεν τῶν ἀνθρώπων, ad apparendum hominibus. What is meant is, that they are not to be done with the object of being seen (comp. on πρός, p. 208). It is thus a θεατρίζειν τὴν ἀρετήν that is disapproved; and then we must also recollect that the word ὑποκριτής originally meant an actor.[1] (On μισθός, see p. 103; on ἔχετε, p. 269.)

I. Warning against a Hypocritical Exercise of Charity, for the sake of the Praise of Men. Vers. 2—4.

Vers. 2. Οὖν, as before remarked, evolves the special admonition out of the general one contained in the first verse: Be it

---

[1] The note of Nic. Lyra here furnishes a striking example of philological barbarity: hypocrita dicitur ab *hypos* quod est *sub* et *crisis aurum,* quia sub auro vel sub *honestate* exterioris conversationis habet absconditum plumbum falsitatis.

far from you to seek to draw the attention of men to your deeds of charity and alms-giving. It may be asked, whether the phrase σαλπίζειν ἔμπροσθέν τινος is to be understood literally. If so, we should have to suppose that the sanctimonious hypocrites were wont to call together the poor by trumpets, blown either by themselves or by their attendants, with a view to direct public attention to their charities. Euthymius: φασὶ δέ τινες, ὅτι ὑποκριταὶ τότε διὰ σάλπιγγος συνεκάλουν τοὺς δεομένους: Lyra, Calvin, Chemnitz, Bengel, Wolf, Moldenhauer, Paulus. A boastful theatrical behaviour was quite in keeping with the character of that class of men. The following trait also bears this impress, although it has a certain facetiousness about it, which the case before us has not. It is related of the Rabbi Abba, who is represented to have been a model of benevolence, that in order not to hurt the feelings of the poor, he used to go about with an open bag on his back, **full of** alms, to which the poor might help themselves unobserved (Wagenseil excerpt. Gemar. in Sota, p. 98). Still it is a suspicious circumstance, that not one instance can be found of this trumpet-summoning of the poor. The laborious Lightfoot confesses: Non inveni, quaesiverim licet multum serioque, vel minimum tubae vestigium in praestandis eleemosynis; a doctioribus libentissime hoc discerem. To this we must add,—at least if συναγωγαί means the "synagogues,"—the consideration, that sounding trumpets ἐν ταῖς συναγωγαῖς must necessarily have disturbed the service there. Besides, we find from the Talmudists, that there was a regular form in the giving of alms in the synagogues. It was this: before the prayers were begun, alms were put into the קופה or alms-boxes. In later times, the congregation, on certain special occasions, were called upon to give their alms, which they handed to the officer (see Lightfoot; and still more fully and accurately, Vitringa, de synag. vetere). In these circumstances, it is preferable to understand the expression figuratively, **as has** been done by Chrysostom, the auctor operis imperfecti, Theodoret, Jerome (apparently), Beza, and most moderns. Chrysostom: οὐχ ὅτι σάλπιγγας εἶχον ἐκεῖνοι, ἀλλὰ τὴν πολλὴν ἐπιδεῖξαι βούλεται μανίαν, τῇ λέξει τῆς μεταφορᾶς ταύτης κωμῳδῶν ταύτῃ καὶ ἐκπομπεύων αὐτούς. Theodoret, in Ps. xcviii. 6 (Opp. i. 1303): σάλπιγγα πολλάκις τὴν βοὴν ἡ θεία καλεῖ γραφή; then on our text: ἀντὶ τοῦ, μὴ κηρύξῃς, μηδὲ δήλην ἅπασι καταστήσῃς· ἵνα μὴ τῇ κενῇ δόξῃ τὸν τῆς φιλανθρωπίας λιμήνῃ καρπόν. In the rabbinical writings, it is true, there occurs no proverbial expression of this kind: a few traces of it may, however, be found in Greek and Latin, in the Church-language of the first century (which may, however, have been influenced by the view taken of our passage); and, especially, in the modern languages. Cicero (fil. ad Tiron. epp. ad diversos L. xvi. ep. 21): quare quod polliceris, te *buccinatorem* fore existimationis meæ; on which Manutius observes: qui quasi buccina canens divulgas laudes meas; adding the remark, that Cicero, in the speech pro Archia, speaks of the father instead of his præco. Prudentius (contra Symm. L. ii. v. 68): talia principibus dicta interfantibus, ille persequitur, *magnisque tubam concentibus inflat.* (A passage from the rhetorician Sidonius, ep. l. iv. ep. 3, which some have adduced, is irrelevant; besides, the reading is corrupt.) Achilles Tatius, L. viii. p. 507: αὕτη δὲ οὐχ ὑπὸ σάλπιγγι μόνον ἀλλὰ καὶ κήρυκι μοιχεύεται. Demosth. I. contra Aristogit. ed. Reiske, T. i. 797: καὶ ἃ τῶν ἄλλων τῶν ἠτυχηκότων ἕκαστος ἀψοφητὶ ποιεῖ, ταῦθ᾽ οὗτος μόνον οὐ κώδωνας ἐξαψάμενος διαπράττεται. Jerome (ep. xxii. ad Eustoch. c. 32, where he describes the corrupt practices of the Christians of his time): quum manum egenti porrexerint, *buccinant.* Quum ad agapen vocaverint, præco conducitur. Vidi nuper (nomen taceo, ne satyram putes) nobilissimam mulierum Romanarum in basilica beati Petri, semiviris antecedentibus, propria manu, quo religiosior putaretur, singulos nummos dispertire pauperibus. Comp. dial. c. Pelag. L. ii. c. 10: ad largiendum frustum panis et binos nummulos præco conducitur, et extendentes manum huc illucque circumspicimus, quæ si nullus viderit contractior fit. Esto unus de mille inveniatur, qui ista non faciat. In the Apostolic Constitutiones, L. iii. c. 14, under the title ὅτι οὐ δεῖ κομπάζειν, it is said of the widows: ἡ μέντοι εὖ ποιοῦσα ἀποκρυπτάτω τὸ οἰκεῖον ὄνομα, ὡς σοφή, μὴ σαλπίζουσα ἔμπροσθεν αὐτῆς. From Basil, Grotius quotes the saying: τῆς εὐποιΐας σαλπιζομένης ὄφελος οὐδέν. So too compare the following expressions in modern languages: in German, ausposaunen und an die grosse Glocke schlagen; in English, to sound one's own trumpet, to trumpet forth, "every man his own trumpeter;" in French, faire quelque chose tambour battant, trompetter; in Italian, trompetar, bucinar. If then σαλπίζειν is not to be taken literally, but figuratively, the verb must denote (just as in the case of the same word, 1 Sam. xiii. 3), not the preliminaries of the act (as Calow, Wolf, Baumgarten-Crusius think), but the act itself. Ἔμπροσθέν σου is pictorial, the sounding trumpet is represented as going before the man.

The two following explanations are peculiar. According to Stephen le Moyne (Notæ in varia Sacra, Ludg. Bat. T. ii. p. 73), our Lord is alluding to the custom of the hypocrites, of throwing their alms into the שׁוֹפָרוֹת,[1] in such a way that the sound attracted the attention of the bystanders. This is also the view taken by Hottinger, Deyling (Observationes Sacræ iii. 175), and Schoettgen. Against it is the following: In the first place, so far as we know, שׁוֹפָרוֹת was the name only of the vessels set apart for the temple-monies; the alms-boxes, on the contrary, were called קֻפָּה; and of what shape they were, is unknown to us. Then it is not easy to see how, even with vessels shaped like the שׁוֹפָרוֹת, the donors could succeed in imparting a louder reverberation to one piece of money than to another. Supposing them to have trumpet-shaped vessels fixed to the ground, one coin must have sounded like another. Then, σαλπίζειν would not be a fitting expression for the ring of a piece of money (tinnire): for this, the word would rather be κροτεῖν, κροτοθορυβεῖν, or ἠχεῖν = צָלַל, 1 Sam. iii. 11; 2 King xxi. 12. And lastly, be it observed, this could apply only to the συναγωγαί, and not to the ῥῦμαι.

There is more to be said in favour of the other view, which was first propounded by the learned Iken (dissert. philol.-theologicæ i. diss. 21), and has been adopted by Michaelis, and C. F. Schulz in his notes to Michaelis. Iken remarks, that among the ancients the servants of Isis and Cybele used to go beating cymbals and asking alms: this is also, travellers tell us, the practice of the monks of Persia and India (comp. on this, Jahn's Archæology, 1. 2, 340; Rosenmueller, altes und neues Morgenland, Th. v. S. 33). If now σαλπίζειν is to be taken transitively, ne patiaris tuba cani, the admonition would be

---

[1] This was the name given to those thirteen γαζοφυλάκια into which the contributions to the temple were thrown. The name was given because in shape they resembled trumpets;—they were narrow at the top, wide at the bottom, in order that the money could not be taken out. See a drawing of them in Reland, de Spoliis Templi Hierosol. Traj. ad Rhen. 1716, p. 116.

not to allow, from a desire of ostentation, the poor to *ask* alms in so noisy a way. Against this view, however, there are several objections. First, there is Iken's own honest avowal, that he could not prove the existence of this custom among the Hebrews: ingenue fateor, me, licet non vulgari studio hanc in rem inquisiverim, quin et alios sive Christianos sive Judæos sedulo consuluerim, nihil hactenus certi invenire potuisse. Yet he then adduces, in support of his opinion, a passage which Lightfoot has quoted from the Jerusalem Gemara of the Codex Demai, fol. xxiii. 2, where it is said that on feast-days the collectors of alms (מַכְרִיזִין) used not to call out for alms as on other days; and from this he concludes, that the persons who made use of the σάλπιγξ were not the givers, but the recipients of charity. But for one thing, it is not of the poor that the passage in question speaks: it is of the public collectors of alms, whose business הִכְרִיז was; and it is very questionable if they were in the habit of performing that office with the sound of trumpets, as Iken supposes. Further, Michaelis says, "If Christ were discoursing among us, He would say, 'Do not allow people to sing before your door;'" and, in truth, the singing of the poor is not something demanded by the alms-givers, but a spontaneous act. Our Lord cannot therefore have said: ne curato buccina cani, but His words would have been: κώλυε τοὺς σαλπιζομένους. Finally, this explanation would apply only ἐν ταῖς ῥύμαις, and nowise ἐν ταῖς συναγωγαῖς.

Then, again, συναγωγή has not been taken here in the sense of "the synagogue" by all the critics: some, as Erasmus, Grotius, Elsner, Wolf, Kuinoel, etc., have taken it in the sense of conciliabula, circuli hominum, as denoting either social gatherings or greater assemblages on the street. But why should ἐν ταῖς συναγωγαῖς καὶ ἐν ταῖς ῥύμαις be understood here otherwise than in ver. 5, we understand the phrase, ἐν ταῖς συναγωγαῖς καὶ ἐν ταῖς γωνίαις τῶν πλατειῶν? And although even that phrase has by some been understood to denote crowds of people or social assemblies, there is nevertheless even less reason to take exception to the ordinary signification of synagogue in that passage than in the one before us. It is very doubtful, too, whether the word used for such a concourse of people would be συναγωγή, and not rather ὄχλος. And besides this, if the latter were meant, the expression would not run: ἐν ταῖς συναγωγαῖς καὶ ἐν ταῖς ῥύμαις, which plainly indicates two different places, but rather: ἐν ταῖς συναγωγαῖς τῶν ῥυμῶν. Finally, be it observed, the synagogues were really, as can be shown, places where alms were collected, just as the Christian churches became afterwards; and when the Jewish writers speak of the places where alms were taken, they usually distribute them into those *within* the synagoge and those *without* it (see Lightfoot; Vitringa, de synag. vet. iii. 1, 13; Buxtorf, de synagogâ, c. xliv.). It is said here, "*in* the synagogues," and alms were actually given in the synagogues: we cannot, therefore, suppose that what is referred to is the alms-giving which took place *before* the doors of the synagogues (Acts iii. 3), as later, before the doors of the Christian churches (Bingham, antiqq. ecclesiast. T. v. p. 273 seqq.).

Ῥύμη, in the Macedonian dialect for στενωπός. It may not be essentially different from πλατεῖαι, Luke xiv. 21: in the East, as in all ancient and in all southern cities, the streets are, in comparison with ours, decidedly στενωποί, in order to exclude the sunshine. In the *narrow* streets, individuals would be more observed.

The antithesis to δοξασθῆναι ὑπὸ τῶν ἀνθρώπων is the thought expressed in ch. v. 16—Ἀπέχειν (Luke vi. 24; Phil. iv. 18) is equivalent to a Præterite: "they have already got what they were to get." So in classic Greek, τὸν μισθὸν ἀπέχειν, τὸν καρπὸν ἀπέχειν (see Wyttenbach, Plut. moral. ed. Lips. ii. p. 124). All they wanted, was the evanescent praise of men: and they have it. Capellus shows the phrase to have been also rabbinical: he quotes from the rabbinical book Liber Timoris the saying: "the man who boasts of a fulfilment of the law הוּא נָטַל שְׂכָרוֹ has taken his reward" (thereby depriving himself of any other). The more usual expression in the Talmud is קִבֵּל שִׂלְמוֹ. Compare also St Luke xvi. 25.

Ver. 3. In order that there may be no room for the motive of human approbation, the deepest seclusion is to be chosen (comp. ver. 6). The placing of σοῦ first is intended to bring out the contrast. This secrecy is expressed in fitting parabolical language. What, indeed, can be more closely connected together than the members of the body, particularly those members which belong to each other, like the two hands, which the Greeks and Latins called ἀδελφός and frater; the Syrians, ܐܚܐ (vide Xenoph. Memor. ii. 3, 19, and Gesenius, thes. s. v. אָח). The right hand gives the alms: the left hand, closely as it is connected with it, is not to know of the alms-giving. This figure must then vividly present the thought, that no one, not even the nearest and most intimate friend, is to know of it: the only witness is to be the Father which is in heaven. Chrys.: εἰ γὰρ οἶόν τέ ἐστι, φησί, καὶ σεαυτὸν ἀγνοῆσαι, περισπούδαστον ἔστω σοι τοῦτο, κἂν αὐτὰς δυνατὸν ᾖ τὰς διακονουμένας χεῖρας λαθεῖν. According to Paulus (also Goethe), what is meant is, that the deed of alms-giving is not to be "counted," from the custom of counting from the right hand into the left. In the Collection of Egyptian proverbs which had been edited from the papers of Burckhardt (Arabic Proverbs of the Modern Egyptians, London 1830, p. 77), there occurs the saying: يمينك ما تدري عن شمالك "Let thy right hand know nothing of thy left." Burckhardt quotes the following parallel saying from the Hadiz or tradition of Mahomet,—which, however, has evidently been borrowed from Christianity,—رجل يمينه تصدق بصدقة فلم تعلم شماله ما انفقت "In alms-giving, the left hand is not to know what the right has given."[1] Some of the Fathers urged the *bad* sense in which the left hand is understood: Augustine says, that several understand it to denote unbelievers, others the unbelieving wife; the auctor operis imperfecti: voluntas carnis semper Deo contraria. Augustine's own view (and he is followed by Schoettgen in his Greek lexicon) is, that the left hand is ipsa delectatio laudis, whilst the right is intentio implendi præcepta divina. Zwingli: Sinistra manus hypocrisis est, quæ semper in benefaciendo accurrit. Luther's view is peculiar: according to him, the right hand is to give in such a way that the left, knowing nothing of it, is not even to stretch itself out in order to receive honour, and so to indemnify itself: "das heisst man Gebers Nehmers, wie die Kinder unter einander spotten."

---

[1] The Greek proverb, αἱ χάριτες γυμναί, expresses the same idea in a manner truly Hellenic. Ὅτι δεῖ τὴν δωρεὰν ἀκενοδόξως χαρίζεσθαι (Arsenius, Violetum, ed Walz, Stuttgart 1832, S. 33).

Ver. 4. What is done only under the eye of God shall not go unrewarded by Him. Chrys.: μέγα καὶ σεμνὸν αὐτῷ καθίζων θέατρον, καὶ ὅπερ ἐπιθυμεῖ, τοῦτο μετὰ πολλῆς αὐτῷ διδοὺς τῆς περιουσίας· τί γὰρ βούλει· φησίν· οὐχὶ θεατὰς ἔχειν τῶν γινομένων τινάς; ἰδοὺ τοίνυν ἔχεις, οὐχὶ ἀγγέλους καὶ ἀρχαγγέλους· ἀλλὰ τὸν τῶν ὅλων Θεόν; εἰ δὲ καὶ ἀνθρώπους ἐπιθυμεῖς ἔχειν θεωροὺς, οὐδὲ ταύτης σε ἀποστερεῖ τῆς ἐπιθυμίας καιρῷ τῷ προσήκοντι ..... ἂν δὲ σπουδάζῃς νῦν λανθάνειν, τότε τε αὐτὸς ὁ Θεὸς ἀνακηρύξει τῆς οἰκουμένης παρούσης ἁπάσης.— Βλέπων is not to be supplemented by τὰ ἐν τῷ κρυπτῷ as the object (Ar. Erp., Ethiop., Grotius, Kuinoel), or by σὲ ἐν τῷ κρυπτῷ (Beza); but ἐν includes both motion and rest; Bengel: qui in occulto et *est* et *videt:* it is the general attribute of God. Αὐτός which is omitted in B. K. L., and rejected by Lachmann and Tischendorf, forms, if genuine, a pointed antithesis to a reward from *men.*—Ἐν τῷ φανερῷ. On the day of judgment, even the hidden thought will be made manifest (Rom. ii 16; 1 Cor. iv. 5): how much more the secret deed,—the judgment, namely, on the results of moral training, in which each isolated act of self-denial forms as essential element! Yet the words, ἐν τῷ φανερῷ, are omitted in B. D. Z, the Vulgate, Coptic, min. and **patres**; these also omit it at ver. 6, and a still greater number at ver. 18. Bengel, accordingly, regards it as doubtful in all the three passages, and Lachmann and Tischendorf omit it. We might wish to retain it for the sake of the rhetorical emphasis, as standing over-against ἐν τῷ κρυπτῷ: as regards the *sense,* **we must always suppose it to be implied.**

II. Warning against Hypocritical and Unworthy praying. Vers. 5—15.

With the Jews of that time prayer held a yet more prominent position than alms-giving and fasting among the outward manifestations of virtue. Thus we read in the Gemara, tr. Berachoth, f. 32, 2, א"ר", אליעזר גדולה תפלה יותר ממעשים, "Great is **prayer,** says the Rabbi Elieser, greater than good works. Who is greater in good works than Moses? and yet it was as a reward for his prayer that it was granted to him to see the land of promise from Pisgah, Deut. iii. 26, 27." But in the period of the fall of the **Hebrew nation prayer** became **more** and **more** a matter of form. Daily prayer was repeated three times, at 9 o'clock, at 12, and at 3; people assembled in the synagogues for prayer on Sabbath, Monday, and Thursday. He who prayed properly was to spend nine hours a-day in prayer. The Mischna, tr. Berachoth, v. 1, states: חסידים הראשנים היו שהין שעה אחת ומתפללין כדי שיכוונו לאביהם שבשמים, "The pious of the old time waited an hour in order to address themselves to their Father in heaven." The Gemara, f. 32, 2, says: תנו רבנן הסידים הראשונים היו שהין שעה אחת ומתפללים שעה אחת וחוזרין ושוהין שעה אחת וכי מאחר ששוהין תשעה שעות ביום בתפלתן תורתן היאך משתמרת ומלאכתן האך נעשית אלא מתוך שהסידים הם תורתם משתמרת ומלאכתן מתברכת, "The Rabbis teach that the pious people of old time waited an hour and prayed for an hour, and then waited another hour. Now, if they spent nine hours a-day at their prayers, how was their doctrine kept up, and their work done? But because they were pious people, their doctrine was preserved (in memory), and their work was blessed."[1] Countless are the prayers which are prescribed in the Mischna, tr. Berachoth (Surenh. T. i. p. 31), for all possible occasions: of these, according to the Rabbi Gamaliel (Berachoth 4, 3), at least eighteen were to be used daily. There are prayers in connection with comets, rain, lightning, tempest; at the sight of the sea, of lakes and rivers; for places where miracles had been performed, where idols had been destroyed; prayers on receiving good news, on using new furniture, on entering a fortified city, and on leaving one, etc. All that was required, indeed, on such occasions were short prayers (Musaphim), short expressions of praise; but a long prayer was regarded as more meritorious, Matt. xxiii. 13 (Lightfoot in loc. cit.; Wettstein on chap. vi. 7). People went to the synagogue not only for public worship, but, as in R. Catholic churches, for private prayer whenever special strength was required; especially to offer the eighteen Musaphim. Prayers offered in the synagogue were supposed to be more efficacious (Wagenseil, Sota, p. 605). Prayer was offered up in the street, above all, at the hour of prayer; at that hour, whoever was riding on an ass was obliged to dismount. Prayer was to be so

---

[1] As Lightfoot remarks on this passage, p. 294, one might think that the object of this waiting was merely hypocritical, in order the lengthen out the time; but the passage in the Mischna shows that the object really was the preparation of the mind for prayer.

earnest, that even if one were saluted by the king when engaged in prayer, one ought not to acknowledge it: if a serpent wound itself round one's foot, still one might not remove it (Berachoth v. 1). Prayer was offered in a standing posture, with the face turned towards the temple.

Instead of the singular, *προσευχῇ, ούκ ἔσῃ*, Lachmann and Tischendorf read the plural, after B, Z, and most translations. It is true that the singular may have originated from a wish to conform the word to the singulars before and after it; but it is also true that the plural might arise from the use of the saying among Christians as an exhortation. The posture in prayer was standing (Maim. constit. de precat. c. v. 2), Mark xi. 25: *ἑστῶτες*, accordingly, is not equivalent to *ὄντες*, as if it were to be connected with the place (Beza, Castell., Pric., Hammond): it is rather to be connected with *προσεύχεσθαι*, which it more definitely characterizes, as in St Mark. The ancient Church also prayed standing. Cyprian: quando stamus ad orationem. In the Koran, Sure V. v. 8, اذا قمتم الي لصلوة, "When ye stand to pray."[1] The posture naturally made one conspicuous, and on this account it is noticed by Christ. "Praying in the streets" is to be explained in part from the obligation to do honour to the appointed hours of prayer: as was also the practice among the Mahommedans (Olearius, Itiner. Pers. p. 683). The *γωνίαι τῶν πλατειῶν* were the corners where two ways met, and where accordingly you would come under the observation of many: it corresponds to the *διέξοδος τῶν ὁδῶν*, Matt. xxii. 9, in triviis; thus it is said of the harlot, in Prov. vii. 12. "She lieth in wait in every corner." The auctor op. imp. thinks, curiously enough, that the allusion is to the narrow recesses in the street, where they might conceal themselves: ut ne, si in plateis oraverint, quasi simultatores religionis vituperarentur, sed in angulis, ut videantur abscondite orare—astuta vanitas. Nothing is intended to be said in blame of praying in the synagogues in itself. Theophylact: *οὐ γὰρ βλάπτει ὁ τόπος ἀλλὰ ὁ τρόπος καὶ ὁ σκοπός*. Erasmus, Beza, Hammond, Elsner, suppose here, as in ver. 2, that by the synagogues are meant the assemblages

---

[1] Comp. Lakemacher de ritibus formulisque precum Pharis., Observ. philol., P. vii. S. 97 In Michaelis ritualia quædam cod. sacri ex Alcorano illustrata. Halis 1739 (in Pott. Sylloge diss. T. II.).

of people in the streets; but this idea is here even less admissible. For them to have stood praying among crowds of people, would have been a piece of hypocritical impertinence which the people could scarce have tolerated.—Φιλεῖν, joined with the infinitive following, and similarly ἀγαπᾶν, expresses the adverbial idea of doing gladly, of liking to do a thing (Luther): similarly אָהֵב לְ, חָפֵץ לְ; comp. LXX., Isa. lvi. 10, Jer. xiv. 10, Hos. xii. 8: in the New Testament, Matt. xxiii. 6. But when a thing is done readily, it is apt to be done frequently: thus the Greek φιλεῖν, and also ἀγαπᾶν and ἐρᾶν, are explained by the scholiasts in the sense of εἰωθέναι, ἔθος ἔχειν, with infinitive and participle (Irmisch Excurs. ad Herold i. 2, 8, T. i. p. 800). Xenophon de mag. equit. c. 7, § 9: φιλοῦσι δέ πως στρατιῶται, ὅσῳ ἂν πλείους ὦσι, τοσούτῳ πλείω ἁμαρτάνειν. Aristotle œcon. 2: τοὺς Λεκίους ὁρῶν ἀγαπῶντας τρίχωμα φέρειν. Frequently in Latin amare in this sense. Horace: "aurum perrumpere amat sacras;" thus Erasmus translates here "solent" (the Dutch translation is Zy pleegen gaarne). It may be doubted, however, if the Greeks themselves converted the idea, to do anything readily, into the feebler idea of "being *wont* to do a thing:" in Matt. xxiii. 6, φιλεῖν is certainly more correctly translated delectari; comp. θέλειν, Mark xii. 38, Luke xx. 46. Luther's rendering is, accordingly, "vorzuziehen."—Ὅπως φανῶσι (infra ver. 16, ὅπως φανῶσι νηστεύοντες). It is not to be translated by the *passive* (as Luther, the Vulgate, and other translations have done); here, as elsewhere, the Aorist 2. pass. ἐφάνη has a middle signification. Beza: ut conspicui sint, "that they may fall under the eye." The words are weighty and impressive: "they wished the praise of *men:* the praise of men they have,—but nothing more."

Ver. 6. The thought, that the observation of men should be shunned, is expressed in a vivid and concrete manner. The houses of the East had then, and still have, upper chambers, עֲלִיָּה, which were set apart for special purposes. They were used as store-rooms, or for lodging strangers, or for religious meditations and disputations (vide Talmud passim), or again for prayer, as frequently in the Acts (see Faber, Archæology of the Hebrews, i. 442). This upper chamber is called in the New Testament ὑπερῷον: the word here is the more general ταμεῖον, or ταμεῖον, which means that upper chamber which was set appart from common use. The thought is further enforced by the advice to close the door. The passage has been distorted so as to make it imply a denial of the blessing attending public worship; on the other hand, it has been quoted against the so-called conventicle: both applications are excluded by a right view of the object of the admonition. Origen, Hilary, Augustine, interpret the text allegorically: **quæ sunt ista** cubicula nisi **ipsa corda**, quæ in Ps. iv. 5 **etiam** significantur. Claudendum est **ostium**, *i.e.* carnali sensui **resistendum**, ut oratio spiritalis dirigatur ad Patrem. That which is done under the eye of God alone, will not fail to be rewarded by Him.

Ver. 7. It was natural to pass from hypocritical prayers to those which were but "vain repetitions." As we have already seen, long prayers themselves form part of the false sanctity of the Pharisees (Matt. xxiii. 14). We need not therefore regard vers. 7, 8, as out of place in this context (see Introduction, p. 26). Baumgarten-Crusius: "Previously He has been speaking of the way in which **they sought to deceive** men: now He shows how they thought to deceive God."

The meaning of βαττολογεῖν has been matter of discussion. We must gather its meaning partly from the πολυλογία, and partly from the context.[1] It was first investigated as to whether the word is derived from the proper name Βάττος, or whether it is an onomatopoetikon, like βατταρίζω (which, however, some also refer to a certain Battus); βαβάκτης, βαττολάλος (which the gloss. **Philox. has**): comp. also the nickname of Demosthenes, βάτταλος, alluding to his stuttering (comp. Schaefer, **appar.** ad

---

[1] Numerous are the philological and antiquarian investigations concerning the phrase: Heinr. Stephan. im Thes.; Dan. Heinsius exercit. sacr. Lugd. Bat. 1639, p. 30; Cl. Salmasius de foen. trapez. Lugd. Bat. 1690, p. 795; Is. Casaubonus exercitt. Anti-Baronianæ, Francof. 1615, exercit. 14, p. 235; Balth. Stollberg im thes. theol.-philol. Amst. 1702, T. ii. p. 112; Joh. Schaller im thes. nov. theol.-philol. Amstelod. 1732. T. ii. p. 183; Guil. Saldeni otia theolog. Amstel. 1684, p. 579; Joh. Sauberti opera posth. Altd. 1604, p. 70; Corn. Adami observatt. philol.-theol. Gron. 1710, p. 108; Selden de Diis Syriis, Lips. 1662, proleg. c. iii.; Deyling Observv. sacræ iii. p. 208; Olearius observ. in Matt. Obs. xix.; J. D. Michaelis comment. de battologia, 1753; Herder, Erlaeuterung des N. T. aus morgenländischen Quellen, S. 109.

Demosth. i. 175). The latter derivation is the one now generally adopted, after the example of Vossius instit. orat. L. v. c. 5, and Salmasius de foen. trapez. p. 796. Moreover, tradition has combined the two derivations; for, according to one form of the tradition, the name of this Battus was originally Aristotle: the other name he received from the Pythia, on account of his stammering (vide Hemsterh. in Aristoph. Plutus v. 926).[1] Ancient critics assumed a vox hybrida, and referred to the Hebrew בטא, effutivit. It is possible that our Lord used the word בטא in the language of the country (it is from it that בטא, futilitas, temeritas in loquendo, a word which frequently occurs in the Rabbis, is taken); and that the translator was consequently let to select this uncommon Greek word.[2] Only a single passage besides the glossaries has as yet been found where this word occurs: it is in Simplicius, in Epict. enchirid. c. 37, p. 212.[3] In Simplicius, βαττολογία is manifestly equivalent to πολυλογία. Βαττολάλος is translated garrulus in the Glossa Philoxeni (ed. Labb. Par. 1679, p. 35); and βατταρίζειν, in Lucian, Dio Chrysostom, and Themistius (vide Wettstein), includes *speaking foolishly and at random*. In a passage in Theod. Opp. v. 47, βατταρισμοί and τὰ ἀτημελῶς εἰρημένα are parallel expressions. The Glossators explain βάττος first by ἰσχνόφωνος, μογιλάλος, and βαττολογία by μόγις λαλεῖν (Etym. M.); next, they give the signification πολυλογία (Suidas); and finally, they have also φλυαρία, ἀργολογία, ἀκυρολογία (Hesych., Alberti Gloss.). These three explanations merge into one another; for the stammerer *repeats* his words; consequently *speaks much*, and

---

[1] Herder begins his inquiry by remarking: "The learned expositors have to answer for having so terribly *battologized* about the word." And what is his own discovery? That the word is taken from the *Zendlanguage!*

[2] The Hebrew translation of the New Testament, edited by the London Society for the Conversion of the Jews, which is usually too literal, has here לֹא תְשַׁנּוּ דִּבְרֵיכֶם. The edition published by Baxter in 1831 has the Hebrew phrase אַל תָּרְבּוּ נְאֻם בְּשָׂפָה רָקָה (בְּשִׂיחֲכֶם).

[3] To this we should have to add, according to Schaller and others, a passage from Plautus: paucis verbis rem divinam facito, centies idem dicere est βαττολογεῖν. But it is by a strange oversight that this sentence has been ascribed to Plautus; for they are the words of Grotius, which he subjoins to a quotation from Plautus: the former words occur in Pœnulus, act. i. sc. 2, v. 196.

often *unskilfully*. Theophylact, indeed, makes this distinction, that only βαττολογία = φλυαρία; whereas βατταρισμός = ἡ ἄναρθρος φωνή: but it can be shown that, in philological usage, this distinction did not exist.

In determining the meaning of the text, it is important to inquire whether it is merely *much speaking* in prayer that is alluded to, or whether, at the same time, *improper and unworthy prayers are condemned*. The Greek Fathers, whose criticism was greatly influenced by a comparison of the text with ver. 32, make but little allusion to the idea of much speaking, whilst they dwell upon that of praying with unworthy and improper motives. Gregory of Nyssa (in the introduction to his exposition of the oratio dominica, ed. Par., T. i. p. 717), has the following remarks: ἄξιον ἐξετάσαι, τί σημαίνει τῆς βαττολογίας τὸ ῥῆμα ... δοκεῖ τοίνυν μοι σωφρονίζειν τὴν χαυνότητα τῆς διανοίας καὶ συστέλλειν τῶν ταῖς ματαίαις ἐπιθυμίαις ἐμβαθυνόντων, καὶ διὰ τοῦτο τὴν ξένην ταύτην τῆς λέξεως καινοτομίαν ἐξευρηκέναι,[1] ἐπὶ ἐλέγχῳ τῆς ἀνοίας τῶν περὶ τὰ ἀνωφελῆ τε καὶ μάταια ταῖς ἐπιθυμίαις διαχεομένων· ὁ γὰρ ἔμφρων τε καὶ συνετὸς καὶ πρὸς τὸ χρήσιμον βλέπων λόγος, κυρίως λέγεται λόγος· ὁ δὲ ταῖς ἀνυπάρκτοις ἐπιθυμίαις διὰ τῆς ἀνυποστάτου ἡδονῆς ἐπιχεόμενος οὐκ ἔστι λόγος, ἀλλὰ βαττολογία· ὡς ἄν τις Ἑλληνικώτερον ἑρμηνεύων εἴποι τὸν νοῦν, φλυαρία καὶ λῆρος καὶ φλήναφος καὶ εἴ τι ἄλλο τῆς τοιαύτης σημασίας. Basil quotes the text in his commentary on Isa. i. 15: καὶ ἐὰν πληθύνητε τὴν δέησιν, οὐκ εἰσακούσομαι: both in the Old Testament passage and in the New, he considers the much speaking to denote praying for manifold σωματικά and ἐπίγεια, and he collates Prov. x. 19: ἐκ πολυλογίας οὐκ ἐκφεύξῃ ἁμαρτίαν, with which he acutely compares Ps. xxvii. 4: μίαν ᾐτησάμην, κ.τ.λ. The word was understood essentially in the same sense by Origen (περὶ εὐχῆς, T. i. p. 330) and by Chrysostom. Origen begins his investigation with the antithesis: μὴ βαττολογήσω-

---

[1] When this Father speaks of *new* words which the Evangelists invented, as in the present case, this must not be understood as if he introduced words which did not occur in the whole range of the Greek language. Gregory, in his sermon on 1 Cor. xv. 28, T. ii. p. 19, characterizes also as καινοτομία λέξεως the Pauline phrase περπερεύεσθαι, 1 Cor. xiii. 4, and ἐριθεία,—words which occur by no means so rarely in Greek: comp. the author's Beitraege zur Spracherklärung des Neu. Testaments, S. 27.

μεν, ἀλλὰ θεολογήσωμεν,[1] and adds: βαττολογοῦμεν δὲ, ὅτε μὴ μωμοσκοποῦντες ἑαυτούς, ἢ τοὺς ἀναπεμπομένους τῆς εὐχῆς λόγους, λέγομεν τὰ διεφθαρμένα ἔργα, ἢ λόγους, ἢ νοήματα ταπεινὰ τυγχάνοντα, κ.τ.λ. Πολυλογεῖν, he thinks, means the same thing, for the good is but *one thing*. Chrysostom says that βαττολογία is in the first instance φλυαρία, οἷον ὅταν τὰ μὴ προσήκοντα αἰτῶμεν παρὰ τοῦ Θεοῦ, δυναστείας καὶ δόξας . . . καὶ ἁπλῶς τὰ μηδὲν ὑμῖν διαφέροντα—μετὰ δὲ τούτων, he goes on: δοκεῖ μοι κελεύειν ἐνταῦθα μηδὲ μακρὰς ποιεῖσθαι τὰς εὐχάς. So too Theophylact and Euthymius. This view is approached in the Ethiopic and Persian translation: "Say nothing unseemly;" on the other hand, the large majority of the translations take βαττολογία in the sense of πολυλογία. The Syriac, with its much criticised[2] phrase ܠܐ ܬܗܘܘܢ ܦܩܩܝܢ. The Vulgate and the Arabic have nolite multum loqui; Ulphilas, filuvaurdjwaith (to make many words); Luther, plappern; the English translation, use not vain repetitions. Almost all the commentators also restrict the meaning to much speaking in prayer. Zwingli: sine verbositate, multa jacula simul emissa tardius volant, pennis impedita, unum solum velocius scopum attigit. There are a few exceptions. Casaubon says, there are two faults βαττολογεῖν—repetitio eorundem verborum and multiloquium: similarly Grotius. Baronius, against

---

[1] Θεολογεῖν has here the meaning which it has received in the language of the Church: Deum laudibus celebrare; vide Eusebius Hist. eccl. L. x. c. 3, and Montfaucon on Anathas. Opp. in indice s. h. v.

[2] Vide Casaub. exercit. Anti-Baron. L. xiv. p. 236; Nic. Fuller, Miscellanea sacra, London 1617, L. ii. c. 16; Ludovicus de Dieu critica sacra, Amsterdam 1693, p. 327. The word ܦܩܩ is undoubtedly the same as occurs in the Targum of Ps. xxxi. 19, and very frequently in the Rabbins, in the sense of to shut up, to close. It is unquestionable that ܦܐܩܐ, which Castellus derived from the same root ܦܩܩ, is used in the Syriac translation of Ps. xxxviii. 14 for אִלֵּם; as, however, the stammerer also is incapable of opening his mouth properly, the word has also received the signification of *blæsus*, which is the common one. The Syrian translator has just used the word which corresponds to the *first* meaning of βαττολογεῖν; whether the Syriac ܦܩܩ ever has the other meaning, πολυλογεῖν, is uncertain.

whom he contends, had remarked that βαττολογία is not like πολυλογία, but denotes φλυαρία; to which his opponent rightly rejoined, that the πολυλογία is itself expressly mentioned immediately after. Salmasius takes the same view with Basil. The heathen, he says, prayed for all manner of earthly goods and possessions, and so far the βαττολογεῖν includes praying **for vain** things. Many, like Chemnitz, combine this allusion with the two significations given by Casaubon.

That view of the text which is found in the Greek Fathers and in Salmasius, has arisen chiefly from a comparison of vers. 8 and 32. In the latter passage it is said, that the disciple of Christ is not, like the heathen, to be careful about earthly things, since his heavenly Father knows that he has need of these things; **and the** antithesis in ver. 8 is taken in the same sense: "Ye need not enumerate to God, one by one, your many earthly wants, for He well knows what ye **have need of.**" This view, in itself, has much to commend it; yet is the following better established by the context: the γάρ after δοκοῦσιν gives the reason why the heathen used those repetitions; it was because they thought to constrain God to hear them by a multitude of words. Polybius quite expresses the feeling of the ancient world, when, in words corresponding to the idea which is here reproved, he says, that the much-praying of the heathen is a μαγγανεύειν πρὸς τοὺς Θεούς, an ἀποκναίειν, καταδυσωπεῖν πρὸς τοὺς Θεούς: in Latin, fatigare, **lassare, obtundere Deos** (Polyb. hist. L. xix. c. 29). From this antithesis it necessarily follows, that here the leading idea of βαττολογεῖν must be πολυλογεῖν, although of course other ideas will be implied in it, **as** that of φλυαρεῖν, ὑθλεῖν. Ver. 8 must accordingly be understood in this sense: "He who is My disciple must not think that it is by the prayers of men that God first learns what they need; hence it is not necessary to enumerate to Him our wants in detail, or to make many repetitions, with the idea that in this way we may **cause** Him at last to hearken to our prayers. The man who prays in a right spirit has, above all, the feeling of a childlike trust **in** God, and therefore prays in words few, but yet full of meaning, in the manner taught in vers. 9—13." In accordance with this view, we should most naturally translate βαττολογεῖν, with Luther, "Plappern," or with Beza, Blaterare,—only, by adding eadem, **he unnecessarily** restricts the compass of the word.

The words of our Lord are not therefore directed against frequent and repeated prayers, neither are they spoken in condemnation of *long* prayers, so long as the many words are a real expression of the soul. In this case we might then apply the words of Philemon (Philemonis reliquiæ, ed. Meinecke, p. 398): Τὸν μὲν λέγοντα τῶν δεόντων μηδὲ ἓν | μακρὸν νόμιζε, κἂν δύ' εἴπῃ συλλαβάς· | τὸν δ' εὖ λέγοντα μὴ νόμιζ' εἶναι μακρόν, | μηδ' ἂν σφόδρ' εἴπῃ πολλὰ καὶ πολὺν χρόνον. Well observes Augustine, in ep. 121, ad Dioscor.: multum loqui in precando est rem necessariam superfluis agere verbis, multum autem precari est ad eum, quem precamur, diuturna et pia cordis excitatione pulsare, nam plerumque hoc negotium plus gemitibus, quam sermonibus agitur.[1] An admirable practical application is made by Luther and by Chemnitz.

As regards the phrase ὥσπερ οἱ ἐθνικοί, it is not exactly to be viewed as in chap. v. 47. In that passage the heathen are mentioned as representing egotistical self-love, and our Lord accordingly assumes the point of view of the Pharisees: here, on the other hand, as in ver. 32, an error is spoken of which was in fact peculiar to the heathen. As has been already noticed, as Matt. xxiii. 14 expressly testifies, and even our passage requires us to assume, long prayers were certainly common among the Pharisees and their followers; although there are many more passages in commendation of concise and pregnant brevity than of the converse (comp. Eccles. v. 1; Sir. vii. 14; see also the numerous expressions in Grotius; Drusius; Schœttgen; Buxtorf, Florileg. p. 280; Scheid in Meuschen N. T. e Talm. illustr. p. 68). Sometimes the sayings are distinctly opposed to one another: in the Gemara, Berachoth, fol. xxxii. 2, we read, the Rabbi Chanina says: כל המאריך בתפלתו אין תפלתו מחזרת ריקם, "He who makes his prayer long, is sure to receive something." On the other hand, the Rabbi Jochanan says: כל המאריך תפלתו סוף בא לידי כאב לב, "He who prays long, falls at last into sadness of heart." The Gemara restricts the latter saying by adding, that this consequence ensues only when he prays long *without hope of being heard.* It is possible that the later Jews may have been more addicted to the use of words. Maimonides speaks in a manner similar to our Lord, of those fools who

---

[1] It follows also from this, that, rightly viewed, Luke xviii. 1 is not really contradictory of the saying under consideration.

thought that they could persuade God by a multitude of words (More Nevoch, i. 59). Saubert (in loc. cit. S. 71) speaks of Jews who used to repeat the last syllable of the word אֶחָד, from Deut. vi. 4, at the Sabbath evening service for half an hour together; but it is especially among the heathen that we find these repetitions in prayer, and this in two ways: first, as διπλασιολογία, κυκλοπορεία, ταυτολογία, and then as πολυλογία in the narrower sense (comp. Casaubon ad locum). In the first place, the number of his gods induced the heathen to practise στωμυλία in his prayers. The Greek, with his 30,000 gods (such is the number that Hesiod reckons, Opera et dies, v. 250), would think it necessary to use many words to insure his being heard. In addressing one, he often mentioned a whole chorus of them. Thus it is said of the Mauritanian priestess in the Æneid, L. 4, v. 510: Per centum tonat ore Deos Erebumque Chaosque (comp. Heyne). To this we must add the ἐπωνυμίαι of the gods which had to be enumerated at solemn prayers; comp. Plato de republica, iii. 394, A.: πολλὰ τῷ Ἀπόλλωνι εὔχετο, τάς τε ἐπωνυμίας τοῦ Θεοῦ ἀνακαλῶν. These enumerations are known to us by the Orphean hymns, and from Lucian, who makes game of them, Timon, c. i. It is, however, a question whether these repetitions of heathen prayers were known to the Jews and to the Saviour. On the other hand, the Jews must have been well acquainted with the recitative form of prayer of the heathen. This would strike even one unacquainted with the language, as in our day in the towns of Italy a stranger is struck with the countless repetitions of the Ave Maria sung by the penitential crowds. The oldest instance that we have of those endless repetitions of one and the same formula occurs in 1 Kings xviii. 26, where we read that the priests of Baal cried out for the space of half a day: O Baal, hear us! Then in the New Testament we read of the Ephesian mob shouting for two hours: Great is Diana of the Ephesians; Acts xix. 34. We read in Terence, Heautont. V. 1, v. 6 et seqq.: Ohe! jam desine deos, uxor, gratulando (to thank) obtundere . . . illos tuo ex ingenio judicas, ut nihil credas intelligere, nisi idem dictum est centies.[1] These repeti-

---

[1] Almost all the commentators quote here, as an instance, the passages from Lampridius and Trebonius Pollio, where the senatus consulta are given with the statement that it was exclaimed sexagies: Auguste Claudi, dii te nobis

tions are much practised by Indian and Mahommedan monks: the former, for days together, echo the sacred syllable Um; and the latter keep repeating the word هو He! or الله, God, going round in circles while they say it, till at last they fall down fainting![1] Now we saw that this meaning of διπλασιολογία, κυκλοπορεία, comes nearest to the original meaning of βαττολογεῖν, to *stammer,* as the stammerer naturally repeats his words, and so uses *many* words. Now, that very abuse of prayer which our Lord here especially reproves, has become authorized and honoured in His own Church by the rosary of the Roman Catholics; and that prayer which He gave as an antidote to those repetitions is the very one which has been most abused by vain repetitions. According to the rosary, the Pater noster (Patriloquia, as it was called) is prayed fifteen times (or seven or five times), and the Ave Maria one hundred and fifty times (or fifty or sixty-three times). Compare the learned treatise against repetitions in the Christian Church, De pseudoprecationibus, rosariis, litaniis, etc., by Gisbert Voetius, disputationes selectæ theol. T. iii. p. 1022.

Ver. 8. Our Lord having already explained that the great end of prayer is not to make God *acquainted* with our necessities, now goes on to point out another object of prayer. But we cannot say that this object is one given by reflection, as Calvin remarks: ut nosmet ipsos expergefaciamus ad eum quærendum; on the contrary, it is implied in the very nature

---

præstent, *quadragies*: principem te semper optavimus, *quinquies;* tu nos a Palmyrenis vindica etc. Vide Trebellius, vita Claudii, c. 4. But, in the first place, these exclamations are civil and not religious; then they belonged to the forms of the latter Roman and Byzantine courts. These acclamations, along with the number of times that they were repeated by the different parties, were registered by a public secretary; hence also the name ἄκτα and ἀκτολογία. Constantine Porphyrog. hist. l. i. c. 38—40, p. 114 ff.; Casaubon ad Vulcat. Gall. in Avid. Cass. c. 13; Reiske and Leich on Constantine Porphyr. Ceremoniale, ed. Lips. S. 27.

[1] These repetitions are carried to the utmost limit among the Mahommedans. Olearius, in his Persian Travels, tells of a Persian in Schammachia, who prayed so loud and so long that he lost his voice, and then groaned out in voiceless accents the name of God fifty times. Compare Henning's profound treatise: Muhammedanus precans, Schleswig 1666, p. 14.

of prayer, which is nothing else but *the lively expression of the feeling of dependence upon God.* And it is because the religious character of a man is shown by the depth of this feeling of dependence upon God, that the gifts of God are connected with prayer.

THE LORD'S PRAYER, vers. 9—13; AND ITS SUPPLEMENT, vers. 14, 15.[1]

I. The proper position of the prayer, and its original form. II. The object with which it was given. III. The original sources. IV. The connection and train of thought.

I. THE PROPER POSITION OF THE PRAYER, AND ITS ORIGINAL FORM.

This prayer, as it occurs here, appears to furnish an example of how *much may be prayed in a few words.* And in this view, it seems to be here quite in its proper place. There would, therefore, have been scarcely a doubt as to this being its proper place if the same prayer did not occur also in St Luke xi. 1, where a definite historical occasion is given to it.

It has been already shown in the Introduction, p. 25, how the historical occasion and chronological place given to the prayer by St Luke was regarded as the correct one by those critics who were less favourably disposed towards the narrative of St Matthew. This view, unfavourable to St Matthew, was carried to its utmost limits by Bruno Bauer, who held that the more elaborate form in which the Lord's Prayer occurs in St Matthew is a proof that this prayer grew up by degrees in the Church, "out of the simple and general religious categories which had been handed down to the Church along with the Old Testament." The petition, "Forgive us our debts, as we forgive our debtors," he holds to have arisen solely from the development of the *Christian* consciousness. This writer denied at the same time that the narrative of St Luke possesses the merit of greater originality, as Schleiermacher maintained: "the occasion of which St Luke speaks, chap. xi., is made up, and is very unfortunate" (Kritik der ev. Geschichte, i. 360). The opinion

[1] For the literature of the subject, see p. 47.

thus expressed by Bauer, which is the utterance of mere uncritical caprice, was also maintained by the critics of the Tuebingen school, from their view of the Gospel narrative as written in the interest of certain doctrines. The words of Baur apply to both Gospels: "It is only the peculiar manner in which the Evangelist has moulded and elaborated the general scheme of the Gospel which he received" (Baur, Kritische Untersuchungen, S. 474; comp. Hilgenfeld, die Evangelien, S. 188). Now, if the historical character of both versions of the prayer was regarded as doubtful, it was natural, in determining their respective claims, to take the shorter form which St Luke gives as the more ancient version (as is done by Bruno Bauer): the account of St Luke itself is regarded as an altered form of the original Marcionitic text (Hilgenfeld). Ewald also feels constrained to regard the shorter form in St Luke as the more ancient (die 3 ersten Evv. S. 286).

We have found no adequate reason either for removing the prayer from the position which St Matthew has assigned to it, or, on the other hand, for setting aside the account of St Luke as unhistorical (Introduction, p. 25). Still less weight have the arguments by which Volckmar and Hilgenfeld have sought to prove the more ancient character of the text of Marcion (the same opinion is held by Ritschl, at least as regards St Luke xi. 2; although this author has retracted his original opinion as to the priority of Marcion, Zeller Jahrb. 1851, S. 530). Hilgenfeld gives what he supposes to have been the text of Marcion's Pater noster. It is, however, almost impossible to determine this, as, with regard to those passages which Tertullian (adv. Marc. iv. 26) omits, it must ever be matter of uncertainty whether the reason of their omission is because they furnished no occasion for a polemical antithesis, or because they did not occur in Marcion. The principal point of difference is in regard to the second petition, which, according to Baur (Marcusev.), Volkmar (Ev. des Marc.), runs thus: δὸς ἡμῖν τὸν ἅγιον πνεῦμα; according to Hilgenfeld, ἐλθέτω τὸ ἅγιον πνεῦμά σου πρὸς ἡμᾶς. The argument derived from the fact that Gregory of Nyssa and Maximus appear to have been acquainted with the reading, ἐλθέτω τὸ ἅγιον πνεῦμά σου ἐφ' ἡμᾶς καὶ καθαρισάτω ἡμᾶς, is not so much insisted on by Hilgenfeld as the internal argument, based upon the doctrinal tendencies of

St Luke. When the disciples of Jesus offered a prayer for some special thing, "how natural was it for an adherent of St Paul to make this into a prayer for the Holy Spirit, the pledge and seal of the adoption of the children of God!" (Zeller Jahrb. 1853, S. 227). We have already seen, in a few other cases, the feebleness of this tendency-argumentation (vide supra, p. 6). As regards the historical evidence however, it must first be observed, that the two witnesses in favour of this reading reduce themselves to *one*, viz. to Gregory alone. For the other, Maximus Confessor (in the seventh century), rests entirely on the authority of Nyssenus. Further, by neither is this petition substituted for the *second* petition, as by Marcion, but for the *third*. Οὕτω γὰρ, says Gregory of Nyssa, T. i. 737, ἐν ἐκείνῳ τ. εὐαγγελίῳ φησὶν, ἀντὶ τοῦ ἐλθέτω ἡ βασιλεία σου, ἐλθέτω, φησὶ, τὸ ἅγιον πνεῦμά σου ἐφ᾽ ἡμᾶς κ. καθαρισάτω ἡμᾶς . . ὁ γὰρ Λουκᾶς μὲν πνεῦμα ἅγιον λέγει, Ματθαῖος δὲ βασιλείαν ἐνόμισε, vide Matthäi, ed. maj. ad Luc., S. 507. Now it is evident that this pretended reading of St Luke, which none of the other Fathers know anything of, and which, moreover, is *different from the reading ascribed to Marcion,* is nothing else but a gloss on that exposition of the third petition, according to which "the kingdom of God" is viewed ethically, not historically (Origen). A scholiast on Matthew has, ἐλθέτω ἐπ᾽ ἐμὲ ἡ βασιλεία σου; from this a reading like that of Maximus might easily arise: ἡ βασιλεία σου, τουτέστι τὸ πνεῦμα τὸ ἅγιον. As regards the reading of Marcion, some excellent remarks have been made on it by Nitzsch in a treatise which has been overlooked by recent critics (Ueber die noch uneroerterte Umstellung der 2ten und 3ten Bitte des Vaterunsers bei Tertullian). Two suppositions are possible. Either Marcion, without being acquainted with the clause on which Gregory bases his opinion, did himself transform the first petition into a prayer for the Holy Ghost. He might have thought himself justified in doing this by what is said in St Luke xi. 13 of the Holy Ghost as the highest blessing, or from such an interpretation of the original text as that which occurs in Cyprian, de oratione dominica: Sanctificamur non modo in nomine domini Jesu Christi, sed et in spiritu Dei nostri. Hæc sanctificatio itaque, dum, ut in nobis permaneat, oramus, *quodammodo spiritum* s. *postulamus;* and Aug. enchir. c. 115: nomen Dei *sanctificetur in spiritu.* Or, on the other hand, supposing that Marcion found the clause of Gregory appended as a marginal note, he may, taking into consideration ver. 13 of St Luke, have determined to add it to the first petition instead of the second. To regard this reading of Marcion as the original text, is a course which will be taken only by one who thinks that the 13th verse of St Luke is also merely the result of a Pauline doctrinal tendency in the author of that Gospel.

Another question which arises, is as to what may be the relation of St Luke's version to that of St. Matthew. If we consider how natural it was for the transcriber of St Luke's Gospel to perfect the text by the addition of materials from the well-known forms of prayer, we cannot help regarding the brief version given in the text of Tischendorf as the correct one; for this version is supposed by the strongest testimony, such as that of the most ancient Codex Vaticanus (comp. Tischendorf, Studien und Kritiken 1847, S. 131), the express and repeated testimony of Origen in the Eastern, of Augustine in the Western Church. Now, if this text is to be regarded as authentic, and if we are to maintain that the prayer was given on two separate occasions, can we believe that on the second occasion it was spoken in *this* form by the Saviour Himself? None of the arguments adduced in support of this view can be considered sufficient. If we are to suppose that the disciples were present on the first occasion, and that all that is intended here, is to remind them of a prayer that they had already heard, it would have sufficed, for *this* purpose, to give merely the first words of the prayer. If our Lord had omitted here the third and seventh petitions, because they were already implied in the former ones, as Augustine says, then the very prayer which was opposed to vain repetitions, would itself contain something tautological: Origen, indeed, who also supposes that the third and seventh petitions were omitted on this occasion, thinks that our Lord may have spoken with greater brevity for an advanced disciple than for the multitude (Opera, T. i. 264). But the addition which St Matthew gives is one essential to the sense: our exposition will show this in the case of the third petition; in the case of the seventh, Neander recognises "that the second clause is necessary to an understanding of the first." Now, as many instances prove the discourses are almost always given more fully by St Luke (see above), can it then be a matter of doubt that the abbreviations here are to be ascribed to this informer? Neander expressly admits this, although he questions the true historical character of the position of the prayer in St Matthew.[1] Nay, he even holds that directions for prayer similar to those in St Matthew, ver. 7, may have preceded the prayer also in St Luke. All the less, then, is there reason to call in question the authenticity of the position of the prayer, as it occurs in St Matthew. As we admit that St Matthew's report of the sayings of Christ is the most faithful, this holds good of the words with which he introduces the prayer, which (especially ver. 8) so well correspond to the character of Christ. And if St Matthew has given these words correctly, a more fitting introduction to the Pater noster could scarcely be conceived.

II. THE OBJECT WITH WHICH THE PRAYER WAS GIVEN.

The primary object of the prayer, as it occurs in St Matthew, is evident: it is to furnish an example of a prayer at once short, concise, and void of repetitions. It may be asked, whether it is also intended as a form of words to be used in prayer. It was customary in the East, especially among the Hindoes and Parsees, to use stated forms of prayer; and, as we gather from St Luke xi. 1, this was also the practice of the Jews at the time of our Lord. We find, for instance, a prayer composed of eighteen sentences, and another briefer version of the same, dating from the times of Gamaliel and John the Baptist (comp. Lightfoot in loco). In reply to the request of the disciple, our Lord says: ὅταν προσεύχησθε, λέγετε; and this certainly shows that, according to that passage, He intended that the *words* should be used. Hence also with regard to the prayer as it stands in St Matthew: it is designed to be used verbally in prayer. The Bogomilans went so far, in their rigorous adherence to the text of Scripture, that they condemned the use of any other prayer. This we learn

---

[1] Although the shorter version of the prayer in St Luke, in which the words "ἡμῶν" and "ὁ ἐν τοῖς οὐρανοῖς" are omitted, were the more original form, it does not follow that this version is the very one which came from Christ. St Luke is usually more correct in giving the chronological and historical connection of Christ's discourses, but St Matthew gives the discourses themselves more fully than St Luke; and this might be the case also with regard to the Lord's Prayer.

from the statement of Harmenopulus (fourteenth century): μόνην ὀνομάζουσιν προσευχὴν τὸ Πάτερ ἡμῶν, τὰς δὲ ἄλλας ἀθετοῦσι βαττολογίαν καλοῦντες. Ernesti says: quód si vobis *formam* præscribi vultis evangelicæ precationis accipite hanc. So especially the expositors of the English Church in opposition to the Puritans, who insisted on the exclusive use of extemporary prayer; Hammond: quotiescunque solennes funditis preces, nunquam hanc precum formulam omittite. Cyprian and Tertullian, in the second century, also characterized the prayer as oratio legitima et ordinaria. Cyprian says of it: quæ potest magis spiritualis esse oratio, quam quæ a Christo nobis data est, a quo nobis et spiritus sanctus missus est; quæ vera apud patrem precatio, quam quæ a filio, qui est veritas, de ejus ore prolata est, ut aliter orare, quam docuit, non ignorantia sola sit, sed et culpa, quando ipse posuerit et dixerit: rejicitis mandatum Dei, ut traditionem vestram statuatis. It is manifest that the Saviour, in setting forth this prayer as a model of a short and pregnant prayer, cannot have intended to exclude the verbal use of the prayer itself.[1] It is equally certain, on the other hand, that He here gives His sanction for the use of other prayers, which in a similar manner combine brevity with fulness of meaning. Further, the brevity of this prayer is only in opposition to a meaningless and vapid verbosity: accordingly, it does not imply that long prayers are condemned when the spirit is sustained throughout. Well observes St Augustine, ad Probam, ep. cxxxi.: absit ab oratione multa *locutio;* sed ne desit multa *precatio,* si fervens perseverat *intentio.* Aliud est *sermo* multus, aliud *affectus* diuturnus. Accordingly, Augustine contends against the verbal use of this prayer being held as obligatory, and argues that the suppliant is bound only to the spirit of it: unde liberum est aliis atque aliis verbis eadem tamen in orando dicere, sed non debet esse liberum, *alia* dicere . . . habes, quantum arbitror, non solum *quale* ores, verum etiam *quid* ores. Hereupon he shows how all Christian petitions may be regarded as contained in the petitions of the Lord's Prayer. Tertullian, showing that the use of other prayers is also permitted,

---

[1] Socinus: quamvis videatur Christus tantum præscribere, quid orare debeamus, cum oramus, non autem præcipere, ut omnino oremus, tamen animadversa qualitate rerum istarum in eam sententiam procliviores sumus, *ut Christus utrumque simul facere voluerit.*

well observes: quoniam tamen Dominus prospector humanarum necessitatum seorsim post traditam orandi disciplinam: *petite*, inquit, et *accipietis*, et sunt, quæ petantur pro circumstantia cujusque. And Euthymius remarks: παραδίδωσι τύπον εὐχῆς, οὐχ ἵνα ταύτην μόνην τὴν εὐχὴν εὐχώμεθα, ἀλλ' ἵνα, ταύτην ἔχοντες πηγὴν εὐχῆς, ἐκ ταύτης ἀρυώμεθα τὰς ἐννοίας τῶν εὐχῶν. So also Bucer: *in hunc modum* orate, **non hæc verba, ut** stulte vulgus hactenus persuasum fuit; Jansenius, a Lapide, Socinus, Grotius, Neander, Baumgarten-Crusius, De Wette. Augustine says that we **must be able to deduce all** prayers from the petitions of **the Lord's Prayer**. This opinion, observes Wolzogen, must be accepted with limitations. Many prayers of a Christian man, he says, are widely removed from these petitions: all that we can say is, that the Lord's Prayer expresses those things which are to be prayed for under *any* **circumstances**. (Comp. also Socinus, Voelkel de vera religione iv. 9.)[1]

How little attention the Christian Church in its first beginnings paid to the mere letter, may **be seen by** the difference of the text of Luke. Hence Ernesti remarks on St Luke xi.: vel hinc palam fit, quam evv. **non** fuerint superstitiosi de verbis .... ubi sunt qui misere trepidant, quoties ex *humanis* preculis vocula fuerit omissa! There appears to have been then no regular use of this prayer, at least it does not occur in the Acts of the Apostles; and in Justin it is said that the προεστώς prays "that strength may be given him" (comp. Augusti, Denkwuerdigkeiten, Th. v.; Joh. Walch, orat. **domin.** apud veteres Christianos (Miscellanea, Amst. 1744). Afterwards the prayer began to be regarded with greater veneration, when it was used in the consecration of the Lord's Supper (Bunsen, Hippolytus ii. 374). Then it became part of the disciplina arcani, and **was** no more permitted to be used by the catechumens; the fourth petition likewise **received a spiritual** signification, and was made to refer to the Lord's Supper. **From** the Apostolic Constitu-

---

[1] We may mention here two now **antiquated** hypotheses regarding **the object of this** prayer. Pfannkuche thought that the intention of our Lord was to give His disciples a symbol of faith. Moeller held that each petition is the beginning of a Jewish prayer then in use, and that our Lord's intention was to point out to His disciples some of the best Jewish prayers, which they might make use of in the meanwhile, until the Spirit was given to teach them how to pray. Augusti also defends this hypothesis. Pfannkuche was answered by Noesselt in his Exercitationes.

tions (L. vii. c. 24), in the beginning of the fourth century, we learn that at that period the Pater noster was used three times in the daily worship of the Church. Since Charlemagne the children learnt it by heart. We have already referred to the repetitions of the Romish Church connected with its use. The Protestant Church likewise accepted the Lord's Prayer as a standing form in public worship, although without any superstitious veneration of the use of the mere words. Luther has some admirable remarks on this prayer. "It is," says he, "the very best prayer that ever came into the world, or was ever invented by man, because God the Father has given it through His Son, putting it into His mouth; we cannot, therefore, doubt that of all others it pleases Him best. And it is a very good practice, particularly among uneducated persons, for the children and people in the house, that the Lord's Prayer should be daily prayed through, both morning and evening, and at meat, and also at other times; that men may thus present before God their common wants." Thus the Lord's Prayer came soon to take the place of a morning and evening prayer, and in the Lutheran service was offered four times on each occasion; thus for the Protestant Church it retained its significance. Yet although it was well to use it as a $\mu \acute{\epsilon} \tau \varrho o \nu\ \tau \tilde{\eta} \varsigma\ \pi \varrho o \sigma \epsilon v \chi \tilde{\eta} \varsigma$, as Chrysostom calls it, which all men might join in offering, it is nevertheless a prayer of such a deep spiritual character, that the number of those who are capable of offering it in its deep spiritual truth must ever be small. Tertul. de orat. c. 1: brevitas ista . . . . . magnæ ac beatæ interpretationis substantia fulta est, quantumque substringitur verbis, tantum diffunditur sensibus, neque enim propria tantum orationis officia complexa est, venerationem dei, aut hominis petitionem, sed omnem pæne sermonem domini, omnem commemorationem disciplinæ, ut revera in oratione *breviarium totius Evangelii comprehendatur*. Cyprian: qualia sunt orationis dominicæ sacramenta, quam multa, quam magna, breviter in sermone collecta, sed in virtute spiritualiter copiosa, ut nihil omnino prætermissum sit, quod non in precibus atque orationibus nostris cœlestis doctrinæ compendio comprehendatur.

III. SOURCE FROM WHICH IT MAY HAVE BEEN DERIVED.

Of course, when we inquire if there were any sources from which this passage may have been derived, we only mean to ask whether our Lord did, in this case as in others, avail Himself of certain elements of truth which already existed among the people. That a sense of poverty of mind should have constrained Him to do so, no one would for a moment maintain. Herder, influenced by his joy at the opening up of a hitherto unknown source of Oriental religious knowledge, somewhat hastily tried to explain this prayer and **other** passages of the New Testament by the Zend Avesta (comp. Erlaeuterungen des N. T.'s aus einer neueroeffneten Urkunde, **Riga** 1776). He failed, however, fully to weigh the possibility of this prayer having an historical connection. He was followed by J. A. Richter, das Christenthum und die aeltesten Religionen des Orients, 1819; Rhode, die heilige Sage der alten Baktrer, 1820; Seyffarth, Beitrag zur Specialcharakteristik der Johanneischen Schriften, 1823. Rhode (in loc. cit. S. 416): "One may, in fact, call the prayer of Jesus a short extract of the prayers of the writings of the Zend Avesta; and for each petition we find there are several valuable passages almost verbally identical." (!) There is only one single passage in the Zend Avesta (B. i. Th. ii. S. 89) which bears a resemblance, and that only an apparent one, to the fifth petition. The refutation of this groundless hypothesis may be found in Gebser: de explicatione script. sacr. præsertim N. T. e libro Zendavesta, Jen. 1824, de oratione dominica, p. 19.

All we can suppose is, that there may be some allusion to the forms of prayer then in use among the *Jews*. Such an allusion would not be surprising. The Psalms themselves are to a great extent prayers, and form the foundation of the Christian liturgical prayers. The religion of the time of our Lord might offer admirable prayers, such as in fact were in use in the Jewish synagogues: only one of the petitions, viz., the fifth, gives more distinct expression to the *new religion*. Why might not the Saviour have collected and combined the best petitions of those well-known prayers? Longe abfuit, observes Grotius, dominus ab omni affectatione non necessariæ novitatis. Especially, might not this be supposed to have been the case, when we consider that a closer examination of the train of thought in the prayer shows that these petitions have not been put together accidentally, but have been formed into a new and peculiar whole by the creative spirit of the Saviour? (The so-called parallell passages from the rabbinical writings are to be found in the remarks on the Pater noster by Drusius, Grotius, Capellus, Lightfoot, Schoettgen, Wettstein; in Vitringa de syn. vet. p. 962; in the treatise by Witsius, de oratione dom.; and in a special treatise by Surenhusius, syll. dissert. p. 31, which is pointed as an appendix to the Paternoster-collection by Chamberlayne.)

Docent autem nos, says Grotius, ea, quæ ex Hebræorum libris ab aliis sunt citata, non tam formulam hanc a Christo suis propriis verbis conceptam, quam in eam congestam quidquid in Hebræorum precibus erat laudabile. So too Wolzogen, Beausobre, Michaelis, and many more. Expositors have especially referred to the prayer of the synagogue, *Kaddisch*, which was very highly prized as one of the sources of the Lord's Prayer (Vitringa, B.-Crusius, Nitzsch in the essay already quoted). This would depend, first of all, on the age of that prayer. Zunz points out, that it is quoted in the Book of Sifri: now the date of the latest authority quoted in that book is in the first half of the third century; accordingly, the prayer Kaddisch might reach back as far as the time of our Lord (Zunz, gottesdienstliche Vortraege, S. 48, 372). Now the prayer commences as follows: יתגדל ויתקדש שמיה רבא בעלמא דברא כרעותיה וימליך מלכותיה בחייכון וביומיכון ובחיי דכל בית ישראל בעגלא ובזמן קריב ואמרו אמן, "Let His (God's) great name be glorified and sanctified in the world which He has created according to His good pleasure. May He cause His kingdom to have dominion in your life and in your days, and in the life of the whole house of Israel now and henceforth; and say ye, Amen." Then the hallowing of the name of God (from which the prayer derives its name קָדִישׁ) is repeated several times; and so great an importance is attached to this petition, and to that for the kingdom of God, that it is reported in the Gemara (tract. Berachoth xl. 2): א״רב כל ברכה שאין בה הזכרת השם אינה ברכה ור׳ יוחנן אמר כל ברכה שאין בה מלכות אינה ברכה, "Rab says: Every prayer in which the name of God is not mentioned, [that is, in which He is not praised] is no prayer. And Rabbi Jochanan says: That prayer in which the kingdom of God is not named, is no prayer." Then, we find in many forms of prayer expressions such as these: "Thy name be hallowed by our works;" "Thy name be hallowed, and Thy memorial glorified." And similarly the petitions for the kingdom are repeated in many ways. If we consider these facts, we shall admit that there is certainly some probability attaching to the opinion, "that his coincidence is not merely accidental, that our Lord adopted and introduced into His prayer these two petitions of the synagogue, which form, as it were, the foundation of all prayer, the one of which contemplates the hallowing of God, and the other the coming of the **kingdom of the Messiah**." We are not, indeed, constrained to accept this view, as in the case of both these petitions we find sufficient points of connection with the Old Testament (comp. on the first and second petitions).

We have now exhausted the number of real parallels, unless indeed we are also to take into consideration the expression, "Heavenly Father," which likewise occurs in the Jewish prayers of the time of Christ (see on ver. 9). With reference to the *third* petition, we might indeed compare the words, "Let Thy name be hallowed in this world, **as it is** hallowed **in** heaven;" and again, "The Israelites are angels on earth; the angels hallow God's name in heaven, and the Israelites upon earth." For the *fourth* petition, the passage from the tractate Berachoth is cited: "Many are the necessities of Thy people; may it please Thee, O God, to grand unto each of them **as** much **as** may be needful for their nourishment, and to satisfy their need." For the *fifth* petition we cannot adduce even one apparent parallel. With regard to the *sixth*, the following words of a Jewish morning-prayer have been quoted: "**O Lord** our God, grant that we may follow Thy laws; lead **us not into** the power of sin, nor into temptation, nor into contempt; remove from us evil desires (יֵצֶר רַע), grant us good desires." It is self-evident that we cannot, from similarities such as these, argue that the Lord's Prayer originated from the rabbinical prayers. Moreover, the similar phrases have been gathered together in the most diverse writings. Some occur in the Talmud and in the Book of Sohar, in an *historical* narrative: others in *moral* writings; others, again, in *collections of prayers*. The most similar are those which we find in a מַחְזוֹר, *i.e.*, a collection of prayers of the Portuguese Jews, and in the סֵפֶר מוּסָר (of which Drusius makes much use), the author of which was a certain Rabbi Jehuda Klatz. Now it is certain that this Portuguese collection is of no older date than the middle ages; and as for this

Rabbi Juda Klatz, *he* flourished, it appears, only at the end of the *fifteenth* century.[1] To conclude anything from the prayers of this Rabbi Juda Klatz and from those of the Portuguese Jews in Amsterdam, on the subject of the prayers in use at the time of our Lord, would certainly be a very rash and unjustifiable proceeding.

We have yet to mention a peculiar view of the pious Knorr von Rosenroth, a man deeply imbued with Hebrew mysticism. He is also known as a writer of sacred poetry (apparatus in libr. Sohar iii., Vorrede, § 2). His idea is, that the petitions of the Pater noster are in the order of the cabbalistic emanation of the four worlds, mundus aziluticus, beriathicus, jeziraticus, and asia: even Buddeus concurs in this view. It is opposed by Wernsdorf vindiciæ orationis dominicæ, Vit. 1708; Schrader: oratio dominica historice et dogmatice proposita, præcipue autem Judaismo opposita (præs. Joh. Andr. Schmid), Helm. 1710.

IV. Connection of the Prayer and Train of Thought.

Even if there were a sure foundation for the opinion that in this prayer we have a combination of certain Jewish forms of prayer at that time in use, we should still have to regard it as peculiar to our Lord, as it forms a perfect whole, bearing the original impress of the spirit of Christ. True, in a time when men could not recognise the depth of the Scriptures, this prayer too was subjected to shallow and superficial criticism, such as the following. J. C. Schulz, in his notes to Michaelis' translation, remarks: It is impossible to suppose that this prayer forms a connected whole. Such an idea is opposed by the absence of all connection, by the want of any combining element among the petitions themselves, such as could be scarcely excused in any suppliant, even in one who gave the utmost reins to his imagination, least of all in one who prayed in the thoughtful and reflecting spirit which Jesus certainly requires.

Moeller (in loc. cit. S. 47) has not scrupled to disclose, by the following decision, his own mental poverty: "*In a word,*

---

[1] Wolf does not give his date: his German name alone shows that he belongs to modern times. De Rossi, however, says in his dizzionario storico degli autori Ebrei, Parma 1802, i. p. 89: That his work Sefer Muser appeared in Constantinople as an opus posthumum in 1537.

whenever one regards the Pater noster as one connected prayer, one sees in it so many imperfections, that one cannot understand why Jesus has not given something more perfect."

Tertullian and Augustine already owned the existence of a progressive sequence in the prayer. This is seen, even on a casual view, from the σοῦ of the three first petitions, and the ἡμῶν, ἡμῖν, ἡμᾶς of the last. At the outset the suppliant appears lost in the contemplation of the Being to whom his spirit ascends: next, he turns his thoughts upon himself and his own wants. Further, it is not difficult to recognise a progression in the first three petitions, and in the three (or four) last. The recognition of the name of God is the basis on which alone the kingdom of God can be established; and again, this kingdom is the sphere in which the will of God is fulfilled. Further, the prayer for the maintenance of the life of man precedes the prayer for the forgiveness of his sins; and again, it is only when the guilt of the past is removed that the thought is directed to the temptations of the future. The thoughtful reader, who has derived from other sources the knowledge of the Trinity, will also find a reference to that truth in the scheme of this prayer. The petitions of the first and second parts refer to God as Creator and Preserver; the second petition of either part refers to God as Redeemer; whilst the third of either part relates to God the Holy Spirit, by whom the Divine will comes to be fulfilled, and through whose power temptation is overcome.

The number of the petitions is, according to the Catholic reckoning, *seven*. Thus Augustine (de oratione in monte); although in his sermo de oratione dominica, he thinks that the two last petitions may be taken together, and so counts six. Luther, and the Lutheran Church, reckon seven; whilst Origen (Opera i. 265) and Chrysostom, taking the two last petitions as one, reckon *six*, as do also the expositors of the Reformed Church, and likewise Socinus.[1] If ἀλλὰ ῥῦσαι were nothing more than the positive expression of the preceding negative prayer, still there could be no objection to take it separately, so

---

[1] Yet some expositors of the Reformed Church, as Aretius, reckon seven, and some R. Catholic and Lutheran commentators leave it doubtful whether the number may not be six, as Maldonatus, Bengel, Chemnitz: qua de re cum nemine contendam.

that we should have seven petitions (comp. ad locum). Some commentators are unwilling to regard the first three petitions as αἰτήματα, and would rather take them for εὐχαί, pia vota, as Grotius and Weber. But does not the wish of the Christian naturally become a prayer (Rom. i. 10, x. 1)? This distinction is therefore groundless. Others, again, have held that the first petition is a votum addressed to the πάτερ ἡμῶν, or a doxology similar to the form εὐλογητὸς ὁ Θεός; Pricæus, Olearius, Wettstein, Michaelis: but were this the case, these words must have been more closely connected, grammatically, with the address πάτερ ἡμῶν. Some original, and in part just, observations on the arrangement of the Pater noster are made by Weber in the Programme already mentioned, p. 51. He gives the following scheme:—

Πρόλογος.	Λόγος.		Ἐπίλογος.
	εὐχαί.	αἰτήματα.	
1) πάτερ.	1) ἁγιασθήτω τὸ ὄνομά σου.	1) τὸν ἄρτον ἡμῶν τ. ἐπιούσιον δὸς ἡμῖν σήμερον.	1) ὅτι σοῦ ἐστιν ἡ βασιλεία.
2) ἡμῶν.	2) ἐλθέτω ἡ βασιλεία σου.	2) καὶ ἄφες ἡμῖν τὰ ὀφειλήματα κ.τ.λ.	2) σοῦ ἐστιν ἡ δύναμις.
3) ὁ ἐν τοῖς οὐρανοῖς.	3) γενηθήτω τὸ θέλημά σου κ.τ.λ.	3) καὶ μὴ εἰσενέγκῃς ἡμᾶς εἰς πειρασμὸν κ.τ.λ.	3) σοῦ ἐστιν ἡ δόξα.

It is a matter of some importance in expounding the Lord's Prayer, to determine the stand-point which Christ here maintains. We see at once that the prayer is given solely for His disciples: this is expressed in the προσεύχεσθε ὑμεῖς. As for the *fifth* petition, it could not have been spoken by Him in this way; comp. the antithesis, vii. 11, εἰ οὖν ὑμεῖς, πονηροὶ ὄντες, κ.τ.λ. Further, that petition appears adapted to disciples who were conscious of having already received forgiveness of sins. The thought, that the willingness of man to forgive those who have trespassed against him, has its real source in the Divine pardon, is also expressed in the parable, ch. xviii. This petition, accordingly, leads us to conclude that the Saviour did not merely consider the state of the disciples at the time, but also adapted Himself to the more advanced stage that they should afterwards attain. And if our Lord had before His eye the Church of the future, then the expositor must not attempt to limit the meaning which He gave to His words to the measure of the comprehension of the disciples at that time (vide supra,

p. 66). The Lord's Prayer, apprehended by a Christian and spiritual understanding, implies such a depth of religious feeling, such an intense sense of our relation to God, and such a strength of faith, that it has been regarded by the large majority of praying Christians as not so much an expression of their actual state of mind, as the type of that condition which they were striving to attain. Comp. the author's Predigten, vol. ii.

The Invocation. Ver. 9.

The use of the name of Father with reference to the Deity, is also found in the extra-biblical religions of the ancient world. The name *Jupiter* is compounded of Deus and Pater, and the Homeric *Zeus* is the Πατὴρ Θεῶν τε ἀνδρῶν τε. What meaning was implied in this name in the view of the heathen world, may be gathered from Diodorus Siculus, bibl. v. c. 72: πατέρα δὲ (αὐτὸν προσαγορευθῆναι) διὰ τὴν φροντίδα καὶ τὴν εὔνοιαν τὴν εἰς ἅπαντας, ἔτι δὲ καὶ τὸ δοκεῖν ὥσπερ ἀρχηγὸν εἶναι τοῦ γένους τῶν ἀνθρώπων. Thus Plutarch (de superstit. c. 6), speaking of the δεισιδαίμων, by whom he understands the *superstitious* man, says that he recognises only the τυραννικόν in the Deity, and not the πατρικόν: two ideas which he opposes to one another. In Acts xiv. 17, St Paul goes upon the supposition that the heathen was in a condition to recognise in the blessings of nature as sign of the fatherly care of God. In Israel, the relation of God as the Father of the nation, though not yet fully realized by the individual, was recognised by the nation; comp. such passages as the following: Deut. xxxii. 6; Isa. lxiii. 16, lxiv. 8; Jer. iii. 4, 19; Mal. i. 6, ii. 10. He was the Father of the people, inasmuch as to Him they owed their existence as a nation (Deut. xxxii. 8 et seqq., xiv. 1, 2); and as the Source to them of blessing and protection (Ps. lxviii. 5; Isa. ix. 6). It is doubtful if the words, "my Father," Job xxxiv. 36, express the *individual* relation: the Targum, Kimchi, and many others, explain it otherwise. In Ps. lxxxix. 26, "He shall cry unto Me, Thou art my Father," the name is a special distinction. The same childlike national feeling we find also in the Apocrypha, Tobit xiii. 4; 3 Mac. vi. 3, 8; but here the *individual* feeling already begins to develop itself; Wisdom ii. 16; Sirach xxiii. 1, 4 (li. 10). The name of Father applied with reference to individuals is very general in the Rabbins of the centuries after Christ. In the national relation, it is used in their prayers, and also in the Kaddisch. Yet it is noteworthy that there appears to be a certain shrinking from the use of the name even in a general and national way. In Jer. iii. 4, 19, the Targumist translates Abba merely by Rabboni; and in Isa. lxiii. 16, he resolves the force of the original into a mere comparison thus: "Thou art our Lord, and Thy blessings are as richly poured out upon us *as* those of a father upon his children." Now, from these circumstances, we may well conceive that the constant use of the words "your Father" in the conversations of Christ with His disciples, must have struck the people of that time as something unusual. Further, it is to be noticed that in none of the four Gospels it is used in addressing the multitude, but only to the disciples, to whom alone, moreover, the term $υἱοὶ\ Θεοῦ$ is applied. In a few passages the relation of childhood is especially appropriated to them. Thus in St Luke xii. 32: "Fear not, little flock; for it is your Father's good pleasure to give you the kingdom;" comp. chap. vi. 26, x. 21: so too in ver. 9, it is that special relation of sonship into which the disciples were to enter that is referred to; a relation, the deepest foundation of which consists in the $τέκνον\ Θεοῦ\ γενέσθαι$, which St Paul characterizes as an $υἱοθεσία$, an adoptatio in filios, the result of which is the participation *in the spirit of adoption;* and St John represents as in the first instance a $καλεῖσθαι\ τέκνον\ Θεοῦ$, 1 John iii. 1, and next as an actual $γενέσθαι$, 1 John i. 12, 13, iii. 9. The name of Father given in the Gospels, points to the new birth spoken of in St John iii. 7, 8, and to men becoming children of God by moral affinity with God, Matt. v. 9, 45.

In the prayer the plural is used. So too in the prayers of the Rabbis. Gemara Berachoth, fol. 30, 1: אמר אביי לשתף איניש נפשה בהדי צבורה היכא נימא יהי רצון מלפניך י" אלהינו שתוליכינו בשלום וכולה, "The Rabbi Abai said: A man must in his prayers always unite himself with the congregation. How is he to speak? Let it please Thee, O Lord *our* God, to lead us," etc. The gloss to this is as follows: אל התפלל תפלה קצודה בלשון יהיד אלא בלשון רבים שנמתוך כן תפלתו נשמעת, "Even a short prayer must not be offered in the singular, but in the plural; for only thus can it be heard." Their prayers were indeed offered, for the most part, as the prayers of the congregation. The Rabbi Chija says: "All my life long have I never prayed the Musaphim (*i.e.*, the benedictions of the eighteen prayers) alone, except on the day when the army of the king took the city, and the congregation could not assemble, so that I was by myself alone" (Gemara, fol. 30, 1). Of course our Lord could by no means discountenance the prayers of individuals for **themselves**: in the Book of Psalms such prayers predominate; **but in a typical and model prayer**, such as He here seeks to give, there must of necessity be an expression of the feeling of mutual fellowship and communion.

Ὁ ἐν τοῖς οὐρανοῖς.—The name of Father had awoke a sense of childlike trust and confidence in the heart of the suppliant (1 St John iii. 1; Rom. viii. 15; Ps. ciii. 13). Luther says in his Shorter Catechism: "By this name God seeks to attract us, that we may believe that He is our true Father, and that we are His true children." The clause, "which art in heaven," directs our thoughts to the difference between earthly fathers and this Father. "We are to have," says the Heidelberg Catechism, "*no earthly thoughts respecting the heavenly majesty of God.*" The religious spirit of all nations has by an unconscious symbolism regarded the ether, in its depth and repose, in its boundlessness and unchangeableness, as the dwelling-place of Deity.[1] This is also the idea of the writers of the Old Testament, although at the same time they take care to give the strongest expression to the truth that God is omnipresent, and is raised above space (1 Kings viii. 27; 2 Chron. ii. 6; Ps. cxxxix. 7; Jer. xxiii. 23). In Job xxii. 13, 14, it is said of the ungodly, that he says, "How does God know? Can He judge through the dark cloud? Thick clouds are a covering to Him, that He seeth not; and He walketh in the circuit of heaven." In Isa. lxvi. 1, where it is said that heaven is the throne of Jehovah and the earth His footstool, it is easy to recognise the symbolical character of the expression. (On the views of the ancients, compare Suicer Thesaurus ii. p. 523.)

The very commencement of the prayer assumes in the suppli-

---

[1] Aristotle, in a remarkable passage (de Cœlo L. i. c. iii.), says: πάντες γὰρ ἄνθρωποι περὶ θεῶν ἔχουσι ὑπόληψιν καὶ πάντες τὸν ἀνωτάτῳ τῷ θείῳ τόπον ἀποδιδόασι, καὶ βάρβαροι καὶ Ἕλληνες, ὅσοιπερ εἶναι νομίζουσι θεούς, δηλονότι, ὡς τῷ ἀθανάτῳ τὸ ἀθάνατον συνηρτημένον.

ant a spirit penetrated with reverence and love,—a spirit which, like the Psalmist, thinks of God as the highest and best portion, Ps. lxxiii. 25, 26. What the suppliant asks is, that God may be glorified, that His kingdom may be perfected on earth; this is an object of his desire which must find utterance, before he can give expression to his own personal wants.

The First Petition.

On the original reading, vide supra, p. 316. Ἁγιασθήτω τὸ ὄνομά σου.—The *Name* in the East was always significant. It expressed that which was peculiar to the individual named: as the name "Jehovah" itself. Already in the Old Testament, and very frequently with the Rabbins, the name of God is accordingly a periphrasis for God Himself: Ps. xx. 2; Isa. l. 10; הַשֵּׁם is even an appellation of God, Lev. xxiv. 11, 16; Deut. xxviii. 58. Hence the name of God here denotes God in those attributes with which He is thought of by men: זֵכֶר is also used in this sense (Isa. xxvi. 8). Origen: ὄνομα τοίνυν ἐστὶ κεφαλαιώδης προσηγορία τῆς ἰδίας ποιότητος τοῦ ὀνομαζομένου παραστατική.

Ἁγιάζειν corresponds to the Hebrew הִקְדִּישׁ and קָדַשׁ; and signifies, primarily, to *make holy an unholy thing*; next, it came to mean to *treat a holy thing as holy, to hold sacred*, i.e., to *honour*: Num. xx. 12; Deut. xxxii. 51; Ex. xx. 8; Lev. xxi. 8. The transitive signification of intransitive verbs is frequently that of *treating*: thus קָלַל *to be light*, קִלֵּל to treat contemptuously; כָּבֵד *to be heavy, to be splendid*, כִּבֵּד *to treat honourably*, etc. So too ἁγιάζειν is used in the New Testament, 1 Pet. iii, 15; in the Apocrypha, Sir. xxxiii. 4, and by the Fathers, *e.g.*, Chrysostom, Hom. in Ps. cxiii.; ὥσπερ ἄγγελοι τὸν Θεὸν ἁγιάζουσι πονηρίας πάσης ἀπηλλαγμένοι, ἀρετὴν δὲ μετιόντες μετὰ ἀκριβείας, οὕτω δὴ καταξιωθείημεν καὶ ἡμεῖς αὐτὸν ἁγιάζειν. Thus the meanings of ἁγιάζειν and δοξάζειν correspond; and these words also occur together: τὸ ὄνομα τοῦ Θεοῦ τὸ ἅγιον καὶ ἔνδοξον, Tob. viii. 5. Chrys.: τὸ ἁγιασθήτω τοῦτο ἔστι δοξασθήτω. Similarly, ἀνέψωσε and ἡγίασε occur together in Sirach xxxvi. 4. In the Old Testament we find אֲכַבֵּד and אֶקָּדֵשׁ used beside each other, Lev. x. 3; so too Ezek. xxviii. 22, xxxviii. 23: in the Jewish prayers the expressions are used together: יִתְקַדַּשׁ וְיִתְגַּדַּל שֵׁם :־״, and יִשְׁתַּבַּח וְיִתְפָּאַר יִתְבָּרַךְ וְיִתְקַדַּשׁ שְׁמֵהּ. In the Semitic dialects, and even in latter Greek, ἁγιάζειν has accordingly received the meaning of εὐλογεῖν. In the rabbinical writing, קִדּוּשׁ is equivalent to בְּרָכָה. In the Ethiopic the doxology is named by a word from the same root. In the Arabic تقديس takdis, is the technical term for praising God: Reland. de rel. Muh. p. 149. In the later Greek Church-language the formulæ commonly used were ἁγιάζειν τὸ ποτήριον = εὐλογεῖν, and ἁγιασμὸς μέγας stood for the benediction of the water (Du Cange, Gloss. Græc. med. s. h. v.). Theodoret (Opp. T. ii. p. 349) expounds, like St Chrysostom, Isa. xlix. 7 thus: τὸ ἁγιάσατε ἀντὶ τοῦ ὑμνήσατε τέθεικεν. οὕτως γὰρ καὶ προσευχόμενοι λέγομεν, ἁγιασθήτω τὸ ὄνομά σου ἀντὶ τοῦ δοξασθήτω. Similarly Origen uses ὑψοῦν for ἁγιάζειν.

Now this hallowing imples two things. The first is, the recognition of God as being what He is; the second is, suffering one's self to be influenced by Him: and the latter is the necessary consequence of a true and hearty recognition of Him; comp. נִקְדַּשׁ Lev. x. 3, xxii. 32; 1 Pet. iii. 15: "*Sanctify* the Lord God in your hearts." Even if its periphrastic meaning were ignored, and ὄνομα were understood simply of the name Jehova, the sense would be the same; inasmuch as the sincere abhorrence of the misuse of the name of God with the lips must proceed from fear of God in the heart. This is expressed by Calvin in his exposition, although he does not bring out clearly the periphrastic signification of the Name: sanctificari Dei nomen nihil aliud est, quam suum Deo habere honorem, quo dignus est, ut nunquam de ipso loquantur vel cogitent homines sine summa veneratione. In this view it is the third commandment which is here made into a prayer.

The petition is taken in the *narrowest* compass of its signification by those who regarded it simply as a prayer that the Name of God may not be profaned, but always named with reverence. This is the view of those commentators who view the clause simply as a kind of doxology, as Pricäus, Olearius, Wettstein, Michaelis. Those again take a larger view of its meaning, who consider the hallowing of the Name by praising and glorifying God *by words* as also implied; as Socinus, verbis, scriptis evidenti honore afficere nomen ipsius; Episcopius, Piscator. Others again consider that the recognition and glorifying of God in the heart, and in the outward walk and conversation, is also implied; and observe, that from such a hallowing of the name of God, others learn to hallow it too (chap. v. 16): thus Chrysostom, Euthymius, Augustine ad Probam: Nos ipsos admonemus ut nomen ejus, quod semper sanctum est, etiam apud homines sanctum habeatur neque contemnatur; quod non Deo sed nobis prodest: Jerome, Beza. The petition is taken in the widest sense of all when the hallowing by word and by deed are both regarded as comprehended in it. Thus Luther: "It is indeed a short saying, but its sense is as broad as the world: it speaks against all false doctrine, and all false living." In his Larger Catechism he says: "Now the saying is somewhat obscure, and not like as *we* should speak; for in our mother tongue we should say, 'Heavenly Father, grant that Thy name alone may be hallowed;' now, how is it hallowed among us? *Answer.* Most plainly one may say, When both our life and our doctrine are truly Christian." So too Zwingli, and similarly the Heidelberg Catechism. Witsius thinks that the glorifying of God even by the lower animals and the works of creation is included in the text, and he refers to such passages as Ps. ciii. 22, cxlv. 10. Calov: Fit sanctificatio nominis divini tripliciter: (1) $\delta o\gamma \mu \alpha \tau \iota \kappa \tilde{\omega} \varsigma$, per sanam doctrinam; (2) $\dot{\epsilon}\nu\epsilon\rho\gamma\eta\tau\iota\kappa\tilde{\omega}\varsigma$, per sanctam vitam: (3) $\pi\alpha\vartheta\eta\tau\iota\kappa\tilde{\omega}\varsigma$, per passiones ob evangelii confessionem toleratas. Cocceius, with the idea of better distinguishing the second petition from the first, takes a peculiar view: Dei nomen sanctificatur (1) per obedientiam servatoris, (2) per verbum evangelii, quo Christi justitia et Dei sanctitas manifestatur.

The Second Petition. Ver. 10.

The beginning of the work of God in us is the acknowledging and hallowing of God: the form in which the Divine work is perfected, as well as the means by which it comes to perfection, is the kingdom of God. This kingdom was prefigured in Israel; it was introduced in its essence by Christ: and through His power it advances ever more and more in the course of the ages towards its perfection. Thus this petition is connected with the first; and again with the third, which indicates the final goal and end of all things, the removal of all distraction, and the perfect harmony of the creature with the will of the Creator.

These three petitions accordingly present to us the beginning, middle, and end of the development of the kingdom of God. Neander explains that the object in thus illustrating the nature of the kingdom of God by these petitions, was to meet the earthly misconceptions then entertained by the Jews concerning the kingdom of God. Already in the Glossa ordinaris this progress of the thought was adverted to: the first petition relates to the humilis adventus regni; the second, **to the glorious** manifestation thereof; the third, to the perfectio nostræ beatitudinis.

As regards the history of the exposition of this petition, the view taken of it has depended much upon the sense in which the "kingdom of God" itself was understood (on which see chap. v. 3): according as the idea of that kingdom was taken in a wider or a narrower, a one-sided or a many-sided sense, so was the petition regarded as more or less comprehensive. The narrowest view is of those who think they are bound, for the sake of the historical interpretation, to adhere to the *Jewish* idea of the kingdom, and explain the words thus: "Let the kingdom of the Messiah appear" (Pfannkuche, Meyer). This explanation adheres to the Jewish and historical idea. On the other hand, Semler, Teller, Kuinoel, entirely lose sight of the historical element, when they bring prominently forward the abstract idea of the spread of Christian truth in the world. The two leading thoughts in the petition, understood in a Christian sense, are, first, that of a kingdom of God *manifested in time;* and, secondly, of the same kingdom destined to be *at last brought to perfection.* Nitzsch has acutely adduced the different views expressed in the Rubrics **with reference to** the moral and spiritual kingdom, and to the kingdom in its future perfection (comp. his essay "Ueber die noch uneroerterte Umstellung der II. und III. Bitte des Vater Unsers bei Tertullian," Studien und Kritiken, 1830, H. 4). The idea that the kingdom here spoken of is the future kingdom of God, was held in the ancient Latin Church by Tertullian, who was hereby induced to place the second petition *after* the third; by Cyprian, Hilary, and the author Operis Imperfecti; also by Augustine: videlicet regnum *gloriæ,* nam de regno *gratiæ* sequitur in petitione tertia. The same view occurs in the Glossa ordinaris, Euthymius, Theophylact, Piscator, Maldonatus; the last of whom collates 1 Cor. xv. 28 and Rev. vi. 9, 10. Similarly Bengel, who remarks that the first petition was already partially fulfilled in the Old Testament, sed adventus regni Dei est Novi Testamenti quodammodo proprius; and he quotes Rev. v. 10. The opinion that the kingdom spoken of is the *moral sovereignty of God* in the hearts of believers, was entertained by Jerome (who dreaded the fanatical abuse of the eschatological view); in the Greek Church by Origen, Cyrill, Isidorus Pelusiota, Gregory Nyssenus; among later writers, by Zwingli, who remarks: Petimus, ut ad nos veniat regnum Dei, *i. e.* justitia, pax, gaudium in Spiritu Sancto; by Bucer, Socinus, Wettstein, Heumann, and others. The kingdom of God would then be understood in the sense indicated in Rom. xiv. 17. Chrysostom ad Matthæum speaks of it as the future kingdom; but in other passages he also gives the moral and spiritual interpretation: $\dot{\eta}$ $\tau\tilde{\eta}\varsigma$ $οἰκειώσεως$ $βασιλεία$, *i. e.*, the sovereignty by means of which man is made the property of God (comp. Suicer, Observationes, p. 219).

Now, the *complete* fulfilment of the second petition can only take place when the kingdom of God is perfected: we cannot therefore separate the reference to the future from the idea of the present moral and spiritual kingdom. Accordingly we find the two views combined by several critics: Luther, Calvin, Chemnitz, Witsius, the Heidelberg Catechism. Luther says: "The kingdom of God comes *first* in the present through the word of God and through faith, and it comes the second time in eternity by being *manifested*." Calvin: Quare summa hujus precationis est, ut deus verbi sui luce mundum irradiet, spiritus sui afflatu corda formet in obsequium justitiæ suæ: quidquid est dissipatum in terra, suis auspiciis in ordinem restituat, exordium vero regnandi faciat a subigendis carnis nostræ cupiditatibus. Jam vero, quia regnum Dei per continuos progressus augetur usque ad mundi finem, necesse est quotidie optare ejus adventum. Quantum enim iniquitatis grassatur in mundo, tantundem abest regnum Dei, quod secum affert plenam rectitudinem. (Compare the exposition given above, p. 78.) The Heidelberg Catechism says: "So govern us by Thy word and Spirit, that the longer we live the more we may submit ourselves to Thee. Preserve and increase Thy Church, and destroy the works of the devil, and every power that lifts up itself against Thee; bring to nought all evil counsels that are cherished against Thy holy word: until the perfection of Thy kingdom come, when Thou shalt be all in all."

When Luther says, that "as the name of God is holy in itself, even apart from our prayer that it may be hallowed, so also His kingdom comes without our asking," this observation does not seem in keeping with the common ideas that are connected with the coming of the kingdom of God. In it he follows the exposition of Augustine ad Probam: seu velimus, seu nolimus, utique veniet, (sed) desiderium nostrum ad illud regnum excitamus, ut *nobis* veniat atque nos in eo regnare mereamur. This explanation accordingly contemplates only the *final* coming. It leads, however, to the question which has recently been discussed on ethical grounds, as to whether the perfected kingdom of God can be regarded as a subject of ethics. Now, this has been denied; and for this reason: because it is said that this kingdom is to be brought to perfection by God Himself, independently of the moral condition of man (see above, p. 75). Such a view, however, could be entertained only by men who ignored the revelation of God in *history,* and the historical coming of His kingdom. Of course, on the other hand, we cannot imagine an historical development into which the causality of God does not enter. The Divine plan for the world must, on the contrary, be realized by means of the moral development of man. Unquestionably the above quoted comment of Luther upon St Augustine's exposition is based on a one-sided view of predestination. The exposition of the three first petitions is permeated by the spirit of that doctrine in the case of all those critics who held it. They have spoken of the fulfilment of these petitions as depending unconditionally on the will of God, and have regarded them as simply the unfolding of the Divine decree. Aretius remarks on the third petition: summa petimus hic, *ut æterna Dei sententia de redemptione generis humani . . compleatur et ad finem denique perducatur.* Quod cum indices in hac vita videmus fieri, tum demum in novissimo judicio Christi judicis finalis sententia his rebus omnibus colophonem imponet, ac deinceps in piis voluntas Dei ad plenum locum habebit. Holding that these three petitions can only be fulfilled in the case of the "elect," Calvin finds a difficulty here, inasmuch as one might be praying for an impossible thing. The only answer he can give to this objection is as follows: sufficit hoc voto (*i.e.*, fiat voluntas tua) *testari*, nobis odio et tristitiæ esse quidquid Dei voluntati adversum cernimus extinctumque cupere, ut non modo omnium nostrorum affectuum sit moderatrix, sed ut nos totos, qua decet promptitudine, ad eam implendam feramur. This one-sided exposition has been opposed by others, and the freedom of the will maintained. Particularly Socinus brings prominently forward the thought, that in all these three petitions what we pray for is not so much that God would *accomplish* the thing asked, as that He would grant the means which are indispensable to its accomplishment. Origen, taking the same line of thought, observes, that He who said, "All power is given to Me in haven and on earth," by this prayer raised His disciples to be fellow-workers with Himself, and to a participation in His own power. In answer to Luther, Stier observes: "Notwithstanding, the kingdom of God comes not without our prayer, but in it and along with it." Similarly Otto von Gerlach.

THE THIRD PETITION.

$\Gamma εν\eta θήτω\ τὸ\ θέλημά\ σου$, κ.τ.λ.—The object for which the redeemed is made a member of this kingdom and a recipient of its blessings, is that he may himself become an instrument of the Divine will, which works by love. "To be holy in love,"—this is stated by St Paul to be the end of man's election in Christ before the foundation of the world, Eph. i. 4. As this end shall be reached only at the close of the development of the kingdom of God (1 Cor. xv. 28), this petition anticipates that final point of time. Quamdiu regnum mixtum est in terra, says the author of the Opus imperfectum, fit quidem voluntas Dei in hominibus, SED NON *sicut in cælo*. It was this ultimate point of time especially that the Old Testament prophecy had before its eye, when, in describing the kingdom of the Messiah, it foretold that in that kingdom the knowledge of the Lord should cover the earth as the waters cover the sea; that neither sun nor moon shall shine there, but the Lord Himself will be the light of His chosen; and that the people who compose it shall all be men in whom the spirit of righteousness dwells: Isa. iv. 3, xi. 9, lx. 19—21, lxi. 10, 11, lxv. 24, 25. These predictions are repeated in the prophetic book of the New Testament, the Book of Revelation, and there they serve to describe the kingdom of Christ in its perfection: Rev. xxi. 3, 22, 23, xxii. 3—5. There is a peculiar view given in a work by an unknown author (who is answered in an essay in Süsskind's Magazine, xiv. S. 39): he regards the "will" here spoken of as denoting simply the purpose of Christ with reference to His kingdom on earth; and what is prayed for is supposed to be the successful establishment of that kingdom: "May Thy kingdom be perfected on earth, **as it lies unfolded before** the eye of God in heaven." This view is both one-sided and philologically incorrect; but, substantially, we may certainly regard it as a petition that the plan of redemption may be perfectly fulfilled and accomplished, as Aretius expresses himself.

Heaven, we have seen, was regarded as the dwelling-place of God in contrast to the restricted and imperfect nature of the earth: so, too, here heaven is viewed as the habitation of pure spirits. The angels are especially called οἱ ἄγγελοι τῶν οὐρανῶν, or ἐν τοῖς οὐρανοῖς, Matt. xxiv. 36; Mark xii. 25; their purity and holiness, and their readiness to do the will of God, are alluded to in Ps. ciii. 21, ποιοῦντες τὰ θελήματα αὐτοῦ; Heb. i. 14; Luke xv. 10. This idea is expressed also in the predicate, οἱ ἅγιοι ἄγγελοι, Mark viii. 38. The latter is the passage in which our Lord most distinctly speaks of a kingdom of pure spirits beyond this earth. Now, in the state of perfection, this world of spirits shall, with the glorified spirits of the earth, be gathered together under one Head, who is Christ, Eph. i. 10; Heb. xii. 22, 23. Chrysostom: δὸς ἡμῖν, δέσποτα, τὴν ἐν οὐρανῷ μιμεῖσθαι πολιτείαν, ἵν᾽ ἃ θέλεις αὐτός, καὶ ἡμεῖς θέλωμεν. In the system of Origen the future element involved in this petition would naturally receive special attention: ἔτι ὄντες ἐπὶ τῆς γῆς οἱ εὐχόμενοι, νοοῦντες ἐν οὐρανῷ γεγονέναι τὸ θέλημα τοῦ Θεοῦ παρὰ πᾶσι τοῖς οἰκείοις τῶν οὐρανῶν, εὐξώμεθα καὶ ἡμῖν τοῖς ἐπὶ τ. γῆς ὁμοίως ἐκείνοις, κατὰ πάντα γενέσθαι τὸ θέλημα τ. Θεοῦ· ὅπερ συμβήσεται, μηδὲν ἡμῶν παρὰ τὸ θέλημα πραττόντων αὐτοῦ. ἐπὰν δέ, ὡς ἐν οὐρανῷ τὸ θέλημά ἐστι τοῦ Θεοῦ, καὶ ἡμῖν τοῖς ἐπὶ τ. γῆς κατορθωθῇ, ὁμοιωθέντες τοῖς ἐν οὐρανοῖς ἅτε φορέσοντες παραπλησίως ἐκείνοις τὴν εἰκόνα τοῦ ἐπουρανίου, βασιλείαν οὐρανῶν κληρονομήσομεν· τῶν μεθ᾽ ἡμᾶς ἐπὶ γῆς καὶ ἡμῖν γενομένοις ἐν οὐρανῷ ὁμοιωθῆναι εὐχομένων. A few, as Ernesti, Aretius, Olshausen, dwell especially upon the future element in the petition, and on the advance from the second petition; the larger number confine their remarks to the continuous fulfilment of the petition.

It was natural that those critics who held the tenet of predestination should understand by the $\vartheta \acute{\epsilon} \lambda \eta \mu \alpha$ merely the voluntas divina decernens (Matt. xxvi. 42), and not the voluntas præcipiens: yet is this done neither by Augustine nor yet by Calvin. Only Aretius, Beza, Witsius, unexpectedly also Rosenmueller, think that we have here not so much a petition as a declaratio animi acquiescentis in voluntate Dei. Yet their view resolves itself into this, that the petition is simply a declaration of the readiness of the suppliant to bear the *Divine chastisement;* thus Grotius, Pricæus, Wettstein, and, long before, Tertullian: jam hoc dicto ad sufferentiam nosmetipsos præmonemus. Radbertus at first agrees with the common interpretation: hoc oramus, ut libertatem arbitrii nostri ejus per gratiam sociemus ipsius voluntati, ut qui vivit jam non sibi vivat. But he seems to incline to this other view when he adds: Nullus igitur ista ex affectu potest dicere, nisi qui pro certo credidit, omnia quæ videntur, vel quæ non videntur, prospera vel adversa, Deum pro nostris utilitatibus dispensare. Oportet enim fide devota credere, magis eum pro nostra salute sine ulla intermissione esse providum, ac dispensatione sollicitum, quam nos ipsos pro nobis. But even if this *readiness* to submit to the will of God were more distinctly expressed in $\gamma \epsilon \nu \eta \vartheta \acute{\eta} \tau \omega$ than is the case, still the words $\dot{\omega} \varsigma \ \acute{\epsilon} \nu \ o \dot{\nu} \varrho \alpha \nu \tilde{\omega}$ exclude the relation to the voluntas decernens: unless indeed we were to suppose, with Grotius, Michaelis, and Stier, that the words $\dot{\omega} \varsigma \ \acute{\epsilon} \nu \ o \dot{\nu} \varrho \alpha \nu \tilde{\omega}$ imply a reference to the constant order which obtains among the stars of heaven, of which Lucan sings:—

> Sicut cœlestia semper
> Inconcusso suo volvuntur sidera motu.

Now, although this modern astronomical reflection was not one which would naturally occur to the Jewish mind, the idea of pure heavenly spirits was.

A few of the Fathers give allegorical expositions. Tertullian gives the following as the interpretatio figurata: Heaven and earth denote the contrast between *spirit and body.* Yet, after his reading in cœlis et in terra, he prefers this interpretation: "Thy will be done in earth and in heaven, in us." They only exposition which Cyprian gives is the allegorical one, that heaven and earth denote either the spirit and the flesh, or the pious and the ungodly. Augustine (Sermo lvi.) brings together a number of allegorical interpretations: (1.) Thy will be done, as in saints, so in sinners; so that sinners **may** be converted. (2.) Thy will be done, as in saints, so also in sinners at the last judgment; so that those may receive their reward, and these the **merited** condemnation. (3.) Thy will be done, as by angels, who are beyond the restrictions of earth, so by men, who are under these restrictions. (4.) As Thy will is done in spirit, so may it also be done in the body, when it shall have been made partaker of glory. (5.) Further, as the earth is made fruitful by the heavens, heaven may be made to signify Christ, and the earth the Church, which through Christ is enabled to perform the will of God.

THE FOURTH PETITION. VER. 11.

The suppliant has hitherto been **lost in the** contemplation of God: now he turns his thoughts to his own necessities. Here, too, there is a progression and a climax: this first petition relates to the supply of temporal wants as necessary in order to the spiritual life.

The exposition depends upon the view taken of $\dot{\epsilon}\pi\iota o\acute{v}\sigma\iota o\varsigma$. Now this word has been the subject of numerous learned disquisitions: yet is there room for new investigations. **Scultetus** calls the interpretation of $\dot{\epsilon}\pi\iota o\acute{v}\sigma\iota o\varsigma$, carnificina theologorum et grammaticorum. Alberti says, that to attempt to ascertain its exact meaning were $\sigma\pi\acute{o}\gamma\gamma\psi$ $\pi\acute{\alpha}\tau\tau\alpha\lambda ov$ $\varkappa\varrho o\acute{v}\epsilon\iota v$. The opinions of philologians and theologians are given in the following works: Wilh. Budaeus, comm. ling. Gr. s. h. v.; Heinr. Stephanus, thes. s. h. v.; Jos. Scaliger, epist. p. 810, in the critics sacris, ad h. l.; Daniel Heinse, exercit. sacræ (ed. 1639), p. 31; Cl. Salmasius, de foen. trap. p. 795; Is. Casaubonus, **exercit.** Antibar. l. xvi. c. 39; Erasm. Schmid, commentary ad locum; Balth. Stolberg, Thes. disp. Amst. T. ii. p. 123; Joh. Phil. Pfeiffer, ib. p. 116; Wilh. Kirchmayer, Nov. Thes. disp. T. ii. p. 189; Grotius in loco; Tanaq. Faber, ep. 2, p. 183, P. 2; Lud. Kuester on Suidas s. h. v.; Toup., epist. crit. p. 140; Alberti, obs. in N. T. ad h. l.; Segaar, obs. philol. et theol. in ev. Luc. 298; Valckenaer, selecta e scholis Valck. T. i. p. 190;

Fischer, de vitiis lex. N. T. prol. xii. p. 312. Theologians: Beza ad locum; Abr. Scultetus, l. ii. c. 32; Gottfr. Olearius, obs. sacræ, ad h. l.; Heinr. Majus, observ. sacræ, p. 5; Calov, Bengel, Wolf, and Fritzsche ad locum. The most worthy of attention are Salmasius, Stolberg, Pfeiffer, Fischer.

The word is one of those New Testament words which occur nowhere else in all the 1200 works of Greek literature which remain to us (Wolf's Museum, i. 25). This is also the case with other words, such as πειθός, 1 Cor. ii. 4; πιστικός (which, however, also occurs in Diogenes Laertius, iv. 6, 4, and Pollux Onomast. iv. 21, where also παραπιστικόν is used), Mark xiv. 3; John xii. 3; παραβολεύομαι, Phil. ii. 30, according to Griesbach, Lachmann; εὐπερίστατος, Heb. xii. 1. Origen, who had so profound a knowledge of Greek literature, already observes: πρῶτον δὲ τοῦτ᾽ ἰστέον, ὅτι ἡ λέξις ἡ ἐπιούσιος παρ᾽ οὐδενὶ τῶν Ἑλλήνων οὔτε τῶν σοφῶν ὠνόμασται, οὔτε ἐν τῇ τῶν ἰδιωτῶν συνηθείᾳ τέτριπται, ἀλλ᾽ ἔοικε πεπλᾶσθαι ὑπὸ τῶν εὐαγγελιστῶν. He notices that the LXX. also use those unclassical words; words, for instance, such as ἐνωτίζεσθαι and ἀκοντίζεσθαι.

The sense must be determined by the derivation. Now the word may come either from εἶναι or from ἰέναι. The derivation from the former is that generally maintained. But to this derivation, there are several grammatical objections. A few critics would regard the word as coming directly from the participle of the verb ἐπεῖναι, as παρουσία, μετουσία, and probably also περιουσία. By far the greater number held it to be a compound of the noun οὐσία and the preposition. To this, however, it has been objected by Olearius and others, that nouns in ια regularly form their adjectives by αιος or ώδης. And indeed this is the rule: e.g., ὡραῖος, ἀγοραῖος, βίαιος; and from οὐσία, not οὔσιος, but οὐσιώδης: wherefore also the adjectives συνούσιος, περιούσιος, ἑτερούσιος, cannot be derived from the substantive οὐσία, but from the participle feminine. But to this rule there are exceptions; adjectives in ιος do occur which are derived from nouns in ια,—e.g.: ἐγκοίλιος; πολυγώνιος, as well as πολύγωνος, from γωνία; ὑπεξούσιος, αὐτεξούσιος, from ἐξουσία; ἐνούσιος and ἐξούσιος, from οὐσία; περιούσιος too many ancients derived from οὐσία; the scholiast on Thucydides, i. 2, ἡ περιουσία—ἡ περιττὴ οὐσία. Now, although we find no adjective οὔσιος from οὐσία, but only οὐσιώδης, still, as these examples testify, it is not impossible that ἐπιούσιος might come from that root. But a weightier objection has been urged, first by Scaliger and Salmasius, and more recently by Grotius and many others. It is alleged by these critics that the word ἐπιούσιος cannot be compounded of ἐπί, for then it must lose its ι. Others have sought to answer this objection by citing numerous instances in which ἐπί retains its ι in composition: ἐπιανδάνω, ἐπίουρα, ἐπιόσσομαι, etc. And although these examples are taken chiefly from Epic language, yet there are instances of this also in prose, as ἐπιεικής, ἐπίορκος, ἐπιόγδοος. With these examples, modern expositors—among others, Kuinoel and Fritzsche—have pronounced themselves satisfied. There remains still, however, this difficulty, that ἐπί, when compounded with this very verb εἶναι, invariably loses its ι; the adjective ἐπουσιώδης, which would correspond to our ἐπιούσιος, occurs without the ι, in Porphyry Isag. c. 15, Jamblichus, Protr. 3. It might indeed be said, that even in prose the rule was not always adhered to[1] as ἐπόπτομαι and ἐπιόπτομαι are both used (also ἐπίοπτος and ἔποπτος); the latter, however, as a special meaning, that of *providing*. (Comp. Buttmann's ausfuehrliche Grammatik, ii. 201, note; Buttmann reads ἐπιόψωνται also in Plato legg. xii. p. 947, c.) This objection has not yet been entirely removed. Many critics have, in consequence of it, preferred to derive the word from ἰέναι.

The philologians who take this view are the following:—Heinse, Scaliger, Salmasius, Faber, Kuester, Valkenaer, Fischer, Passow (5th ed.); the theologians are: Grotius, Wettstein, Calov, Bengel, Wahl, Bretschneider (Lexicon, 3d ed.), Winer, Fritzsche and Meyer. It is also to be found in the Coptic translation: panem nostrum crastini (diei),[2] and in some of the Fathers, with an allusion to the αἰὼν μέλλων. The adjective is by some derived from the participle feminine ἡ ἐπιοῦσα, sc. ἡμέρα, by others from ὁ ἐπιών, sc. χρόνος. It has become customary to derive the adjective and substantive in ούσιος and ουσία from

---

[1] In the citations of the passage from the Dialogus cum Tryphone, c. 95, viz.: οὐδ᾽ ὑμεῖς τολμήσετε ἀντειπεῖν, sometimes ἀντιειπεῖν is given instead; the Paris and Cologne editions have ἀντειπεῖν.

[2] Is not this also the idea of the singular translation of the Syriac-Jerosolym. Version, which has ܠܚܡܢ ܕܣܘܢܩܢܢ, "our plentiful, abundant bread?"

the feminine of the participle, yet the form thereof is derivable from the Genitive-form of the masculine (Salmasius, de foen. trapez. p. 812; Balth. Stolberg, Thes. nov. dissert. T. ii.; Buttmann, ausfuehrliche Grammatik, ii. 337; Lobeck ad Phryn. p. 4). Compare ἡ πιγών, πιγούσιος; Ἀχέρων, Ἀχερούσιος; Πηλιών, Πηλούσιον; γέρων, γεροσία; and the following forms which both occur: πιγούσιος and πιγωναῖος, Ἀχερόντιος and Ἀχερούσιος, ἑκοντί and ἑκουσίως, γεροντία and γερουσία. Thus, *etymologically*, there is nothing to be said against this derivation. The derivation from ἐπιοῦσα is, however, more natural in a philological point of view, because the use of ἡ ἐπιοῦσα with ellipsis of ἡμέρα is very common in the New Testament, in the LXX., and in Josephus; just as elsewhere we find the phrases ἡ παροῦσα, ἡ προσιοῦσα, ἡ παρελθοῦσα[1] (Lobeck ad Phryn. 464). To this we must add, that, as St Jerome informs us, in the Gospel of the Hebrew ἐπιούσιος is translated by מחר, which Jerome appears to refer to the future life; an argument on which Grotius lays great weight. From an etymological point of view, it was urged by Salmasius and Suicer, that it is only adjectives in αῖος that are formed from the elliptical feminines of the numbers, as ἡ δευτέρα, ἡ τρίτη, viz., δευτεραῖος, τριταῖος, δεκαταῖος, etc., and the interrogatory ποσταῖος. But then this form belongs *only* to the proper words of numbers (except perhaps in the case of ἡ ὑστεραία, ἡ προτεραία); and further, this ending of ιος imparts to the adjective a wider compass of meaning than the ending in αιος does. Accordingly, we conclude that, philologically, the word is derivable from ἡ ἐπιοῦσα, or ὁ ἐπιών; and no doubt the statement of St Jerome is to some extent in support of this derivation.

But the *sense* is decidedly opposed to such a derivation. Indeed, if we translate the words in accordance with it, thus: *"Give us this day our bread for to-morrow,"* are we not inclined

---

[1] One might imagine that St Chrysostom also points to this derivation, when, in the homily on our passage, after explaining the word by ἐφήμερος, he adds: ὥστε μὴ περαιτέρω συντρίβειν ἑαυτοὺς τῇ φροντίδι τῆς ἐπιούσης ἡμέρας. However, that he uses the expression, ἡ ἐπιοῦσα ἡμέρα, in this connection, is merely accidental; we see also subsequently, from his exposition of chap. vi. 25—34, that he does not derive ἐπιούσιος from ἐπιέναι; also, in that paragraph, he once more explains the word by ἀναγκαῖος.

to say, with Salmasius: "quid est ineptius, quam panem crastini diei nobis quotidie postulare?"[1] Caninius indeed remarks, and similarly Meyer: Christ has indeed forbidden us, in the sixth chapter, to *care* for the morrow; but on account of our infirmity, præcipit, ut Patrem *rogemus,* qui nostræ infirmitati prospiciat nobisque pridie præbeat, quantum sufficere possit postridie. This view is, however, scarcely adequate. We might, with Augustine, rejoin, that a prayer which the suppliant has not seriously at heart, is really and truly no prayer; moreover, this explanation leaves the σήμερον out of sight. The Arabic proverb says: رزق الغدا لغدا, "the bread of to-morrow for to-morrow" (Burckhardt, "Arabic Proverbs of the Modern Egyptians," p. 298). The notion of Ernesti, that the prayer was to be offered in the *evening,* so that then one would literally pray to-day for the bread of to-morrow, looks like jesting. In this view, the petition would necessarily include somewhat of the sense thus expressed by the Chevalier Michaelis: "To have some foresight, some concern for the future, so as not to live merely for one day with the prospect of being without food or shelter on the next, this is itself no doubt, a great gift of God."

The greater number of this class of expositors take refuge in the solution of the difficulty which Grotius has suggested, viz., that ἡ ἐπιοῦσα is to be regarded as denoting the future in a wider sense. In support of this view, Grotius adduces the use of the Hebrew מָחָר in a wider sense. He might have at once adduced the Greek usage, as ἡ ἐπιοῦσα in Greek denotes the future generally, almost more frequently than the morrow. Σήμερον, again, Grotius regards as equivalent to the plenior hebraismus, the double σήμερον σήμερον; so that the word would have to be translated *postridianus,* and to be taken in the sense of *quotidianus.* Thus Bengel, Olearius, Rosenmueller, Kuinoel, and many more. The *sense* of quoditianus is given in the Itala, Ulphilas, Persian Polyglott, and apparently also in the Ethiopic,

---

[1] It almost looks like a satire on the explanation "crastinus dies," when Erasmus, who ad Matt. vi. and ad Luc. xi. defends this view, says in the latter place: We may well imagine this prayer was intended to be used in the evening, so that people might pray truly for the bread of the *morrow:* et qui vesperi petit pro victu postridiano, quid aliud petit, quam victum quotidianum.

which has: cibum nostrum uniuscujusque diei nostri. Thus viewed, the petition would express the following thought: "Give me this day, and every day to come, that which I need in the present and in the future."

The sense is not objectionable, but this interpretation of σήμερον is philologically inadmissible. Σήμερον is not equivalent to St Luke's τὸ καθ᾿ ἡμέραν; and the Hebrew writer would not use the phrase σήμερον σήμερον to express the idea τὸ καθ᾿ ἡμέραν, because the Hebrew for σήμερον is הַיּוֹם with the article, whereas the Hebrew for "daily," "day by day," is יוֹם יוֹם, or יוֹם בְּיוֹם, which the LXX. translated ἡμέραν ἐν ἡμέρᾳ (Nehem. viii. 18), or ἡμέραν ἐξ ἡμέρας (Gen. xxxix. 10). But if we cannot take σήμερον in the sense of τὸ καθ᾿ ἡμέραν, there is no fitting sense deducible from the interpretation of ἐπιούσιος under consideration (viz., as derived from ἐπιοῦσα). Socinus, Chemnitz, Pasor, Elsner, and others, translate thus: succedaneus, adventitius, quem non suffict semel accepisse, sed quem in hac vertentium temporum vicissitudine quotidie necesse est nobis advenire. Pasor: demensum nostrum, quod nec superfluit nec deficit, da nobis hodie, *i.e.* hac quoque die. But all this is not expressed in the text; and further, if this were the meaning, we should at least expect to find καὶ σήμερον. Alexander Morus' explanation may be mentioned, but only as a curiosity. The allusion, he thinks, is to the manna falling on the Friday in sufficient quantities to serve for the Sabbath, and the sense: Give us bread enough to-day to serve for to-morrow. Calov expounds: quod spirituali nostræ necessitati supervenit, nam non primarium est.

Our conclusion then is this: Great as are the difficulties in the way of deriving ἐπιούσιος from εἶναι, yet, even were they greater, we must still give the preference to that derivation; and for this reason, that it is impossible, on the supposition of its derivation from ἐπιοῦσα, to find in it any meaning in keeping with the context. (Comp. also Ewald.) Some support is afforded to it, further, by the judgment of Origen, who was no mean philologian, and who mentions, although he rejects, the derivation from ἰέναι: it is favoured also by the Peschito. The difficulty of the hiatus disappears if we may assume, what is not improbable, that the word is formed on the model of the current περιούσιος. There still, however, remains the question,

What meaning is to be attached to the word? Amongst philosophers, οὐσία signifies "substance, essence," in distinction from ποιότητες, "qualities"—a meaning which, according to Heindorf (see the Phaedo, p. 41), was introduced subsequently to Plato: Plutarch, Arrian, and others use it also in the sense of "matter." Origen gives the word the same meaning: "that which serves for the nourishment of the *substance*" (that is, the spiritual). So also Chrysostom, ἄρτον ἐπιούσιον, τουτέστιν, ἐπὶ τὴν οὐσίαν τοῦ σώματος διαβαίνοντα καὶ συγκρατῆσαι ταύτην δυνάμενον ("de instit. sec. Deum vita"); Gregory of Nyssa, ζητεῖν προσετάχθημεν τὸ πρὸς τὴν συντήρησιν ἐξαρκοῦν τῆς σωματικῆς οὐσίας ("orat. iv. in orat. dom."); and Basilius, τὸν ἐπιούσιον ἄρτον, τουτέστι, τὸν πρὸς τὴν ἐφήμερον ζωὴν τῇ οὐσίᾳ ἡμῶν χρησιμεύοντα. The most current meaning was, "property, wealth," to which περιουσία also may be referred, and which belongs also to the Talmudical word אסיא. This meaning is adopted in a treatise by Steck, "Tempe Helv. Fig." 1741, T. v. fasc. 4, Lamb. Bos, and Alberti. The latter renders, "that which forms a part of the property of the children of God." But are we not rather taught by Luke xvi. 11, 12, that the ἀληθινόν is the peculium of God's children, whereas temporal good they only have in common with the children of the world? We should therefore rather explain, with Steck, "that which is added to the patrimonium of the children of God;"—only that we may not further says with this expositor, "which we earn for ourselves by our own efforts." But how obscurely would the thought be expressed! It would be easiest and most agreeable to take οὐσία in the sense of "existence," were it allowable. Theophylact uses the term in this sense: on this passage he remarks, ἄρτος ἐπὶ τῇ οὐσίᾳ καὶ συστάσει ἡμῶν αὐτάρκης; and on Luke xi., ὁ ἐπὶ τῇ οὐσίᾳ ἡμῶν καὶ συστάσει τῆς ζωῆς συμβαλλόμενος· οὐχ ὁ περιττὸς πάντως, ἀλλ' ὁ ἀναγκαῖος: Euth. also, ἐπιούσιον δὲ προσηγόρευσε τὸν ἐπὶ τῇ οὐσίᾳ καὶ ὑπάρξει καὶ συστάσει τοῦ σώματος ἐπιτήδειον: further, Suidas and Etym. Magn., ὁ ἐπὶ τῇ οὐσίᾳ ἡμῶν ἁρμόζων. The Peschito and Philox. appear to understand it thus also: in the former we read ܠܚܡܐ ܕܣܘܢܩܢܢ "the bread of our need," and Pers. Wheloc.

On searching, however, for illustrations of this usage from the classical writers, we find that, as far as has hitherto been shown, they are limited to one—the passage, namely, in Sophocles' "Trach." v. 911: ἔκλαιεν ἡ δύστηνος εἰσορωμένη | αὐτὴ τὸν αὑτῆς δαίμον' ἀνακαλουμένη | καὶ τὰς ἄπαιδας ἐς τὸ λοιπὸν οὐσίας. By most οὐσίας is here translated, "existence, life:" even by the most recent editor of Sophocles, Schneidewin. The scholiast, indeed, in accordance with a usage, the existence of which in Sintipas also, Dindorf was the first to point out (see Steph. Thes. s. h. v.), renders, κοίτας, συνουσίας: nay Dindorf, without, however, approving this explanation, is disposed to expunge this verse as unworthy of Sophocles. This example is the more uncertain, as οὐσία might here be rather taken in the sense of "property, household" = οἶκος. Toup, however, in his edition of Suidas, has adduced a passage open to no objection, namely, Porphyr. "de Abstin." 2, 34: ἀπαρχὴ γὰρ ἑκάστῳ ὧν δέδωκεν ἡ θυσία καὶ δι' ὧν ἡμῶν τρέφει καὶ εἰς τὸ εἶναι συνέχει τὴν οὐσίαν. Still, even were there no such example, we ought not to give up this meaning. If the Christian commentators, being Greeks by birth, could use the word in that sense, why not the translator of Matthew? We need not therefore maintain that Christ made use of the Aramaic word אוּסיא, or of the exactly corresponding expression כְּדֵי לַהֲוָיָה, כְּדֵי לַהֲוָיִת.[1] The translator might have used ἐπιούσιος in the sense referred to, even if Christ had only employed the expression כְּדֵי פַרְנָסָתֵינוּ, "according to our needs." The same expression occurs in the Talmudic prayer (Berach. f. 29, 2): אחרים אומרים צרכי עמך ישראל מרובין ודעתם קצרה יהי רצונך מלפניך י" אלהינו שתתן לכל אחד ואחד כדי פרנסתו, "Others avail themselves of prayer: the needs of Thy people Israel are great, and they have little insight. May it please Thee to give to every one according to his needs." The ἐπιούσιον is something between τὸ ἐλλιπές and the περιττόν or the περιούσιον, and denotes that which is just enough. So understood, this prayer has many analogies in the Old and New Testaments: compare, for example, Prov. xxx. 8, where Solomon prays, "Keep far from me poverty and riches," הַטְרִיפֵנִי לֶחֶם חֻקִּי; which corresponds to the passage under consideration: חק denotes a portion assigned to any one. Such also is the explana-

---

[1] Jacob of Edessa (at the end of the seventh century) remarks, that the Syrians first, two hundred years previously, adopted the Greek word ܐܦܝܣܘܢ into their language (see Assemani "Bibl. Orient," i. 479).

tion of Jarchi in his comment on Gen. xlvii. 22. Symmachus translates, δίαιτα ἱκανή (comp. James ii. 15). This view of the petition not only involves no contradiction to Matt. vi. 25, but is in perfect agreement with ver. 34, where care for the present day is allowed. Should it, however, be objected, that in vers. 25 and 31 all care about temporal matters is forbidden, and that in ver. 33 a promise is given that temporal things shall be provided by way of supplement, we may appeal to ver. 34, where the words, ἀρκετὸν τῇ ἡμέρᾳ ἡ κακία αὐτῆς, show that the preceding sayings are not to be understood quite absolutely. Moreover, in ver. 33, emphasis may be laid on πρῶτον in proof that though the kingdom of God is to be sought first of all, care for temporal things is not entirely forbidden. Only by adopting such an explanation can justice be done to the expression σήμερον. It is not identical with Luke's expression, τὸ καθ᾽ ἡμέραν. The translation, "quotidianus," in the "Versio Itala" was not intended to be an exact rendering of σήμερον,—this word is rather rendered by "hodie:"—nor, as many have thought, was it adopted with reference to the passage in Luke: the translation is rather according to the sense, as Chrysostom, Suidas, and others render, ἐφήμερος, following the spirit, rather than the letter. Indeed, a literal rendering is impossible. Beza and Castellio translate, "panis cibarius," and "victus alimentarius." Σήμερον exactly characterizes the mood of one who prays truly, and whose soul is entirely absorbed in the present moment. So does Chrysostom justly explain the term: οὐκ εἰς πολὺν ἐτῶν ἀριθμὸν αἰτεῖν ἐκελεύσθημεν ἀλλὰ τὸν ἄρτον σήμερον ἡμῖν ἀρκοῦντα μόνον, "for," says he, "who knows whether he shall be alive on the morrow?" Isidorus also remarks, "The fixing of such a period as this, enables us to rise to the very highest pitch of wisdom."

That this petition should have been regarded as one for spiritual bread, can excite no wonder, when we take into consideration that in the symbolical language of the Scriptures the gift of the Spirit is so frequently compared with food and drink (comp. John vi. 33—35; Heb. vi. 4, 5 ff.). Nay, even the more special reference thereof to the Eucharist, was suggested by John vi. 51, 53—55, and by the employment of the Lord's Prayer during the consecration. Quoting John vi., Origen explains the passage of the ἄρτος ἐξ οὐρανοῦ καταβάς, which is changed into the οὐσία of the Spirit, as natural bread is changed into the οὐσία of the body.¹ Owing to the preference for mystical interpretations of Scripture, this view spread very widely, and made its appearance occasionally, even after the Reformation. So Tertullian, Cyprian, Cyril of Jerusalem, Athanasius, Isid. Pel., Ambrose, Augustine, Jerome: in the middle ages, Erasmus, Zegerus, Bellarmin, Luther (in his two expositions of the Lord's Prayer, of 1518; otherwise in the Catechisms), Zwingli,² Heinr. Majus, Peter Zorn ("vindiciæ pro perpetua veteris ecclesiæ traditione de Christo pane ἐπιουσίῳ," in his "Opusc. sacr." i.):³ in more recent times, Pfannkuche, Olshausen, Stier, Delitzsch. The passages which bear upon this matter are given more in detail in Suicer's "Observat." (p. 248) and "Thesaurus ecclesiasticus" (p. 1173); still more fully by Pfeiffer in his "Thes. Theol. Philol." (T. ii. p. 120). Several of these commentators allow a reference to spiritual bread, as well as that of physical.⁴ Some understand by spiritual bread, merely the "doctrina Christi," the "verbum Dei:" some, the spiritual influence of Christ: some refer it also to the food of the Eucharist, others exclusively. The reference to the spiritual nourishment of Christ in general, and to the Eucharist in particular, may be found even in Irenæus

---

¹ He explains other passages also, which relate to bodily nourishment, of spiritual. Ps. lxv. 9, ἡτοίμασας τὴν τροφὴν αὐτῶν he refers to the τροφὴ πνευματική which was prepared in Christ πρὸ καταβολῆς κόσμου (compare Corder. Catena in Ps. T. ii. 270).

² Zwingli says: "Græce dicunt *supersubstantialem*. Deus enim substantiam nostram vere pascit et sustinet, idque vero et substantiali cibo.... Nihilo tamen minus vitæ nostræ necessitatem hac petitione apud Dominum quærimus. Panis enim Hebræis omnem cibum significat. Qui animam pascit, quomodo idem non etiam corpus pasceret?"

³ By strict Lutherans this interpretation was rejected as mystical. A citizen of Wittenberg, who interpreted the fourth petition of spiritual bread, had to choose between renouncing his error and leaving the city. Majus in Giessen, and Zorn, were opposed by Wernsdorf of Wittenberg in the above-mentioned treatise. Compare Spener's "Theolog. Bedenken," i. S. 144, and Walch's "Religionsstreitigkeiten in der Luth. Kirche," Th. v. 1167.

⁴ The Greek Collectors also, who derived the reference to natural nourishment from the Fathers of their Church, added afterwards that to spiritual food. In an appendix Theophylact and Euthymius explain of the Eucharist.

(see his "Adv. Haer." 4, 18): whether at the time of Justin Martyr. (see his "Apol." i. 66), is not quite clear; but certainly in Tertullian and Cyprian, probably also in Cyprian of Jerusalem (see Touttée ad Catech. 24, Mystag. 5) In his treatise on the "Sermo in monte," Augustine rejects all decided reference of the petition to the Eucharist, for one reason, because the prayer could not then be offered up in the evening. In his sermon on the Lord's Prayer (Tom. v. 234), he refers the panis quotidianus, (1.) to physical bread, "victus et tegumentum;" (2.) to the food of the word of Christ; (3.) to the food of the sacrament. That this explanation should become more and more common, is explicable from the ever-increasing reverence for the sacrament, which led to its receiving a name which readily brought the Lord's Prayer to mind: ὁ ἄρτος ἅγιος, ἄρτος ζωῆς, εὐλογηθείς, ἱερουργούμενος (see Casaubon's "Exerc. Anti-Baron." xvi. c. 39). The Eastern writers were encouraged in their mystical view of ἐπιούσιος by the infrequency of its use. But even the very plain term employed in the Latin translation (quotidianus), which was, strictly viewed, unfavourable to the reference to the Eucharist, led to much the same result; for the Western Churches, down even to the time of Augustine, celebrated the Eucharist *daily*. Although at a later period the Western commentators of the Catholic Church still vacillated between the reference to spiritual food in general and the sacrament in particular, the latter predominated, and is adduced as the primary one in the "Glossa Ordinaria:" "panis *corpus Christi* est, ut verbum Dei, vel ipse Deus, quo quotidie egemus."

Two modifications of this view may, in the first place, be mentioned. A number of Fathers, especially of the Greek Church (Athanasius, Damascenus, Pseudo-Ambrosius, and others), derive the word from ἐπιέναι, and understand by it the ἄρτος τοῦ αἰῶνος μέλλοντος, that heavenly bread which will be the portion of believers in the life to come (comp. Luke xiv. 15), and is even now bestowed on them (σήμερον). The Coptic rendering breviously alluded to, both the Memphitic and the Sahidic (see ed. M. G. Schwartz), is undoubtedly based on this mystical explanation, which Matthäi, in his anger at the mysticism of the Church Fathers, denominates "mad" (ed. maj. ad Luc. p. 510). An objection to this modification is the inadmissible antithesis then existing between σίμερον and ἄρτος τοῦ ἐπιόντος χρόνου or αἰῶνος. Should it even be granted that ὁ ἄρτος ὁ μέλλων might, without further ado, be termed "the future heavenly bread," we must decidedly understand by it that blessedness which does not yet begin in the present life: and then the question arises, In this case, how can it be bestowed on us now, and that every day?

Others regard the word as a compound of οὐσία. Accordingly Jerome, for example, translated ἐπιούσιος, "supersubstantialis:"[1] following his example, Emser translates, "the superindependent bread" ("das überselbstständige Brot"): Luther also, in his explanation of 1518, gives the three renderings, "superessential" (überwesentlich), select, morning-bread (panis crastinus); and seeks to combine all the three meaning. In this case ὑπέρ ought evidently to be used, instead of ἐπί, just as the adjective ὑπερούσιος is employed in a mystical-speculative sense by Dionysius Areopagita (see his "de div. nomm." c. xi. § 6), and by Maximus in his Scholia on the same work (see c. xi. § 11). It is an error to appeal to ἐπίλογος, and ἐπίμετρον, which is ὑπέρμετρον; for ἐπί there only denotes that which is added to the just measure. Even on the spiritual view we must then explain ἐπί in the same way as on the physical, namely, "that which is serviceable and necessary to existence, that is, to a true existence." So Origen and Cyril of Jerusalem: ὁ ἐπιούσιος ἀντὶ τοῦ ἐπὶ τὴν οὐσίαν τῆς ψυχῆς καταταασσόμενος.—What now is the foundation of this spiritual explanation? Olshausen adduces the following reasons: (1.) Because the whole prayer comprises only spiritual petitions. But if the pious receives the fruit of his labour from the hand of God, and is sensible of his dependence in this particular, why may he not also beg the Divine blessing on the work of his hands, in accordance with Ps. cxxvii. 1? If our food first becomes holy when we have by thanksgiving expressed our feeling of dependence on God, should not the same thing hold true of

---

[1] Compare also Jerome's remarks on Titus ii. 12, where he treats more in detail of the words ἐπιούσιος and περιούσιος. He quotes John vi. 5, and reports that "some believe it to be the bread which is super omnes οὐσίας." In commenting on Matthew he mentions, besides, that others preferred, "in accordance with 1 Tim. vi. 8, to refer the words simpliciter to physical nourishment."

petitions (1 Tim. iv. 5)? Auct. op. imp.: "Ita ergo intelligendum est, quia non solum ideo oramus: panem nostrum da nobis, ut habeamus, quod manducemus, sed ut, quod manducamus, de manu Dei accipiamus. Nam habere ad manducandum commune est inter justos et peccatores, frequenter autem et abundantius peccatores habent, quam justi. De manu autem Dei accipere panem non est commune, sed tantum sanctorum." Luther remarks: "God gives bread every day, even without our praying for it, to all evil men: but in this prayer we beg Him to let us recognise it, and receive our daily bread with thanksgiving." Comp. Spener's "Bedenken," i. 1, 16. (2.) Because in what follows (chap. vi. 25) all care for the body is set in the background. But is it not also put into the background by this very petition;—firstly, in that only one petition refers to earthly matters; and secondly, in that no more is asked for than is necessary for subsistence,—subsistence, too, during the present day? as Chrysostom says: ἄρτον ἐκέλευσεν αἰτεῖν ἐπιούσιον, οὐ τρυφὴν ἀλλὰ τροφήν. (3.) Because ἐπιούσιος directs attention to spiritual food. This, however, is questionable. It might, indeed, be answered, that we could not expect a distinct and peculiar term to be employed for the expression of so popular an idea. But if the word is formed on the model of, and by way of antithesis to, the current περιούσιος, the choice of this expression is at once explained.

Ἄρτος is used in the New Testament, like לחם, in a wider sense: for example, in 2 Thess. iii. 12. With this wider meaning the word passed into later usage: compare, for example, ἄρτον βεβαρημένον ἐσθίειν in Du Cange's "Gloss. Græc. Med." s. h. v. In this general way do the modern Greeks also employ ψωμί. From the appended word ἡμῶν some have drawn a conclusion favourable to the spiritual, others, one favourable to the physical, application. Neither of these conclusions is warranted. It simply indicates that the bread is such as we need, as is intended for us. Euth.: ἄρτον δὲ ἡμῶν εἶπεν, ἀντὶ τοῦ, τὸν δι' ἡμᾶς γενόμενον.

The Fifth Petition. Ver. 12.

The petitioner now passes on to his spiritual needs. The soul, considering itself in the presence of God, becomes conscious, first, of the guilt cleaving to it, and begs that it may be pardoned. Τὰ ὀφειλόμενα signifies, according to the Aramaic use of חוב, moral debts: Luke has τὰς ἁμαρτίας. Greek authors use the term merely of "money-debts," to which, Augustine tells us, some foolishly referred it in this place. A literal contrast to his prayer of Christian humility is presented by that of Apollonius of Tyana, which used to be: ὦ Θεοὶ, δοίητέ μοι τὰ ὀφειλόμενα (see Philostratus' "Vita Apoll." l. i. c. 11). In opposition to the Pelagians, the Church justly appealed to this prayer in proof that the general sinfulness still continues to be shared even by believers. To which was given the bungling reply—if Jerome gives a faithful report (see his "c. Pel." iii. c. 15),—that the saints present this prayer *humiliter*, but not *veraciter*. How different are Luther's words: "In the third place, we must remark how here again the indigence of our miserable life is indicated: we are in the land of debts, we are up to the ears in sin," etc.

Ὡς καὶ ἡμεῖς ἀφίεμεν.—The Textus receptus here reads, after D.E.L.Δ. al., ἀφίομεν, as in Luke; Cod. B.Z. Lachm., Tischend., and Meyer, read ἀφήκαμεν. The rendering of the Peschito ought not to be adduced in favour of the Aorist. Both it and Philox. have ܫܒܩܢ,—which Perfect, however, expresses the Present. Luke xi. also is thus used by the translator, who read the Present; the Persian translation of the Polyglot, too, which owed its origin thereto, expresses the Present. Origen is not reliable here: at the commencement he quotes (T. i. 252) the text of Matthew and Luke with ἀφήκαμεν, but afterwards adduces ἀφίεμεν as the text in both Evangelists. In favour of the Present in Matthew are not only D.E.L.Δ., but also Chrysostom, Codd. Mtth., Itala, Vulgate, Ulfilas, Coptic, and the Æthiopic; to which, according to the observation just made, the Peschito and Philox. may be added. Reflection might have led to the substitution of the Aorist for the Present in the command contained in vers. 14, 15, and in chap. v. 24: —no reconciliation with God without previous reconciliation with the brethren. Origen says: μεμνημένοι γὰρ ὧν ὀφειλέται ὄντες οὐκ ἀπεδεδώκαμεν ἀλλὰ ἀπεστηρίσαμεν παραδραμόντος τοῦ χρόνου .... πραότεροι ἐσόμεθα πρὸς τοὺς καὶ ἡμῖν ὀφλήσαντας. Add to this, that the Present is used by Luke also, and we think we may fairly prefer it to the Perfect, suiting, as it does, the context better. It would surely be more in accordance with the intention of Christ, to direct attention to the necessity for the petitioner's constantly cherishing a conciliatory spirit, than to make the single acts of forgiveness in the past a condition of being heard. The subjoined words, ὡς καὶ ἡμεῖς ἀφίομεν, have usually been regarded as containing a condition. Hence the anonymous writer in Stephen le Moyne says: ταῦτα λέγων, ἄνθρωπε, ἐὰν οὕτω ποιῇς (προσεύχῃ), ἐννόησον τὸ φάσκον λόγιον, φοβερὸν τὸ ἐμπεσεῖν εἰς χεῖρας Θεοῦ ζῶντος! Chrysostom gives us to understand that many, when praying, entirely suppressed the clause in question.

We ask, therefore, in the first place, whether the words do contain a *condition;* or rather, a *presupposition?* We might undoubtedly take them as expressive of the proportion observed by God in the bestowal of forgiveness. Ὡς is sometimes employed where a more accurate usage requires ὅσον (see Passow s. v. ὡς, p. 1488, 4th ed.). So also the ampler word τοιοῦτος is sometimes used inaccurately for τοσοῦτος, and talis for tantus (see Xenoph. Cyrop. L. iv. c. 2, § 41, ed. Born.; and Bremi on Cornel. Nep. Vitæ, p. 367). In the New Testament, it is so used in the parable recorded Matt. xx. 14: θέλω τούτῳ τῷ ἐσχάτῳ δοῦναι ὡς καὶ σοί = τοσοῦτον ὅσον σοί: also in Rev. xviii. 6, where ἀπόδοτε αὐτῇ, ὡς καὶ αὐτὴ ἀπέδωκε, denotes the corresponding measure of retribution, and the words διπλώσατε αὐτῇ διπλᾶ, which follow immediately afterwards, denote the double measure (compare Rev. ix. 3). On the other hand, καθ' ὅσον (and τοσοῦτον), which assigns the measure, and institutes a comparison, is used in comparisons which relate merely to actions; thus being equivalent to ὡς, and therefore followed by οὕτω in the minor clause (see, for example, Heb. ix. 27). In the Hebrew, also, כְּ is equivalent to tot (see Ex. x. 14; Judges xxi. 14). As far as the language, therefore, is concerned, the word may be taken as expressive of proportion. Chrysostom remarks: "God makes thee arbiter of the judgment: as thou judgest thyself, He will judge thee." Chrysostom and Luther (see his Commentary of 1518) compare Luke vi. 38, "With what measure ye mete, shall it be measured to you again;" and Luther goes on to remark: "Psalm cix. 7 says, his prayer will be a sin in the sight of God; for what else canst thou mean when thou sayest, 'I will not forgive,' and yet standest before God with thy precious Pater noster, and babblest, 'Forgive us our debts, as we forgive our debtors,' than, 'O God, I am Thy debtor, and I also have a debtor; I am not willing to forgive him, therefore do Thou also not forgive me: I will not obey Thee though Thou shouldest declare me pardoned; I would rather renounce Thine heaven and everything else, and go to the devil'?" B.-Crusius also explains, "in the measure, in which we." Grammatically, it is quite as admissible to take merely the similarity without laying stress on the proportion. A strong proof for this is Matt. xviii. 33: οὐκ ἔδει καὶ σὲ ἐλεῆσαι τὸν σύνδουλόν σου, ὡς καὶ ἐγώ σε ἠλέησα: in this parable the master had shown the servant greater compassion than the servant showed his fellow-servant. Two considerations induce use to adopt this sense in the present instance: first, the doctrine which lies at the basis of the parable: and secondly, the view taken of the sentence by Luke in chap. xi. 4: καὶ γὰρ αὐτοὶ ἀφίομεν. This is quite correctly explained by Cyrill, ad Luc., καὶ, ἵνα οὕτως εἴπω, τῆς ἐνούσης αὐτοῖς ἀνεξικακίας μιμητὴν ἐθέλουσι γενέσθαι τὴν Θεόν. We must assume that he who speaks thus, cherishes constantly a conciliatory disposition,—be it in consequence of his own need of forgiveness, or in consequence of forgiveness received. So far these words are designated by Zwingli, not so much an „oratio," as a "publica Christianorum confessio." On the other hand, they can scarcely be interpreted as a condition, inasmuch as in vers. 14 and 15 the same thought is expressed in the form of a condition. The very parable, therefore, in Matt. xviii. warrants us rather in affirming that we are not doing any violence to the words when we regard ὡς καὶ and καὶ γὰρ αὐτοί as referring to grace already received. Chemnitz and Hunnius retain the "conditio" view: substantially, therefore, Sarcerius explains more correctly, "sicut certitudinis adverbium hic est, non similitudinis. Nos enim quando remittimus aliis, hoc certissimum nobis signum esse debet, quod et Deus nobis reliquerit (?) nostra peccata" (compare Calov).[1] So also the Heidelberg Catechism: "Impute not to us poor sinners all our iniquity: as we also feel within ourselves the *witness of Thy*

---

[1] The philological makeshift by which Olearius justifies grammatically this meaning is ingenious. He takes ὡς in the adverbial sense of the demonstrative pronoun, as in the epic poets = "in such a manner, in this way." Whereas most commentators make our forgiveness the condition of the Divine, on this view, Divine forgiveness would become the condition of ours.

grace, in that our whole heart is set to forgive our neighbours;" and Luther in his Larger Catechism remarks, that this addition is made "in order that we may have as sign by which to decide whether we are true children of God; and then, whether our sins are forgiven." But as the consciousness of deliverance never becomes complete in the minds of believers, we may, with Cyprian, Luther, and Chemnitz, regard the ground assigned merely as a relative "sponsio;" or, with Calvin and Melanchthon, as a "commonefactio publica."

THE SIXTH, OR THE SEVENTH PETITION. VER. 13.

Relieved of the burden of his past guilt, the man looks forward to the future, and, conscious of his weakness, wishes to be kept from temptations, yea, to be freed from all evil and sin.

There are two difficulties in connection with this petition: (1.) How can we pray that πειρασμοί may be turned away from us, when at the same time they arise out of the unalterable course of the world (John xvii. 15: compare Acts xiv. 22; Job vii. 1); and when they, moreover, effect the δοκιμή of Christians, so that James exhorts them to rejoice when they fall into all manner of πειρασμοί? This difficulty was raised even by Origen. (2.) In what sense can God be said to lead us into temptations?

It is necessary to begin with the idea of πειρασμός (compare Suicer's "Observ. Sacræ," p. 260, Thes. s. h. v.; specially Witsius, p. 220, and Pott's Exc. 1, ad ep. Jac.). The idea of *trial* is expressed in Greek by the words δοκιμάζειν and πειράζειν. Δοκιμάζειν, from the etymon δέχεσθαι, signifies originally, "to investigate wheter a thing be acceptable:" πειράζειν, connected primarily with "perior, experior," and later with πείρω, signifies originally, "to penetrate, to scrutinize." But, like the word בָּחַן in Hebrew (נִסָּה, on the contrary, should rather be compared with δοκιμάζειν), *tentare* in Latin, and "versuchen" ("to attempt," then, "to tempt") in German, πειρᾶν acquired a bad secondary meaning. Πειρᾶν, πειρᾶσθαι, πειράζειν τινός (at a later period, frequently τινά), was originally used synonymously with πεῖραν λαμβάνειν, πεῖραν ποιεῖσθαι, of any attempt whatever made on any one. Very early, however, the substantive πεῖρα designated specially a bold undertaking: for example, πεῖραν ἐχθρῶν ἁρπάσαι (Sophocles' Ajax, v. 2) simply in the sense, "to trace out a bold undertaking:" afterwards πεῖρα denoted "Piracy," and πειρατής, "Pirate." Suidas: πεῖρα ὁ δόλος καὶ ἀπάτη καὶ ἡ τέχνη. The verb πειρᾶν with γυναῖκας, like the Latin "tentare Junonem" (Tibullus i. 3, 73), is used of the enticement and seduction of women (for example in Polybius, "Hist." 1, 10, c. 26, § 3). Even the Biblical writers use the word primarily in its wider sense of, "to attempt, to make an attempt" (see Acts xvi. 7, where Cod. Cantab. has the gloss ἤθελον: Acts xxiv. 6). It is questionable whether in 2 Cor. xiii. 5, it is synonymous with the following δοκιμάζετε. Still, in the Septuagint it occurs in parallelism with δοκιμάζω in Ps. xcv. 9, and thence in Heb. iii. 9: or the codices alternate with δοκιμάζειν, as in Dan. i. 12; compare also Wisdom ii. 3. In Ps. xvii. 3, some read, ἐπύρωσάς με, instead of, ἐπείρασάς με. It is, however, more commonly used in malam partem, of men who try God by mistrust (Acts xv. 10, v. 9; 1 Cor. x. 9). In Wisdom i. 2, it is synonymous with ἀπιστεῖν τῷ Θεῷ. (2.) It is used of God, who puts men to the test, not with an evil design, but in difficult circumstances, so that it may easily come to pass that they stumble, though it is never a necessity (see 1 Cor x. 13; Heb. ii. 18, iv. 15, xi. 37). In the Old Testament this usage is frequent, especially in the history of Abraham; see Gen. xxii. 1, ὁ Θεὸς ἐπείραζε τὸν Ἀβραὰμ καὶ εἶπεν αὐτῷ. Compare Ex. xv. 25; Deut. xiii. 3. (3.) It is used of men who make attempts on others with a malicious purpose and intent (Matt. xvi. 1, xix. 3, xxii. 35; Mark viii. 11, xii. 15; John viii. 6). (4.) Hence is it specially used of the attempts which the devil—ὁ πολυμήχανος ὄφις—makes on men, which always originate in evil designs (Matt. iv. 1 and 4; 1 Cor. vii. 5; 1 Thess. iii. 5; Rev. ii. 10). For this reason he is, by way of pre-eminence, designated ὁ πειράζων = ὁ πειραστής, whereas God is called, ὁ δοκιμαστὴς τῶν καρδιῶν (Ps. xvii. 3). In all these passages we might also translate, "seduce;" and such is the rendering adopted in James i. 13, 14. There is nothing, however, to prevent us abiding by the meaning, "to put into circumstances of temptation:" nor can we, in James, take πειράζειν in an essentially different sense from πειρασμός previously, in ver. 12. Consequently, even in James the usual meaning must be retained: "Let no man say, when he comes into circumstances of temptation, that it is God's fault: it is our inward evil inclinations that make the circumstances of life temptations to us." The substantive πειρασμός is formed from the Perfect passive of the verb πειράζειν, and is frequently synonymous with the active πείρασις. Following the anology of the verb, the noun denotes, (1.) Trial in general, and is so far undistinguishable from δοκιμασία (1 Pet. iv. 12). (2.) A state of trial *where there is the danger of falling:* here belong the passages in which lexicographers and commentators have rendered the word by "calamitas" (Luke viii. 13, xxii 28; Acts xx. 19; Gal. iv. 14; James i. 12, etc.). (3.) Many assume the meaning, "inward allurement, enticement of the ἐπιθυμία," and base it on Matt. xxvi. 41; 1 Tim. vi. 9; Luke iv. 13. In the latter passage, however, it is used actively = δοκιμασία; in the others, it denotes a position of temptation, a σκάνδαλον: Paul adds, by way of explanation, εἰς παγίδα. It designates consequently, not the δελεάζειν of the ἐπιθυμία, but the seductive state produced by the δελεάζειν. The word thus corresponds exactly to the classical περίστασις, often used by Epictetus, Max. Tyrius, and others, which signifies, strictly, simply "circumstance," and then "a suspicious, seductive condition." The passages classed under this third head must therefore be regarded as belonging to the second. When πειρασμός is used concretely, it is equivalent to σκάνδαλον; for this latter word also denotes a πρόσκομμα, an ἔγκομμα, over which one may easily fall. מוקש also is equivalent to ἡ παγίς, and is connected with σκάνδαλον in Josh. xxiii. 13, and 1 Macc. v. 4. The same usage is observable in the classical authors: Amphis, for example, in Athenæus calls courtezans, παγίδας τοῦ βίου. In the Sept. (see Job vii. 1, x. 17), in the Pseudo-epigraphs (see Testament. Isaschar 627, in Fabric. Tom. ii.), and in the Church Fathers, for πειρασμός is used πειρατήριον, the ending of which shows that, like κριτήριον, it denotes a means of trial. Ὄχλησις is employed also by the Church writers in the sense of πειρασμός (see Photius in Wolf. Anecd. Gr. i. 145).

If, then, πειρασμός designates the circumstances by which the Christian is tried of God; if the Scriptures represent these Divine trials as the means by which we are established and grounded in the faith (Rom. v. 3; James i. 2—4; 1 Pet. i. 6, 7); if, as Chrysostom says in Epist. 157, πειρασμὸς τοῖς γενναίως φέρουσι πολλὰ κομίζει τὰ βραβεῖα καὶ λαμπροὺς τοὺς στεφάνους, so that, in the consciousness thereof, Clemens represents the true Christian as crying out, ὦ κύριε, δὸς περίστασιν καὶ λάβε ἐπίδειξιν; if it is impossible to be kept free from all σκανδάλοις so long as the course of this world lasts (1 Cor. v. 10); and finally, if Christ expressly prays the Father not to take His own people out of this world, but only to preserve them from the evil (John xvii. 15); then the question arises: How can Christ put into the mouths of His disciples the petition, "Lead us not into πειρασμοί"?

In order to be able to answer this question, some commentators take πειρασμός emphatically; others, εἰς; most, however, εἰσενέγκῃς. By exegets of the Predestinarian school, πειρασμοί are referred to "tentationes Satanæ in perniciem," such as are sent to "reprobis" for judgment. Calvin remarks, "hic notatur interior tentatio, quæ *diaboli* flabellum apte vocari potest:" Aret., "aliter Deus tentat reprobos, dum eos incitat ad lapsus æternos .... sic in Pharaone, Juda, Juliano. De hac et similibus tentationum speciebus hic agitur, quas iratus Deus immittit, Satanæ committit, aliisque organis iræ concedit." But a particular species of πειρασμοί is not here spoken of. To the question, whether sickness and suffering are included in the prayer, Basil. answers ("Resp. ad interr." 221): οὐ διέκρινε πειρασμοῦ ποιότητα, καθολικῶς δὲ προσέταξε· προσεύχεσθε μὴ εἰσελθεῖν εἰς πειρασμόν. The Pelagians weakened the force of the expression quite as arbitrarily, when, as Augustine affirms (Ep. 178), they explained, "ne quisquam irruens corporaliter nos humanus casus affligat." Beza lays stress on the preposition: "est vis præpositionis εἰς diligenter observanda:" Christoph. Starke also, "εἰς, ἐνέγκῃς—lead us not *into*, that is, *too deeply into*." In support of this increased stress laid on the word, Grotius, Drusius, Wettstein, and Witsius compare the rabbinical term לִידֵי "into the hands," which expresses therefore total surrender = "given over as a prey to" (Rom. vii. 14);—for this the rabbinical phrase הֵבִיא בְיַד נִסְיוֹן is adduced. But even in the Old Testament, לִידֵי בְּיַד had lost its strict meaning; much more in rabbinical usage. It would be another thing only in case συγκλείειν εἰς (Rom. xi. 32) were used.—Most commentators, however, lay stress on the verb εἰσφέρειν. Origen says, διόπερ εὐχώμεθα ῥυσθῆναι πειρατηρίον, οὐκ ἐν τῷ μὴ πειράζεσθαι (τοῦτο γὰρ ἀμήχανον μάλιστα τοῖς ἐπὶ τῆς γῆς) ἀλλὰ ἐν τῷ μὴ ἡττᾶσθαι πειραζομένους. The same distinction is drawn by Isid.

Pel. i. 5, ep. 226, between ἐμπεσεῖν εἰς πειρασμόν, and εἰσελθεῖν τουτέστι καταποθῆναι ὑπὸ τοῦ πειρασμοῦ: so also Theoph. and Augustine ("de Sermone in monte" and Ep. 121), "aliud est *tentari*, aliud *induci in tentationem*."[1] Luther observes: "We cannot help being exposed to assaults, but we pray that we may not fall and perish under them." Bengel: "non precamur, *ut ne sit*, sed ut ne nos ea *tangat et vincat*." So Melanchthon, Chemnitz, Socinus, Grotius, Clericus, Olearius, Michaelis, Stier. Grammatically, such an emphasis cannot be justified.[2] Olearius only was disposed to substitute ἐν for εἰς, and to explain the expression, ἐν τῷ πειρασμῷ φέρεσθαι, by the Homeric φέρειν, in the sense "drag away." Chrysostom arbitrarily imports the idea of the voluntary into εἰσελθεῖν, so that εἰσφέρειν designates the Divine permission of a free ἐπιπηδᾶν into sin.

By the majority of the older exegets—as, for example, by Augustine, Jerome, Melanchthon, Este, and others—the positive view of the petition is either expressly or tacitly substituted for the negative: "adjuva nos adjutorio spiritus tui," which, strictly taken, is only permissive, if by πειρασμός we understand the sinner δελεασμός. Hence Cornel. a Lapide expresses himself more accurately, when he says, "non solum *ne vincamur* petimus, sed etiam ne in certamen descendamus, *ne forte vincamur*."

Chrysostom remarks justly, that the petition is the expression of the feeling of weakness and danger, causing a man, not indeed to flee from the temptations brought upon him, but still to avoid seeking such as are not put in his way; ἑλκυσθέντας μὲν γὰρ δεῖ γενναίως ἑστάναι· μὴ καλουμένους δὲ ἡσυχάζειν καὶ τὸν καιρὸν ἀναμένειν τῶν ἀγώνων, ἵνα καὶ τὸ ἀκενόδοξον καὶ τὸ γενναῖον ἐπιδειξώμεθα. So also Cyril ("in Luc." ed. Maii): οὐκ ἀνάνδρους ἡμᾶς, οὔτε δειλοὺς εἶναι βούλεται, νεανικοὺς δὲ μᾶλλον . . . πρὸς δὲ αὖ τούτοις καὶ μετριόφρονας καὶ μὴ νομίζειν

---

[1] Similar is the view taken by Donatus of „inducere" in his explanation of the passage, "duci falso gaudio," in Terence's "Andria" (act. 1, sc. 2, v. 9), which he explains, first by "prolatari falsa spe," and then by "induci, ut feræ in retia."

[2] In Latin, a distinction is made between inferre and inducere, in so far as the latter word has the bad secondary meaning of "to entice" (see Nich. Heinsius on Ovid's "Metamorph." viii. 123). The Vulgate, therefore, did well to translate, "ne nos inducas:" Augustine's rendering, "ne nos inferas," though, as he says, in accordance with the greater number of the MSS., is less happy.

ὅτι πάντῃ δὲ καὶ πάντως παντὸς περιεσόμεθα πειρασμοῦ (see further, Augustine, "de dono persev." c. 6; auctor op. imp., Euth., Mald., and a Lapide). Specially to be compared is the exhortation in Matth. xxvi. 41, προσεύχεσθε, ἵνα μὴ εἰσέλθητε εἰς πειρασμόν; for which is assigned the reason, τὸ μὲν πνεῦμα πρόθυμον, ἡ δὲ σὰρξ ἀσθενής. The opposite disposition would be that expressed by Job in chap. xxiii. 10: "Let Him tempt me, I will come forth as gold." Inasmuch, moreover, as πειρασμός designates a state of passivity, and as a passive state is felt by human nature to be one of antagonism and limitation, the dread of suffering, which is natural to, and justifiable in human nature, justifies this petition. On this principle, the prayer of the Redeemer in Gethsemane is a type and example for us. In connection with James' exhortation to rejoice at temptations (chap. i. 2), we may compare the eighth beatitude—"Blessed are they which are persecuted" (Matt. v. 10)—; which does not, however, forbid, but rather admits of the command to flee from persecution where it is possible (Matt. x. 23). Ewald says: "All suffering and all insecurity is a temptation, and it is not every one that can bear up against it: it is, at all events, in no case to be desired."

The other question, as to how God can be regarded as the cause of the εἰσφέρειν εἰς πειρασμόν, presents less difficulty. Augustine mentions that many deemed themselves bound to pray, "ne nos *patiaris* induci," which, according to his account (de dono persever. c. vi.), several codices read; Cyprian also has it. If, with most expositors, we are to regard πειρασμός as equivalent to δελεασμός, and as denoting the inward impulse, and are to understand πονηρός to mean the devil as tempter, we can certainly go no further than the idea of *permission*, as Euthymius, Theophylact, Luther expound; Theophylact: μὴ συγχωρήσῃς ἡμᾶς ἐμπεσεῖν. If, however, πειρασμός has no other meaning than the "occasion in which temptation arises," then it is one's own ἐπιθυμία which makes the περίστασις become a πειρασμός; the περίστασις itself, however, is to be ascribed to the Divine causality. Gregory of Nyssa rightly apprehends the meaning of πειρασμός; he observes: ἐν τοῖς κοσμικοῖς πράγμασιν αἱ τῶν πειρασμῶν ἀφορμαί· καλῶς καὶ προσηνῶς ὁ ῥυσθῆναι ἀπὸ τοῦ πονηροῦ εὐχόμενος ἔξω τῶν πειρασμῶν γενέσθαι παρακαλεῖ· οὐ γὰρ ἄν τις καταπίῃ τὸ ἄγκιστρον, μὴ κατασπάσας ἐν λιχνείᾳ τὸ δέλεαρ.

Ἀλλὰ ῥῦσαι ἡμᾶς ἀπὸ τοῦ πονηροῦ.—These words are wanting in St Luke. Bunsen's opinion (Hippolytus ii. 181) is, that, like the clausula, they were originally a response by the people, and in this way came to be inserted in the text of St Matthew. Compare, however, what has been already remarked on the text of St. Luke (p. 318). Whether they are to be regarded as forming a seventh petition, depends partly on the view we take of them. If ἀπὸ τοῦ πονηροῦ **refers** to Satan, and the previous petition to *devilish* temptations, these last words would only be a positive expression of what had been formerly expressed negatively, and there would be no reason to regard them as a separate petition. Thus Tertullian already determines: Respondet clausula, *interpretans quid sit* "ne nos deducas in temptationem;" hoc est enim: sed devehe nos a malo (in his "de fuga in persec." c. 2: sed erue nos a maligno). The words are explained as referring to the devil—and consequently the same view is taken of the division of the petitions,—for the most part, by Origen, Chrys., Greg. Nyss.,[1] Zwingli, Calvin; the last, however, in his Instit. Christ. iii. 20, 46, does not reject the view of πονηροῦ as the neuter (comp. Rienaecker, "ueber die Abweichungen im Gebete des Herrn, in Luthers und im Heidelberg. Katechism.," Studien u. Kritiken, 1837, H. 2); also by Socinus, Chemnitz, Ernesti, Schmid, Bengel, Kuinoel, Fritzsche, Olshausen, Meyer, Hofmann (Schriftbeweis i. 394). The Sixth petition appears to coincide with this view: there *Divine* assistance is asked, while here that assistance is explained to mean deliverance; comp. Origen: ῥύεται δὲ ἡμᾶς ὁ Θεὸς ἀπὸ τοῦ πονηροῦ. On the other hand, the Vulgate translates *malum*, which Cyprian explains as a neuter, thus: omne malum sive peccatum sive quidvis aliud, quod detrimentum nobis afferat; so Augustine, auct. op. imp., Glossa ordinaris: a malo omni visibili et invisibili; Luther, Melanchthon, Camerarius, Olearius, Stier, Ewald. Now although this πονηρόν and the πειρασμοί may be regarded as correlative ideas, yet the petition for redemption from the circumstances of temptation is a more comprehensive thought, and one better fitted for the conclusion of

---

[1] Gregory explains thus: μὴ εἰσενέγκῃς ἡμᾶς εἰς τὰ τοῦ βίου κακά; but, in this inaccurate way of expressing himself, πειρασμός, μαμωνᾶς, ὁ πονηρός are *equivalent* terms: consequently he regards the last votum as identical with the sixth.

the prayer, than that for deliverance from the allurements of the devil. Accordingly Augustine regards *that* as the closing votum, in which view he is followed by Luther. Aug. ad Probam: Cum dicimus: libera nos a malo, nos admonemur cogitare, nondum nos esse in eo bono, ubi nullum patiemur malum. Et hoc quidem ultimum, quod in or. Dom. positum est, tam late patet, ut homo Christianus in qualibet tribulatione constitutus in hoc gemitus edat, in hoc lacrymas fundat, hinc exordiatur, in hoc immoretur, ad hoc terminet orationem. Melanchthon: vult autem Deus in hac misera massa in hac vita inchoari hoc summum beneficium, vid. restitutionem justitiæ et vitæ æternæ, in qua deinceps, prorsus abolito peccato et deleta morte, *ipse erit omnia in omnibus*. Luther (Kleiner Katechism.): "In this prayer we ask our heavenly Father to set us free from all evil of body and soul, honour or estate; and finally, when our last hour comes, to vouchsafe us a happy end, and to take us from this valley of tears to Himself in heaven."[1] Now, if there is any reference whatever to this final terminus of life in the words, they have decidedly a claim to be regarded as an independent petition. They recall 2 Tim. iv. 18: καὶ ῥύσεταί με ὁ κύριος ἀπὸ παντὸς ἔργου πονηροῦ, καὶ σώσει εἰς τὴν βασιλείαν αὐτοῦ τὴν ἐπουράνιον. For although, from the context, the ἔργον πονηρόν refers here only to the wicked attacks of enemies, yet this is only one species of the πειρασμοί, to which is immediately added the anticipation of deliverance from *all* πειρασμοί. Therefore Stier is wrong in saying that there is no *liturgical* significance in the view of these closing words of the prayer taken by the Reformed Church. As the succeeding clausula, Ὅτι σοῦ ἐστιν ἡ βασιλεία, κ.τ.λ., is unauthentic, and accordingly is not a conclusion, we are almost compelled to read *these* words as forming the conclusion: as De Wette, also, with his æsthetical and religious insight, feels constrained so to regard them.

This wider view of the meaning of the words, ἀπὸ τ. πονηροῦ, will not be found inconsistent with the interpretation of πονηροῦ as a masculine, viz., of the wicked one, if, as Hofmann thinks, the whole domain even of the outward πειρασμοί is regarded as the work of Satan. Nor is there in the text

---

[1] In the Larger Catechism Luther explains the words "of the wicked one," which does not, however, prevent his regarding them as the close.

anything against regarding τοῦ πονηροῦ as masculine,—only against the neuter no objection need be raised; for, as Matt. xv. 19 shows, Christ does not invariably refer back to the ultimate cause of all sin, much less of all evil (confer supra, p. 265).

The Epilogue.

'Ότι σοῦ ἐστιν ἡ βασιλεία, κ.τ.λ.—It is scarcely correct to call these words a doxology: they are rather in form an ætiology. Their genuineness has been very strongly called in question by criticism. There are no valid *internal* arguments against their authenticity: although B.-Crusius, following Wettstein, urges the objection, that this ἐπιφώνημα severs too much the 12th verse from the 14th, which is joined to it; yet the sixth and seventh petitions come in between them. He further objects, that this conclusion is of a character too brilliant for so simple a prayer. But the words are not to be regarded as a mere doxological outburst of feeling: they are rather the emphatic expression of the ground of hope on which the whole prayer is based; and at the close of such a prayer a greater elevation of expression would not appear strange. Well remarks Calvin: neque enim ideo solum addita est, ut corda nostra ad expetendam Dei gloriam accendat, et admoneat, quisnam esse debeat votorum nostrorum scopus, sed etiam ut doceat, preces nostras, quæ hic nobis dictatæ sunt, non alibi quam in Deo solo fundatas esse, ne propriis meritis nitamur. Bengel urges that a doxology like this is scarcely fitted for prayers offered in this earthly status militans: but here he also overlooks the ætiological form. The only objection which can be made against it on *internal* grounds is, that, in accordance with the symmetry of the rest of the prayer, one would expect to find the δύναμις, in relation to the kingdom of the Father, preceding the βασιλεία.

External arguments, however, must decide against the genuineness of these words. Comp. Bengel, Appar. crit., p. 459; Jak. Breitinger, Museum Helveticum, xi. 370, xvi. 591, xviii. 719; Wettst., Griesbach comment. crit., p. 68 seqq. Few codices indeed omit them: these, however, are the best Greek codices, Vat. and Cantab.: Cod. Alex. is imperfect here. The majority of these codices belong to those of the Western

Church: that in them the words are wanting, is confirmed by the Latin translation and the earliest Latin Fathers. Neither Tertullian, who calls the sixth petition the clausula of the Prayer, nor Cyprian, nor Jerome (who, however, retains the *Amen*), nor Augustine, read the doxology. Neither were the words in the Alexandrine codices: they are not to be found in Origen, or in the Coptic translation; not in the Arabic translation of the ed. Rom. and Pol.; not in the Persian translation by Wheloc, in Cyrillus Hieros., Gregory Nyssenus, Maximus, Cæsarius. Euthymius[1] charges the Bogomilans with rejecting the ἐπιφώνημα of the Lord's Prayer, which *the Fathers of the Church had added:* τὸ παρὰ τῶν θείων φωστήρων καὶ τῆς ἐκκλησίας καθηγητῶν προστεθὲν ἀκροτελεύτιον ἐπιφώνημα—τὸ ὅτι σοῦ ἐστιν ἡ βασιλεία καὶ ἡ δόξα τοῦ πατρὸς καὶ τοῦ υἱοῦ ἁγίου πνεύματος, οὐδὲ ἀκοῦσαι ἀνέχονται. In conclusion: Although in other cases St Luke has borrowed materials to fill up his shorter edition from the more perfect narrative of St Matthew, yet *it is certain that this clausula is wanting in St Luke in all the codices of his Gospel.*

It is not difficult to see how this clausula has originated. From the earliest times, responses were used in Divine service, after the example of Jewish worship (1 Chron. xxix. 11): this was especially the case in the use of the Lords's Prayer in the celebration of the Eucharist (Bunsen's Hippolytus, ii. 179, 374). Here a doxology was introduced to satisfy liturgical requirements; and traces of its gradual origin can still be pointed out. Whilst in the Peschito, which retains the doxology, the Amen is omitted; Jerome and Cyprian, who ignore the doxology, retain the Amen. The Cod. Bobbiensis of the Itala, edited by Tischendorf, has: quoniam est tibi virtus in sæcula sæculorum. The Sahidic translation has: quod tuum est robur et potentia in ævum ævi Amen (ed. Schwartz quatuor evv. Copt.).

---

[1] Paulus gives incorrectly *Euthalius* instead of *Euthymius* (Exeg. Handbuch, ii. 661). No doubt the passage of the latter is not to be found in the Commentary; but it occurs in the fragments of the Panoplia, edited by Toll. In the Commentary, he explains the formula like Chrysostom, without any critical remark; nor does he add the words: τοῦ πατρὸς καὶ τοῦ υἱοῦ καὶ τοῦ ἁγίου πνεύματος. Hence it is probable that the Bogomilans, who felt always a concern for the pure text of Scripture, rejected these last words alone; and that Euthymius' ἀκροτελεύτιον ἐπιφώνημα *relates exclusively to these words.*

The const. apostol. 7, 24, have: ὅτι σοῦ ἐστιν ἡ βασιλεία εἰς τοὺς αἰῶνας· ἀμήν; on the other hand, in 3, 18, there is the perfect formula. The mention of the Trinity was added still later. Cod. 157 and 225 place after δόξα: τοῦ πατρὸς καὶ τοῦ υἱοῦ καὶ ἁγίου πνεύματος; to which Lucian (Philopatris, c. 27) seems to make allusion in the words: τὴν εὐχὴν ἀπὸ τοῦ πατρὸς ἀρξάμενος, καὶ τὴν πολυώνυμον ᾠδὴν εἰς τέλος ἐπιθείς. Hence already in the ed. Complutensis, Ernesti, Beza,[1] the suspicion was expressed, that the formula had been transferred to the text of the New Testament from liturgical use. In a similar way, in the Ave Maria, there was added to the words, benedicta tu in mulieribus, the clause, quia peperisti servatorem animarum nostrarum. So, too, in our own day the Mosaic benediction[2] is expanded in various ways by clergymen; and so the Catholic Church, in using this very prayer, often added to the words, libera nos a malo, the formula: per Jesum Christum dominum nostrum. This view of the origin of the words is further supported by the circumstance already alluded to, **that the internal constitution of the prayer would lead us to expect the** δύναμις to precede the βασιλεία: if the epilogue came from Christ Himself, we should in all probability find that its three members corresponded to the arrangement of the petitions. Thus the authenticity of these words came to be denied by the following theologians: Zwingli (not Calvin), Œcolampadius, Pellican, Bucer, Melanchthon, Camerarius, Drusius, Scultetus, Walton, Grotius, Mill, Grab, M. Pfaff, who have been followed by almost all modern writers: Luther, too, has passed over the doxology in his Larger and Smaller Catechisms.[3]

The authenticity of the words was defended by Wolf, Olearius, Witsius, Heumann, J. Baumgarten de auth. doxol.

---

[1] Beza observes that the clausula is not explained by St Chrysostom, which is a misstatement.

[2] Which is used in the Lutheran Church at the close of Divine service. —ED.

[3] That the Pater noster came to be offered in the Protestant Church without the doxology in the celebration of the Lord's Supper, was simply the effect of the use of the Vulgate. Heumann, who defends the authenticity of the epilogue, urges the abolition of this abuse. Moreover, that custom was not universal [e. g., in the English Communion Service, the Lord's Prayer is used once without the epilogue, and once with it]. See on this point Brem. and Verdische Bibliothek, ii. 530, iv. 1026.

Halac 1753, Benzenberg Symbolæ Duisb. 1784, T. ii. P. 1, p. 97, the capricious critic Matthæi (ed. maj. in appendix), Weber (in his angef. Diss.). The most important testimony in favour of the authenticity of the words is the Peschito version; next, the Philoxen. and Hieros., the Pers. Pol., Ethiopic, Armenian, Ulfilas. Yet this evidence is inadequate to throw a sufficient weight into the scale. In the most recent investigations on the antiquity and critical value of the Peschito (in Wichelhaus de N. T. vers. Syr. 1850), the highest antiquity and critical value are ascribed to that version. But even there, alterations at least of a doctrinal character are not denied. Griesbach (meletemata) de vetustis N. T. recensionibus, p. li.) seeks to show traces of interpolations in it. Even supposing that it is as old as the beginning of the second century, still the liturgical use is yet more ancient. Besides, the absence here of the ἀμήν seems to show that the addition is noth authentic, since Christ would not have given the doxology without this ἀμήν. It is, however, impossible, with Griesbach, to place the addition of the words in this form in the fourth century, as the testimony of the Peschito is opposed to this.—The arguments adduced by the latest apologists only serve to make the matter worse. According to Matthæi, Origen and his superstitious disciples must bear the blame of the mutilation. Benzenberg conceives that all those Fathers in whom the words are wanting have been corrupted by their Parisian editors, after the Vulgate!—Absolute necessity on liturgical grounds for this conclusion there is none, if the immediate object of the prayer be kept in view. If, however, by *a liturgical need* be meant the religious and psychological desire on the part of the suppliant for a fitting close, this purpose is abundantly answered by the seventh petition, if it is understood as indicated above.

Vers. 14, 15. That which in the fifth petition has already been presupposed, is here expressed as a condition. This is necessary, inasmuch as, although presupposed, it would not always be found to exist. Expressed as a condition, it is confirmed first by a positive, next by a negative statement. The conjunction by γάρ, referring as it does to the remote ver. 12, is certainly surprising. This peculiarity of construction has induced

Calvin to suspect that the saying does not belong to this context: comp. Mark xi. 25. As, however, γάρ is not ætiological, but explanatory, the interposition of the sixth petition offers no reason why it should not refer back to the fifth. What importance the Saviour attached to the thought, that men should display towards one another the same dispositions of mercy which God manifests towards sinful men, may be seen also from other passages, such as v. 24; Luke vi. 37; Matt. xviii. 35. The frequent recurrence of this thought renders it all the more likely that the saying here occurs in its original position, especially as it here fits in so well with the context. A similar thought occurs in Sirach xxviii. 2: ἄφες ἀδίκημα τῷ πλησίον σου, καὶ τότε δεηθέντος σου αἱ ἁμαρτίαι σου λυθήσονται. Alluding to this saying, Chrys. (de compunctione 1, § 5) says: "To ask forgiveness from God as at great benefit, and to deny the same to others, is to mock God."

It is self-evident that a condition of forgiveness such as this, is not to be taken by itself, and regarded as opposed to other conditions, such as penitence, etc., as the Rationalists would have it.[1] Augustine, de civitate Dei, L. xxi. c. 22, observes, that such a carnal method of expounding Scripture would lead one to conclude from Matth. xxv. 34, 35, that alms-giving is the sole condition of salvation. He then ingeniously combines that condition with the one given in our passage, and remarks, that forgiving the trespasses of our neighbour is a "spiritual alms-giving."

WARNING AGAINST A HYPOCRITICAL EXERCISE OF FASTING.

Vers. 16—18.

Vers. 16—18. By the law, private fasting was left to be determined according to the necessity of each individual. After

---

[1] Wegscheider (Institutiones, § 137), after admitting that the Bible teaches the forgiveness of sins on the ground of the death of Christ, goes on to say: "haud tamen prætermittendum est, in iisdem libris alias quasdam hac de re formulas deprehendi ab illa supra proposita *plane abhorrentes*, vel ei *repugnantes*. Sic gratiam Dei remissionemque peccatorum Matt. vi. 12, 14, animo placabili precibusque obtineri edocemur."

the Exile the custom became more and more general: Judith viii. 6; Tob. xii. 9; Lightfoot, p. 318; Winer, Realwoerterbuch Article "Fasten." The Pharisees used to fast regularly on the second and fifth days of the week (Luke xviii. 12). A few placed fasting above alms-giving. R. Elieser, in Gem. Berach. f. 32, 2: "Fasting is greater than alms-giving: the former takes place on one's own body, the latter only on one's property." Among the Hebrews, fasting was one of those outwards acts which betokened grief and inward self-abasement: hence also ענה נפש. It usually appears accompanied with other signs of humiliation, such as abstinence from the use of water, of anointing oil, of razors, with the besprinkling of ashes, the putting on of mourning: Isa. lxi. 3; Dan. x. 3; 2 Sam. xii. 20; 1 Mac. iii. 47; Maimon. on tr. Thaanith, c. iv. 7. The hypocrites here spoken of, used more especially, as the antithesis shows, these other outward signs of humiliation,—their object being to draw attention to their fasting, as these signs would more readily catch the eye of an observer than the mere pallor caused by fasting, to which Chrysostom here alludes.—Σκυθρωπός, from σκύζομαι, to be gloomy, sad. Basil, de jejunio I., well puts στυγνάζων in its place. Luther: "sauer sehen," "to be of a sad countenance."[1]—Ἀφανίζουσι ὅπως φανῶσι,—a play of words scarcely to be regarded as intentional. Ἀφανίζειν, Chrysostom: διαφθείρουσι, ἀπολλύουσι; Hombergk, Hammond: colorem auferre; he compares Antiochus, hom. 55, de invidia: τὸ πρόσωπον ἐξαφανίζει, pallorem inducit; Er., Fr.: e conspectu tollere; Elsner, Meyer: to cover, conceal, *i.e.*, in the garb of mourning. But, in accordance with later usage of the word, the meaning is rather deformare, to disfigure; which is also expressed by the exterminare of the Vulgate: this signification is established from a number of examples by Clericus, in loco; Valck. Phœniss. at v. 373; Schaefer, ad Dion. de comp. verb. p. 124. Stobaeus, Serm. tit. 74, 62, quotes what Nicostratus

---

[1] The Sophists of the time of the Roman Empire assumed a similar hypocritical appearance, which is a theme of lamentation and derision to the writers of that period; particularly, Lucian adverts to it, using the derisive expression, φιλοσόφου τὸ χρῶμα ἔχειν. Seneca, ep. v.: asperum cultum et *intonsum caput*, et negligentiorem barbam ... et quidquid aliud ambitionem perversa via sequitur, evita; comp Corn. Adami observ. theol.-philol. Gron. 1710, p. 114.

says of the women who adorned themselves: πόρρω δ' ἂν εἴη καὶ τοῦ διηγῆναι γυνὴ ὑγιαίνουσα καὶ ψιμμιθίου καὶ ὑπ' ὀφθαλμοῦ ὑπογραφῆς καὶ ἄλλου χρώματος ζωγραφοῦντος καὶ ἀφανίζοντος τὰς ὄψεις: Far be it that a healthy woman should rouge herself or stain her eye-lashes, or use any other colour which paints and *disfigures* the face. The allusion, accordingly, is not to a covering of the countenance, which could only be regarded as an expression of mourning, but to **the *squalor* of the unwashed** face and undressed hair and beard, as is seen from the antithesis in ver. 17: "Thou, when thou fastest, anoint thine head and wash thy face." So, too, the outward expression of humiliation is opposed by an outward sign of cheerfulness: which may be regarded as a concrete expression of a cheerful appearance. The idea of Hilary, and of some others quoted by Jerome, that there is here an allegorical allusion to the washing and anointing **for** the remission of sins, **is utterly erroneous.**— Φαίνω intransitive, joined not with an infinitive but with a participle, because they wish not to seem **what they are not** (ut videantur jejunare), but to appear what they are (ut appareant jejunare).

GOD THE SUPREME OBJECT OF HUMAN DESIRE AND ENDEAVOUR, TO WHICH ALL ELSE MUST BE ENTIRELY SUBORDINATED.

Vers. 19—24.

Whatever probability may exist, a priori, that the proper connection of this passage is that in which it occurs in St Luke, still we could not but acknowledge that its place in St Matthew is the correct one (see Introd. p. 24). The principal ground of this conclusion is to be found in the general character of Christ's **discourses in St Luke in** relation to those in St Matthew, **and** more particularly as regards this Sermon on the Mount. Nor do we altogether fail to find a point of connection between this passage and what precedes. Three times, the last in ver. 18, occur the momentous words: καὶ ὁ πατὴρ ὑμῶν ὁ βλέπων ἐν τῷ κρυπτῷ (κυφαίῳ) ἀποδώσει σοί. The one idea, that "good works" are to be performed alone with a reference to the Invisible, might naturally lead to the other, that in all human labour and endeavour the eye should be fixed upon the Invisible. So, too, at the close in ver. 33, the fixing of the mind upon the things unseen is, although in a modified form, again set forth as a leading requirement. It can scarcely be insisted that, in a popular discourse, which is really not of the nature of a treatise, the transition should be formally expressed: nevertheless this may have been the case, and the connecting link have been lost, as in vii. 1—5. The indirect connection of thought which we have pointed out is supposed by Hilary to be immediately contained in the words of the 19th verse, for he understands the treasures upon earth to mean the praise of men. The Glossa ordinaris on ver. 19 also hints at this connection: qui jejunat vel servando quod non edit vel gloriam quærendo, in terra thesaurizat.

Vers. 19, 20. The laying up treasures in heaven denotes, inasmuch as God is regarded as in heaven, the laying up treasures with God; as likewise in Matt. xix. 21; Luke xii. 33; 1 Tim. vi. 18, 19. Accordingly, the more accurate expression in πλουτεῖν εἰς Θεόν, Luke xii. 21. The favour of God is the alone imperishable treasure, inasmuch as, when all else comes to an end, ὁ ποιῶν τὸ θέλημα τοῦ Θεοῦ μένει εἰς τὸν αἰῶνα, 1 John ii. 17. Whatever of this world's goods may be sacrificed in a strong faith in the invisible world remains, inasmuch as the eternal destiny of the man is determined by the spirit in which the sacrifice has been made. The prohibition to amass wealth, or other goods, is by no means to be regarded as absolute, as the Chevalier Michaelis has been peculiarly careful to point out. He shows that the negation is to be understood rather in the sense of "not so much, as rather;" and further states, that the treasures here spoken of are treasures of corn, not to collect which would expose the country to the peril of famine. Undoubtedly the words of the text, in this popular form of exhortation, express the thought with a certain one-sidedness (conf. supra, p. 164); in consequence of which, we must frequently take into consideration other passages besides, in order to apprehend the proper limitation. As regards the present case, it must be borne in mind, that it is possible so to gather together earthly treasures that the sovereign treasure of the favour of God is thereby multiplied and increased: everything depends on the object in view. The duty of parents to gather up for their children is especially recognised by the Apostle, 2 Cor. xii. 14. The words are intended to convey no other meaning than that expressed in 1 Cor. vii. 30, 31: "They that **possess** as though **they** possessed not." This is apparent from ver. 21: what the Saviour there warns against, is having one's *heart* in the treasures. Accordingly, Clement of Alexandria observes (i. 578, Pott.), that it is only the φιλοκτήμονες and μεριμνηταί whom the words oppose. To confine the laying up treasures in heaven to alms-giving, as in Luke xii. 33, is a one-sided restriction: so Basil. (?) de baptismo i. 1; auct. op. imp.; Glossa ord.; Jansenius, and others.

The treasures of the East consisted in ancient times, and still do, in part, of valuable articles of apparel (Ezra ii. 69; Neh. vii. 70; Job xxvii. 16; James v. 2), which might be destroyed by *moths* (Job xiii. 28; Isa. l. 9, li. 8). Accordingly, the mention of the moth is in reference to this species of treasure. It were then natural to expect that βρῶσις, and perhaps also κλέπται, are used in respect of some specific kind of property. As for βρῶσις, it can be proved that it has here only the general signification, *canker, corrosion*. Clericus, however, Michaelis, Kuinoel,[1] maintain that it signifies the *corn-worm;* a rendering which, if it could be defended, would give this advantage, that the second **kind of treasure might be** supposed to be corn (with regard to which Luke xii. 18 may be consulted); while a third species would be gold and silver, to which the κλέπται might correspond.[2] Kuinoel fortifies his opinion by Mal. iii. 11, where the LXX. have translated אכל by βρῶσις. This, however, proves as little that βρῶσις means just the corn-worm, as the circumstance that Aquila has translated βρωτήρ for moth in Isa l. 9, proves that βρωτήρ signifies moth. The

---

[1] Whether Theophylact also holds this **view** is doubtful. He **has:** σὴς μὲν καὶ βρῶσις ἀφανίζει βρώματα καὶ ἱμάτια, κλέπται δὲ χρυσίον καὶ ἀργύριον. The Ethiopic translation, however, understands βρῶσις to signify an insect similar to the moth; Bode, ev. Matth. ex vers. æthiop. interpr. p. 54.

[2] In a fragment by Menander are classed together as three **internal destroyers** of things: οἷον ὁ μὲν ἰός, ἂν σκοπῇς τὸ σιδήριον, τὸ δ' ἱμάτιον οἱ σῆτες, ὁ δὲ θρίψ τὸ ξύλον, Menandri reliquiæ, ed. Meineke, p. **198**.

LXX, have translated as though the word were לֶאֱכֹל, and they do the same at Isa. lv. 10, where לֶחֶם לְאֹכֵל is translated ἄρτον εἰς βρῶσιν. Clericus defends this explanation, comparing חָסִיל, really the *eater*, subsequently the *locust*.[1] But this proves nothing, further than that in the Greek of the New Testament βρωτήρ might stand for *locust*.

It were more in point to refer, with Bretschneider, to the ep. Jer. ver. 12, where it is said of the false gods: οὐ διασώζονται ἀπὸ ἰοῦ καὶ βρωμάτων. Here one might, perhaps, with Bretschneider, suppose the rust to refer to the metallic idols, and the βρώματα, in the sense of moths, to be in allusion to the garments which the images wore; but it is more probable that βρώματα refers to the *wooden* statues, which were spoilt by rotting, by wood-worms, etc.[2] The view of the other special signification of *rust* is very widely maintained: so the Vulgate, Coptic translation, Ulfilas, Erasmus, Luther, Grotius, Bengel. Thus, in the classics, moths and rust occur frequently side by side, when the perishable character of earthly goods is depicted;[3] so too in James v. 2, 3, where the rusting of even the nobler metals is spoken of. It is possible that the Hebrew language had no special word for *rust*; in the Syriac, the word ܚܒܠܐ, corruptio, is carried over from the species to the genus.[4] Yet the view is very questionable. In the passage quoted, cp.

---

[1] Michaelis, in his annotations for the learned, endeavoured, but without success, to justify this signification.

[2] The moth is also spoken of in the Arabic as proverbial for a destructive animal, افسد من السوس "more destructive than the moth;" see Meidani, Proverb. ed. Freytag, ii. c. 20, n. 79, 80.

[3] The Münster Hebrew translation of Matthew has also הֶחָסִיל; that of the London Society for spreading Christianity among the Jews has הָאֹכֵל; that of the Bible Society has הַאֲכִילָה (which probably stands for הֶחֳלִי), after the English translation, which has "moth" and "rust."

[4] At our passage the Peschito and the Philox. have ܐܟܠܐ. When, however, Mich. (as does also Castellus) places tinea and ærugo side by side, this is incorrect, for the word cannot have both meanings at once. The Syriac, on the other hand, has sought to express only the sense erosio; so likewise the Arabic, which has اكل, which, with Kesre under the Elif, means corrosion, more particularly in Avicenna, the corrosion of bone; but with the threefold Fatha it might also signify the *destroyers*.

Jer. ver. 12 (Baruch vi. 12), βρώματα occurs beside ἰός; and the Rabbinic at least has a distinctive word for rust, הֲלֻדָּה. It is therefore safest, with Bretschneider and Wahl, to abide **by the** general signification; perhaps in specie the reference is to corruption, as Basil. in Luc. (Opp. iii. 49): τὰ ἐκεῖ ἀποτιθέμενα (sc. ἐν οὐρανῷ) οὐ σῆτες καταβόσκονται, οὐ σηπεδὼν ἐπινέμεται. Thus Euthymius; also the Itala, which Augustine and the auct. op. imp. follow, has *comestura*. Beza already exchanges the ærugo of the Vulgate for erosio. To suppose, with Casaub., Drusius, Hombergk, that there is a hendiadyoin = σὴς βρώσσουσα, is inadmissible, were it only for this reason, that not καί occurs, but οὔτε—οὔτε. Neither can we think that the consumption referred to is by *human* agency (see auct. op. imp. and de Dieu), for the treasures spoken of are laid up, such as (as the Calembourg of Greek etymologists says), τίθενται εἰς τὸ αὔριον (Luke xii. 19).

There are thus two kinds of insecurity and perishableness mentioned as concerning these earthly treasures. First, they are liable to destruction, in the ordinary course of nature, by animals, and by internal corruption; next, they may be forcibly abstracted. That the idea, "the very smallest thing may destroy then," is intended to be brought forward (Baumg.-**Crusius**), we can scarcely believe. Διορύσσειν, here used of the thieves, occurs similarly in Greek even without the οἰκίας (like the German *einbrechen*); along with it we find τοιχωρυχεῖν **and** ἐκτοιχωρυχεῖν: comp. Job xxiv. 16.

Ver. 21. St Luke (xii. 34) gives this saying in an isolated form; but its connection here with ver. 22, 23, imparts to it a profound significance. The **preceding context** had indicated the perishable nature of earthly treasures **as** the reason why they should not form **the great** object of human desire. Here a fresh reason is **added**, viz., that **the object** of desire assimilates to itself the mind of him who strives after **it**. Chrys.: ὥσπερ οὖν εἰς τὸν οὐρανὸν ἀποτιθέμενος, οὐ τοῦτο καρποῦσαι μόνον τὸ τυχεῖν τῶν ἐπὶ τούτοις ἐπάθλων, ἀλλ' ἐντεῦθεν ἤδη τ. μισθὸν λαμβάνεις, ἐκεῖ μεθορμιζόμενος. In every impulse there exists a certain affiance, a certain sympathy with the object towards which it is directed. Aug.: sordescit aliquid, cum inferiori miscetur naturæ, quamvis in suo **genere** non sordidæ.

Similarly, too, knowledge is based upon love: men must love what they would know, a dictum which holds good in reference to other things besides that knowledge of *eternal* truth which alone is contemplated in the well-known saying of Pascal: "Il faut aimer les choses divines pour les connoître." As previously the nature of the treasures had been characterized by the two spheres in which they respectively exist, the one *above*, the other *beneath*, the thought is expressed thus: the καρδία, *i. e.*, the seat of the affections and desires,[1] moves either in the one sphere or in the other; that is, it assimilates itself to the one or to the other. This profound truth admits also of more special applications. Thus it has been said, the miser becomes like a stone, the self-indulgent becomes assimilated to the beast, the vain-glorious to the devil. Jerome remarks: huic *servit* unusquisque a quo vincitur; still more appropriately might we say here: huic assimilatur a quo vincitur. Luther: "What a man loves, that is his God. For he carries it in his heart, he goes about with it night and day, he sleeps and wakes with it: be it what it may, wealth or pelf, pleasure or renown."—The reading σου of Cod. D. J. adopted by Lachmann, Tischendorf, is to be regarded as the more authentic, ἑμῶν having been probably introduced from Luke xii. 34. Bengel: sing. Græcis ad sermones asceticos aptus fuit.

Vers. 22, 23. According to Calvin, Kuinoel, Paulus, Br. Bauer, Neander, this saying is added on without having any internal connection with what precedes. "Here," says Br. Bauer (in loc. cit. S. 364), "the Evangelist begins to grow tired, his powers abandon him, and he is in despair to think how he shall impart to the reader the rich treasury of sayings, that precious string of pearls, which he is determined to turn to the account of the Sermon on the Mount." Undoubtedly the saying occurs in St Luke (chap. xi. 34—36) in an entirely different context. Yet even supposing that its connection there imparts to it a more satisfactory signification, still Olshausen owns that it is by no means self-evident that that signification is the authentic one, and Hilgenfeld recognises the Sermon on

---

[1] Stirm, Tueb. theolog. Zeitschrift 1834, S. 53; Beck, bibl. Seelenlehre, S. 88. Justin, in his apol. i. 15, cites ὁ νοῦς, but in the same *practical* sense as denoting "the disposition."

the Mount as its original place (Olshausen, Neander, S. 423, Hilgenfeld, S. 189). Then, the wealth of words introduced in Luke ver. 36, in the description, seems to indicate its derivation to be second- or third-hand. How Ewald could think that these verses were more fitly placed after ver. 16, is, however, still more difficult to conceive (Ewald, Jahrb. 1848, S. 129). Certainly the only way in which a manifest and strict connection with ver. 21 could be made out, would be to regard ὁ ὀφθαλμὸς τῆς ψυχῆς as identical with καρδία, as Augustine, auct. op. imp., Bucer, Melanchthon, Druthmar, Zeger, Episcopius, and Stier have done. The last says, "It is that *practical* reason which regulates action,—so to speak, the fundamental purpose of a man." Aug.: oculus ipsa intentio, qua facimus quidquid facimus. Further, he considers the tenebræ to be the *outward actions*, quia incertum habent exitum, inasmuch, namely, as the results are not within human control; for which reason the value of all actions is to be judged of by their intentio. (On the abuse of this canon in Roman Catholic practice, compare Gerh. loci viii. 68; Quenstedt, Theol. didact. polem. v. 320.) But, then, this practical faculty, even if it could be characterized by the term ὀφθαλμός, could not be designated τὸ φῶς τὸ ἐν σοί; **as** Stier explains: "Even the unconverted has some honest striving after the eternal inheritance." Besides, the eye, in the figurative language of Scripture, always denotes the organ of inward knowledge: Ps. xiii. 3, cxix. 18; Mark viii. 18; Luke xxiv. 31; Eph. i. 18, etc. So, too, here the inward eye must be the *faculty* of knowledge of things eternal,—the same with what in Pauline phraseology is called, in a psychological sense, πνεῦμα. So Chrys., Maldonatus, Grotius, Olearius, Michaelis, Fritzsche, Olsh., De Wette, Meyer, and Delitzsch (bibl. Psychol. 1855, S. 69): and the sense would be in the words of St Chrysostom: ὅταν γὰρ ὁ κυβερνήτης ὑποβρύχιος γένηται . . ποία λοιπὸν τοῖς ὑπηκόοις ἐλπίς; . . ὥσπερ γὰρ τὴν πηγὴν ἀνελὼν καὶ τὸν **ποτα**μὸν ἐξήρανεν· οὕτως ὁ τὸν νοῦν ἀφανίσας πᾶσαν αὐτοῦ τὴν ἐν τῇ ζωῇ ταύτῃ πρᾶξιν ἐτύφλωσεν. Hofmann (Schriftbeweis, ii. 296) takes a different view: "The light signifies the holy nature of Good which seeks to illumine men."—The 21st verse warns men against the *tendency* to regard earthly things as the highest good; in vers. 22—24, they are exhorted to preserve the inward light of spiritual discernment clear and unobscured, in order that they may retain a right consciousness of what is the highest good. The real point of transition could be mistaken only by those who treated the subject in an abstract pedantic manner. Unquestionably לֵב and καρδία denote, in biblical phraseology, not merely the organ of impulses of the will, but equally the organs of knowledge and feeling (comp. Delitzsch in loc. cit. S. 215 f.). To the καρδία itself, ὀφθαλμοὶ ἐπιγνώσεως are ascribed (see Harless on Eph. i. 18). Accordingly, the devotion of the καρδία to earthly things, spoken of ver. 21, must be regarded as including that obscuration of the faculty of spiritual discernment which accompanies such devotion; in accordance with what has been remarked above in connection with the saying of Pascal.—Certain writers, Pisc., J. Gerhard, Beausobre, Hammond, referring the text to the covetousness which springs from devotion to earthly things would understand the ὀφθαλμὸς πονηρός as the *covetous* eye (רַע עַיִן Prov. xxiii. 6), by which man becomes enslaved to the things of the world, and the ὀφθαλμὸς ἁπλοῦς, on the other hand, as the liberal, benevolent disposition; an explanation which must be pronounced erroneous.

Thus the Redeemer ascribes to man, *as* man, the possession of an inward eye capable of discerning the true end of life. And this circumstance certainly implies, as the Rationalists contended, the recognition, on His part, of the existence even in fallen man of an efficacious principle of affinity to the Divine. This truth is also stated in St John viii. 47, xviii. 37. The Church system of doctrine, however, does not deny this; it expressly contends for a lumen naturæ, for notiones de Deo innatæ, quae nihil aliud sunt quam reliquiæ imaginis divinæ (Gerhard loci, T. i. 93). Calvin: lumen vocat Christus rationem, quantulacunque hominibus reliqua manet post lapsum Adæ. And yet no use has been made of our text in this interest, either by Socinians and Arminians, or yet by orthodox theologians. By Sarcerius the conditional clause of ver. 23 is thus unwarrantably metamorphosed into a distinct assertion: oculus seu judicium in homine tenebræ sunt: ergo nihil vere docere de ratione thesaurizandi potest. Beza, Chemnitz, Gerhard, Calov, substitute "the eye enlightened by the word and Spirit of God." Episcopius, again, who takes the eye to denote the appetitus and affectus, argues merely that the tenebræ fieri is not to be taken in an absolute sense, as though implying an assertion of the total corruption of the tendencies of the natural will. Now, this idea is not directly expressed in the text—at least if our explanation of ὀφθαλμός be correct—but, considering how knowing and loving act and react upon each other, and as the ὀφθαλμός is, according to Eph. i. 18, the ὀφθαλμὸς τῆς καρδίας, it is indirectly involved in the words (comp. the expression, συνήδομαι τῷ νόμῳ κατὰ τὸν ἔσω ἄνθρωπον, Rom. vii. 22, and Mueller, Lehre von der Suende, ii. 325).

Not a few expositors take an incorrect view of the logical progression of the sentences, and of the relation of metaphor and application. The application does not begin with ἐὰν οὖν ὁ ὀφθαλμός, κ.τ.λ., as Aug., Erasmus (Commentary), Luther, Piscator, Beausobre, Hammond, Clericus, and Wettstein suppose; still less with ὁ λύχνος, as the auct. op. imp. thinks, who, by the way (like Luther), by restricting the thought to an admonition against *covetousness,* mistakes the sense. The first clause, ὁ λύχνος—ὁ ὀφθαλμός, is a proverb; the next, ἐὰν οὖν, κ.τ.λ., is an inference drawn from the first; the last, εἰ οὖν, κ.τ.λ., is the *spiritual* application of that inference. The sense of seeing is used more frequently than that of hearing for mental and spiritual apprehension, because the eye is the organ of most acute perception: *e.g.,* Aristotle, topic. i. 14, ὡς ὄψις ἐν ὀφθαλμῷ, νοῦς ἐν ψυχῇ; comp. Grotius, Wettstein; comp. also the antithesis of ἀκούειν an ὁρᾶν, John vi. 45, 46. Light, as the medium of physical perception, is here the designation of the sensible eye (thus τὰ φάεα in Homer, lumina in Latin); it is then taken over into the spiritual sphere, and applied to spiritual perception. Τὸ φῶς τὸ ἐν σοί is accordingly equivalent to ὁ ὀφθαλμὸς ὁ ἐν σοί. It is next said of the eye that it is the source of light, which makes the whole body light. For the members of the body are so knit together that each separate member does not need to have an eye of its own, but every one has part in the light of the one organ of vision, 1 Cor. xii. 14—18.[1] **But if the eye is to perform this service for the whole body, it must not** be evil, πονηρός. The word πονηρός, used thus of the outward eye, can mean only diseased, sickly; as the people say, "a

---

[1] Hence the thought would be still more pungently expressed thus: ὅλον τὸ σῶμά σου ὀφθαλμὸς ἔσται. Maldonatus: erit veluti oculatum, nam oculus perexiguus orbiculus ita toti corpori necessarium lumen praebet ut, cum oculus purus est, totum omnino corpus oculus esse videatur.

bad eye:" so, too, the Hebrew רָע; in Greek, πονηρῶς ἔχειν means κακῶς ἔχειν, the opposite of ὑγιαίνειν. This must also determine the meaning of ἁπλοῦς. In the sense of *healthy*, this word occurs nowhere: hence we may think that it is to be taken here in its proper sense (Elsner, Olshausen), viz., an eye that does not *see double;* the eye which sees double is diseased; and so we might, with Quesnel, expound the words: "the heart which knows but one object of love, that is, God." We must, however, begin by inquirinig what the Hebrew word is for which ἁπλοῦς is here used. Now, in Aquilas and in the LXX. we find ἁπλοῦς as the translation of תָּם, יָשָׁר = ὁλόκληρος: this is, however, related in sense to integer, sound, healthy; accordingly, Theophylact renders ἁπλοῦς and πονηρός by ὑγιής and νοσώδης. Accordingly, the inward eye is here declared to be diseased, whenever it ceases to be directed towards the highest good.

The clause τὸ σκότος πόσον is thus explained by Olshausen, who supplements ἐστί: "The condition of spiritual darkness is then more fearful than bodily darkness, than blindness." Meyer: "If the outward eyesight is destroyed, the body is in darkness; how great then is that (spiritual) darkness in which thou art!" Thus Grotius, Wolzogen, Olearius, Baumgarten-Crusius, Neander, and De Wette. But may not the comparison be carried somewhat further? As in the physical body, the eye is the single member which gives light to all the rest, which, without it, would remain in darkness, may it not be so also in the spiritual sphere? If so, the darkness would denote the blind appetites and passions of nature, which must be permeated by the light of the λόγος. The Vulgate translates: tenebræ *ipsæ,* which Jerome and Augustine explain in the sense just indicated. The Syriac, Armenian, and Ethiopic translations have, "thy darkness," *i. e.,* "that which in thee is darkness." Thus the words are expounded by Euthymius, Erasmus, Bucer, Luther, and Stier. We must then regard the clause as supplemented thus: τὸ σκότος, πόσον σκότος ἔσται! Erasmus: si ratio excæcata id judicat imprimis esse expetendum, quod vel contemnendum, vel neglectui habendum, in quas tenebras totum hominem rapiet ambitio reliquæque animi pertubationes, quæ suapte natura caliginem habent! Luther: "The man who has avarice in his heart, has in his heart a darkness. But if he goes away and flatters himself that he is not avaricious, and **hood-winks** his conscience, that it may not interfere with him, **then** is he indeed doubly in darkness."

Ver. 24. The soundness of the inward eyesight consists, as we have seen, in this, that the true and highest good be apprehended as the only good: hence it follows, that to this highest good all else must be subordinate, and that the love of it must take precedence of all other love. Every species of ἐπαμφοτερίζεσθαι in the province of religion, every attempt to give to any other thing a prominence and importance equal to that highest good, tends to impart to these other coveted blessings an indepedence which does not of right belong to them, and to elevate them to the dignity of something divine. Hence this is called in Scripture εἰδωλολατρεία (Col. iii. 5; Phil. iii. 19), μοιχεία, comp. James iv. 4: μοιχοὶ καὶ μοιχαλίδες, οὐκ οἴδατε ὅτι ἡ φιλία τοῦ κόσμου ἔχθρα τοῦ Θεοῦ ἐστιν; Δουλεύειν denotes precisely that relation to a good in which the latter is raised to the position of absolute κύριος, being subordinated to no other power. St Chrysostom: πῶς οὖν ὁ Ἀβραάμ, φησι, πῶς ὁ Ἰὼβ εὐδοκίμησε; μή μοι τοὺς πλουτοῦντας εἴπῃς, ἀλλὰ τοὺς δουλεύοντας. ἐπεὶ καὶ ὁ Ἰὼβ πλούσιος ἦν· ἀλλ᾽ οὐκ ἐδούλευε τῷ μαμμωνᾷ, ἀλλ᾽ εἶχεν αὐτὸς καὶ ἐκράτει, καὶ δεσπότης (αὐτοῦ) οὐ δοῦλος ἦν. Also in the classics, δουλεύειν τινὶ πράγματι denotes absolute *devotion* to a thing, as in Plato (Phaedon. p. 66, D.; de Repub. l. vi. 494, D.). Now, **when the** things of this world are regarded as the highest **good, and** are not pursued in subordination to God and His will, **these call** forth efforts opposed to the Divine will. There are **thus two** κύριοι **corresponding** to the two different tendencies of the will, **according** as God or the earthly good is master. That the two κύριοι **indicated** different tendencies of the will, is plain; for, as Chrysostom rightly observes, two masters who had but one will, were not two but one: and we know that the desire for earthly possessions, whenever it becomes subordinated to the Divine will, by no means excludes the desire **for** heavenly blessedness. Now, two masters who are so essentially unlike as God and Mammon, cannot be served together **without** the one being set below the other, consequently subordinated to that other, and deprived of its κυριότης: and this is true of either of them, for both lay claim **to** absolute mastership: so that if God is Master, Mammon can no longer be so; and if Mammon, then no longer God. No man can serve two masters so essentially different: only one of them can be his real lord.

Ὁ εἷς and ὁ ἕτερος are placed in opposition to each other; and no doubt the εἷς and the ἕτερος in the second clause of the verse, are the same with those in the first. We should certainly have expected τοῦ ἑνός, which would more clearly have referred us back to the preceding εἷς: yet εἷς, without the article here, is intelligible. With Meyer, we might understand it thus: "Or he will hold to one (not both), and despise the corresponding other." But then it is held by many, that if καταφρονεῖν is to be taken quite in the same sense as μισεῖν, and ἀντέχεσθαι in the sense of ἀγαπᾶν, the sentence would be tautological. But since, in modern parlance, καταφρονεῖν is not so strong as μισεῖν, it was natural also to regard ἀντέχεσθαι as feebler than ἀγαπᾶν: and accordingly Grotius, who is followed by Kuinöl, translates thus: futurum enim, ut aut hunc amet, illum oderit, aut certe alterum curet neglecto altero. On the other hand, several commentators (Casaub. and Raphel, followed by Schmid and Baumgarten-Crusius, who refer to 1 Thess. v. 14) have endeavoured to vindicate for ἀντέχεσθαι a stronger meaning than ἀγαπᾶν, making the meaning of the passage as follows: vel unum odio habebit alterum amans, aut etiam, licet amet utrumque, fieri poterit, ut, dum in alterius voluntate exsequenda erit intentior, erga alterum se gerat negligentius. But that ἀντέχεσθαι, to hold to one, is a stronger expression than ἀγαπᾶν, is what cannot be maintained. If then ἀγαπᾶν and ἀντέχεσθαι are parallel expressions, we shall expect this to be also the case with καταφρονεῖν and μισεῖν; and then, in order to bring the sentence to perfect conformation, we shall not have to intensify the idea of καταφρονεῖν, but rather to modify that of μισεῖν. Since Bohl (Thesaurus phil.-theol.) and Hackspan (notæ philologicæ), it has been commonly observed that the Hebrew, in comparisons, would use the positive expression "hate," where we should rather employ the negative one, "to think little of." Fritzsche and Meyer, in their philological rigour, ignored this circumstance, and maintain the full force of the antithesis: as does De Wette in commenting on Rom. ix. 12, although here he recognises the correctness of the remark. But when one account of the

Saviour's words gives, in St Matt. x. 37, the words, "He who loveth father or mother *more* than Me," and the other (St Luke xiv. 26), "He who cometh to Me, and *hateth not*,"—is not the difference merely a difference in expression, just as certainly as is the difference in the words immediately following those just quoted, viz., between "He is not worthy of Me," and "he cannot be My disciple?" And the following passages from Moses render this yet more evident. In Gen. xxix. 30, we read, וַיֶּאֱהַב גַּם־אֶת־רָחֵל מִלֵּאָה, and in the 31st verse, וַיַּרְא יְהֹוָה כִּי־שְׂנוּאָה לֵאָה. Of course the latter expression is to be read by the light of the former.

Μαμωνᾶς is an expression occurring frequently in the Targum, in rabbinical and also Syriac writers.[1] Augustine: lucrum Punice mammon dicitur: so, too, the Targum has it for the Hebrew בֶּצַע. Although the word is found spelt which double μ in the codices and the Fathers, the spelling with one μ, as in Syriac and Chaldaic, which is found in St Luke xvi. 9, is alone correct. Regarding its derivation, preference is to be given to the opinion of Drusius and Castellus, that it comes from אָמַן, and signifies accordingly, "what a man puts his trust in;" after the Samaritan ܐܰܡܺܝܢ manens, sibi constans. In Isa. xxxiii. 6, Ps. xxxvii. 3, אֱמוּנָה is translated by the LXX. θησαυροί, πλοῦτος. This signification might also explain how it happens that the Aramaic word comes to be retained in the Greek gospels, viz., because the word served to mark riches as the idol of man. And doubtless this is the ground of the assertion of the ancients, that the Syrians had a god corresponding to Plutus, who went by the name of Mammon. This Tertullian is supposed to say; but in the passage relating to it, adv. Marcion. l. iv. c. 33, nothing of the kind occurs. Schleusner further refers in proof of the assertion to Barth (adversariorum l. lx. Francof. 1648). Barth unquestionably, after the example of certain ancient writers, understands by Mammon the devil: but, in proof of this, he quotes only Papias (the grammarian, of the eleventh century), who says in his Glossarium: mammona dæmon ille dicitur, qui divitiis et lucris carnalibus præest.

Ver. 25. On the position of this passage here and in Luke

---

[1] Assemani, Biblioth. orient. iii. 2, 122, 123.

xii. 22, vide Introduction, p. 24. The transition from the foregoing verse is evident. The warning against devotion to the quest of earthly possessions, is followed by the admonition to make our desire for the perishing goods of this world subordinate to the great end of life. Now the most common excuse for men's striving after earthly possessions, is the *care* they have about the necessaries of life: therefore must this care be subordinated to the high end of life. Aug.: ne forte, quamvis jam *superflua* non quærantur, propter ipsa *necessaria* cor duplicetur. That this is the right aspect in which to view the prohibition of μεριμνᾶν, is proved by the ζητεῖτε δὲ πρῶτον of ver. 33. Yet μεριμνᾶν is not equivalent to ζητεῖν, σπουδάζειν. The common meaning of the word is (although Meyer groundlessly denies this), a restless, anxious care; comp. μέριμρα, μεριμρίζω, derived from μερίζομαι, "to have a divided mind:" so in St Luke x. 41: μεριμνᾷς καὶ τυρβάζῃ περὶ πολλά. The antithesis to this anxious concern, this ὀλιγοπιστία (ver. 30), is given in the manner of the light and joyous race of birds, which have no human provider, as, further on, κρίνα τοῦ ἀγροῦ, "the lilies which no gardener tends;" compare also St Luke xxi. 34, μήποτε βαρηθῶσιν ὑμῶν αἱ καρδίαι . . μερίμναις βιωτικαῖς, and Sirach xxxiv. (xxxi.) 1, ἀγρυπνία πλούτου ἐκτήκει σάρκας κ. ἡ μέριμνα αὐτοῦ ἀφιστᾷ ὕπνον. Those questions, τί φάγωμεν; τί πίωμεν; are the questions of an anxious faintheartedness. St Luke has in addition the unmistakeable expression, μὴ μετεωρίζεσθε. The only care of which the Saviour speaks here, is such as proceeds on the belief that God *does not care* (ver. 32; 1 Peter v. 7). The same thought is to be found in these Old Testament word: "It is vain for you to rise up early, to sit up late, to eat your bread with *care:* to His beloved He giveth it when they sleep:" Ps. cxxvii. 2. Here the antithesis suggests the thought: we are not so to work as if God could not give it to us without our working for it. The 26th and 28th verses plainly show that this admonition, μὴ μεριμνᾶν, does not exclude work, but rather presupposes and involves it: work, which is a Divine appointment enjoined as far back as Gen. iii. 17. These vers. 26, 28, contain this thought, that "even *without* the means of supporting life which work supplies to *you,* the beasts and the flowers receive nourishment and clothing." And that this is indeed the case, we have the testimony of the Psalmist, derived from his own experience, in the words, "I have been young, and now am old," etc.: Ps. xxxvii. 25. The clergyman will indeed find the comforting assurance of the text met by the sceptical complaint, Has it then never happened that a man who has sought first the kingdom of God, and His righteousness, has died of starvation? And the **proper** answer to this cavil is assuredly not to be found in De Wette's remark, that the consolation of the text is not to be looked into too *microscopically:* rather in remembering that Christ is speaking here only of the ordinary course **of human** life, in which that "sowing, reaping, and gathering into barns," of which ver. 26 speaks, can take place. Assuredly, in the ordinary course of life, he who strives after the righteousness of God,—which $\delta\iota\varkappa\alpha\iota o\sigma\acute{v}\nu\eta$, of course, includes diligence in his calling in life,—will experience the truth of the consolation of the text: for *extraordinary* cases there are other extraordinary texts of consolation.

The exhortation is based, in the first place, upon the reflection: He who gives the greater, is He likely to withhold the lesser gift? Luther: "Who can conceive greater folly than for a man to be careful about what he is to eat and to drink, who has no care about where he is to get his body and his soul?" $\Psi v \chi \acute{\eta}$ is the animal soul, the principle of life: hence Luther and De Wette translate "life." Bengel: cibo sustentatur anima *in* corpore, quod ipsum cibo pascitur: veste corpus solum tegitur. This reflection is carried out in vers. 26—30, with an intervening argument at the close of ver. 26. In ver. 31, we are recalled to the admonition of ver. 25. Let us sum up the various arguments here given **in** support of the $\mu\grave{\eta}$ $\mu\varepsilon\varrho\iota\mu\nu\tilde{\alpha}\nu$: they **are the following:**—1. He who has given the greater, the body and the life, shall He not also bestow the lesser, to wit, the means to support that body and that life? 2. Does He not actually do this in the case of the creatures around you, of beasts and of flowers, although these cannot use for this purpose the means of working which are placed at your disposal? 3. Besides, human care and concern cannot accomplish anything without the help of God. 4. Your necessities are known unto God.

Vers. 26, 27. Arguing a majori ad minus, ver. 25 had shown that God, who had been pleased to bestow on man body and life, could not leave him destitute of the means of supporting them. The consideration is now further confirmed by a reference to the orders of being beneath man, which, although they have no power to use the means of work, are yet maintained by God. Now, that God *can* support life even without work, is a statement which assumes that work is for man the appointed means by which life is to be supported: this sufficiently refutes the foolish notion, that the text recommends a slothful passivity, which would manifest the strength of faith by a total suspension of labour. With regard to the means by which the life of animals is upheld, viz., brute-instinct, this is a subject which, the more it is studied, the more worthy of admiration will it appear (see Kirby's Animal Kingdom, 1838). Luther: "Here He supplements the admonition by an example and illustration, to the shame and confusion of all that miserable avarice and gluttony, and to draw us from them, and show us what we ourselves are; and that He may make us ashamed of ourselves, to think that, although we are so much higher and nobler and better than the fowls of the air, inasmuch as we are lords not alone of them, but of all things which He has created to serve us, we yet have not faith to trust Him to feed us. And yet shall not He who maintains the smallest bird, yes, and the meanest worm of the dust, our humblest servants, and who, without any care or thought of theirs—for they can gather in nought, nor make any provision for their wants, nor sow, nor reap what is sown—daily gives them food,—shall not He also supply the wants of His children?" The argument is further strengthened, ver. 27, by the reflection, that all our care is useless and ineffectual.

In these sayings we cannot fail to recognise a healthy appreciation of the manifestations of nature, both in the animal and vegetable kingdoms. Similar to this is the train of thought in some of the Psalms; *e.g.*, on the care of God for beasts in Ps. civ. 27, cxlvii. 9, compare Job xxxviii. 41. But this love of nature, and these allusions to her operations, were something very uncongenial to the spirit of the pharisaic religion. Of Gamaliel it is recorded, as an exceptional case, that he was a lover of the beauties of nature.—The Saviour makes use of the animal kingdom to illustrate the care of God in providing food, as subsequently He adduces the vegetable kingdom to exemplify

His care to clothe. Instead of the genus τὰ πετεινά, St Luke has here a species, the *ravens* (xii. 24): a circumstance which may be regarded as a proof of the inferior degree of originality of his account (see p. 24). The Genitive, τοῦ οὐρανοῦ, denotes generally the relation of participation: the birds, "whose element is the air;" as elsewhere we read: "the beasts of the field," "the fish of the sea." The addition τοῦ οὐρανοῦ is not superfluous: it helps us to realize the careless freedom of these creatures, as further on τὰ κρίνα τοῦ ἀγροῦ is used with similar import. These animals cannot, like man, procure for themselves food by labour, and yet they are fed by the hand of Him who is called the Father of men (ὁ πατὴρ ὑμῶν, comp. this ὑμῶν in chap. x. 29). The labour relative to food is mentioned in its three principal functions, of sowing, reaping, and gathering into barns. Hilary gives the following allegorical interpretation: The fowls of the air are, according to Eph. ii. 2, the unclean spirits; the lilies are the good angels, who, without their own exertions, enjoy in eternal innocence the glory of God; the grass destined for the oven represents the heathen doomed to damnation.

In ver. 27 the argument is enforced by the consideration, that care is moreover bootless, it can accomplish nothing. Ἡλικία has a twofold signification: *stature*, or *length of life*. It is rendered stature in the Vulgate and in the Syriac version, by Chrysostom, Erasmus in his Paraphrase, Luther, Calvin, Beza, Grotius, Fritzsche; the other meaning, of "length of life," is ascribed to it here by Erasmus in his Annotationes, Gusset (Vesp. Gron. p. 398), Hammond, Wettstein, and all recent commentators, except Fritzsche. Meyer thinks that the context speaks for the translation, "length of life," because we read previously of τροφή, the support of life. In any case this consideration is decisive in favour of this interpretation, that here is manifestly meant a *small* measure; but a yard of additional height to one's stature would form a very considerable addition: compare in chap. v. 36, οὐ δύνασαι μίαν τρίχα λευκὴν ἢ μέλαιναν ποιῆσαι. Moreover the clause added in St Luke xii. 26 points to the capacity to do a small thing: εἰ οὖν οὐδὲ ἐλάχιστον δύνασθε, τί περὶ τῶν λοιπῶν μεριμνᾶτε; With regard to the figurative application of this measure by yards to the length of life, Fritzsche says we have no decided examples of the practice in classic writers: something similar, indeed, he says, occurs in their writings, but only by way of jest. Yet life was often regarded as a stadium (Job ix. 25; Acts xiii. 25; 2 Tim. iv. 7). Also in Ps. xxxix. 5, man's life is compared to a hand-breadth (טְפָחוֹת). Compare the following passages from the classics: Diogenes Laert. 8, 16, σπιθαμὴ τοῦ βίου; Alcaeus in Athenæus l. x. c. 7, δάκτυλος ἁμέρα; Mimnermus in Stobæus, Sermones tit. 98, ed. Gaisf. T. iii. 282, ἡμεῖς .... πήχυιον ἐπὶ χρόνον ἄνθεσιν ἥβης τερπόμεθα.

Vers. 28—30. With reference to clothing, the Saviour might a second time have taken an illustration from the animal kingdom; for instance, He might have alluded to the peacock, as Solon did to Crœsus when he sought to humble him: but the figure He selects is more tender, and at the same time better suits His purpose. For He points out the glorious adornment in which one of the most unassuming of the products of creation is invested. The lily, which in this country is usually white, in the East is more commonly red, orange, and yellow: its finest species is the Crown Imperial, κρίνον βασιλικόν. In the East it grows wild in the fields: specially in Palestine were the broad, fertile pasture-lands on the plain of Sharon covered with it: comp. Cant. ii. 1, and Iken de lilio saronitico, dissertatt. Tom. ii. The ancient classic poets, too, sing the beauty of the lily, with the epithets alba, candida, argentea. Now the glory of the clothing of this flower is all the more striking, when we think how poor and trivial is its life: it grows wild (κρίνα τοῦ ἀγροῦ); it comes speedily to bloom, and as quickly fades. Often in the East, one south wind sweeping across the plain will, in four and twenty hours, leave all its beauty faded, parched, and dead (Ps. xc. 5, 6; 1 Peter i. 24; Horace, Carm. i. 36, 16 [breve lilium]); and when the dried grass is gathered to heat the baker's oven, then is the withered lily gathered among it. Jerome, Thren. 5, 10; solebant autem furni incendi non tantum ramalibus arborum, sed et floribus, postquam exaruerunt, quemadmodum et paleis et lolio. For χόρτος in ver. 30 comprehends the whole class of plants which grow in the field and meadow, and thus includes also the flowers, like הָצִיר, עֵשֶׂב.—We might (with the auct. op. imp.) regard κοπιᾶν and νήθειν as denoting, the one, the labour of men, the other, that of women, for in 2 Tim. ii. 6 κοπιᾶν is used of field-labour. The reference is, however, rather to the different tasks of the planting and preparing of the flax for clothing; the meaning is thus: "**the flowers cannot prepare themselves their clothing.**" The varied colours of the flowers are, so to speak, their robe, just as it is said of man's mortal body, that it shall *put on* ἀθανασία (1 Cor. xv. 54). This glorious vestment of the lily is now brought into comparison with the Jewish ideal of glory. As such Solomon and Esther were regarded: Solomon's magnificence, and particularly **his ivory throne, are dwelt upon** in 1 Kings x. 18 ff.; 2 Chron. ix. 17. (**On the latter** compare Cassel, "Weltgeschichtliche Fragmente," in the Transactions of the Academy of Sciences at Erfurt, 1853.) Οὐδέ, *not even,* marks out king Solomon as the height of human glory. By δόξα we are to understand the whole royal solemn magnificence of the king in state,—more especially, however, the rich, gold-embroidered robe of royalty. The reader may compare Sirach l. 8, where it is said of the high-priest Simon, who has been previously compared to the rose and the lily: ἐν τῷ ἀναλαμβάνειν αὐτὸν στολὴν δόξης, καὶ ἐνδιδύσκεσθαι αὐτὸν συντέλειαν καυχήματος, ἐν ἀναβάσει θυσιαστηρίου ἁγίου ἐδόξασε περιβολὴν ἁγιάσματος.—Ὡς ἕν, Bengel: quodvis, nedum uti sertum. Τούτων, δεικτικῶς.

Vers. 31, 32. In these verses our Lord resumes the exhortation of ver. 25, and censures the state of mind of which He speaks. **That is** represented as characteristic of the heathen. To what extent is this to be so regarded? The answer to the question must be determined by the view take of the causal relation expressed by the twofold γάρ. According to some writer, *both* the γάρ-clauses give the ground of the admonition,—the one giving the principal ground, the other a subordinate: so Cocceius; recently Fritzsche, Wahl, Käuffer, and Meyer (2d edition). Such a use of γάρ to introduce a second reason is certainly classical (Bornemann ad Xen. symp. iv. 55; Krueger, griechische Grammatik, § 69, 14, 2). The Hebrew כִּי is also used similarly (Gesenius, thesaurus, p. 679, and further on to chap. vii. 14). But we are not warranted in assuming such a use here, any more than in St Matt. xxiv. 27, 28, to which passage Käuffer refers: comp. Rom. viii. 6. For if we are to assume that *this* is regarded as the characteristic feature of the heathen, that they have not the knowledge of God (1 Thess. iv.

5), then the second causal clause must be viewed as an explanation of the first: "*You* believe, indeed, truly in a heavenly Father, who is concerned about the affairs of men." Auct. op. imp.: gentes, quæ vitas suas incerto duci eventu æstimant. At the same time, it is certainly true that a marked feature of the heathen world was, that they lived only for the present: and even Goethe (Winkelmann's Leben, S. 397) gives this as its great characteristic. Chrysostom says: τὰ ἔθνη, οἷς ὁ πόνος ἅπας κατὰ τὸν παρόντα βίον, οἷς λόγος οὐδεὶς περὶ τῶν μελλόντων οὐδὲ ἔννοια τῶν οὐρανῶν.—As, according to ver. 8, our Lord's disciples are to pray, although their heavenly Father knows their wants, so His care of them cannot supersede their working.

Ver. 33. The leading thought of the whole passage, from ver. 19, is here summed up and expressed in a command. To the question concerning what is the highest good, Christian ethics has, especially since St Augustine, replied, that the highest good is God,—more definitely, is *fellowship with God,*—and the realization of the Divine idea of man by means of such fellowship with God. But this end is not attained by any man as isolated and alone, but by each one solely as a member of that organized body of the *kingdom of God,* the perfection of which is referred to in the Lord's Prayer (ver. 10) and 1 Cor. xv. 28. On the other hand, in the restoration of the will of man to harmony with God, *every* blessing is involved: accordingly, the righteousness of that kingdom is pre-eminently brought forward. To this righteousness reference had already been made in chap. v. 20. Unquestionably δικαιοσύνη is not here to be understood to mean the righteousness of faith, as by Luther, Calov, Crusius, and Stier: on the contrary, it is the fruit of that righteousness of faith, viz., the righteousness of the life, of which St Paul himself speaks (Rom. viii. 4, v. 18, 21): this is recognised even by the Lutheran divines, Sarcerius, Hunnius, Bengel, who refer to Rom. xiv. 17. Bengel: cœlestis cibus et potus opponitur terreno. Still more emphatic would this δικαιοσύνη be, if, according to Codex B., we were to read, with Lachmann and Tischendorf, τὴν δικαιοσύνην καὶ τὴν βασιλείαν αὐτοῦ. But that βασιλεία is the leading idea here, is seen from St Luke xii. 31, where we have only ζητεῖτε τὴν βασιλείαν αὐτοῦ, and from Rom. xiv. 17, *οὐ γάρ ἐστιν ἡ βασιλ. τοῦ Θεοῦ βρῶσις κ. πόσις, ἀλλὰ δικαιοσύνη*.

Προστίθεσθαι denotes the *πρόσδομα, μέτρον προσθήκης* (Tobit v. 16, xii. 1; Epictetus i. 8, 9); Latin, corollarium, mantissa, superpondium, that which was given in addition to the purchase or the loan,—so to speak, "into the bargain." Strictly taken, the idea of this additional gift corresponds to the *πρῶτον* here used, which term **certainly** seems to authorize a relative seeking after other things. On this very account, probably,—because the *πρῶτον* seems to allow this,—it was omitted in Cod. 61, Ethiop., opus imp. Stier would explain away this meaning of *πρῶτον* in a manner similar to that of Bengel, who remarks: qui id *primum* quærit, mox id *unum* quæret. Yet all that the *πρῶτον* is intended to indicate is, that all other striving is to be *subordinated* to this, as ver. 24 has already shown that this requirement is paramount: and in this view, the thought, that everything else is given as something over and above, may be taken in a literal acceptation. In this sense, says St Augustin: *hæc omnia apponentur vobis*—ne cum ista quæritis illinc avertamini, aut ne *duos fines constituatis,* ut et regnum Dei propter se appetatis et ista necessaria, sed hæc (terrena) potius propter illud, ita vobis non deerunt.

The promise that piety shall be accompanied with all other blessings, is also expressed in 1 Tim. iv. 8; St Mark x. 30. And, as a concrete ratification of the same thought, may be adduced the Divine reply to Solomon's prayer for wisdom, 1 Kings iii. 11 et seqq.: "Because thou hast asked this thing, and hast not asked for thyself long life; neither hast asked riches for thyself, nor hast asked the life of thine enemies,—lo, I have given thee a wise and understanding heart,—and I have also given thee that which thou hast not asked, both riches and honour." We may accordingly well regard as a further amplification of the words of Christ, the remark of Clement of Alexandria (Strom. i. 346), and of Origen (T. iii. de la Rue, p. 762): *αἰτεῖτε τὰ μεγάλα καὶ τὰ μικρὰ ὑμῖν προστεθήσεται, καὶ αἰτεῖτε τὰ ἐπουράνια καὶ τὰ ἐπίγεια προστεθήσεται ὑμῖν*.

Ver. 34. In ver. 33 we have seen the leading thought of the whole passage condensed and expressed. That the admonition is repeated here, can only be with a direct practical purpose.

What strikes one in this verse, however, is, that to the μέριμνα is assigned a wider sphere of influence, inasmuch as it is prohibited here also as regards the morrow, the future. Moreover the motive on which the argument is here based is more trivial, as it regards only individual interest. But then the form of this utterance is so thoroughly Oriental, so fresh, so popular, that it cannot in the least have destroyed the impression of the passage, if spoken precisely as it occurs in the text: a remark which applies to the whole discourse as reported by St Matthew. St Luke omits the saying; but this is only an additional proof of the less perfect character of his account of this whole passage, from ver. 19.

Attempts have been made to remove the apparent incongruity by a forced exegesis. According to the auctor op. imp., the crastinum means what is superfluum, and ἀρκετὸν κ.τ.λ. he forcibly explains: superflua quantacunque congregaveris, illa seipsa curabunt. Te quidem non eis fruente, ipsa autem invenient dominos multos, qui ea procurent sicut placuerit ipsis. According to St Augustine, the crastinum is the temporale, simply, non enim dicitur crastinus dies, nisi in tempore, ubi præterito succedit futurum. The explanation he subjoins of ἡ αὔριον μεριμνήσει τὰ ἑαυτῆς is acute but subtle: ut, cum oportuerit, sumas cibum vel potum vel indumentum, *cum ipsa scilicet necessitas urgere cœperit*, aderunt enim hæc, quia novit pater noster, quod horum omnium indigeamus. Maldonatus thinks there is here an allusion to the prayer for daily bread; hence what is added here he supposes to be a sollicitudo petendi a Deo quam industria nostra quærendi.

If we are to expound the passage argute, we might certainly say that care really concerns itself always with the morrow, if by this we understand generally the future; for the present moment engages all the energies of the soul by the κακία (*i.e.*, the occupations) which belongs to it (similarly Olshausen). But then, if αὔριον really comprehends a *longer* period than merely the next day, then it does not mean a *shorter*. Further, if κακία expresses more than occupation, then, in contrast to the μέριμνα of the following day, it denotes that μέριμνα which is connected with the labour of the present day. Hence Jansenius more correctly: ne putaremus, quoniam præcepit, ne simus solliciti, non debere nos laboribus parare quæ ad victum et vestitum sunt necessaria, *quales labores non possunt omnino esse sine aliqua cura et sollicitudine,* totam hanc de abjicienda sollicitudine doctrinam terminaturus, tandem infert: nolite ergo, etc. In the same sense writes Chrysostom, making allusion to the petition for *daily* bread in ver. 11: ὅπερ οὖν καὶ ἐνταῦθα ποιεῖ. οὐ γὰρ εἶπε, μὴ μεριμνήσητε, ἀλλά, μὴ μεριμνήσητε ὑπὲρ τῆς αὔριον, ὁμοῦ καὶ τὴν ἐλευθερίαν ἡμῖν παρέχων καὶ τὴν ψυχὴν ἡμῶν προσηλῶν τοῖς ἀναγκαιοτέροις. But if from the permission of μέριμνα for the present day, we would infer that μέριμνα cannot then denote an anxious care, the inference is not admissible; for even the κακία which is ascribed to the present day, suggests the idea of some anxiety in providing for the wants of the day. This κακία involves the element of care; and if our Lord allows the present day to have its κακία, we can rightly interpret His meaning only by bearing in mind, that it is perfectly consistent with the character of a popular speaker to content himself occasionally with reducing a sin to its minimum, especially when, as in the present discourse, He has shown that carefulness should really be *entirely* done away with. A disquietude which is confined to the present day and its concerns, would at least diminish with its every fleeting hour. Bengel: qui hoc discet, curas tandem a die ad horam contrahet, vel plane dediscet. By μέριμνα we are not to understand all care and foresight, but only anxious carefulness. Else our Lord violated His own precept not to care for the morrow, by having a γλωσσόκομεν (St John xii. 6). Else was Joseph wrong in laying in his stock of corn (Gen. xli.); and Solomon's allusion to the example of the ant (Prov. vi. 6) must be held to be a mistake. The Saviour's use, here, of the inferior motive of self-interest, could be disapproved only if the highest motive were passed by. Now, however, that He has done full justice to that higher motive, we cannot fail to see, in this allusion to the meaner one, something very human: it is an expression of the Saviour's sympathy with the daily care of man. Very different is Elsner's idea of the passage: he would explain κακία morally, as the vice of μέριμνα which, out of indulgence to human weakness, is allowed for the day, but confined by ἀρκετόν to a certain measure.

Wettstein, Paulus, and others abound in parallel quotations from Horace, as: carpe diem, quam minime credulus postero, and: lætus in præsens animus, quod ultra est, oderit curare.

But between a want of care which springs from the thoughtless vanity of the Epicurean ἡμερόβιοι, and that which has its source in the knowledge that "your heavenly Father knoweth that ye have need of all these things," what *can* there be in common? The one philosophy throws care to the winds, the other casts it upon the Lord (1 Peter v. 7). Rightly then says Olearius: *Verbis* igitur non *sensu* plerasque illas sententias cum salutari salvatoris doctrina conspirare arbitramur. Hilary well remarks: The freedom from care which Christ commends incuria sollicitudinis relaxatæ non *negligentiæ* est sed *fidei*.

Ἡ αὔριον is commonly regarded as denoting the future generally. What holds good for the morrow, holds good also for the future the general. But we must not blunt the point of the apophthegm by regarding αὔριον here as merely a vague term for the future: it is rather to-morrow as opposed to to-day. The prosopopœia by which the day is represented as caring for its own wants, is full of meaning: the idea is, that within the sphere of each new day, new means of help are in wainting for us,—a truth which many biographies, such as those of Francke, Stilling, amply illustrate for Christian edification. Zwingli: adferet crastinus dies eas res, pro quibus tu sollicitus es, ut videas Deum tui curam gerere. Chrysostom: ὅταν δὲ λέγῃ, ὅτι ἡ αὔριον μεριμνήσει περὶ ἑαυτῆς, οὐχ ὡς τῆς ἡμέρας μεριμνώσης ταῦτά φησιν, ἀλλ' ἐπεὶ πρὸς δῆμον ἀτελέστερον ὁ λόγος ἦν αὐτῷ, βουλόμενος ἐμφατικώτερον ποιῆσαι τὸ λεγόμενον, προσωποποιεῖται τὸν καιρόν, κατὰ τὴν τῶν πολλῶν συνήθειαν φθεγγόμενος πρὸς αὐτούς. The genuinely Oriental character of such prosopopœia is shown by Schultens on Job iii. 3, and by Gesenius on Isa. viii. 23. Cod. B. G. L. S. read ἑαυτῆς merely, and after them (Cod. A. C. D. being here incomplete), Griesbach, Lachm., Tischend. adopt this reading. A few codices minores have ἑαυτήν, ἑαυτῇ, περὶ ἑαυτῆς: the Latin translations, ipse cogitabit, or ipse cogitabit sibi, or de se cogitabit. If τὰ ἑαυτῆς had been the original reading, these alterations would assuredly never have arisen. Yet there was occasion for them, for the construction of μεριμνᾶν with the Genitive, although not without analogy in the use of the language (Bernhardy, Syntax, S. 176), is not usual.—Κακία, evil, denotes not so much the μέριμνα itself, as that by which it is called forth. The Vulgate has malitia; on account of which, Augustine finds an allusion here to labour considered as penal; but Tertullian rendered it more correctly by vexatio: for even in the classics κακία, κακότης signify misfortune. Ἀρκετόν, adjective in the neuter, construed with feminine substantive, is "something sufficing:" in Latin also it is often so used, chiefly (according to Kühner griech. Gramm. ii. S. 45) in maxims and proverbs.

CHAPTER VII.

SUNDRY ADMONITIONS.

Vers. 1—12.

That there is no connection of thought to be traced in the first twelve verses of this chapter (comp. Introduction, p. 23), is admitted by the older commentators, Calvin, Bucer, Pellicanus, Chemnitz, Maldonatus, Jansenius, as well as by most recent writers. A few have indeed attempted to discover here a consecutive train of thought. According to Olshausen, the connecting idea of the passage is: "to set forth the character of the disciples of the Messiah in its peculiar features as in opposition to the prevailing ideas, in order that He might thus exhibit what is new and Divine in the revelation of the Gospel." But the same might be said, with equal truth, of many other sections of this discourse. Stier says, there is here a sudden but intentional transition from a reference to inward feelings, to a reference to outward demeanour. According to Baumgarten-Crusius, the object of our Lord in chap. vi. 1—18 was to rebuke hypocrisy; in vi. 19—34, to rebuke covetousness; while in this passage, vii. 1—12, He exposes the sin of arrogance. But, in the first place, the view here taken of vi. 19—34 is plainly incorrect, while in the seventh chap., vers. 7—11 have manifestly nothing to do with arrogance. Ewald thinks the object here is, that the Christian, having been instructed in the perfect religion, may be taught "to treat those who are less enlightened with a proper measure of reserve." Nor can it, on the other hand, be maintained, that here a different class of hearers is addressed. According to the author of the opus imperfectum, in vers.

1—6, Christ addresses Himself chiefly to the teachers, consequently the Apostles: this idea seems to have been suggested by ver. 6, which certainly has a special reference to the teachers of the truth. Yet must the isolated utterances which make up this section have found a place in the discourse as originally delivered, since at least vers. 1—15 occur in St Luke's account. If now we are to pronounce conjecturally upon the subject of this section of the sermon, we shall find a clue in the 12th verse, if we do not, with Ewald, displace it. (See p. 292.) That verse seems to bear the character of a final summary of one's duties towards one's neighbour: this, then, we may suppose to be the general subject of the section. With regard to ver. 5, although much in that verse also bears upon this subject, yet unquestionably it occurs there as a rebuke of pharisaic righteousness: vers. 7—11, however, belong to this subject; for they are to be regarded as a final reference to that source from whom alone the power to keep these commands proceeds.

Vers. 1, 2. These verses are not to be viewed apart. They form with vers. 3—5 one connected thought. It is self-evident that the prohibition of κρίνειν does not mean that we are never to pronounce upon the conduct of others: κρίνειν is expressly *required* where church-discipline is necessary, as we find in St Matt. xviii. 15—17; 1 Cor. v. 12. That what is meant here is a faulty judgment, is manifest from the fact that the words, ἐν ᾧ γὰρ κρίματι, κ.τ.λ., point to an unjust standard of judgment; and likewise from this, that in ver. 3 (τότε διαβλέψεις), in opposition to a wrong judgment, a right judgment is placed and authorized. The only question here is the lexical one, as to whether κρίνειν is to be taken as meaning judging with some other notio adjuncta, or whether we are to accept the meaning *condemning*. The former is held by Chrysostom: μὴ πικρὸς γένου δικαστής (with the addition, that our Lord is not speaking of gross transgressions); Bengel with this addition: sine scientia, amore, necessitate; Fritzsche: judicium *præceps, temerarium*; De Wette: "to judge; then, secondarily, to judge wilfully and unfairly, whilst we are ourselves faulty." Aug., Druthmar, Radbert, Gl. ord. obtain the idea of a judicium temerarium by confining the sphere of the judgment to the facta, quæ dubium est quo animo fiant, which ought to be interpreted in meliorem partem. Undoubtedly, in Rom. xiv. 13, St Paul speaks of a judging of those things which lie within the sphere of the *conscience* of each individual; but there is no ground thus to limit the judging spoken of in the text. These commentators, then, accept as the meaning of κρίνειν, to *judge*, while each superadds to this some one or other idea. But by far the majority of expositors prefer the meaning, **to condemn.** Gregory of Nyssa: Οὐ τὴν κρίσιν καὶ τὴν εὐγνωμοσύνην ἐκβάλλει· κρίσιν δὲ ὀνομάζει τὴν τραχυτέραν κατάκρισιν: Theophylact, Euthymius, Beza, Piscator, Olshausen. As judges are a φόβος τῶν κακῶν ἔργων, the idea of condemning and punishing always clings to the Hebrew שׁפט; and this idea likewise attaches to κρίνειν in the New Testament, St John iii. 19, v. 29; Rom. ii. 1, xiv. 3 (comp. Winer de verborum simpl. pro compositis in N. T. usu et causis, 1833, p. 19). That this is the meaning which the word here bears, will however appear doubtful, if we consider that St Luke (ver. 37) **has** both μὴ κρίνετε and μὴ καταδικάζετε, one after the other. Remembering this, it were better (with Paulus, Baumgarten-**Crusius,** and Meyer) to translate κρίνειν, to pronounce upon with judicial authority; comp. Cyrill in Luc.: φιλοψογίας ἀφορμὴν ποιεῖσθαι τὰς ἀσθενείας τῶν ἀδελφῶν. Then the admonition would be directed against setting oneself up as judge, against judging for the pleasure of judging. For in this is both temeritas and supercilium: the wise and humble Christian will never wish to become a judge of others without good cause. At the same time, where there is occasion, he may also judge: in such a case, this is not only permitted him, it is his prerogative as an enlightened Christian; indeed, the gift of the διάκρισις τῶν πνευμάτων is numbered among the special χαρίσματα, and proceeds from the inward working of the Spirit of God; 1 Cor. xii. 10, ii. 15; 1 John iv. 1; 2 John 10; 1 Thess. v. 21.

The clause ἵνα μὴ κριθῆτε and κριθήσεσθε is explained by Aug., Erasmus, Kuinöl, Paulus, Fritz., De Wette, as **referring to** human retribution. Augustine: temeritas, qua punis alium, eadem ipsa te puniat necesse est. It is certainly not to be interpreted as a rule of worldly policy, as by Paulus: "By judging others we expose ourselves to the cavils of every light and foolish talker;" but rather according to the law of moral reci**procity (ver. 12).** With this view St Luke (vi. 38) would accord, if, with Euthymius, we could understand his μέτρον καλὸν δώσουσιν εἰς τὸν κόλπον ὑμῶν of the εὐεργετηθέντες. But the idea of a return made by *God* for good done to men is constantly recurring in the New Testament; and Euthymius himself comes back to this when he says: τοῦ Θεοῦ γὰρ ἀποδιδόντος ὑπὲρ αὐτῶν αὐτοὶ δοκοῦσιν ἀποδιδόναι (comp. Luke xvi. 9). St Augustine quotes as a parallel expression Matt. xxvi. 5 (?); yet is the meaning there different from this. The Divine measure of judgment cannot, however, be made use of to *threaten;* for it corresponds to human judgment, not in the unrighteousness by which the latter is often marred, but in the severity of its retributive justice. Comp. the proverbial rabbinical phrase, מִדָּה כְּנֶגֶד מִדָּה, "one measure for another" (vid. Capellus); Hariri, Consessus iv., p. 38, ed. Schultens: وكلت للكيل كما كال لي على وفا الكيلي او بسعة, "I measure my friend as he measures me, with overflowing or with scanty measure;" St Mark iv. 24, in a different connection.—Ἐν is not "according to," but instrumental; for μέτρον is not the standard rule, but a dry measure: comp. St Luke, εἰς τὸν κόλπον ὑμῶν δώσουσιν.

Vers. 3—5. Reference to the way of judging common among men, viz., how each one has a much quicker eye for the faults of other than for his own. This meaning is evident, and has been expressed in numerous sayings of the ancients.[1] The figure used has not, however, been rightly understood by commentators, as they all, the most recent not excepted, have confined the simile to a comparison between a great fault and a small one. But if this were all, how should it happen that the small fault is compared to something in the brother's *eye?* How much more pointed would be a comparison like that which Seneca makes, de vita beata, c. 27: papulas observatis alienas, obsiti plurimis ulceribus.[2] The splinter in the eye denotes something which

---

[1] Comp. Grot., Priceus, Alberti, Wettstein, and Vorst (adagia N. T.) Menander: οὐδεὶς ἐφ' αὑτοῦ τὰ κακὰ συνορᾷ, Πάμφιλε, σαφῶς, ἑτέρου δ' ἀσχημονοῦντος ὄψεται. Sosicrates: ἀγαθοὶ δὲ τὸ κακόν ἐσμεν ἐφ' ἑτέρων ἰδεῖν, αὐτοὶ δ' ὅταν ποιῶμεν, οὐ γινώσκομεν.

[2] Ingenious, but subtle, is the remark of Erdmann in one of his sermons He notices that the splinter and the beam are of the same substance; by which, he thinks, it is intended to show that often a man is ready to blame another for the very fault with which he is most chargeable himself.

gives pain, but which the sufferer cannot himself take cognizance of; which he therefore requires to have pointed out to him by others, and from which he requires to be relieved by others. The beam is a cross-beam. In the Hamassa we read: "He saw my concealed poverty, and was as deeply moved at the discovery as *if he had seen a splinter in my eye*" (Freytag, Hamasæ carmina, T. ii., p. 541); repeatedly in Hariri; "the eyelids close on a splinter **therein**" (Consessus Hariri, ed. Schultens, cons. vi. 236). In **Kamus**, يقضي علي القذي, "he is silent about a splinter," *i.e.*, a slight injury (vid. Freytag, lex. Arab.). Again in the Bava Bathra we read (f. 15, 2): "In the days when the judges were judged themselves, said the judge to one of then: 'Take the splinter out of thine eye,' whereat he made reply: 'Take thou the beam out of thine eye.'" In Meidani (ed. Freytag, ii. c. 22, n. 115), we read, literally as in the Gospel: كيف تبصر القذي في عين اخيك و تدع لجذع المعتض في عينك, "How seest thou the splinter in thy brother's eye, **and seest noth the cross-beam in thine** eye? Samachschari has: "in thy throat." The same figure occurs again **in the** Hamassa (Freytag, as quoted, p. 483). From all this the meaning of our passage would be: "Wherefore art **thou** keen-sighted enough to **wish to** free thy brother from a painful fault, and knowest not that thou thyself art suffering the while from one much greater and more painful?" In the injunction ἄφες πρῶτον, however, is implied: This do, and leave not the other undone. This also is expressed in the proverb of the Gem. Sanhedrim, fol. 19, 1, where we find the same τότε followed by an imperative: אחר הוא לקיש קשוט עצמך ואחר כן קשוט אחרים, "Thus spake Resch Lakish, Trim thyself, and then begin to trim others." The Future, τότε διαβλέψεις, **is potential or permissive,** "then canst thou see clearly" (διαβλέπω occurs in this sense in Aristotle, De Somniis, c. 3, Plutarch, Alex. c. 14). Yet as both the κάρφος and the beam, but especially the latter, must hinder one from seeing, a question may occur as to whether there is not here some allusion to the mote and the **beam** as an obstacle to the vision, which must be removed ere it be possible to look into the other's eye. And this is the leading thought of the old writers in their exposition of the verse: an unamiable, fault-finding temper is, according to them, the splinter which must be removed.

St Augustine, followed by the Glossa ordinaris, says that the odium, conjoined with the censure of the man who falls into ira, is just such a *trabs:* for odium is defined *inveterata ira;* and where this disposition exists, no improvement of the offender can at all be anticipated. In the main, St Chrysostom's view is the same: he argues, that if one does not begin the judgment with himself, the rebuke will be administered without love, and therefore without effect: εἰ κηδόμενος ποιεῖς, σαυτοῦ κῆδου πρότερον—εἰ δὲ σαυτοῦ καταφρονεῖς, εὔδηλον ὅτι καὶ τὸν ἀδελφόν σου οὐ κηδόμενος κρίνεις ἀλλὰ μισῶν καὶ ἐκπομπεῦσαι βουλόμενος. So, too, Jansenius, Este, Erasmus: ut oculo judicamus ea, quae sunt corporis, ita animo judicamus ea, quae sunt animi. Proinde vitio careat oportet illud quo vitium alterius judicamus. Chemnitz: propria emendatio docebit, quomodo illa sit quaerenda et exaedificanda in proximo. So, after my example, Baumgarten-Crusius, von Gerlach, Stier. Further the circumstance, that a man cannot himself see the mote in his own eye, suggests an additional view of the text: "Wouldst thou be to others a master, and help to rid them of their faults, then first prove thy humility by suffering others to help to rid thee of thine." This idea is not, indeed, immediately and directly in the text. In all the many examples of the splinter in the eye in the Arabic, not one of them speaks of it as an obstruction to the sight, but only as a painful defect in the eye. The address of Christ, ὑποκριτά, which might seem to contain an allusion to this idea, refers only to dishonesty of intention in rendering the seeming service of love: the source of the reproof so administered being merely the love of finding fault. But although this meaning is not directly conveyed in the text, it is nevertheless indirectly implied: he who allows himself to be told by others of his evil tendencies, and strives to get the better of them when he knows them, will have a surer eye to mark the sins of others, and a milder tone to rebuke them.

Κατανοεῖν, to perceive, descry. Ἤ serves to combine connected ideas, and thus indicates here that the same thought is about to be enforced from another point of view (see ver. 9). The Future ἐρεῖς is poetical; ἐκβάλω, the conj. of encouragement, also in sing. (Kühner ii. S. 101); τότε διαβλέψεις is explained by Meyer (third ed.): The results of the improvement of self will be the wise endeavour to improve others.

But τότε διαβλέψεις can be regarded only as potential, as in St Matt. xii. 29, τότε διαρπάσει; St Luke xiv. 10, τότε ἔσται σοι δόξα; St John viii. 28, τότε γνώσεσθε.

Ver. 6. Several expositors think they can trace the connection between this verse and the preceding. According to some (Bengel, Olshausen, Stier), the discourse, from speaking of severe judging, passes to the other extreme of a too great laxity in judgment: according to others (Erasmus, Rus, Meyer), the exhortation implied in διαβλέψεις, to reprove faults, is here restricted. But it is impossible to determine the connection; as Bucer remarked: qua consequentia subjecta sint superioribus, non plane video. If the object of the verse were to offer either an antithesis to the preceding verses, or a limitation of them, we should certainly find this indicated by a particle.—There is no reason for restricting the verse to teachers or Apostles exclusively: as the auct. op. imp., Chemnitz, Maldonatus, and many others, would do,—they refer to chap. x. 14, and the apparently contradictory saying, chap. x. 27.

In our exposition we have first to determine what the character is which is here typically represented by two kinds of animals. Dogs and swine were often classed together in antiquity as unclean beasts. Horace, Ep. i. 2, 26: vixisset canis immundus vel amica luto sus; ii. 2, 75: hac rabiosa fugit canis, hac lutulenta ruit sus. Priapeia 84: canisque sæva susque ligneo tibi lutosus adfricabit luteum latus. In the Septuagint, 1 Kings xxi. 19, xxii. 38, we read: ἐξέλειξαν αἱ ὕες καὶ οἱ κύνες τὸ αἷμα αὐτοῦ καὶ αἱ πόρναι ἐλούσαντο ἐν τῷ αἵματι, κ.τ.λ. Comp. Prov. xxvi. 11; 2 Peter ii. 22. Besides, they were both counted unclean by the law, and are consequently mentioned in Scripture with contempt: 2 Sam. iii. 8, ix. 8; 2 Kings viii. 13; St Matt. xv. 26; Rev. xxii. 15; Prov. xi. 22; St. Luke xv. 15, 16. The predicates applied by the Greeks, Romans, Hebrews, and Arabians to the dog were: λοίδορος, ἀναιδής, ἰταμός, and to swine: ἀσελγής, ῥυπαρός, ἀκάθαρτος (comp. Bochart hieroz. ii. c. 56, 57; Wettstein on Phil. iii. 2; and Meidani Prov., ed. Freytag, iii. n. 789, 413). The question we have to determine is, Are those animals used here as typical of two different characters, and as denoting, accordingly, two different classes of men? The affirmative is the opinion

26

generally held. The distinction made by St Chrysostom is, that one animal denotes unbelievers, the other unworthy Christians; κύνας τοὺς ἐν ἀσεβείᾳ ζῶντας ἠνίατῳ ..... ᾐνίξατο, καὶ χοίρους τοὺς ἐν ἀκολάστῳ βίῳ διατρίβοντας; Isidorus Pelus. lib. i. cap. 143, Euthymius, Theophylact, Grotius. Origen in Josuam ii. 447: qui fidei nostræ secretioribus scrutatis, conversi postmodum impugnant nos. Jerome: quidam per canes eos intelligi volunt, qui post fidem Christi revertuntur ad vomitum peccatorum suorum, porcos autem eos, qui necdum crediderunt. Hilary: canes, gentes; porci, hæretici, quia acceptam Dei cognitionem non ruminando disponunt. Augustin: canes pro oppugnatoribus veritatis, porcos pro contemtoribus. Erasm.: canis profanum animal, sus immundum. When the animals are thus distinguished, a distinction is also supposed to be implied in the account of their treatment of the gift. Thus by the dogs, which in the East are wild beasts (see Commentary on Ps. xxii. 16), furious persecutors would be denoted, who, when the holy thing is presented to them, tear the gift to pieces: by the swine, again, such as fall away into lust, and drag the gift into the mud. In defence of this exposition, an appeal is made to the form of speech which goes by the name ἐπάνοδος or ὑστέρησις, according to which, when two connected verbs occur, preceded by two connected nouns, the first verb does not relate to the first of the nouns (as is usually the case), but to the second, and the second verb to the first noun. In support of this construction, Matt. xii. 12 is quoted (see Wolf, Hammond); but the case is different there. For there nouns and verbs are connected in one clause, whereas here they form two distinct clauses: certainly, were this distinction intended here, we should expect ἢ στραφέντες instead of καὶ στραφέντες. If the clause καὶ στραφέντες κ.τ.λ., can possibly be referred to the last subject, then to it, it must of necessity be referred, because the other construction has something forced about it. Now it not only may, but can most naturally, be referred to the χοῖροι. Στραφέντες is precisely the word which vividly depicts the attach of the boar [1] (verres et aper); or, if this be not what it is intended to describe, then it depicts the conduct of the boar towards the gift, to which follow the ῥήξωσιν ὑμᾶς, describing

---

[1] Horace, carm. iii. 22: verres *obliquum* meditans ictum. Ovid. Heroid. iv. 154: obliquo dente timendus aper (comp. Plautus, Trucul. ii. 2, 13).

his demeanour towards the giver. The picture is perfectly natural: the brute sees the gift which has been thrown to him, and treads it forthwith under foot; then, seeing that he has been deceived, he turns him to *the side,* and rushes at the giver. But while these verbs apply perfectly to the boar, they do not so well correspond to the dog: it is not common to represent that animal as the type of the ravenous destroyer. In Jer. xv. 3, dogs are indeed threatened as a plague, but then it is that they may tear in pieces dead bodies: in the Bible, **as in classical** usage, the dog is the type of ἀναισχυντία, while the emblem **of** the furious persecutor is rather the wolf (ver. 15). But is it likely that wild boars are meant here? is it not more natural to understand by χοῖροι domestic swine than the wild animals of the desert? Now the word itself may easily mean tame animals; for even these, especially when fed on acorns in the wood, acquire a certain wildness, which **renders** them sometimes dangerous, not only to dogs, **but to men.** But here the χοῖροι must denote wild swine, because that with the Jews the rearing of swine was quite unknown: dogs were occasionally domestic animals; swine never. In the Mischna Bava Cana, **c. vii. 7,** we read; "No man may rear a dog except he fasten **him by a** chain: swine a Jew may never rear." In Galilee, too, among people not Jews, the pig was never domesticated, whereas wild swine are still very common in Palestine (Robinson, iii. 39, 456). More accurate usage would no doubt **have** required σῦς ἄγριος here: yet χοῖροι and σῦς **include both** kinds. Thomas M. s. v. χοῖροι; Aelian, hist. animal. vii. 47; and in Ps. lxxx. 13, **where the boar of the wood is** spoken of, the LXX. **have translated by** χοῖρος.

According to Chrysost., Euthym., Grotius, Hammond, Lösner, στραφέντες is to be taken here as equivalent to μετενεχθέντες, μεταβληθέντες: "suddenly become wild, they tear." Euth.: εἶτα στραφέντες ἀπὸ τῆς ἐπιπλάστου ἐπιεικείας εἰς φανερὰν ἐναντίωσιν. According **to** this view, hypocritical men are meant here, who show the disposition of a lamb before they have been introduced into the Sanctum of Christianity, but, once admitted there, **they** becomes wolves: and in this sense the sentence was applied to heretics. To this view Fritzsche opposes the observation, that then the word would have been τραπέντες; but στρέφεσθαι occurs in Hellenistic Greek as a translation of הפך, in its secondary meaning of *to change one's mind*, in Lam. v. 15; Isa. xxxiv. 9; Ps. xxx. 11; Exod. vii. 15; Rev. xi. 6. Yet this view must be rejected: it agrees neither with the figurative nor with the strict sense of the passage;—not with the figurative, for those animals are not supposed to be first seized with a disposition to tear and destroy when the gifts have been thrown to them; not with the strict sense, as denoting profane men, for it is far from true that they appear friendly before the Holy is presented to them.

We come now to speak of the gift itself: and here we begin with the second clause as the most explicit of the two. Μαργαρῖται is here used in its ordinary acceptation, viz., something of value (St Matt. xiii. 45); specially, in the East, precious, valuable discourses (Gesenius, in Rosenmüller's Repertorium i. 128). The ἡμῶν annexed to it might lead us to infer that the word is here used in a secondary (metaphorical) sense; but if this were true of μαργαρῖται, it must be likewise the case with regard to χοῖροι: this, however, is not so, for the predicates show that the animals here are to be taken really as such. Βάλλειν seems to hint that it is *food* that is thrown. Hence we must assume that there is some resemblance between what is thrown to them and the ordinary food auf the animals, and to hold that the reason why pearls are here chosen, is because they are somewhat similar to the common meat of swine, to wit, peas and acorns. Nor need it cause surprise that the figure should be so exact, if we remember how in Matt. xiii. 22, Luke viii. 14, the μέριμναι καὶ ἡδοναὶ τοῦ βίου are used to denote *thorns,* because by them people prick themselves; or how, in vers. 9, 10, the stone resembles bread, the fish a serpent; or, again, the comparison in ver. 16.—The generally received explanation of τὸ ἅγιον is that which takes it abstractly for "the holy:" hence the ecclesiastical apophthegm, τὰ ἅγια τοῖς ἁγίοις: hence too the circumstance, that the Fathers, in their quotations of the passage, use τὰ ἅγια much oftener than the singular (Griesbach quotes only Origen and Chrysostom; but see also, *e.g.,* Theodoret, Opp. i. 1049, 1441, ii. 1300, and even in the MSS. of the Vulgate). But if χοῖροι is not to be regarded as a *direct* predicate of men whom it figuratively characterizes, then neither is this the case with κύνες, and τὸ ἅγιον does not *directly* denote spiritual holy things. Rather should we expect to find that the precious thing, parallel to the μαργαρίται, would have some resemblance with the food of dogs. Michaelis was the first to whom it occurred that there might be here a mistake in the translation from the Aramaic. His idea was, that Christ used the word קְדָשָׁא, which means an *amulet*, or specially an *ear-ring*. This word the translator is supposed to have confounded with the more common word, and rendered by τὸ ἅγιον. Similarly Eichhorn, Bertholdt, Bolten, and Kuinoel. This is **unquestionably the meaning of the word in Aramaic, as Gesenius shows on Isa. iii. 20; also in the Sama**ritan the allied word ꟿꝗꝙP occurs in the sense of ear-ring. But to suppose a mistake in the translation, is always a precarious proceeding. Besides, if we adopt an error in translating, we must also suppose an error in the transcribing: for ear-ring is קְדָשָׁא, קְדָשָׁא, קַדַּשָׁא, קַדִּישָׁא, in Syriac ܩܕܫܐ, whereas the Holy is קְדוּשָׁא, הַקְדֵשׁ, ܩܘܕܫܐ. Moreover, if ear-ring had been the word intended, Christ would not have employed the singular, but the plural, which could not be misunderstood. And finally, we have not sufficient proof that ear-rings were used as proverbially as pearls and precious stones to denote a thing of value,—the passage quoted from Prov. xi. 22 cannot prove this.

Now, however, the two clauses are not so formally balanced as to warrant us in expecting that what is mentioned in the first, will be a thing of value corresponding to the μαργαρίται in the second. All we shall **expect is, a word denoting food given to dogs which has some connection with holy things**. Now animal food is of this nature. Flesh is "cast to the dogs," Exod. xxii. 31. Hence τὸ ἅγιον is explained by Herm. von der Hardt to mean **sacrificial meat (Tempe anecdota sacra, ed. Winkler. Halæ 1758, p. 483)**. This view is elaborately defended in the Tempe of Helvetius, **1736, T. ii. p. 271**; likewise by Paulus. In Hebrew, קֹדֶשׁ signifies everything consecrated to the service of the sanctuary, **especially** the flesh offered in sacrifice: Lev. xxii. 2—7, בְּשַׂר קֹדֶשׁ in Jer. xi. 15, Hag. ii. 12. In the rabbinical writings certain sacrifices are called קָדְשֵׁי קָדָשִׁים (see Buxt. Lex. Talm. p. 1980, Tract. Schekalim, ed. Wülfer, p. 166). Any priest who would have dared to throw to the unclean beast the meat of sacrifice consecrated to God, had been doomed to death! Certainly, according to this view of the τὸ ἅγιον, we could not regard the ῥήξωσι (and the καταπατεῖν as little) as relating to the dogs; for the sacred meat would have been to them welcome food, as well as any other: we must therefore take the clause μὴ δῶτε τὸ ἅγιον τοῖς κυσί entirely by itself. The idea here expressed is accordingly: "Give not that which is holy to him who is unworthy of it." This thought is further expanded in the second clause, which points out the demeanour of the unworthy recipient alike towards the gift and the giver. The gift is despised, and, because its value is not appreciated, the giver is maltreated. All the less reason have we now to regard the two species of animals mentioned as representing two distinct classes of character. Both of them are examples of ἀναισχυντία, as the two are placed together in this sense in the passages quoted above.

Having thus explained the figure, let us now inquire into its meaning. There is no difficulty about the general idea. Even the Pythagoreans taught, μὴ εἶναι πρὸς πάντας πάντα ῥητά, Diog. Laert. L. viii. c. 15; figuratively, σιτίον εἰς ἀμίδα μὴ ἐμβάλλειν; and in this sense we read in the γνῶμαι πυθαγορικαί of Demophilus, in Gale's Opuscula mytholog. p. 623: λόγον περὶ Θεοῦ τοῖς ὑπὸ δόξης διεφθαρμένοις λέγειν, οὐκ ἀσφαλές· καὶ γὰρ τἀληθῆ λέγειν ἐπὶ τούτων καὶ τὰ ψευδῆ, κίνδυνον φέρει. And the word of the text were frequently interpreted in this Pythagorean acceptation, from which arose the distinction of the Esoterics and Exoterics, in the time when the doctrine of the disciplina arcani was in vogue in the Church. Tertullian, quoting our passage, blames the heretics for making no distinction between catechumeni and fideles (de præscript. hæret. c. 41). Alluding to this passage, Clement of Alexandria says (Strom. i. 348, Pott.): τοὺς περὶ τοῦ φωτὸς καθαροῖς ὄντως καὶ διαυγεῖς ἐπιδεῖξαι λόγοις ἀκροατῶν τοῖς ῥυθμοῖς τε καὶ ἀπαιδεύτοις. In the Treatise de Trinitate (by Theodoret, according to Garnier; according to Combefisius, by Maximus): τὸ μὲν γὰρ εἰπεῖν, ὅτι Χριστοῦ δοῦλός εἰμι, ἀναγκαῖον εἰπεῖν· τὸ δέ, τί ἐστιν ὁ χριστιανισμός, οὐκ ἀσφαλές, ἐὰν μὴ γνῶ, τίς ἐστιν ὁ ἐρωτῶν, μήποτε εὑρεθῶ βάλλων τὰ ἅγια τοῖς κυσὶν ἢ τοὺς μαργαρίτας ἔμπροσθεν τῶν χοίρων. Comp. Suicer Thes. T. ii. 301. By Roman Catholic theologians the text was used to justify the withholding of the Bible from the laity! (vid. Quenstedt, Theol. polem.-didact.

i. 225). Grotius understands also the ἅγια to mean the *interiora praecepta sapientiæ Christi*: Vitringa takes them to mean the allegorical interpretations (Obs. Sacræ, L. vi. c. 20, § 7). Many of the Fathers comprehended in the term not only the higher doctrine, but also the sacrament of the Supper, which in church-language was called τὰ ἅγια or τὰ ἅγια τῶν ἁγίων (vide Suicer, as above, and Fabricius, Cod. apocr. v. T. i. 566).

If we are to confine ἅγιον and μαργαρῖται to the Christian mysteries, it will be most natural to understand by them (along with Christ. Starke and Olshausen) the doctrine proper of salvation as taught in the Gospel, comparing our passage with St Matt. xiii. 46: to communicate this doctrine before the preaching of repentance has preceded, awaking the feeling of a need of redemption, is always dangerous. Bull.: valeat *admonitio* atque *increpatio* inter fratres et eos quoque, qui nondum sese Satanæ totos dediderunt (2 Tim. ii. 25). Thus it is observed by J. Wesley, a preacher who was himself undaunted before these very dogs and swine (Explanatory Notes to the New Testament): "But our Lord forbids us in no wise to *reprove,* as occasion is, both the one and the other." The Holy and the Pearls he explains, however, to be the deep things of God, such as perfection; and the great things of God, such as one's own experience. Similarly, Bengel acutely remarks: ἐμῶν, antithetum implicitum: sanctum res *Dei,* margaritæ *fidelium,* quæ his a Deo **committuntur** *secreta* **bona**. But this is more allegory than exposition.

But as regards this whole explanation, we may well ask, what right there is to limit in this way τὸ ἅγιον and οἱ μαργαρῖται? The pearls are not the same with that *one* pearl of great price, spoken of in Matt. xiii. 49, as the more general expression, τὸ ἅγιον, sufficiently shows. In 2 Peter ii. 22, it is said of those who are there called κύνες and ὕες, that it had been better for them **never** to have known the ἁγία ἐντολή; and parallel to that occurs the more general expression, ὁδὸς δικαιοσύνης, and surely that expression must include under it μετάνοια. In Mark xvi. 15; Matt. x. 27; 2 Tim. iv. 2, the command is given to preach the Gospel to every one without distinction; and the Gospel there spoken of is evidently the Gospel in its narrower sense. On the other hand, it cannot be said even of the preaching of repentance, that it is to be addressed to every one without distinction, at all times, or in any circumstances. To confine, with Bengel, the exhortation to quotidiana conversatio—publice cum talia proponuntur, leviter isti transeunt, is an arbitrary restriction: nor could we expect such an admonition in an address to *Apostles*. The interpretatio which deserves preference is that which obtained in the Older Protestant Church, and which is thus expressed by Pellican: *quando autem et quibus loquendum verbum Dei incremento gloriæ Dei, nemo sine spiritu patris recte intelliget.* According to Zwingly, Luther, Calvin, Chemnitz, Rus, it is only from the *effects* of the preaching that we are to decide who are the dogs and the swine; Luther: "Because they trample the pearls under their feet, we take back our pearls." It is impossible to determine a priori, even concerning the most depraved, that he is among the κύνες and χοῖροι in Christ's sense: from the depths even of the most abandoned soul a confession may be wrung, like that of the thief on the cross. The man's treatment of the Divine gift conveyed to him, alone can determine whether he belongs to the κύνες and χοῖροι; and only after we have seen his treatment of it, can we decide whether the Divine truths are to be further communicated to him, or whether, proving impenitent and insensible, he is to be abandoned to the judgment of spiritual hardening, according to the words, "He that hath not, from him shall be taken even that he hath." That this is the sense in which we are to understand the words of Christ, is confirmed by a reference to St Matt. x. 12—14, where it is said that the salutation of peace is to be given even to the unworthy, and only when the message is rejected, is the hardened man to be left self-condemned: for St Paul says of such, that by not receiving the repeated admonition they are αὐτοκατάκριτοι (Titus iii. 11; Acts xiii. 46. As parallel passages may be compared Prov. ix. 6, xxiii. 9).

Vers. 7, 8. The exhortation contained in these verses is regarded by several expositors as a direction as to the way in which this peculiar wisdom is to be obtained (Chrysostom, Augustine, Luther, Stier). It is, however, rather to be regarded (as formerly hinted, p. 396) as a final admonition, as to how men may attain strenght to fulfil their duties towards their neighbours.—In practical application, αἰτεῖτε frequently relates to prayer, ζητεῖτε to one's own exertions, κρούετε to careful reflection on the Scriptures. St Augustine, with stricter reference of the words to the preceding commands, understands αἰτεῖτε to mean a desire for strength, ζητεῖτε of the needful wisdom. In the Retractation his exegesis is more correct; operose quidem tria ista, quid inter se differant, exponendum putavi, sed longe melius ad *instantissimam petitionem* omnia referuntur (comp. Bengel). There is here a climax: ζητεῖν is the earnest longing (like בקשׁ Jer. xxix. 13, 14); κρούειν is the patient waiting, even when the petition seems denied (St Luke xiii. 25). Chrys.: ἀπὸ δὲ τοῦ κρούειν τὸ μετὰ σφοδρότητος προσιέναι κ. μετὰ θερμῆς διανοίας ἐδήλωσε—παραμένειν δεῖ, κἂν εὐθέως μὴ ἀνοίξῃ τὴν θύραν. De Wette: "Yet in the two last sayings the thought is obscurely implied, that the desire of prayer is not passive merely, but active."—Of course the promise is given under certain conditions and presuppositions (comp. Melanchthon in loco). For in other similar promises, the answering of our petitions is expressly connected with conditions; for instance, that the prayer be offered in the name of Christ, in faith, and with a clear conscience (Matt. xxi. 22; Mark xi. 24; John xiv. 13, xv. 7, xvi. 23, 24; 1 John iii. 22; James i. 6). The condition as respects him who prays is, that he pray with a right disposition: the condition as regards his prayer (which indeed is implied in the former) is, that he pray for right things. The central point of all prayer is to be found in this: "Thy kingdom come." This is the highest good, and all other things are subordinate in excellence to this: consequently, when other things are asked, it must only be as means towards this end; and if one blessing is asked as a means to this end, it may be refused, that one more conducive to the end may bestowed. St Augustine says (ep. xxxiv. ad Paulinum): bonus autem dominus, qui non tribuit sæpe quod volumus, ut quod mallemus, attribuat; and of this truth his own life supplies a most striking illustration. Monica, dreading the persecutions which were then threatening the metropolis, prayed to God that He would not suffer her son to go to Rome: he went notwithstanding, and it was in Italy that he found Christ: quid a te petebat, Deus meus, tantis lacrymis, nisi ut navigare me non sineres? Sed tu alte consulens, et exaudiens *cardinem desiderii ejus,* non curasti, quod tunc petebat, ut in me faceres, quod semper petebat (Confess. L. v. c. 15).

Vers. 9—11. The promise is confirmed by a comparison. Τίς ἐστιν—μὴ λίθον, κ.τ.λ., comprehends a twofold question, viz.: "Who is the man who would give?" and, "if one were asked, yet would he not give?" (comp. Luke xi. 11; Winer, 6 ed. S. 454). Ἄνθρωπος is not a pleonasm here, any more than in Luke ii. 15, as Elsner maintains; on the contrary, it serves to place the human father, characterized as πονηρός, in contrast to God. Stier remarks: This saying appears to me the strongest dictum probans of original sin in the whole Bible, while it is at the same time one of the attestations of the superhuman excellence of the Saviour, who could thus stand out from the whole human race and say to them, Ye are evil (John viii. 23, 24). For although, by the word, ye being evil, the Lord addressed, doubtless, those who were fathers among His hearers, still it was simply as ἄνθρωποι that He so characterized them. And who, reflecting on the whole impression of Christ's sayings, could for a moment expect to hear from Him ἡμεῖς πονηροὶ ὄντες? Episcopius proposes the milder expression, etiamsi mali essetis.

Οἴδατε, according to Bengel, in the strict sense of to *understand:* discriminantes panem a lapide etc., mirum est mansisse in nobis hanc *intelligentiam;* so, too, Meyer. But even in Homer (comp. Passow) οἶδα means to know, so that it implies the capacity (as Luke xii. 56; Phil. iv. 12). It is man's natural φιλοστοργία which gives him this insight and this capacity.

Here, again, we find in St Luke a later form of Christian tradition (see Introduction, p. 6, 7), which marks him as a follower of St Paul; viz., he has (ver. 13) the more precise τὸ πνεῦμα ἅγιον instead of the more general δόματα ἀγαθά.—In opposition to the ὑμεῖς πονηροὶ ὄντες is the πατὴρ οὐράνιος. Luther observes: "And had we none other call or reason (to pray) but this rich gracious saying, it had of itself been sufficient to drive us to prayer: not to say how graciously He exhorts us, and how greatly we require it." The comparison holds even to the minutest details: the bread bears some resemblance to the stone (which cannot be eaten), and the fish to the serpent (which is deadly).[1] And if from the relation of man to God, as His child, it follows that He will not give a stone to him who asks for bread, then we may also conclude that the converse holds good, and that He will not give a stone to him who asks for a stone. St. Luke (xi. 12) has in addition the contrast of an egg and a scorpion (here, too, if we speak of the contracted scorpion, there is a certain external similarity), which suggests the able remark of St Augustine: the *fish,*—that is, *faith* amid the stormy billows of this life; bread,—that is, the nourishing power of *love;* an egg,—that is, the believing *hope* which anticipates the future.

Ver. 12. Πάντα οὖν ὅσα, κ.τ.λ.—On the force of οὖν in this passage very different opinions have been held. Wolzogen regards it as superfluous: vocula *ergo* nullam hic vim habet inferendi, sed redundat. According to the auctor op. imp., οὖν refers back to ver. 1; according to St Augustine, to ζητεῖν, which he had explained to mean firmiter ambulare per sapientiæ viam. Przipcov, who interprets the preceding exhortation to prayer as an exhortation to love God above all things, thinks that this is succeeded in our text by the command to love to neighbour. According to St Chrysostom, οὖν introduces here one of the conditions of prayer being heard: τὸ γὰρ οὖν τοῦτο οὐχ ἁπλῶς προσέθηκεν, ἀλλ᾽ αἰνιττόμενος. εἰ βούλεσθέ, φησιν, ἀκούεσθαι, μετ᾽ ἐκείνων, ὧν εἶπον, καὶ ταῦτα ποιεῖτε, whereas, according to St Paul, the love of man flows rather from the love of God. According to Kuinoel, Neander, and Baumgarten-Crusius, it refers to vers. 1—5: "In this way ye are to prove yourselves, lest ye belong to that class of hypocrites: by putting yourselves in the place of others." Luther regards the verse as forming a summary of the whole preceding discourse: "With these words He concludes the exposition of His doctrine set forth in these three chapters, and gathers them all up in a little bundle, that each man may take and put in his bosom, and keep easily." Similarly De Wette, Stier. But as in chaps. v. vi. men are not viewed so much in relation to their fellow-men as in their relation to God, this general sentence will be better interpreted as having a comprehensive reference only to the preceding part

---

[1] Comp. Matt. iv. 3. Phædrus: qui me saxo petierint, quis panem dederit. Plautus: altera manu fert lapidem, panem ostendit altera.

of this seventh chapter (vide 396). At the close of chap. v. the οὖν in ver. 48 has also, as we have seen, been regarded by many as similarly comprehensive and conclusive.

The maxim which the Saviour gives as the sum of His injunctions touching the love of our neighbour, flows, as He explains, from the whole of the Old Testament, which is substantially based upon the command to love God and man: Matt. xxii. 40. Euth.: ὅπερ ταὐτόν ἐστι τῷ ἀγαπᾶν τὸν πλησίον ὡς ἑαυτόν. If love is truth to *oneself*, if it is the finding of oneself anew in others, then he who loveth does to the other what he wishes that other to do unto him; wherefore love is said by St Paul to be the πλήρωμα of the law, Rom. xiii. 10. The reply is well known which Hillel the Jew gave to one who wished to embrace the Jewish religion, and who made this the condition of his proselytism: "Teach me the law while I stand on one foot": "What thou hatest thyself, that do not thou to another: זה היא כל התורה כלה ואידך פירושא הוא זיל גמור, that is the whole of the law, all the rest is only a comment on it" (Schabbath, f. 31, 1). Incorrectly, therefore, has this command been extolled as a peculiar excellence of the "doctrine of Jesus." Gibbon (Decline, chap. liv. note 36) after expending his indignation on the condemnation of Servetus, adds: "Calvin violated the golden rule of doing as he would be done by; a rule which I read in a moral treatise of Isocrates (in Nicocles, tom. i. p. 93), four hundred years before the publication of the Gospel: Ἃ πάσχοντες ὑφ᾽ ἑτέρων ὀργίζεσθε, ταῦτα τοῖς ἄλλοις μὴ ποιεῖτε." And undoubtedly there are many parallels to be found besides this (see Grotius, Wettst., Pricaeus, Alberti, and Tobit iv. 16). Yet, where love is not, the command is not worth much. The egotist who, absorbed with his own concerns, makes no claim upon the interest of his neighbour, will be satisfied with but feeble manifestations of affection. And in its negative form still more, the saying may become merely the maxim of egoistic self-love, thus: "What thou wilt not have done to thee, see thou do it not to others;"—and it is noteworthy that in *all* the parallel sayings from the classics and the rabbinical writings, like that just quoted from Isocrates, there is to be found the *negative* expression: comp. Tob. iv. 16, ὃ μισεῖς, μηδενὶ ποιήσῃς. Nowhere is this egoism more freely expressed than in that epitaph which Wettstein unsuspiciously quotes among his parallels: Apusulena Geria vixi an. xxii., quod quisque vestrum optaverit mihi, illi semper eveniat vivo et mortuo. The true depth and the full import of this saying of Christ can accordingly be apprehended, only when he who receives it has been already filled with that spirit which can be happy only when it enjoys the devoted love of others. In other words: the full apprehension of the maxim requires Christian *faith*.

Epilogue.—Vers. 13—27.

It is easy to perceive that the Sermon is approaching towards its close. Luther: "Our blessed Lord, having now finished His discourse, **adds a few** warnings to arm us against every obstacle and difficulty."

Vers. 13, 14. Injunction to follow the way which He has pointed out, difficult as it is.

Vers. 15—20. Warning against false teachers, who seek to lead astray from that way.

Vers. 21—27. How that nothing but a unity of the will with God manifested in the conduct of our life, can secure us an entrance into the kingdom of God.

Vers. 13, 14. The $δικαιοσύνη$ which conducts to the final goal of all man's efforts, to $ζωή$ (Lev. xviii. 5), had been exhibited, in this discourse, before the disciples in severer colours than they had ever been taught to view it before: all the more needful, then, was the admonition not to allow this severity of its aspect to drive them from its pursuit. These verses accordingly come in here in their proper place, as Neander admits (Leben Jesu, 404, 5. Aufl.), and even Schleiermacher does not assail their position. In St Luke, however (xiii. 24), the thought occurs in a different connection, but, at the **same** time, also with a somewhat modified application.

Life was even in the law the final end presented to the obedient (Lev. xviii. 5). It is one of those Old Testament conceptions which amplify and expand as the revelation proceeds, acquiring ever a deeper and more spiritual significance; and still for us the word (regarded as $ἡ\ ὄντως\ ζωή$ [1 Tim. vi. 19]) is the most adequate expression of absolute contentment and repose. *Life* is the unimpeded development of a nature, in accordance with its indwelling principle. Wherever there is this free unfolding of a nature, there is harmony, peace, and blessedness (see Commentary on Romans, S. 220, 5. Aufl.). In the progressive development of Judaism in Palestine, the promise of life which Moses had given, had in the time of our Lord already come to be apprehended as a promise of *eternal* life. When Onkelos translates בְּחַיֵּי עָלְמָא, Jonathan adds: הֻלְקְהֵיהּ עִם צַדִּיקַיָּא, "and his portion will be with the righteous." In this sense the young man we read of in St Matt. xix. 16 said, ἵνα ἔχω ζωὴν αἰώνιον. That by the life spoken of in our text is also meant the future perfection of life in the other world, is shown by the opposite ἀπώλεια, and likewise from the parable of the virgins in St Luke xiii. 24.

A question may be raised, as to whether the *gate* and the *way* represent different ideas. According to Bengel and Meyer, the *gate* mentioned is supposed to stand at the entrance of the *way:* the gate accordingly represents the beginning, the way the continuation, of the journey. But paths enclosed by gates (as may be found in pleasure-grounds) are comparatively rare: more commonly, the kingdom of heaven is compared to a palace or a city (Rev. xxii. 14; St Matt. xvi. 18); also in the passage in St Luke (xiii. 25) the θύρα is the θύρα τῆς βασιλείας τοῦ Θεοῦ. The exposition of Calov is not more correct: the way he would explain as the way of life spoken of v. 25, the gate (and this is also the opinion of Maldonatus) as the end of life; but when life is ended, it were surely too late to solve the problem of life. Some, taking a new view of the whole teaching of the passage, thought they must explain the strait gate to mean the gate of faith. Thus, in fact, did Sarcerius, whose idea is, that the strait gate is the evangelium, the broad the lex operum! And Gerhard: angusta salutis porta, quia ostium est solus Christus, a maxima hominum parte spretus (loci tom. xx. 519). According to Grotius, the straitness of the gate and narrowness of the way, and the wideness of the gate and breadth of the way, denote different ideas: the strait gate referring to the *self-denial,* the narrow way to the *difficulties,* of a Christian life: the way might be broad and yet not εὐρύχωρος, which means level, smooth, the antithesis to which here is τεθλιμμένη, via confragosa, an uneven way; but not only is the way narrow, it is also rough. But all that the predicate τεθλιμμένη is meant to say is, that the way is narrow. Beza would interpret τεθλιμμένη metaphorically for θλίβουσα, causing θλίψεις: but this interpretation the parallel word εὐρύχωρος renders inadmissible.

The large majority of commentators, as Jerome, Chrysostom, Clem. Alex., Este, Er., Hunnius and recent writers, maintain that the two figures contain but *one* thought. The *meaning* of the figurative expression is to be found indicated even in the Mosaic admonition to "turn neither to the *right hand* nor to *the left*" (Deut. v. 32; Prov. iv. 27; Isa. xxx. 21); it is this: the commandments are severe in order that they may curb the caprice of human self-will. Clem. Alex. Strom. v. 664: τὴν στενήν, τὴν κατὰ τὰς ἐντολὰς κ. ἀπαγορεύσεις περιεσταλμένην. Hence the self-denial represented as necessary in those who follow this way, while those who are on the broad way wander along unencumbered, Luke vi. 25; Wisdom ii. 6—9. Doubtless there is also some allusion here to the enmity of the world against the followers of Christ, and the effects of its hostility (Acts xiv. 22; John vii. 7).—Not only is it said that there are few who walk in the narrow way, but that "few there be that *find* it." Gl. ord.: si pauci inveniunt, pauciores per eam intrare contendant. For, from the narrowness of the entrance, and the small number of those who go in thereat, the way is unobserved by the multitude; and the little that is known of it is not liked, and deters men from entering it; whereas the many passengers crowding down the other broad highway, entice others to follow them. Justly remarks the Gl. ord. of the via lata: hanc etsi non quaerant, omnes tamen inveniunt, *quia in ea nati*.

Εἰσέρχεσθαι occurs here, as in Rom. xi. 25, without any determining clause: this is explained by the fact that cognate forms of expression were well known, such as εἰσελθεῖν εἰς τὴν βασιλ., Matt. xix. 23, Luke xviii. 17, John iii. 5; εἰς τὴν χάραν, Matt. xxv. 21, 23.—Ὅτι, ver. 13, gives the ground of the exhortation, taken a ratione contraria.—Ver. 14. Τί is read, instead of the ὅτι of the Recept., by Cod. B. second hand (A. D. are imperfect), C.E.G.K.L.M.S.U.V.Δ., Pesch., Vulg., Ulf., Arabic Pol., Persian Wheloc.[1] Beza: quia tamen in codd. *impressis* legimus ὅτι, nihil mutandum putavi. In favour of ὅτι, there is only, among the codices, Cod. B first hand: a second hand has struck out the ὁ of the ὅτι—comp. Birch, prol. to the quatuor

---

[1] The testimony of the Ethiopic comes in here, which has *valde angusta*: Suidas explains τί καλή ἡ τάξις by λίαν.

Evangel. p. xv.; of translations, the Memphitic (the Sahidic, on the contrary, has τί, see ed. Schwartz) and the Armenian. Some codices have καὶ τί, others τί: these Luther follows. External authority seems therefore to decide for τί. Internal arguments, however, are in favour of ὅτι. Tischendorf also retains it (2d Ed.). If retained, it must be translated by *sed*, in accordance with the Hebrew כִּי אִם (de Dieu, Bengel, Kuinöl). It is not desirable, though this is commonly done, to attach the second ὅτι to πολλοί εἰσιν εἰσερχόμενοι διὰ τῆς πλατείας, in a subordinate relation. For then would this 14th verse hold a too subordinate position to ver. 13, although the thought it contains is in no respect less forcible and emphatic. On the other hand, to understand ὅτι in the sense of *and*, as those codices do which here have καί, is perfectly justifiable on philological grounds. This classical use of γάρ is well known: a second clause following the conditional clause is introduced by a second γάρ, where *we* should carry on the construction with *and*; comp. above, vi. 32; James i. 6, 7, according to Fritzsche. There is the same use of the Hebrew כִּי; where as double כִּי, it means *then* (strictly, *because*, see Ewald, Lehrbuch, 5. Aufl. §. 340 a.) and *and:* of which Gesenius quotes the following examples: Isa. vi. 5, i. 29, 30, iii. 1, 6, ix. 3—5; Job iii. 24, 25, viii. 9, etc.

On the other hand, the reading τί affords no suitable sense. It is no doubt philologically true that τί, like the Hebrew מָה, is used in Hellenistic Greek for ὡς (LXX., 2 Sam. vi. 20; Cantic. vii. 6; Luke xii. 49). If it were so used here, the passage would form one of those rare utterances of Christ which, in the form of expression, disclose deep emotion (as elsewhere Mark ix. 19; Luke xii. 49; Matt. xi. 25). But when we consider that the preceding clause has given expression to the same thought without any exclamation of this kind, we must admit that it would appear strange and abrupt if the Saviour thus expressed Himself in this repetition of it. Surely, if in uttering this thought the Lord was moved, we should rather expect to find τί instead of the *first* ὅτι. And even then there would not present itself a sufficient reason for such emotion. It could not have arisen from a feeling of surprise at the rigour of the Divine law: this is as little probable as the notion that in St Matt. xxvii. 46 the ἱνατί is a question addressed to Fate. The only other possible supposition is, that it may have been an exclamation of surprise at the sinfulness of man, which rendered a gate, otherwise so easy, so narrow and difficult of entrance. Thus Photius: διὸ καὶ ὁ σωτὴρ τεθαύμακε λέγων· τί στενὴ κ.τ.λ., ὡσανεὶ ἔλεγεν· οὐ στενή ἐστιν, ἀλλ᾽ ὑμεῖς πονηροὶ ὄντες στενὴν πεποιήκατε. The question would then rather be regarded as an exclamation, and that not so much of surprise as of sorrow: a view which follows also, if, with Fritzsche, τί is translated *wherefore*. Such an exclamation would doubtless be a deep expression of sympathy with human sinfulness and its consequences. But in a discourse in which Christ speaks as the Lawgiver and the Judge of men, a Brother's expression of sympathy would seem rather out of place (comp. vers. 23 and foll.). The expositor is therefore constrained to reject the reading τί, and to conclude—in which conclusion he is borne out by the other readings, καὶ and καὶ τί—that τί must have been substituted for the original ὅτι by certain transcribers who were unacquainted with that abnormal Hebraistic usus loquendi.

The expression appears hard and severe. From it, not only the Reformed theology, but even the Lutheran, sought to prove the paucitas salvandorum (Quenstaedt, theol. polem. didact. iii. 23). Episcopius calms the reader by a reference to the circumstances of that time, when Christianity had not yet become the dominant religion: ex his verbis videtur servator potissimum de statu illius temporis loqui. It must not be forgotten that on one occasion, when asked εἰ ὀλίγοι οἱ σωζόμενοι, Christ declined to give a direct answer (St Luke xiii. 23). Here He describes simply the actual facts of the case at the time when He spoke, and neither generally of the present αἰών, nor of that which is to come (Matt. xii. 32). Moreover, as has been observed, the difficulty here spoken of in connection with the Christian way, would appear to be in contradiction to what He says in Matt. xi. 29 of the easiness of His yoke, which saying is endorsed by St John (1 Epist. v. 3): "His commandments are not grievous." But the apparent inconsistency is reconciled by a right understanding of the relation of this sermon to the Christian scheme of salvation (see Introduction, § 5).

Ver. 15. The difficulty that there is even in *finding* this way, requires that right guides should point it out to us. This is the idea which dictates the admonition of this verse: προσέχετε δὲ ἀπὸ τῶν ψευδοπροφητῶν. Chrysostom: καὶ γὰρ πρὸς τὸ στενὴν αὐτὴν εἶναι πολλοί οἱ ὑποσκελίζοντές εἰσι τὴν ἐκεῖσε φέρουσαν εἴσοδον.—The question now arises, whether by these false prophets we are to understand teachers, and if so, whether Christian or Jewish teachers are meant. The latter point is not discussed by the recent commentators, Kuinoel, Paulus, Fritzsche, Olshausen, or Stier. The former question, as to whether the false prophets are teachers, is to be answered in the affirmative: the term προφῆται shows this, and likewise the context, which naturally suggests a reference to those who are to point out the way. With regard to the latter question, most writers think the teachers spoken of are Christian teachers; and they quote as a parallel passage Acts xx. 30. Unquestionably the Old Testament term προφῆται is used of Christians, Matt. xxiii. 34, and also ψευδοπροφῆται, 1 John iv. 1; Matt. xxiv. 11; 2 Peter ii. 1. If ver. 21 is a continuation of the subject of this verse, there can be little hesitation about referring this to Christian teachers. And, among recent writers, this view is held by Meyer. The objections to it were first propounded by de Wette: "Were this the case, Jesus would here say something which was superfluous, not only in that period, but in all His lifetime: and said it too without any reference to the future, such as is to be found, *e.g.*, in ver. 22. But the question here is touching the way into the kingdom of God, not as to how men are to distinguish the true from the false in Christianity itself. Consequently it must be to Jewish deceivers that Christ here alludes, like those of whom Josephus speaks, Antiq. xx. 5, 1. 8, 6; de bello Jud. ii. 13, 4. 5." If we rightly apprehend the character of this sermon, in which everything is in exact relation to the circumstances of that time, we shall feel that it would appear very little in keeping, if in this last section we were to find a prophetic warning against false teachers of the Christian Church,—a Church which was to be founded only a considerable time subsequently. Hence Neander (?), Baum.-Crusius, as long before them Druthmar, think the allusion is to goetic deceivers and messiahs. So it is undoubtedly in chap. xxiv. 11. But would not this explanation altogether cut asunder the connection of our verse with the foregoing, and still more with the succeeding 21st verse? If we are to preserve the connection of the verse with the circumstances of the time, would it not be more natural to refer it to the *pharisaic* guides of the people, even to such as, in John x. 8, Christ calls κλέπται καὶ λῃσταί? So accordingly Michaelis, Rosenmüller, and Riegler. Was it not they who, under the πρόφασις of piety, left undone τὰ βαρύτερα τοῦ νόμου, τὴν κρίσιν, τὸν ἔλεον, τὴν πίστιν (xxiii. 14. 23); who said, "I go, sir," and yet went not into the vineyard (xxi. 30); who therefore led men into the broad way? **Taking this view,** the transition to the subject **of** ver. 21, where more specially *Christian* teachers are spoken of, is easy and natural (comp. on ver. 21). The words of Matt. xxiii. 3 might, indeed, seem to raise an objection to this explanation: for there it is said that the doctrine of those pharisaic teachers is to be accepted by the people, and from that statement it might appear that the *doctrine* of these ψευδοπροφῆται did not form part of the ψεῦδος. But the words, πάντα ὅσα ἂν εἴπωσι τηρεῖτε, in so far as they relate to the Pharisees, it is impossible to take so literally: otherwise such precepts as that of theirs quoted in Mark vii. 11, and condemned, would fall to be included. All that is intended, is to show the inconsistency of their practice and their teaching: "you may, perhaps, follow their doctrine, but not their practice."

The figure of the Wolf and the Lamb, which Æsop has rendered familiar to all, is one which occurs in the symbolical representations of all nations. It is found elsewhere in Scripture, in Isa. xi. 6, lxv. 25; Sir. xiii. 17; Matt. x. 16: on the natural qualities of the two animals, their ἀντιπάθεια, and the symbolical signification attached to them by different nations, see Bochart, Hieroz. L. ii. 46, iii. 10. False teachers and deceivers are specially characterized as wolves in St John x, 12; Acts xx. 29. The predicate ἅρπαγες, **rapaces,** was classically applied to wolves, see Pricæus. Ἔσωθεν, not "in heart," but "underneath their exterior." Now, as in John x. 12, and Acts xx. 29, the false teachers are called wolves in relation to the πρόβατα, the ποιμνίον which is the true fold of the Church, it might be thought that by ἐνδύματα τῶν προβάτων was here meant the feigned, assumed appearance, on the part of the false teacher, of a member of the *Christian* Church. But the Church is not here, as in those passages, represented under the figure of a flock (Meyer); and, moreover, we have seen that by the wolves, Pharisees must be meant. We must therefore con-

27 *

sider the expression as intended as a sensible representation of innocence. Under this innocent exterior, the false teachers gained admittance to the people, and proved as dangerous and deadly as wolves in sheep's clothing, finding their way into an unsuspecting flock of sheep. This idea is expressed, John x. 8, 11, in reference to the Old Testament theocracy. What the appearance they put on, the sheep's clothing, consists in, we shall further consider at ver. 16. Καρποί has generally been regarded as placed in contradistinction to ἔνδυμα προβάτων: if by καρποί doctrine be meant, then the sheep's clothing would denote an immoral life; if again the former were to be understood to mean works, the latter would stand for the ostensibly correct teaching,—according to some, the ostensibly correct teaching *along with the works,* according to others, dissimulation in introducing doctrine. On the other hand, several expositors have understood by ἐνδύματα προβάτων, the garb of the prophets: who were wont to appear in μηλωταῖς, in garments made of sheep's skins, Heb. xi. 37. Justinus, dial. c. Tr. c. 35, quotes ἐνδεδυμένοι δέρματα προβάτων. The false prophets come in the garb of true prophets; the antithesis to the wolves might then be this: Christ meant to characterize the garb of the prophets as the garb of innocence. (Thus Maldonatus, Bochart, Grotius, A. Schott adagia sacra N. T. p. 19; Er. Schmid, Krebs, Rosenmüller, Kuinöl, Stier.) To this it cannot be objected that we should then have expected to find the Genitive of the subject,—viz., not προβάτων, but μηλωτῶν, not clothing of sheep, but clothing of sheep-skins,—because ἐνδύματα προβάτων may easily be explained as the clothing which sheep have, *i.e.,* skins. In opposition to the opinion, however, it must be considered that the garb of prophets was not exclusively sheep-skins; they wore also goat-skins, and raiment of camels' hair, like John the Baptist (iii. 4): further, the supposed symbol would have been without any significance in those times; for, from the age of Malachi to the Baptist, no prophet had appeared in Israel (1 Mac. ix. 27; comp. iv. 46, xiv. 41): and finally, it cannot be shown that that prophetic garb was specially regarded as the symbol of innocence: it was merely the rough garb of the common man.

Ver. 16. *First half.* What are we to understand by those καρποί, those evidences of the false prophet? This is a question of great practical importance. The designation ψευδοπρο-φῆται can only refer to those who *teach* wrong; and the sheep's clothing, what can that be, but the correct walk and conversation of those false teachers? If so, the καρποί must then be the *doctrines:* by their doctrines those apparently correct men are to be judged; as Moses, in Deut. xiii. 1—4, made sound doctrine the touchstone of the false prophets. Moreover, **the** figure of Matt. xii. 33—35 supports this view; for there, **as in** Sirach xxvii. 6, the doctrines are spoken of as fruits: especially Luke vi. 45, where this dictum of the Sermon on the Mount is introduced before the 21st verse of St Matt. To the **latter** circumstance, indeed, no weight can be attached, when the peculiar construction of St Luke's account is considered: still less can we find in this alteration traces of an anti-Pauline tendency (Hilgenfeld, S. 173). Nevertheless, the grounds just mentioned were deemed strong enough to **warrant all** expositors down to Michaelis, with few exceptions, in understanding by καρποί doctrines, and more particularly, Christian **doctrines.** The ancient Church, more especially the Church of Rome, un-terstood by the pseudo-prophets, heretics: now, as the heretics were generally distinguished by purity of life, even more than the members of the Church they left,—*e.g.,* Jovinian, the Waldensians and other dissenters from the Church **of Rome,—this** explanation of καρποί, **as not** a bad life but a false creed, **was** all the more confirmed by this circumstance. Thus Tertullian, de præscript. hær. **c. 4: quænam istæ** sunt pelles ovium, **nisi** nominis Christiani extrinsecus superficies? Jerome: specialiter de hæreticis intelligendum est, qui **videntur** continentia, castitate, jejunio, quasi quadam pietatis **se veste** circumdare, intrinsecus vero habentes animum venenatum, simpliciorum fratrum corda decipiunt. **Nic. a Lyra:** qui falsam doctrinam palliant apparentia virtutum; comp. Glossa ord. The auctor op. imp. expressly contends against those **who** would make the passage refer to doctores Christiani, qui sunt peccatores: these, he says, can never have the intention of destroying the Christian Church; he then says: fructus hominis est confessio fidei ejus;—he does certainly add: et opera conversationis ipsius, but to **this** he makes no further allusion. With all **the** bitterness **of** an old inquisitor, Maldonatus thus comments on ἐν ἐνδύμασι προβάτων: falsi prophetæ **sunt omnes** hæretici, omnium vero maxime Calvinistæ. Primum, quia non missi venerunt; deinde quia ovina induti pelle; nihil enim in eorum erat ore, nisi Dominus, nisi Pater noster cœlestis, nisi Christus, nisi fides, juramentum inauditum; nihil in eorum factis apparebat, nisi eleemosyna, nisi temperantia, nisi modestia. Quo habitu pastores ementiti magnam in grege Domini fecerunt stragem. Similarly Este,[1] Jansenius, Tirinus, Cornel. a Lapide. These do not, however, understand by the καρποί, doctrines *exclusively:* Jansen., Corn. a Lapide, Calmet, include "doctrines and works." Maldonatus, the last even exclusively: "at the end," he says, "their vileness will be apparent." Among the Fathers, the only exceptions to this view are Hilary, Chrysostom, and Augustine. Origen does indeed say (Opp. iv. 683), that an exact knowledge of Scripture is necessary to enable one to decide: it cannot, however, be exactly determined whether or not he regards the fruits as doctrine. Hilary: blandimenta verborum et mansuetudinis simulationem admonet fructu *operationis* expendi oportere. Chrysostom understands by the pseudoprophetæ only hypocrites, οὐ τοῖς αἱρετικοῖς, παρὰ γὰρ αἱρετικοῖς ἐστι πολλάκις βίον (καλὸν) εἱρεῖν: so too Aretius, in opposition to the Anabaptists. Augustine, however, regards the spiritual fruits of a Christian life, spoken of in Gal. v. 22, as the sign by which teachers are to be known, and adds, with a true Christian feeling: cætera quæ hic posita sunt, habent quasdam imagines suas in malis hominibus et deceptoribus, ut omnino fallant, *nisi quisque jam mundum oculum et simplicem habuerit, quo ista cognoscat.* Among the Reformers, the fruits are regarded as practical by Zwingli and Luther. Zwingli: si gloriam Dei spectat propheta, si justitiam, veritatem, pacem et salutem publicam, certum est, eum esse verum prophetam. Luther regards the sentence now in the one aspect, now in the other, according to circumstances. In Walch's 22d volume of his works, at page 2098, we read: "False prophets are very injurious. For, albeit they may be regarded as pious, devout, honest people, yet these things are virtues of the man, not of the prophet—whose doctrine must chiefly be looked to, not his life." In his remarks on Ps. xxii. (Walch, v. 1297), he quotes ver. 15 of our passage, and argues,

---

[1] Among the evil fruits, Este assigns the first place to disobedience to the Church; the second place, to the sensuality which originates in neglect of fasting, and so forth.

against those who maintain salvation by works, that it is all the more difficult to know them by their works, because they imitate the example of pious men, and thus concludes: "In truth, we Christians must look more to *faith,* as St Paul requires in 2 Cor. iv. 13." On the other hand, speaking of Gal. v. 19, "The works of the flesh are manifest," he says (viii. 2736): "This text agrees with Matt. vii. 16, 18." In his exposition of the Lord's Prayer (vii. 1040), referring to our text, he **speaks** of those whose conduct is **very pious and holy, but if any one will not listen to them, they demean** themselves most unmannerly. In his **commentary** on the Sermon on the Mount he recurs finally to the single criterium, that *"if we hold fast the leading article of our faith, and have the Lord Christ truly in our heart,* the Spirit will be given us to lead us in the right way." Calvin, on the contrary, distinctly explains the passage to refer to *doctrine:* falluntur meo judicio qui ad vitam restringunt; nam cum sæpe fucosa sanctimonia, ac nescio quibus etiam austerioris vitæ larvis se venditent pessimi quique impostores, valde incertum esset hoc examen. Fateor quidem, hypocrisin tandem patefieri, quia nihil difficilius est, quam virtutis simulatio, etc. Similarly Pellican, Melanchthon: agnoscendi sunt ex fructibus, *ex manifesto aliquo impio dogmate,* quod impossibile est cadere in ecclesiam. Sed falsam doctrinam prophetarum postea comitantur alii fructus in *vita* et *moribus.* Bucer comprises together doctrine and life. In the Protestant exegesis also, this reference of the text to works was predominant. Chemnitz considers that, in deciding upon Christians in general, the criterium of works is sufficient, but not so in the case of Christian teachers: so too Gerhard (loci xi. 198, xii. 2, p. 87), Er. Schmid; even Calixt, who at least allows vita and mores to count as merely criteria secundaria; likewise Spener (theol. Bedenken, Th. iv. S. 201[1]). Several, however, have understood the sheep's clothing as not only denoting bona vita generally, but as containing a special allusion to that insinuating character ($\chi\rho\eta\sigma\tau o\lambda o\gamma i\alpha$) which St Paul ascribes to false teachers,

---

[1] "The fruit is that which is produced by him whose fruit it is called. That, therefore, is the fruit of a teacher and prophet, which as teacher and prophet he produces, consequently his *doctrine:* by this, according to Christ's words, we know him. When, however, we speak of **a Christian** in general, then we know that his fruit is faith and good living."

Rom. xvi. 18. Chemnitz, wo in his exposition makes use of ver. 22, mentions as *vestimenta ovium* the following: (1) titulus, vocatio, officium. Dicunt enim se prophetare in nomine Christi. (2) Verba pietatis et ædificationis zelus. Dicunt enim: domine, domine. (3) Externa species vitæ; mollior lana potest significare χριστολογία Rom. xvi. 18. (4) Peculiaria et illustria dona posse se prophetare, dæmones ejicere, etc. Only by the Socinian and Arminian writers (Grot., Episcop., Cleric.) was the *practical* criterium maintained.

Even after Bengel, leading in the van of the Church-exegesis, explained the passage of the *practical* fruits, the earlier orthodox opinion was still held. Bengel: doctrina non est fructus, ex quo propheta cognoscitur, sed est forma, quæ ei dat esse veri falsive prophetæ et ipsa ex fructu cognoscitur. Bonitas arboris ipsius est veritas et lux interna. Bonitas fructuum est sanctitas vitæ. On the other hand, it is explained as referring to doctrine and life by Christ. Starke, to doctrine and its consequences by Elsner, to doctrine exclusively by Michaelis: "To determine whether a teacher is true or false from his life, is impossible: his doctrines must be tested by the word of God." But if it appears that the γνώρισμα of works is one which it is impossible to apply, it must not be forgotten that the same objection may be made regarding the fruits of *doctrine*. Particularly so, if we are not to regard the warning as intended merely to the future, but also for the time when Christ spoke it. Was it possible for Christ to entrust the deciding "according to the word of God" upon true and false teachers to the people at large, or even to His disciples, when the majority of them knew scarcely anything about that word of God besides what they heard from the lessons of the synagogue? In Matt. xxiii. 3, at least, He enjoins upon them the general observance of the traditional teaching (compare also ver. 23); leaving it to the further development of the Christian principle to form afterwards the true criterium. But also, in general, is there not a heretical teaching against the *spirit* of God's word, which may co-exist with the most scrupulous fidelity to its letter, which may be far more destructive to the souls of men than any deviation from the letter, such as might be shown to be contradicted by the creeds? And is it not therefore manifest that the command to test teachers by their doctrine, requires in him who proves them a certain state of advancement in spiritual things, as much as the command to prove them by their works?

Thus in both explanations there is the same difficulty in applying the criterium. A reference to the following context must then decide whether of the two is right, and such reference appears to decide for the *practical* fruits. We have, namely, to consider the connection of our text with verses 21 and following, where we find creed, prophecy, and working of miracles placed in opposition to ποιεῖν τὸ θέλημα τοῦ πατρός. True, if we were to understand here the θέλημα τοῦ Θεοῦ, as in John vi. 29, to mean *faith* (the auct. op. imp. and the critics mentioned in the Introduction, p. 36) our difficulty would not yet be removed. And it would be only somewhat lessened if we were to regard ver. 21 as introducing a new section of the discourse, the subject of which is to be, not the προφῆται, but the members of the Church in general. But it is self-evident that we have here no fresh subject introduced: the same thought which has been expressed in a particular relation is continued here, although now with a more extended application. Then we must bear in mind, that in those sayings of John the Baptist, to which the thoughts of His hearers would naturally revert, the same figure of a tree and its fruit is used in reference to works (Matt. iii. 10). Consequently that exposition must also be rejected, which, meeting the other two halfway, explains καρποί as the fruits of doctrine,—"the power of amendement of life, the consolation of faith," which doctrines may impart. This is the view of Piscator, Rus, Doddridge, Wesley,[1] Fritzsche, B.-Crusius, and Heubner (in praktisch. Erklärung des N.T.). No doubt the practical effects of preaching—which is the satisfying of the religious necessities of man, —as it is made by Christ a criterium of His own doctrine (Matt. xi. 29; John vii. 17), is also a criterium of the doctrine of the προφῆται; but this meaning here would destroy the connection of our text with ver. 21. We must accordingly conclude, that what is here meant by the fruits is precisely what is subsequently called ποιεῖν τὸ θέλημα τοῦ πατρός: the same καρποὶ τοῦ πνεύματος which St Paul sets forth in Gal. v. 22.

---

[1] Wesley: "A short, plain, easy rule, and one that may be applied by people of the meanest capacity. True prophets convert sinners to God, or at least strengthen and confirm those that are converted."

The sheep's clothing we must regard as denoting not so much works which appear good, as the show of inward piety, the look of harmless innocence, by which the false teacher deceives, as St Paul expresses it, τὰς καρδίας τῶν ἀκάκων, Rom. xvi. 18. With regard now to the difficulty about applying this test, we must say, with St. Augustine, that Christ assumed that those who should prove the teachers, should have in them the presence of the guiding Spirit of God, and should thus possess a spiritual discernment. He spoke of those who belong to His πρόβατα, and who therefore hear His voice (John x. 27). For, even in the time of Christ, what drew impressible spirits away from the Pharisees to Him and His disciplina, was certainly not His doctrine alone, but also the καρποὶ τοῦ πνεύματος manifest in His life (Matt. xi. 29). We find that of those who have the μόρφωσις of godliness, but deny its power (2 Tim. iii. 9), it is further said that they shall have no long continuance, ἡ γὰρ ἄνοια αὐτῶν ἔκδηλος ἔσται πᾶσιν.

Ver. 16, *second half*,—ver. 18. The figure of which Christ here makes use, is one which occurs repeatedly in the classics under various forms. (Compare in Scripture, Sir. xxvii. 6, and James iii. 11.) St Luke (vi. 44) joins ἄκανθαι with σῦκα, and he has βάτος instead of τρίβολοι joined with σταφυλή. Here, as elsewhere (see above on vers. 9, 10), St Matthew's figure is very exact. Ἄκανθαι or ἄκανθα is the generic term for all thorn-plants, the best of which is the buckthorn (?), אָטָד, which bears small black berries similar to those of the vine; the τρίβολοι have a flower which might be likened to a fig. In addition to which, it must be remembered that these fruitless plants are the very ones which have the finest flowers, that of the buckthorn resembling the Oriental hyacinth. Theophylact thinks that by the thorns is intended to be figuratively represented the secret wound inflicted by the false teachers; by the thistles, the indoles versatilis: but these plants are chosen simply on account of their unfruitfulness. It is with men as with trees: in the produce of the tree only, its innermost nature is revealed; and in the outward acts of men, their inner nature, their spirit, *must* manifest itself. The words were quoted in support of the Manichæan idea of a twofold origin of all things; but the Fathers, Origen (T. i. 820), Augustine, Jerome, refuted such an application.

Ver. 19, 20. According to Neander, De Wette, and Meyer, ver. 19 is not in its proper place here, having no connection with the context. In the same form, the same thought occurs in the discourse of the Baptist, Matt. iii. 10. But is not this word of threatening spoken here of the $\psi\varepsilon\upsilon\delta o\pi\rho o\varphi\tilde{\eta}\tau\alpha\iota$, who to all appearance teach the truth, exactly in keeping with the words spoken in vers. 26, 27, of those who apparently make a good profession? Ver. 20 refers back to ver. 16.

Ver. 21. **Here a question emerges, as to whether the discourse has still in view the same persons, the pseudo-prophets.** Hilary, Chrys., Aug., the auct. **op. imp.**, Radbert, Luther, Zwingli, Chemnitz, Przipzov, Wolzogen, Mald., and many others, are of this opinion. According to Calvin, the discourse still relates to the pastores gregis, but with this difference, that here it is no longer those qui rapiendi et vorandi causa in gregem insiliunt who are spoken of, but the mercenarii. On the other hand, Jerome, whose words the Glossa ord. adopts, makes a marked distinction: sicut supra dixerat, eos qui haberent vestem bonæ vitæ, non recipiendos propter dogmatum nequitiam: ita nunc e contrario asserit, ne his quidem accommodandam fidem, qui quum polleant integritate fidei, turpiter vivunt, et doctrinæ integritatem malis operibus destruunt. It is plain that those expositors who understand $\varkappa\alpha\rho\pi oί$ to be the criterium of pure doctrine, could not, if they maintained the identity of the sub**jects now spoken of, explain** $\pi oιεῖν\ τὸ\ \vartheta έλημα\ \Theta εοῦ$ of works, but were necessitated to find some other explanation of the words. Hence arose the $\pi\alpha\rho\varepsilon\rho\mu\eta\nu\varepsilon ία$ repeatedly alluded to, "the fulfilling the command of God in reference to belief" (Introduction, p. 35). That this view, **however, is inadmis**sible, may be seen from the phrase in ver. 23, $oἱ\ ἐ\rho\gamma\alpha\zeta όμενοι\ τὴν\ ἀνομίαν$, and also from $\pi oιεῖ$ in ver. 24.

If ver. 16 speaks of the same subject, then the $\psi\varepsilon\upsilon\delta o\pi\rho o$-$\varphi\tilde{\eta}\tau\alpha\iota$ must there have been understood exclusively of Christian teachers. Against this interpretation, however, are the considerations already urged on ver. 16. Hence we hold it more correct to maintain, that in this verse the subject spoken of is expanded so **as to** include Christian $\pi\rho o\varphi\tilde{\eta}\tau\alpha\iota$, who belong to the same category. And now **the** admonition relates less to teaching, **and more** to life: **and the** contrast of confession of faith with practice comes more prominently forward. Προφῆται, we said, not teachers, are here spoken of; for at that time, in the beginning of Christianity, there was really no very clear line of demarcation drawn between teachers and congregation: indeed, in such a time, when Christianity was comprised in a single article of faith, viz., that Christ was the Messiah, there was no very marked distinction even between Christian and Jewish προφῆται and exorcists: as may be seen from such examples as Mark ix. 38; Simon Magus; the Jewish-Christian Churches, such as those to whom St James and the author of the Epistle to the Hebrews wrote: and from the various phases of Ebionitic thought.[1] Nor is this view contradicted by the κύριε κύριε. The expression is not mere repetition: here, as in other places (comp. on v. 37), the diplasiasmus denotes *zeal*. This was the term of honour popularly applied to the Messiah (xx. 30, 31), as it is also in this passage, where the Redeemer appears as the Judge of the world, ver. 23. In John xiii. 13, Jesus *requires* it from the disciples: in the Church, this confession forms the fundamental article of the Christian faith; in this name the early Church baptized (Neander, Pflanzung i. 32). But under the banner of this confession (as Neander has historically set forth) were united, at first, men of great variety of opinion, and diversity of life. And this remark is true also of that subsequent period in the history of the Church, when the first dimness and obscurity had been succeeded by something

---

[1] Many scraps of information concerning the various phases in which this mixture of Jewish and Christian ideas presented itself, may still be obtained from the Talmud. Take, for instance, the following trait from the time of Gamaliel (Gemara Shabbat, f. 115, 1):—"In the neighbourhood of Ema Shalom, daughter of the R. Gamaliel, dwelt a philosopher who enjoyed the reputation of incorruptibility. She, wishing to expose him, brought him a golden candlestick, that he might adjudicate to her a portion of the paternal inheritance. He answered, "Divide thou it then." She replied: "But it is written in the Scriptures, that the daughter shall not inherit along with the son." To which he replied: "Since your captivity the Thora of Moses is abolished, and son and daughter inherit equally" (as according to Roman law). Next day came the brother, bringing a Lybian ass: then to him he answered: "Read on to the end. There you find: I am come not to destroy the law, but to fulfil it." Now this can scarcely have been a heathen philosopher, although he says "*your* captivity." He was probably a Jewish eclectic, who was neither unacquainted with Christianity nor unfriendly to it, but yet a Jew.

like clearness, and when that fundamental article had been elaborated into a formulary of beliefs, but when also the Church, by her alliance with the State, did more or less loosen her hold of the reins of discipline.

Τὸ θέλημα τοῦ Πατρός μου (comp. xii. 50, and John vii. 17), the moral requirements of God. On the dissimilar form in which St Luke has the expression (vi. 46), compare Introduction (p. 6). It affords a fresh instance of how little grammatical accuracy forms an adequate bulwark against erroneous exposition, when we find Fritzsche availing himself of the οὐ πᾶς here only to hurl another anathema against the so-called "Pietists:" illud genus hominum quotquot sunt: so too David Schulz (in 1st ed. of his work "vom Glauben"), and B.-Crusius. The πᾶς is not absolutely negatived: it could only be so if the negation were joined with the *verb;* rather compare the subsequent πολλοὶ ἐροῦσί μοι. It is a mistake to regard the "saying Lord, Lord," as denoting merely a lifeless, formal profession: this sense it has not necessarily. Rightly, therefore, in the main remarks Justin: οὐ γὰρ τοὺς μόνον λέγοντας, ἀλλὰ τοὺς καὶ τὰ ἔργα πράττοντας σωθήσεσθαι ἔφη.

Ver. 22. The Messiah is the Judge on whose award the ultimate destiny of the race depends (John xii. 48, comp. John iii. 36): so was He regarded alike according to Jewish and Christian dogma, Rom. ii. 16; Acts xvii. 31. On the anachronism supposed to be involved in this appearing of Christ as Judge of the world, see Introduction (p. 11). The form of dialogue is used here, as in Matt. xxv. 12 ff., to make the scene more vivid and forcible. The men who appear before us, are such as have the assurance to demonstrate the sincerity of their profession by the effects of their charismata. The προφητεύειν, *i.e.,* λαλεῖν ἐν ἀποκαλύψει εἰς οἰκοδομήν (1 Cor. xiv. 6), is placed at the head of these, as in 1 Cor. xii. 28. In Eph. iv. 11, the προφῆται are ranked next to the Apostles, who united in themselves a multitude of charismata. Next come the exorcists, who possessed manifold miraculous powers,[1] 1 Cor. xii. 10. The threefold σῷ is emphatic: it is dativus medii (Winer 694, 6. Aufl.). Ποιεῖν δυνάμεις, comp. LXX. Ps. lix. 12 (lx. 12), in

---

[1] Bengel subjoins: adde commentarios et observationes exegeticos ad libros et loca V et N. T. scripsimus, homilias insignes habuimus, etc.

the sing. for הָיָה עָשָׂה. De Wette: Observe the self-glorifying way in which they vindicate their own merits, as the unholy are wont to do (xxv. 24). But what σῷ expresses, is rather the intimacy of the relations in which they seem to have stood to the Saviour. Hence in St Luke the words used are: ἐφάγομεν ἐνώπιόν σου κ. ἐπίομεν καὶ ἐν ταῖς πλατείαις ἡμῶν ἐδίδαξας. Justin's memorable quotation is based upon a mixing together of the two: ἐν τῷ σῷ ὀνόματι ἐφάγομεν καὶ ἐπίομεν (dial. c. Tr. c. 76). But this mixing the two disturbs the sense: as φαγεῖν (ἐν) τῷ ὀνόματί σου can be rightly understood only of that eating and drinking spoken of in 1 Cor. x. 31,—that is to say, eating and drinking with that feeling of dependence upon God, which is precisely wanting here.

We have now to inquire in what light those charismatical workings are to be regarded. Origen (in Matt. iii. 853) thus decides: si nunquam eos Christus cognovit, virtutes autem se fecisse gloriantur in Christo ... ab eo, qui non solum transfiguraverat se in angelum lucis sed in ipsum Christum (factæ sunt), by which Antichrist is meant. But we cannot think that the reference here is to such apparent, or even real miracles, as, according to St Augustine, Satan, by virtue of his knowledge of the semina occultiora, can accomplish (de Trin. 3, 4.): for the works spoken of here, indicate a high relation to Christ: as St Chrys. forcibly remarks: ὃ γὰρ δεῖξαι ἐσπούδακε τοῦτό ἐστιν, ὅτι οὔτε πίστις, οὔτε θαύματα ἰσχύει, βίου μὴ παρόντος. Hence Chys., Aug. (sermo 38, T. i. 468), and Jerome regard these as really miraculous works; Jerome: prophetare et virtutes facere interdum non ejus est, qui operatur, sed vel invocatio nominis Christi hoc agit, vel ob condemnationem eorum, qui invocant et utilitatem eorum, qui vident et audiunt conceditur. Accordingly, both the R. Catholic and the Protestant exegesis—Mald., Jansenius, a Lapide, Hunnius, Gerhard, Spener (letzte theol. Bedenken i. 136), and others—maintain that the wonderful works were real, referring in support of this opinion to the case of Judas, Matt. x. 8, and the disciples, Mark ix. 38. Only a few, as Chemnitz and Wolzogen, think that the persons here spoken of were those who, after performing such works, had apostatized.

Now, not only in order to make the text intelligible, but, indeed, in order to find in it any meaning at all for that time, we must first of all note, that the phraseological expression, οὐδέποτε ἔγνων ὑμᾶς and οἱ ἐργαζόμενοι τὴν ἀνομίαν, cannot be taken so strictly as to imply an absolute denial of *all* influence in those persons of the Christian principle. Further must be considered the isolating influence which sin has upon the powers of mind (although, of course, they were all intended to work together): as in all time experience abundantly testifies that faith may be in pretty lively exercise in the domain of feeling, imagination, and knowledge, while the will and disposition are little affected by it:— how many a gifted preacher is there, for instance, carrying with him the rapt interest of his hearers, who preaches least of all to his own heart! Then we must not leave out of account the fact, that, according to **1 Cor.** xiv. 1, 39, the attaining of certain charismata was more or less determined by the efforts which the spiritual man gave himself in the direction of one grace or gift, or another: that one he sought after, set himself to win, that was likely to become his. And, finally, the ancients sought to explain the circumstance, that miraculous powers were imparted to "the unworthy," from the final object in view, viz., the Divine purpose to advance the spread of the Church among unbelievers: how much more will this phenomenon appear intelligible from a consideration of the peculiar causes operating at that time! History shows how, at different times, and in diverse communities, extraordinary supernatural phenomena, evoked by extraordinary exciting circumstances, have been exhibited: with regard to which, is not seldom happened that it was **no easy** matter **to distinguish how much was to be** ascribed to divine, and how much to demoniac influence.[1] Instances of this in more limited spheres are to be found in the ecstatic phenomena of the Seven-years' War, in the prophets of the Thirty-years' War, in the ecstasia of the first period of Wesleyanism and of Irvingitism: most of all, however, it is in the apostolic times that we come into contact with an atmosphere in which the powers of the upper and the under worlds are vehemently stirred. In those times, when miracles had become an everyday occurrence, how natural was it that those

---

[1] That the wonders of the dark region of the life of the somnambulist may co-exist with moral depravity, is an established fact: on this subject some interesting remarks will be found in Kieser's System des Tellurismus, ii. 227, 241.

very persons in whose case the enkindling ray of the Gospel had not really penetrated to the heart, or had only glanced from its surface, should direct their regards with the greatest longing to those extraordinary manifestations by which the first preaching of the truth was accompanied! In proof that it was so, we have only to recall the case of Simon Magus on the one hand, and of the vain Corinthians on the other, with their earnest longings to possess the gift of tongues. So, too, even in the time of our Lord, healing was performed in the name of Jesus, even by those in whom were scarcely even the very dawnings of faith. This is seen from the case of the man spoken of in Mark ix. 39, who must, according to Christ's own words concerning him, be regarded as one of these; from the account, too, of the sons of the high priest, recorded in Acts xix., in whom there does not appear to have been even the beginning of faith. While thus the words of Christ with reference to these spurious manifestations of faith apply with special force to those times, they are equally true of all times, and contain the condemnation of all who, leaving out of account the great object of the Gospel, which is to restore the will to obedience to God, allow His religion to affect only the understanding, feelings, or imagination. Accordingly, De Wette well observes: A man might, it is true, be a prophet by his faith, but it was also possible for him to allow his faith to influence only his mind and his imagination, and so, because it does not reach his heart, his faith might be found conjoined with an ungodly life.

Ver. 23. Ὅτι is recit. (v. 31); Meyer regards is as causal, as do Origen and Chrysostom, who place ὅτι—ὑμᾶς after ἀποχωρεῖτε. Ἐργαζόμενοι τὴν ἀνομίαν is with reference to Ps. vi. 8: ἀπόστητε ἀπ' ἐμοῦ πάντες οἱ ἐργαζόμενοι τὴν ἀνομίαν; so that the expression is not to be pressed. Ἔγνων is not necessarily to be taken in the secondary sense of *love* which ידע has (Aug., Kuinoel): they had laid claim to an intimate acquaintance with Christ; but their acquaintance with Him (as expressed in Luke xiii. 26) was merely an outward one, whereas that inward knowledge of Him, that relationship of soul to Him of which St John speaks, x. 14, was wanting. We can scarcely mistake a reference to this passage in the words, 2 Tim. ii. 19: "ἔγνω ὁ κύριος τοὺς ὄντας αὐτοῦ," καὶ "ἀποστήτω ἀπὸ ἀδικίας πᾶς ὁ ὀνομάζων τὸ ὄνομα κυρίου." The Calvinistic exegesis takes the passage to mean, that the persons spoken of may have belonged to the *awakened,* but could not be of the number of the *chosen* (Bucer). —A paraphrase of the text is formed by that passage in the unauthentic 2d Epistle of Clem. Romanus (which cannot be earlier than the end of the third century), c. 4: ἐὰν ἦτε μετ' ἐμοῦ συνηγμένοι ἐν τῷ κόλπῳ μου καὶ μὴ ποιῆτε τὰς ἐντολάς μου, ἀποβαλῶ ὑμᾶς καὶ ἐρῶ ὑμῖν· ὑπάγετε ἀπ' ἐμοῦ, οὐκ οἶδα ὑμᾶς, πόθεν ἐστε, ἐργάται ἀνομίας: comp. **Olearius, Obs.** xxiii.

Vers. 24—27. **The close is in the form of a** parable. Οὖν shows what thoughts suggest such a close, viz., those of vers. 21—23. That which must decide the final **issue,** is not a man's creed, but the sincerity of his will: hence, in this discourse, whose object is to unfold the Divine will, everything is made to depend upon a man's actions and life.—Πᾶς ὅστις—ὁμοιώσω αὐτὸν, the Nominative absolute, placed first with rhetorical emphasis, x. 14, 32; Rev. iii. 12. Ὁμοιώσω, ὁμοιωθήσεται, incorrectly regarded by Kuinoel as a Present: futura indicant continuationem, atque adeo accipienda sunt ut præsentia. Fritzsche, B.-Crus., De Wette, make it have reference to what **comes** immediately after: comp. Luke vi. 47, ὑποδείξω ὑμῖν, τίνι ἐστὶν ὅμοιος. But the relation here is different. For whereas, in St Luke, the comparison really follows, here it is already begun. Ὁμολογήσω refers, accordingly, not to the comparison, but to the time of judgment, as does ὁμοιωθήσεται, ver. 26, and in xxv. 1. It is the Judge who will institute this comparison, and He will do so by the judicial sentence given by Him here. The comparison will involve the sentence of acquittal or condemnation, and the execution will accompany the sentence.

Φρονίμῳ, prudent. Wisdom appoints the object of pursuit, prudence **uses the right means towards** its attainment. The Gospel enjoins the latter as well as the former, Matt. xxiv. 45, xxv. 1 ff., x. 16; Luke xvi. 8 (compare Neander's excellent remarks, Leben Jesu, S. 476, 5. Auflage). In accordance with x. 16, this prudence, having in view the attainment of the highest ends, must also be pure in the choice of the means. In our passage, prudence shows itself also in the use of the right means in establishing the building upon a *sure foundation.*

The description of the test which the building undergoes

is truly rhetorical both in form and matter. As regards the form, attention is due to the πολυσύνδετον, the frequent repetition of καί. As regards the matter, let it be observed, the rain descends upon the roof, the swelling waters rage around the foundations and undermine them, the winds storm against the walls and overthrow them (Bengel). The description will gain in force and vividness if we realize the force of Eastern tempests, as travellers represent them to us: *e.g.*, the account of Rae Wilson, in his Travels in the Holy Land, vol. ii. p. 155. That the walls of the lightly-built houses of the East fall in when thus assailed, is an event which not unfrequently occurs: indeed it happened in Wilson's case, on the occasion he speaks of.

Of course no special signification is to be attached to the isolated elements of the test to which the building is subjected, as the object is merely to show the severity of the trial, and its impetuosity in assailing the building on every side. Nevertheless the ancient commentators have endeavoured to find a special significance in the several details. According to Theoph., Euth., the quick-falling rain denotes the assaults of the devil; the streams, the passions assaulting men; the storm-blasts, the injuries endured at the hands of men or of devils. The foundation of rock upon which the building rests securely, might, according to the analogia fidei, be understood to mean Christ, as Orig., Hilary, Jerome, Chrys., Luther, Zwing., Olsh.: but all that is intended to be thus represented, as seen from the whole context, is that moral earnestness which combines knowledge of the truth with practical obedience. Calvin: perinde est igitur ac si dixisset, veram demum esse fidem, quæ profundas habet radices in corde, et serio constantique affectu quasi fundamento nititur, ut tentationibus non cedat.

The profound impression which the discourse, especially in all probability its close, produced upon the hearers, was chiefly due, the Evangelist declares, to the Divine power with which Jesus spoke. The people recognised in Him at least a Prophet, nay more, the Messiah-Prophet, Deut. xviii. 15,—as expressions such as v. 17, vii. 22, 23, might lead them to conclude. Ἐξουσία is explained by many to mean His power as a speaker, δεινότης; Bengel: non poterant se subducere. So Bretschneider, Olsh., etc. Assuredly ἐξουσία might be used here of the **power of words, as it is** used elsewhere (Mark iii. 15) of the power of healing; and in support of this, Luke iv. 32 might be compared: ἐν ἐξουσίᾳ ἦν ὁ λόγος αὐτοῦ. But the parallel passage to this in St Mark **i. 22** is: ἦν γὰρ διδάσκων αὐτοὺς ὡς ἐξουσίαν ἔχων καὶ οὐχ ὡς οἱ γραμματεῖς: and from this it seems probable that the ἐν ἐξουσίᾳ in St Luke has no other meaning. But the contrast of His **teaching to that of the Scribes compels us to** understand by **this** ἐξουσία the direct **and irresistible power of** the Prophet (comp. **the contrast in John vii. 15, 16).** But the intention cannot **be to institute a contrast between His teaching as** a Messianic Lawgiver speaking forth out of His own **omnipotence (comp.** the phrase ἐγὼ λέγω) **and** the *Prophets* **(as Chrysostom,** Erasmus, Beza, Paulus think), **for then the expression would have been:** καὶ οὐχ ὡς οἱ προφῆται.

INDEXES.

I. GREEK WORDS ILLUSTRATED OR EXPLAINED.

	Page		Page
Ἀγαπάω,	173	Ἡλικία,	387
Ἀγγαρεύειν,	273 n.	Θέλημα τοῦ Θεοῦ,	37
Ἁγιάζειν,	332	Ἱμάτιον,	272, etc.
Ἅγιον, τό,	405, etc.	Ἰῶτα,	132
Ἀδελφός,	181	Καλὰ ἔργα,	114
Ἄκανθαι and ἄκανθα,	426	Καρδία,	378
Ἀνατέλλειν,	288	Καρποί,	420, etc.
Ἀνίστημι,	271	Καταλλάσσειν,	195
Ἀνοίγειν τὸ στόμα,	57, etc.	Κληθήσονται,	99
Ἀντέχεσθαι,	382	Κολαφίζειν,	272
Ἀντίδικος,	201	Κρίνειν,	396
Ἁπλοῦς,	380	Κρίσις,	181
Ἀπολύειν,	218	Λόγος,	228
Ἀποστρέφεσθαί τινα,	274	Λύειν,	126
Ἄρτος,	353	Λύχνος,	114
Ἀρχαῖοι,	162	Μαμωνᾶς,	383
Ἀσπάζεσθαι,	291	Μαργαρίτης,	404, etc.
Αὔριον, ἡ,	294	Μεριμνᾶν,	384
Ἀφανίζειν,	370	Μισθός,	103
Βασιλεία τῶν οὐρανῶν,	71	Μισεῖν,	382
Βαττολογεῖν,	307, etc.	Μοιχεύειν,	206
Βρέχειν,	288	Μωρέ,	179
Βρῶσις,	373, etc.	Μωρός,	110
Γέεννα and γ. τοῦ πυρός,	181, 182, etc.	Οἴδατε,	410
Γῆ,	84, 85	Ὅλως,	249
Διαλλάγηθι,	194, 195	Ὄνομα,	332
Διαλλάσσειν,	195	Ὀργίζεσθαι,	173
Δίκαιον,	86	Οὐρανοῖς, ὁ ἐν τοῖς,	331
Δικαιοσύνη,	294, etc.	Ὀφειλόμενα, τά,	354
Δοκιμάζειν,	357	Ὀφθαλμός,	377
Δόξα,	389	Παρεκτὸς λόγου πορνείας,	228
Δῶρον,	194	Παρέρχεσθαι,	132
Ἔγνων,	432	Πειράζειν,	357
Εἰκῆ,	174	Πειρασμός,	357, etc.
Εἰρηνοποιός,	97, etc.	Πληροῦν,	126
Ἐλάχισται,	145, etc.	Πλησίον, ὁ,	280
Ἔλεος, τό,	88, 89	Πνεῦμα,	36, 70
Ἔνοχος,	184	Πονηρός and ἐκ τοῦ πονηροῦ,	264, etc.
Ἐξουσία,	434		363, etc.
Ἐπιθυμεῖν γυναικός,	207, etc.	Πορνεία and μοιχεία,	206
Ἐπιούσιος,	341, 342, etc.	Πράκτωρ,	202
Εὐνοεῖν,	198	Πραΰς,	81
Ἦ,	121	Προστίθεσθαι,	391

438 INDEXES.

	Page		Page
Πτωχοί,	67	Υἱός,	99
Ῥακά,	177	Φανερῷ, ἐν τῷ,	303
Ῥύμη,	301	Φιλεῖν,	306
Σαλπίζειν ἔμπροσθέν τινος,	297	Φρονίμῳ,	433
Σκανδαλίζειν,	212	Φυλακή,	202, etc.
Σκυθρωπός,	370	Χιτών,	272
Συναγωγή,	300	Χοῖροι,	403
Συνέδριον,	182	Χόρτος,	388
Τέλειος,	292	Ψυχή,	385
Τί,	194		

II. TEXTS OF SCRIPTURE INCIDENTALLY ELUCIDATED.

Genesis i. 27,	222	Luke x. 30,	282, etc.
xxix. 30,	383	xi. 1,	319
Leviticus v. 4,	257	xii. 26,	387
Deuteronomy xix. 15,	220	xvi. 17,	132
2 Kings xxiii. 10,	187	John i. 17,	130
Psalm xiv. 1,	180	iii. 20,	101
xv. 3,	27, 282	v. 45,	200
xviii. 15,	92, 93	vii. 7,	101
lxxiii.,	90, 96	xi. 5,	285
cxxvii. 2,	384	Acts xiv. 17,	329
Proverbs xii. 20,	98	1 Corinthians vi. 16,	224, 227
xxiii. 6,	378	vii. 23,	231, etc.
Isaiah lxiii. 16,	330	xiv. 1, 39,	431
Jeremiah iii. 4, 19,	329	2 Corinthians viii. 21,	114
Matthew xii. 42,	200	Ephesians iv. 26,	174
xiii. 49,	201	v. 28, 29,	225
xviii. 33,	356	1 Timothy vi. 19,	413
xix.,	220, 226	2 Timothy iv. 18,	364
xix. 8, 9,	158	James i. 20,	173
xix. 9,	227	iv. 12,	38
xix. 10,	234	v. 12,	257
xxv. 31,	37	1 Peter v. 7,	384
Mark i. 22,	435	v. 8,	201
ii. 27,	142	2 Peter ii. 22,	407
x. 12,	219 n.	1 John ii. 17,	372
Luke ix. 15,	269	iii. 15,	177

III. PRINCIPAL MATTERS MORE OR LESS FULLY DISCUSSED.

Adulterers and adulteresses, Constantine's enactments respecting, 234; Luther's views of, 234, note.

Adultery, order in which the prohibitions of murder and, are cited in the Sermon on the Mount, 68; commandment forbidding, 204, etc.; Attic and Roman law respecting the husband who did not divorce his wife, when guilty of, 235, note.

Adversary, thine, 201.

INDEXES.

Alms and Almsgiving. importance attached to, by the Rabbis, 294; why alms called righteousness, 295; warnings against hypocrisy in connection with, 296; sounding a trumpet before, 297, etc.
Altar, bringing the gift to, 193.
Ancients, the, 160, etc.
Anger, 173, etc.; a kind of, right, 174.
Anxiety, or anxious care about worldly things, forbidden, 383, etc.
Aramaic words in the New Testament, a peculiarity of, 179.
Asking and borrowing, 273.
Asking, seeking, and knocking, their import, 408—410.
Augustine, St, and his **mother Monica**, interesting circumstance respecting, 409.
Authenticity and genuineness **of the Sermon on the Mount, 17, etc.**

Beam in the eyes, 398, etc.
Beatitudes, the relation of Matthew's narrative of the, to that of Luke, **59, etc.;** why **our Lord opened** His discourse with, 62; distribution of the, 63.
Blessedness, **gradations** of, 38, etc.; faith the condition of, 38; dependence of, on **obedience, 40.**
Bogomilans, the **peculiar** custom of the, in relation to prayer, 319.
Bread, daily, the petition for, 342, etc.

Canons, **two** hermeneutical, 163, etc.
Capernaum, 51; its site determined, 54, etc.
Careans, the forerunners of the, 152.
Charity, hypocritical, condemned, **296, etc.**
Cheek, smiting on the 271, 272.
Christ, His peculiar relationship to **the human race, not that of a lawgiver,** 35; His address, that **of a** popular orator, 165.
Chronological order of the Sermon on the Mount, 8, etc.
Clairvoyant criticism of Ewald, the, 9.
Council, liable to the, 182.
Courts of judgment among the Jews, according to rabbinical records, 184, etc., and Josephus, 185, note.
Cutting off the right hand, 212.

Daily bread, the petition **for,** 342, etc.; is it spiritual or physical? 352, 353.
Darkness, spiritual, 380.
Divorce, 221; among the Jews in the time of Josephus, 219, note; the ground of, variously interpreted, 220; restrictions on, 227, etc.; the only valid ground of, 230, etc.; marriage after, 233, etc.
Divorce, collisions of the Church with the State respecting, 241; different opinions within the Church respecting, 241, etc.
Divorce and marriage, **according** to Moses and the **traditions of** the Pharisees, 217; according to the Christian πλήρωσις, 221, etc.; Paul's doctrine on 231, etc.; survey **of the** history of, 238—245.
Dogs, and swine, the **symbolic import** of, 401, etc.

Earth, to inherit the, meaning of the words, 82, 85.
Eating and drinking in the name of Christ, 430.
Enemy, the command to love our, 277: hating **our, 278, 284.**
Epilogue to the Lord's Prayer, 365, etc.
Evangelists, the synoptical, do not jumble their materials, 8.
Evil, resisting, 164, etc.
Evil, prayer to be delivered from, 363, etc.
Evil thoughts, 209.
Eye, the, the light of **the** body, 377; an evil, 379; **a** single, 380.
Eye, **seeing a** mote in our brother's, 398, etc.

Eye, plucking out the right, 212.
"Eye for an eye," meaning of the phrase, 266—270.

Faith, the condition of the blessedness, 38; in Christ, the living fountain of obedience, 39.
False prophets, 427, etc.
Fasting, warnings against hypocritical, 369, etc.
Father, our, use of the formula in Biblical and extra-Biblical religions, 329.
Fellowship with God, the highest good, 390.
Fool, import of the word, 179.
Forgiveness of trespasses, 353, etc.
Fruits, the test of true or false teachers,—what they are, 420—426.
Fulfilling the law and the prophets, 126, etc.; how accomplished by Christ —various ways enumerated, 131, etc.

Galilean Lake, the beauties of the environs of the, 55.
Gate, the strait, 414, etc.
Gehenna, 186, etc.
Gemara, the, quoted as to a compendium of the law, 139—141.
Gift brought to the altar, 193.
God, the object of supreme desire, 371, etc.
Good, the highest, 381, etc., 390.

Hallowing God's name, 333, etc.
Hand, cutting off the right, 212, etc.
Hate, to, 382.
Hatred of our enemies, 278, etc., 284.
Heart, the, where the treasure is. 376.
Heaven, 102; Our Father in, 331, etc.; the dwelling-place of pure spirits, 339, etc.
Heaven, the kingdom of, 71, etc.
Heaven and earth passing away, 132.
Hebrew vocals, great irregularity of the rendering of, in the LXX., 178, note.
Hell-fire, liability to, 182, etc., 186; to be cast into, 187.
Hillelites and Shammaites, the schools of the, 220.
Holy, that which is, not to be given to dogs, 405, etc.
House, the, upon the rock, 433, etc.
Hungering and thirsting after righteousness, 87.
Hypocrisy, warnings against, in charity, 296, etc.; in prayer, 303, etc.; in fasting, 369, etc.
Hypocrite, N. Lyra's curious derivation of the word, 296, note.

Injuries, the Mosaic and Christian law respecting retaliation for, 266—270.

Jot, or tittle, 132.
"Judge not," meaning of the precept, 396, etc.
Judgment according to works, 37, etc.
Judgment liable to the, 181, etc.
Judgment, courts of, among the Jews, 184, etc.
Jupiter, the etymology of the name, 329.
Jus talionis, the 266.

Kaddish, the Jewish prayer so called, 324.
Kingdom of God, seeking the, 390.
Kingdom of heaven, the, 71—78, 149, etc.; the least in, 145, etc.; prayer for the coming of, 334, etc.
Know, to, 432.

Lamp, covering a, with a vessel, 114.
Law, the Mosaic, relation of the Sermon on the Mount to, 34; and the prophets, relation of Jesus to, 116, etc.; in various ways fulfilled by Christ, 131, etc.; the *Gemara* quoted as to, 139—141.
Lawgiver, how far is Christ a, 35.
Lawgiving of Christ, the, in what respect antagonistic with the *dicta* of the law, 154, etc.
"Least in the kingdom of heaven," 147, etc.
Letter, bad results of veneration for the, 164.
Life 413.
Light, and salt, distinction between the figurative meaning of the words, 109; the Apostles called, 113, etc.
Likeness to God, 286; the Platonic idea of, 287.
Lily of the field, the, 388.
Literature, exegetical, of the Sermon on the Mount, 41—49.
Lord's Prayer, the, position of in the Gospels, 25, 315, etc.; works on the, 47, etc.; original from of, 316, etc.; relation of Luke's recension of, to that of Matthew, 318; object for which it was given, 319, etc.; source of, 322, etc.; was it, in part, derived from the *Zend Avesta?* 323; or from Jewish forms? 323; connection of, and train of thought, 326, etc.; number of petitions in, 327; arrangement of, 328; invocation, 329, etc.; first petition, 332—334; second, 334—338; third, 338—341; fourth, 341—353; fifth, 353—357—365; epilogue, 365—368.
Love of God and our neighbour, 412.
Luke, his incorrect arrangement of the Sermon on the Mount,—how to account for it, 30; Ewald's view of the documentary character of his Gospel, 32; a Pauline object ascribed to him, 32.
Lusting after a woman, the precept respecting, 207, etc.
Luther the popular character of his writings, 166, 167.

Mammon, 383.
Marriage and divorce, according to Moses and the tradition of the Pharisees, 217; according to the Christian πλήρωσις, 221, etc.; Paul's doctrine of, 231.
Marriage, second, 233—245; polemic of the Protestant Church against the sacramental view of, 243.
Matthew, the Gospel of, its relation to Judaism, 12; was it constructed on the plan of the Pentateuch? 13; assigned the position of first Evangelist by modern critics, 21.
Meek, the, 81; their blessedness, 82—85.
Monica, the mother of Augustine, her prayer for her son, how answered, 409.
Morrow, taking thought for the, 392, etc.
Moth, and rust, 373.
Motives of Christian works, 293, etc.
Mountain, the, on which the Sermon on the Mount was delivered, 51, etc.
Mourn, those who, 79, etc.
Murder, and adultery, the order in which the prohibitions of, are cited in the Sermon on the Mount, 168.
Murder, the commandment relating to, expounded by Christ, 169, etc.

Name, the signification of the word, 332.
Neighbour, loving our, 278, etc.

Oaths, literature of the subject, 245, 246; the law of, discussed, 246—257; the use of, necessarily conceded in certain cases, 253; irreverent and frivolous, alone, forbidden, 255, etc.; historical view of opinion on the subject in the Christian Church, 257—261; by created things, 261, etc.; come of evil, 264, etc.
Obedience, faith the fountain of, 39; dependence of blessedness on, 40.

"Officer, the," 201.
Open the mouth, to, force of the phrase, 57, etc.

Peacemakers, 97.
Pearls, to cast, before swine, 404.
Peccata venalia et mortalia, Luther's view of, 190.
Persecution for Christ's sake, 100.
Pharisees, the, 15; seven classes of, enumerated by the *Gemara*, 152; the righteousness of the Scribes and, 153, etc.
Piety, false, exposed, 294.
Poor in spirit, the, who? 67, etc.
Popular style of Christ's address, 165.
Power, the, with which Jesus spoke, 434. etc.
Prayer, warnings against hypocritical, 303, etc.; standing in the streets, 305; much speaking in, 309—312.
Prayer, the Lord's, the position of, 315, etc.; from of, 316; relation of Matthew and Luke's versions of, 318, etc.; object of, 319, etc.; sources, 322, etc.; connection and train of thought of, 326, etc.; number of petitions in, 327; arrangement, 328; invocation, 329, etc.; first petition, 332—334; second, 334—338; third, 338—341; fourth, 341—353; fifth, 353—357; sixth, 357—365; epilogue, 365—368.
Prison, to be cast into, 202, etc.
Prophets, 428.
Protestant theology, its conclusions respecting the Sermon on the Mount, 34, etc.
Providence of God over the inferior creation, an argument for His care of man, 385, etc.
Punishment, degrees of, assigned to angry speech, 181.
"Pure in heart," the, 89, etc., 95, etc.
Purgatory, 202, etc.

Quakers, their false method of interpreting Scripture, 164.

Raka, import of the word, 177, etc.
Reconciliation to one's brother, 195.
Reformation view of the Gospel, the, 35.
Retaliation, Old Testament sayings about, 266; bad sense in which the word has been applied by the Scribes, 267; views of the Fathers respecting, 267, etc.
Reward, 103; the Romish doctrine of, 104.
Right hand, cutting off the, 212.
Right hand, and left, in almsgiving, 302, etc.
Righteousness, 86; hungering and thirsting for, 87; of the Scribes and Pharisees, 153; in the sense of almsgiving, 295.
Rock-built house, the, 434.

Sacrificial ceremonial, the, under what circumstances it might be interrupted, 193.
Salt, the disciples called, 105, 106; its properties, 107; as a religious symbol, 107, 108; distinction between, and light, as to their figurative import, 109, etc., losing its savour, 110, etc.; Maundrell quoted on the subject, 111, note.
Salute, to, 291.
Sanhedrim, the, 185.
Satan, the New Testament idea of, in respect to evil, 265.
Scribes and Pharisees, the, 151.
Seeing God, 91, etc.
Sermon on the Mount, the, comparison of Matthew and Luke's report of, 1; which report to be preferred, 2, etc.; source of Luke's report of, 5, etc.;

amplifications in Luke's report, 6, 7; chronological order of, 8, etc.; why assigned its present position, 12, etc.; occasion of, 13; object, 14; division of, 15; train of thought in, progressive, 16, etc.; distinction of the parts of, 17; authenticity and genuineness of, 17, etc.; passages of, in which it is difficult to trace a train of thought, 22—25; arrangement of, by Matthew, in the main correct, 27; how explain the erroneous arrangement of, by Luke, 30, etc.; relation of, to the Mosaic law, 34; conclusions of Protestant theology respecting, 35, etc.; exegetical literature on, 41—49.

Sixth commandment, quoted by our Lord along with the rabbinical gloss, and expounded, 169, etc.

Sounding a trumpet before giving alms, 297, etc.; peculiar interpretations of the phrase, 299, etc.

Splinter in the eye, 398, 399.

Standing, an attitude of prayer, 305.

Stature, adding a cubit to one's, 387.

Swine, and dogs, figurative import of, 401—403.

Synoptical Evangelists do not jumble their materials, 8.

Talmud, the, quoted, 205.

Tax-gatherers, their character among the Jews, 289; how regarded, 289, 290.

Tempests, the force of Eastern, 434.

Temptation, 357, etc.

Third commandment, the, 246, etc.

Thorns and thistles, 426.

Thoughts, evil, rabbinical views of, 205, etc.; Luther's views of, 209.

Tophet, 187.

Treasure, to be laid up in heaven, 372, etc.

Treasures, what they often consisted of in the East, 373, etc.

Trespasses, the forgiveness of, 353, etc.

Trumpet, to sound a, before one in almsgiving, 277; peculiar interpretations of the words, 299, etc.

Visio Dei, 94.

Way, the broad and narrow, 414; few find the narrow, 417.

Will, the petition that God's, may be done on earth as in heaven, 338, etc.

Wolves in sheeps' clothing, 419, etc.

Women, the demeanour required by the Talmud towards, 205.

Works, judgment according to, 37, etc.

Yea, yea, and Nay, nay, 263, etc.

THE END.

T. and T. Clark's Publications.

(TEMPORARY) CHEAP RE-ISSUE OF
STIER'S WORDS OF THE LORD JESUS.

To meet a very general desire that this now well-known Work should be brought more within the reach of all classes, both Clergy and Laity, Messrs. CLARK are now issuing, for a limited period, the *Eight* Volumes, handsomely bound in *Four*, at the *Subscription price* of

TWO GUINEAS.

As the allowance to the Trade must necessarily be small, orders sent either direct or through booksellers must *in every case* be accompanied with a Post Office Order for the above amount.

'The whole work is a treasury of thoughtful exposition. Its measure of practical and spiritual application, with exegetical criticism, commends it to the use of those whose duty it is to preach as well as to understand the Gospel of Christ.'—*Guardian.*

New and Cheap Edition, in Four Vols., Demy 8vo, *Subscription price* 28s.

THE LIFE OF THE LORD JESUS CHRIST:

A Complete Critical Examination of the Origin, Contents, and Connection of the Gospels. Translated from the German of J. P. LANGE, D.D., Professor of Divinity in the University of Bonn. Edited, with additional Notes, by MARCUS DODS, D.D.

'We have arrived at a most favourable conclusion regarding the importance and ability of this work—the former depending upon the present condition of theological criticism, the latter on the wide range of the work itself; the singularly dispassionate judgment of the author, as well as his pious, reverential, and erudite treatment of a subject inexpressibly holy. . . . We have great pleasure in recommending this work to our readers. We are convinced of its value and enormous range.'—*Irish Ecclesiastical Gazette.*

BENGEL'S GNOMON—CHEAP EDITION.
GNOMON OF THE NEW TESTAMENT.

By JOHN ALBERT BENGEL. Now First Translated into English. With Original Notes, Explanatory and Illustrative. Edited by the Rev. ANDREW R. FAUSSET, M.A. The Original Translation was in Five Large Volumes, demy 8vo, averaging more than 550 pages each, and the very great demand for this edition has induced the Publishers to issue the *Five* Volumes bound in *Three*, at the *Subscription price* of

TWENTY-FOUR SHILLINGS.

They trust by this still further to increase its usefulness.

'It is a work which manifests the most intimate and profound knowledge of Scripture, and which, if we examine it with care, will often be found to condense more matter into a line than can be extracted from many pages of other writers.'—*Archdeacon Hare.*

'In respect both of its contents and its tone, Bengel's Gnomon stands alone. Even among laymen there has arisen a healthy and vigorous desire for Scriptural knowledge, and Bengel has done more than any other man to aid such inquirers. There is perhaps no book every word of which has been so well weighed, or in which a single technical term contains so often far-reaching and suggestive views. . . . The theoretical and practical are as intimately connected as light and heat in the sun's ray.'—*Life of Perthes.*

T. and T. Clark's Publications.

In Twenty-four Handsome 8vo Volumes, Subscription Price £6, 6s. 0d.,

Ante-Nicene Christian Library.

A COLLECTION OF ALL THE WORKS OF THE FATHERS OF THE CHRISTIAN CHURCH PRIOR TO THE COUNCIL OF NICÆA.

EDITED BY THE

REV. ALEXANDER ROBERTS, D.D., AND JAMES DONALDSON, LL.D.

MESSRS. CLARK are now happy to announce the completion of this Series. It has been received with marked approval by all sections of the Christian Church in this country and in the United States, as supplying what has long been felt to be a want, and also on account of the impartiality, learning, and care with which Editors and Translators have executed a very difficult task.

The Publishers do not bind themselves to *continue* to supply the Series at the Subscription price.

The Works are arranged as follow :—

FIRST YEAR.

APOSTOLIC FATHERS, comprising Clement's Epistles to the Corinthians; Polycarp to the Ephesians; Martyrdom of Polycarp; Epistle of Barnabas; Epistles of Ignatius (longer and shorter, and also the Syriac version); Martyrdom of Ignatius; Epistle to Diognetus; Pastor of Hermas; Papias; Spurious Epistles of Ignatius. In One Volume.
JUSTIN MARTYR; ATHENAGORAS. In One Volume.
TATIAN; THEOPHILUS; THE CLEmentine Recognitions. In One Volume.
CLEMENT OF ALEXANDRIA, Volume First, comprising Exhortation to Heathen; The Instructor; and a portion of the Miscellanies.

SECOND YEAR.

HIPPOLYTUS, Volume First; Refutation of all Heresies, and Fragments from his Commentaries.
IRENÆUS, Volume First.
TERTULLIAN AGAINST MARCION.
CYPRIAN, Volume First; the Epistles, and some of the Treatises.

THIRD YEAR.

IRENÆUS (completion); HIPPOLYTUS (completion); Fragments of Third Century. In One Volume.
ORIGEN: De Principiis; Letters; and portion of Treatise against Celsus.

CLEMENT OF ALEXANDRIA, Volume Second; Completion of Miscellanies.
TERTULLIAN, Volume First: To the Martyrs; Apology; To the Nations, etc.

FOURTH YEAR.

CYPRIAN, Volume Second (completion); Novatian; Minucius Felix; Fragments.
METHODIUS; ALEXANDER OF LYcopolis; Peter of Alexandria; Anatolius; Clement on Virginity; and Fragments.
TERTULLIAN, Volume Second.
APOCRYPHAL GOSPELS; ACTS AND Revelations, comprising all the very curious Apocryphal Writings of the first Three Centuries.

FIFTH YEAR.

TERTULLIAN, Volume Third (completion).
CLEMENTINE HOMILIES; APOSTOlical Constitutions. In One Volume.
ARNOBIUS.
DIONYSIUS; GREGORY THAUMAturgus; Syrian Fragments. In One Volume.

SIXTH YEAR.

LACTANTIUS; Two Volumes.
ORIGEN, Volume Second (completion). 12s. to Non-Subscribers.
EARLY LITURGIES AND REMAINing Fragments. 9s. to Non-Subscribers.

Single Years cannot be had separately, unless to complete sets; but any Volume may be had separately, price 10s. 6d.,—with the exception of ORIGEN, Vol. II., 12s.; and the EARLY LITURGIES, 9s.

T. and T. Clark's Publications.

The Works of St. Augustine.

EDITED BY MARCUS DODS, D.D.

SUBSCRIPTION:

Four Volumes for a Guinea, *payable in advance* (24s. when not paid in advance).

FIRST YEAR.

THE 'CITY OF GOD.' Two Volumes.
WRITINGS IN CONNECTION WITH the Donatist Controversy. In One Volume.
THE ANTI-PELAGIAN WORKS OF St. Augustine. Vol. I.

SECOND YEAR.

'LETTERS.' Vol. I.
TREATISES AGAINST FAUSTUS the Manichæan. One Volume.

THE HARMONY OF THE EVANgelists, and the Sermon on the Mount. One Volume.
ON THE TRINITY. One Volume.

THIRD YEAR.

FIRST ISSUE.

COMMENTARY ON JOHN. Vol. I.
ON CHRISTIAN DOCTRINE, ENchiridion, etc. **One** Volume.

Messrs. CLARK believe this will prove not the least valuable of their various Series, and no pains will be spared to make it so. The Editor has secured a most competent staff of Translators, and every care is being taken to secure not only accuracy, but elegance.

The Works of St. AUGUSTINE to be included in the Series are (in addition to the above)—

The remaining TREATISES in the PELAGIAN CONTROVERSY.

The LECTURES on the GOSPEL OF ST. JOHN, Vol. II., and the CONFESSIONS.

The Series **will** include **a LIFE** of ST. AUGUSTINE, by ROBERT RAINY, D.D., Professor of Church History, New College, Edinburgh.

The Series will extend to about Eighteen Volumes. The Publishers will be glad **to receive** the *Names* of Subscribers **as** early **as** possible.

It is understood that Subscribers are bound to take at least the books of the first two years. Each Volume is sold separately at (on an average) 10s. 6d.

'For the reproduction of the "City of God" in an admirable English garb we are greatly indebted to the well-directed enterprise and energy of Messrs. Clark, and to the accuracy and scholarship of those who have undertaken the laborious task of translation.' —*Christian Observer.*

'The present translation reads smoothly and pleasantly, and we have every reason to be satisfied both with the erudition and the fair and sound judgment displayed by the translators and the editor.'—*John Bull.*

T. and T. Clark's Publications.

In Demy 8vo, price 10s. 6d.,

Christian Dogmatics: A Compendium of the Doctrines of Christianity. By H. MARTENSEN, D.D., Bishop of Seeland, Denmark.

'Every reader must rise from its perusal stronger, calmer, and more hopeful, not only for the fortunes of Christianity, but of dogmatical theology.'—*British Quarterly Review.*

BY THE SAME AUTHOR.
Just published, in Demy 8vo, price 10s. 6d.,

On Christian Ethics. Translated from the Danish.

In Demy 8vo, 10s. 6d.,

Biblical Theology of the New Testament. Translated from the German of C. F. SCHMID, D.D.

'The first part is preceded by an historical review of the life of Jesus, and the second by a fruitful and suggestive sketch of the lives of the apostles. The strength of learning and highly analytical powers of the author are reserved for the doctrinal review, and very beautifully does he bring forth the teaching of our Lord.'—*British Quarterly Review.*

In Demy 8vo, price 7s. 6d.,

Handbook of Church History to the Reformation. From the German of Professor KURTZ.

Handbook of Church History, from the Reformation to the present Time. Second Edition, translated from Sixth German Edition.

'A work executed with great diligence and care, exhibiting an accurate collection of facts, and a succinct though full account of the history and progress of the Church, both external and internal. . . . The work is distinguished for moderation and charity, and for a spirit which is truly Christian.'—*English Churchman.*

In Three Volumes, Royal 8vo, price 36s.,

History of the Christian Church; From the Birth of our Lord to Gregory the Great. By PHILIP SCHAFF, D.D.

'We can heartily commend this work as learned, scholarlike, and thorough. There is throughout a breadth of view, a calmness of spirit, an occasional beauty of reflection, and, above all, a religiousness of tone.'—*Freeman.*

BY THE SAME AUTHOR.
In Demy 8vo, price 10s. 6d.,

History of the Apostolic Church; with a General Introduction to Church History.

'Worthy of a German scholar, and of a disciple of Neander, and of a believing and free Christian and Protestant.'—BUNSEN's *Hippolytus.*

In Two Volumes, Demy 8vo, price 21s.,

The Church of Christ: A Treatise on the Nature, Powers, Ordinances, Discipline, and Government of the Christian Church. By the late Professor BANNERMAN.

'We are thankful for this goodly gift, and we trust its reception will show that the Church knows how to use it. We commend these learned and masterly volumes to the careful study, not only of the scientific divine, but of all thoughtful men who would desire to understand some of the greatest and most vital questions of our time.'—*Presbyterian.*

In Demy 8vo, price 10s. 6d.,

Analytical Commentary on the Epistle to the Romans, tracing the Train of Thought by the aid of Parallelism; with Notes and Dissertations on the Principal Difficulties in the Epistle. By JOHN FORBES, D.D.

'In every point of view it is a valuable addition to critical biblical literature, and possesses many attractions even for the unlearned reader. For full satisfaction on every difficulty, we have referred with complete satisfaction to this modest yet learned and exhaustive work.'—*Contemporary Review.*

T. and T. Clark's Publications.

MEYER'S
Commentary on the New Testament.

MESSRS. CLARK beg to announce that they have in course of preparation a Translation of the well-known and justly esteemed

CRITICAL AND EXEGETICAL
COMMENTARY ON THE NEW TESTAMENT,
By Dr. H. A. W. MEYER,
OBERCONSISTORIALRATH, HANOVER,

Of which they have just published—

ROMANS, Vol. I.
GALATIANS, One Volume.

The Subscription will be 21s. for Four Volumes Demy 8vo.

By arrangement with Dr. MEYER, Messrs. Clark have obtained the sole right of translation into English, and they have the very great advantage of Dr. Meyer's emendations to the time of his death. In order to secure perfect accuracy, the Publishers have placed the whole work under the editorial care of Rev. Dr. DICKSON, Professor of Divinity in the University of Glasgow.

The Volumes will vary in number of pages according to the size of the original, but an average of about 400 pages may be assumed. Each Volume will be sold separately at (on an average) 10s. 6d. to Non-Subscribers.

Intending Subscribers will be kind enough to fill up the accompanying Form, which may be returned, either direct to the Publishers at 38 George Street, Edinburgh, or through their own Booksellers.

'I need hardly add that the last edition of the accurate, perspicuous, and learned commentary of Dr. Meyer has been most carefully consulted throughout; and I must again, as in the preface to the Galatians, avow my great obligations to the acumen and scholarship of the learned editor.'—BISHOP ELLICOT *in Preface to his Commentary on Ephesians.*

'The ablest grammatical exegete of the age.'—PHILIP SCHAFF, D.D.

Mr. _____

BOOKSELLER,

Will please enter my Name as a Subscriber, and forward, as published, the above Translation of

MEYER'S COMMENTARIES.

FOREIGN THEOLOGICAL LIBRARY.

ANNUAL SUBSCRIPTION:

One Guinea (payable in advance) for Four Volumes, Demy 8vo.
When not paid in advance, the Retail Bookseller is entitled to charge 24s.

N.B.—Any *two* Years in this Series can be had at Subscription Price. *A single Year's Books* (except in the case of the current Year) *cannot be supplied separately.* Non-subscribers, price 10s. 6d. each volume, with exceptions marked.

1864—
- Lange on the Acts of the Apostles. Two Volumes.
- Keil and Delitzsch on the Pentateuch. Vols. I. and II.

1865—
- Keil and Delitzsch on the Pentateuch. Vol. III.
- Hengstenberg on the Gospel of John. Two Volumes.
- Keil and Delitzsch on Joshua, Judges, and Ruth. One Volume.

1866—
- Keil and Delitzsch on Samuel. One Volume.
- Keil and Delitzsch on Job. Two Volumes.
- Martensen's System of Christian Doctrine. One Volume.

1867—
- Delitzsch on Isaiah. Vol. I.
- Delitzsch on Biblical Psychology. 12s.
- Delitzsch on Isaiah. Vol. II.
- Hengstenberg on Daniel. 12s.

1868—
- Keil's Commentary on the Minor Prophets. Two Volumes.
- Delitzsch's Commentary on Epistle to the Hebrews. Vol. I.
- Harless' System of Christian Ethics. One Volume.

1869—
- Hengstenberg on Ezekiel. One Volume.
- Stier on the Words of the Apostles. One Volume.
- Keil's Introduction to the Old Testament. Vol. I.
- Bleek's Introduction to the New Testament. Vol. I.

1870—
- Keil's Introduction to the Old Testament. Vol. II.
- Bleek's Introduction to the New Testament. Vol. II.
- Schmid's New Testament Theology. One Volume.
- Delitzsch's Commentary on Epistle to the Hebrews. Vol. II.

1871—
- Delitzsch's Commentary on the Psalms. Three Volumes.
- Hengstenberg's History of the Kingdom of God under the Old Testament. Vol. I.

1872—
- Keil's Commentary on the Books of Kings. One Volume.
- Keil's Commentary on the Book of Daniel. One Volume.
- Keil's Commentary on the Books of Chronicles. One Volume.
- Hengstenberg's History of the Kingdom of God under the Old Testament. Vol. II.

1873—
- Keil's Commentary on Ezra, Nehemiah. and Esther. One Volume.
- Winer's Collection of the Confessions of Christendom. One Volume.
- Keil's Commentary on Jeremiah. Vol. I.
- Martensen on Christian Ethics.

MESSRS. CLARK allow a SELECTION of TWENTY VOLUMES (*or more at the same ratio*) from the various Series previous to the Volumes issued in 1870 (*see next page*),

At the Subscription Price of Five Guineas.

They trust that this will still more largely extend the usefulness of the FOREIGN THEOLOGICAL LIBRARY, which has so long been recognised as holding an important place in modern Theological literature.

T. and T. Clark's Publications.

CLARK'S FOREIGN THEOLOGICAL LIBRARY—*Continued.*

The following are the works from which a Selection may be made (non-subscription prices within brackets):—

Dr. Hengstenberg.—Commentary on the Psalms. By E. W. HENGSTENBERG, D.D., Professor of Theology in Berlin. In Three Vols. 8vo. (33s.)

Dr. Gieseler.—Compendium of Ecclesiastical History. By J. C. L. GIESELER, D.D., Professor of Theology in Göttingen. Five Vols. 8vo. (£2. 12s. 6d.)

Dr. Olshausen.—Biblical Commentary on the Gospels and Acts, adapted especially for Preachers and Students. By HERMANN OLSHAUSEN, D.D., Professor of Theology in the University of Erlangen. In Four Vols. 8vo. (£2, 2s.)

Biblical Commentary on the Romans, adapted especially for Preachers and Students. By HERMANN OLSHAUSEN, D.D. In One Vol. 8vo. (10s. 6d.)

Biblical Commentary on St. Paul's First and Second Epistles to the Corinthians. By HERMANN OLSHAUSEN, D.D. In One Vol. 8vo. (9s.)

Biblical Commentary on St. Paul's Epistles to the Galatians, Ephesians, Colossians, and Thessalonians. By HERMANN OLSHAUSEN, D.D. One Vol. 8vo. (10s. 6d.)

Biblical Commentary on St. Paul's Epistle to the Philippians, to Titus, and the First to Timothy; in continuation of the Work of Olshausen. By Lic. AUGUST WIESINGER. In One Vol. 8vo. (10s. 6d.)

Biblical Commentary on the Hebrews. By Dr. EBRARD. In continuation of the Work of Olshausen. In One Vol. 8vo. (10s. 6d.)

Dr. Neander.—General History of the Christian Religion and Church. By AUGUSTUS NEANDER, D.D. Translated from the Second and Improved Edition. Nine Vols. 8vo. (£2. 11s. 6d.)

This is the only Edition in a Library size.

Prof. H. A. Ch. Havernick.—General Introduction to the Old Testament. By Professor HAVERNICK. One Vol. 8vo. (10s. 6d.)

Dr. Müller.—The Christian Doctrine of Sin. By Dr. JULIUS MÜLLER. Two Vols. 8vo. (21s.) New Edition.

Dr. Hengstenberg.—Christology of the Old Testament, and a Commentary on the Messianic Predictions. By E. W. HENGSTENBERG, D.D. Four Vols. (£2, 2s.)

Dr. M. Baumgarten.—The Acts of the Apostles; or the History of the Church in the Apostolic Age. By M. BAUMGARTEN, Ph.D., and Professor in the University of Rostock. Three Vols. (£1, 7s.)

Dr. Stier.—The Words of the Lord Jesus. By RUDOLPH STIER, D.D., Chief Pastor and Superintendent of Schkeuditz. In Eight Vols. 8vo. (£4, 4s.)

Dr. Carl Ullmann.—Reformers before the Reformation, principally in Germany and the Netherlands. Two Vols. 8vo. (£1, 1s.)

Professor Kurtz.—History of the Old Covenant; or, Old Testament Dispensation. By Professor KURTZ of Dorpat. In Three Vols. (£1, 11s. 6d.)

Dr. Stier.—The Words of the Risen Saviour, and Commentary on the Epistle of St. James. By RUDOLPH STIER, D.D. One Vol. (10s. 6d.)

Professor Tholuck.—Commentary on the Gospel of St. John. By Professor THOLUCK of Halle. In One Vol. (9s.)

Professor Tholuck.—Commentary on the Sermon on the Mount. By Professor THOLUCK. In One Vol. (10s. 6d.)

Dr. Hengstenberg.—Commentary on the Book of Ecclesiastes. To which are appended: Treatises on the Song of Solomon; on the Book of Job; on the Prophet Isaiah; on the Sacrifices of Holy Scripture; and on the Jews and the Christian Church. By E. W. HENGSTENBERG, D.D. In One Vol. 8vo. (9s.)

Dr. Ebrard.—Commentary on the Epistles of St. John. By Dr. JOHN H. A. EBRARD, Professor of Theology. In One Vol. (10s. 6d.)

Dr. Lange.—Theological and Homiletical Commentary on the Gospel of St. Matthew and Mark. Specially Designed and Adapted for the Use of Ministers and Students. By J. P. LANGE, D.D. Three Vols. (10s. 6d. each.)

T. and T. Clark's Publications.

CLARK'S FOREIGN THEOLOGICAL LIBRARY—*Continued.*

Dr. Dorner.—History of the Development of the Doctrine of the Person of Christ. By Dr. J. A. Dorner, Professor of Theology in the University of Berlin. Five Vols. (£2, 12s. 6d.)

Lange and Dr. J. J. Van Oosterzee.—Theological and Homiletical Commentary on the Gospel of St. Luke. Specially Designed and Adapted for the Use of Ministers and Students. Edited by J. P. Lange, D.D. Two Vols. (18s.)

Dr. Ebrard.—The Gospel History: A Compendium of Critical Investigations in support of the Historical Character of the Four Gospels. One Vol. (10s. 6d.)

Lange, Lechler, and Gerok.—Theological and Homiletical Commentary on the Acts of the Apostles. Edited by Dr. Lange. Two Vols. (21s.)

Dr. Hengstenberg.—Commentary on the Gospel of St. John. Two Vols. (21s.)

Professor Keil.—Biblical Commentary on the Pentateuch. Three Vols. (31s. 6d.)

Professor Keil.—Commentary on Joshua, Judges, and Ruth. One Vol. (10s. 6d.)

Professor Delitzsch.—A System of Biblical Psychology. One Vol. (12s.)

Professor Delitzsch.—Commentary on the Prophecies of Isaiah. Two Vols. (21s.)

Professor Keil.—Commentary on the Books of Samuel. One Vol. (10s. 6d.)

Professor Delitzsch.—Commentary on the Book of Job. Two Vols. (21s.)

Bishop Martensen.—Christian Dogmatics. A Compendium of the Doctrines of Christianity. One Vol. (10s. 6d.)

Dr. J. P. Lange.—Critical, Doctrinal, and Homiletical Commentary on the Gospel of St. John. Two Vols. (21s.)

Professor Keil.—Commentary on the Minor Prophets. Two Vols. (21s.)

Professor Delitzsch.—Commentary on Epistle to the Hebrews. Vol. I. (10s. 6d.)

Dr. Harless.—A System of Christian Ethics. One Vol. (10s. 6d.)

Dr. Hengstenberg.—Commentary on Ezekiel. One Vol. (10s. 6d.)

Dr. Stier.—The Words of the Apostles Expounded. One Vol. (10s. 6d.)

Professor Keil.—Introduction to the Old Testament. Vol. I. (10s 6d.)

Professor Bleek.—Introduction to the New Testament. Vol. I. (10s. 6d.)

And, in connection with the Series—

Alexander's Commentary on Isaiah. Two Volumes. (17s.)

Ritter's (Carl) Comparative Geography of Palestine. Four Volumes. (32s.)

Shedd's History of Christian Doctrine. Two Volumes. (21s.)

Macdonald's Introduction to the Pentateuch. Two Volumes. (21s.)

Ackerman on the Christian Element in Plato. (7s. 6d.)

Robinson's Greek Lexicon of the New Testament. 8vo. (9s.)

Gerlach's Commentary on the Pentateuch. 8vo. (10s. 6d.)

The series, in 120 Volumes (including 1873), price £31, 10s., forms an *Apparatus*, without which it may be truly said *no Theological Library can be complete;* and the Publishers take the liberty of suggesting that no more appropriate gift could be presented to a Clergyman than the Series, in whole or in part.

⁎⁎* In reference to the above, it must be noted that NO DUPLICATES can be included in the Selection of Twenty Volumes; and it will save trouble and correspondence if it be distinctly understood that NO LESS number than Twenty can be supplied, unless at non-subscription price.

Subscribers' Names received by all Retail Booksellers.

LONDON: (*For Works at Non-subscription price only*) HAMILTON, ADAMS, & Co.

www.ingramcontent.com/pod-product-compliance
Lightning Source LLC
Chambersburg PA
CBHW031957300426
44117CB00008B/796